LANDMARK CASES IN REVENUE LAW

In an important addition to the series, this book tells the story of 20 leading revenue law cases. It goes well beyond technical analysis to explore questions of philosophical depth, historical context and constitutional significance. The editors have assembled a stellar team of tax scholars, including historians as well as lawyers, practitioners as well as academics, to provide a wide range of fresh perspectives on familiar and unfamiliar decisions. The whole collection is prefaced by the editors' extended introduction on the peculiar significance of case-law in revenue matters. This publication is a thought provoking and engaging showcase of tax writing that is accessible equally to specialists and nonspecialists.

Landmark Cases
in Revenue Law

Edited by
John Snape
and
Dominic de Cogan

Foreword by
Lord Walker of Gestingthorpe

·HART·
OXFORD · LONDON · NEW YORK · NEW DELHI · SYDNEY

HART PUBLISHING

Bloomsbury Publishing Plc

Kemp House, Chawley Park, Cumnor Hill, Oxford, OX2 9PH, UK

HART PUBLISHING, the Hart/Stag logo, BLOOMSBURY and the Diana logo are
trademarks of Bloomsbury Publishing Plc

First published in Great Britain 2019

A catalogue record for this book is available from the British Library.

Library of Congress Cataloging-in-Publication data

Names: Snape, John, editor. | De Cogan, Dominic, editor.

Title: Landmark cases in revenue law / edited by John Snape and Dominic de Cogan.

Description: Oxford [UK] ; Portland, Oregon : Hart Publishing, [2019] |
Includes bibliographical references and index.

Identifiers: LCCN 2018038296 (print) | LCCN 2018038552 (ebook) |
ISBN 9781509912254 (Epub) | ISBN 9781509912261 (hardback : alk. paper)

Subjects: LCSH: Taxation—Law and legislation—Great Britain—Cases.

Classification: LCC KD5355 (ebook) | LCC KD5355 .L36 2018 (print) | DDC 343.4104—dc23

LC record available at https://lccn.loc.gov/2018038296

ISBN: HB: 978-1-50991-226-1
        ePDF: 978-1-50991-227-8
        ePub: 978-1-50991-225-4

Typeset by Compuscript Ltd, Shannon
Printed and bound in Great Britain by CPI Group (UK) Ltd, Croydon CR0 4YY

To find out more about our authors and books visit www.hartpublishing.co.uk.
Here you will find extracts, author information, details of forthcoming events
and the option to sign up for our newsletters.

Foreword

IT IS A pleasure to welcome the latest volume in the *Landmark Cases* series. Unlike all the earlier volumes this work is primarily – indeed, almost exclusively – concerned with statute law. One of its central themes is the changing attitude of the courts to the construction of revenue statutes, especially in the context of artificial tax-avoidance. Here we can revisit the magisterial (but, as its author emphasised, in no way revolutionary) speech of Lord Wilberforce in *Ramsay* and the reassuringly collegiate decision of the House of Lords in *Barclays Mercantile*.

But the problems of construing revenue statutes are by no means limited to artificial tax-avoidance. When engaged in construing statute law, rather than developing the doctrines of the common law and equity, the courts are often dealing with issues that have a constitutional element and may find themselves in conflict with Parliament. That was certainly true in the *Case of Ship-Money*, the most venerable of the decisions considered by the contributors to this volume. As DL Keir wrote more than 80 years ago, the familiar statement that the Court of Exchequer Chamber had been almost evenly divided obscures the real significance of the case: 'The discord between the legislature and the judiciary could hardly have been more complete. But Parliament did not content itself with righting a mistaken decision. It treated the error as culpable. Seven judges were impeached or threatened with impeachment'.

Other cases in the volume have an important constitutional element, including *Bowles v Bank of England* (provisional collection of taxes), the *National Federation of Self-Employed and Small Businesses* case (extent of Revenue's management powers and access to judicial review) and *IRC v Commerzbank AG* (touching on the international law of treaties), *Pepper v Hart* (reference to Hansard, as to which the general opinion, 25 years on, seems to be that Lord Mackay of Clashfern was right in his sole dissent).

Other contributors revisit familiar problems including the tax residence of companies, generally accepted accountancy practice, and the fact-finding function of the General or Special Commissioners (now the First-tier Tribunal). A curious and forgotten perspective on the pitfalls of statutory construction is uncovered in the chapter on the tax on quack medicines introduced and then amended by various statutes in the reign of King George III, an early example of taxation serving the dual and conflicting purposes of raising revenue and at the same time discouraging unhealthy or wasteful consumption.

Together the contributors to this volume cover not merely the development of our present-day tax system, but also a good deal of social, political and economic history. I hope that it will be read and enjoyed by a wide audience, not limited to tax specialists.

Robert Walker

Notes and Acknowledgements

THIS BOOK IS dedicated to Angela Kershaw, John Snape's wife, who died of cancer in June 2018. Compassionate, honest, funny, clever, elegant, wise, conscientious, and beloved of friends and family, not least her nieces, Katy and Helena Snape, Ange was an unfailing inspiration, steadfast companion and loving wife to John, whom she never failed to astonish. Ange, a senior lecturer in French studies at Birmingham University, continued to supervise her research students into the spring of 2018 and had, before her death, finished responding to copy-editor's queries on her last book, *Translating War: Literature and Memory in France and Britain from the 1940s to the 1960s* (Palgrave Macmillan, 2018).

As is to be expected with a project of this size, our gratitude is spread widely. The idea of a *Landmarks* volume dealing with revenue law was first discussed between John Snape and another now-departed friend, John Tiley of the Centre for Tax Law in Cambridge. There was some American precedent for the idea, in the two *Tax Stories* books,[1] but the proximate spur came from the approaches taken in other volumes in the *Landmarks* series. Many of our contributors knew Professor Tiley well, and something of his spirit breathes through the various contributions. Profound thanks are also owed to the other two members of our four-person editorial panel, Chantal Stebbings and John Avery Jones. They have been instrumental in shaping the project and have been on hand with invaluable advice, often at very short notice.

The contributors to the volume were selected for their experience, the value of their insights and also for the diversity of their perspectives on revenue law. This last point was underlined by a workshop that was held at the University of Warwick on 6 October 2017, in which drafts of a number of the chapters were presented. This provided an opportunity for contributors to gain robust feedback on their chapters, but also forced us, as editors, to refine our understanding of what it can mean to pinpoint 'landmark' cases in revenue law. Much of the content of the Introduction was solidified in the aftermath of this often challenging yet always thought-provoking event. It goes without saying, also, that the constraints of publication only allowed us to represent a fraction of the wonderful and increasingly varied range of tax scholarship currently being carried out in the UK, and we can only hope that this book provides a spur to further research.

---

[1] PL Caron (ed), *Tax Stories* (2nd edn, New York, Foundation Press, 2009); SA Bank and KJ Stark (eds), *Business Tax Stories* (New York, Foundation Press, 2005).

The team at Hart Publishing has been supportive throughout, and we are extremely grateful for the advice provided by Sinead Moloney, Roberta Bassi and Bill Asquith. Thanks, too, are due to Linda Staniford at Hart, for her work on the proofs, and to Kim Harris for the beautifully detailed index. Our copy-editor, Anne Bevan, has been painstaking and responsive, also going well beyond the call of duty in helping with detailed editing. When Ange's illness meant that John had to hand over the remaining editorial tasks to Dominic in late May 2018, Dominic took on this responsibility willingly and unhesitatingly. John records here his deep gratitude to him for this. John also thanks family, friends and clergy supporting him just now, not least John's brothers, Andrew Snape and Michael Snape.

There is insufficient space to do full justice here to everyone who has helped with this book, but the editors would like to thank Lord Walker of Gestingthorpe, for writing the Foreword, and the anonymous reviewers for Hart Publishing, who supported this project in the first place and who provided excellent advice in the process. We are grateful, too, to the following members of Warwick Law School, who helped with the workshop: Jennifer Paterson; Sandra Phillips; Sunil Chudasama, who provided on-the-spot IT assistance on the day; Professor Roger Leng, who welcomed the Workshop participants; and the Warwick Law School Legal Research Institute, who funded the workshop.

Finally, the editors would like to reiterate our thanks to our families and in particular to Felicity de Cogan; to Ruth de Cogan, an eagle-eyed six-year old who has helped her father to avoid a range of editing mistakes; and, of course, to Ange.

JS,
DdC,
July 2018

Contents

Table of Cases

Table of Legislation

UK STATUTES

US LEGISLATION

FRENCH LEGISLATION

CANADIAN LEGISLATION

SOUTH AFRICAN LEGISLATION

EU LEGISLATION

INTERNATIONAL TREATIES AND CONVENTIONS

Notes on Contributors

Dr John Avery Jones CBE is a member of the Alternative Dispute Resolution Unit of Pump Court Tax Chambers, a retired judge of the Upper Tribunal (Tax and Chancery Chamber) and a retired Visiting Professor at the London School of Economics. He was formerly a practising solicitor. He is a member of the Editorial Advisory Panel and former editor of the British Tax Review.

Philip Baker is a barrister and QC practising from Field Court Tax Chambers in Gray's Inn. He was called to the Bar in 1979, began practising in 1987 and took silk in 2002. He is Visiting Professor in International Taxation at Oxford University and also a Senior Visiting Research Fellow at the Institute for Advanced Legal Studies, London University.

Dr Victor Baker is a senior policy and technical adviser to HM Revenue and Customs and HM Treasury specialising in corporation tax and corporate structure. He has held a number of Head Office policy and technical roles in direct tax and was a District Inspector and Area Director in the former Inland Revenue London Region.

Michael J Braddick is Professor of History at the University of Sheffield. He has published extensively on the political, social and economic history of England and the wider territories of the Tudor and Stuart Crown. His most recent book is *The Common Freedom of the People: John Lilburne and the English Revolution* (Oxford University Press, 2018).

Dr Dominic de Cogan is a University Lecturer in Taxation Law at the University of Cambridge, Assistant Director of the Centre for Tax Law and a Fellow of Christ's College, Cambridge. His research on the National Federation of Self-Employed was supported by travel grants from the Yorke Fund.

Martin Daunton is Emeritus Professor of Economic History at the University of Cambridge. He published *Trusting Leviathan: The Politics of Taxation in Britain, 1799–1914* and *Just Taxes: The Politics of Taxation in Britain, 1914–1979* with Cambridge University Press in 2001 and 2002. His most recent publication is *The Political Economy of State Finance: Taxation, State Spending and Debt since the 1970s*, edited with Marc Buggeln and Alexander Nutzenadel (Cambridge University Press, 2017).

Anne Fairpo MA (Oxon), CTA (Fellow), is a barrister at Temple Tax Chambers, with a practice in UK and international corporate tax planning and disputes. She has a particular interest in the taxation of technology, and is the author of Bloomsbury Professional's *Taxation of Intellectual Property*. She is also a part-time judge in the First-tier Tax Tribunal, a lecturer at Queen Mary University of London, a PhD candidate at the Institute of Advanced Legal Studies, University of London, and a former President of the Chartered Institute of Taxation.

Judith Freedman CBE, FBA, Hon CTA (Fellow) is the Pinsent Masons Professor of Taxation Law at the Oxford University Faculty of Law, a Fellow of Worcester College, Oxford and one of the founders of the Oxford University Centre for Business Taxation. She was a member of the Aaronson General Anti-Avoidance Rule Study Group and has served on many other corporate and tax law committees, including a consultative committee of the Office of Tax Simplification. Judith is a member of the IFS Tax Law Review Committee and joint general editor of the *British Tax Review* and has published widely on tax and corporate law issues.

Malcolm Gammie CBE, QC, is a barrister at One Essex Court, Temple. He is a judge of the First-tier Tribunal (Tax Chamber) and deputy judge of the Upper Tribunal (Tax and Chancery).

Dr Johann Hattingh is Associate Professor of the Faculty of Law in the University of Cape Town, South Africa. He was educated at the Universities of Cambridge, Cape Town, Leiden and Stellenbosch. His research for this book was financially supported by the Research Committee of the Faculty of Law in the University of Cape Town.

Glen Loutzenhiser BComm (Sask), LLB (Toronto), LLM (Cantab), MA (Oxon), DPhil (Oxon) is Associate Professor of Tax Law at the Faculty of Law, University of Oxford and Tutorial Fellow in Law at St Hugh's College, Oxford. Glen teaches on the undergraduate and graduate tax law courses at the Oxford Law Faculty and is also a course director for the MSc in Taxation. He is an assistant editor of the *British Tax Review*, and is sole editor of a leading UK textbook on tax law – *Tiley's Revenue Law* (Hart Publishing, 2016).

Geoffrey Morse is the Professor of Corporate and Tax Law at the University of Birmingham. In addition to numerous articles, he is the joint editor of *Davies: Principles of Tax Law*. In the corporate field he is the general editor of *Palmer's Company Law* and *Palmer's LLP Law* (all Sweet and Maxwell). He has also written eight editions of *Partnership and LLP Law* (Oxford University Press).

Ann Mumford is a Professor of Taxation Law at the Dickson Poon School of Law, King's College London. Ann's research interests include fiscal sociology, tax and equality, and historical perspectives on tax law. She is the author of two monographs and several articles.

Abimbola Olowofoyeku is Professor of Law and Head of the Division of Public and International Law at Brunel University, London. He is an Associate of the Chartered Institute of Taxation of Nigeria.

Christiana HJI Panayi is a Professor in Tax Law at Queen Mary University of London and an Adjunct Professor of European Union Tax Law at New York University. Christiana is also an expert member in the European Commission's Joint Transfer Pricing Forum and in the Platform for Tax Good Governance. She has published extensively in the area of EU and international tax law and is considered a leading expert in her field. Christiana is a solicitor of England and Wales and an Advocate of the Cyprus Supreme Court.

Dr John Pearce worked for many years in the Office of the Solicitor of Inland Revenue. He is now retired and has recently completed a PhD at the University of Exeter.

Philip Ridd, a solicitor, joined the Inland Revenue Solicitor's Office in 1971. From 1993 to 1995 he was Head of Litigation in the Treasury Solicitor's Department. From 1998 to 1999 he was Solicitor to the Bloody Sunday Inquiry. From 1999 to 2005 he was the Solicitor of Inland Revenue. He is currently a part-time law reporter.

David Salter is an Emeritus Reader at the University of Warwick. After a spell in practice, he spent his career in higher education (retiring from the University of Warwick in 2012). His teaching and research interests over the years lay, principally, in the law of taxation (UK and international). He has written widely and continues to write on the subject. Presently, he is one of the two general editors of *Revenue Law: Principles and Practice*. He is a member of the European Association of Tax Law Professors and he has had a long association with the Tax Research Network.

Dr John Snape is an Associate Professor of Law at the School of Law, University of Warwick. He is the author of *The Political Economy of Corporation Tax* (Hart Publishing, 2011).

Chantal Stebbings is Professor of Law and Legal History at the University of Exeter, UK. She is editor of the *Journal of Legal History* and chair of the Hamlyn Trust.

Dr John Vella is an Associate Professor of Tax Law in the Faculty of Law at the University of Oxford, a Fellow of Harris Manchester College and a Programme Director at the Oxford University Centre for Business Taxation.

Table of Abbreviations

AG	Advocate General
A-G	Attorney-General
ALBA	Administrative Law Bar Association
ASB	Accounting Standards Board
ASP	Alliance of Small Firms and Self-Employed People
ATAD	Anti-Tax Avoidance Directive
ATC	Annotated Tax Cases
ATO	Australian Taxation Office
ATP	Aid and trade provision
BAILII	British and Irish Legal Information Institute
BBC	British Broadcasting Corporation
BCA	British Constitutional Association
BCC	Butterworth's Company Cases
BEPS	Base erosion and profit shifting
Bl Comm	Blackstone's Commentaries
BSA	British South African Company
BTR	British Tax Review
Burr	Burrow's King's Bench Reports
CA 2006	Companies Act 2006
CAT	Competition Appeal Tribunal
CB	Chief Baron
CAA 2001	Capital Allowances Act 2001
CBI	Confederation of British Industry
CBNS	Common Bench Reports, New Series
CCE	Commissioners of Customs and Excise

CD	Certificate of Deposit
CEC	Commissioners of Customs and Excise
CFC	controlled foreign company/corporation
CGT	capital gains tax
CGTA	Capital Gains Tax Act 1979
Ch	Law Reports, Chancery Division
CIR	Commissioners of Inland Revenue
CJ	Chief Justice
CJCP	Chief Justice of Common Pleas
CJEU	Court of Justice of the EU
CIRA	Customs and Inland Revenue Act
CLJ	Cambridge Law Journal
CLP	Current Legal Problems
CMG	Companion of the Most Distinguished Order of St Michael and St George
CMLR	Common Market Law Reports
COM	EU Commission Communication
CPAG	Child Poverty Action Group
CRC	Customs and Revenue Commissioners
CTA	Corporation Tax Act
CTT	Capital Transfer Tax
DBCFT	destination-based cash flow tax
DEFRA	Department for Environment, Food & Rural Affairs
DSO	Distinguished Service Order
DTC	Dominion Tax Cases
DTI	Department for Trade & Industry
ECHR	European Convention on Human Rights
ECJ	European Court of Justice
ECOFIN	Economic and Financial Affairs Council
ECR	European Court Reports

EEA	European Economic Area
EEC	European Economic Community
ER	English Reports
ESC	Extra Statutory Concession
EU	European Union
Eu LR	European Law Reports
EWCA	England and Wales Court of Appeal
EWHC (Ch)	Chancery Division of the High Court of Justice of England and Wales
EWHC (Fam)	Family Division of the High Court of Justice of England and Wales
ExD	Exchequer Division
FA	Finance Act
FII	franked investment income
FRS	Financial Reporting Standard
FTT	First-tier Tribunal
GAAP	Generally Accepted Accounting Principles
GAAR	General Anti-Abuse Rule
GDP	gross domestic product
GLC	Greater London Council
GLO	group litigation order
GmbH	Gesellschaft mit beschränkter Haftung
GWR	Great Western Railway
HC	House of Commons
HKFCA	Hong Kong Court of Final Appeal
HKLRD	Hong Kong Law Reports and Digest
HL	House of Lords
HMRC	Her Majesty's Revenue and Customs
IACEW	Institute of Chartered Accountants in England and Wales
IASB	International Accounting Standards Board

IBFD	International Bureau of Fiscal Documentation
ICLQ	The International & Comparative Law Quarterly
ICTA 1970	Income and Corporation Taxes Act 1970
ICTA 1988	Income and Corporation Taxes Act 1988
IDA	International Development Act
IEA	Institute of Economic Affairs
IFRS	International Financial Reporting Standards
IFS	Institute for Fiscal Studies
ITA	Income Tax Act
ITAA 1870	Income Tax Assessment Act 1870
ITEPA 2003	Income Tax (Earnings and Pensions) Act 2003
ITLR	International Trade Law Reports
ITL Rep	International Tax Law Reports
ITTOIA 2005	Income Tax (Trading and Other Income) Act 2005
JSC	Justice of the Supreme Court
KB	Law Reports, King's Bench
LGFA 1988	Local Government Finance Act 1988
LJ Bcy	Law Journal, Bankruptcy Reports
LLC	limited liability company
LLP	Limited Liability Partnership
LMCLQ	Lloyd's Maritime and Commercial Law Quarterly
LPA 1907	Limited Partnerships Act 1907
LQR	Law Quarterly Review
LR PC	Law Reports, Privy Council Appeals
LSG	Law Society's Gazette
MLR	Modern Law Review
MP	Member of Parliament
MR	Master of the Rolls
NAFF	National Association for Freedom

NASE	National Association of Self-Employed
NATSOPA	National Society of Operative Printers and Assistants
NCT	National Chambers of Trade
NHS	National Health Service
NI	Northern Ireland Law Reports
NICs	National Insurance Contributions
NLJ	New Law Journal
NIRC	National Industrial Relations Court
NFSE	National Federation of Self-Employed and Small Businesses
NGA	National Graphical Association
NSWLR	New South Wales Law Reports
ODA	Overseas Development Agency
ODCA	Overseas Development and Cooperation Act
OECD	Organisation for Economic Co-operation and Development
OJLS	Oxford Journal of Legal Studies
OTS	Office of Tax Simplification
PA 1890	Partnership Act 1890
PAC	Public Accounts Committee
PAYE	Pay-As-You-Earn
PC	Privy Council
PE	permanent establishment
PL	Public Law
PSC	personal service company
PSI	personal services income
PTCA	Provisional Collection of Taxes Act
QB	Law Reports, Queen's Bench
R	Rex (King) or Regina (Queen)
RUPA	Revised Uniform Partnership Act
SA	société anonyme

SACF	Supreme Administrative Court of Finland
SARL	société à responsabilité limitée
SC	Session Cases
SCA	société en commandite par actions
SCM	Structured Capital Markets
sch	schedule
SCS	sociétés en commandite simple
SEPA	Sole Enterprise with Protected Assets
SIB	Stanford International Bank Limited
SLR	Statute Law Review
SLT	Scots Law Times
SNC	sociétés en nom collectif
SOGAT	Society of Graphical and Allied Trades
SpA	Società per azioni
SSAP	Statement of Standard Accounting Practice
STEP	Society of Trust and Estate Practitioners
St Tr	State Trials
Stat LR	Statute Law Review
STC	Simon's Tax Cases
STC (SCD)	Simon's Tax Cases (Special Commissioners' Decisions)
SWTI	Simon's Weekly Tax Intelligence
TC	Tax Cases
TCEA	Tribunals, Courts and Enforcement Act
TCGA	Taxation of Chargeable Gains Act
TCPA	Town and Country Planning Act
TFEU	Treaty on the Functioning of the European Union
TLR	Times Law Reports
TLRC	Tax Law Review Committee
TMIJ	Tax Management International Journal

UK	United Kingdom of Great Britain and Northern Ireland
UKFTT (TC)	UK First-tier Tribunal, Tax and Chancery Chamber
UK	United Kingdom
UKHL	UK House of Lords
UKPC	UK Privy Council
UKSC	UK Supreme Court
UKUT (TCC)	UK Upper Tribunal, Tax and Chancery Chamber
UNESCO	United Nations Educational, Scientific and Cultural Organization
UPA	Uniform Partnership Act
U Pa L Rev	University of Pennsylvania Law Review
US	United States
VAT	value added tax
V-C	Vice-Chancellor
VATA 1994	Value Added Tax Act 1994
WDM	World Development Movement
Wake Forest L Rev	Wake Forest Law Review
WTD	Worldwide Tax Daily
WLR	Weekly Law Reports

Introduction: On the Significance of Revenue Cases

JOHN SNAPE AND DOMINIC DE COGAN

T HE EXPRESSION 'the public services revenue', or 'the revenue' for short, comprises the entirety of sums raised by the government of the state through 'taxes and duties' and 'from the sale of goods and services'.[1] For the UK in 2015–16, those sums totalled £693.9 billion.[2] The UK's revenue-levying and expenditure processes are, as in all developed states, structured by legislation. That legislation is both voluminous and complex, especially for the most important category of revenue, namely taxation. Judicial decisions concerning the interpretation and application of revenue legislation, including tax, are known as revenue law cases. What makes a very small number of them 'landmarks' is the fact that, every now and again, a case contains discussions of legal and factual issues that for whatever reason become critically important resources for future debate.

The £693.9 billion of public services revenue raised in the UK in 2015–16 was expended on a range of objects,[3] all controversial to different people in different ways, in a marketised and highly conflictual public sphere. In broad terms, those who emphasise property rights,[4] balanced budgets and small government will object in principle to public spending on civil service salaries and overheads; on social welfare; on transfer payments from rich to poor;[5] on subsidies to utilities, transport undertakings, commerce, industry, and cultural institutions; to public spending on running a large deficit; to interest payments on the

---

[1] Government Resources and Accounts Act 2000, s 9; HM Treasury, *Whole of Government Accounts: Year Ended 31 March 2016* (HC 2016–17, 254) 49.

[2] *Whole of Government Accounts* (above n 1) 9; and see the (now repealed) ICTA 1988, s 45.

[3] Expenditure exceeds this, of course, but recall that 'public services revenue' does not include the proceeds of public borrowing.

[4] J Locke, 'Of Civil Government. Book II: Second Treatise' in I Shapiro et al (eds), *Two Treatises of Government* and *A Letter Concerning Toleration* (New Haven, CT, Yale University Press, 2003) 161; and see RA Epstein, *Design for Liberty: Private Property, Public Administration, and the Rule of Law* (Cambridge, MA, Harvard University Press, 2011) esp 16–18, for Locke's place in this liberal legal tradition.

[5] T Piketty, *Capital in the Twenty-First Century* (A Goldhammer trans) (Cambridge, MA, Harvard University Press, 2014) 477–78.

National Debt, and so on. Especially, they are likely to object to redistribution in the form of direct transfer payments. By contrast, those who emphasise solidarity, individual duties as opposed to rights,[6] fiscal stimuli and a large state tend to mock balanced budgets as 'economic illiteracy'. In turn they are likely to accept the various incidents of large government, not simply as a necessary evil, but as virtuous in themselves, giving 'spiritual depth to economic and political life'.[7] These incidents make society happier, the argument goes, as well as more moral. Little, if anything, could unite such divergent beliefs about what HM Government now refers to as the 'public services expenditure' of public services revenue. Even areas of expenditure that might be thought to unite them turn out to be freighted with incipient conflict: national defence (maintenance of a nuclear weapons deterrent); healthcare (scope and cost at the point of use);[8] free public education (selectiveness); state pensions (women's eligibility age); policing (staffing levels); and development aid (the relative claims of expedience and justice).

These types of intense rival political claims are mediated by revenue law in both its 'raising' and 'expending' sides. On the raising side, revenue law provides for a range of taxes (importantly, income tax, corporation tax, value added tax and national insurance contributions);[9] for the sale of governmental services, such as local authorities' charges for development and planning or social care (together totalling £35.5 billion in 2015–16); for other charges, fees and levies, such as prescription and dental service fees (£12.8 billion); and for profits on the sale of public assets, especially (in recent years) those on the sale of shares in banks nationalised since the crisis of 2007–08 (£6.3 billion).[10] On the expenditure side, revenue law helps to structure the payment of civil service salaries, the buying-in by HM Government of goods and services, the provision of subsidies and grants, the payment of interest on sovereign debt, the payment of social security benefits[11] and perhaps even the fairness and reasonableness of accounting provisions and depreciation conventions on government assets.[12] What is clear is that, in a broad understanding of revenue law, even social security law and

---

[6] Often Christian in inspiration (see, eg, Catholic Church, *Catechism*, rev edn (London, Geoffrey Chapman, 1999) paras 1939–42; and A Briggs, 'Birmingham: The Making of a Civic Gospel' in A Briggs, *Victorian Cities* (London, Penguin, 1968)), 'human solidarity' – or 'solidarism' – was secularised, notably, in Émile Durkheim's 'political sociology' (see A Ryan, *On Politics: A History of Political Thought from Herodotus to the Present* (London, Allen Lane, 2012) 983–84).

[7] Ryan (above n 6) 983, citing, *passim*, E Durkheim, *Professional Ethics and Civic Morals* (C Brookfield trans) 2nd edn (London, Routledge, 1992).

[8] For starkly contrasting passions, even about the National Health Service, see Danny Boyle's choreographed depiction of the NHS at the Olympics opening ceremony (London, 2012, available via YouTube) and media reactions to it (available at: www.bbc.co.uk/news/uk-19025686).

[9] See, eg, S Adam, J Browne and C Heady, 'Taxation in the UK' in S Adam and T Besley et al (eds), *Dimensions of Tax Design: The Mirrlees Review* (Oxford, Oxford University Press, 2010).

[10] HM Treasury (above n 2) 13, 68 (all items in this list).

[11] ibid, 49.

[12] ibid.

public procurement law may be said to fall within its ambit. Currently, however, the focus of political and societal debate on public services revenue is almost solely on taxation. Public discussion has thereby excluded or distorted a whole range of legitimate other worries,[13] as well as failing to encourage scholars from drawing relevant analogies between taxation and linked fields. Meanwhile, the issues that taxation raises have a profile greater than could have been imagined even a decade ago. For lawyers, such a transformation of a legal subject from technical preoccupation to a matter of widespread public concern is bound to raise fundamental questions. The ongoing transformation of revenue law, with its implications for tax and welfare, raises fundamental questions like no other subject. The more that discussions of tax and welfare could be linked, the better informed discussions of each would be.

These general points on the nature of revenue law may be elaborated by examining three issues that are of central importance to the book. First, the purposes served by fine-grained legal analysis of revenue law cases. Most public discussion of revenue law is framed in non-jurisprudential terms, and most contributions are not distinctively legal ones. It is important in particular to clarify what detailed legal study of tax cases can add to the study of taxation more generally. Secondly, the role of case law in revenue law and, specifically, the qualities that might give a particular case 'landmark' status. In certain other legal subjects, case law forms the bedrock of the subject itself; not so in revenue law, where instead *legislation* has centre stage. Thirdly, whether and to what extent revenue law cases may have wider significance. Tax law in particular has often been presented by lawyers, perhaps opportunistically, from the point of view of the taxpayer. Yet this is far from inevitable. How do the landmark cases on taxation throw light on questions of personal freedom and collective wellbeing respectively? If the emphasis is shifted from the former to the latter, even to a limited extent, the preoccupations of revenue law discussion change correspondingly. Indeed, these decisions may reconfigure fundamental aspects of how we understand our own subject. The strict division that can be made between tax and welfare law on a certain understanding of property rights dissipates if entitlements to benefits and liabilities to taxes are reconceived as equally dependent on law, rather than being referable to some pre-legal property entitlement. In the book as a whole, we do not adopt any editorial view on how these three questions ought to be answered. On the contrary, our objective has been to be highly tolerant of different conceptions of revenue law, accepting a certain open-endedness in the process rather than seeking to over-define the discipline. The contributions to this book illustrate this point by taking a wide variety of approaches to the three questions just set out. This variety is apparent even in respect of what is most significant in denoting 'landmark' status, although there is wide agreement that the cases selected are ones that raise perennial questions.

---

[13] eg, value-for-money in public asset sales.

I. REVENUE LAW CASES AND FINE-GRAINED LEGAL ANALYSIS

As is to be expected, tax litigation frequently engages fundamental features of revenue law.[14] The compulsory nature of taxation[15] gives rise to cases dealing with the extent of that compulsion, and thus with tax evasion and tax resistance, as well as tax avoidance. The need for legislative authority[16] when taxes are imposed throws up cases concerned with the proper role of Parliament and approaches to interpreting tax legislation. The fact that tax revenues are ultimately paid to the government, or to a governmental agency,[17] occasions cases examining both why and how government brings coercion to bear in tax matters. By contrast, hardly ever do the rights and wrongs of the purposes for which tax proceeds are applied fall for adjudication before a court, which is not the same as saying that legal philosophy has nothing to say about the application of tax revenues.

The main motivations for the detailed study of revenue law cases, and the various approaches that may be taken, are examined in the next section. Here, we merely emphasise that legal and legal historical skills are very much to the fore in the study of revenue law cases, albeit that the study of taxation in general draws on a range of disciplines. Unlike in some other areas of law, however, such skills are not the sole preserve of those who specialise as lawyers and legal historians. Tax specialists originate in a range of disciplinary backgrounds – including law, accounting, economics, history and politics[18] – but they are united by their focus on the close reading and interpretation of legislative texts. Besides, it is not only a lawyer's understanding of binding precedent that informs a contextual understanding of tax cases, but also a sense of how those cases relate to wider historical and political ideas. This, in turn, means that, in revenue law, legal analysis may validly and valuably be undertaken by those who are tax specialists but whose home discipline is not law.

In the legal analysis of revenue law cases, vivid impressions of the implications of the compulsory nature of taxation run like a thread through judicial pronouncements. Indeed, state compulsion has possibly greater resonances in tax law than in any other area of revenue law, except perhaps for those rare occasions when the conditions placed upon welfare claimants come to wider notice.[19] One consolation with tax law is that compulsion is grounded in its

---

[14] See G Loutzenhiser, *Tiley's Revenue Law*, 8th edn (Oxford, Hart Publishing, 2016) 3–7, esp discussion of *Re Eurig* (1998) 165 DLR (4th) 1, 10.

[15] eg *Armour Packing Co v United States* 209 US 56 (1908); *Brocklebank Ltd v R* [1925] 1 KB 52, CA; *Congreve v Home Office* [1976] 1 QB 629, CA.

[16] Bill of Rights 1689, Art 4; V Thuronyi, *Comparative Tax Law* (The Hague, Kluwer Law, 2003) 70–71.

[17] *Armour Packing Co v United States* (above n 15); Thuronyi (above n 16) 45.

[18] See the contributions to M Lamb et al (eds), *Taxation: An Interdisciplinary Approach to Research* (Oxford, Oxford University Press, 2005).

[19] We owe the observation about conditions imposed on welfare claimants to Shani Wijetilaka, one of Dominic de Cogan's research students.

statutory character, parliamentary consent being the necessary and sufficient condition under which taxes are levied, exemptions detected and reliefs afforded. The volume and intricacy of this statute law contrasts strikingly with the wide administrative discretions conferred on government officials in other areas of revenue law. That said, the contrast between tax and other areas of revenue law may be more apparent than real, since new tax legislation is introduced with alarming frequency and HM Revenue and Customs (HMRC) is closely involved in its design. In any case, it is undeniable that tax legislation exhibits a distinctive complexity and instability. Statutory complexity is widely believed to invite the manipulation of exemptions and reliefs, such as to prevent a tax liability arising in the first place (successful tax avoidance).[20] It is also reported to invite non-compliance, such as to encourage non-satisfaction of a liability that has already arisen (tax evasion).[21] Statutory complexity and instability offends against Adam Smith's certainty maxim for the prudential compliance of tax legislation with natural law.[22] It may also offend, directly or indirectly, against Smith's equity maxim, which in turn may give rise to a third category of behaviour typically described as principled 'tax resistance'.[23] However speculative some of these claims may be, the potential links between Smith's maxims are certainly striking.

In many of the near-legends associated with principled refusal to pay various levies (Lady Godiva, Wat Tyler, Beatrice Harraden, Mahatma Gandhi, and so on),[24] the conflict between equity and certainty has played a significant part. There is, for example, the strange story of a Newcastle old-age pensioner, Mr Kempton Bunton,[25] who in 1961 refused to pay for a television licence on the basis that it constituted a form of indirect taxation.[26] His objection was one of regressivity, that the tax was unfair as taking a greater proportion of pensioners' income than would have been taken from people less poor.[27] When, subsequently, Mr Bunton (or his son) removed Francisco de Goya's portrait of the Duke of Wellington from the National Gallery, it was with the apparent

---

[20] L Oats, A Miller and E Mulligan, *Principles of International Taxation*, 6th edn (London, Bloomsbury Professional, 2017) 14–16.

[21] ibid.

[22] RH Campbell et al (eds), *Adam Smith: An Inquiry into the Nature and Causes of the Wealth of Nations*, 2 vols (Carmel, IN, Liberty Fund, 1981) II, 827 (V.ii.b.7). See J Snape, *The Political Economy of Corporation Tax: Theory, Values and Law Reform* (Oxford, Hart Publishing, 2011) 198.

[23] See the wide-ranging compilation in DM Gross, *We Won't Pay! A Tax Resistance Reader* (North Charleston, SC, Createspace, 2008) and RD Huret, *American Tax Resisters* (Cambridge, MA, Harvard University Press, 2014).

[24] Gross (above n 23).

[25] A Travis, 'Revealed: 1961 Goya "Theft" from National Gallery was a Family Affair' *The Guardian* (30 November 2012), available at www.theguardian.com/artanddesign/2012/nov/30/1961-goya-crime-national-gallery. BBC R4, 'Kempton and the Duke' Afternoon Drama (21 November 2017), details available at www.bbc.co.uk/programmes/b06flmdp.

[26] As to which, see *Congreve v Home Office* (above n 15).

[27] T Grant, *Jeremy Hutchinson's Case Histories* (London, John Murray, 2015) ch 7; A Hirsch, *The Duke of Wellington Kidnapped: The Incredible True Story of the Art Heist That Shocked a Nation* (Berkeley CA, Counterpoint, 2016).

purpose of eventually redressing this particular balance.[28] So compulsoriness does not always seem to outweigh the combination of regressivity and volatility that offends the tax resister. This was so with the failure of the community charge, introduced by the Local Government Finance Act 1988 (LGFA 1988).[29] There, civil unrest was directed, not against taxation in general, but specifically against the community charge as a form of poll tax. Nor, in a different way, can compulsion always withstand the intricate tax-avoidance activities of multinational groups.[30] By definition, though, what compulsoriness must withstand is tax evasion. All of these activities – tax avoidance, tax evasion and tax resistance – variously illustrate the *absence* of a common sense that taxes in general, or particular taxes, are virtuous in themselves so as to give to political and economic life the spiritual depth referred to at the start.[31]

The principle that taxes are imposed by legislation, rather than by executive fiat, has two clear implications in the legal analysis of revenue law cases and it also raises at least one deep ambiguity. First, the principle makes legislation – statute law created by Parliament – foundational to revenue law. This ancient constitutional principle[32] was at issue in the *Case of Ship Money (R v Hampden)*,[33] discussed by Michael Braddick in chapter one. Charles I, having previously been assured by the judges that the principle admitted of some exception, levied contributions by royal prerogative for the provision of ships for national defence. In chapter four, Martin Daunton analyses the story of *Bowles v Bank of England*,[34] which carried the principle to its logical conclusion and, in doing so, established beyond doubt the legislative basis of taxation. The principle remains relevant even today to supporters of small government who deplore any attempt to impose taxes without what they regard as sufficient parliamentary involvement. Secondly, the principle of parliamentary taxation expresses the importance of representative consent to taxation and, in so doing, places statutory interpretation at the heart of cases on revenue law. By the same token, it discourages judicial activism. *WT Ramsay Ltd v CIR*,[35] discussed by John Snape in chapter ten and one of the most famous of all revenue law cases, has always occupied an uneasy constitutional position. The case sets out a judicial approach to striking down benefits from tax avoidance but is *Ramsay* a case on statutory interpretation only, as the judicial committee of the House of Lords

---

[28] 'The case became so famous that a copy of the picture appeared in a 1962 Bond film, with Sean Connery remarking: "So there it is," when he sees it in Dr No's Jamaican lair. It was actually in a cupboard in Kempton Bunton's council flat in Newcastle' (Travis (above n 25)).

[29] D Butler, A Adonis and T Travers, *Failure in British Government: The Politics of the Poll Tax* (Oxford, Oxford University Press, 1994).

[30] Oats, Miller and Mulligan (above n 20) ch 19.

[31] See text around n 7 above.

[32] Thuronyi (above n 16) 70.

[33] *Case of Ship Money (R v Hampden)* (1637) 3 St Tr 825 (see ch 1 below).

[34] *Bowles v Bank of England* [1913] 1 Ch 57.

[35] *WT Ramsay Ltd v CIR* (1981) 54 TC 101.

in *Barclays Mercantile Business Finance Ltd*[36] seemed to affirm, or a constitutional exception to parliamentary control of taxation? Moreover, despite the unease, judges have shown a certain willingness to develop principles as opposed to applying statute law robotically. *De Beers Consolidated Mines Ltd v Howe (Surveyor of Taxes)*,[37] discussed by John Avery Jones and Johann Hattingh in chapter three, is a remarkable instance of statute leaving a foundational concept – that of the 'residence' of companies – for determination by the judges. In doing so, the judicial committee based its decision entirely upon the case law of lower courts, one case drawing on German jurisprudence. Again, the Lords Justices in *Conservative and Unionist Central Office v Burrell (HM Inspector of Taxes)*,[38] which Victor Baker discusses in chapter twelve, took a similarly audacious approach. They held – creatively – that an unincorporated 'body of persons', lacking the mutual undertakings of members, created for non-business purposes, and holding funds subject to a mandate for certain purposes, was not liable to corporation tax. These judicial interpretations of the legislative basis of taxation are important but are hardly obscure.

A deeper question, though, involves our underlying conception of revenue law: as positive law akin to any other type of legislative regulation or as something much deeper, something fundamental to the very fabric of the state itself. There is a rather complex relationship between these conceptions and the ideas of small and large government aired at the beginning. On the one hand, proponents of large government tend to regard revenue law as special in the sense of being an irreducible part of the environment within which individual lives are possible. On the other hand, proponents of small government often emphasise the restrictions that revenue law places on supposedly natural property rights. Curiously, on a practical level, this leads the former to treat tax legislation as *normal* in the sense that it ought to be interpreted purposively in the manner of any other legislation, and the latter to treat it as *exceptional* and deserving of a literalistic interpretation that provides particular protection to property rights. A number of the cases discussed in this book track these issues in a manner that acknowledges the late-twentieth century transformation of the state. In *CIR v Commerzbank*[39] and the litigation of which it formed part, discussed by Philip Baker in chapter fifteen, Mummery J ostensibly took a purposive approach to the interpretation of a double taxation agreement. In chapter sixteen, Philip Ridd contends that *Pepper (HM Inspector of Taxes) v Hart and Others*[40] was the first case to validate a purposive approach to the construction of domestic tax legislation, an aspect of the case that in his view may be even more significant than its statement of the basis on which a court may have recourse to the

---

[36] *Barclays Mercantile Business Finance Ltd v Mawson* [2004] UKHL 51; [2005] STC 1.
[37] *De Beers Consolidated Mines Ltd v Howe (Surveyor of Taxes)* (1906) 5 TC 198.
[38] *Conservative and Unionist Central Office v Burrell (HM Inspector of Taxes)* (1981) 55 TC 671.
[39] *CIR v Commerzbank* [1990] STC 285.
[40] *Pepper (HM Inspector of Taxes) v Hart and Others* (1992) 65 TC 421.

parliamentary record. *Barclays Mercantile*, as discussed by John Vella in chapter eighteen, is a confirmation of the idea that *Ramsay* is really about purposive interpretation.

For the legal analysis of revenue law cases, the fact that taxes are, by definition, paid[41] to the government, or to an agency thereof, is their most obvious public law characteristic. Considerable numbers of revenue law cases are concerned with *how* and *why* a taxing authority exercises its coercive powers. What Smith notoriously called 'the frequent visits, and the odious examination of the tax-gatherers'[42] feature heavily in some important cases on revenue law-enforcement procedure.[43] The chief interest of such cases to an economist might lie in what they incidentally say about the efficiency, or cost-effectiveness, of the tax or taxes concerned. As the subject of *legal* analysis, though, a close reading of them provides much interpretative insight about the tensions around the revenue discussed at the beginning. An individualistic attitude inclines to taking Smith's comments at face value; at least certain types of solidaristic attitude do not. Either way, the nexus of government and subject is crucial and the incapacity or other failure of government and its agencies to enforce levies eventually spells the end of the state. This necessity of taxes to the state's continued existence seems to be WH Auden's burden *in The Fall of Rome* (1937). Though the poem had contemporary resonances, for us, it neatly pinpoints the dependence of the state and of political order on continued flows of successfully-raised revenue. The poet depicts a collapsing regime, with a people's morale decaying ('Fantastic grow the evening gowns'), as '[a]bsconding tax defaulters' are pursued by '[a]gents of the Fisc'[44] along '[t]he sewers of provincial towns'.[45]

These points came to the fore in *R v CIR, ex parte National Federation of Self-Employed and Small Businesses Ltd*,[46] discussed by Dominic de Cogan in chapter eleven. It concerned a complaint about the failure by one of the then revenue departments, the Inland Revenue, to enforce tax obligations even-handedly as between employed and self-employed people. The interesting feature of this case is that it can be seen in two different lights. In an individualistic light, the complaint was that the Revenue was acting oppressively against self-employed people and ought not to. In a solidaristic light,[47] the problem was

---

[41] Payment is significant and explains why, though an economist might think of inflation as a tax, because it 'appropriates resources to the government', inflation is not a tax in legal analysis (see Thuronyi (above n 16) 45).

[42] Campbell (above n 22) II, 827 (V.ii.b.6).

[43] eg, *R v CIR and Quinlan (ex parte Rossminster Ltd and Others)* (1979) 52 TC 160.

[44] Literally, basket, purse, *etc* (OED).

[45] E Mendelson (ed), *WH Auden: Selected Poems* (London, Faber & Faber, 1979) 183. The implication, too, is that the sewers themselves exist only because of (typically local) tax revenues.

[46] *R v CIR, ex parte National Federation of Self-Employed and Small Businesses Ltd* (1981) 55 TC 133.

[47] M Loughlin, *Public Law and Political Theory* (Oxford, Clarendon Press, 1992) 110–11 traces the translation of solidarism or solidarity into French public law. See, too, Pontifical Council for Justice and Peace, *Compendium of the Social Doctrine of the Church* (London, Burns and Oates, 2004) 98–101.

that employed people were not pulling their weight and that the Revenue was colluding with them.

While the chosen application of tax proceeds to further one public purpose rather than another is almost entirely a matter of political judgement (whether or not informed by economic analysis) there is at least one revenue law case in which that political judgement has been called in question. This is *R v Secretary of State for Foreign and Commonwealth Affairs, ex parte World Development Movement*,[48] also known as 'the *Pergau Dam* case'.[49] As Abimbola Olowofoyeku explains in chapter seventeen, 'the Divisional Court held that the [UK] government's decision' to apply revenue in the funding of the eponymous dam in Malaysia 'was unlawful, causing the UK government considerable embarrassment and diplomatic and international trade difficulties'. However, even in *Pergau Dam*, the judge's discussion of the issues was confined to whether a given purpose was a proper one. It could not range more widely over questions of possible alternative purposes. Controversies over the full range of alternative purposes are irreducibly political. Judges cannot address these issues, not so much because of the issues' political nature, but because, unlike Parliament and HM Treasury, judges have no funds to distribute.[50] Along similar lines, the ultimate decision whether taxes are efficient to collect is a political question, whereas whether revenue collectors acted properly in a particular case is a legal one. Whether the redistribution of societal goods is a proper purpose for taxation is a political question, whereas whether one taxpayer is liable to higher-rate income tax, and another entitled to universal credit, are legal ones. Whether taxation should always have revenue raising as its primary function or whether there are certain situations in which a regulatory function may take precedence are political questions, whereas whether the provisions of a particular environmental tax constitute unlawful state aid or whether a particular good falls within one or other customs classification, are legal ones. Whether taxes should be used for macroeconomic policy purposes, or only for very limited purposes are political questions, whereas whether a local authority is entitled to fix rates of local taxation for ideological reasons is a legal one. The point is that the legal questions in each case are a function of earlier political judgements, or to be more precise the expression of those judgements in revenue statutes. As Snape has argued in detail,[51] this is fundamental to a proper understanding of revenue law as a patchwork of political judgements reduced to legislative form.

---

[48] *R v Secretary of State for Foreign and Commonwealth Affairs, ex parte World Development Movement* [1995] 1 All ER 611.

[49] See T Prosser, *The Economic Constitution* (Oxford, Oxford University Press, 2014) 114–16.

[50] '[T]he judiciary', writes Martin Loughlin, 'acquires its legitimacy from an independence derived from its own powerlessness', and he invokes both Alexander Hamilton, in *Federalist No 87*, and Montesquieu in *The Spirit of the Laws*: 'The judiciary … has no influence over either the sword or the purse; no direction either of the strength or of the wealth of the society; and can take no active resolution whatever' (Hamilton) and '[o]f the three powers of which we have spoken, that of judging is in some fashion, null' (Montesquieu) (see M Loughlin, *Foundations of Public Law* (Oxford, Oxford University Press, 2010) 454, fn 71).

[51] Snape, *The Political Economy of Corporation Tax* (above n 22) esp ch 5.

II. LANDMARK QUALITIES AND REVENUE LAW CASES

The role of the judge in a revenue law case, as most would concede, is primarily to interpret legislation in the light of the facts found. Accordingly, to describe a case as a 'landmark' suggests either that there was something special about the interpretative insights of the judges who decided it, or that there was something within the judgments that inspired special interpretative insights in subsequent cases. This last point, as elaborated, has at least three important resonances, to which we will shall return shortly. It is worth considering, though, how observers' perspectives on revenue law cases may be conditioned by their beliefs about the nature of the revenue and its relation to tax law.

Revenue law cases, as already noted, can be studied with skills developed in various disciplines. For skilled people, personal beliefs about the revenue and its relationship with tax law may be no less important than their study of the cases and the ways in which that study is undertaken. A scholar's antagonism to some aspect of a revenue law case, whether to one or more of the parties, the decision, the political consequences or something else, may be the precise reason for their interest in the case. A historian, or historically minded lawyer, writing about a constitutionally significant case, such as *Ship-Money* or *Bowles*, may personally deplore the values articulated in it, if not the conduct of the parties. Snape found himself in this position (see chapter ten) in trying to weigh the merits of the losing side's arguments in *Ramsay*, arguments that he finds deeply unattractive. By contrast, a revenue law specialist seeking to use a case as the basis of an argument before a court or tribunal will be more interested in the doctrinal insights the case offers than any moral ambiguity. Tax accountants engaged in compliance work will simply want to know whether a particular case supports or undermines a particular accounting treatment. For most purposes, however, an understanding of the context of revenue law issues is everything and the imparter of context is history. It was Sir Winston Churchill who once told a gathering of professionals that '[t]he longer you can look back, the farther you can look forward. This is not [he continued] a philosophical or political argument – any oculist will tell you this is true'.[52] To lack this historical background is to have a rule but not to grasp why it exists in the first place.[53] A sense of history, as Churchill went on to say, provides people with a 'greater ... sense of duty ... to ... the society of which they are members'.[54] It may, for sure,

---

[52] WS Churchill, 'The Royal College of Physicians. March 2, 1944' in R Rhodes James (ed), *Winston S. Churchill His Complete Speeches 1897–1963*, vol 7 (New York, Chelsea House Publishers, 1974) 6895, 6897.

[53] 'Current politicians are so awful ... because ... they've never seriously studied history. Whereas the thing that makes Churchill great is the fact that he's a great historian' (David Starkey discussing the performance of Chloe Smith, MP (Economic Secretary to the Treasury) in a television interview with Jeremy Paxman on 26 June 2012, available via YouTube (*BBC R4, Loose Ends* (30 June 2012), details available at www.bbc.co.uk/programmes/b01k9lvl.

[54] Churchill (above n 52) 6897.

involve reflecting on documents and events, such as Malcolm Gammie's study of the House of Lords appeal files (see chapter six), or it may involve reflecting on the history of ideas. Many of the contributions to the book strive to do both.

To return to the role of the revenue judge, her work is peculiarly sensitive both to factual nuance and legislative complexity, but is also likely to be informed with one or other of the two views of the revenue with which we began. The primarily interpretative role of the judge means that her priority is to resolve disputes in the light of the legislation and, perhaps less obviously, of the factual circumstances that legislative provisions show to be relevant. *Zim Properties Ltd v Proctor*,[55] discussed by David Salter in chapter fourteen, is a good example of a case that involves a combination of highly abstract legislative provisions and abstruse facts, and a judge – Warner J – willing to extend the scope of the relevant tax by adopting a particular statutory interpretation. The starting point of *Zim* is the kind of statutory wording[56] that seems to 'dance before ... [the] eyes in meaningless procession: cross-reference to cross-reference, exception upon exception – couched in abstract terms that offer no handle to seize hold of'.[57] Moreover, the facts to which *Zim* related seem far removed from anything the legislative wording, or the purpose of the legislature, could have envisaged. The case illustrates how, in relation to the conceptual structure of taxation, the judge is engaged in what is fundamentally a 'bottom-up' exercise. The particular dispute is resolved, leaving it to the tax authority, academics and other commentators to argue over whether the ruling supports or impedes a rational understanding of the tax in question. All this is far removed from case in fields governed purely or largely by common law, where judges are deeply conscious that their decision on the facts may have the consequence of refining an existing rule or even creating a new one. In such a context, the judge brings to mind myriad case law precedents, winnowing *rationes* from *dicta* uttered in countless draughty courtrooms, far scattered in time and space. The contrast in conceptions of the judicial role is palpable and has set the culture of revenue law apart even from that of other lawyers. 'I still recall', a famous revenue judge once wrote,

> the mingled horror and pity which crept into my tutor's voice when commenting on the news that I was ... going into tax chambers ... [N]o respectable lawyer would study tax ... It is ... a subject for eccentrics, weeds and swots ... An English lawyer is a man who has studied the English *common law*.[58]

---

[55] *Zim Properties Ltd v Proctor* (1985) 58 TC 371.

[56] In what is now s 21(1) TCGA 1992.

[57] Judge Learned Hand, 'Thomas Walter Swan' (1947) 57 *Yale Law Journal* 167, 169.

[58] HH Monroe, 'Fiscal Statutes: A Drafting Disaster' [1979] *BTR* 265, 271, quoted, slightly adapted in R Kerridge, 'The Taxation of Emoluments from Offices and Employments' (1992) 108 *LQR* 433, 458. In the original, the second sentence precedes the first as quoted, and Monroe's apparently sexist language is actually designed to caricature English institutional attitudes of which, '[a]s an Irishman', he was himself wary (ibid).

Furthermore, the specificity and complexity of the revenue judge's task may lead one to conclude that the results to which it leads are completely, or virtually completely, incomprehensible. John Prebble would have us believe this, arguing that even revenue lawyers may be baffled by revenue legislation, creating, as it does, artificial concepts such as 'chargeable gains', 'deemed disposals' and so forth, which are incapable of being understood except by reading across from other similarly artificial concepts.[59] Bret Bogenschneider invokes Ludwig Wittgenstein,[60] to argue on the contrary that 'tax law is just as comprehensible as it ought to be', since, '[f]or those that [*sic*] speak the language, it provides the basis for legal actions'.[61] However, each of these arguments is made solely in relation to the logical potential of unmediated legislative texts. Snape prefers to assess the judicial interpretation of tax legislation in the broader context of the function of tax legislation within the state.[62] He argues that judges disposed to take a somewhat collectivist view of taxation are open to purposive construction, while those of an individualist bent opt for the more literal. A different type of response (because, unlike Snape's, which is interpretative only, it is a normative one) is to observe that the statutory nature of taxation law places a special onus on those responsible for designing and drafting legislation to create and maintain coherence.[63] If no existing institutions are capable of ensuring this coherence, it is argued, they ought to be established. This line of thought is significant because it attacks directly the bottom-up mode of reasoning in revenue law, while absolving judges from primary responsibility for it.

In any case, we maintain that 'landmark' status either implies the articulation of distinctive interpretative judicial insights, or that the judicial opinions expressed have inspired special interpretative insights in subsequent cases. What we do not imply, at least in any unguarded sense, is that any of the cases in this book form the basis of a *self-contained* common law or equitable doctrine. This may seem obvious given the statutory basis of revenue law, but the often-discursive approach of judges in revenue cases has often disguised the fact. The traditional free-ranging style of judicial pronouncements in legal systems based on the English common law does not differ greatly depending on whether common law or statutory interpretation is at stake. For example, there is the old question of whether *Ramsay* is simply a case on statutory interpretation

---

[59] J Prebble, 'Why Is Tax Law Incomprehensible?' [1994] *BTR* 380; J Prebble, 'Ectopia, Tax Law and International Taxation' [1997] *BTR* 383.

[60] In L Wittgenstein, *Philosophical Investigations* (trans GEM Anscombe et al), 4th edn (Chichester, Wiley-Blackwell, 2009) *passim*.

[61] BN Bogenschneider, 'Wittgenstein on Why Tax Law is Comprehensible' [2015] *BTR* 252, 256.

[62] J Snape, 'Legal Interpretation of Tax Law: United Kingdom' in RF van Brederode and R Krever (eds), *Legal Interpretation of Tax Law*, 2nd edn (The Hague, Wolters Kluwer, 2017).

[63] A particularly forceful variant on this argument was put forward by Peter Harris in the unpublished paper 'A 200-page Income Tax Constitution for the UK?' presented at the conference 'Celebrating the End of the Rewrite' (HM Treasury, October 2010), available at www.law.cam.ac.uk/people/academic/pa-harris/39.

or whether it contains an anomalous judicial doctrine for combating tax avoidance. The failure to distil a correct answer to this question has not been for lack of trying; it would be hard to overstate the significance of the case within the culture of tax specialists. Even among non-specialists, as Judith Freedman has written, the case raises glimmers of recognition.[64] *Ramsay* has been as cited, as scrutinised and rationalised, over the three decades since it was decided, as any common law decision. Despite this, or perhaps because of it, the true meaning of the case remains highly contested. Indeed, this contested quality is in part exacerbated by the differences in background beliefs and experiences discussed above. For example, it is inherent in the nature of a landmark case that Ridd states of *Pepper v Hart* that 'it was the first occasion on which the House of Lords recognised that purposive interpretation had superseded literal interpretation in relation to tax cases',[65] whereas de Cogan would tend to emphasise the continuities in interpretative approach between this and previous House of Lords decisions. The former is a valuable descriptive point for which evidence exists; the latter is an interpretative argument which can be argued against but not disproven. Both scholars are discussing the same case, and the same set of facts, but they cannot even agree on the character of the case's importance. This in turn offers an indication why the case is worth reading, re-reading and arguing over; in other words, why it is a landmark. Legal analysis draws on many experiences and understandings. Neither law-in-context nor analytical jurisprudence is inferior. The importance of the rigorously analytical mode adopted by Geoffrey Morse, writing about *Mallalieu v Drummond (HM Inspector of Taxes)*[66] in chapter thirteen, cannot be overstated at a time when legal science and legal education is threatened by a move away from the close scrutiny of legal texts. Moreover, even if a particular case is widely agreed to be seminally important, different commentators will argue for different aspects of the case as betokening landmark status. Even while doing so, some may even acknowledge reasons why the case should not be considered a landmark at all! Our editorial role, with advice from John Avery Jones and Chantal Stebbings, has not involved us in instructing contributors on what perspective they ought to adopt on any such matters. Indeed, the common denominator in the cases explored here, at the highest level of abstraction, may be that they all contain some 'breath of … inspiration'[67] for special insights in later cases. They are precisely the cases that provoke enduring disagreement on what the interpretative insights of the judges

---

[64] J Freedman, 'Interpreting Tax Statutes: Tax Avoidance and the Intention of Parliament' (2007) 123 *LQR* 53.

[65] See 357, this volume.

[66] *Mallalieu v Drummond (HM Inspector of Taxes)* (1983) 57 TC 330.

[67] The reference is to 'A breath of our inspiration/Is the life of each generation', from the 'Ode' (1873), by Arthur O'Shaughnessy (see, in part, A Quiller-Couch (ed), *The Oxford Book of English Verse 1250–1918*, 2nd edn (Oxford, Clarendon Press, 1939) 1006), as set by Elgar, in *The Music Makers* (Birmingham, 1912).

mean, why they do so, and the extent of their significance. Landmark cases tend to be especially difficult and intractable, and therefore to stand in need of full scholarly elucidation.

From what has been said we might draw out at least four further intriguing resonances. First, because tax statutes are so often replaced or modified, a landmark cannot depend for its status on whether the legislation under consideration remains unrepealed. *Ship-Money* is a landmark case, not because of what it decided – because it was statutorily reversed in 1641 – but because of what it came to stand for, and for the range of issues canvassed in detail in its pages. The *Ship-Money* judges came to epitomise a judiciary supine in the face of royal levies and the case was a totemic warning to succeeding judges minded to help the Crown's argument along in revenue cases. Snape senses, for instance, that judges' unwillingness to interpose a judicial view of profit-measurement on prevailing accounting practice still owes something to institutional memory of the *Ship-Money* judges.[68] This is notwithstanding the fact that judgments such as Pennycuick J's, in *Odeon Associated Theatres Ltd v Jones (HM Inspector of Taxes)*[69] – as discussed by Judith Freedman in chapter nine – seem to leave open the possibility of judicial intervention. *Ship-Money*, like other landmarks, can only be appreciated from a distance. That distance is such that only history offers.[70]

Secondly, the conflictual and politicised nature of taxation supports our view that landmark status cannot depend, as with certain private law cases, on being universally admired. Universal admiration would, on the basis of what has been said above, deprive a case of landmark status all on its own. Far from being a landmark, it would simply decide a point, which in the context of a field of law based mainly on statute is likely to be mundane. There would be no point revisiting the case over and over again. It would be enough to cite it and move on. Thirdly, the deep variation among our authors not only on the substantive legal issues but on how to tell the stories contained within the cases is, so to speak, a design feature of the book rather than a defect. The fact that their approaches are not the only possible ones, and may even provoke strong reactions in some readers, is intimately linked to our arguments for the landmark status of the cases covered. To put the same point the other way around, a book entitled *Landmark Cases in Revenue Law* is, in a profound sense, the ideal forum in which to showcase the enormous variety of opinions, interests, perspectives and methods used by revenue law specialists. So, then, no one should be surprised to find John Pearce, as a former member of the Office of the Solicitor of Inland Revenue, find hidden subtleties in a case often referred to only as the origin

---

[68] Snape, *The Political Economy of Corporation Tax* (above n 22) 95.

[69] *Odeon Associated Theatres Ltd v Jones (HM Inspector of Taxes)* (1971) 48 TC 257.

[70] That said, revenue law's role in the state's very existence means revenue law is much older than many other areas of law. Even income tax is a good century and a bit older than the tort of negligence and it is by no means the oldest tax. Nevertheless, the cases covered in this book are newer than in almost any other *Landmarks* book.

of the definition of 'office' for income tax purposes.[71] *Great Western Railway Company v Bater (Surveyor of Taxes)*,[72] discussed in chapter five, turns out to provide a lucid explanation of the original significance of the schedules of income tax. As we discover, schedules did not so much classify income according to its type as provide the very basis of the tax-collection mechanism. No less insightful, though different, is Olowofoyeku's analysis of *Pergau Dam*. Olowofoyeku is an academic tax and public lawyer, whose meticulous analysis of the case draws on a range of social and political source materials. Ann Mumford (see chapter seven) judiciously and insightfully assesses an impressive variety of source material, in discussing what might otherwise have seemed a rather dry case on the quantification of the value transferred for estate duty purposes, *CIR v Crossman*.[73] The chapter refers, for instance, to the journal *Business History*, to an official history of the concern whose shares were the subject of the case, to the background of the protagonists, and to cultural histories of the area in which the brewing company's premises were situated. Finally, it follows from the contentiousness of many of these cases, and also from the contributors' diverse approaches, that readers may not necessarily find here their own particular favourite. A notable absentee, for example, is *CIR v His Grace the Duke of Westminster*.[74] On this case, our editorial decision was that the jurisprudential controversies to which it gave rise were best discussed in relation to those cases that 'glossed' it. Rather than being the subject of its own chapter, therefore, the case is discussed in chapters nine and eighteen, in relation to those cases most closely shaped by it, *Ramsay* and *Barclays Mercantile*.

III. THE WIDER SIGNIFICANCE OF REVENUE LAW CASES

Revenue law cases offer a focal point for the nexus between collective wellbeing and personal freedom. How broadly and deeply collective wellbeing is conceived relates, in some sense, to the breadth and depth of a conception of personal freedom. The reader will appreciate immediately that this relationship is the subject matter of centuries of legal and political thought relating, first, to the interplay of the necessity of raising revenue and the subject's constitutional rights, and secondly, to the nature and scope of revenue law. The position that an observer takes on these fundamental questions is likely to inform her views on whether landmark cases show that revenue law is best conceived as a public law subject, as private law, or whether indeed such dichotomies are best avoided altogether.

---

[71] ITEPA 2003, s 5(1).

[72] *Great Western Railway Company v Bater (Surveyor of Taxes)* (1922) 8 TC 231.

[73] *CIR v Crossman* (1936) 15 ATC 94.

[74] *CIR v the Duke of Westminster* [1936] AC 1. See A Likhovski, 'Tax Law and Public Opinion: Explaining IRC v Duke of Westminster' in J Tiley (ed), *Studies in the History of Tax Law: Volume 2* (Oxford, Hart Publishing, 2007).

Despite the intellectual traditions just alluded to, the ability of revenue law to pinpoint the nexus between personal freedom and collective wellbeing has not been as widely appreciated as might be expected. The concept of a tax, as analysed earlier, requires political institutions to hold resources in a fiduciary capacity, in the absence of immediately identifiable beneficiaries, and on the basis of a general accountability to the nation's representatives. The echo of these arrangements in charity law, where private persons (trustees or corporations) hold resources to be applied for 'public purposes', is instructive.[75] With both tax proceeds and charitable funds, the purposes and the mechanics of the arrangement are thought to require the clearest justifications and also the closest scrutiny. The possible justifications for the accumulation of resources by HM Government are, in effect, the justifications for the controversial range of objects discussed at the beginning. Note that few, if any, of those objects straightforwardly satisfy the conception of what economists refer to as a 'public good'.[76] Nevertheless 'public money for public goods'[77] is a slogan that is currently gaining ground among populist elements. It appeals in particular to those on the libertarian Right because one way of reading it is to strip back the functions of government, and hence the purposes of taxation, to a bare minimum. It also appeals, though somewhat less so, to those on the hard Left because, suitably widened, the slogan can alternatively be read as justifying radical redistribution through the tax system. Most governing parties have deliberately shunned these stark alternatives:[78] as is well known, public and private purposes have become closely intertwined. Sol Picciotto sees deeper problems in this state of affairs, writing that 'tax "planning" has become routinized; and … [multinational groups] in particular can take advantage both of competition [*sc* from states] to offer incentives to attract investment, and opportunities for international avoidance'.[79] This conflict was at the root of *Cadbury Schweppes and Cadbury Schweppes Overseas*,[80] discussed by Christiana HJI Panayi in chapter nineteen. *Cadbury Schweppes* was the case in which an Ireland-based subsidiary

---

[75] Indeed, in traditional Chancery-speak, charitable trusts are often referred to as 'public purpose trusts', which are in general valid, in contrast with 'private purpose trusts', in general void (see J McGhee (ed), *Snell's Equity*, 33rd edn (London, Sweet & Maxwell, 2017)).

[76] D Hume, *A Treatise of Human Nature* (first published 1739–40; Oxford, Clarendon Press, 1978) 538–39. See also S Picciotto, *Regulating Global Corporate Capitalism* (Cambridge, Cambridge University Press, 2011) 77: 'Public goods are said to have either or both of two characteristics: they are (a) non-rival in consumption (enjoyment by one person does not detract from enjoyment by another); and (b) non-excludable (it is inherently difficult or impossible to restrict their use or consumption'. See, further, HJ Kiesling, *Taxation and Public Goods: A Welfare-Economic Critique of Tax Policy Analysis* (Ann Arbor, MI, University of Michigan Press, 1992).

[77] See, eg, DEFRA, 'Once-in-a-Generation Opportunity to Shape Future Farming Policy' (London, 27 February 2018), available at www.gov.uk/government/news/once-in-a-generation-opportunity-to-shape-future-farming-policy.

[78] Perhaps responding to the imperatives of 'ordoliberalism' (see J Snape, 'Stability and its Significance in UK Tax Policy and Legislation' [2015] *BTR* 561, 566).

[79] Picciotto (above n 76) 452.

[80] Case C-196/04 *Cadbury Schweppes and Cadbury Schweppes Overseas* [2006] ECR I-7995.

of Cadbury Schweppes in the UK had invoked the fundamental freedoms of the EU treaties, both to claim the benefit of Ireland's very low corporate income tax rate and to shelter group income with a non-UK source. In ruling unfavourably on the validity of the UK's controlled foreign companies' (CFC) regime,[81] the European Court of Justice sought to balance two considerations. The first was the rightness of 'the specific objective of such a restriction', namely 'to prevent conduct involving the creation of wholly artificial arrangements' that did not reflect 'economic reality'. The second was the right of a 'controlled company' actually to establish itself in any EU Member State and to carry on 'genuine economic activities there'.[82] The outcome was a classic technocratic 'fudge'[83] and it has won few supporters either on the libertarian Right or hard Left. At least to some, *Cadbury Schweppes* might be seen as an exemplar of a 'centrist' orthodoxy in which the big controversies around the proper expenditure of revenues were progressively ignored in favour of technocratic arguments over matters of detail and process. In somewhat different ways, the orthodoxy has been accepted by both left-and right- of-centre political parties over recent decades. In the UK, for example, both the New Labour administration and the Conservative–Liberal Democrat Coalition had long accepted the inevitability of so-called 'public–private partnerships' in the provision of public services. The orthodoxy has, though, been decisively rejected on both the populist Right and the populist Left. Britain's Labour Party, under the leadership of Jeremy Corbyn, has called for the bringing 'in-house', that is, the renationalisation, of public services currently supplied under the public–private partnership model, though few think this realistic.[84] On the other side of the Atlantic, the 2010 Patient Protection and Affordable Care Act ('Obamacare') was created firmly in the spirit of close co-operation between public and private, and President Trump has repeatedly, though so far unsuccessfully, attempted to remove all traces of it.[85] The UK's reform to its CFC regime in FA 2012, which in various ways embodies a close intertwining of public and private, has become the subject of an EU Commission state-aid investigation. The recent erosion of the centre ground of technocratic orthodoxy is one possible reason why it is possible to find condemnation of the *status quo ante* on both Left and Right. Increasingly, then, the justifications for taxation that commend themselves to partisans of

---

[81] Then contained in ICTA 1988, ss 747–56 and schs 24–26.

[82] Case C-196/04 [2006] ECR I-7995, para 76.

[83] For some implications of the argument that, especially since 1992, EU law has ordoliberalism, rather than neoliberalism, at its core, see Prosser (above n 49) 11–14 and (regarding tax) Snape, 'Stability and its Significance in UK Tax Policy and Legislation' (above n 78) 566.

[84] J Ford and G Plimmer, 'Public Service, Private Gain' *Financial Times* (23 January 2018) 9.

[85] The validity of the so-called 'individual mandate' component in Obamacare was accepted by the US Supreme Court in *National Federation of Independent Business v Sebelius* 132 S Ct 2566, 2600 (2012), not under the Commerce Clause, but pursuant to the taxing competence of US Congress (see BN Bogenschneider, 'The Taxing Power after *Sebelius*' (2016) 51 *Wake Forest L Rev* 941).

one or other side of these arguments are so varied that it is difficult to identify common ground. That said, perhaps all sides might agree on the necessity for the prevention of corruption in the design and administration of tax laws and the promotion of the broadly based public good of national self-defence. Examples of outright corruption are easily exposed in developed nations under the rule of law, although equivocal examples are much more troublesome. What has been alleged in some quarters as the capture of public policy by the Gupta brothers in South Africa,[86] for example and, possibly, too, *Pergau Dam*, might be viable examples of the latter. Weaker although still passionate allegations have been against the close involvement of the 'Big Four' professional services firms with the design of new tax legislation. The UK's replacement CFC legislation, introduced in FA 2012 in the wake of *Cadbury Schweppes*, has come in for particularly strong criticism in this respect.[87] National defence, indeed, provides a strong example of a public good the nature and purpose of which have traditionally commanded wide acceptance. It might be objected that controversies such as the non-renewal of Trident, or the question of what percentage of gross domestic spending should be devoted to defence, show that, even on the latter, there is no consensus. These may be disputes about means rather than ends. On this perspective, taxpayers do not disagree about the existential significance of the British state but on how best to ensure its continued existence. Either way, it is tolerably clear that national defence is typically the paradigm case of common ground between otherwise divergent approaches to public services revenue and expenditure. What underlies these examples and counter-examples is an understanding of how common and individual interests interact and what tax has to do with it.

In drilling down into this last point, we need to pause to reflect on the relationship between collective wellbeing and personal freedom and how, if at all, this relationship comes through in revenue law cases. At stake here are two contrasting ideas. One of them is that *personal freedom* is both foundational and best expressed by the state's *non-intervention* in the life of the individual. In the dissenting words of the libertarian judge Douglas J in a non-revenue context, '[t]he right to be let alone is indeed the beginning of all freedom'.[88] The other is that *collective wellbeing* is both foundational and best expressed by the very opposite: by the state's extensive intervention in individual lives. Each finds some expression in the cases discussed within this book. Admittedly, historical and jurisprudential factors mean that judicial opinions consonant with the former are much more frequent, at least in the last three-and-a-half centuries

---

[86] D Pilling and J Cotterill, 'The Selling of South Africa' *FT Weekend Magazine* (2/3 December 2017) 12.

[87] R Brooks, *The Great Tax Robbery: How Britain Became a Tax Haven for Fat Cats and Big Business* (London, Oneworld Publications, 2013) ch 4.

[88] *Public Utilities Commission of the District of Columbia et al v Pollak et al* 343 US 451, 467 (1952).

since *Ship-Money*, than those echoing the latter. Because no two people agree precisely on what personal freedom entails, and because, however it is mapped, tax is crucial to it, these questions have never conclusively been resolved. In fact, it is almost impossible to imagine that they ever will be. Economically liberal ideology which is ultimately traceable (though in different ways) to the political philosophies of both John Locke (1632–1704) and David Hume (1711–76), finds expression in many of the cases. Entirely expectedly, in its insistence on representative consent by legislation to the interference with property rights, *Bowles* is a paradigm of this tradition. Less expectedly, perhaps, so also is *Jones v Garnett (HM Inspector of Taxes)*,[89] discussed by Glen Loutzenhiser in chapter twenty. Important incidents of the right of property are freedom to dispose of it[90] and a distrust of purposive statutory interpretation.[91] Sure enough, *Jones v Garnett* vindicates one spouse's right to alienate an income stream in favour of the other (and thereby to take the consequent tax advantage) and it does so by refusing to accept HMRC's strained construction of the relevant legislation. The liberal ideas just illustrated assign a limited role to the state, including its legislation, as being brought into existence primarily to protect property rights. These are in a sense 'natural' and therefore pre-political,[92] a position which is explicitly rejected in the collectivist view. Instead, the collectivist view regards the state as being the source of rights and views legislation as the means of bringing them into existence.[93] 'There'll be creative business leaders', the Shadow Chancellor, John McDonnell MP acknowledged to an interviewer in 2018, 'but actually, when it comes down to it, they can't do anything unless they're part of a collective'.[94] In revenue law terms, the latter view has the potential exponentially to increase the range of objects that revenue law might seek to promote. Navigating a middle way, Sir Isaiah Berlin (1909–97) referred to 'positive liberty': not simply being let alone (what Berlin called 'negative freedom' or 'negative liberty') but being equipped by the state with the means to act.[95] Such positive liberty has given rise to the concept of 'basic income'.[96] With these extremes and one example of a middle way in mind, it is productive to think of 'individualistic' and 'collectivist' ideas – not as alternatives – but as struggling

---

[89] *Jones v Garnett (HM Inspector of Taxes)* [2007] UKHL 35; (2007) 78 TC 597.

[90] K Gray and SF Gray, *Elements of Land Law*, 5th edn (Oxford, Oxford University Press, 2009) 103.

[91] See above (text around n 41).

[92] See, eg, R Nozick, *Anarchy, State, and Utopia* (New York, BasicBooks, 1974) 174–82.

[93] See, eg, L Murphy and T Nagel, *The Myth of Ownership* (Oxford, Oxford University Press, 2000).

[94] J Pickard, 'Is Britain Ready for John McDonnell?' *FT Weekend Magazine* (3/4 March 2018) 12, 14.

[95] I Berlin, 'Two Concepts of Liberty' in I Berlin, *Four Essays on Liberty* (Oxford, Oxford University Press, 1969).

[96] As to which, see G Standing, *Basic Income: And How We Can Make It Happen* (London, Pelican Books, 2017).

tendencies within every system of public finance. The political struggle between ideologies can then be seen, not in terms of a choice between models, but in terms of the emphasis in practice to be placed on the rival ideologies. This analysis has the great benefit of shifting attention away from extreme depictions of revenue law that would be intolerable in practice and that have not survived unimpeded even in communist or hyper-capitalist societies. Instead the focus is placed on the variations of opinion that are most likely to have a concrete influence in developed jurisdictions. For exactly the same reasons, it is a framework that is useful in clarifying the outlook of at least some of the parties to the cases discussed within this book, not to mention judges, officials and indeed our own contributors. Few if any adopt either of the extreme positions, but it is often possible to see individualism or collectivism being brought into slightly sharper relief than the other.

These considerations resonate down the centuries, though bloody struggles over the Crown's need to raise revenue and the constitutional rights of the subject have given way to less bloody but often still violent debates about the nature and scope of the very concept of revenue law. When, in the eighteenth century, Sir William Blackstone (1723–80) described 'the rights of the people of England', he 'reduced [them] to three principal or primary articles; the right of personal security, the right of personal liberty; and the right of private property'.[97] The last of these, drawing on Locke, he defined as consisting 'in the free use, enjoyment, and disposal of all his acquisitions, without any control or diminution, save only by the laws of the land'.[98] That meant, in turn, that 'no subject of England can be constrained to pay any aids or taxes, even for the defence of the realm or the support of government, but such as are imposed by his own consent, or that of his representatives in parliament'.[99] By the late nineteenth century,[100] AV Dicey (1835–1922) had developed Blackstone's teaching about rights into a particular threefold conception of the rule of law: 'the absolute supremacy or predominance of regular law as opposed to the influence of arbitrary power, and excludes the existence of arbitrariness, of prerogative, or even of wide discretionary authority on the part of the government';[101] 'equality before the law, or the equal subjection of all classes to the ordinary law of the land administered by the ordinary Law Courts';[102] and the fact that 'the principles of private law have with us been by the action of the Courts and

---

[97] William Blackstone, *Commentaries on the Laws of England* (first published 1765; Oxford, Oxford University Press, 2016) I, 88 (I.1). See HH Monroe, 'The Constitution in Danger' [1969] *BTR* 24, 24–26.

[98] Blackstone, ibid, 93–94 (I.1).

[99] ibid, 94.

[100] M Loughlin, *The British Constitution: A Very Short Introduction* (Oxford, Oxford University Press, 2013) ch 5 (esp 88–9); Loughlin, *Foundations of Public Law* (above n 50) 316.

[101] AV Dicey, *Introduction to the Study of the Law of the Constitution* (first published 1885; Carmel, IN, Liberty Fund 1982) 120.

[102] ibid.

Parliament so extended as to determine the position of the Crown and of its servants; thus the constitution is the result of the ordinary law of the land'.[103] While these Blackstonian and Diceyan ideas find expression throughout this book, three cases stand out as illustrating different aspects of their views. The story of *Bowles*, already mentioned, involved an action by Bowles against the Bank of England for paying him interest net of income tax without legislative authority. The bank, on the advice of Freshfields, their solicitors, had relied on the Budget resolutions of the House of Commons. The judge, Parker J, held that the resolutions were not enough. An Act of Parliament was required to authorise the net payment. The case was followed briskly by the enactment of the Provisional Collection of Taxes Act 1913, designed to provide the requisite temporary statutory authority for the collection of taxes. While neither Blackstone nor Dicey is referred to in the *Bowles* case report, the latter had, in 1908, affirmed that 'no-one can nowadays fancy that taxes can be raised otherwise than in virtue of an Act of Parliament'.[104] A second, counterintuitive, example is *Farmer v Glyn-Jones*,[105] since it illustrates Diceyan principles in a somewhat backhanded way. 'At stake', as Chantal Stebbings explains in chapter two, was 'the chemist's privilege', namely, whether a qualified chemist and druggist was the 'first vendor' of a 'known, admitted and approved remedy' and thus that the medicine sold was exempt from medicine stamp duty under the Medicine Stamp Act 1812. Although the Divisional Court held, on a literal interpretation, that the chemist was indeed within the exemption, the Revenue's subsequent practice was not only too wide but was the exercise of an unlawful discretion. The case illustrated both the limitations of Dicey's 'judge-made constitution'[106] and the idealism implicit in his statement that 'every official, from the Prime Minister down to a constable or collector of taxes, is under the same responsibility for every act done without legal justification as any other citizen'.[107] Finally, there is *Baker v Archer-Shee*,[108] analysed by Malcolm Gammie in chapter six. There, the issue was whether money received by Lady Archer-Shee (the life tenant under an American will trust governed by English law) constituted 'income from a foreign possession' (that is to say, the right to due administration of the trust) or income from shares, securities or foreign property. If the former, her husband (Sir Martin Archer-Shee) was liable for income tax only when the amounts were remitted to the UK. If the latter, he was liable for income tax whether they were remitted or not. The judicial committee of the House of Lords, by a bare majority, held that that the amounts were income from shares, securities or foreign property. Sir Martin was taxable on them, even though they had never been remitted to

---

[103] ibid, 121.
[104] ibid, 201.
[105] *Farmer v Glyn-Jones* [1903] 2 KB 6.
[106] Dicey (above n 101) 116.
[107] ibid, 114.
[108] *Baker v Archer-Shee* [1927] AC 844.

the UK. Possibly, what *Archer-Shee* illustrates is Dicey's claim that, in interpreting legislation, judges tread a distinctive path, one 'which would not commend itself either to a body of officials, or to the Houses of Parliament, if the Houses were called upon to interpret their own enactments'.[109] In all three cases, indeed, the judges' constitutional propriety highlighted the consequences, for better or worse, of the Diceyan rule of law in the early-twentieth century constitution.[110]

By the mid-twentieth century, the constitutional values expressed by Blackstone and Dicey were, for many, no longer sufficient. This is because they had nothing to say about the purposes of taxation in a state transformed beyond anything they would have recognised. A radical transformation took place in what is still the most extensive expansion of revenue law, namely the revenue legislation of the 1964–70 Labour government. Significantly, the sweep of theorists to whom this expansion could be traced – Sidney and Beatrice Webb, William Beveridge, John Maynard Keynes, Nicholas Kaldor, Robert Neild and so on[111] – were not primarily *legal* theorists. The terms of mainstream debate had moved away from Diceyan values.[112] At the same time, the legal foundations of the tax system became increasingly divorced from observable commercial phenomena.[113] This was, in part, a result of the sheer range of purposes to which it was put, in part a result of the need to make the system watertight against tax avoidance. One of the most important of these purposes was greater social justice by redistribution through the tax system.[114] This had been a source of unease for Friedrich von Hayek and his followers for some time,[115] and it remains contentious to this day. The main planks of the transformation were the introduction of corporation tax and capital gains tax (CGT) in FA 1965. *Zim Properties*, already referred to, illustrates the judiciary's willingness to ensure that the base of CGT was robust but fair. The chargeable gains legislation[116] states that '[a]ll forms of property shall be assets ... whether situated in the United Kingdom or not'. Warner J held that a claim in negligence against a law firm, regarding a property transaction, was itself such an asset. In turn, the settlement of the claim for £69,000 was a chargeable disposal involving a 'capital

---

[109] Dicey (above n 101) 273.

[110] Interestingly, Terence Rattigan's play, *The Winslow Boy* (1946), was inspired by *Archer-Shee v R*, involving a petition of right for breach of contract, and affirms the values of the Diceyan view of the constitution (see ER Keedy, 'A Petition of Right: Archer-Shee v The King' (1939) 87 *U Pa LR* 895; T Rattigan, *Collected Plays*, vol 1 (London, Hamish Hamilton, 1953) 391–92; Dicey (above n 101) 417).

[111] RC Whiting, *The Labour Party and Taxation* (Cambridge, Cambridge University Press, 2000) esp 43, 107, 160–68, 191.

[112] That said, legal scholars did eventually engage with the welfare state thus created, eg: JAG Griffith, 'Comment' [1963] *PL* 401; H Street, *Justice in the Welfare State*, 2nd edn (London, Stevens, 1975); JAG Griffith, 'The Political Constitution' (1979) 42 *MLR* 1.

[113] See text around n 59 above, and n 59 itself, in relation to Prebble's comments. He describes this dislocation as 'ectopic'.

[114] Whiting (above n 111) 179–95.

[115] FA Hayek, *The Constitution of Liberty* (first published 1960; Abingdon, Routledge, 2006) 266–81.

[116] TCGA 1992, s 21(1) (ex CGTA 1979, s 19(1); ex FA 1965, s 19(1)).

sum derived from an asset'.[117] As Ridd has explained elsewhere,[118] this brought the £69,000 within CGT's scope (the robust aspect) but permitted the deduction of a base cost (the fairness aspect). Interestingly, Ridd attributes 'this broad approach' to the fact that 'Sir Jean-Pierre Warner ... had, prior to his appointment to the Chancery Division, been an Advocate-General [*sic*] in the European Court of Justice'.[119]

So unexpected was the decision in *Zim*, and so wide-ranging its potential ramifications, that the Inland Revenue eventually responded with an Extra-Statutory Concession (ESC D33), attempting to clarify the circumstances in which *Zim* would apply. This raised its own controversies. Extra-Statutory Concessions had only recently attracted trenchant criticism from judges in the Diceyan mould and particularly from Walton J.[120] 'One should be taxed by law, and not be untaxed by concession',[121] he said, later adding that in publishing ESCs, the Crown was claiming the prerogative to dispense with laws.[122] Walton J's association of prerogatival levies in the would-be absolutist state of James II, with the discretions of tax administration in the welfare state, is commonly invoked by libertarians. So too is the invocation, also in connection with intolerable discretion, of *Ship-Money* in the reign of James' father, Charles. *Bowles*, decided over 250 years later, and to precisely the opposite effect, just follows the end of a period when hardly any revenue cases came before the higher courts. The main exceptions were stamp duty cases, and then only because '[d]ocuments which ought to be, but were not, stamped, could not be used in any judicial proceeding. And enforcement therefore required a judicial determination on the stamp laws'.[123]

Whether landmark cases demonstrate that revenue law is best thought of as public law or private law, or that indeed such categories are best avoided, are hard questions. Public law, in David Walker's definition,

> comprises the principles and rules which relate to the structure, activities, rights, powers and immunities, duties and liabilities of the State ... save ... in circumstances where the State ... enjoys no special rights or powers.[124]

Private law, at an equally high level of generality,

> comprises the principles and rules dealing with the relations of ordinary individuals with one another [traditionally, property, contract and tort], and also those dealing

---

[117] TCGA 1992, s 22(1) (ex CGTA 1979, s 20; ex FA 1965, s 19(3)).

[118] P Ridd, 'Statutory Interpretation in Early Capital Gains Tax Cases' in P Harris and D de Cogan (eds), *Studies in the History of Tax Law: Volume 8* (Oxford, Hart Publishing, 2017) 279–80.

[119] ibid, 280.

[120] S Daly, 'The Life and Times of ESCs: A Defence?' in P Harris and D de Cogan (eds), *Studies in the History of Tax Law: Volume 8* (Oxford, Hart Publishing, 2017) 170–74.

[121] *Vestey v CIR (No 1)* [1979] Ch 177, 197G.

[122] *Vestey v CIR (No 2)* [1979] Ch 198, 203F–H.

[123] D Williams, 'Taxing Statutes are Taxing Statutes: The Interpretation of Revenue Legislation' (1978) 41 *MLR* 404, 408–09.

[124] DM Walker, *The Oxford Companion to Law* (Oxford, Oxford University Press, 1980) 1013.

with the relations of the State … with an individual in circumstances where the State … does *not* have any special position.[125]

For Dicey, neither the public law/private law dichotomy nor the allocation of revenue law to either category is permissible, since the rule of law requires one law for state and subject alike.[126] Though possible, a Diceyan position on revenue law is both controversial and difficult to maintain in the face of modern realities. It is possible because the courts in *Bowles*, *Glyn-Jones*, *Archer-Shee* and, surprisingly, *Garnett*, took a Diceyan line. It is controversial because Dicey's position, that of a (liberal) idealist, is partisan.[127] Dicey's view is/was always hard to maintain in reality, because of the long growth in the administrative state discussed above.[128] Granted these objections, and being willing therefore to admit the dichotomy, we might nonetheless emphasise that there is an irreducibly private law component to taxation because property rights are foundational to private law and tax necessarily interferes with them. Revenue law might then be *negatively* characterised as the (state) law that, by its very precision, shores up and supports the sharp edges of property law. The nature of revenue law's interference with property rights is quite distinct from that of human rights or equalities law. With revenue law, this interference needs to be concretised and measured in every single case. In passing judgment, the revenue law judge is meticulously mapping the boundaries between public right and private right. With human rights or equalities law, however, it is only in relatively rare cases where that law is engaged and property rights are constrained. For economic liberals and libertarians, this recognition of the intimate connection between property rights, taxation and private law, is transformed into an insistence on the axiomatic nature of property rights. 'Tragically',[129] though, in UK revenue law, the *quietus* of this particular view was *Ramsay*. As regards the internal workings of property law, the constructive trust case of *Lloyd's Bank plc v Rosset*[130] might possibly be said to occupy a similar position.[131]

That leaves us to examine the claim that, rather than either of the foregoing, the cases tend to illustrate revenue law's public law quality. This claim is often made in other jurisdictions.[132] From this perspective we would point out that, without revenue law, there would be no United Kingdom of Great Britain and

---

[125] ibid, 994. (Both are sophisticated definitions, because they say what public law or private law *does*, not what it *is*.)

[126] See text around n 99 above.

[127] Loughlin, *Public Law and Political Theory* (above n 47) 140–53.

[128] ibid, 153–56.

[129] '"My dear Spencer, I should define tragedy as a theory killed by a fact", HUXLEY', quoted in G Chapman, *A Passionate Prodigality: Fragments of Autobiography* (London, MacGibbon & Kee, 1965) 68.

[130] *Lloyd's Bank plc v Rosset* [1991] 1 AC 107 (HL).

[131] Despite the foregoing discussion, this suggestion does not go so far as to treat property law as a subset of revenue law.

[132] See, eg, *Ferrazzini v Italy* [2001] STC 1314, 1319c, 1320g–j; (Thuronyi (above n 16) 60).

Northern Ireland. We might then consider the linked question whether revenue law should be regarded as ordinary positive law or whether it has some special constitutional status. This point needs some careful historically minded thought. A narrow view might be that revenue law is, for the most part, positive law, but that some of it has constitutional status.[133] Thus, *Bowles* would involve a 'constitutional statute' (the Bill of Rights 1689), whereas *Bater* would not (the Third Rule of Schedule E in the Income Tax Act 1842). Both would, however, be public law cases because of their close engagement with the relationship of tax, citizens and government. A wider view might be that no part of revenue law can be regarded *solely* as positive law; that tax is 'a set of practices embedded within, and acquiring its identity from, a wider body of political practices'.[134] On this view, not even the detail of tax legislation could be separated from its contribution to a set of political practices, understandings and relationships that were not exclusively legal and not even exclusively about tax. On this view, too, there would be no intrinsic difference between the statutes in *Bowles*, say, and in *Bater*. Both would be recognised as embedded within broadly the same practices, understandings and relationships. Not only would this obviate the need to sift constitutional statutes from others, it would acknowledge that Schedule E, Rule 3, ITA 1842 had no coherence or morality outside this political and public law context. It would also recognise the interconnection of revenue law and the administrative state, even as far back as the mid-nineteenth century. In our own time, social security legislation underlines this point even more forcefully. This is because, although it benefits poorer people, it also enmeshes them. In short, the poorer you are, the more intimate your connection is with the state. Because revenue law is existential to the state, its public law dimension is not restricted to regulating how HM Government conducts tax policy and promulgates revenue legislation. Instead, revenue law moulds how goods in society are distributed in the furtherance of political decisions. The question, in the broad terms outlined at the beginning, is that of what kind of state this law will shape.

A further resonance between tax and public law is the sense that it is not only the substance of a decision that is important but the sensitivity of the judges to the political consequences of their judgments. This point has rather come to the foreground since the abolition of the General Commissioners and Special Commissioners fundamentally changed the character of tax litigation. Not only has the qualification for hearing revenue law cases been professionalised; under the new system, revenue law issues only fall for consideration by the higher courts once an appeal has been made from a decision of the Upper Tribunal. In future, therefore, tax law is likely to receive more input from tax-trained judges at the lower tiers of the appeals system, and less input from generalist

---

[133] *Thoburn v Sunderland City Council* [2002] EWHC 195 (Admin), para [62]; [2003] QB 151, 186F–G (Laws LJ). Generally, see F Ahmed and A Perry, 'Constitutional Statutes' (2017) 37 *OJLS* 461.

[134] M Loughlin, *The Idea of Public Law* (Oxford, Oxford University Press, 2003) 43.

appeal judges. As Anne Fairpo points out in her discussion of *Edwards (HM Inspector of Taxes) v Bairstow and Harrison*,[135] older judicial examinations of the courts' review and appellate jurisdictions retain much of their force despite these recent reforms; it still makes sense to refer to this 1955 case as a landmark. Arguments over the circumstances in which a higher court can review the lower court's fact-finding, and when it can substitute its own decision for that of the latter, will continue to involve this case. Meanwhile, the likelihood that the enhanced importance of the Upper Tribunal will foster a distinctive revenue law jurisprudence provides yet another reason for doubting the continued relevance of a Diceyan view of revenue law.

IV. CONCLUDING COMMENTS

A full conclusion would not be fitting for an exploratory essay such as this. However, we would make three very brief concluding points. First, the detailed study of revenue law cases gives wisdom as to the origin and purposes of particular revenue law rules. Secondly, landmark cases are those that, in one way or another, illuminate particularly intractable issues. Thirdly, the significance of that illumination is not limited to the particular rules and principles: it can reveal much about the nature and purpose of a whole system.

[135] *Edwards (HM Inspector of Taxes) v Bairstow and Harrison* (1955) 34 ATC 198.

1

Case of Ship-Money (R v Hampden) *(1637)*

Prerogatival Discretion in Emergency Conditions

MICHAEL J BRADDICK

MANY OF THE instruments of rule used by Charles I were subsequently abolished (not least of course, albeit temporarily, the monarchy, House of Lords and the Church of England), a fact which has done little for his posthumous reputation. Ship-money was among them, abolished by statute in 1641[1] and never revived. In fact, the system of public finance with which it was associated was swept away in the crisis of the mid-seventeenth century, with the result that ship-money has subsequently seemed an anachronism, a doomed attempt to make the existing arrangements work and merely a prelude to the construction of something better. Part of the charge sheet against Charles has been, in effect, that he tried it at all. As a result, ship-money has had few defenders among modern historians, usually seen as an outdated expedient employed by a king with flawed political judgement.

However, in 1637 Charles I's judiciary had twice given ship-money a clean bill of health: first in an extra-judicial opinion and then in opinions in a prominent test case, *R v Hampden*.[2] As we will see most of the judges gave unambiguous views on very large constitutional issues about necessity, the collective good and individual property rights but were more divided in their rulings on more

---

[1] An Act for the declaring unlawful and void the late proceedings touching Ship-Money, and for the vacating of all records and process concerning the same 16 Car I cap 14; J Raithby (ed), *Statutes of the Realm* (Great Britain Record Commission, 1819) V, 116–17; reprinted in SR Gardiner (ed), *The Constitutional Document of the Puritan Revolution 1625–1660*, 3rd edn (Oxford, Oxford University Press, 1906) 189–92.

[2] *R v Hampden* (1637) 3 St Tr 825.

narrowly defined questions about the writ for collection and the means of its enforcement. In 1641, when those big questions were fully in play in very different circumstances, ship-money was abolished by Parliament, apparently delivering a damning verdict on the judiciary. However, although the judges were condemned for having failed to settle these questions in a reasonable way the parliamentary Act did not give any kind of answer at all to those same questions: nonetheless the condemnation of the judges as tools of a corrupt administration, or at least as craven or time-serving in their opinions, has been very influential.

I. THE FISCAL CONTEXT AND THE KING'S CASE

The arguments in *R v Hampden* belong to a world of royal finance that is now lost. Charles I inherited a financial system in which the king was expected to 'live of his own'. He was possessed of lands, revenues and rights to demand service of various kinds, and these were intended to supply the ordinary needs of government. He could resort to other sources for extraordinary purposes – notably parliamentary taxation, but also rights to demand service in extraordinary conditions. Overall, therefore, parliamentary taxation formed a small part of the overall income of the Crown – just one component of the extraordinary revenues – and was probably in decline during the first three decades of the seventeenth century.[3]

This set of arrangements had been under pressure during the Tudor and Stuart periods. Inflation had reduced the value of many Crown assets which, in any case, had to be managed in a way that met expectations about benevolent paternal rule. So, for example, the Crown lands yielded far less than their market value because the Crown was hampered by sticky rents from long leases and also sometimes by a reluctance to extract the market rate from its tenants.[4] Other assets had simply been neglected – the boundaries of royal forests had been encroached upon and the Crown had simply lost track of some of what it owned. The latter situation was summed up in the need to employ the excitingly named 'hunters after concealed lands'.

Inflation and inattention were not the only difficulties, however. If we think of this as a royal estate, with revenues and services attached, we can see how the Crown, like other landlords, was increasingly keen to commute services into payments. A good example of that is purveyance – the legal right enjoyed by the King to demand supplies for the royal court at the King's price rather than

---

[3] MJ Braddick, *The Nerves of State: Taxation and the Financing of the English State, 1558–1714* (Manchester, Manchester University Press, 1996). For the following paragraphs, see also MJ Braddick, 'The Rise of the Fiscal State' in B Coward (ed), *A Companion to Stuart Britain* (Oxford, Blackwell, 2003).

[4] For the Crown lands see RW Hoyle (ed), *The Estates of the English Crown 1558–1640* (Cambridge, Cambridge University Press, 1992).

the market price. From the late sixteenth century onwards, this was increasingly commuted into a simple cash payment of the difference between the King's price and market price.[5]

The pressure to raise cash rather than impose service was more marked in military matters, as military skills and equipment became more specialised. At root, the adoption of hand-held gunpowder weapons was transforming land battles, while in the early seventeenth century the possibilities for arming ships led to a much sharper separation of merchant and military ship design. On land, troops needed specialist equipment, training in its use and to be thoroughly drilled to enable effective collective action. The result was the selection of trained bands from the general muster, and for many people the duty of service in the militia was commuted into a payment to support the trained band. These were also years of more or less incessant warfare: one estimate is that during the sixteenth century there were 34 European wars, lasting on average 1.6 years and, during the seventeenth century, 29 wars each lasting 1.7 years. In effect there was a war somewhere in Europe 95 per cent of the time in the sixteenth century, and 94 per cent of the time in the following century. As Elizabeth's privy council had put it, 'all forrain princes, beinge neighbours to this Realme be in armes, and the manner of the present warres doe differ from warres in former tymes'.[6]

At sea the crucial development was the evolution of broadside fire. In the sixteenth century it had been possible to convert a merchant ship for war by mounting a gun at the bow. It would recoil along the centre of the ship, posing no particular challenge to its balance, and did not take up cargo space. Many long-distance merchantmen had some capacity to defend themselves in any case. The bow-mounted gun was used to fire directly ahead as the ship bore down on the enemy. The development of the broadside had dramatic implications for ship design – weakening the hull with multiple gun-ports, posing greater problems of stability and taking away cargo space. The broadside however was far more effective, and there was an increasing advantage to those powers with specialised military vessels. The ship-money fleets were developed as this process accelerated and one of the ornaments of the Royal Fleet was to be the *Sovereign of the Seas* – completely unsuited to mercantile use (and also to military use, as it happens, after Charles I elaborated on the original designs). The fleets mobilised against the Spanish Armada in 1588 and during the subsequent mobilisations of the 1590s had consisted largely of requisitioned merchant ships adapted for the purpose. From 1650 onwards, the state had a large fleet of specialised naval vessels.[7]

---

[5] For purveyance see A Woodworth, *Purveyance for the Royal Household in the Reign of Queen Elizabeth* (American Philosophical Society, 1945).

[6] Quoted from MJ Braddick, *State Formation in Early Modern England c 1550–1700* (Cambridge, Cambridge University Press, 2000) 61–62. Figures for frequency of wars quoted from C Tilly, *Coercion, Capital and European States AD 990–1992* (Oxford, Blackwell, 1992) 73.

[7] Braddick, *State Formation* (above n 6) 202–13.

In this context, ship-money was a plausible expedient, taking an established right to demand service in the form of provision of a ship and commuting that into a payment to support the building of a ship fit for modern purposes. It was analogous to the commutation of purveyance and to developments in the militia; and like the militia promised to allow the King to secure a military resource fit for the new purposes from his 'own' rights.

That was not the only way to see it, however. First, the precedents supported the use of ship-money in emergency conditions but during the 1630s it came to resemble an infinitely recurring annual charge, of potentially unlimited scale, imposed as long as the King perceived the kingdom to be in danger. This was the key issue in responses to the judicial opinions of 1637, as we will see. More generally, though, many of the landed classes, at least if the opinions expressed in Parliament are any guide, thought the whole problem was royal extravagance, not rising costs. Parliaments urged active engagement in European wars but balked at the predicted costs, and in the meantime gave vent to many grievances about strategies the Crown developed to live of its own. Reluctant to grant extraordinary revenues on the wished-for scale, Parliament was also highly critical of attempts to improve ordinary revenues or to enforce the Crown's other legal rights.[8]

An attempt had been made to cut through this in 1610, with the Great Contract, that would have granted recurring parliamentary taxation intended to support the ordinary expenses of the Crown in return for a renunciation of unpopular existing rights, duties and rates. The settlement was undermined by a lack of faith that the Crown could be trusted with money and this persisted into the 1620s but was not accompanied by a similar proposal for a new financial arrangement. Instead, during the frequent parliamentary meetings of that decade James I and then Charles were met with relatively stingy extraordinary supply, demands for active warfare and for a restriction of ordinary expenditure. Coupled with increasingly sharp criticism of Charles I's religious policy and of his choice of favourites as advisers, by 1629 Parliament had come to seem more trouble than it was worth. It did not offer a solution to either the ordinary or extraordinary revenue problems, and the inadequate 'supply' came at the expense of sometimes trenchant criticism of royal government.

II. SHIP-MONEY DURING THE 1630s

Ship-money derived from an earlier provision for port towns to supply a ship for royal service in times of danger. Ports benefited particularly from the defence against threats at sea, and their service in this sense was justified by their direct

---

[8] For this and the following paragraph see C Russell, *The Causes of the English Civil War* (Oxford, Oxford University Press, 1990) ch 7.

benefit from it. During the 1590s, in the aftermath of the Armada, it had been a regular feature of life, and it was used again during the 1620s, when England renewed engagement in wider European conflicts. There had been a proposal in 1628 to make it a national levy on the grounds that the whole kingdom benefited from naval defence, not just the port towns, although the proposal was dropped. Following the failures of the Parliaments of the 1620s it was deployed rather differently, with serious political consequences.[9]

Ship-money in its fatally controversial form took shape after 1634. It was raised initially from the port towns, but as a compulsory payment, levied by the sheriff and enforced by distraint. In 1635 it was extended inland, and this departure from precedent was recognised to be significant. In June that year Lord Keeper Coventry had included the enforcement of ship-money as a priority in his charge to the Assize judges, noting that 'Christendom is full of war, and there is nothing but rumours of war', that defence of the kingdom in such circumstances was clearly a royal duty, and for the 'general good of his kingdom'. '[S]ince … all the kingdom is interested both in the honour, safety and profit', he continued, 'it is just and reasonable that they should all put to their helping hands'.[10]

Nonetheless, at this point the initiative had several key features that might attract legal attention: whether it could indeed be raised from inland counties; under what circumstances; and how it could be enforced. On the first point, Charles had received very encouraging legal opinion in November 1635: 'when the good and safety of the kingdom in general is concerned, and the whole kingdom in danger (of which His Majesty is the only judge), then the charge of the defence ought to be borne by all the realm in general'.[11] This view was not publicised for a full year after it was made.[12]

Ship-money in this new form was pretty clearly less popular than other rates and taxes, being as far as we can tell more prone to rating disputes and its officers more subject to legal challenge for their actions. Respectable rates of return were achieved until its final year, but it was dogged by delays and relatively slow payment.[13] The greater difficulty of collection was partly a reflection of the fact that the ratings were more contestable: it rested on ratings made by individual sheriffs working without precedents or the commissions that apportioned some other burdens. There remains a sneaking suspicion however that rating problems

---

[9] For the history and precedents see MD Gordon, 'The Collection of Ship-money in the Reign of Charles I' (1910) 4 *Transactions of the Royal Historical Society, Third Series* 141.

[10] 3 St Tr 825, 837–38. See, in general, AAM Gill, 'Ship-Money during the Rule of Charles I: Politics, Ideology and the Law' (PhD thesis, University of Sheffield, 1990) ch 1; K Sharpe, *The Personal Rule of Charles I* (New Haven, CT, Yale University Press, 1990) ch 9.

[11] J Rushworth, *Historical Collections of Private Passages of State*, 8 vols (London, 1721 edn) III, Appendix 249.

[12] Gill (above n 10) 169–70; JS Hart Jr, *The Rule of Law, 1603–1660* (Harlow, Pearson, 2003) 150.

[13] H Langelüddeke, '"I finde all men & my officers all soe unwilling": The collection of Ship-Money, 1635–1640' (2007) 46 *Journal of British Studies* 509; Gill (above n 10) ch 3.

were a symptom of a more serious malaise. Simonds D'Ewes, a Suffolk gentleman with detailed legal and antiquarian knowledge, certainly had profound concerns about the legality of the levy, although he didn't say anything publicly. When he was eventually put in charge of collecting ship-money he made some show of trying to raise it but threw up his hands in the face of the scale of the administrative problems, perhaps a little easily defeated by these difficulties.[14] Certainly in this case, what D'Ewes recorded privately was far more critical of the basic legality of the levy than what he said publicly, and this may have been true more generally.[15]

Charles sought to clear the way for ship-money in February 1637, a strong hint one would think that his government suspected that more was at stake in this rash of apparently minor disputes. The King put three key questions to his judges very clearly:

> [W]hen the good and safety of the kingdom in general is concerned, and the whole kingdom in danger, whether may not the King, by writ under the Great Seal of England, command all subjects of our kingdom at their charge to provide and furnish such a number of ships, with men, victuals and munition, and for such time as we shall think fit for the defence and safeguard of the kingdom from such danger and peril?

In such circumstance could he

> by law compel the doing thereof?

Finally, and crucially,

> is not the King the sole judge both of the danger, and when and how the same is to be prevented and avoided?

Charles got an unambiguous affirmative on the first two, and an equally unambiguous opinion 'that in such case your Majesty is the sole judge both of the danger, and when and how the same is to be prevented and avoided'. Some of the judges later claimed to have been pressured into this view, but Charles could hardly have hoped for a more supportive answer. The names attached to the judgment were all of the men who were later to sit in *R v Hampden*: Sir John Bramston, Sir George Croke, Sir John Finch, Sir Thomas Trevor, Sir Humphrey Davenport, Sir George Vernon, Sir John Denham, Sir Edward Crawley, Sir Richard Hutton, Sir Robert Berkeley, Sir William Jones and Sir Francis Weston.[16]

When Coventry returned to ship-money in his charge to the Assize Judges in February 1637, he had this letter and legal judgment read out. The first writ, he said, had been unproblematic but once the duty had been extended inland

---

[14] SP Salt, 'Sir Simonds D'Ewes and the Levying of Ship-Money, 1635–1640' (1994) 37 *Historical Journal* 253.

[15] For public discussion of the issues more broadly see Gill (above n 10) chs 2–4.

[16] Gardiner (above n 1) 108–09. For the pressure some judges felt see Hart (above n 12) 151; Gill (above n 10) 170–72.

resistance had increased – there had been refusals not just inland but in some maritime places too and legal action taken against those trying to enforce the levy. However, the legality of the writ had now been vindicated by all the 'Judges of England, with one voice, and set under their own hands'. It was to be entered in the courts of Star Chamber, Exchequer, Chancery, Common Pleas and King's Bench and published throughout the kingdom. The King had no desire to halt or stop legal cases, but he did hope that 'his subjects who have been in error, may inform themselves, or be reformed'. At the same time, counsel in any cases relating to ship-money should not now be 'surprized'.[17]

III. R v HAMPDEN

John Hampden, a relatively significant Buckinghamshire gentleman, had refused to pay the ship-money demanded by the 4 August 1635 writ and faced punishment as a consequence. It was consciously intended as a test case and may have been the brainchild of opponents of broader aspects of Charles I's religious and secular policy.[18] On the face of it, however, the formal position was more limited: that, having refused, the sum had been certified as due by Chancery by writ of *Certiorari*, and sent by writ of *Mittimus* to the Exchequer, where Hampden and other refusers were to show cause why they should not pay. This was recited in a writ of *Scire Facias* directed to the Sheriff of Buckinghamshire, empowering him to make Hampden show cause why he should not obey the orders of the Court. In response to this process, Hampden had demanded *Oyer* of the *Scire Facias*, the Schedule of the original writ, the *Certiorari* and the *Mittimus*.[19]

Potentially at least, the case related to the process of enforcement rather than the legality of the demand for ship-money itself. As Hampden's counsel Holborne put it, there were three questions: whether on 4 August 1635 Charles had been able to charge Buckinghamshire to 'find a ship at their cost and charges'; if he had that power, whether he could give the Sheriff the power to assess the county for those costs and charges; and, if so, whether charges assessed but unpaid could be recovered using *Certiorari*, *Mittimus* and *Scire Facias*.[20] The result was pleading on both the broader issue – whether ship-money in this form was legal at all – and the narrower question – whether it could be enforced by these means. As a result, there was some variety among the 12 judicial opinions about what was critical to this case. However, all of those sitting had already given an opinion 'with one voice' on the declaration of an emergency, and so it is hardly

---

[17] 3 St Tr 825, 841–46, quotations at 845.
[18] Sharpe (above n 10) 721. For a clear account of the legal arguments, see DL Keir, 'The Case of Ship-Money' (1936) 52 *LQR* 546; Hart (above n 12) 148–57. The government had also been interested in prompting a test case: Gill (above n 10) 173–74.
[19] 3 St Tr 825, 856–57.
[20] ibid, 963.

surprising that neither counsel nor they dwelt on the principle of the King's duty to recognise danger, and responsibility to defend the kingdom from it.

A. Arguments for the Parties

Oliver St John, opening for Hampden, dwelt mainly on the first issue: the writ of 4 August 1635. He conceded the King's case that the duty to provide for the security of the kingdom was the King's alone, but concentrated instead on the means by which he should carry out that duty. There was no question over where the powers given to the Sheriff in the ship-money writ lay – 'for that is in the King' – but only over the means by which he exercised those powers. He also conceded that individual property rights were protected, but that these protections were subordinate to the collective interest of the whole kingdom – if that was not safeguarded there would be no individual property.[21] This lies close to a longer-term reading of Hobbes, that the collective interest in the preservation of sovereign authority outweighs individual rights since without that sovereign authority a return to the state of nature is threatened. The sovereign has reciprocal moral obligations to impose the duty equally and so on, but there is no fundamental doubt about the sovereign's right to taxation.[22] The question St John needed to argue, then, was how to balance the King's highest duty – defence of the realm – with the subject's highest interest – in his property. In allowing this argument he had apparently made a very large concession to the royal case, with dramatic implications for the exercise of prerogative discretion. Rather than challenge this argument, his limitation on the King was based instead on a distinction between the monarch's *potestas volunta* or *interna* and his *potestas legalis* or *externa*. Although he was the fountain of justice, for example, or could give bounty, he did that through the known channels of legal process – by his *potestas legalis*, not simply by his own will. This opened the door to discussion of the role in assisting him of his judges and also the Great Council in Parliament. Parliament was another of his courts, given life by his summons, and what was done in Parliament was done by the King; and it was in Parliament that the King had power over the subject's property.

---

[21] ibid 857–61, quotation at 861. The following discussion is based on the printed record rather than the abundant manuscript material. I was not able to make use of the very careful discussion of the discrepancies between on the one hand the printed record and on the other the draft notes and submissions in N Perkins, 'The Judiciary and the Defence of Property in the Law Courts during the Personal Rule of Charles I' (PhD thesis, University of Cambridge, 1997) 4–9 and ch 2. I am grateful to Dr Saunders (née Perkins) for discussing these issues with me. Her forthcoming work on St John and Littleton will give important new insight into the shaping of their arguments in particular.

[22] D Jackson, 'Thomas Hobbes' Theory of Taxation' (1973) 21 *Political Studies* 175. For Hobbes's views on taxation in a much broader and more immediately historical context see N Dauber, *State and Commonwealth: The Theory of the State in Early Modern England, 1549–1640* (Princeton, NJ, Princeton University Press, 2016) ch 5.

The writ gave power to alter the property of the subject but no sign that it was issued by the King 'sitting in his estate royal in Parliament'.

Since the law could not demand something impossible, it was also clear that the King must have resources with which to fulfil his duty to defend the realm. Many precedents showed that the King could call on feudal tenures and employ prerogative rights, some of which generated revenue for defence – tonnage and poundage and customs duties, for example. Where St John opened space to justify Hampden's refusal was by claiming that where further resources were needed, the King must go to Parliament. By demanding access to further resources he was affecting property rights, and those could only legitimately be altered in Parliament. This was not to argue that Parliament shared the duty of defence, only that it shared in the provision of the means of defence; and this did not reduce the King's power, since he was here exercising his power in Parliament. The danger specified in the writ was apprehended by the King in time of peace, not war, and could apparently be met by payment brought in seven months later. In this case, he clearly could have called a parliament. St John's most dubious move, however, was to claim that in an emergency the King had to summon a parliament – there was no emergency in which that could not be done: as the later arguments began to put it, he had to do this even with Hannibal at the gates. By all the precedents he had laid out, St John hoped to have demonstrated that previous monarchs could not have imposed such a charge on a subject as that imposed on Hampden, 'without assent in parliament'.[23] If in need of urgent assistance the King could borrow, and repay when Parliament met to supply the additional assistance. As Keir pointed out long ago, this was in effect to say, despite his initial statement, that the property rights of the individual did indeed trump the threat to the collective.[24]

Opening for the King, Sir Edward Littleton accepted much of St John's legal and antiquarian scholarship but dismissed its significance to the case: 'I shall now discard many things as impertinent to the question'.[25] The critical difference between them was about how the King should act in an emergency – if the King thought his own resources insufficient to meet some great danger then he had the right to act at his discretion to secure further resources, and only he could be the judge of that. If he felt that the nature or immediacy of the danger rendered resort to Parliament inappropriate, then he had no legal obligation to make such a resort. To say otherwise was in effect to say that he could only fulfil his duty to provide security with the assent of his subjects. St John's review of the King's various rights and financial sources therefore, 'though it was done with advantage and policy, yet the bulk and mass of [it] shall appear to fall quite off as nothing to the purpose'.[26]

---

[23] 3 St Tr 825, 923; Keir (above n 18) 557–58.
[24] 3 St Tr 825, 557.
[25] ibid, 924.
[26] ibid, 925.

If St John's argument seemed to threaten all property by offering essentially unqualified defence of individual property, the danger here was the unlimited discretion Littleton seems to give the King to interfere with the property of his subjects. The key claim of St John's case, or at least political sensitivity revealed by it, was that if the King could charge 20 shillings on Hampden by these means, he might in future charge £20, or any other sum, 'whereby it would come to pass, that if the subject had any thing at all, he is not beholden to the law for it, but it is left entirely in the mercy and goodness of the King'.[27]

Littleton's argument that the security of the Commonwealth is to be preferred to the private rights of the subject seems to raise this spectre: all private estates depend on the security of the Commonwealth, of course, so it makes logical sense, but the implication that the King's judgement about the needs of the security of the Commonwealth overrides specific legal protections for individual estates gives no obvious remaining defence to the subject. He was conscious, in fact, that he was at a disadvantage arguing in this way, 'every man being a party interested that hears me'.[28] In law, though, it was better to run this risk, than to rob the King of the power to act without Parliament in an emergency. Without security of the kingdom there were no laws; the King's obligations were prior to the particular protections of national law.

Having established this general position Littleton then cited precedent and example to show that the whole kingdom had a shared responsibility for the security of the land and the seas, that the King had powers over property in emergency conditions and so on, and to undercut the relevance or accuracy of St John's account. His emphasis was on the constant usage of previous monarchs, rather than 'scattered judgements here and there, or judicial proceedings in any court'.[29]

Richard Holborne, for Hampden, placed much greater emphasis on the legal sufficiency of the writ of 4 August, and the *Mittimus* which recited its burden: neither of which gave evidence of the danger to the safety and preservation of the kingdom that the King perceived. The writ did not set out what this danger was beyond the threat of piracy, and through it to the King's dominion of the seas. Many of the judges were therefore later forced to comment on the statement of the danger in the writ, and its sufficiency in law, even while they studiously disclaimed any power to second guess the King on his perception that the kingdom was in danger. Everyone, in fact, was bound to avoid questioning the judgement of this particular king: as Holborne put it, Hampden and his counsel 'believe there was such a danger [on 4 August 1635], though not apparent to us', but it was dangerous to leave such a matter simply to the King's affirmation: 'lest what his majesty in his own worth deserves, by after princes might turn to a disadvantage'.[30]

[27] ibid, 886.
[28] ibid, 925.
[29] ibid, 937.
[30] ibid, 967.

Holborne also went well beyond this technical issue though, arguing (having sought permission of the judges) on the more sensitive question: in his view the King could not charge the subject out of Parliament except in special cases which were different from the current one; not even for necessary defence, even though the King judged the danger to be 'instant and unavoidable'.[31] Of course, he did not dispute the King's word that there was an imminent danger but set even tighter restrictions than St John had done around what the King could do in such circumstances: since he could only alter property in Parliament, he was required to resort to Parliament. Only in a case of instant and apparent danger can these defences of individual property be ignored, but in such circumstances any subject might do the same, including with the King's property – building defences and so on. If the King wanted to lay a *charge*, however, he had to do so by law, and that required resort to Parliament.

His point was that this levy was not governed by law – whereas law decided the king had to be restrained, and that was why kings had such a good record in relation to their subjects' property. Requiring them to submit to this restraint was better than the alternative – to risk the effectiveness of the response in conditions of extreme danger was preferable to removing these protections of individual estates. He did though concede that service could be demanded in an emergency, but not money – and this was a distinction which proved of some importance to the judges' opinions.

These arguments served to throw doubt on the sufficiency of the process – the role of the sheriff and the appropriateness of the procedure of debt recovery: how could a sheriff know enough to allocate a rate equally among all the people of a county (parliamentary taxes used commissions, or customary allocations, neither of which applied in this case), and how could he tax himself, as an inhabitant of the county? And how could such a rating for a contribution to a ship provided by the county be enforced by distraint to the king? The ship belonged to Buckinghamshire and had been provided for service in emergency conditions. This latter point is briefly made in the record but was crucial to at least two of the judgments: that the writ *Scire Facias* would bring money to the Exchequer (as a debt to the King) and so was not obviously an appropriate remedy for Hampden's failure to bear his charge for the county's ship.[32]

Sir John Bankes, for the King, took a stronger line than Littleton on prerogative powers in times of danger, responding to Holborne's stronger line on the essential restraint of the King. The prerogative to provide for defence and security of the realm was intrinsic to the royal dignity. It was confirmed by natural law, the civil law and the law of the realm, and where the law assumed the good intentions of a monarch, it was not appropriate for subjects to doubt that. Since kings had existed before parliaments, it must be the case that they could

---

[31] ibid, 969.
[32] ibid, 1014.

choose whether to exercise their power in or out of Parliament. Here, the threat of absolutism and untrammelled royal discretion is very clear: this power was 'inate in the person of an absolute king, and in the persons of the kings of England'. He was equally unequivocal that 'the king is the sole judge, both of the danger, and when and how it is to be avoided'. Bankes had little time either for the procedural questions: 'the power of punishing those that neglect such commands hath been always in the king', exercised by his commissioners or by his writs.[33] Procedure by *Scire Facias* was appropriate since there was a debt to the Commonwealth. Reason and precedent supported the view that the King, as head of the Commonwealth, could pursue that debt.

Although no one had questioned the King's judgement of the existence of danger (or power and duty to make that judgement), counsel had taken rather different positions on what the King could or should do in such conditions. Littleton and Bankes gave him discretion in that; St John argued that he had to act in concert with Parliament if he was going to demand access to property and not just service; Holborne that it was essential to restrain the King in this way. There was a related question, of how immediate a danger would have to be in order to prevent the very desirable resort to Parliament.

B. Judgment

A number of the judges agreed with Crawley, who said that this was 'one of the greatest cases that ever was in judgement before the judges of law', putting the royal prerogative in the balance with the subject's property rights.[34] Crawley regretted that it had been brought to a court rather than a public assembly, echoing the response of some in the provinces to news of the earlier extra-judicial opinion.[35] Vernon (who found for the King) and Denham (who found for Hampden) both excused their non-attendance and brief judgments on grounds of ill-health.[36] There was certainly great interest in the provinces, and news of the judgments was subsequently to circulate widely.

The judgments are lengthy and detailed, and we will here divide the arguments in two: the legality of the demand and sufficiency of the original writ; and the legality of the means taken to administer the writ and enforce payment. Both, of course, were critical to Crown policy, but it is the first question that has attracted most attention subsequently. Most of the judges restricted themselves to what they considered legal questions, leaving matters of statecraft to masters

---

[33] ibid, 1017, 1025, 1029.
[34] ibid, 1073, 1089, 1125. For further insight into the political sensitivities, which are revealed more clearly by comparing draft and manuscript materials with the public account of the trial, see Perkins (above n 21) ch 2.
[35] 3 St Tr 825, 1127–28; Fincham, Twisden.
[36] ibid, 1125, 1201–02.

of 'policy', philosophy or history, although Finch and Berkeley both delivered judgments that contained very strong statements about royal prerogative power. There was little disagreement among the judges that the law provided the King with the means for the normal defence of the kingdom and if they proved insufficient then he could borrow or resort to Parliament. The clear implication was that ship-money could not be used for the normal needs of defence – it was an emergency measure.

Similarly, the earlier ruling that the King was the sole judge of danger, and that the law had to provide the means for him to carry out that duty, had not been contested by counsel, and was upheld by all the judges. For Weston and Trevor this was simply a matter of legal procedure – in demurring the writs Hampden had accepted the facts. Demurrer led to a hearing of the law, only a jury could have judged the facts.[37] Others though accepted it as a matter of fact simply because the King had said there was a danger, in line with the earlier extra-judicial opinion, and Weston pointed out that it was a matter of common sense – one only had to look around to see that war was everywhere in Europe.[38] There was some difference about whether the writ sufficiently specified the danger, although most of the judges agreed that the threat of piracy and the implied threat to the King's control of the seas, were real dangers, and that the latter posed a serious threat to the kingdom's international standing at a time of more or less universal European war. Trevor made the positive argument that the *Sovereign of the Seas* provided exactly this kind of demonstration of power, and hence protection from the dangers perceived by the King.[39] On narrower questions too, the judges agreed that the demand was legal: there were precedents, for example, for inland charges for coastal defence[40] although Croke pointed out that the precedents were for charges on particular places and not for a general inland rate.[41]

A key point of argument though, was that in such circumstances the King could demand service, not impose a charge. A number of judges pointed out that if he needed money and could not call a parliament he could indeed borrow and pay the money back once Parliament met. Hutton took an advanced position on this, arguing that the King could only raise cash in times of actual war, and that the threat of piracy was insufficient.[42] It is critical for understanding the rulings as a whole though to understand the question the judges were answering, or felt that they should answer: it is not a decision about the legality of 'non-parliamentary taxation', which was not supported by any of them, but about the powers of the King to demand service in conditions of danger; and whether

[37] ibid, 1066, 1126.
[38] ibid, 1067–08 (Weston); 1087 (Crawley).
[39] ibid, 1127.
[40] ibid, eg, 1069–73.
[41] ibid, 1137.
[42] ibid, 1191–92, 1198.

ship-money fell within the bounds set by law in such conditions. Deeming it a service not a charge was one way of containing it within those bounds.

Hutton and Croke were outliers, in that respect. Croke declared the rate to be against common law as well as statute. It was a common charge and no such common charge could be imposed without consent. Necessity might allow the King to demand men's physical service, but not their property – no danger permitted a breach of the laws governing property.[43]

On the whole though the judges accepted the general principle that space had to be left in times of danger for the King to act without Parliament, although they were divided on whether the immediacy of the danger mattered – Hampden's counsel had argued that only in the case of the most immediate danger was it justifiable for the King to act without resort to Parliament.[44] The urgency of the danger could really be very extreme before the King had to impose charges out of Parliament – as Weston and Berkeley both acknowledged in judgments very favourable to Charles, the King could borrow *in extremis* and repay once conditions permitted the summons of a parliament. It was generally agreed it was preferable to take emergency measures through Parliament, but that it could not be right to require this by law.[45] Both Berkeley and Finch, however, made very strong statements in opposition to any 'King-yoking' policy on this point which have become notorious.[46]

But if there was no requirement in law to resort to Parliament, what should we make of the statutory protections of the subject's property? If the King was not yoked by the means Croke hoped, what did give subjects security in their property? One line of argument here is almost platitudinous – that the law is the King's friend, and so we are wrong to assume any tension. Others are more narrow – that ship-money is not mentioned in the Acts against taxation without consent, or that those statutes related to the King's ordinary expenses, rather than emergency conditions. Here the most advanced position was that in extreme conditions statutes could not restrain a king – in a case of necessity, law and reason must come before statute.

Pushed to these extremes – what powers did a king have in the face of danger, immediate or apparent – it was hard to argue differently from the majority of the judges. But this did of course raise the more obvious question: did this situation pertain to England in 1635, when the writ contested by Hampden was issued? To some extent this argument had been forestalled by the concession that only the King could judge, but Croke and Hutton both pointed out that the original writ had not spelt out the danger. That this seemed to matter was manifest in the fact

---

[43] ibid, 1128–34. Keir thought that in admitting that a charge might be imposed on individuals for a common benefit that Croke was in fact selling the pass to ship-money (above n 18) 566, 568.

[44] This thread of argument is discussed at length, ibid.

[45] See Weston, eg, 3 St Tr 825, 1075.

[46] ibid, 1096–99, 1235.

that the *Mittimus* that had brought Hampden to court in 1637 had tried to fill in the gap. The other judges felt the writ sufficient, that Hampden had demurred to writs that did mention the danger thereby acknowledging the fact, or that the *Mittimus* explained but did not expand on the earlier writ.

As already noted, there was a further ground for supporting the writ, and one that proved of critical importance – ship-money was a demand for service (the supply of a ship), not a charge. This is on the face of it, a hard one to swallow, but as Weston pointed out the writ demanded supply of a ship, and any unused money was not to be detained by the assessors or used for any other purpose. This was in fact true: the money was accounted for separately, all of it went to support the fleet except a very small amount loaned in the final year of the levy, and it does not seem to have replaced normal navy spending to any significant degree, since that remained fairly stable through these years.[47] It was clear, in other words, that the money was simply the means by which the service of providing these ships could be performed. A number of judges contented themselves with this line of argument, and it allowed Berkeley to judge that ship-money was clearly not a tax or charge. On this basis Weston argued that statutes and charters against imposing charges without consent were intended against *illegal* charges – it was surely not necessary for the King to resort to Parliament every time he made a charge on his subject for some particular purpose.[48] Others though could not follow him. Davenport's starting point was that it was impossible for Buckinghamshire to supply a ship, the law could not demand anything that was impossible, and so it must in fact be a charge, and Croke also argued this way. Hutton was similarly unconvinced that it could really be seen as a service not a charge.[49]

Agreed that the King was the sole judge of danger, and more or less agreed, that the writ had been sufficient on this point, the question remained whether the enforcement of the obligation had been legal. It was on this point that the outcome was genuinely close. Five of the judges found, one way or another, that Hampden could not be prosecuted for failure to pay – he had been asked for a service not for money. The strong view was that it was not practically possible for Hampden to perform the service of providing part of a ship in an inland county – Hutton and Croke doubted the existence of such a ship, and Croke suggested that if there was no such ship then the Sheriff owed everyone in Buckinghamshire a refund. The issue was also a more limited one: the ship, if there was one, belonged to Buckinghamshire, so how could the King recover a debt owed to him? What interest did he have in the money? Those in favour of the King had to admit the point, arguing that the money was a means of apportioning the burden of the service, or the means to provide it, but that the case

---

[47] Gordon (above n 9) 141–45.
[48] 3 St Tr 825, 1068 (Weston); 1095 (Berkeley).
[49] ibid, 1206 (Davenport); 1139 (Croke).

could not properly be considered one of debt. Weston, who found for the King, admitted 'this point ... is of most difficulty'.[50]

A secondary question on the means of enforcement was whether a sheriff could perform this task, of assessing the rate and recovering sums unpaid by defaulters. Again, Weston put the case that he was able to impose the rate, as did Berkeley, although Davenport and Croke were much more doubtful: could he know enough on his own to impose an equal charge, and if he was himself an inhabitant, how could he assess himself fairly?[51] The question about whether they could recover unpaid sums was critical to the future of the rate, of course, and here the judges found the King's case particularly difficult. Sheriffs were appointed annually, so there was a related issue that the *Scire Facias* was directed to men who were not sheriff at the time the assessment was made. Neither did it state who the money should be paid to: if it was simply paid into the Crown's general funds it was a tax not a service and therefore illegal; but on the other hand, if there was already a Buckinghamshire ship, Hampden's money should be part of a refund to the county. If there was no Buckinghamshire ship, then the Crown's energy should be directed at the sheriff who had failed to carry out the writ.[52]

There were other technical concerns. Davenport found for Hampden partly because the original writ was not returnable, and doubted that the *Certiorari* and *Mittimus* could revive it. He also objected that a *Scire Facias* could not be issued except on the record of another court, but the *Mittimus* had only communicated the tenor of the record. Denham found for Hampden on the grounds that the King could only take goods on the basis of a judgment in court, and there was no such judgment in this case.[53]

If some of this sounds a little like trying to find loopholes it might be because the biggest question could not be politely posed, and in any case had been foreclosed: was there really an imminent danger that justified imposing a general rate without consent? All the judges agreed in principle that the King was the sole judge of danger and that the law must provide him the means to carry out his duty. Nine of them agreed, on slightly different grounds, that he could not be required to resort to Parliament in times of danger and that in a case of necessity the standard protections of property did not apply. With slightly less conviction they also agreed that the 1635 writ had given sufficient notice that the King judged there to be a danger to the realm. The view of the court then was that ship-money was a legitimate means by which the King could deal with apprehended danger and, by implication, that the subject's property rights were

---

[50] ibid, 1140 (Croke); 1212–13 (Davenport); 1077 (Weston). For the argument that money was the means of service and so enforceable ibid, 1095 (Berkeley).

[51] ibid, 1077 (Weston); 1139–40 (Croke); 1207 (Davenport).

[52] ibid, 1200 (Hutton); 1250–51 (Bramston). The implications of Bramston and Davenport's opinions on this issue are drawn out by Conrad Russell, in C Russell, 'The Ship-Money Judgments of Bramston and Davenport' (1962) 77 *English Historical Review* 303.

[53] 3 St Tr 825, 1212, 1213–14 (Davenport); 1201–02 (Denham).

not threatened, by such extraordinary powers. The issue on which the King's case nearly foundered, however, was whether compliance with this service was enforceable by these means. Here the balance, was very fine, just shading 7:5 for the King. Jones gave the least resounding judgment for the King, concluding on condition that none of Hampden's 20 shillings should end up in the King's purse, 'for it do, my opinion is against it'. In fact, his whole judgment was rather measured, so that one contemporary wrote to Thomas Wentworth that Jones 'had handled the business so that no man could tell what to make of his argument'.[54]

Although the judges had not seriously questioned the existence of an emergency, Weston noted the wider political problem: 'The subject suspects this is only a pretence and that the kingdom is not really in danger'. As a legal question though, he dismissed this, as we have seen, and he did himself think the danger was obvious.[55] The judges had really been asked to comment on the King's powers when he judged there to be a danger affecting the whole realm. There was broad agreement among counsel that he could demand service, but deep disagreement about the means by which he could get access to his subjects' property. The judgments, on the whole, favoured the King's position. The implication though was that the King had discretion to identify a danger, and to take assets in which subjects' property subsisted without parliamentary sanction if he saw such a danger: this made it imperative that monarchs be trustworthy in identifying such danger.

IV. THE ABOLITION OF SHIP-MONEY

The judges had given opinions within a relatively narrow frame – set by the opinion of 1635 and by an unwillingness to say as a matter of law that the King's judgement could not be trusted as to the existence of danger. As things stood in 1637 it is hard to think a judge could say much other than that the King was the sole judge of an emergency, and it must have seemed hard to gainsay the pressure to say that in such an emergency he had to have freedom to act. Parliament at that stage 'was an event and not an institution', and not well equipped to act as an executive.[56] The rulings however may have been counterproductive: Clarendon thought that prior to the ruling people had been willing to pay even though they did not have to; after the ruling they were more reluctant to pay because that might mean, potentially, condoning the more extreme statements of Finch and Berkeley. And given the reluctance of the judges to question the facts of the case, these high claims about the prerogative could seem to require only that the

---

[54] ibid, 1191; Gill (above n 10) 175.
[55] 3 St Tr 825, 1067.
[56] C Russell, *Parliaments and English Politics 1621–1629* (Oxford, Oxford University Press, 1979) quotation at 3.

King 'perceiveth' danger. These statements, Clarendon subsequently said, had been gravely against the King's real interests.[57] Certainly ship-money seems to have continued to provoke more rating disputes than other seventeenth-century taxes.[58]

Soon after the judgment on Hampden's case events moved against Charles, and the unravelling of his regime led to a more fundamental change in the role of Parliament. As the judges were deliberating in the summer of 1637 Charles faced an escalating rebellion in Scotland, prompted by the imposition of a new prayer book. Failure to defeat the Scots led to the summoning of a parliament, the Short Parliament, to rearm the Crown for war but instead it gave vent to many grievances, ship-money among them.

By then, of course, ship-money had been levied year after year on the King's judgement that a danger existed, and without the need to have recourse to Parliament. Charles, sensing the hostility, had offered to exchange his power to raise ship-money for the grant of 12 parliamentary subsidies, and in so doing one might think he had sold a pass. Unlike the judges, the politicians saw in the ship-money judgments an open door for Charles simply to impose a charge, claiming he perceived a danger, with no parliamentary control. George Peard, for example, argued that the ruling gave the absolute royal prerogative, exercised by the King's will alone, priority over common law defences of property:

> [I]f wee have noe property, noe man will marry that cannot leave his estate, noe man industrious if not sure to enjoy his labours, noe man sowe he may reape, but not sure to sowe. Noe may provid for his daughter, nor bring up a sonne at university, but must pay shipmoney. Noe man eate but in danger to have his meate taken away or to be taken away from his meate.[59]

Patently, his subjects (unlike the law) did not trust the King. Charles dissolved Parliament, took on the Scottish Covenanters once again without parliamentary support, and lost. An occupying Scottish army demanded payment of their expenses on a scale that only Parliament could meet, so that the defeated King was forced to call a parliament that could not be dissolved until the Scottish army had left. Ship-money was not a principal cause of the crisis, although it was an early victim of it. One reason for that was that the polite fiction that there might be regal misgovernment only in principle was now revealed to be just that: a fiction. Charles's judgement was now in question on a whole range

---

[57] Edward Hyde, Earl of Clarendon, *History of the Rebellion and Civil Wars in England* WD Macray (ed), 6 vols (first published 1702–04; Oxford, Oxford University Press, 1888) I, 86–90. He singled out Finch's judgment, and its unnecessary logic, for raising rather than settling fears: ibid, 89–90. For 'when he perceiveth danger to be imminent … and a necessity of defence' see, eg, 3 St Tr 825, 1182 (Jones, conceding this point in a judgment that found for Hampden on other grounds).

[58] Langelüddeke (above n 13).

[59] G Burgess, *The Politics of the Ancient Constitution: An Introduction to English Political Thought* (Basingstoke, Macmillan, 1992) quotation at 216; see also Hart (above n 12) 167–70.

of issues, and openly so, and it was no longer plausible to claim that this was a simply theoretical possibility: the fig leaf now was that it was the people around him, rather than the King himself, that could not be trusted.

The ship-money judges who found against Hampden figured in this list of enemies of good government. The way that the questions had been framed now seemed to have avoided the key question: this king was so patently capable of misjudgement that it was clear that the law must offer defence against the absolute royal prerogative. They had refused to consider whether or not there was an emergency, resulting in a 'judgement of law grounded upon matter of fact of which there was neither inquiry or proof'.[60] The extra-judicial opinion, which had forestalled much discussion in *R v Hampden*, and which some thought would have been better coming from a Parliament, was as much a target as the judgments delivered on Hampden's case.[61] The royalist historian Clarendon observed that the judges earned 'deserved reproach and infamy [having been] made use of in this and the like acts of power'.[62] Seven of them were impeached or threatened with it. All the judges had signed the extra-judicial opinion, of course, which was now seen as a major threat to the integrity of the laws of the kingdom, and so Bramston and Davenport were in trouble even though they had found in Hampden's favour: they had done so only on the narrow issue of debt recovery. Jones, Vernon and Denham were already dead, so the only surviving judges to escape this vengeance were Croke and Hutton, both having found for Hampden on the grounds that ship-money was illegal. Finch, who was now accused by others of having pressured them over the extra-judicial judgment, had fled to Holland as his impeachment was being prepared.[63]

The levy itself was abolished by An Act for the declaring unlawful and void the late proceedings touching Ship-Money, and for the vacating of all records and process concerning the same. By implication it can be thought to have limited the King's discretionary power to determine a national emergency, and has stood for the repudiation of non-parliamentary taxation, but the text says nothing directly about this.[64] The body of the Act simply declared the extra-judicial opinions and the judgments in *R v Hampden* 'utterly against the law of the land', 'contrary to the laws and statutes of this realm, the right of property, the liberty of the subjects, former resolution in Parliament and the Petition of Right'. It also called for the full execution of 'every the particulars prayed or desired' in the Petition of Right, and the destruction of all records relating to the various judgments in favour of ship-money or process on them.[65] But there

---

[60] Clarendon (above n 57) I, 87.

[61] Much of this material is reproduced in 3 St Tr 825, 1254–1306. For broader discussions see Burgess (above n 59) 215–20; M Mendle, 'The Ship-Money Case, *The Case of Shipmony*, and the Development of Henry Parker's Parliamentary Absolutism' (1989) 32 *Historical Journal* 513.

[62] Clarendon (above n 57) I, 88.

[63] Keir (above n 18) 546–47; Gill (above n 10) 170–72.

[64] Hart (above n 12) 187–88.

[65] Gardiner (above n 1) quotations at 191.

really is nothing else beyond this: the Act simply overturns the judgments; it does not explain how they were illegal, or how the subject should understand the relationship between necessity and the common law, or how the prerogative should be exercised in or out of Parliament. Although many of the main players in these debates clearly rejected the arguments of necessity accepted by the judges,[66] the Act of abolition did not state an alternative position on the prerogative powers in cases of emergency.

However, a practical position took shape in the rest of the legislation from this period: the abolition of a whole host of particular prerogative powers, including for example, the power to set the rates at which many import duties had been collected. It is hard to think of any practical powers remaining to the King which allowed him to alter a subject's property. All those powers now rested in Parliament. Further reversal was to follow as Parliament assumed the power to declare emergency conditions in 1642, as England was sliding into civil war.

In the spring of 1642 Parliament took charge of military and financial resources without royal assent, on the basis of arguments about an emergency, and the parliamentary apologist Henry Parker returned to some of the issues in *R v Hampden*. Despite the rhetoric surrounding the impeachments, the judges had really justified ship-money as necessary for the benefit of the Commonwealth (of which the King was in such conditions the sole judge) and not the benefit of the King: a number of them saw themselves as arbitrating between Hampden's rights in his own property and the collective interests of the community as determined by the King. In his commentary on the case Parker accepted these arguments about necessity, individual rights and the public good, but turned them: it was the King who was pursuing an individual benefit and Hampden who stood for the collective good in resisting a misguided King. Parker retained the view that necessity could trump the individual interest, but now vested that executive interest in Parliament, not the King's will – the *dominium politicum*, where matters of state could be fully considered alongside matters of law. This was the origins of a parliamentary absolutism (some would say tyranny) that licensed dramatic new measures, without legal precedent, enacted by Parliament in Ordinances without royal assent.[67]

Armed with these arguments Parliament quickly erected a massively more effective revenue system, with allied powers to seize and dispose of property as well as (for example) powers to suspend religious ministers and imprison authors of publications they found distasteful. To some radicals, notably John Lilburne, the leading Leveller, it looked as if there had been an *Animal Farm* moment, in which the parliamentary pigs had simply started behaving like their predecessors, the royalist humans. The war was not between Crown and

---

[66] Mendle (above n 61) 520–21.
[67] R Ashton, 'From Cavalier to Roundhead Tyranny, 1642–9' in J Morrill (ed), *Reactions to the English Civil War 1642–1649* (Basingstoke, Macmillan, 1982); J Morrill, *Revolt in the Provinces: The People of England and the Tragedies of War 1630–1648*, 2nd edn (Harlow, Longman, 1999) ch 2.

Parliament, Lilburne came to think, but between the people and tyranny. The struggle now was to make Parliament accountable, or subject to some mechanism of restraint: the Leveller answer was an *Agreement of the People*, although Lilburne also fought successive governments in print, parliamentary committees and the courts.[68]

Much of the parliamentary war machine was retained after the Restoration, so that parliamentary taxation came to dominate the much larger revenue flows that underpinned England's (and then Britain's) emergence as a world power: this truly was a revolution in government. Across the seventeenth century these developments made it clear that expedients such as ship-money belonged to a lost world, as royal finances were transformed into public finances. This allowed a doubling of the proportion of GDP being taxed during the 1640s, followed by a further doubling in the 1690s. That greatly increased tax-take was associated with more or less complete parliamentary control over revenue: rising to 97 per cent of the total in 1690s. The invention of the civil list in 1697 was symbolic of this – allocating a royal income from the public finances.[69] More secure tax flows, underpinned by parliamentary sanction and powers of audit, secured borrowing on a hitherto unimaginable scale. The growth of the Royal Navy after 1650 made the pride in the *Sovereign of the Seas* look unambitious to the point of quaintness. Meanwhile Parliament, by far the biggest spender and consumer in the economy, began to use that power more coherently to manage the national economy, for example, by encouraging and discouraging particular forms of production or consumption.[70]

This was not though because the Act abolishing ship-money had outlawed 'unparliamentary taxation', or even the ideal of a king living of his own and resorting to Parliament for extraordinary revenues. Still less had it settled the balance of the executive judgement of the collective interest and individual property rights. These developments did though clearly put the ship-money judges on wrong side of history, and so clearly on that side that it is understandable that their sincerity or courage has subsequently been called into question. However, the questions in 1635 and 1637 were rather different, and Keir can be thanked for salvaging the questions as they were actually posed at that point, rather than at a very different political conjuncture only three, five or 10 years later.[71] It was perhaps equally true of the parliamentary cause in 1642 that hard cases make bad law: the parliamentarian answers to these questions in the 1640s were no more decisive than *R v Hampden* had proved, and were equally repugnant to a new generation of champions of individual protections from executive power.

[68] M Braddick, *The Common Freedom of the People: John Lilburne and the English Revolution* (Oxford, Oxford University Press, 2018).

[69] EA Reitan, 'The Civil List in Eighteenth-Century British Politics: Parliamentary Supremacy Versus the Independence of the Crown' (1966) 9 *Historical Journal* 318.

[70] Braddick, *The Nerves of State* (above n 3) ch 1; Braddick, *State Formation* (above n 6) 213–26.

[71] Keir (above n 18).

2

Farmer v Glyn-Jones *(1903)*
The Perils of Revenue Practice

CHANTAL STEBBINGS

I. THE CASE

T HE CASE OF *Farmer v Glyn-Jones*[1] was heard in the Divisional Court of the King's Bench Division in the spring of 1903. It was an appeal by way of case stated by a Metropolitan police magistrate,[2] and the tax it concerned was the medicine stamp duty. Abolished in 1941, this was a tax first introduced in 1783 on proprietary medicines – essentially commercial medicines purchased from a range of retailers without the need for a physician's prescription – in order to tap that very lucrative trade in times of acutely straitened public finances. The bottles or packets of those medicines liable to the tax, namely those which were secret, proprietary, patented, or recommended for the relief or cure of any human ailment, would have to be wrapped in a medicine stamp of the correct value purchased from the Stamp Office. The tax was charged under the Medicine Stamp Act 1812,[3] and was enforced by means of an information laid by officers of the Inland Revenue against any vendor selling such medicines unstamped.[4]

In the *Farmer* case, an information was laid against the respondent, William Glyn-Jones, for having sold unstamped a bottle of medicine which was liable to

---

[1] *Farmer v Glyn-Jones* [1903] 2 KB 6 (KB).
[2] The first stipendiary magistrates.
[3] 52 Geo 3 c 150, s 2.
[4] See generally, C Stebbings, *Tax, Medicines and the Law: From Quackery to Pharmacy* (Cambridge, Cambridge University Press, 2017).

the tax. The medicine in question was *Tincture of Quinine*. The label on the bottle read:

Ammoniated

TINCTURE OF QUININE B.P.

A well-known and highly recommended remedy

for

INFLUENZA AND COLDS

Dose – One teaspoonful in water every four hours until relieved

The action was a test case, deliberately initiated by Glyn-Jones as the Secretary of the Chemists' Defence Association[5] in order to provoke a definitive judicial ruling on a particular statutory provision. In his view that provision had always been misinterpreted by the Inland Revenue authorities so as to deny qualified chemists and druggists[6] an exemption from the tax which was rightfully theirs. He acted in the interests of the trade, to have the question settled once and for all. To that end, Glyn-Jones corresponded beforehand with the officials of the Board of Inland Revenue, sending them two copies of the medicine label and stating that he intended to sell a bottle of the medicine, unstamped, at his shop in East India Road, Poplar. He duly made the sale to a certain Mr Powning, who was an officer of the Board. An information was subsequently laid against him by the Inland Revenue, and thus began the litigation.

The background to the case was the interpretation of a statutory exemption from the medicine stamp duty in favour of *known, admitted and approved remedies* sold by a qualified pharmacist. The *Tincture of Quinine* in this case was prima facie liable to the medicine stamp duty because it came within the words of the general charge to tax. This provided that every enclosure containing any preparation to be used as a medicine 'for the prevention, cure, or relief of any disorder or complaint incident to, or in anywise affecting, the human body' and sold in Great Britain was chargeable, if the maker or seller made or sold it under letters patent, or claimed a secret art, or an exclusive right in doing so, or recommended it to the public as an effective remedy, or if it was expressly named in the schedule to the Act. The *Tincture of Quinine* was clearly a medicine sold to relieve a human ailment, and there was no doubt that the wording of the label amounted to an unambiguous written recommendation for the medicine's efficacy. The *Tincture of Quinine* was undoubtedly within the charge to tax.

---

[5] William Samuel Glyn-Jones (1869–1927), barrister, pharmacist, secretary and registrar of the Pharmaceutical Society, founder of the Proprietary Articles Trade Association in 1896, Liberal Member of Parliament for Stepney in 1910.

[6] The title was a conjunctive one. Chemists prepared and sold chemical substances, while druggists were concerned with the sale of drugs of vegetable rather than mineral or chemical derivation. Originally chemists and druggists were distinct occupations, and although they were indistinguishable by the eighteenth century, the dual title remained in use.

The Medicine Stamp Act, however, provided for the exemption of composite medicines which were *known, admitted and approved remedies* for illnesses. Three conditions had to be satisfied for the exemption to apply. Two were positive: the medicine had to be sold by a qualified individual, which class included chemists and druggists; and it had to be known, admitted and approved as a medicine relieving or curing a human ailment. The third condition was negative, to the effect that for the exemption to apply the medicine should not be secret, proprietary, patented or recommended in writing as an effective remedy by the 'owners, proprietors, makers, compounders, original or first vendors thereof'.

Glyn-Jones was a qualified chemist and druggist, the medicine's composition was not secret because its formula was included in the *British Pharmacopoeia*, and he claimed no proprietary rights in it as owner or maker, and so the only material legal issue was his status when he made the unequivocal written recommendation on the label. He was certainly the vendor, but the question was whether he was 'an original or first vendor'. If he was, then he was in breach of the express words of the exemption and would be liable. If he was not, then the exemption applied and he was not guilty of an offence in selling the medicine unstamped.

When the case was first heard in the Thames Police Court in May 1902,[7] Glyn-Jones was defended by Cyril Kirby, who was the solicitor to the Chemists' Defence Association which Glyn-Jones had founded in 1899. He argued that the aim of the Act was to tax only proprietary, secret and recommended medicines, and not medicines sold by a chemist and druggist which were recognised in the *Pharmacopoeia* as beneficial to illness, and to which no claim to ownership or recommendation had been made by the original or first vendor. The key issue was, therefore, the identity of the original or first vendor, and Glyn-Jones was not that individual. The meaning of 'original or first vendor' could be ascertained from other sections in the Act, and referred to the owner or proprietor of the medicine and not the retailer. Kirby had managed to trace the history of the *Tincture* back to 1853 and confirmed it had never been a proprietary or recommended medicine. His argument was that if the original proprietor of a medicine had never recommended it, no subsequent recommendation could make it liable. Any other construction would result in the exemption for *known, admitted and approved remedies* being nugatory. Chemists and druggists had the right under the exemption to recommend and sell free of duty *Pharmacopoeia* medicines. Mr Dennis, the solicitor representing the Inland Revenue, argued that Glyn-Jones was the first vendor of the bottle bearing the label which was liable to the duty. The medicine became liable to duty as soon as the recommending label was put on it, and it was Glyn-Jones who had done that when he put the medicine on sale in his shop.

---

[7] For the report to the profession of the *Farmer* case in the magistrate's court see Anonymous (*Pharmaceutical Journal* Editors), 'Legal Intelligence, Medicine Stamp Duty Acts' (1902) 68 *Pharmaceutical Journal* (series 4) 443, 523, 562.

In order to settle on any points which could be agreed, and leave only debatable ones for the trial, the hearing was adjourned for the two solicitors to confer. When the trial resumed three weeks later, a number of points had been agreed between the parties: essentially that the defendant was a qualified chemist and druggist; that the *Tincture* was well known, admitted and approved as a remedy for influenza; that it was prepared in accordance with the formula and directions published in the *British Pharmacopoeia*; and that the defendant claimed no secret, proprietary or exclusive right in the medicine and was not its originator. Since its widespread sale began in 1853 the *Tincture* had never been a proprietary medicine and anyone could make it. The point at issue was thus narrowed to just one: whether Glyn-Jones was or was not the 'original or first vendor'.

The magistrate, John Dickinson,[8] dismissed the information. The *Tincture* was unquestionably liable under the Medicine Stamp Duty Acts as coming within the words of the general charge, and the only question was whether it had been recommended by the original or first vendor, and whether Glyn-Jones was that person. He held that the first vendor was not, as the revenue authorities had contended, the person who first sold the medicine to the public, so it was not Glyn-Jones. It was the person who first introduced the product as a medicine, and in this case that was the manufacturer and wholesaler, Messrs Gale and Co, from whom Glyn-Jones had purchased the medicine. As the wholesaler did not recommend or advertise the medicine for the relief of influenza, it was not liable to the duty. So, when Glyn-Jones recommended the medicine through affixing a label at the retail stage, it was the first and only recommendation, and it could not and did not make the medicine liable. A contrary interpretation, namely that favoured by the Inland Revenue, would mean the exemption gave chemists and druggists no advantage. 'If the first person selling the article did not recommend it', observed the magistrate, 'then chemists were not liable to duty; but if, by recommending, a chemist became the first vendor, no chemist could ever sell with a recommendation'.[9] He accordingly found for Glyn-Jones and dismissed the summons.

The Inland Revenue appealed from this decision by way of case stated.[10] The appeal was heard in March and April 1903 in the Divisional Court of the King's Bench Division by Lord Alverstone CJ, Wills J and Channell J.[11] Both parties had the most distinguished counsel. The Inland Revenue's case was argued by Sir Edward Carson, who was the Solicitor General, and Sidney Rowlatt, who was then junior counsel to the Inland Revenue and was later to become a High

---

[8] He became the chief magistrate of the Metropolitan Police Courts, retiring in 1920.

[9] Anonymous (*Pharmaceutical Journal* Editors), 'Legal Intelligence, Medicine Stamp Duty Acts' (1902) 68 *Pharmaceutical Journal* (series 4) 563.

[10] Under the Summary Jurisdiction Act 1857 (20 & 21 Vict c 43) s 2; Summary Jurisdiction Act 1879 (42 & 43 Vict c 49) s 33.

[11] For the report to the profession of the *Farmer* case in the Divisional Court see Anonymous (*Pharmaceutical Journal* Editors), 'Legal Intelligence, Medicine Stamp Duty Acts' (1903) 70 *Pharmaceutical Journal* (series 4) 503, 630.

Court judge with a notable expertise in revenue matters.[12] Glyn-Jones was represented by HH Asquith KC, the future Prime Minister, and Henry Bonsey, who later became a county court judge.

The arguments on either side were lengthy in court though only briefly recorded in the Law Reports. The only issue was whether Glyn-Jones was the 'first vendor': if he was not, then he came squarely within the exemption for *known, admitted and approved remedies*. Sir Edward Carson, leading, argued that Glyn-Jones was the 'first vendor'. The word 'thereof' in the phrase 'owners, proprietors, makers, compounders, original or first vendors thereof' referred to the bottle containing the medicine and not the medicine itself. The Act, he said, intended to tax the medicine only once it was sold in a container with a written recommendation, and so until that point it was not dutiable. When Glyn-Jones affixed a label on the bottle recommending the medicine, the preparation became liable to duty and so he was its 'first vendor'.[13]

Asquith, leading for Glyn-Jones, argued that the duty had indeed to be paid on the enclosure,[14] but the legislation also provided that it was to be paid by the 'owners … and first vendors' of the medicine.[15] This suggested that the same phrase in the exemption clause must refer to the same subject matter, namely the medicine and not the bottle. The first vendor was, therefore, the person who first prepared the medicine and put it on the market.[16]

The Divisional Court, in a reserved judgment delivered one month later, affirmed the magistrate's decision and found against the Inland Revenue. Its judgment, delivered by Wills J, was unanimous, closely considered and reflected a concern fully to justify the decision. The judge began by dismissing the Crown's argument that the word 'thereof' in the phrase 'owners, proprietors, makers, compounders, original or first vendors thereof 'in the exemption could relate to each particular bottle, since that was patently absurd. It could only relate to the medicine itself. It was for the court to decide which person was meant within that phrase. The words of the exemption also made it clear that once that individual had made the written recommendation of the medicine, the medicine became liable to the duty and that liability was perpetual.[17] The words of the exemption alone showed that an ordinary retail chemist buying in the ordinary course of his trade a medicine which hitherto was within the exemption, could not be its owner or proprietor.

This finding on the basis of the words of the exemption alone was confirmed by other provisions in the legislation. Section 3 of the Medicine Stamp Act 1802[18]

[12] See R Thomas, 'Sir Sidney and Sir John: The Rowlatts and Tax' [2011] *BTR* 210.
[13] *Farmer* (above n 1) 9.
[14] Medicine Stamp Act 1802 (42 Geo 3 c 56) s 2.
[15] ibid, s 3.
[16] *Farmer* (above n 1) 10.
[17] Medicine Stamp Act 1812 (52 Geo 3 c 150) schedule.
[18] 42 Geo 3 c 56.

regulated the incidence of the tax, providing that the duty was to be paid by the 'owners and proprietors, or makers and compounders, or original and first vendors' of the medicine[19] in respect of every enclosure containing such medicine and should be paid before such medicine was first sold or delivered out of their possession and offered for sale. The Court took the view that the 'original or first vendors' mentioned in the exemption were the same as those mentioned in the charging portion of the schedule to the Act of 1812 and section 3 of the 1802 Act[20] – namely those individuals who first put the medicine into circulation and who were to pay the tax. It was for them, said the judge, to decide whether or not they wanted to increase their sales of the product by advertising it as an effective remedy, but as a consequence subjecting the medicine for ever to the burden of the duty.[21] In this case the first vendors – the manufacturers who had sold the medicine to Glyn-Jones, had made no recommendation, and so the medicine was not liable to duty when Glyn-Jones purchased it. Glyn-Jones' recommendation at the retail stage could have no effect on the liability of the medicine. It was not liable. It was a *known, admitted and approved remedy* which had not been recommended by the first vendor. The exemption thus applied and Glyn-Jones was not guilty. Furthermore, were the Crown's argument to be accepted that Glyn-Jones must be the 'first vendor thereof' because he was the first person to sell the medicine with a recommendation, the exemption for *known, admitted and approved remedies* would be entirely nugatory, as no chemist and druggist could come within it.

The case of *Farmer v Glyn-Jones* was, on the face of it, one in which the Court addressed a challenging issue of statutory interpretation, trying to find the meaning of the words as expressed in overlapping, obsolete and poorly drafted legislation. The construction of the language was to affirm what came to be known as the 'Chemists' Privilege', namely the statutory right of qualified chemists and druggists to recommend and sell recognised medicines free from duty. In assigning a definitive meaning to the words of the *known, admitted and approved remedy* exemption in the Medicine Stamp Duty Act, the case was of real substantive technical importance to the contemporary understanding of the law relating to the tax. Indeed, the consensus among chemists and druggists was that the decision 'supported the simple common-sense view' that the exemption would be 'little better than a sham' if the original approach of the revenue authorities was adopted. 'So far, therefore, important progress has at last been made towards a rational interpretation of the Medicine Stamp Acts'.[22] Its landmark status lay not so much in its technical clarification of the law,

---

[19] ibid, s 3.
[20] *Farmer* (above n 1) 18.
[21] ibid, 15.
[22] Anonymous (*Pharmaceutical Journal* Editors), 'Legal Intelligence, Medicine Stamp Duty Acts' (1902) 68 *Pharmaceutical Journal* (series 4) 561.

important though that was, but in its significance for the administration of the tax, the development of the pharmacy profession, and the very viability of the tax itself.

II. AN ADMINISTRATIVE LANDMARK

The decision in *Farmer v Glyn-Jones* was of technical importance in that it was the first judicial interpretation of one of just three exemptions to the medicine stamp duty, and that interpretation demonstrated that the meaning assigned to it for over one hundred years by the revenue authorities had been wrong. It thus clarified the law. However, it was in its impact on the administrative practice of the revenue authorities that it constituted a landmark case, and in its stark revelation of the nature and extent of that practice as it operated within the administration of the medicine stamp duty. Its administrative impact was immense and had two aspects. First, it caused a change from a practice which denied any kind of exemption for *known, admitted and approved remedies* to one which allowed it in its full vigour with minimal restriction and in so doing disregarded the statutory provision itself and aspects of the court decision which purported authoritatively to interpret it. Secondly, the decision in *Farmer* had long-term consequences which illustrate with unique clarity the dangers of bureaucratic law-making.

From its inception in the Medicine Stamp Duty Act 1785,[23] the *known, admitted and approved remedies* exemption had consistently been interpreted by the revenue authorities as merely declaratory, as a 'dead letter'[24] not involving any substantive exemption. Indeed this interpretation was a rational one: the statute provided that when a qualified chemist and druggist sold a *known, admitted and approved* medicine it was exempt from the tax, but that the exemption would not apply if the medicine was secret, proprietary, patented or recommended in writing as an effective remedy by the 'owners, proprietors, makers, compounders, original or first vendors thereof'.[25] Since a preparation that was not secret, proprietary, patent or recommended would not have been subject to duty anyway, the exemption was implicit in the charging provision itself. The exemption could accordingly be regarded as legally otiose, and not a true exemption in the sense of taking a medicine that would otherwise be within the charge, out of the charge. The revenue authorities interpreted the provision in the genuine belief that the draftsmen had intended a declaratory provision, that it was part of the pattern of the Act and other similar legislation which was deliberately repetitive in order to make the point clear. For over a hundred

---

[23] 25 Geo 3 c 79.

[24] Board of Customs and Excise and Predecessor: Private Office Papers, The Medicine Stamp Duties 1783–1936 (hereafter Private Office Papers), The National Archives CUST 118/366, 56.

[25] Medicine Stamp Duty Act 1785 (25 Geo 3 c 79) s 4.

years, the provision was thus understood by both the pharmaceutical profession and the revenue authorities. Chemists and druggists had to accept that they had no choice but to disregard the provision. Indeed, so far did this interpretation prevail that a consolidation of the stamp duties proposed in the 1830s would have repealed the exemption entirely, while the Board's *Instructions* to its officers of 1848 and 1897 both ignored it.

The decision in *Farmer v Glyn-Jones,* however, entirely overturned this established and consistent revenue interpretation of the exemption and in so doing it was perceived as having 'fundamentally altered the whole administration of the medicine stamp duty'.[26] The decision affirmed that the provision was not merely declaratory of the law, but was a material exemption in that *known, admitted and approved remedies* sold by qualified individuals, even if recommended for human ailments, were exempt from the duty as long as that recommendation had not been made by the owner, proprietor, maker, compounder, original or first vendor.[27] Although the decision was reported very briefly and without comment in the annual report of the Commissioners of Inland Revenue,[28] in reversing an established revenue practice which was well understood by the revenue authorities and the trade, it was received by the revenue authorities with concern bordering on horror and provoked the dry reflection that 'it might appear that an interpretation of a statute sanctioned by a century of practice was that intended by Parliament'.[29] Their alarm was not merely at the need to change established practice, but because they immediately understood that the literal interpretation of the provision adopted by the court was unworkable. This was because it was in practical terms impossible to determine at what stage, if any, a recommendation was attached to a remedy. In current trading conditions a chemist and druggist would simply be unable retrospectively to prove that the original or first vendor had never recommended the medicine. Indeed, when Glyn-Jones argued before the magistrate in the first hearing of the *Farmer* case that the medicine had never been recommended before, the solicitor representing the Board of Inland Revenue said that Glyn-Jones could not possibly prove that.[30] As a result of predictable difficulties, the Board was 'not anxious to raise questions as to recommendations by the original vendor'.[31]

Whatever their misgivings, the revenue authorities had no choice but to implement the court's decision. The practical impossibility of proving that the original or first vendor had never recommended the medicine would have meant

---

[26] Private Office Papers (above n 24) 80–81.

[27] For a contemporary analysis of the *Farmer* decision, see CH Kirby, 'The Recent Medicine Stamp Duty Decisions' (1903) 71 *Pharmaceutical Journal* (series 4) 75.

[28] Inland Revenue, *Forty-seventh Annual Report of the Commissioners of Inland Revenue* (Cd 2228, 1904) xviii, 401, 552.

[29] Private Office Papers (above n 24) 77.

[30] Anonymous (*Pharmaceutical Journal* Editors), 'Legal Intelligence, Medicine Stamp Duty Acts' (1902) 68 *Pharmaceutical Journal* (series 4) 524.

[31] Private Office Papers (above n 24) 82.

that in practice the exemption could never be claimed. And yet the decision in *Farmer* clearly stated that the exemption was a material one. They had to make the best of it and they proceeded to create an operational method to make the law workable in practice. From motives of necessity and practicality, and adopting the advice of the chairman, Sir Henry Primrose, the Board framed a straightforward and feasible practice.[32] The Board took the view that the exemption could be claimed if just two conditions were satisfied. The first was that the vendor should be a qualified chemist and druggist and the second was that the ingredients should be disclosed. In terms of the required qualification, the Board allowed chemists and druggists qualified by registration following examination to do so. This was of course a recognition by the Board of the reality of the situation whereby in 1903 few chemists and druggists were qualifying by traditional apprenticeship. In relation to the requirement to disclose the composition of the medicine, the revenue authorities at first insisted on a complete and precise description of the quantity of each ingredient on the medicine label itself.[33] It then modified this requirement so as to allow the exemption to be claimed if either the principal active ingredients were named on the label,[34] or the label indicated that the medicine had been prepared in accordance with the formula published in the *British Pharmacopoeia*.[35] So simple and inexpensive was this process of disclosure that it enabled all qualified chemists and druggists to satisfy the requirement and claim the benefit of the exemption. They could do so, however much and however extravagantly they then proceeded to recommend the medicine. By the year after the *Farmer* decision, the Board had modified its practice on the basis of the decision and formulated it so as to appear in its *Instructions* to its officers.[36] Under the revised practice a chemist and druggist, even if qualified by examination rather than regular apprenticeship, could sell any medicine without a stamp, even if the medicine was secret, patent, proprietary or recommended, as long as the label disclosed the principal ingredients or a reference to its formula in an approved publication.

The Board's revised practice gave the exemption the widest possible scope. Indeed, it was extraordinary in its breadth and nature when set alongside the decision of the court in *Farmer* and the statutory provision itself. It departed so far from both that it bore little resemblance to either. The revenue authorities simply ignored the central point in the judicial decision, namely that the person who claimed the exemption had to establish that the original or first vendor had

---

[32] ibid, 88–89.

[33] Anonymous (*Pharmaceutical Journal* Editors), 'The Incidence of Medicine Stamp Duty' (1903) 71 *Pharmaceutical Journal* (series 4) 233–34.

[34] Anonymous (*Pharmaceutical Journal* Editors), 'Known, Admitted, and Approved' (1903) 71 *Pharmaceutical Journal* (series 4) 293.

[35] Disclosure could be in the *British Pharmacopoeia* or other book of reference. The letters 'BP' would suffice to indicate this. Note that some of these books of reference were compiled by the professional press and so chemists could submit their own formulae for inclusion in them.

[36] *Precedents and Instructions*, 1904: The National Archives IR 78/60; IR 83/61.

never recommended the medicine. It should have been the case that the onus was on the chemist and druggist who claimed it to prove that his or her medicine satisfied the precise terms of the exemption, but the Board decided that the claimant would only have to provide that proof if there were clear grounds for thinking that the medicine in question had been recommended by the first vendor.[37] Even this requirement became nominal, and was soon dropped entirely. With respect to the statutory provision itself, the Board disregarded it in two important respects: the Act stated that the exemption could not be claimed if the medicine was recommended, but the practice clearly allowed a recommendation to be made by subsequent vendors; and whereas the statute expressly allowed qualification only by regular apprenticeship, the Board permitted chemists and druggists qualified by examination and registration to claim the exemption.

The reason for the Board's apparent indifference to both the definitive judicial decision and the words of the statute was clear: it was necessity. The revenue authorities were under a statutory duty to administer the medicine stamp duty.[38] The legislation they were obliged to implement was, however, complicated, archaic and flawed. It retained the same structure as it had at the inception of the duty in its modern form in 1785, a structure which even then had been based on other stamp duty Acts of the early eighteenth century. Key terms had been left undefined, loose wording and repetitive clauses had not been rationalised, the elaborate design of the charge had not been simplified, contradictory provisions remained unreformed, and no attempt had been made to ensure that all concepts it addressed – including the *known, admitted and approved remedies* provision – were kept up to date to reflect modern commercial and professional realities. Judges too were bound to interpret the legislation before them, and enjoined by the constitutional imperatives of taxation, they interpreted the legislation, however flawed, strictly. So, when the court in *Farmer* revived this outdated provision which the revenue authorities had always regarded as superfluous and had ignored for so long, and gave it a strict and literal construction, it was bound to cause acute difficulties with the administration of the tax. The revenue authorities, uniquely aware of what was feasible in everyday tax administration – and fully appreciating the importance of practicality in tax – were left with no choice but to develop a practice which almost inevitably could not accurately reflect either the court's legalistic interpretation of the legislation or the muddled provisions of the statute.

Farmer unequivocally demonstrates the pitfalls of a literal interpretation of a tax statute and, it follows, the desirability in some respects of the application of a purposive approach. Tax law had always rejected a purposive approach, insisting instead that recourse to the words of the enactment was the only permitted course to reveal the intention of Parliament. Indeed, the judges interpreted

[37] Private Office Papers (above n 24) 82.
[38] Medicine Stamp Duty Act 1785 (25 Geo 3 c 79) s 6.

taxing Acts 'with no guide except a grammar book and a dictionary'.[39] The reason lay in the fundamental constitutional principle that a subject could be taxed only by Parliament and, it followed, by express and clear words of charge. Only a literal interpretation was consistent with this principle, since a purposive approach would permit instances of taxation where the case was not within the letter of a statute. In theory, a literal construction ensured legitimacy certainty and predictability in taxation, and this was the governing principle, with very few exceptions, throughout the nineteenth century. In practice, particularly where the taxing Act was antiquated and poorly drafted, it frequently caused hardship to the taxpayer and presented the revenue authorities with an impossible administrative task. There was, nevertheless, little option. Constitutional considerations apart, *Farmer* was decided at a stage in the development of tax law where a purposive approach to the interpretation of tax statutes was not possible: appeals to the courts of law in relation to the principal taxes were yet relatively few and the development of principles through regular judicial consideration of tax Acts as a whole, and in their wider context, was still in its infancy. This, and other factors,[40] ensured that while Edwardian judges might appreciate the desirability of an approach ascertaining the purpose of tax legislation, the time had not yet come for its overt or general implementation.[41]

The effect of the decision in *Farmer* unequivocally demonstrated the interaction between tax legislation and executive practice and showed that revenue practice was the inevitable result of flawed legislation. Indeed, revenue practice was the measure of legislative inertia – of the failure of legislators to express themselves clearly and to ensure the legislation was kept up to date. The gap between the legislative provision and the revenue practice demonstrated how far apart necessity had driven them. While this applied to all tax legislation in the formative period of British tax law in the long nineteenth century, the medicine stamp duty legislation was the most extreme example of an unsound statutory code, and accordingly that tax's administration became dominated to an exceptional degree by revenue practice. The decision also demonstrated that when faced with conflicting imperatives – a judicial decision it was impossible to implement and a statutory duty to administer the tax – pragmatism inevitably won. It reveals a tacit acceptance that a workable practice was the only solution if the legislation and the judicial decision were to be implemented at least to some degree. A workable practice conceived by the executive, however, brought with it considerable dangers especially when it was, as in the case of the *known, admitted and approved remedies* exemption, not a minor aspect of a tax, but had become its defining characteristic and the exemplar of other practices developed

---

[39] J Vinelott, 'Interpretation of Fiscal Statutes' (1982) 3 *Stat LR* 78, 80.
[40] C Stebbings, *The Victorian Taxpayer and the Law: A Study in Constitutional Conflict* (Cambridge, Cambridge University Press, 2009) 122. See too ibid, 31–35, 111–22.
[41] This had changed by the middle years of the century: see Vinelott (above n 39) 81.

to implement the tax in all its aspects. The principal danger was that although it flowed from a perfectly legitimate judicial decision, it was illegal.

The task of assigning a meaning to statutory language was the sole prerogative of the judiciary, for only the judges of the courts of law were constitutionally permitted to discern the true intention of Parliament from the words of a statute. However, the nature of the common law system in developing substantive law through a reactive judiciary, with judicial decisions occurring if and when appropriate litigation was begun, and the paucity of appeal provision in tax law in particular, meant that judicial decisions on the interpretation of the medicine stamp duty – and indeed all the taxes – were few and far between in the nineteenth century. The practical demands of daily implementation of a tax in a dynamic professional context required the immediate interpretation of statutory provisions, and so the task of assigning a meaning to the words of tax statutes necessarily fell in the first instance to the officers of the revenue department of the executive charged with the administration of the tax. It followed, too, that the interpretation adopted by the revenue authorities and circulated through official instructions to their officers with an insistence that they implement it nationally, would endure for many years as the operationally definitive meaning. But since the revenue authorities had no discretion, having to adhere to the words of the statute and the decisions of the regular courts interpreting those words, by adopting the interpretation of the statute and the judicial decision that they did after *Farmer*, and thereby affecting the liability of the taxpayers, they were taking upon themselves the functions of the judges contrary to the most fundamental constitutional principles of tax law. The practice was illegal and therein lay the danger.

The revenue authorities had always known that their practice in implementing the *known, admitted and approved remedies* exemption after *Farmer* was illegal in that it was not authorised by the statute, and successive solicitors of Inland Revenue made it clear in the 1920s and 1930s that this was so, though this view had only ever been aired privately within their department. Within government circles the Board admitted that 'it might be represented as a glaring instance of legislation by Executive action and an unauthorised assumption, or usurpation, of the functions of Parliament'.[42] In 1934, however, FW Woolworth, keen to claim the benefit of the *known, admitted and approved remedies* exemption to place themselves on an equal footing with Boots and Timothy Whites in the sale of commercial medicines,[43] decided to challenge the legality of the practice,[44] and counsel's opinion was sought. The outcome was an expert and uncompromising confirmation that the practice was illegal: no corporate body could legally claim the exemption because it could not have become qualified

---

[42] Private Office Papers (above n 24) 86.

[43] Boots and Timothy Whites had been permitted to sell such medicines free of duty on the basis that they were under the control of a qualified chemist.

[44] Private Office Papers (above n 24) 119–21.

through regular apprenticeship as the statute required, and the requirement that the medicine should never have been recommended to the public by the first vendor – the crux of the *Farmer* decision – was a material one which had to be proved to claim the exemption. The revenue practice in failing to institute proceedings when these requirements were not satisfied – indeed in not expecting them to be satisfied at all – was illegal.[45] This practice by the revenue authorities, the opinion stated, 'amounts to taxation at their discretion, and also to an assumption by them of a power to grant general exemptions from taxes which Parliament has expressly decreed shall be imposed. In our opinion this procedure is illegal, and unconstitutional'.[46] The decision in *Farmer* was an administrative landmark in that it was a judicial decision which could only be implemented by developing an executive practice which was strikingly dislocated from its judicial or statutory foundations, and whose illegality, it will be seen, could not be hidden from public and professional view.

III. A PROFESSIONAL LANDMARK

It is always tempting when analysing a legal decision, in order to ascertain its landmark status in revenue law, to address primarily its impact on the substantive law or on revenue practice. There is a further possible and valid dimension to landmark status, and that is the impact of a judicial decision on the occupational sphere in which the tax operated in practice – in this instance, the profession of pharmacy. The wider social impact of a legal decision is not always readily discerned, but in the case of *Farmer v Glyn-Jones* it was recognised and welcomed at the time as a landmark case in the history of the profession of chemists and druggists. It was significant socially, in the sense that it raised the status of chemists and druggists by officially affirming their status as a group given a fiscal privilege because of their recognised expertise, and provided a much more definite differentiation between the qualified chemist and standard medicines on the one hand, and unqualified makers of secret remedies on the other. The decision went far 'to secure public recognition of the pharmacist's claim to be regarded as a professional man'.[47] Its greater professional significance, however, was an economic one. While the revenue authorities did not necessarily foresee the extent of the consequences of the *Farmer* decision, the more informed and astute of the chemists and druggists certainly understood it as potentially extremely valuable, and did so almost as soon as the decision was published. In an article in the *Pharmaceutical Journal* a few weeks after

---

[45] ibid, 179–81.

[46] ibid, 181.

[47] Anonymous (*Pharmaceutical Journal* Editors), 'Liability to Medicine Stamp Duty' (1903) 70 *Pharmaceutical Journal* (series 4) 828.

Farmer, Cyril Kirby pointed out that by the decision 'the trade have obtained a very substantial benefit'.[48]

Economically, in establishing the *known, admitted and approved remedies* provision as a material exemption, *Farmer* was largely responsible for the survival of the profession because it made it commercially robust. The 'Chemists' Privilege', as it was known, as laid down in substance in the decision and in practice by the revenue authorities gave chemists and druggists, for the first time, a material advantage over other retailers in selling commercial medicines. From the eighteenth century such medicines had been sold by a wide variety of vendors including booksellers, printers, grocers, hairdressers, stationers, tobacconists and, by the end of the nineteenth century, department stores. Throughout the nineteenth century there was intense competition between these various vendors for the sale of these medicines, at a time when the trade was booming. The effect of the revenue practice after *Farmer* in 1903 meant that of all these retailers, only qualified chemists and druggists could sell commercial medicines free of duty while all the other vendors selling the same products had to sell them with the tax attached. Qualified chemists and druggists needed every privilege they could obtain: dispensing work had become insufficient to maintain a business, and chemists and druggists were increasingly being forced to engage in the sale of a number of sidelines. Commercial medicines formed a potentially important part of their retail work, and by 1936 qualified vendors of commercial medicines were outnumbered by unqualified ones by 10 to one. There were 135,000 unqualified vendors, mainly grocers, and 15,000 qualified registered chemists and druggists. Since unqualified vendors only had to pay five shillings for an annual licence to sell the medicines, which would have to be stamped, their numbers alone, and the economies of scale available to the large department stores, meant they were still potent competition. The potential to undercut their unqualified commercial rivals and claim a significant share of the trade in commercial remedies was accordingly of immense importance to the retail chemists. They immediately began to claim the exemption, as evidenced by the lists of declared medicines in the *Pharmaceutical Formulae* published by the pharmacists' trade journal, the *Chemist and Druggist*, being one of the 'well-known books of reference' allowed for the formal disclosure of the ingredients. In 1904, for example, it contained the formulae of nearly 700 mixtures for coughs, for diarrhoea and for neuralgia alone.

In developing its practice in relation to the exemption, the Board of Inland Revenue was inevitably choosing not to tax those falling within its remit, namely qualified chemists and druggists, and accordingly to leave untouched the tax burden on those unqualified vendors falling outside it. However, the Board was not thereby imposing a direct charge on those falling outside the exemption so as to infringe the fundamental constitutional principle of taxation only by

---

[48] Kirby (above n 27).

parliamentary consent, but the illegal nature of revenue practice undoubtedly fuelled a powerful perception of partiality and unfairness among unqualified vendors.

The landmark status of the *Farmer* case in pharmaceutical circles was clear from the publicity the decision received in the professional press, publicity rarely seen in relation to tax cases in other spheres where the notoriety of a judicial decision tended to be limited to a rarefied circle of tax lawyers and accountants. In pharmacy, all chemists and druggists could not help but know about the decision and thereby immediately recognised its profound potential impact. The two principal professional journals, the *Pharmaceutical Journal* and the *Chemist and Druggist* gave the case the most intensive coverage from its first hearing in the Police Court where they reported the trial verbatim[49] to the final settling of revenue practice in the months following the judgment in the Divisional Court. The decision occupied hundreds of pages of editorial comment, readers' correspondence and reports of local and national associations' discussion, in both journals throughout the summer of 1903. It is clear from the retrospective article at Christmas 1903 in the *Chemist and Druggist* how important the year was to chemists and druggists as result of the decision.[50] The editor described the judicial decision as nothing less than 'epoch-making'.[51]

IV. CONCLUSION

The features that made the case of *Farmer v Glyn-Jones* an administrative and professional landmark combined to create an unstoppable dynamic which led to its third claim to landmark status. The case clearly and directly led to the abolition of the tax itself. The full damage caused by the *Farmer* decision and the Board's interpretation of it became apparent some 30 years later. The practice was so widely conceived that from the 1920s the exemption was legitimately exploited by the large manufacturing chemists, who were a far cry from the individual qualified retail chemist who was the original intended beneficiary of the exemption. This resulted in a dramatic collapse of the yield in the 1930s, which first caused the revenue authorities some alarm. But the legal foundations of the practice were equally and evidently vulnerable. The illegality of the practice, so starkly revealed by counsel's opinion in 1934, made it abundantly clear that the practice could not survive scrutiny by a court of law or public opinion. When FW Woolworth threatened just that, the Law Officers of the Crown knew the position of the revenue authorities was untenable. The government could not risk public exposure of the illegitimacy of the practice. The ammunition

---

[49] Anonymous (*Pharmaceutical Journal* Editors), 'Legal Intelligence, Medicine Stamp Duty Acts' (1902) 68 *Pharmaceutical Journal* (series 4) 443, 523, 562.

[50] Editor, 'A Glance Back' (1903) 63 *Chemist and Druggist* 1051.

[51] ibid.

of illegality was deadly. A select committee was appointed in 1936 to look into the whole question of the medicine stamp duty and see if it could be reformed so as to put it on 'a modern and defensible basis',[52] namely unambiguous legislation free from anachronism and anomaly, and to pacify Woolworths,[53] but such reform was found to be impossible. Over the next four years of intensive discussion and investigation it became clear that repeal was the only option. The determination of the chemists and druggists to retain the valuable *known, admitted and approved remedies* exemption emerged as the main political obstacle to be overcome. Having grown in power and status over the previous 30 years, a development due in no small degree to the effect of the exemption, they argued they had a 'legal and moral right' to it[54] because their expertise, achieved at their own effort and expense, protected the public from dangerous drugs and secret remedies.[55] Indeed, they considered themselves 'the main bulwark between the public and quackery'.[56] They felt threatened by the loss of their historic fiscal and commercial privilege.[57] Indeed, the level of outrage and objection to any proposal to get rid of the exemption practice itself was a measure of how it was valued by the profession. After several years of testy and politically challenging negotiations, the duty was finally abolished in 1941.[58]

The case of *Farmer v Glyn-Jones*, with its extreme administrative consequences, highlights more starkly than any other case the causes, imperatives and dangers of bureaucratic law-making and the extent to which an indifference to the quality of tax legislation made such practices inevitable in the real context of its practical implementation. The decision placed the revenue authorities in an impossible position and led them to lose control of the tax. Unable to retain its anchorage in judicial precedent or enacted law, the medicine stamp duty depended entirely on administrative practice to make it work at all. Its administration had become its substance, and that was untenable. A reactive judiciary, apathetic legislature, complacent executive and astute taxpaying body combined to produce a legally unsound, politically indefensible and fiscally unsustainable tax exemplified above all by the *known, admitted and approved remedies* exemption. The landmark case of *Farmer v Glyn-Jones* not only set in train a chain of events that led to the abolition of the very tax it addressed, but in so doing provided the most acute window onto the nature, role and dangers of tax practice.

---

[52] *Medicine Stamp Duty*, 1936: The National Archives T 172/1844.
[53] The Woolworths proceedings were withdrawn.
[54] Anonymous (*Pharmaceutical Journal* Editors), 'Medicine Stamp Duty Acts' (1903) 71 *Pharmaceutical Journal* (series 4) 8.
[55] *Report and Minutes of Evidence before the Select Committee on Medicine Stamp Duty* (Cmd 54, 1937) viii, 129, 195, q 785.
[56] ibid, q 787.
[57] ibid, qq 694–702.
[58] Pharmacy and Medicines Act 1941, s 14.

The consequences of the post-1903 revenue practice developed after *Farmer* were wide-ranging and perilous both with respect to the medicine stamp duty itself in that it led, ultimately, to its abolition, but also as an exemplar of the perils of revenue practice to the administration of tax in general. Regarded as de facto law, as of equal or indeed greater importance than the enacted law, and with its consistent use by the revenue authorities and its necessary acceptance by the taxpaying public, revenue practice possessed a degree of status, authority and permanency. In the early twentieth century, while the fundamental illegality of such bureaucratic law-making was understood, its implications were not yet fully appreciated. It would be left to the judges and legal scholars of the middle years of the century to begin addressing the profound legal questions as to the legitimacy and control of revenue practice, the interface of law and administration in modern government committed to accessibility and openness, to consider the consequences of traditional literal interpretation of tax legislation and how far it served the interests of law and justice, and to do so in the context of a judiciary constrained by constitutional imperatives.

3

De Beers Consolidated Mines Ltd v Howe *(1906)*

Corporate Residence: An Early Attempt at European Harmonisation

JOHN AVERY JONES AND JOHANN HATTINGH[*]

'Both are cases raising, I believe for the first time, a question of great importance both in its nature and the extent of its operations, and involving important principles of great weight as affecting the law of this country, and, I may almost say, the international law of the world.'[1]

D*E BEERS* MIGHT be thought to have the weakest possible claim to be a landmark case: it did not appear to decide anything new, the speeches in the House of Lords occupy a mere three-and-a-quarter pages, only one authority was cited, the Revenue was not even called upon to argue, the circumstances of the company were unique, and the taxpayer found a way of

[*] We gratefully acknowledge the valuable assistance given to us by Professor Birke Häcker, Linklaters Professor of Comparative Law, Oxford University, and Dr Andreas Fleckner, Max Planck Institute for Tax Law and Public Finance, Munich, in drawing our attention to the article by C Trautrims, for answering many questions about Savigny and German legal history and for helpful comments on a draft of section V 'What would Savigny have made of that?'. The views expressed are ours. We gratefully acknowledge Mr Bruce Cleaver, chief executive officer of De Beers Consolidated Mines Ltd for allowing us access to the De Beers archives in Kimberley and the staff in Kimberley, particularly Mr Eben van Heerden for his tireless assistance and warm hospitality. Archival research for this chapter was financially supported by the Research Committee of the Faculty of Law in the University of Cape Town. We gratefully acknowledge Richard Thomas and Professor Jennifer Roeleveld, Emeritus Professor of the Faculty of Commerce in the University of Cape Town in making useful comments on a draft of this chapter, and Victor Baker, HMRC, for his help to reconcile the original assessments with financial information (n 44).

[1] This was said not in *De Beers* but in the only authority cited and upheld in that case: *The Calcutta Jute Mills Co Ltd v Nicholson* and *The Cesena Sulphur Co Ltd v Nicholson* (1876) 1 TC 83, 92 (Kelly CB) (with drafting differences between the two reports). There is no equivalent of this passage in the (1876) 1 ExD 428 report, which suggests that the Chief Baron may have had second thoughts about the influence of the decision on the international law of the world when revising his judgment.

avoiding the tax imposed by the decision less than two years later. And yet its influence has been, and over a century later, remains, enormous throughout the Commonwealth as the foundation of determining corporate residence for tax. It has influenced other fields of law in a number of countries too. Ask any lawyer in any Commonwealth country about corporate residence and he will immediately say '*De Beers*' or 'central management and control'.[2] The paradoxical feature is that the unique circumstances of the company helped to create a test for residence that has stood the test of time and as recent cases show is virtually impossible to use to avoid tax.

I. BACKGROUND

As is well known, De Beers[3] was found to be UK resident because London directors had a controlling voice. The existence of London directors of a company incorporated in the Colony of the Cape of Good Hope[4] and ostensibly carrying on the whole of its business there, needs some explanation. It came about because Rothschilds in London had financed De Beers' acquisition of its rival diamond mining companies,[5] resulting in Rothschilds and Lord Rothschild himself becoming large shareholders in the resulting combined company, De Beers Consolidated Mines Limited.[6] The London directors[7] were appointed to look after their interests and those of the English and French shareholders.[8] Their importance was that they controlled the principal source of finance, which was crucial because it was then customary to pay out the entire profits of a

---

[2] Many countries have since added incorporation as a criterion for residence (including the UK in 1988) leaving central management and control to operate for companies incorporated elsewhere. The US has used only incorporation from the start.

[3] *De Beers Consolidated Mines Ltd v Howe* [1906] AC 455. Howe was the Surveyor of Taxes, the forerunner of the Inspector of Taxes (who was historically the Surveyor's superior, an example of grade inflation).

[4] See the map in the Appendix.

[5] They were principally a French company, Compagnie Française des Mines de Diamant du Cap de Bonne Espérance, under the control of Jules Porgès & Cie whose leading members were Wernher and Beit who were later Life Governors of De Beers, and its larger rival, Kimberley Central Diamond Mining Co, under the control of the Barnato brothers.

[6] By 1899 Rothschilds held 31,666 shares in De Beers, the family of the former major shareholder in Kimberley Central, Barnato, 33,576 shares, and Rhodes 13,537 shares (N Ferguson, *The World's Banker: The History of the House of Rothschild* (London, Weidenfeld & Nicolson, 1998) 883). Rothschilds originally advanced £200k in debentures, then £2.25m, 17.8% of an issue of £1.75m, and then the whole of £3.5m issue in 1894.

[7] This expression is used both to denote the directors appointed by Rothschilds and those directors who were in London at any particular time.

[8] According to RV Turrell, 'Review Article: "Finance ... The Governor of the Imperial Engine": Hobson and the Case of Rothschild and Rhodes' (1987) 13 *Journal of African Studies* 417, 428 by 1899 French shareholders dominated De Beers, the two largest individual shareholders being the London and Paris Rothschilds.

company as dividends[9] and investment in South African diamond mining was speculative in the 1880s.[10] The London directors, whose protagonist was Carl Meyer, Rothschilds' chief clerk,[11] did not see eye to eye with Cecil John Rhodes, the chairman. One of the first disagreements arose after the financiers demanded (and got) an undertaking from the Kimberley directors in 1891 to limit diamond production, which was essential to create price stability.[12] Turrell explains that the basic difference between Rhodes and Rothschild over De Beers was that the former, who had no other vehicle for investment, wanted to use the company for colonial development while the latter, who had other vehicles like the Exploration Company,[13] wanted to restrict its field of operation to diamond mining alone and to 'judicious investments' that reduced the costs of production, like cheap coal[14] or cheap meat.[15] Rhodes as one of the Life Governors, who between them were entitled to 25 per cent of the profits above 36 per cent on the issued capital,[16] also had a conflict of interest in wishing to expand De Beers' profits.

We shall first examine the relationship between the London and Kimberley directors in more detail, followed by the tax situation in the Cape to demonstrate the double taxation that the decision caused. Next, we shall deal with the law as the House of Lords decided, including a discussion of Savigny who had been relied on in the only authority cited. Finally, and unusually, we are in a position to review the facts as presented to the court.

---

[9] In 1900 Rothschilds were complaining about De Beers not paying out everything as dividends (Ferguson (n 6) 894), presumably in relation to 1899. Dividends were affected by the Anglo-Boer War (see text at n 35 below). The proportion of profit (plus Life Governors' remuneration) was 95% (1898), 82% (1899), 28% (1900: Life Governors only), 71% (1901) and 98% (1902).

[10] Historians suggest that the creation of monopoly conditions by De Beers through syndication of diamond sales after 1891 can be attributed to the insistence of financiers to create a framework for price stability because the deep-level method of mining Kimberley diamonds required significant capital expenditure compared with the much lower cost associated with winning alluvial diamonds (D Innes, *Anglo American and the Rise of Modern South Africa* (New York, Raven Press, 1984) 36); and see n 22 below for the monopoly pricing.

[11] Later Sir Carl, who was on the board from 1888 to 1922 and deputy chairman from 1901.

[12] C Newbury, *The Diamond Ring* (Oxford, Clarendon Press, 1989) 132–33: Rhodes was forced to reveal to Lord Rothschild that he directed the build-up of a secret reserve of diamonds in London for 'clandestine sales' to merchants outside the syndicate prior to 1891, causing the London directors to take 'great exception'.

[13] RV Turrell and JJ van Hilten, 'The Rothschilds, the Exploration Company and Mining Finance' (1986) *Business History* 181. Turrell (n 8) 429 lists investments denied to De Beers that were taken up by the Exploration Co.

[14] The company had a 'considerable interest' in the Vierfontein colliery. The 1904 accounts mention De Beers contributing to the cost of a railway to transport the coal. See HA Chilvers, *The Story of De Beers* (London, Cassell and Company, 1939) 165 regarding building of railways, and text at n 103 below.

[15] Turrell (n 8) 429.

[16] The calculation is shown in the 1901 accounts. The Life Governors received a share of profits from 1896 rising to £159,851 in 1899 and £316,593 in 1902, 1899 and 1902 Accounts, *The Times* (20 March 1900) 15, (11 December 1902) 15). Their rights were bought out in 1901 (as mentioned in the case stated, para 13) at Rothschilds' insistence. The accounts from 1902 onwards write-off each year £100,000 Life Governors Interest Purchase Account.

II. THE LONDON AND KIMBERLEY DIRECTORS

We emphasise that there was only one board comprising directors who at any one time were meeting weekly in both London and Kimberley,[17] the location of the mines in the Cape Colony. It is necessary to go into more detail about the two sets of directors in order to understand which activities of the London directors led the City of London General Commissioners[18] to find that they were dominant and hence led the House of Lords to decide that the company was UK resident. Two out of three Life Governors and nine of the other 16 directors were resident in the UK (and the Articles required at least four to reside in England),[19] two directors travelled between the two, and one was resident in both countries; the chairman (Rhodes) and six directors were resident in the Cape only but Rhodes frequently attending London meetings and also sent cables to the directors from wherever he was.

The London directors appointed four committees: (a) the finance committee in November 1888; (b) the diamond committee in June 1889; (c) the machinery committee in December 1888; and (d) the dynamite committee, to act in London and to deal with matters falling respectively under such headings.[20] The finance committee made weekly reports to the London directors on the company's finances; most receipts and payments went through the London office.[21] The diamond committee negotiated successive agreements from 1895 (with one earlier one in 1890) for the sale of the entire output of diamonds to a Syndicate of seven London diamond merchants which demonstrates the effect of monopoly pricing.[22] This was done at Rothschilds' suggestion to avoid the company

---

[17] The city is named after Lord Kimberley, the Secretary of State for the Colonies, who declined to be connected with such a vulgarism of New Rush, as it was known after the discovery of diamonds, and as for the Dutch name, *Vooruitzigt* ... he could neither spell nor pronounce it (B Roberts, *Kimberley, Turbulent City* (Cape Town, David Philip, 1976) 115).

[18] The first stage in a tax appeal was generally to a lay tribunal, the General Commissioners, an important constituent of which was the City of London General Commissioners who were noted for their commercial expertise.

[19] *De Beers Consolidated Mines Ltd v Howe* [1905] 2 KB 612, 647. It is interesting that in 1890 there was a proposal by shareholders that London directors should spend three months of the year in South Africa, Annual Report 1907 (below n 81), 40.

[20] *De Beers* (above n 19) 620, case stated, para 12.

[21] Year ended 30 June 1900, receipts and payments about £5.7m each. Year ended 30 June 1901, receipts and payments about £3.7m each (case stated, para 12). (In view of the siege (below n 35) we suspect that the figures may relate to one year earlier.)

[22] This originally started in 1890 but did not continue (Chilvers (above n 14) 265). From 1895 there were annual agreements until 1899 under which the Syndicate agreed to purchase the entire output (subject to a maximum) for the first six months and then had an option to purchase for the next six months, of, initially, the production of the De Beers and Kimberley mines, and from 1897, the Wesselton mine (Chilvers (above n 14) 101). There was a break during and immediately following the siege of Kimberley in December 1899, then another agreement with successive two- or three-month periods from April 1900 to July 1901. This was followed by a five-year agreement from October 1901 to June 1906 with successive six-month options to continue at a price of 12% less than the actual or estimated selling price, with sharing equally of any profit or loss after allowing £30,000 plus 5% of sales and interest incurred to the Syndicate. The prices for the De Beers and Kimberley mines

speculating in diamonds, thus ensuring price stability. Director control from London over the Syndicate agreements potentially could lead to tax problems as the contracts were made by the London office with the Syndicate members all having UK addresses which would surely have meant that the sales (as opposed to the mining) profit would have been liable to UK tax.[23] Indeed this was the Revenue's alternative argument in the case.[24] The machinery committee and the dynamite committee were less important as they merely controlled the purchase of machinery and dynamite requisitioned from Kimberley through the London office.[25]

Some extracts from the London directors' minutes are included in the case stated[26] and give a flavour of their type of activity which relate only to finance and expansion and not to the mining activities; more extracts are annexed to it but are available only in the House of Lords archives.[27] The Kimberley directors' minutes, also annexed to the case stated but not referred to in it, of which we include a few extracts below as they are not generally available, contain a number of disagreements with the London directors and, as was no doubt intended in choosing them in order to bolster the case for the company's not being managed in London, show that they were far from willing to agree anything that London wanted:[28]

29 June 1897. Resolved that reply be sent to London that the Board cannot agree to their proposal to reduce the value of the surplus stock of diamonds to 10s per carat.

24 February 1898. Re shares in Bechuanaland Railway Company. Resolved to inform the London Board that they cannot favour the view their London colleagues have taken; and with regard to the application of the Burma Ruby Mines for permission to

started at 26s 0d per carat in 1895 and rose steadily to 50s 0d per carat in 1901, ultimately rising to 64s 9.74d in the 1907 accounts; for the Wesselton mine they ranged between 20s 6d and 37s. 6d, ultimately rising to 43s 9.26d in the 1906 accounts. The Syndicate agreements from 1895 onwards are in an Appendix to the case stated, which is available in the House of Lords archives, and the last agreement of 2 December 1901 is summarised in the case stated at [1905] 2 KB 612, 615. Members of the Syndicates included Wernher Beit & Co and Barnato Brothers (associated with Beit and Barnato, two of the directors and Life Governors) with 29.5% each (with annual changes from 1899 resulting in 1901 with 34% for the former and 27.5% for the latter). How the Syndicate operated in practice is described by A Hocking, *Oppenheimer and Son* (New York, McGraw-Hill, 1973) 29.

[23] Newbury (above n 12) quotes Lord Rothschild's prescient warning in 1901 against commission sales through dealers: 'any attempt to centre company sales on London would attract the attention of the Inland Revenue, which might claim tax on all DBCM's profits'.

[24] *De Beers* (above n 19) case stated, para 17.

[25] ibid, 620, case stated, para 12. In 1898 the company resolved to manufacture their own explosives (Chilvers (above n 14) 172).

[26] *De Beers* (above n 19) 623, case stated, para 14.

[27] Because they are extracts there is little point in analysing them statistically, but the approximate breakdown of the items considered by the London directors is financial (accounts, debentures, bills of exchange, payments) 38; dividends 17; renewal of sales contracts with the diamond Syndicate 20; new and existing investments 36; internal governance (directors, Life Governors, annual meetings) 13; other matters 10.

[28] Parliamentary Archives, *Appeal Cases, series 3 – 1906, D*, HL/PO/JU/4/3/541. The language is interesting in showing that the Kimberley directors regarded themselves and the London directors as separate boards.

use the automatic sorter, it was resolved to inform the London Board that the Board are not disposed to accede to it.

8 August 1901. Resolved to inform the London Office that the Board here are not in favour of the proposal, and are of opinion in fairness to the Life Governors[29] if Consols are to be written down other securities which are taken into accounts at merely nominal figures should be written up to their value as at 30th June 1901, and the Kimberley Board suggest that the Consols be taken into the balance-sheet after the year ended 30th June last at cost, and that the other securities be dealt with as heretofore. [A London minute of 9 October 1901 says: it was agreed ... to write down the Reserve Consols, to leave shaft, machinery and plant account at last year's figures ...]

15 May 1902. With reference to the London office letters of 18th and 25th April, the Board gather from them that it is not the intention of the London Board to proceed immediately with the flotation of the Butterfly Gold Mining Company, but as the Board here thinks that prompt flotation is necessary, the Secretary was instructed to cable London office, urging them to act without delay.

The by-laws approved by all the directors provided that the technical management of the company's work and operations at its mines was under the control of the Kimberley directors.[30] The case provides a particularly clear example of the London directors not being involved at all in day-to-day management of the business of the company (even if that were possible at the distance involved in the then state of communication) but nevertheless causing the company to be UK resident.

Lord Loreburn summarised the facts found by the General Commissioners as first, there was one trade carried on in the UK, and secondly, that the directing power of the affairs of the company was in London.[31] The logic of the first may not be immediately obvious. It equates the place of business with the place of intellectual control, not the place of the business operations for the reasons given in the discussion below of the earlier cases.

III. TAX IN THE CAPE AND THE UK

By 1898 everything was going in De Beers' favour. It had acquired all its rivals and enjoyed a virtual monopoly of the diamond market through the central selling mechanism, the Syndicate in London. It was making profits of

---

[29] Their profit share (above n 16) would be reduced if the value of the Consols (British government securities) were written down.

[30] *De Beers* (above n 19) 617–18, case stated, para 10. The by-laws were made pursuant to art 119 of the Articles of Association (at 648). The actual technical management was in the hands of the General Manager who spent six months of the year in each of England and South Africa (at 619) who made extremely detailed reports in each annual report; many of the Kimberley directors were politicians and industrialists who were not involved in the day-to-day management either.

[31] *De Beers* (above n 2) 459.

£2 million,[32] and owned 538,000 acres of land regarded as actually or potentially diamondiferous.[33] But in 1899 production was affected by the Boer War. Kimberley was in a vulnerable geographical position eight kilometres from the western border of the Boer Republic, the Orange Free State, with the Transvaal 72 kilometres to the north-west.[34] At the outset of war it came under siege in October, necessitating the cessation of diamond production in December; it was not relieved until February 1900.[35] Rhodes involved himself in the war[36] and De Beers resources were used in the relief effort.[37] This caused much tension with important constituents of De Beers shareholders.[38] As we will explain (see the heading 'The Real Facts' below), this tension had been present since 1890 and manifested in continuous disagreement between the London directors with Rhodes and the Kimberley directors which gave rise to the decision that the ultimate control was exercised in London even though this was not fully reflected in the factual record before the English courts.

The immediate prelude to De Beers' income tax travails at the Cape and in the UK arose after Rhodes' standing was diminished as a result of the Boer War; he passed away on 26 March 1902. In this period De Beers lodged a claim against the Imperial government for war losses of £54,641,[39] which seems somewhat

---

[32] Equivalent to £234m in 2017 (Bank of England inflation calculator). The number of employees in 1896 was 1,371 white and 6,669 black, Annual Report 1906, 46.

[33] Innes (above n 10) 42.

[34] DE Peddle, 'Long Cecil: The Gun made in Kimberley during the Siege' (1977) 4 *Military History Journal* 1.

[35] During the siege 120 citizens of Kimberley were killed or wounded (*The Times* (27 February 1900) 5). The British forces sent to end the siege under Lord Methuen suffered a series of defeats at the Battles of Modder River (28 November 1899) and Maggersfontein (11 December 1899) in what became known back in England as 'Black Week'; approximately 1,500 of Lord Methuen's forces were killed (A Conan Doyle, *The Great Boer War* (London, Smith, Elder & Co, 1900) 150; M Davitt, *The Boer Fight for Freedom* (New York, Funk & Wagnalls, 1902) 222).

[36] Rhodes took the last train to reach Kimberley before the siege and was personally stationed there for the entire period, overseeing with General Kekewich the local garrison made up mostly of De Beers employees (Peddle n 34).

[37] The De Beers workshops at Kimberley were turned into a munitions factory to assist with the relief effort after the defeat of the British forces at the Battle of Maggersfontein – shells had 'DE BEERS' and a diamond shape cast into the base, whilst some even had 'WITH COMPTS CJR' (Rhodes' initials) stamped on the body (Peddle n 34); this all explains why mining ceased by December 1899. A famous field gun named 'Long Cecil' was designed and built by De Beers' chief engineer in these workshops after Rhodes gave his approval on 24 December 1899; the gun was tested on 19 January 1900. See Appendix for a picture.

[38] Rhodes delivered a speech on 19 February 1900 shortly after Kimberley was set free in which he appealed to shareholders, many of whom being French and German, were opposed to British policy in South Africa. He set out to reconcile them to the use of De Beers' funds for political purposes to which they objected. In this speech, he referred to the British flag as a 'commercial asset', which drew much criticism at the time. (WT Stead (ed), *The Last Will and Testament of Cecil John Rhodes with Elucidatory Notes to which are Added Some Chapters Describing the Political and Religious Ideas of the Testator* ('Review of Reviews' Office, 1902) 173–74).

[39] A newspaper reported that the De Beers general report for 1903 showed the War Office tendered £30,000 in respect of the claim and a 'detailed statement of the war losses showed that the company's actual loss amounted to £272,904, in addition to the fact that it paid no dividend in 1900' (*Poverty Bay Herald* (New Zealand, 8 January 1904) 4).

audacious given that Rhodes shouldered part of the cause of the war and that many lives were lost in the expensive relief effort to set Kimberley free. One of the De Beers bankers and Rhodes' biographer,[40] Sir Lewis Michell, succeeded him as chairman of De Beers and served in the Cape Colony's cabinet until 1905. In 1904, Dr Leander Starr Jameson, Rhodes' close confidant of the raid fame and a director of De Beers, became Prime Minister of the Colony. Yet political influence by De Beers representatives did not stem the inevitability of income tax. The trailblazer for imposing income tax in the Colony was John X Merriman, treasurer in Rhodes' cabinet from 1890 to 1893, again from 1898 to 1900 and from 1908 to 1910, when he also served as Prime Minister.[41]

Merriman put forward a Bill proposing a 5 per cent tax on the profits of a trade carried on in the Colony, which would be De Beers' whole trading profits. That Bill failed in the Legislative Council but a similar Bill was passed in 1904.[42] De Beers appeared to have accepted by this point the inevitability of an income tax in the Cape Colony.[43] Meanwhile in May 1902[44] De Beers received assessments to UK tax on their profits for the tax years ending 5 April 1901 and 1902, both of £1,557,693 with tax at 5 per cent which after the appeal process were confirmed by the House of Lords in 1906.[45] Then in 1907 the Cape tax was increased to 10 per cent for diamond mining companies,[46] about which the chairman[47] expressed considerable anger at the 1907 Annual General Meeting (AGM) saying: 'People in South Africa were tired at this nagging at the mining

[40] L Michell, *The Life and Times of the Right Honourable Cecil John Rhodes, 1853–1902* (New York, Mitchell Kennerley, 1912).

[41] E Jansen van Rensburg, 'The History of Income Taxation in the Cape Colony: A Story of Dangerous Beasts and Murderous Fathers' in J Hattingh, J Roeleveld and C West (eds), *Income Tax in South Africa: The First 100 Years 1914–2014* (Cape Town, Juta & Co, 2016) 49.

[42] Additional Taxation Act 1904 (No 36, 1904) s 50; and see van Rensburg, ibid, 50. The Cape Supreme Court held that the company's share of profits from the Syndicate (see n 22 above) were taxable as Cape source income, being deferred consideration for sale, as it was dealt with in the accounts: *Colonial Government v De Beers Consolidated Mines Ltd* (1905) 22 SC 452.

[43] The chairman, Sir Lewis Michell is reported to have said at the De Beers general meeting in Kimberley on 14 November 1903 that 'The company were willing to pay their full share of taxation, but objected to be singled out above others' (*Poverty Bay Herald* (New Zealand, 8 January 1904) 4).

[44] After the Revenue had investigated the minute books (presumably including Kimberley) and other documents: Annual Report 1907, 34. The first year's is a supplementary assessment and the second year's is an additional assessment (case stated, para 1), implying that there were existing first assessments. We have almost been able to recreate the figure assessed from the accounts by taking three months proportion of the trading profit in the accounts to 30 June 1899 and nine months proportion of the 30 June 1900 profits after adding back apparently capital expenditure giving £1,565,483 (a difference of only £7,790 from the assessment). Alternatively, the Revenue may have started from the dividend figure of £1,579,582 for the years ended 30 June 1898 and 1899 and made some adjustment, but as there was no dividend in 1900 this seems less likely.

[45] The reports are contained in *De Beers* (above n 19) (case stated, Phillimore J and Court of Appeal) and *De Beers* (above n 2) (House of Lords).

[46] Income Tax Continuance and Mining Profits Tax Act 1907, s 3. Tax rates were changed in the Income Tax Act 1908 but not so as to change the rate on diamond mining companies, of which a definition was now inserted in s 9(a).

[47] Francis Oats succeeded Sir Lewis Michell who had succeeded Rhodes.

industry and everyone connected with it'.[48] De Beers was then paying a total of 15 per cent tax (or 14.5 per cent assuming that the UK gave relief by way of a deduction for the South African tax as was then thought to be the law,[49] although there is no evidence in the accounts whether this was the case) and assuming that the tax base was the same in both countries (which it was not as depreciation was deductible in computing Cape tax). While these rates may not sound high one should remember that seven years earlier they paid no tax on profits and three years earlier only the UK 5 per cent (assuming they lost their appeal).

IV. THE LAW

Addington's 1803 income tax was extremely short on definitions, and the position was no different on the reintroduction of income tax in 1842; the legislation contained no definition of residence, which was left to the tribunals and courts to work out. We do not know much about how they operated before 1874 because the tribunals (the General and Special Commissioners) met in private and no appeal lay to the courts, presumably to prevent taxpayers from delaying paying tax. Importantly, there were two cases heard together in 1878, involving UK incorporated companies, one operating entirely in Calcutta and the other in Italy,[50] to which we shall return. UK tax and corporate law was not connected because the applicable corporate law was determined by country of incorporation. A UK incorporated company was therefore free to do business anywhere else and to be managed from anywhere, which gave rise to the tax cases on corporate residence. *De Beers* is a good example of such a separation but applied to a company incorporated in the Cape Colony.

Lord Loreburn's (the Lord Chancellor's) reasoning on the law is short and can be set it out in full:

> In applying the conception of residence to a company, we ought, I think, to proceed as nearly as we can upon the analogy of an individual. A company cannot eat or sleep, but it can keep house and do business. We ought, therefore, to see where it really keeps house and does business. An individual may be of foreign nationality, and yet reside in the United Kingdom. So may a company. Otherwise it might have its chief seat of management and its centre of trading in England under the protection of English law, and yet escape the appropriate taxation by the simple expedient

---

[48] Annual Report 1907 (below n 81) 30 and see *The Times* (16 December 1907) 5 under the heading 'De Beers and the Politicians: Chairman's Reply to Attacks'.

[49] In view of *Stevens v The Durban-Roodepoort Gold Mining Company Ltd* (1909) 5 TC 402 where the deduction of a 1902 Transvaal tax on the profits of mining companies was conceded in computing the profits of a UK resident company, it is likely that the UK gave a deduction for the South African tax. Later, *CIR v Dowdall O'Mahoney* [1952] AC 401 decided that the deduction was wrong but was restored by statute in 1969.

[50] See above, n 1.

of being registered abroad and distributing its dividends abroad. The decision of Kelly CB and Huddleston B in the *Calcutta Jute Mills v Nicholson* and the *Cesena Sulphur Co v Nicholson*, now thirty years ago, involved the principle that a company resides for purposes of income tax where its real business is carried on. Those decisions have been acted upon ever since. I regard that as the true rule, and the real business is carried on where the central management and control actually abides.[51]

'Management and control' was an expression that was already associated with control by the directors.[52] It will be argued that 'central' was (perhaps partly) derived from Savigny's *Mittelpunkt der Geschäfte* or *le centre de l'entreprise*,[53] which, as will be seen below, is quoted in the *Calcutta Jute* and *Cesena Sulphur* cases,[54] the sole authorities cited. The analogy with an individual seems right and Savigny too proceeded on that base, as will be discussed. An individual may have a foreign nationality at birth and come here to do business; so may a company be incorporated abroad and come here to do business.

Lord Loreburn reviewed and approved the two earlier cases, *Calcutta Jute* and *Cesena Sulphur* in the latter of which he, then Mr RT Reed,[55] had been the third counsel for the taxpayer.[56] The cases were heard together and involved similar facts to *De Beers* with one important difference, that the company was incorporated in the UK rather than in the country where the business was carried on, but, like *De Beers* most of the directors were in the UK.[57] For convenience, only *Cesena* will be referred to. In that case residence was agreed by both parties to be where the real trade and business is carried on,[58] which was interpreted in the same way as for the county court jurisdiction over railway companies, from

---

[51] *De Beers* (above n 2) 458.

[52] In *Universal Life Assurance Society v Bishop* (1899) 4 TC 139 it was held that 'The real management and control of the whole of the business and operations of the Society both in and out of the United Kingdom is vested in and exercised by the Board of Directors, which meet at the head office in London, and the meetings of the proprietors are also held in London, and the Dividends are declared and paid there'. Also *St Louis Breweries Ltd v Apthorpe* (1898) 4 TC 111; *R v Special Commissioners ex parte Essex Hall* (1911) 5 TC 636; and *Kodak Ltd v Clark* (1903) 4 TC 549.

[53] Friedrich Carl von Savigny (1779–1861) was a Prussian minister and professor who taught Roman law and its importance for the development of German civil law.

[54] See above, n 1.

[55] He was called to the bar in 1871 (QC 1882) and was 7 years' call when he appeared in *Cesena* (above n 1). He became a liberal MP and was appointed Solicitor General (1894) and Attorney General (1894–95), becoming Lord Chancellor in 1905. As Attorney General (in the House of Lords with his successor in that office) he appeared for the Crown in *San Paulo (Brazilian) Railway Ltd v Carter* [1896] AC 31, (1895) 3 TC 407 (HL), [1895] 1 QB 580 (1895) 3 TC 344 (CA) in which a similar test was applied to determine whether a trade was a foreign one.

[56] Another similar connection with the future is that the Revenue's junior counsel in *De Beers* was the future Rowlatt J.

[57] In *Cesena* (above n 1) eight directors of which two or three (including the managing director) were in Italy; in *Calcutta Jute* (above n 1) five directors of which one (a large shareholder in the company and acting partner in the company's agents in Calcutta) was in Calcutta.

[58] *Cesena* (above n 1) (1876) 1 ExD 428, 452 (see the passage quoted in the text below at n 63). 'But I do not think that the principle of law is really disputed, that the artificial residence which must be assigned to the artificial person called a corporation is the place where the real business is carried on' (Huddleston B) 454.

which many of the authorities cited were taken.[59] The analogy may seem surprising but the logic is the same. One did not want a railway company to be sued in any county court with jurisdiction over any station along the line, wherever the cause of action arose, so a rule developed that railway companies were sued at the head office.[60] Savigny also considered continental railway companies when developing the concept of *Mittelpunkt der Geschäfte*.

Kelly CB equated the place where both the directors and shareholders met with the seat of the company, the same expression that he had used in an even earlier case, *Alexander*,[61] thus whether consciously or not, also relying (inappropriately, as this would be in the country of incorporation) on the mainland European concept of seat.[62]

Huddleston B's judgment was the one which had the greater lasting influence both because of his reference to Savigny and his greater emphasis on the directors, which was critical for *De Beers*. He started with the definition of residence agreed by the parties of where the real trade and business is carried on: 'There is a German expression applicable to it which is well known to foreign jurists – *der Mittelpunkt der Geschäfte*; and the French term is '*le centre de l'entreprise*,' the central point of the business'.[63]

It is not clear what the source of this reference to Savigny was as there is no record of it in the report of the arguments. The *Dictionary of National Biography* describes Huddleston B as an accomplished man, and well read in French literature, so he may have known about Savigny through French sources, hence his addition of the French expression. His reasoning also concentrated on

---

[59] The Revenue relied on *Taylor v Crowland Gas Co* (1855) 11 Ex 1, 24 LJ (Ex) 233; *Adams v Great Western Railway Co* (1861) 6 H&N 404, 30 LJ (Ex) 124; *Shiels v Great Northern Railway Co* (1861) 30 LJ (QB) 331; *Brown v London and North Western Ry Co* (1863) 4 B&S 326, 32 LJ (QB) 318; and *Aberystwith Promenade Pier Co v Cooper* (1865) 35 LJ (QB) 44. The taxpayer relied in Cesena on a non-railway case for which a different rule for jurisdiction applied, *Keynsham Blue Lias Co v Baker* (1863) 2 H&C 729, 33 LJ (Ex) 41.

[60] *Cesena* (above n 1) (1876) 1 ExD 428, 446.

[61] *AG v Alexander* (1874) LR 10 Exch 20.

[62] Compare Savigny: 'One may … consider the corporation as the owner of its business and, consequently, the individual shareholders as the corporation's creditors or mere beneficiaries. – But one may also (as I do) consider the shareholders as the co-owners of the business, limiting the corporate structure's function to making its legal representation easier and more comprehensive' (FK von Savigny, *Das Obligationenrecht als Theil des heutigen Römischen Rechts* Vol 2 (Berlin, Veit, 1853) S 113 n f).

[63] *Cesena* (above n 1) (1876) 1 ExD 428, 452. The last quoted sentence reads in the (unrevised) report at [1874–80] All ER 1102, 1118 'There is a German word which is applicable to it, which means "the middle point" of the business carried on. The French term, adopted from Savigny, is "*le centre de l'entreprise*", the central point of the business, that is to say, the real place where it is carried on'. One therefore needs both reports for the name Savigny and for the German *Mittelpunkt der Geschäfte*. The 1 TC 88, 103 (unrevised) report reads: 'There is a German word which is applicable to it, which means the point of the business carried on. The French term, adopted from Saugne [obviously a misprint or mishearing by the reporter], is "*le centre de l'Enterprise*", the central point of business, that is to say, the real place where the business is carried on'.

the company's constitution but the emphasis in his judgment on the directors with only a passing reference to the shareholders' meetings in contrast to Kelly CB's approach, is noticeable. Although Lord Loreburn refers to both judges it was Huddleston B's that he was really approving because Kelly CB's approach would have resulted in De Beers' residence in South Africa where the shareholders' meetings took place. After considering the facts, Huddleston B returned to Savigny and concluded that *le centre de l'entreprise*, the central point, was in England.

Accordingly, he looked at the constitution which showed that the directors 'called the shots' and so the location of the directors was where the real and substantial business was carried on. Huddleston B's emphasis on the directors was the point that was followed in *De Beers*. One suspects it was because after *Salomon v Salomon*[64] the shareholders were no longer regarded as the company and so the importance of the place of their meetings was much reduced. Even only nine years later it was by then too obvious to need a mention.

V. WHAT WOULD SAVIGNY HAVE MADE OF THAT?

The section in Savigny's celebrated work *System des heutigen römischen Rechts* (volume 8, 1849) to which Huddleston B referred dealt with domicile as one of two ways in which a natural person may be attached to a community. In the passage that uses the expression *Mittelpunkt der Geschäfte*, Savigny described how a natural person may have more than one domicile due to divided 'centres of his connections and affairs'. He then explained that these ideas of domicile relate to natural persons

> and is not, therefore, properly applicable to legal persons. Yet even to these it may become necessary to assign something corresponding or similar to the domicile of natural persons, – as it were an artificial domicile, especially in order to fix their forum. In most cases all doubt will be removed by the natural connection of the legal person with the soil: so it is in the case of towns and villages, churches, schools, hospitals, etc. There may be doubt in the case of industrial associations, if their activity is either fixed to no locality, or extends over great distances, as *eg* the case of railway companies, or steamboat companies, or companies for the building of bridges over great rivers, whose banks are often subject to different jurisdictions, different legislatures, or even different states. In such cases it is advisable at the first establishment of such a legal person to fix its artificial or constructive domicile; if this is neglected, the judge must endeavour to discover by construction the centre of its affairs [*Mittelpunkt der Geschäfte*].[65]

---

[64] *Salomon v Salomon* [1897] AC 22.

[65] FK von Savigny, *A Treatise on the Conflict of Laws, and the Limits of their Operation in Respect of Place and Time*, vol 8, translation with notes by W Guthrie (Edinburgh, T & T Clark, 1869) §354 (footnotes suppressed).

In this passage Savigny extended the Roman law concept of domicile to legal persons to establish court jurisdiction and the person's personal law.[66] Savigny would probably have regarded *Mittelpunkt der Geschäfte* as primarily relevant to determine court jurisdiction within a kingdom comprised of several provinces, which was the exact equivalent to county court jurisdiction over railway companies in the UK; jurisdictional problems over railway companies were clearly not peculiar to the UK. The primary rule that he was proposing was that the document constituting the company should fix its domicile, similar to a natural person's domicile of choice, and in a footnote he gave two examples of railway companies. In other words, the location of a company's seat was the choice of the incorporators failing which 'the judge must endeavour to discover by construction the centre of its affairs [*Mittelpunkt der Geschäfte*]'.[67] Savigny gave two examples of statutes of Prussian railway companies, which required the directors to reside at the locations of the stipulated seat.[68] In modern terms, one could speculate that the residence of the boards of these railway companies was at the same location as their domicile and seat of choice.

Savigny's approach compared with that of Lord Loreburn in *De Beers* shows further similarities than the mere indirect reference. Both saw artificial residence of companies as involving a process of statutory construction. This is significant because unlike drawing on general jurisprudential considerations to establish domicile for natural persons, which is the process followed by Savigny in much of his treatise, establishing corporate residence will rather be informed by the context of the statute that requires residence to be assigned. Lord Loreburn in *De Beers* appeared to have considered statutory context when he said that residence taxation would be appropriate if a company receives the protection of English law for its 'centre of trading' and 'chief seat of management'.[69] It is perhaps as profound a statement as may be made about the reason why a foreign person should become subject to comprehensive income tax.

Savigny's idea about a company's domicile was not immediately put to the test in practice in Germany; rather foreign developments over the next century meant that German authors and courts would eventually return to the topic.[70] The main developments were the enactment in England of the Joint Stock Companies Act 1844, and in 1855, the Limited Liability Act, which caused

---

[66] ibid, §358 and §362.

[67] ibid, §354.

[68] ibid, §354 fn (g). The Statute (or Charter) for the Berlin–Saxony (Anhalt) Railway Company 1839, §1 (Statut der Berlin-Sächsischen (Anhaltischen) Eisenbahn-Gesellschaft in (1839) 1 *Gesetzsammlung für die Königlich-Preußischen Staaten* 178) stipulated 'domicile and seat' in Berlin and the Statute for the Berlin–Stettin Railway Company 1840, §3 (Statut der Berlin-Stettiner Eisenbahn-Gesellschaft in (1840) 1 *Gesetzsammlung für die Königlich-Preußischen Staaten* 306) in Stettin (Szczecin in Poland today); further, it was required that directors all had to 'reside' in Berlin (§48) or Stettin (§31). See also C Trautrims, 'Geschichte und Bedeutung von Sitz- und Gründungstheorie im deutschen Recht' (2012) 176 *Zeitschrift für das gesamte Handels- und Wirtschaftsrecht* 435, 439.

[69] *De Beers* (above n 2) 458.

[70] Trautrims (above n 68) 441–43.

so-called forum shopping to arise: for example, the French used English incorporated companies to avoid matters such as minimum capital in the second half of the nineteenth century.[71] English incorporated companies became particularly suitable as there was no minimum capital, they were free to conduct their business operations outside England, were not taxed as long as they were managed and controlled from outside and they could be created through a process of registration because private Acts of Parliament or Royal Charters were no longer required.[72] It seems that the forum shopping problem did not arise in practice in Germany until much later. It was not a phenomenon that Savigny considered, but German authors later started to discuss it: Savigny's views were still current around the turn of the twentieth century with authors not being specific about what they meant by 'seat'.[73] Trautrims summarises German jurisprudence after 1904: (1) the governing law was that of the corporation's 'seat'; (2) by 'seat' the Supreme Court normally meant the registered seat; (3) in default of a registered seat the Court would look to the administrative seat.[74] Preference for the administrative seat over the registered seat did not become current until the 1960s.[75]

Savigny conceived *Mittelpunkt der Geschäfte* as a fallback to the facts if a company's constitution does not state a domicile or seat in situations where its 'activity is either fixed to no locality, or extends over great distances, as *eg* the case of railway companies'.[76] In relation to bridge-building Savigny envisaged that the two banks might be in different states. This suggests that he was looking at the centre of the business activity rather than, as Huddleston B had concluded, the place of the highest-level decision-making. Savigny also wrote that '[i]n most cases all doubt will be removed by the natural connection of the legal person with the soil',[77] which suggests that he would not have applied *Mittelpunkt der Geschäfte* to a mining company. However as will be discussed below, *De Beers* was no ordinary mining company, even for its time.

While Huddleston B had the laudable intention of harmonisation, the conclusion is that Savigny did not in fact influence the development of UK tax law on corporate residence. Indeed, one might go further and say that it was unhelpful for future cases to introduce the *Mittelpunkt* or 'central' in 'central management

---

[71] ibid, 440.
[72] The motive for the 19th-century English reforms was not to stimulate forum shopping; rather these measures were aimed to regulate unincorporated Deed of Settlement Companies that were used since the start of the 19th century for genuine and fraudulent purposes. Gower explains that these were partnerships that combined trust features (LCB Gower, 'The English Private Company' (1953) 18 *Law and Contemporary Problems* 535). See also MS Rix, *Company Law: 1844 and To-Day* (1945) 55 *The Economic Journal* 242; JF Avery Jones, 'Defining and Taxing Companies 1799 to 1965' in J Tiley (ed), *Studies in the History of Tax Law: Volume 5* (Oxford, Hart Publishing, 2011) 4–7.
[73] Trautrims (above n 68) 441.
[74] ibid, 443.
[75] ibid, 451–52.
[76] Savigny, *A Treatise on the Conflict of Laws* (above n 65) §354.
[77] ibid.

and control' because the next case before the House of Lords after *De Beers* raised the difficulty of two equal centres.[78] One judge who was dissenting in the House of Lords said 'I presume the French lawyers when using this expression [*le centre de l'entreprise*] did not entertain the opinion that an enterprise might at the same moment have two or more different and separate "centres"'.[79]

When Savigny developed his ideas the German states imposed impersonal taxes on the business income of companies; although it is fair to say that when later a modern income tax on companies was imposed in Germany as it is today, the basis of residence was usually the same as the personal law.[80] More importantly, there is a significant difference between domicile and tax residence. Domicile asks the question: 'where is the person domiciled?'; tax residence asks 'is the person resident or not?' English law may say that the person is domiciled in, say, France and apply French law to some aspect such as the essential validity of the person's will; but UK tax law does not say that a person is resident in France, only that he is not resident in the UK, it being understood that each state makes its own determination of residence for tax purposes. This distinction arises out of the context of the statute for which residence must be assigned. It is therefore worth stressing that Lord Loreburn in *De Beers* approached the question of tax residence from that perspective, namely assigning residence under the applicable English income tax statute.

VI. THE REAL FACTS

The courts had to rely, of course, on the facts found by the General Commissioners. We are able to go behind those facts because historians have analysed the actual minutes and other contemporary documents and we had access to some of these.[81] The extracts from board minutes that were before the General Commissioners were selective, which led to criticism by the Kimberley directors as early as 1905 after the High Court judgment on 17 April.[82] It is difficult to understand

---

[78] *The Swedish Central Railway Co Ltd v Thompson* [1925] 1 AC 495.

[79] ibid, Lord Atkinson 509–10.

[80] Various experimentations in the German states at this time with income tax failed (ERA Seligman, *The Income Tax: A Study of the History, Theory and Practice of Income Taxation at Home and Abroad*, 2nd edn (New York, Macmillan, 1914) 236–42); Prussia adopted an income tax imposed expressly on the basis of residence only in 1891 (Seligman, 251; J Hattingh, 'On The Origins of Model Tax Conventions: Nineteenth-Century German Tax Treaties and Laws Concerned with the Avoidance of Double Taxation' in J Tiley (ed), *Studies in the History of Tax Law: Volume 6* (Oxford, Hart Publishing, 2013) 76).

[81] We had access in the De Beers archives in Kimberley to the board minutes of the Kimberley directors' meetings and other contemporaneous materials such as annual reports, accounts and rough minutes; however we have been unable to find the minutes of the London directors' meetings in London or Kimberley and we suspect that they no longer exist.

[82] The Kimberley directors' minute records: 'With regard to the Income Tax decision the Secretary was instructed to mention to London office that the Board here too consider that our Counsel's

the basis for selecting the extracts. For example, the minute of 8 August 1901 mentioned above[83] also dealt with coal and copper mines in Rhodesia; depreciation of the buildings at the explosives works and cold storage;[84] purchase of a site for storage of supplies at Port Elizabeth; approval of tenders for the power plant for the dynamite factory; leases of local building plots; prospecting rights for coal mining over a local farm; economising on the use of coal; acquisition of more mules from the Imperial Government/military for working in the mines and to stop refinement at one of the mines and ease down refinement at others in view of the situation about coal and mules.[85] One would have expected that the items up to and including coal mining at a local farm which related to businesses other than diamond mining would have been relevant to the courts. The extracts before the courts contained absolutely nothing for either set of directors for the period during which Kimberley was besieged by Boer forces during which extraordinary measures were taken by the Kimberley directors. For example, on 26 November 1899 the Kimberley directors resolved to purchase 800 horses and instructed the chief engineer, Labram, to manufacture shells in the company's workshops.[86] The minute for 8 December 1899 records that Rhodes informed the board that he received news from Lord Methuen, who was in charge of the relief effort, that no coal or dynamite supplies could be delivered to Kimberley. As a consequence, the Kimberley directors resolved to dismiss all

---

arguments were feeble, and tended to create the impression that either Counsel did not sufficiently prepare the case or that our Solicitors were at fault in not bringing out the principal points' (De Beers Consolidated Mines Ltd, *Minute Book No 6* (25 February 1904–1 June 1905, Kimberley) 500 (1 June 1905)). At the General Meeting of 1905, and again at an Extraordinary General Meeting in 1907, the chairman extensively discussed the English income tax decisions by the Court of Appeal and the House of Lords saying that the factual nature of the company and how it was managed, were misunderstood. The Kimberley directors further instructed counsel in South Africa to provide a second view on the Court of Appeal's judgment about the merits of an appeal to the House of Lords (De Beers Consolidated Mines Ltd, *Minute Book No 7* (1 June 1906–17 January 1907, Kimberley) 84–88 (8 September 1905)).

[83] See text at n 28 above.

[84] There are several earlier references in the minutes to investment by De Beers in cold storage, initially mostly at the main ports, Cape Town and Port Elizabeth, and later at Kimberley. Rhodes referred to these investments as examples of 'public acts' by De Beers as they illustrate the role De Beers played in the industrialisation of Southern Africa: aided by investment in the railways, cold storage enabled the large-scale exportation of agricultural goods from Southern Africa as well as constant supplies for a rapidly increasing population due to the discovery of diamonds and gold.

[85] De Beers Consolidated Mines Ltd, *Minute Book No 4* (19 May 1900–23 June 1902, Kimberley) 262–66 (7 February 1901). We have also noted errors in the extracts, such as the extracts stated to be in the minutes of 11 and 18 May 1899 in fact being in the 4 and 11 May 1899 minutes respectively, and there is a reference in the extract for 9 May 1900 to a pension to Mr Labram which should have been to Mrs Labram, the widow of the chief engineer who was killed during the siege, suggesting that the extracts were prepared by somebody not acquainted with the company and were not reviewed by the company.

[86] De Beers Consolidated Mines Ltd, *Minute Book No 3* (August 1897–May 1900, Kimberley) 437–39 (26 November 1899).

employees and close the mines.[87] The Kimberley minute continues informally up to February 1900 with an extensive transcription of the correspondence between the board and Colonel Kekewich, the military commander at Kimberley, who disagreed about military strategy. These actions of the Kimberley directors go far beyond the powers delegated to them to deal with 'the technical management of the company's work and operations at its mines'.[88] There was no mention of London during this period (communication lines were evidently inoperative).

After the siege ended, the Kimberley directors resolved to request Lord Methuen to establish a commission to look into the De Beers special war account since the directors were 'anxious to know what portion of the account the Imperial Government were responsible for'.[89] The profit and loss account for 1900 showed £167,733 as extraordinary war expenditure (£29,551 for 1901).[90] On 7 February 1901, telegrams from Rhodes containing a proposal to the Cape Government in regard to the Boer War were laid before the Kimberley board. In terms of the proposal, De Beers was to supply 200 mounted men to protect the Bechuanaland railways on the border with the Transvaal (in which the company had invested), which was to be matched by the Cape Government supplying 400 mounted men – the Kimberley directors approved the proposal without any reference to London.[91] Other examples of financial decisions taken by Rhodes and the Kimberley directors during the Boer War show a looser attitude to the London directors.[92]

If we had had access to the London directors' minutes we suspect that these would show similar deficiencies in the extracts before the courts. Even without these we can conclude that the summary of minutes in the case stated did not always paint the full picture either because there is nothing in the extracts about the particular issue, or because, despite noting disapproval by the London directors of actions undertaken by the Kimberley directors as a basis for holding that control was exercised in London, some of these disapproving resolutions were retracted or changed, for example after representations by Rhodes or during board meetings where London directors were present in Kimberley. A further complication is that Rhodes often communicated by cable with the

---

[87] ibid, 440 (8 December 1899).

[88] Above n 30. The timing is particularly interesting because these events occurred during the period on which the assessments to UK tax were based: see above n 44.

[89] De Beers, *Minute Book No 3* (above n 86) 473–77 (22 March 1900).

[90] *The Times* (25 January 1901) 13; (17 December 1901) 15.

[91] De Beers, *Minute Book No 4* (above n 85) 157–62 (7 February 1901).

[92] eg, the Kimberley minutes record that the company's gold interest in Mashonaland was left in Rhodes' judgment by the London directors and the board further considered the Rhodesia copper offer (De Beers, *Minute Book No 3* (above n 86) 498–500 (9 May 1900)). On 29 June 1900 the Kimberley directors, except for Francis Oats, resolved that no dividend should be declared after receiving Rhodes' agreement by cable; they merely informed London about the decision (De Beers, *Minute Book No 4* (above n 85) 25–27 (29 June 1900)). And see also the extract from the Kimberley minutes of 8 August 1901 (262–66) and 15 May 1902 (450–54) in Parliamentary Archives (above n 28).

boards when he was not present at a meeting and was in neither location. The Kimberley minutes are replete with examples where the board requests his view by cable.

References in the minutes before the courts alluded to what was a key cause of tension between Rhodes and the London directors, namely Rhodes' aspirations for imperial expansion in Southern Africa for which he sought to use the resources of De Beers. This adds an extraordinary dimension when appraising the workings of the board since De Beers was no ordinary company. Rhodes during his chairmanship of De Beers was Prime Minister of the Cape Colony from 1890 to 1896 when he was forced to resign following his involvement in the Jameson Raid on the Transvaal Republic, a key cause for outbreak of the South African war (Boer War) in 1899. The London directors represented the interest of financiers, shareholders and the marketing Syndicate, and were naturally concerned with a more orthodox profit-seeking mandate. A good example of these divergent interests transpires from positions the London and Kimberley directors adopted at times in regard to Rhodes' ambitions for territorial expansion of British interests in Africa. On 21 April 1891 the Kimberley directors resolved that a cable be sent to Rhodes to make no further speculative investments in Mashonaland (later Rhodesia, the present Zimbabwe) 'without fully consulting London'.[93] On 10 June 1891, the Kimberley directors however agreed with Rhodes that a suggestion by the London directors to distribute 10,000 shares in the British South African Company (BSA) should be rejected, and on 17 December 1891 the Kimberley directors approved Rhodes' special request that monthly advances should be made by De Beers to the BSA; no reference was made to London.[94] The London directors unanimously resolved on 21 January 1892 to 'not approve of the advances made to the Chartered Company',[95] which was a reference to the BSA. This last resolution was the only extract before the English courts about advances to the BSA and evidently could lead to a misleading picture. Indeed two weeks later on 3 February 1892 the Kimberley board approved further advances to the BSA.[96] On 7 March 1892 Carl Meyer was present at a Kimberley directors' meeting where the whole matter was resolved: a policy for lending by De Beers to the BSA was formulated and approved in terms of which De Beers could lend up to £113,000 provided that it received the sole mandate over diamond exploitation in the BSA territories.[97] Further advances were approved

---

[93] De Beers Consolidated Mines Ltd, *Minute Book No 1* (1885–24 April 1891, Kimberley) 374–77 (21 April 1891).

[94] De Beers Consolidated Mines Ltd, *Minute Book No 2* (April 1891–August 1906, Kimberley) 12, 57–61 (17 December 1891).

[95] *De Beers* (above n 19) 623, para 14.

[96] De Beers, *Minute Book No 2* (above n 94) 80–81 (3 February 1892).

[97] ibid, 90–91 (7 March 1892).

in 1893 and 1894.[98] The BSA was created by Royal Charter on 20 December 1889 with 'its principal field of operations in that region of South Africa lying to the north of Bechuanaland and to the west of Portuguese East Africa' (nowadays Zimbabwe, Zambia and Malawi), its purpose being 'to carry into effect divers concessions and agreements which have been made by certain of the chiefs and tribes inhabiting the said region'.[99] The concessions referred to land upon which the artisanal Mashonaland gold mines were located and this territory provided the geographical corridor for Rhodes' vision of British commercial and political influence from the 'Cape to Cairo'. Two of the three first directors of the BSA included founding Life Governors of De Beers (Rhodes and Alfred Beit) and the shareholders included De Beers directors.[100] In 1893 Rhodes and Jameson (Chief Magistrate of the BSA at the time) prepared for conflict with the Ndebele in Mashonaland. This resulted in the First Matabele War in the winter of 1893 leading to the defeat of Lobengula, King of the Ndebele.[101] Shortly thereafter Rhodesia (now Zimbabwe) was established in the territory of the BSA. Apart from holding shares in and providing advances to the BSA,[102] De Beers also invested in the railways required by the BSA, a further cause of tension with the London directors as can be seen, for example, from the minutes of 24 February 1898.[103] Rhodes referred to these financial transactions by De Beers as 'public acts'[104] in respect of which Lord Rothschild warned Rhodes in 1894:

[Y]ou are the only judge as to whether the Cape Government ought to take over the Northern Territories; that is not our business and we do not wish to offer any opinion on the subject ... But what we do say is, that if that is your policy, and you require money for the purpose, you will have to obtain it from other sources than the cash reserve of the Debeers [sic] Company. We have always held that the Debeers Company is simply and purely a diamond mining company.[105]

When reading the larger historical context with the benefit of hindsight, one can question whether it was Rhodes or the London directors who were controlling the policy of De Beers. Although it appears that the Kimberley directors

[98] ibid, 217, 310, 403 (3 April 1893; 15 January 1894; 21 October 1894); see also Newbury (above n 12) 151–52.

[99] Charter of the British South Africa Company, *London Gazette* (20 December 1889).

[100] RI Rotberg, *The Founder: Cecil Rhodes and the Pursuit of Power* (Oxford, Oxford University Press, 1988) 286.

[101] ibid, 436–44.

[102] De Beers was the main financier of the BSA (ibid, 286).

[103] See text at n 28.

[104] At the 10th AGM on 10 December 1898 Rhodes described De Beers' interest in the land under control of the BSA: 'You have a large amount of land, and finally you have the first right to diamonds in the whole of that territory, so that your connection with the north which was begun as a public act, has, I consider, turned out very satisfactorily from a business point of view' (Chilvers (above n 14) 114).

[105] Ferguson (above n 6) 888; Newbury (above n 12) 151.

often supported the policy of Rhodes, there are clear examples in the minutes where they also did not. As far as creating and maintaining a monopoly over the diamond market was concerned, the London directors appeared to hold sway over the negotiation and renewal of Syndicate contracts as this was essentially insisted upon by the original English and European financiers who were major shareholders. Some of the Kimberley directors were also merchants and associated with Syndicate members, but the Kimberley directors took an active part in debates with the London directors and on many occasions their views prevailed. The views of Rhodes expressed by cable when he was in neither location may have been more important than the views of either set of directors. While it appears from the minutes of the Kimberley directors that they made more decisions affecting the company as a whole than appears from the extracts, in the absence of the minutes of the London directors we are unable to speculate whether the General Commissioners might have come to a different decision had they seen the full minutes rather than the extracts presented to them.

VII. AFTERMATH

The confirmation by the House of Lords of the imposition of UK tax coupled with the doubling of the rate of Cape tax could not have come at a worse time for De Beers. The 1906 San Francisco earthquake triggered recession by 1907 resulting in large outflows of gold from the US and London, where about half of the insurance was written, leading to significant falls in share prices.[106] At the same time a failed attempt to corner the market in the United Copper Company led to a panic in October 1907 when the New York stock exchange almost collapsed. The recession that followed clearly affected diamond sales as the US was the major diamond market of the time.

Shortly after the decision by the House of Lords, the Kimberley directors on 2 August 1906 resolved that two directors, Francis Oats and Leander Starr Jameson (who was then Prime Minister of the Cape Colony) should consider 'steps to remedy the situation'.[107] The minute of 29 November 1906 refers for the first time to a proposal to close the London office but the board resolved to postpone the matter pending representations 'to Asquith' (the British Prime Minister) and an Imperial Conference.[108] Asquith was unsympathetic to any change in the law and said it was open to the company to determine from

---

[106] KA Odell and MD Weidenmier, 'Real Shock, Monetary Aftershock: The 1906 San Francisco Earthquake and the Panic of 1907' (2004) 64 *Journal of Economic History* 1002.

[107] De Beers, *Minute Book No 7* (above n 82) 389–91 (2 August 1906).

[108] ibid, 459–66 (29 November 1906).

where it was managed by the directors.[109] Discussion of the proposed closure again took place on 14 March 1907 in Kimberley with Carl Meyer present as representative of the continental shareholders (mostly French), who opposed the proposal.[110] On 20 March 1907 the Kimberley directors resolved to send a cable to London regarding its closure saying 'remedy according to Asquith in our hands'.[111] Preparations were thereafter begun and at the meeting of 3 October 1907 the Kimberley directors resolved to call a special general meeting to vote on the closure of the London office.[112] At the AGM on 14 December 1907 the chairman said that, in the light of the recession in the diamond market and in order to provide for the additional Cape and UK taxes 'the directors deemed it necessary to curtail expenditure by reducing operations'.[113] The accounts to 30 June 1908 confirmed his predictions. Reduced sales resulted in a much-reduced profit of £724,000 (compared with £2,607,000 for the previous year), and a combined tax charge provided in the accounts amounting to 66 per cent of the accounting profit.[114]

The directors considered that the UK tax 'was unjustifiable when directed against a Colonial Company registered and conducting its operations and having its Head Office in the Cape Colony'.[115] After considering and rejecting the possibility of moving the London office to New York,[116] following the advice

[109] Letter quoted in Annual Report for 1907 at 33 as part of Mr Hawksley's (the company's London solicitor's) detailed presentation about the case to the EGM.

[110] De Beers Consolidated Mines Ltd, *Minute Book No 8* (24 January 1907–24 June 1909, Kimberley) 33–37 (14 March 1907).

[111] ibid, 103–07 (20 March 1907).

[112] ibid, 158–62 (3 October 1907); on 17 October 1907 the Kimberley directors invited the London directors to attend the 1907 general and special meetings; on 14 November 1907 they received the approval of the sole surviving Life Governor, Sir Julius Wernher; and on 21 November 1907 a resolution was passed to increase advertisement of the 1907 special meeting in local newspapers.

[113] Production was reduced by 35%, Annual Report 1908, 27, *The Times* (16 December 1907) 5). It appears from the report of the EGM on 14 March 1908 that no dividend had been paid on the deferred shares, *The Times* (16 March 1908) 13.

[114] The tax provided in the accounts was £64,574 (UK), and £412,857 (Cape) (comprising not only tax on the previous year's profits paid in the year (£302,174) but also tax for the current year (£110,683)): *The Times* (15 December 1908) 19 (1907 comparisons, *The Times* (23 December 1907) 11. The effect was that the UK tax was reduced and the Cape tax was inflated: the UK because of the deduction for tax charged to shareholders and debenture holders which would have been payable on the profits anyway (but their thought process was that since they were paying the dividends anyway the only tax they had to find was tax on the difference between the profit and the dividend: see De Beers, *Minute Book No 8* (above n 110) 35 (14 March 1907), and the retention of tax deducted from interest is merely a method of obtaining tax relief for the interest, and because the report also states that a refund was being claimed as the current year's profit was less than the three-year average; and the Cape because two years' tax was provided, the directors describing the tax on the previous year's profits as 'an extremely heavy burden on your company', which of course it was when applied to the reduced current year's profit.

[115] 1907 Directors' Report, *The Times* (23 December 1907) 11.

[116] Chilvers (above n 14) 157.

of Mr Cohen KC and Mr Danckwerts KC who had appeared in the appeal[117] an Extraordinary General Meeting (EGM) was called at the same time as the 1907 AGM to alter the Articles to reduce the powers of the UK directors in order to stop paying UK tax. The notice of the meeting stated that these powers would in future be limited to 'the transfer of shares, the issue of bearer shares, the payment of dividends and interest, the purchase of machinery and supplies as may from time to time be indented from Kimberley, and other matters of a formal character'.[118] It recorded that

> the decision of the directors in London to relinquish their powers to the Kimberley board had been arrived at with great reluctance,[119] but … that the directors in London have been unable to resist the force of the arguments brought forward by their colleagues in South Africa.[120]

Ironically it was the Kimberley directors who had the last word when it came to ending the UK tax charge. The EGM was adjourned because in view of the world financial situation it was not the time to make drastic changes.[121] The resolution was unanimously passed at the adjourned meeting on 14 March 1908 and the decision was taken that all sales to the Syndicate had to be concluded in Kimberley after that date.[122] What is strange is that most of the London directors seem to have remained in post, including Carl Meyer who remained deputy chairman until 1922.

Thus, less than two years after the House of Lords decision De Beers had avoided its effect, having paid UK tax for only eight years. But the effect of the decision on everyone else lives on. The judgment continues to be cited, always with approval, by courts in the UK in tax and non-tax cases (often dealing with civil jurisdiction), and similarly by courts in South Africa, Australia, Canada, Hong Kong and on occasion Ireland, India and the US.[123]

---

[117] Annual Report 1907, 39.

[118] *The Times* (14 November 1907) 13. The alterations to the Articles deal only with the transfer of shares and issue of bearer shares. The directors were given powers of attorney to deal with these and also with banking transactions in the UK (De Beers, *Minute Book No 8* (above n 110) 297 (14 March 1907)). While the retention of some powers of the directors resulted in the company remaining UK resident in *Swedish Central Railway* (above n 78), the difference is that there was more activity in London than with De Beers, including making up the accounts and having them audited.

[119] Chilvers (above n 14) 288 records that at the February 1907 Kimberley directors' meeting Carl Meyer 'expressed himself as strongly against closing the London Office as he was of opinion it was against the best interests of shareholders'.

[120] *The Times* (14 November 1907) 13. Carl Meyer attended a directors' meeting in the Cape in 1907 arguing that the London office was in the best interests of shareholders (Chilvers (above n 14) 288).

[121] *The Times* (16 December 1907) 5; Chilvers (above n 14) 289.

[122] De Beers, *Minute Book No 8* (above n 110) 249–54 (14 March 1908); *The Times* (16 March 1908) 13; Chilvers (above n 14) 158–59, 289.

[123] We traced 126 citations (by 2017), of which 34 were in UK tax cases (which excludes the first-tier before 1994 when reporting started) and 15 in non-tax cases; 12-1 for South Africa, 11-4 Australia, 23-17 Canada, 3-3 Hong Kong and one tax case each for Ireland, India and the USA.

APPENDIX

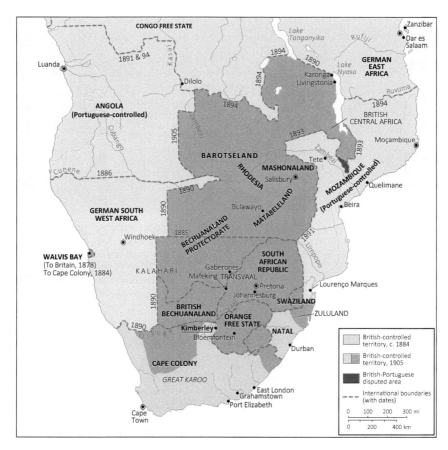

Map showing European penetration into Southern Africa, 1884 to 1905. Much of
the expansion of British control over the region took place in the period when Cecil
Rhodes was in the driving seat as chairman of De Beers and Prime Minister of the Cape
Colony.

'Long Cecil' and the De Beers men who made it (c 1900). Second row standing, left to right: George Paley (Assistant Mechanical Engineer); William Berry (Workshop Foreman); at right of second row: George Labram (Chief Engineer) and Edward Goffe (Chief Draughtsman) (from Peddle n 30). Image courtesy of the McGregor Museum, Kimberley.

4

Thomas Gibson Bowles v Bank of England *(1913)* A Modern John Hampden?*

MARTIN DAUNTON[1]

T HOMAS GIBSON BOWLES (1842–1922)[2], the self-proclaimed reincarnation of John Hampden,[3] was at first sight an implausible champion of the rights of the subject against unauthorised taxation. He was the illegitimate son of Thomas Milner Gibson (1806–84), a wealthy landowner with estates in Suffolk and Islington who was returned as Conservative MP for Ipswich in 1837. He left the Party in 1839 on his conversion to free trade, joining the Anti-Corn Law League to the initial scepticism of Richard Cobden. He regained a seat in Parliament in 1841, initially for Manchester, and remained a MP until his defeat in 1868; he held office in the Board of Trade and played a role in the implementation of free-trade policies, the repeal on taxes on knowledge, and opposing imperialistic adventures. Milner Gibson was a mixture of Tory and radical sentiments, and his son had the same independent approach to politics.[4]

Bowles was accepted into his father's family and was partly educated in France with a short spell at King's College London before he left to take a

---

*I am grateful to Colin Lee, Clerk of Bill, House of Commons, and Professor Chantal Stebbings for helpful comments on an earlier draft.

[1] HC Deb 18 March 1913, ser 5, vol 50, col 995 (F Cassel).

[2] Biographical details are from A Cochrane and HCG Matthew, 'Bowles, Thomas Gibson (1842–1922)' in *Oxford Dictionary of National Biography* (Oxford, Oxford University Press, 2008) and LE Naylor, *The Irrepressible Victorian: The Story of Thomas Gibson Bowles, Journalist, Parliamentarian and Founder-Editor of the Original Vanity Fair* (London, Macdonald, 1965).

[3] eg, in TG Bowles, *Bowles v the Bank of England: The Proceedings in Court* (from the shorthand writer's notes) and official court documents, with an introduction by T Gibson Bowles (London, Butterworth, 1914) xii.

[4] HCG Matthew, 'Gibson, Thomas Milner (1806–1884)' in *Oxford Dictionary of National Biography* (Oxford, Oxford University Press, 2011). There is also a family history at 'The Milner-Gibsons' (1806–1986), available at milnergibson.wordpress.com.

position at the Legacy and Succession Office of the Inland Revenue in 1861, on the nomination of his father. Despite his greater interest in the theatre and journalism, and a casual attitude to official duties as a fast young man about town, the experience gave him technical knowledge of taxation. In 1866, he left to become a leader writer at the *Morning Post*, for whom he wrote despatches on the defence of Paris during the Franco–Prussian War.[5] In 1868, he started *Vanity Fair*, a magazine known for its caricatures of leading politicians and its witty gossip about current affairs; its title derived from the place of vacuity and vice in John Bunyan's *Pilgrim's Progress*. He sold the magazine after the death of his wife in 1887, but he retained *The Lady* which he started in 1884.[6]

His main interest turned to politics, and he stood, unsuccessfully, for the first time at Banbury in 1880, as an 'independent Conservative'. Although he offered support to the government, he informed the electors that he would

> on all occasions prefer the interests of my country to those of my party … I would have England defend her rights and perform her duties at all hazards. History shows that those nations alone are stable and secure whose citizens are ready to defend the institutions of their country at home against rash change, and its honour abroad against violent assault.[7]

In 1880, he expressed admiration for the so-called 'Fourth Party' of young MPs around Lord Randolph Churchill who criticised the party hierarchy. In *Vanity Fair*, Bowles virulently attacked the 'worn-up old relics whose only notion of leading the Party is to prevent anybody else from leading it', blocking all attempts at activity and keeping the spoils of office for themselves.[8] These sentiments continued throughout his career.

Eventually, Bowles was returned as Conservative Member for King's Lynn in 1892. He remained more an independent than a party man, for he was deeply sceptical of the party system as

> the cause, proximate or remote, of most of the recent changes in Constitutional practice … . Parties have become more and more frankly organisations without any colourable pretence of principle, but only with appetites. The principles repudiated today are professed tomorrow without turning a hair. What is never repudiated is the claim to power.[9]

His hostility to the party leadership remained as strong as in the 1880s, now directed against both the Cecil family clique of the Prime Minister, the Marquess

---

[5] TG Bowles, *Defence of Paris; Narrated as it was Seen* (London, Sampson Low, Son and Marston, 1871). He had close links with James Tissot who worked with him at *Vanity Fair* from 1869; Bowles provided him with shelter when he fled Paris in 1871: see Naylor (above n 2) 12, 17, 24–36, 37.

[6] Naylor (above n 2) ch 2.

[7] ibid, 60; see also Bowles's comments in the election of 1906, 156.

[8] Naylor (above n 2) 66–67.

[9] TG Bowles, 'The British Constitution' in *Report of the Constitution Congress in Connection with the Franco-British Exhibition, Being a Special Number of 'Constitution Papers'* (London, British Constitution Association, 1908) 116.

of Salisbury, and his nephew Arthur Balfour who also became Prime Minister in 1902; and Joseph Chamberlain who turned away from free trade to tariff reform. Here he made common cause with Lord Randolph's son, Winston, whom he helped in his maiden speech in 1900.[10] Although Bowles showed considerable knowledge of financial issues and made telling interventions against William Harcourt's Budget in 1894, his critical, often vitriolic, stance meant that any hope that he would be appointed Financial Secretary to the Treasury in 1895 was disappointed. Despite his grasp of financial issues and parliamentary procedure, he was easily dismissed as 'simply a merry wag or jester' – and as the *Morning Leader* pointed out he was neither a Cecil family man, nor 'of the tribe of Joseph'.[11]

Bowles remained a free trader, decrying the conversion of the free-trade Conservative Party into 'a spurious, perverted Protectionist Party, betrayed by Mr Balfour, dominated by Mr Chamberlain'.[12] He was so critical of tariff reform and Balfour's lack of strong leadership that he lost the Conservative whip, and in 1904 he voted against the government on several occasions, on tariff reform, the cost of the army, licensing laws, and Chinese labour in the Transvaal.[13] In the general election of 1906, when Bowles stood on a free-trade platform at King's Lynn against an official Conservative candidate, he attacked Chamberlain in 'an amazing piece of invective which sears its victim in every bitter, remorseless phrase'.[14] Chamberlain stood accused of blackmailing his leader, deceiving workers with promises of social welfare, and insisting on the appointment of his 'abjectly incapable son' Austen as Chancellor of the Exchequer. Joseph was condemned as 'at most but a tradesman-minded man, and incapable of rising to the heights of statesmanship'. If this were not enough, in comparison 'the Thugs of India are faithful friends, and Judas Iscariot himself entitled to a crown of glory'.[15] Winston Churchill was impressed, commending the diatribe as 'the way to knock the stuffing out of the Brummagem scarecrow'.[16] Bowles lost his seat and then stood against Balfour in a by-election in the City of London, before joining the Liberals for whom he was returned at King's Lynn in the first election of 1910. He lost the seat in the second election that year and rejoined the Conservatives, but he mainly concentrated on extra-parliamentary activities that culminated in his legal victory over the Bank of England in 1912 and the subsequent passing of the Provisional Collection of Taxes Act (PTCA) 1913.[17]

---

[10] Naylor (above n 2) 146–47, quoted WS Churchill, *My Early Life: A Roving Commission* (London, Butterworth, 1930).

[11] Naylor (above n 2) 144, 145 quoting *Morning Leader* (18 June 1901); see also 152.

[12] ibid, 161.

[13] ibid, 149–50.

[14] ibid, 155, quoting the *Daily News* (undated).

[15] ibid, 153–54.

[16] Churchill Archives Centre, Cambridge, CHAR 2/3/34, note on cutting of the speech.

[17] There is an excellent account of the legal reasoning in the case in J Jaconelli, 'The "Bowles Act" – The Cornerstone of the Fiscal Constitution' (2010) 69 *CLJ* 582, which does not cover Bowles's motivations in depth.

Bowles's action attracted differing assessments. To AV Dicey, there was 'No better demonstration of the power of the rule of the law'.[18] To others, he was a nuisance and troublemaker who threatened the basis of the collection of income tax. The Chancellor of the Exchequer, David Lloyd George, who had to deal with the consequences of the case, rejected his claim to be a new Hampden as 'rather a poor view to take of that great man'.[19] *Bowles v Bank* was not a leading case in the same way as Hampden's attack on ship-money which raised a fundamental principle of a threat to his landed property by the Crown. By contrast, Bowles deliberately went out of his way to purchase a form of stock that would test the right of the Bank of England to deduct tax on behalf of the Inland Revenue prior to the passing of legislation for the next financial year. He was aware of the basis on which taxation was levied, and he put himself knowingly in the position of being liable to taxation which he then contested.

Bowles's action arose from two concerns: one procedural that raised issues about crown prerogative; the other partisan and ideological. The two were inextricably connected. On the first, he had a very good case that governments – both Conservative and even more Liberal – were playing fast and loose with parliamentary process by relying on resolutions to collect income tax, prior to the passing of legislation. He took a stringent view of the role of legislation and Parliament in circumscribing executive discretion in taxation, a legal point that justifies *Bowles v Bank* as a leading case in tax law. Like Camden CJCP in *Entick v Carrington* [1765] he wished to ensure that the prerogative powers of the Crown and government were subordinate to the law. In Camden's words:

> The great end, for which men entered into society, was to secure their property. That right is preserved sacred and incommunicable in all instances, where it has not been taken away or abridged by some public law for the good of the whole.[20]

The procedural issue was resolved by legislation in 1913 which tidied up an acknowledged shortcoming, but Bowles was also using this point of parliamentary process in pursuit of a wider, highly partisan, attack on the role of the state in dealing with the social problems of Britain. Essentially, the principle at issue was the circumstances in which the right to property could be circumscribed for the good of the whole.

The Liberal government that came to power in 1906 introduced new welfare schemes of old-age pensions, national insurance, labour exchanges and minimum wages, funded in part by higher levels of progressive income tax and an assault on 'unearned' income from land. These schemes offered a free trade alternative to Conservative proposals for tariff reform which would produce revenue and, so it was believed by Chamberlain, create employment, raise wages

---

[18] AV Dicey, 'Lectures Introductory to the Study of the Law of the Constitution' in JWF Allison (ed) *The Oxford Edition of Dicey: Volume I*, rev edn (Oxford, Oxford University Press, 2013) 450.

[19] HC Deb 18 March 1913, ser 5, vol 50, col 998 (D Lloyd George).

[20] *Entick v Carrington* [1765] 19 Howell's State Trials 1029.

and fund welfare – the deceitful promise of which Bowles complained. To Lloyd George, the value of landed property was created by society rather than by the actions of the owners and was therefore a legitimate subject of taxation that could be 'taken away or abridged by some public law for the good of the whole'. This view came to be accepted by Bowles's erstwhile ally Churchill who saw the pragmatic, political need for a free trade solution to social problems based on redistributive taxation as a counter to tariff reform – a view that made political sense when the Liberal Party was needing to find a way of reacting to the rise of the Labour Party. Bowles rejected both Liberal fiscal and social reforms, and Conservative tariff reform. Instead, he advocated lower levels of spending, the free market and self-reliance. What was at stake was an argument about the nature and size of the state and the purposes for which public revenue should properly be raised, and Bowles was using the courts to advance his wider political ideology. Bowles was therefore using a genuine shortcoming in parliamentary process in pursuit of a deeply contentious position on the role of the state. His success contributed to the failure of his wider claims, for he removed a genuine grievance against tax collection on the basis of resolutions, and so restored the legitimacy of the fiscal regime.[21]

Bowles's campaign started when he was issued with a return in September 1911, during his absence abroad, relating to his liability to pay supertax for the tax year ended 5 April 1912. Supertax was an additional income tax of 6d in the pound on incomes of £5,000 and above that was introduced in the 'People's Budget' of 1909. The return was accompanied by a notice relating to the 'Finance (1909–10) Act 1910. Super-tax regulations made by the Commissioners of Inland Revenue under section 78(2)'. Legislation to give force to the Budget of 1909 had been delayed as a result of the constitutional crisis arising from resistance from the House of Lords to the People's Budget, so that the Finance Act authorising the tax measures for 1909/10 was only enacted on 29 April 1910, a year after David Lloyd George's Budget speech. In *Bowles v Attorney General*, Bowles argued that the return and notice were null and void, for at the time they were issued, the Budget resolutions had not been given effect in a Finance Act relating to supertax for the financial year 1911/12, which only passed in December 1911 – an unusually long delay. The question was whether the Inland Revenue could assess and demand payment of a tax before the Act imposing the tax had passed.[22]

[21] eg, A Offer, Property and Politics, *1870–1914: Landownership, Law, Ideology and Urban Development in England* (Cambridge, Cambridge University Press, 1981); BK Murray, *The People's Budget 1909/10: Lloyd George and Liberal Politics* (Oxford, Clarendon Press, 1980); M Daunton, *Trusting Leviathan: The Politics of Taxation in Britain, 1799–1914* (Cambridge, Cambridge University Press, 2001). On Churchill, see WS Churchill, *Liberalism and the Social Problem* (London, Hodder & Stoughton, 1909).

[22] *Bowles v AG* [1912] 1 Ch 123, 125–31; Jaconelli (above n 17) 583.

The income tax was generally imposed for a year at a time, except in 1842 (for three years), 1848 (for three years) and 1853 (for seven years). When the income tax was introduced, it was presented as a temporary tax to be abandoned when expenditure was cut and finances placed on a sound basis.[23] Before long, it was a fiction that stood in the way of efficient collection of the tax, for authority to collect the tax expired on 5 April – and the tax authorities needed to commence collecting information for the next tax year starting on 6 April, despite the fact that the Finance Act was not usually passed in time. As Parker J pointed out, the income tax was legally a temporary tax which had to be reimposed every year; in practice, it was a permanent tax with permanent officials, and the convenience of both officials and taxpayers meant that there had to be continuity of assessment and collection.[24]

There were a number of ways of dealing with the inconvenience of a lack of authority. The first approach was to pass an Act before the end of the financial year, applying the provisions for assessment before the income tax was renewed. Hence, the Income Tax Assessment Act 1870 laid down that all statutory provisions then in force 'shall have full force and effect' for the next year, as if authority for the tax had been granted. This device was used again in 1871, 1872 and 1873. The second approach was adopted by the Customs and Inland Revenue Act (CIRA) 1874 which imposed the income tax for the year ending 5 April 1875, but kept the machinery in operation for the year starting 6 April 1875 before legislation was passed to impose the income tax and determine the rate. This mechanism was used until the CIRA 1890 which contained the provision in section 30 that

> in order to ensure the collection in due time of any duties of income tax which may be granted for any year commencing on the sixth day of April, all such provisions contained in any Act relating to income tax as were in force on the preceding day shall have full force and effect.

This measure bridged the gap between the start of the financial year in April and the actual imposition of the tax, usually by August. As Parker J remarked, this general and perpetual power 'prevents a law officer from being obliged to demonstrate that such a provision is not a new instrument of oppression'. To be doubly sure, every Act reimposing income tax also contained a clause applying the provisions in force on 5 April to the ensuing year. Hence the Finance (1909–10) Act 1910, section 72(2) required anyone served with a notice to make a return for assessment of supertax, whether or not they were chargeable.[25]

Bowles contended that section 30 of the CIRA 1890, did not apply to the supertax, on the grounds that it was different from the income tax, and that the

---

[23] Daunton (above n 21) ch 4.

[24] *Bowles v AG* (above n 22) 132.

[25] As explained by Parker J in *Bowles v AG*, ibid, 133–34; C Stebbings, *The Victorian Taxpayer and the Law: A Study in Constitutional Conflict* (Cambridge, Cambridge University Press, 2009) 57; s 30, Customs and Inland Revenue Act 1890; s 72(2), Finance (1909–10) Act 1910.

Act of 1909–10 only imposed supertax for the year commencing 6 April 1909, with no subsequent enactments. Parker J held that the demand was lawful: the supertax was an income tax, for it was referred to as an 'additional duty of income tax' and was collected by the ordinary machinery of the income tax. Like the income tax, it was imposed annually but intended to be a permanent tax. In the Finance (1909–10) Act 1910, it appeared in the section headed 'Income Tax' and was construed alongside other Acts relating to income tax, including section 30 of the Act of 1890. The supertax was therefore 'a duty of income tax'. Parker J further argued that section 72(3) of the Act of 1910 regulated the collection of the supertax not only for 1909/10 but also for subsequent years. Although Bowles's action failed, Parker then gave him an opening:

> It must not be understood that I am expressing any opinion as to how far the Special Commissioners have power, before the tax for any financial year is actually imposed, to go beyond the preliminary work such as the demand for returns necessary for its assessment. If, for example, they assess and demand payment of the super-tax before it is actually imposed, different conditions might and probably would arise.[26]

Bowles soon pursued this point, for there were indeed circumstances in which the Inland Revenue demanded payment of income tax before it was imposed.

Bowles's opening came from the practice of deducting tax at source that lay at the heart of the efficient collection of a large part of the income tax. When reintroduced in 1842, the income tax followed the procedure of the wartime system of 1803: income was divided into different schedules, and in many cases tax was deducted at source. Hence under schedule A, tax due on rental income was withheld by the tenant; and on schedule C, tax was deducted by the Bank of England before payment to the bondholder. Tax was paid in advance of authority being granted by an Act after the start of the financial year – and the sums involved were considerable. In 1910/11, tax collected at source through schedules A (rent), C (dividends) and E (public employment) amounted to 36.0 per cent of the net receipts from income tax. In addition, an increasing proportion of dividends from companies under schedule D were collected at source, and the Revenue was attempting to collect tax on private employment at source under Schedule E – a practice that led to challenge in *GWR v Bater* (see John Pearce's chapter five). Deduction at source, in the words of one official, 'is of paramount importance lying as it does at the very root of the British Income Tax system'.[27] Richard Hopkins of the Inland Revenue pointed out to the Royal Commission on Taxation in 1919 that no less than 70 per cent of the income tax was collected at source, and 'it is this feature of the Income Tax which constitutes its peculiar

---

[26] *Bowles v AG* (above n 22), 132–37; Jaconelli (above n 17) 583–84.
[27] Daunton (above n 21) 186–87; *Report of the Departmental Committee on Income Tax* (Cd 2575, 1905) 223; Papers of Sir Otto Niemeyer: Copies of papers submitted to Committee on National Debt and Taxation, Undated and unsigned typescript on the tax privileges of various government loans, The National Archives, T176/18, f17.

distinction and has been responsible for the success which has attended the collection of the tax throughout its history'.[28] By contrast, Bowles saw collection of income tax at source before legislative authority as a 'lawless levy' that was 'no casual error perpetuated through inadvertence, and abandoned as soon as recognised. It was deliberate, considered, persistent and obstinate'. The government knew it was breaking the law which was scandal enough – but an even greater scandal was their persistence in defying the law. In his view, the government was no better than criminals: 'Had these been pearls stolen by thieves in the post instead of millions lawlessly filched by the Inland Revenue from the pocket of the tax-payer, there would have been a loud outcry. As it was there was none'.[29]

The collection of taxes without legislative authority could be justified by the fact that the Committee of Ways and Means passed resolutions, and that an Act would follow very soon. The issue arose in the 1840s at a time of major changes in customs duties. In 1846, Robert Peel suggested that the reduction in tariffs on some foodstuffs should be implemented on the basis of resolutions, with the understanding that 'a bond should be taken in the case of every remittance, providing that the whole amount of duties shall be paid in the event of the Bill not receiving the sanction either of the Lords and Commons'.[30] In 1848, the Chancellor of the Exchequer explained that the same principle of implementing a change in duty on the basis of resolutions prior to legislation applied to an increase in the sugar duty.[31] The Attorney General argued that

> a resolution of that House would be recognised by the subsequent passing of the Bill which had been founded upon it. The rule would be this – if the House of Commons resolved that a given duty should be imposed upon goods before they were entered for home consumption, it was fairly to be presumed … that the House would pass a Bill founded upon that resolution … The Government would therefore give an order to officers to act on that resolution. He admitted that an action would lie; but before it would be ripe for investigation the Act of Parliament would have received Her Majesty's assent … and that would be a perfect answer to the action.[32]

In 1851, Erskine May, the authority on parliamentary process, referred to these statements of 1846 and 1848, remarking that the practice of relying on resolutions was customary, but that imposition or collection of taxes 'in anticipation of statute' was 'remarkable' and 'not strictly legal', so that the government was 'acting on its own responsibility' and bearing the risk that the duties would not be authorised. Reference to the legal weakness of the practice disappeared from

---

[28] Royal Commission on the Income Tax, *First Instalment of the Minutes of Evidence with Appendices* (Cmd 288, i–viii, 1919) 2, para 14, evidence of Richard Hopkins.

[29] Bowles, 'Bowles v the Bank of England: The Proceedings in Court' (above n 3) vii, ix–x.

[30] HC Deb 9 March 1846, ser 3, vol 84, col 784 (R Peel); with thanks to Colin Lee.

[31] HC Deb 29 June 1848, ser 3, vol 99, cols 1314–15 (C Wood); with thanks to Colin Lee.

[32] Stebbings (above n 25) 55; HC Deb 29 June 1848, ser 3, vol 99, col 1316 (Attorney General).

later editions which merely referred to customary practice.[33] Certainly, Gladstone relied on customary practice, arguing in 1860 that resolutions on customs duties 'for immediate practical purposes ... have the force of law when the resolution itself has been adopted', and he took this approach in 1861 when he asked the Committee of Ways and Means to pass a resolution 'without prejudice to their ultimate decision' to impose an increase in duty.[34]

The authority of resolutions for changes in customs duties was tested in two cases in Australia – in Victoria in 1865 and in New South Wales in 1892, in relation to the collection of customs duties. The first case arose from the resolution of the Legislative Assembly in Victoria to introduce a duty which was levied on goods imported the next day. The Crown contended that the resolution was 'an absolute and unconditional grant of the taxes imposed', in line with the 'practice and universal custom' of the Commons. The judge did not agree, claiming that it was 'without precedent' and 'in direct violation of the established principle that no tax can be imposed save with the full consent of the three estates of the realm'. The duty was accordingly repaid. In 1892, the Supreme Court of New South Wales came to a different conclusion. The Collector of Customs refused entry of goods until the importer paid duties for which the Assembly passed a resolution but not legislation. The Court accepted that the importers had a legal right to the goods but refused to grant a discretionary right of mandamus on the grounds of public policy, specifically the need to protect public revenues. Darley CJ held that granting the legal right of the importers to the goods entailed discretion

> of the most pernicious and mischievous kind, tending to subvert an invariable practice followed by the ablest exponents of our Constitution – a practice based on sound reason and good sense, and devised by able and wise men in the public interest.[35]

The courts in Australia came to different conclusions on similar issues relating to the authority of resolutions for customs duties. In the United Kingdom, the issue was removed in respect to customs duties by the Customs Consolidation Act 1876, which gave explicit authority to resolutions.[36] But the issue had not been similarly settled for the income tax. In 1894, the Liberal Chancellor of the Exchequer, William Harcourt admitted that 'it was perfectly true that until the Budget Bill was passed the actual authority for levying any taxation was not complete', but he noted that 'it had always been the practice with reference to

---

[33] T Erskine May, *A Practical Treatise on the Law, Privileges, Proceedings and Usage of Parliament*, 2nd edn (London, Butterworths, 1851) 406; Stebbings (above n 25) 55 cites the 3rd edn of 1855 at 425. I owe this point to Colin Lee.

[34] Gladstone to Gwyn (16 February 1860), quoted in *Morning Advertiser* (17 February 1860) 8; HC Deb 15 April 1861, ser 3, vol 162, cols 593–94 (W Gladstone); with thanks to Colin Lee.

[35] Stebbings (above n 25) 55–56; Jaconelli (above n 17) 585; *Stevenson v Queen* (1865) 2 Wyatt, W and A'B 176; and *Ex parte Wallace and Co* [1892] 13 NSWLR 1.

[36] Stebbings (above n 25) 56; s 18, Customs Consolidation Act 1876.

the duties of Customs and Excise, that they should be levied from the date of the Resolutions. If that were not done the Revenue would be seriously injured'.[37]

Of course, the matter had been resolved for customs duties in 1876, but the issue had not been tested for the income tax in Britain, and it now fell to Parker J to decide on the action brought by Bowles in relation to the deduction of income tax at source. Unlike in other leading cases, Bowles's action did not involve the taxation authority directly, and was against the Bank of England. In May 1912, Bowles purchased £65,000 2¾ per cent Irish Land Stock, for which interest was paid in full twice a year. On 26 June 1912, he sought an injunction to restrain the Bank from deducting tax when interest became due on 1 July. His choice of this stock was influenced both by the date of payment and also by a particular concern about this stock. It was issued under the Irish Land Act 1903 to fund the transfer of land from large (often absentee) landowners to tenants, covering the difference between the higher price for which the owners were willing to sell and the lower price the tenants could afford. In the debate in July 1903, Bowles worried that the British taxpayer was not given sufficient security for the loan, and the amount would soar to huge sums:

> If he were to describe the present condition of things from the fiscal point of view, he should picture up a remote and inaccessible cave in which a band of brigands was engaged in cutting the throat of the British taxpayer, and complaining that he did not bleed to death quickly enough.[38]

Bowles was highly critical of Balfour's government for weakening the credit of the British state by guaranteeing loans not only for the purchase of Irish land, but also to local authorities and the Transvaal. As he put it in 1908,

> the more you pledge it for your friends, the less you have left for yourself; and that to guarantee Irish Land Stocks paying 2¾ per cent … is to depreciate the value of Consols paying only 2½ per cent.[39]

His choice of stock was therefore significant. Furthermore, Bowles was concerned that the financial settlement with Ireland would be a major issue in the discussions of the third Home Rule Bill.[40]

When Bowles's action against the Bank appeared before Swinfen Eady J, he declined to grant the injunction but accepted that the matter should be considered speedily and agreed to serve notice of the writ. When it came before Parker J on 28 June, he decided that the case was so important that it should be decided

---

[37] HC Deb 28 June 1894, ser 4, vol 26, col 467 (W Harcourt); Stebbings (above n 25) 54.

[38] HC Deb 1 July 1903, ser 5, vol 124, cols 1090–92 (T Gibson Bowles).

[39] TG Bowles, *National Finance in 1908 and After: Being a Review of the Past, a Forecast of the Future, and Appeal for True Accounts, a Plea for Retrenchment, a Protest Against Debt, and a Warning Against False Taxation* (London, T Fisher Unwin, 1908) 28; TG Bowles, *National Finance: An Imminent Peril* (T Fisher Unwin, 1904) 20.

[40] P Jalland, 'Irish Home Rule Finance: A Neglected Dimension of the Irish Question, 1910–1914' in A O'Day (ed), *Reactions to Irish Nationalism, 1865–1914* (London, Hambledon Press, 1987) 298.

once and for all. Meanwhile, the Bank would pay any deduction from the interest into court. Bowles requested that the same relief should be offered to 'fellow victims', but Parker refused. On 1 July 1912, interest of £900 12s 6d was due, the Bank of England deducted tax of £52 10s 8d and paid £848 1s 10d to Bowles. On 4 July Bowles claimed that the Bank had no authority to make the deduction, for no income tax had yet been imposed. He applied for repayment. The solicitors for the Bank, Freshfields, continued to insist that the Bank had sufficient authority under resolutions of Ways and Means on 2 April 1912 approving income tax for 1912/13; that the Bank had always relied on these resolutions to deduct tax since 1842; that Bowles was aware of the practice when he bought the stock. When the case was heard on 23–24 July, Parker J ruled that the Crown should be allowed to appear in any civil action where its rights were affected. Bowles protested against the postponement of the case:

> I am a little surprised to find an Attorney-General not prepared off-hand to defend a practice which he admits has been very long continued, for which I say there is no defence. I, on my side, am prepared now *stans pede in uno* to defend the Statute of the realm from Magna Charta to the Bill of Rights.

The case was finally heard on 21 October 1912, with Bowles pursuing the case himself as a non-lawyer.[41]

The matter before the court was therefore to decide whether the various devices introduced to cover the period between the passing of resolutions and legislation to reimpose the income tax permitted the collection of tax as well as the preliminary gathering of information. The outcome was open to doubt, and during the interlude between the initial hearing in July and its coming to trial in October, the Chancellor of the Exchequer decided that the situation should be regularised. On 26 July 1912, Lloyd George moved a resolution to be confirmed by a clause in the Finance Bill 1912, that would give statutory effect to resolutions for a limited period, on condition that the Finance Act was enacted before 31 August in any year. Lloyd George showed the resolution to Austen Chamberlain, the 'abjectly incapable' Chancellor in the previous Conservative government, before presenting it to the Commons. Although Chamberlain saw difficulties of dealing with the matter at short notice and late in the session, he accepted that reliance on resolutions was 'for the general convenience of everybody, of tax-gatherer and tax-payer alike, of the trader as much as of the tax-gatherer'. Chamberlain's practical ministerial experience meant that he was willing to accept the proposal on pragmatic grounds as legalising an established, convenient, practice – precisely Bowles's complaint about the attitude of the executive to the rights of Parliament. At the same time, Chamberlain criticised

---

[41] *Bowles v Bank of England* [1913] 1 Ch 57, 6 TC 136, 137–40; Bowles, *Bowles v the Bank of England: The Proceedings in Court* (above n 3) 2–65, Bowles quote at 63; Jaconelli (above n 17) 584–85. The resolution on income tax is at HC Deb 2 April 1912, ser 5, vol 36, col 1131.

Lloyd George who 'grossly abused' normal practice in delaying the Finance Bill for 'non-fiscal purposes':

> I am glad that the Chancellor of the Exchequer has at the present time no intention of sinning again ... [A]s he is willing to prevent any one sinning as he has sinned, I think we had better take advantage of this temporary frame of mind, and before he falls again into temptation we had better put it out of his way to yield.

This combination of support for the government with an attack on its misdemeanours was a clever political tactic. It did not work. Critics on the back benches complained that Lloyd George was rushing through a major change without the resolution being seen by the House. They saw no reason for haste. On one view, the existing practice was not illegal, so a decision of the courts should be awaited before acting. On another view, the Finance Bill was about to pass so the resolution would not have any force in 1912. Lloyd George withdrew the resolution.[42]

When Bowles's case finally reached the courts on 21 October 1912, his rhetoric reached new heights. He traced the history of 'no taxation without consent' back to King Alfred, William the Conqueror, Magna Charta, the Petition of Rights and the Bill of Rights:

> The principles ... are of vast importance. They have existed for centuries. They have been enforced from time to time in the great crises of our history; they have survived tumult and tyranny. Their existence is a great constitutional reality; they still remain safeguards of the subject; and I ask your Lordship to affirm today that they are an essential and unalterable part of the laws of this Kingdom.[43]

There was no doubt that the government was in a weak position, for the Act authorising the income tax for the financial year from 6 April 1911 only passed in December 1911. The constitutional crisis over the People's Budget of 1909 had been some justification for a year-long delay at that time, but there was less reason for the delay to the Finance Act 1910 which only became law on 28 November, or of 1911 which became law on 16 December. Usually, the gap between the resolution and legislation was much shorter, with Acts passing in May or June and occasionally in August – as in 1912 when the Finance Bill completed all stages by 7 August.[44] Chamberlain pointed out that if the Act followed soon after the resolution, any action to question the authority of resolutions would only be heard after they were given force by legislation.[45] The problem was that parliamentary procedure was in disarray at a time of serious

---

[42] HC Deb 26 July 1912, ser 5, vol 41, cols 1521–39; Jaconelli (above n 17) 589.
[43] Bowles, *Bowles v the Bank of England: The Proceedings in Court* (above n 3) 77–79.
[44] Stebbings (above n 25) 58; Jaconelli (above n 17) 588.
[45] HC Deb 26 July 1912, ser 5, vol 41, col 1525 (J Chamberlain).

tension over major issues such as the People's Budget, Home Rule, social reform and land taxation.

Parker J's hint of his views in the earlier case was confirmed when he delivered judgment on 4 November 1912. Resolutions had no legal effect in providing authority for the collection of taxes not yet imposed by an Act of Parliament. His reasoning was that the Bill of Rights

> finally settled that there could be no taxation in this country except under authority of an Act of Parliament ... and no practice or custom however prolonged or however acquiesced in on the part of the subject can be relied on by the Crown as justifying any infringement of its provisions.

In his view, the purpose of resolutions was to protect the subject against the hasty imposition of taxes, allowing an initial discussion before they were confirmed in legislation. Hence resolutions could not be used to impose the tax. Neither did he accept that section 30 of the CIRA 1890 gave authority. In order to deduct interest, the Bank must know the rate of income tax – and once the amount due had been assessed, it was immediately deducted and handed to the Inland Revenue, so that the tax had been levied. He accepted that section 30 allowed officials to carry out preliminary work for assessment and collection but denied that it gave them power to assess and collect the tax. He argued that no assessment is possible without knowing the rate – and even if resolutions were passed by 6 April, the rate could still be changed by the Commons. He reasoned that if the Commons intended to collect taxes on the basis of resolutions, it would have made explicit provision to allow his practice. He also denied that section 30 allowed the imposition of tax at the rate of the preceding year, for that would make it a permanent tax with no need for an Act to reimpose the tax, despite the fact this was explicitly required. Parker claimed that such an interpretation

> would be a serious matter, for ... it would very largely diminish the revenue for which the Crown depends on the annual assent of Parliament, and consequently the power of the House of Commons to bring financial pressure to bear on the Ministers of the Crown.

This was a significant political or constitutional point that was at the heart of subsequent debates.

Parker rejected the contention that assessment and collection under section 30 could be provisional, with any variation in the rate imposed by the Finance Act being refunded. In his opinion, the difficulties were insuperable. How long could the subject be uncertain about the amount levied? How could the subject enforce repayment when the tax might already have been spent? Indeed,

> if the money had been deducted and paid over to the Crown and spent, the unfortunate subject who had the right to return of the money would have to raise the money himself to pay it ... . He would have to pay it again in order to pay himself back.

In his view, a provisional levy would require earmarking the money for return in the event that no Act was passed. Hence the only proper interpretation of section 30 was that

> although it keeps alive the machinery of the Income Tax Acts for the purposes of all the preliminary work necessary for the collection of any income tax which may be imposed for any financial year, it does not authorise any assessment or collection of a tax not yet imposed by Parliament.

He took 'due time' to refer to

> the time when the tax becomes due and payable under the Act which actually imposes it ... though before such Act be passed it is possible to do such preliminary work which will facilitate and expedite the collection of the tax if and when it becomes due and payable.

He supported this interpretation by reference to the Income Tax Assessment Act 1870 which stated that it did not continue the rate of income tax imposed in the previous year. The practice of the Bank in deducting tax 'can only be explained by the tacit assent of the persons from time to time entitled to such dividends'. He therefore ordered the payment out of court of the sum of £52 10s 8d, with costs against the Bank.[46]

The consequences were potentially disastrous, throwing into doubt the practice of deduction of tax at source prior to the passing of the Finance Act, and potentially leaving the government open to claims for repayment of tax deducted without authority.[47] As Felix Cassel pointed out to the Commons in March 1913, collection at source

> is based upon the feeling of human nature that it is easier for a Government to collect its revenue by making a man pay somebody else's tax than it is by making a man pay his own tax ... [T]he deduction in many cases is an advantage to the Income Tax payer himself, because it is a convenience to him to have the deduction made than to deal with it himself.

It would be 'a matter of great dislocation and inconvenience to the whole country if the scheme of continuous deduction of the Income Tax is interrupted even for the shortest possible time'. Yet, despite this danger, the government did 'nothing except sit content on the Treasury Bench'.[48] What was the government to do to resolve its difficulties?

Lloyd George placed the blame on others for creating the problem. He admitted that relying on resolutions was 'always more or less of doubtful legality' but had been accepted as convenient. The normal pattern of the Act passing before any action was heard was overthrown by the unconstitutional action of the Lords in throwing out the Budget in 1909. Then the attempt to regularise the

---

[46] *Bowles v Bank of England* (above n 41) 90, 140–48; Jaconelli (above n 17) 585.
[47] Jaconelli (above n 17) 589.
[48] HC Deb 18 March 1913, ser 5, vol 50, cols 994–95 (F Cassel).

situation in August 1912, with the support of Austen Chamberlain, encountered hostility from the opposition.[49] Although Chamberlain remained sympathetic to the plight of the government, he felt that it was the author of its own misfortunes in delaying the Finance Bill:

> The Government deliberately delayed the financial business to serve party exigencies. They treated finance not as the first business of the House of Commons, as by historic tradition it is, but as the last and least important. They passed the Insurance and Home Rule Bills before they dealt with the Budget. Accordingly at last a citizen intervened to stop this abuse of the latitude that has been allowed to Governments ... The law is even more decisive and unquestioned on the side of Mr Gibson Bowles than it was on the side of John Hampden, and I am not at all prepared to say that Charles I was a more despotic monarch than the present Cabinet is a despotic Cabinet.

These were extraordinarily strong words, reflecting the febrile state of the Commons in 1913. Nevertheless, Chamberlain had genuine grounds for criticising Lloyd George for defending the legality of relying on resolutions, and then requesting legislation at the last moment. Now Lloyd George had the effrontery to return to the Commons six months later to blame the opposition, when 'the truth is it is owing to the necessities of purely party objects as distinct from National objects that the House of Commons has never had time fairly to consider it'.[50]

The desire to regularise existing practice was accepted by men with ministerial experience on both sides of the House, but the issue became a matter of heated discussion when an initial resolution was debated on 7–8 April and a Bill on 14–15 April. On 7 April 1913, Lloyd George moved that a resolution passed by Ways and Means for the imposition of any new tax or variation of an existing tax, or renewal of a temporary tax (that is, the income tax), should have temporary statutory effect for a limited time; that a resolution renewing a temporary tax would give full force to all statutory provisions as last imposed by an Act; and deductions on account of a temporary tax be deemed to be legal payments within two months of the date of expiry of the tax. Lloyd George argued that 'What we are proposing is not an innovation ... On the contrary, it is a means of regularising and legalising the usage and custom which has been followed by every Government for at least sixty years'.[51] Chamberlain was sympathetic:

> [A]s an old Treasury man ... with that desire which must be strong in one who has held the positions I have held, that the King's Government should be carried on with the greatest advantage to the State and the minimum inconvenience to the subject. I am therefore more concerned with the practical working of such proposals ... than I am with the very interesting, but more theoretical, constitutional considerations which naturally arise out of them.

---

[49] HC Deb 18 March 1913, ser 5, vol 50, cols 998–1001 (D Lloyd George).
[50] HC Deb 18 March 1913, ser 5, vol 50, cols 1004–05 (A Chamberlain).
[51] HC Deb 7 April 1913, ser 5, vol 51, cols 835–36 (D Lloyd George).

He welcomed the end of delays to passing the Finance Bill and the imposition of clear rules on both sides of the House. But he also issued a warning. Both parties had their own radical fiscal proposals for which they wished to 'secure the greatest facilities, whilst there are certain other proposals we oppose, and that those we should subject to the greatest disabilities'. His point was a good one, for Lloyd George was interested in a radical new land tax – and equally, the Conservatives were advocating tariff reform. Lloyd George saw the danger and retreated, confining the power to existing customs, excise and income taxes, which would limit the ability of both sides of the House to make radical innovations. Chamberlain felt that this retreat went too far. Although some new taxes should be excluded, others should be included 'because they would be levied in time of urgency, when revenue is of the utmost importance' – and he promised that he would never use the powers to introduce tariff reform.[52] Liberals had doubts whether he could be trusted – and the Conservatives had equally good reason to doubt Lloyd George's self-control.

Chamberlain's 'sympathetic spirit' and pragmatism was shared by Michael Hicks-Beach, Lord St Aldwyn, a former Conservative Chancellor, who admitted that 'if ever there was a sinner in this respect, I am the greatest sinner'. The view of both front benches was that the practice was sensible, but vocal backbenchers saw it as a major constitutional issue – something that Hicks-Beach said 'leaves me quite cold'.[53] Opponents of the proposal argued that the existing procedure had to be used with 'great caution, precisely because it was known or suspected to be illegal. The Government always knew that they could not go beyond a certain point'. A return to timely passing of the Finance Act would solve the problem. Might a more radical granting of legislative authority to resolutions permit arbitrary taxation and an abuse of power? William Hayes Fisher, a leading Conservative MP and former Financial Secretary to the Treasury, castigated the resolution as 'one of the most revolutionary proposals which have ever been proposed to the House of Commons', leading to a loss of control over public expenditure and taxation, and giving power 'to entirely alter the fiscal system of this country without any notice, without any adequate discussion' by means of a single resolution in Ways and Means in the small hours of the morning, under a guillotine.[54] Similarly, Alfred Cripps, a Conservative MP and lawyer (and later Labour cabinet minister), worried that everything was being sacrificed to speed which meant 'accepting the ipsi dixit of the Treasury without any discussion'. By settling everything at the time of the resolution, subsequent discussion in the Commons would be 'merely theoretical and would lose any conditional power'. He argued that the resolution would give the government autocratic power – and he insisted that it was necessary to retain 'the old constitutional safeguards',

[52] HC Deb 7 April 1913, ser 5, vol 51, cols 845–47, 849, 850–51, 852 (A Chamberlain).
[53] HL Deb 23 April 1913, ser 5, vol 14, col 287 (St Aldywn).
[54] HC Deb 7 April 1913, ser 5, vol 51, cols 856, 857, 858–60 (WH Fisher).

and to reject the 'most reactionary and retrograde resolution' that placed the Commons at the feet of the executive.[55]

The case was made even more forcefully by Lord Hugh Cecil, a son of the former Conservative Prime Minister the Marquess of Salisbury, who complained of 'the aristocratic theory of government' – a jibe at the two front benches

> who cannot bear to be interfered with by an ignorant House of Commons or a still more ignorant people … The moment you make a procedure statutory, you destroy all its elasticity, and you enable the Government of the day to use it unreasonably if they please.

Cecil feared the Commons would cede 'supreme control over finance' to the Treasury:

> It is a question of the rights of the House of Commons against the permanent officials, who are exceedingly clever and skilful men, and, like all clever and skilful men, they are extremely anxious to have their own way … I would rather have the finances of the country mismanaged by the House of Commons than well managed by the Treasury. Unlike the Chancellor of the Exchequer, I am a convinced democrat – at any rate in regard to finance – and upon this matter I think the House of Commons ought to have an effective voice.[56]

Despite these constitutional concerns, the resolutions were passed and the matter was returned to the Commons as a bill. After further detailed discussion,[57] the measure passed through the Commons. Crucially, the Speaker defined the measure as a 'money bill' under the terms of the Parliament Act 1911. The Act took a wide definition of a money bill in section 1(2), referring not only to the imposition of taxation, but more generally to 'provisions dealing with all or any of the following subjects, namely, the imposition, repeal, remission, alteration, or regulation of taxation' and still more generally 'subordinate matters incidental to those subjects or any of them'.[58] The point was important, for the Lords could only delay a money bill by a month; otherwise, it might have been delayed until 1915. The last thing the government needed, given the difficulties with Home Rule, was any further opportunity for parliamentary mischief.

Bowles's intervention in 1911 and 1912 removed an anomaly and prevented further slippage in discussion of finance bills, regularising a procedure that both Conservative and Liberal governments knew to be of dubious legality. The PTCA 1913 or 'Bowles Act' allowed resolutions for the imposition of income tax and customs duties to come into immediate operation, on condition that time limits were observed. The resolution of Ways and Means had to be approved

---

[55] HC Deb 7 April 1913, ser 5, vol 51, cols 869–73; and HC Deb 8 April 1913, ser 5, vol 51, cols 1033–06 (A Cripps).

[56] HC Deb 7 April 1913, ser 5, vol 51, cols 877–79, 882 (H Cecil).

[57] HC Deb 14 April 1913, ser 5, vol 51, cols 1661–784; and HC Deb 15 April 1913, ser 5, vol 51, cols 1829–901.

[58] Jaconelli (above n 17) 590–92; Parliament Act 1911, cl 13, s 1(2).

by the Commons within 10 working days; and the Finance Bill had to have its second reading within 20 sitting days, and the power of resolutions ceased if the Act were not passed within four months. During the intervening period, the resolution had 'statutory effect as if contained in an Act of Parliament'. The power was limited to existing customs duties and income tax – a point that both Chamberlain and Hicks Beach thought unwise, for new taxes might be needed to cover increased expenditure, above all in the event of war, as indeed soon proved to be the case.[59]

Why did Bowles raise the issue? He was a stickler for parliamentary process and scrutiny that lay at the heart of the Victorian fiscal constitution. He was, as Austen Chamberlain remarked in 1912, 'a most watchful and vigilant guardian of the proprieties of finance ... a jealous guardian of the old traditions and the statutory procedures which governs such financial business'.[60] William Joynson-Hicks, a Conservative MP, concurred that he was 'a purist in matters of Parliamentary etiquette and procedure'.[61] Another way of putting the point was that he was obsessive and pedantic, turning small points into major constitutional principles. He did, however, sometimes have a point, for he had a firm grasp of parliamentary procedure, and saw dangers of executive authority eroding the Commons' ability to monitor spending.

Chantal Stebbings remarks that Bowles was deeply committed to careful and rigorous scrutiny of financial measures. He was, she notes, 'an exceptional and excellent critic' of Harcourt's death duties in 1894, grasping the intricacies of the measure, and subjecting it to serious and well-founded criticism.[62] Edward Hamilton, a leading official at the Treasury, thought that Bowles was 'an extremely sharp little Parliamentary ferret', whose discovery that the resolutions did not cover increases in succession duties potentially threatened the entire Budget. The risk was only averted when the Speaker allowed the Commons to revert to the Committee of Ways and Means in order to pass a supplementary resolution. Hamilton named Bowles as one of three 'firebrands who have taken best advantage of their opportunities'.[63] In 1896, he sided with Harcourt against the proposal of Balfour, the First Lord of the Treasury, to impose a 'guillotine' and a 'gag' on debates on supply. He could not resist turning the issue into a highly personal attack that caused considerable hilarity in the Commons. In Bowles's view, the rights of the Commons 'were being filched from them by the exclusive oligarchies that successively occupied the Front Ministerial Bench'.

---

[59] Stebbings (above n 25) 60–61; Jaconelli (above n 17) 592–94, 599, 601; Provisional Collection of Taxes Act 1913.

[60] HC Deb 26 July 1912, ser 5, vol 41 col 1525 (J Chamberlain).

[61] HC Deb 8 April 1913, ser 5, vol 51, col 1037 (W Joynson-Hicks).

[62] Stebbings (above n 25) 58, 75.

[63] D Brooks (ed), *The Destruction of Lord Rosebery. From the Diary of Sir Edward Hamilton, 1894–1895* (London, The Historians' Press, 1986) 27; diary entry for 21 May 1894, 144; and diary entry for 26 August 1894, 167, with thanks to Colin Lee; HC Deb 24 May 1894, ser 4, vol 24, cols 1200–03 (T Gibson Bowles, Speaker and W Harcourt).

Where Peel, Russell and Palmerston could manage the Commons by 'persuasion and dexterity' as a good horseman handled a high-spirited steed, with a light hand and firm seat, now things had changed:

> The bungler [Balfour] came, having neither seats nor hands, and he had recourse to gag bits, martingales, and horrible ironmongery, and cast the horse and sat on its head, and said that he too forsooth was a horseman, he too a Leader of the House … These new methods would not improve, but would destroy the House … He could not but place on record his earnest protest against a plan which tended to destroy the rights, impair the dignity, and end the usefulness of the most venerable deliberative Assembly the world had ever seen.[64]

Bowles continued to take a close interest in finances and procedure as a vocal member of the Public Accounts Committee which was, in his view, the only body that was capable of scrutinising expenditure as a result of the weakening of the Commons.[65] In 1903, he was dropped from the Committee, a decision that was attacked by the *Daily News* as a blatant attempt to silence 'a veritable watchdog of the public and the House in their struggle with the slipshod extravagance of the Executive'.[66] He accepted reappointment, on condition that the resolution of the Select Committee on National Expenditure be adopted to create a new committee to inspect the estimates. He was making common cause with Churchill in 'worthily continuing' Lord Randolph's ambition of imposing control on finances. Lord Randolph had campaigned for a committee to examine estimates and increase the Commons' control in 1884:

> I should like to turn the House of Commons loose into our public departments on a voyage of discovery. I should like to see every one of our public departments rigorously inquired into by small committees of about seven experienced and practical Members of Parliament.[67]

In 1904, Bowles urged Winston Churchill that 'we must really make a determined stand now for Retrenchment', which required that 'the People force the Government. And here is the danger. That neither the People nor Parliament take due interest in Finance'.[68]

Bowles feared that national expenditure and debt were rising quickly, and that the checks on 'extravagant expenditure and outrageous debt' were inadequate. His aim was to 'disclose the inadequacy of the control of Parliament, and the

---

[64] HC Deb 24 February 1896, ser 4, vol 37, cols 987–90 (T Gibson Bowles).

[65] Matthew, 'Gibson, Thomas Milner (1806–1884)' (above n 4); Bowles, 'The British Constitution' (above n 9) 115.

[66] Naylor (above n 2) 148 quoting *Daily News* (11 March 1903).

[67] Quoted by C Lee, 'A Road not Taken: Select Committees and the Estimates, 1880–1904' in P Evans (ed), *Essays on the History of Parliamentary Procedure in Honour of Thomas Erskine May* (Oxford, Hart Publishing, 2017) 273–74 from LJ Jennings (ed), *Speeches of the Right Honourable Lord Randolph Churchill MP, 1880–1888, Volume II* (London, Longman, Green and Company, 1889) 105–06.

[68] Churchill Archives Centre, Cambridge, CHAR 2/18/86, Bowles to Churchill, 23 November 1904 and CHAR 2/3/131, Bowles to Churchill, 14 December 1904.

urgent and pressing need for prompt action'.[69] He insisted that the control of Parliament over finance had been impaired so that the increase in government spending arose from 'a want of due control of ambitious departments, from a disregard of economies, a contempt for frugality, and a lavish, wanton, and unnecessary expenditure all around'. It was difficult for the Commons to resist a Chancellor of the Exchequer with the backing of the Prime Minister who commanded a majority of the House – and even if they did resist these 'wanton and extravagant' plans, '[t]he power of Parliament over, and its power of checking, the growth of Expenditure and Debt have been most seriously diminished in several important respects'. He had a long list of concerns. The financial accounts were 'deceptive and false'. Appropriations in aid had been withdrawn from the control of the Committee of Supply. Capital spending was diverted to loans approved by various Acts, and supplementary estimates were used in a way that was a 'scandal and danger'. The growing use of votes on account reduced parliamentary control. New standing orders in 1902 reduced the time available to private members from 60 per cent to 10 per cent, limiting the consideration of supply to 20 days, with the imposition of a 'guillotine' that removed the ability to bargain with the government for concessions in return for a vote. Even worse, since 1887 a minister 'may any moment peremptorily stop debate and take the division on the question ... In short, at any moment the Minister, though created by the House of Commons, may say to it: "*Assez parle*" – "that's enough, you shall debate no more. Shut up!"'. Further, there was an increase in the proportion of permanent to annual revenue which did not need the annual consent of Parliament.[70] He complained about the lack of an adequate sinking fund to cover the funded debt, and the growth of a large unfunded or floating debt without any provision for repayment which was the 'most serious and dangerous item of all' in undermining national credit, and harming trade by taking money from the market for legitimate business. In addition, the government guaranteed loans to New Zealand, Canada and South Africa, as well as covering the Irish land loans, local authority loans, and the liabilities of the savings banks. The liabilities of the British government, in his view, 'beggar all comment'.[71]

One of Bowles's major complaints was the weakening of the Appropriation Act which allocated every grant to a specific purpose and lay at the heart of parliamentary control. The Public Accounts and Charges Act 1891 authorised the Treasury to make appropriations in aid, and to divert surplus funds from the army and navy to other purposes. Although these actions were to be authorised by the Commons after the event, Bowles argued that the matter was taken late in the session and as a matter of course.[72] In 1902, he launched an attack on the

---

[69] Bowles, *National Finance: An Imminent Peril* (above n 39) 3.
[70] ibid, 9–14, 25; Bowles, *National Finance in 1908 and After* (above n 39) 9; Bowles, 'The British Constitution' (above n 9) 115.
[71] Bowles, *National Finance: An Imminent Peril* (above n 39) 17, 18, 20, 24, 26, 27, 28.
[72] ibid, 14–15.

Conservative government's Appropriation Bill which contained a clause to allow the Chancellor to borrow from the Bank of England on condition that he repaid in the next quarter or issued Treasury bills which did not need to be paid off until the end of the financial year, a period that could be as long as 12 months. He felt that this was a new and extraordinary power that required scrutiny by the Commons. Further, he complained that the Bill was proposed in the middle of the session and not, as normal, at the end which would give an opportunity to discuss any new questions relating to supply in the interim.[73] He could not resist linking his critique of the Appropriation Bill to an attack on the leadership of his own party which was under the malign domination of the kin of Salisbury and radicals led by Joseph Chamberlain. He foresaw 'a disaster more general and complete than has ever yet befallen any Minister or any Party, and for the country a period of unrest and uncertainty, of strife and confusion'.[74] His speech was considered by the *Daily News* to be 'the most brilliant of a series of essays in irony, more searching than anything which the House has heard since Disraeli set himself to destroy Sir Robert Peel'.[75]

Both Bowles and Churchill had a deep contempt for Balfour, Chamberlain and their families which was constantly repeated, and they combined to revive interest in scrutiny of public finances by establishing an Estimates Committee that would examine one class of spending in each session. When the idea was first floated in 1901, Hamilton pointed to the danger of 'aggravating an existing tendency on the part of Parliament to usurp the functions of the Executive, which is destructive of all good administration' – the very thing against which Churchill and Bowles fulminated. Balfour agreed with Hamilton's line, and opposed the idea as a potential source of disruption.[76] When no action was taken to establish a committee, Bowles declined to serve on the Public Accounts Committee in 1905.[77] The proposal for a new committee was eventually adopted in 1912 when Churchill was a member of Cabinet.[78] By then, their political paths had diverged, for Bowles was horrified by the spending plans of the Liberal government and disappointed in his hopes that they would be a force for retrenchment.

Bowles denounced much of the additional spending as wasteful. More money for education did not lead to 'a real increase in the real education of the people' but instead to the 'extra cost of an inadequate system'. Similarly, spending on the army and navy was 'certainly not represented by a corresponding increase of the influence of Britain in the counsel of Europe, or of her power in the world'.[79] One of his *bêtes noires* was the cost of the defensive works at Gibraltar which

---

[73] HC Deb 6 August 1902, ser 4, vol 112, col 808 (T Gibson Bowles).
[74] HC Deb 6 August 1902, ser 4, vol 112, cols 817–18 (T Gibson Bowles).
[75] Naylor (above n 2) 147 quoting *Daily News* (6 August 1902).
[76] Lee (above n 67) 280–83.
[77] Naylor (above n 2) 149.
[78] Lee (above n 67) 83.
[79] Bowles, *National Finance: An Imminent Peril* (above n 39) 7.

were expensive and useless, on which he secured a select committee.[80] Above all he argued for the importance of naval power:

> The lesson of all history is that, whether in peace for trading or in war for fighting, the sea has always dominated the land; that in war most especially, navies are more potent than armies, the Trident is a mightier weapon than the Sword.

But naval defence did not mean building more battleships to meet the size of the next two largest fleets, of an ally as well as potential enemy. In his view, the naval race and rearmament were the result of a sacrifice of the constitution and public purse to a 'military oligarchy'. The real problem was that the government was supinely allowing changes in the law of war at sea. The process started with the Declaration of Paris in 1856 which 'filched' Britain's right to seize enemy merchandise carried in neutral ships. The Declaration meant that Britain was 'debarred from the use of the most potent and merciful method of the capture and confiscation of merchandise; and is driven to rely alone upon the far less potent and most unmerciful method of the slaughter and destruction of men'. Retention of these powers would have made the war in South Africa shorter and less costly. Nevertheless, the surrender of maritime power went still further in the convention at The Hague in 1907 and the naval conference in London in 1909, without consulting Parliament. Britain had the world's most powerful navy but would be

> forbidden by new laws from using its powers in the only effectual manner; to submit every act of that navy to the final judgments of a foreign court; to enforce these judgments itself; and to strangle its own fleet with its own hands.[81]

Bowles's insistence on parliamentary scrutiny cannot be separated from his ideological hostility to spending. The opening epithet to his pamphlet on national finance in 1908 summed up his concerns: '*C'est la fiscalité qui a tué l'Empire Romain, la fiscalité pesant sur le possesseur*'.[82] The importance of finance

> cannot be over-rated. It lies at the very root of the national capacities of every kind. The extravagances of our expenditure, the dangers of our financial system, are gross

---

[80] TG Bowles, *Gibraltar: A National Danger, being an Account of the Nature and Present State of Certain Works Now Being Constructed on the Western Side of Gibraltar; an Exposition of the Danger which These Will Create for Great Britain; An Argument for Certain Alterations Calculated to Diminish the Danger Attached to Them; and a Plea for the Suspension of the Works Until a Re-examination and Reconsideration Has Been Made of the Whole Matter* (London, Sampson Low, Marston & Company, 1901).

[81] TG Bowles, *The Declaration of Paris: Being an Account of the Maritime Rights of Great Britain, a Consideration of Their Importance; a History of Their Surrender by the Signature of the Declaration of Paris; and an Argument for their Resumption* (London, Sampson Low, Marston & Company, 1900) v–vii, 209; Bowles, *National Finance in 1908 and After* (above n 39) 41–43. See also TG Bowles, *The Public Purse and the War Office. Being a Vindication of Parliamentary Control Over National Expenditure, and a Protest Against the Sacrifice of the Constitution to a Military Oligarchy* (London, T Fisher Unwin, 1907); and TG Bowles, *Sea Law and Sea Power as They Would be Affected by Recent Proposals with Reasons Against the Proposals* (London, Murray, 1910) v, vii–xiii; TG Bowles, *Maritime Warfare* (London, W Ridgway, 1877).

[82] Bowles, *National Finance in 1908 and After* (above n 39) title page – from E Lavisse and A Rambaud, *Histoire Générale du IVe siècle á nos jours, I* (Paris, Armand Colin, 1894).

and palpable … The nation is wealthy, prosperous, and able to bear a great deal of taxation. But no nation can long continue to bear such loads, so increased, so increasing, and so adjusted as these.[83]

The danger was that unsound financial practices, false accounts and even corruption,

pass unperceived, save by a few, until a situation is reached when disaster is unavoidable. Then, and then only, do people in general become aware of the evil when it is too late to apply any remedy. And then, as all History shows, there ensue Panic, Rage, Revolution, and the destruction of Empires'.[84]

Bowles's attack on Harcourt's Budget in 1894 went beyond technical criticism to an impassioned attack on its underlying principles. Harcourt claimed that the state had an anterior title to share in the property of deceased persons – a claim that Bowles rejected as dangerous, potentially allowing the state to take the entire property of an individual at death. What Harcourt was proposing was 'perfectly monstrous. No Eastern despot, no Robin Hood, not even Robert Macaire himself, ever conceived such as contribution as this'. The Budget was not proposing a tax but sought to 'oppress a class'. Harcourt was unfavourably compared with Charles I who accepted that freedom and liberty depended on 'having of government those laws by which their life and goods may be most their own'. Harcourt was 'less liberal than the least liberal of all the Stuarts', for

the principle to be now acted upon was that a man's life and goods were to be least his own, and that the State had the right to claim all the goods of every man who died possessed of property. That was not the law of England or the practice of the English people. The principle of English law was that what was contributed to the State was given as a benevolence.[85]

This critique of Harcourt's death duties applied even more to the approach of Lloyd George and the new Liberals for whom increments in land value were socially created and therefore liable to taxation, and in whose view the income tax should be differentiated between 'earned' and 'unearned' income, with graduation to impose higher rates on large incomes. Bowles argued that neither the death duties nor income tax were 'any longer a tax at all in the strict and only proper sense of the term. For a tax means a rate of contribution, while here there are various rates, or in other words various taxes'. The issue, he argued, was not whether it was 'fair' to take a greater proportion from large estates and incomes – rather, it was whether those paying the highest rates considered it fair. If they thought the tax was unfair, they would avoid or evade the tax – and they had the ability to do so by divesting themselves of assets during their life or

---

[83] Bowles, *National Finance: An Imminent Peril* (above n 39) 28–29.

[84] Bowles, *National Finance in 1908 and After* (above n 39) 8–9.

[85] HC Deb 10 May 1894, ser 4, vol 24, cols 831–34 (T Gibson Bowles); on Charles I see also Bowles, 'The British Constitution' (above n 9) 112. Robert Macaire was a fictional character in French melodramas, a swindler and villain; he was revived in a spectacular stage production incorporating film in 1905, running for over 500 performances; in 1906, a version was released as a silent film.

investing overseas. The result would be a serious loss of revenue, which might even fall as rates rose. Neither did the poorest members of society below the tax threshold derive any benefit from graduation which reduced the burden on the 'modestly well-to-do' at the expense 'of hatred and envy towards the rich, increasing with their riches, and culminating, when their riches are greatest, almost in confiscation'. Bowles's solution was not to introduce new taxes on the rich, but retrenchment.[86] Such a policy meant tackling the spending departments which were at the heart of the problem and the 'weakest point of our financial system':

> To each member of it, the Department is a sort of divinity, only to be worshipped with sacrifices of public moneys. The well-understood duty of the Department is to get as much money as possible, and above all to spend the last penny that is got. Nothing must be economised, nothing must remain unspent, for whatever does so remain has to be 'surrendered', to go in diminution of the National Debt, a ridiculous despised shadow, the greater or less bulk of which matters nothing.[87]

These views were propagated by the British Constitution Association (BCA), of which Bowles was a member. It was established in November 1905 in opposition both to Conservative tariff reform and new Liberal social reform, drawing together opponents of Irish Home Rule, supporters of free trade, often with academic interests and a reputation for independence. Its first President was Lord Hugh Cecil, leader of the 'Hughligans', a group of Conservative MPs who were critical of Balfour's leadership, supporters of free trade, and opponents of the Parliament Bill.[88] Other leading members were Liberals who left the party over Irish Home Rule in 1886 but remained supporters of free trade. John Lubbock (Lord Avebury) was a banker who wrote extensively on financial issues, as well as a leading archaeologist and zoologist. One of his main complaints was the rise of municipal trading, with its danger of local indebtedness, inefficiency, unfair competition with private firms, and a threat to freedom.[89] Leonard Courtney served as Financial Secretary to the Treasury in the Liberal government in 1882, but left the party over Home Rule in 1886; on his retirement from the Commons in 1900 he adopted the role of 'political sage', publishing *The Working Constitution of the United Kingdom and its Outgrowths* in 1901.[90]

---

[86] Bowles, *National Finance in 1908 and After* (above n 39) 44–51.

[87] ibid, 8.

[88] K Rose, 'Cecil, Hugh Richard Heathcote Gascoyne-, Baron Quickswood (1869–1956)' in *Oxford Dictionary of National Biography* (Oxford, Oxford University Press, 2004).

[89] TL Alborn, 'Lubbock, John, first Baron Avebury (1834–1913)' in *Oxford Dictionary of National Biography* (Oxford, Oxford University Press, 2004); see Lubbock's contribution: J Lubbock, 'Municipal and Government Trading' in MH Judge (ed), *Political Socialism: A Remonstrance. A Collection of Papers by Members of the British Constitution Association, with Presidential Addresses by Lord Balfour of Burleigh and Lord Hugh Cecil* (London, PS King, 1908) 106; and J Lubbock, *Municipal and National Trading* (London, Macmillan, 1907).

[90] HCG Matthew, 'Courtney, Leonard Henry, Baron Courtney of Penwith (1832–1918)' in *Oxford Dictionary of National Biography* (Oxford, Oxford University Press, 2004).

Courtney argued that 'the fundamental fact of our Constitution is the absolutely unqualified supremacy of Parliament', with the Commons as the prime organ of the national will resting on 'the expression of the right of a free nation to self-government'. The authority of the Commons rested on its exclusive rights over taxation, and in particular its express consent through annual votes for each service, with no money unspent under one vote to be transferred to another heading. Here were the fundamental principles of the fiscal constitution.[91]

The most intellectually significant member of the BCA was AV Dicey, a Liberal who left the party over Home Rule, while remaining a firm supporter of free trade. In his view, the English common law was the bastion of freedom and individualism, unlike in French administrative law where liberty depended on the government. In *Lectures on the Relation between Law and Public Opinion in England during the Nineteenth Century* (1905), he decried the emergence of collectivism from the mid-1860s. The main oppression to be feared, he explained to the BCA in 1908, was not royal or aristocratic tyranny – it was

> the passing of laws, and still more the administration of the law, in accordance, not with the deliberate and real will of the majority of the nation, but with the immediate wishes of a class, namely the class – to use an inoffensive term – of wage-earners. *We fear class legislation.*[92]

The BCA took a very different approach to social reform from the Liberal government. In the words of its President, Lord Balfour of Burleigh, the correct approach was

> to increase liberty and to inculcate responsibility, and as we believe that self-help is the mainstay of national character, we desire to maintain the freedom of the individual … We resist the usurpation of power by Government, or the subjection, either of the individual or of the minority, to coercion on the part of the majority of the community. We believe that the only safe path of progress lies in the continued advance of that freedom, and in the ever-increasing emancipation of the individual from interference by the community in the management of his personal affairs.

As he saw it, both main parties were threatening liberty by increasing the power of the state 'with its inevitable accompaniment of increase of taxation', in place of the principle that an individual's earnings were for his own use. The aim of the BCA was to oppose reckless socialist experiments which threatened 'the moral fibre of our people' by destroying self-help and personal liberty. In Lord Balfour's view, individual freedom encouraged those members of society who were efficient and prevented them from 'being unduly burdened

---

[91] LH Courtney, *The Working Constitution of the United Kingdom and its Outgrowths* (London, JM Dent & Co, 1905) 2, 29, 30, 32, 33.
[92] RA Cosgrove, 'Dicey, Albert Venn (1835–1922)' in *Oxford Dictionary of National Biography* (Oxford, Oxford University Press, 2004); AV Dicey, 'Address' in *Report of the Constitution Congress in Connection with the Franco-British Exhibition, Being a Special Number of 'Constitution Papers'* (London, British Constitution Association, 1908) 117.

for the benefit of those less capable', and by an ever-expanding apparatus of unproductive 'Government officers, inspectors, and other classes of officials'. Everything depended on character – and not on municipal trading, attacks on the rich as a class, or on increments in land value. In his view, Christianity rested on two principles: those who would not work should not eat; and love of those who fall by the wayside, rather than envy of the rich.[93] The social system should rest on hard work and personal responsibility, complemented by philanthropy rather than state aid.

The BCA approach rested on personal responsibility or 'moral regeneration' associated with the Charity Organisation Society and the Majority Report of the Royal Commission on the Poor Laws of 1905–08, against the new Liberal approach of 'moral reform' to remove the structural impediments that prevented individuals from taking charge of their own lives. The BCA and Bowles rejected 'moral reform' as pursued by David Lloyd George and Winston Churchill through the introduction of old-age pensions, minimum wages, decasualisation of the labour market and national insurance, as well as fiscal policy.[94] The BCA disagreed with the government's approach:

> To suppose that we can alter the structure of society by sudden and arbitrary legisla-
> tive action is greatly to err. Most of our social difficulties come from moral weaknesses
> in human nature or from physical defect rather than from imperfections in our social
> system … The solution must come through the individual, and not through the State.

Their preferred solution was 'a completely free labour market' that could 'automatically carry labour to that point where it could be most beneficially employed and at the highest remuneration'. Anyone who was not capable of competing in the open market should be left to coordinated charitable agencies working in cooperation with the poor law, and support for the elderly should rely on existing voluntary friendly societies rather than tax-funded old age pensions.[95] State action to reduce poverty and unemployment would merely lead to more poverty in a downward spiral. In the opinion of Hugh Cecil,

> new burdens are placed upon the community, a new set of people are dragged down to
> be in their turn new claimants for new schemes of social reform and new expenditure

---

[93] 'Presidential Address of Lord Balfour of Burleigh' in MH Judge (ed), *Political Socialism: A Remonstrance. A Collection of Papers by Members of the British Constitution Association, with Presidential Addresses by Lord Balfour of Burleigh and Lord Hugh Cecil* (London, PS King, 1908) 1, 2, 3, 5, 7, 14, 19, 26–27. He was not related to Arthur Balfour.

[94] P Clarke, *Liberals and Social Democrats* (Cambridge, Cambridge University Press, 1978) 4–5; AM McBriar, *An Edwardian Mixed Doubles: The Bosanquets versus the Webbs. A Study in British Social Policy, 1890–1929* (Oxford, Clarendon Press, 1987).

[95] PSG Propert, 'The Problem of Unemployment' in MH Judge (ed), *Political Socialism: A Remonstrance. A Collection of Papers by Members of the British Constitution Association, with Presidential Addresses by Lord Balfour of Burleigh and Lord Hugh Cecil* (London, PS King, 1908) 72; W Chance, 'Old Age Pensions: The Better Way. A Question for Friendly Societies' in MH Judge (ed), *Political Socialism: A Remonstrance. A Collection of Papers by Members of the British Constitution Association, with Presidential Addresses by Lord Balfour of Burleigh and Lord Hugh Cecil* (London, PS King, 1908) 125.

… Thus there is a circle of burden, suffering, agitation, expenditure, fresh burden and fresh suffering.

In Cecil's view, liberty in the past was menaced by the divine right of kings; now it was menaced by the divine right of the state, with a need for 'the English spirit of the past to prevail now as then'.[96] Here was the challenge that was taken up by Bowles. His action against the Bank of England was, in his mind, an attack on the Liberal government's persistence in defying the law as a result of its refusal 'to postpone for a day the torrent of its own innovating inventions'. Bowles was exploiting the issue of parliamentary procedure and authority in pursuit of a much wider agenda of opposition to the Liberal welfare and fiscal reforms to which Churchill was converted.

Bowles saw one ground for hope in defending the British constitution, that it 'depends upon the character and the spirit of every individual who exercises under it any power'. 'Men of honour and men of courage' were needed to uphold the laws of England – and clearly Bowles felt he was such a man in acting to rescue the constitution:

> Portions of the ancient and splendid fabric may have suffered … But even they may and will yet be repaired. The Constitution itself remains. Its plan, its principles are there still. And so soon as the mischief reaches its essential foundations, so soon will some remedy be found in our days as of old. For the British People have not lost their spirit. What corruption failed to do will not finally be done either by ignorance, by carelessness, or even by faction.[97]

Bowles's language had much in common with seventeenth-century arguments about the restoration of the 'ancient constitution' in opposition to the royal prerogative.[98] The 'power of the people' could achieve what the leaders of the Conservative party could not.

In Bowles opinion, Balfour lost the general election of 1906 because of the 'wanton extravagance, unbridled expenditure, and profligate increase of debt' of his government, even more than his vacillation between free trade and tariff reform. Together, the two issues of spending and trade policy created alarm for the 'Determining Elector – the commonplace, moderate, sensible, timid man of Tory Temper and Liberal Leanings'. The Liberals were 'united in promising Retrenchment, reduction of Debt, and a firm adherence to Free Trade', but soon disappointed the Determining Elector with the prospect of 'financial extremity and of false and dangerous expedients'. Bowles felt that the Determining Elector would turn against the Liberal government with still more disastrous

---

[96] 'Presidential Address of Lord Hugh Cecil' in MH Judge (ed), *Political Socialism: A Remonstrance. A Collection of Papers by Members of the British Constitution Association, with Presidential Addresses by Lord Balfour of Burleigh and Lord Hugh Cecil* (London, PS King, 1908) 39, 48–49.

[97] Bowles, 'The British Constitution' (above n 9) 117.

[98] JGA Pocock, *The Ancient Constitution and the Feudal Law: A Study of English Historical Thought in the Seventeenth Century*, 2nd edn (Cambridge, Cambridge University Press, 1987).

results – the fall of a free-trade government and its replacement by a protectionist government that would raise revenue by taxing the poor. The outcome would be 'to sacrifice Free-Trade to False Taxation; and to lay the foundations of Protection in the ruins of False Finance ... Convinced that Protection would ruin the country, and that False Finance is the road to Protection, I would avoid both'.[99] Here was the challenge for Bowles, to become a new John Hampden leading an attack on profligate spending and a loss of parliamentary control, against untrustworthy politicians and spending departments. In his mind, what was at stake was far more than a return to proper parliamentary procedure: it was the entire future of Britain.

Bowles v Bank of England exposed the ambivalence of resolutions in providing the authority to collect taxes that had been relied on for many years as a matter of custom and convenience, and accepted by the front bench of both parties. The difficulties of the People's Budget and the slowness of the passage of the Finance Acts in 1911 and 1912 meant that what had been tolerated was no longer sustainable. On one level, the result was a necessary and desirable tightening up of parliamentary procedure, for the government was calling into question the legitimacy of taxation that relied on careful parliamentary scrutiny and control.[100] However, much more was at stake at a time when political controversies were at a high level over fiscal policy between Liberal progressive taxation and Conservative tariff reform; over welfare measures to deal with the labour market, health, support of the elderly; over Home Rule for Ireland; and over the naval race and military expenditure. Bowles was involved with these debates, straddling both sides of the House with his support for Liberal free trade but hostility to their social policies and to graduation and differentiation of taxation. In some ways, he was more like his father and Richard Cobden – a supporter of free trade and minimal government, with some sympathy for radical hostility to militarism and adventures in South Africa. Equally, he was seen by the front benches on both sides of the House as a nuisance – a man who disrupted well-established customs that were convenient to taxpayers and officials alike. His self-description as a modern Hampden was exaggerated. Hampden was acting on a fundamental principle, fearing that his land was being threatened by the government. By contrast, Bowles went out of his way to purchase stock knowing that it was liable to taxation. He was exploiting a weakness in parliamentary procedure to challenge the policies of a legitimate, elected government. He won his narrow point and removed a flaw in the administration of the income tax. The wider attack of the BCA on the role of the state was lost.

---

[99] Bowles, *National Finance: An Imminent Peril* (above n 39) 29; Bowles, *National Finance in 1908 and After* (above n 39) 10, 38–40, 52.
[100] Daunton (above n 21) ch 7.

5

Great Western Railway
Co v Bater *(1922)*

A Question of Classification

JOHN HN PEARCE

I NCOME TAX HAS existed continuously since 1842; and continuity in form masks major changes in substance. Income tax, on its reintroduction in 1842, was a flat-rate tax, paid only by a few and had a local administration: income tax, today, is a graduated tax, paid by many millions and is administered centrally.

Other major changes have also taken place. The charge to income tax is now classified according to the nature of the profit or gain:[1] but, from 1842 until after the end of the twentieth century, the charge to income tax was classified according to a number of schedules. Schedules A, B, C, D and E were those in existence from 1842 until 1965.[2] The income tax schedules had not been a feature of the tax during its brief first period of existence from 1799 to 1802: they appeared in 1803 on the reintroduction of the tax; and were a feature of the tax during the second period of its existence up until 1816.[3] When income tax was reintroduced in 1842, the income tax schedules reappeared as well.[4]

The key to understanding the income tax schedules is to appreciate that the schedules did not classify income according to the nature of the profit or gain. The classification was by reference to the collection mechanism. After its

---

[1] A classification of income according to the nature of the profit or gain replaced the classification according to schedules in Acts prepared by the Inland Revenue's Tax Law Rewrite project: see the Income Tax (Earnings and Pensions) Act 2003 and the Income Tax (Trading and Other Income) Act 2005.

[2] A Schedule F was added by FA 1965.

[3] The income tax schedules as they existed during the Napoleonic period are examined in A Farnsworth, *Addington: Author of the Modern Income Tax* (London, Stevens & Sons, 1951).

[4] It has been said that the ITA 1842 (5 & 6 Vict c 35) 'can justly be called a "reprint"' of an Act of 1806 (46 Geo 3 c 65). BEV Sabine, *A History of Income Tax* (London, George Allen & Unwin, 1966) 62.

reintroduction in 1842 (as earlier during the Napoleonic period), Schedules A and B dealt with income arising from land; and, among other things, permitted tenants to deduct income tax from the rent they paid to their landlords. Schedules C and E dealt with sums paid out of public funds, and hence directly amenable to government control: interest and dividends in the case of Schedule C and the emoluments of an office or employment in the case of Schedule E. Schedule D dealt with all other income. In this case, there was no alternative except to apply to the taxpayer for information – what Gladstone called 'the objectionable principle of self-assessment'.[5] Schedule D, accordingly, was the residuary schedule. It did not apply if some other schedule, with its superior collection mechanism, could be used instead.

On a classification of income by reference to the collection mechanism, some employment income would fall within Schedule E and some within Schedule D. Schedule E would apply, for example, to the earnings of those in the armed forces or the civil service; and Schedule D to the earnings of those working in private firms. In the case of employment income, therefore, Schedules D and E shared a frontier.

Another major change during the history of income tax, therefore, is the replacement of the classification of income according to the collection mechanism by a classification according to the nature of the profit or gain. A further major change concerns the relative importance of the various schedules: for, during the period from 1842 to 1965, sums charged to income tax under Schedule E achieved a total ascendancy over those charged under the other schedules. The question arising in the case of *Great Western Railway Co v Bater* (*Bater*)[6] was whether the earnings of Mr WH Hall, a clerk employed by the Great Western Railway (the GWR), were properly assessed under Schedule D or Schedule E; and the decision of the House of Lords in 1922[7] constituted a staging post of the utmost importance for both these major changes – thus justifying the view that this case was a landmark case in revenue law.

I. THE BACKGROUND TO THE CASE

A. The Law from 1842 to 1864

In *Bater*, the arguments advanced and the decisions given had three essential legal components, and all three were in place by 1864. There were general statutory provisions relating to income tax, dating from 1842 and 1853; statutory provisions relating to railway companies dating from 1860; and a decided case dating from 1864. All three components presented difficulties.

---

[5] HC Deb 18 April 1853, vol 125, col 1364.
[6] It is unusual to refer to a tax case by reference to the Inland Revenue's representative; but '*Bater*' was the usage adopted by the House of Lords in *Edwards v Clinch* [1982] AC 845.
[7] *Great Western Railway Co v Bater* (1922) 8 TC 231.

The charge to income tax in the Income Tax Act (ITA) 1842[8] was restated in the ITA 1853.[9] The 1853 Act provided that the subject matter of the charge under Schedule D included 'the annual profits or gains arising or accruing to any person residing in the United Kingdom from any profession trade employment or vocation'; it was also provided that Schedule D should 'extend to … every description of employment or profit not contained in Schedule E'. If it did not fall within Schedule E, therefore, employment income fell within Schedule D – and this was a distinction that had consequences. Employment income assessed under Schedule D was assessed on the average earnings of the three preceding years; employment income assessed under Schedule E was assessed on the earnings of the current year of assessment.

The 1853 Act also provided that income tax should be charged under Schedule E 'in respect of every public office or employment of profit and upon every annuity, pension or stipend payable by Her Majesty or out of the public Revenue of the United Kingdom'; and, in the 1842 Act, the Third Rule of Schedule E (the Third Rule) set out the ambit of that Schedule. As originally enacted, the Third Rule consisted of a single passage of 270 words – a hostile block of type. To make the structure of the Third Rule easier to grasp, it is now set out in a form in which paragraphing has been supplied:[10]

The said duties shall be paid on all public offices and employments of profit of the description hereafter mentioned within Great Britain; (videlicet,)

(a) any office belonging to either House of Parliament, or to any court of justice …;

(b) any public office held under the civil government of her Majesty …;

(c) any commissioned officer serving on the staff, or belonging to her Majesty's army …;

(d) any officer in the navy, or in the militia or volunteers;

(e) any office or employment of profit held under any ecclesiastical body, whether aggregate or sole, or under any public corporation, or under any company or society, whether corporate or not corporate;

(f) any office or employment of profit under any public institution, or on any public foundation, of whatever nature or for whatever purpose the same may be established;

(g) any office or employment of profit in any county, riding or division, shire or stewartry, or in any city, borough, town corporate, or place …; and

(h) every other public office or employment of profit of a public nature.

The wording primarily considered in *Bater* may be found in paragraph (e).

---

[8] ITA 1842, 5 & 6 Vict, c 35.

[9] ITA 1853 16 & 17 Vict, c 34. In that Act, the charge to income tax was set out in s 2; and s 5 made the rules and regulations of the 1842 Act applicable for the purposes of the schedules as set out in the 1853 Act.

[10] The paragraphing supplied has been governed by the appearances of semi-colons in the original text. Paragraphing was also supplied when the Third Rule was consolidated in the ITA 1918, sch 1, sch E, r 6.

Two conflicting views may be advanced as to how the components of the Third Rule worked together. The first view (called 'the overall view' in this chapter) was that the opening and closing words of the rule showed that the provision applied only to *public* offices and employments. But, if that should be correct, there was no need for the word 'public' to make all of its other appearances (for example at the beginning of paragraph (b)). These further appearances of the word 'public' were capable of indicating that the ambit of the rule was rather more miscellaneous; and that there was no overall restriction to offices and employments of a public nature.

The other, contrary, view (called 'the detailed view' in this chapter) was that the appearance or omission of the word 'public' in the various components of the Third Rule indicated a distinction to which effect should be given. It followed, accordingly, that some offices and employments were of a public nature – and that some were not. In paragraph (e), in particular, the words 'any office or employment of profit held under … any company' should be taken at face value – and no 'public nature' was necessary. But, if that should be correct, the use of the word 'public' near the beginning and end of the Third Rule had to be downgraded or explained away. Two conflicting views, therefore, were possible. Both had difficulties.

Further statutory provisions relating to railway companies were introduced in the ITA 1860.[11] Section 5 of that Act transferred the power to make assessments relating to railways from the General Commissioners to the Special Commissioners; and the section also provided that 'the amount of such assessment shall be paid, collected and levied in like manner as any other assessment' made by the Special Commissioners. Section 6 of the1860 Act then provided that:

> In like manner as aforesaid the commissioners for special purposes shall assess the duties payable under Schedule E in respect of all offices and employments of profit held in or under any railway company, and shall notify to the secretary or other officer of such company the particulars thereof; and the said assessment shall be deemed to be and shall be an assessment upon the company, and paid, collected, and levied accordingly.

Two conflicting views may be advanced as to how section 6 should be construed. No contemporary material relevant for demonstrating the intentions of those who promoted this legislation is known, but it is considered likely that the intention was that all payments of employment income made by railway companies should be brought within the ambit of Schedule E.[12] This construction is called 'the wider construction' in this chapter. But, if that should be correct, the drafting of section 6 was lamentably defective. The legislative intention would surely

---

[11] ITA 1860, 23 & 24 Vict, c 14.

[12] See, eg, the opinion of the Commissioners of Inland Revenue referred to in the Case Stated in *Lancashire and Yorkshire Railway* (text before n 14 below).

have been better served if the words 'under Schedule E' had been placed not after 'the duties payable', but a little later after 'any railway company'.

In *Bater*, however, the majority of the judges construed section 6 of the 1860 Act very differently. On this second construction (called 'the narrower construction' in this chapter) Schedule E was mentioned, not in connection with the characteristics of an assessment made, but in connection with the conditions to be met before any assessment could legitimately be raised. Section 6 of the 1860 Act, in other words, was only engaged if an individual was chargeable to income tax under Schedule E by virtue of some other provision (a condition that led straight to the Third Rule). The fact that section 6 existed at all made it legitimate to infer that some such individuals might be so chargeable – but how numerous they were in comparison with other individuals who did not meet this condition (and who were accordingly liable to be assessed under Schedule D) remained to be ascertained. Once again, two conflicting views were possible.

A case decided in 1864, *AG v Lancashire and Yorkshire Railway Co* required the consideration of the statutory provisions enacted in 1842, 1853 and 1860.[13] The case reached the Court of Exchequer in the form of a special case for the opinion of the Court, which stated that the defendants had been called upon to provide information for income tax purposes:

> [A]nd the defendants and their officers were furnished with the proper forms for that purpose, and were at the same time informed, by the direction of the Commissioners of Inland Revenue, that the said list, declaration or statement ought, in the opinion of the Commissioners of Inland Revenue, to comprehend all the officers, clerks and servants ... in the employment of the defendants, during the year commencing on the 6th of April, 1860, whose salaries or wages amounted to the sum of 100l per annum or upwards.
>
> ... The defendants, however, although willing to comply with this requisition as regards such of their officers, clerks, and servants as are engaged at annual salaries, have refused to comply with it in respect of those engaged at weekly wages.[14]

The question for the decision of the Court was stated to be 'whether the Defendants are liable to be assessed under Schedule E in respect of their officers, clerks or servants so ... engaged ... at weekly wages as well as in respect of those engaged at annual salaries'.[15] One of the Crown's points of argument was that section 6 of the 1860 Act applied to all officers and servants of railway companies actually receiving £100 or more per year;[16] and the Attorney General is recorded as arguing, on behalf of the Crown, that a railway company came within the words 'any company or society, whether corporate or not corporate' in the Third Rule; and that, if there were any doubt about the matter, it was removed by sections 5

[13] *AG v Lancashire and Yorkshire Railway Co* (1864) 2 H & C 792, (1864) 10 LT 95.
[14] ibid, 793.
[15] ibid, 793–94.
[16] *Lancashire and Yorkshire Railway* (above n 13) (1864) 10 LT 95, 96.

and 6 of the 1860 Act, which expressly extended to the taxation of employments of profit under a railway company. Nothing (according to the Attorney General) turned on the nature of the employment or the period of hiring.[17] The Crown, therefore, argued in favour of the detailed view of the Third Rule and the wider construction of section 6 of the 1860 Act.

The Court of Exchequer, however, gave judgment in favour of the railway company. Pollock CB is recorded as stating that,

> persons who are employed by a railway company merely in such offices as that of porters or engine drivers, or indeed any class who are paid merely as weekly servants from week to week are not persons filling a 'public office', or occupying 'an employment of profit of a public nature.[18]

The other members of the Court held the same opinion. The Court, therefore, decided in favour of the overall view of the Third Rule and the narrower construction of section 6 of the 1860 Act. There was no appeal.

The employees of this railway company engaged at weekly wages, therefore, were not within Schedule E. Beyond this point, however, the position was less clear. The company was willing, in practice, to treat employees engaged at annual salaries as within Schedule E; but the question whether, as a matter of law, this treatment was correct had not been decided. Other, wider, propositions, not decided in *Lancashire and Yorkshire Railway*, remained for argument.

More than half a century later, in *Bater*, the Third Rule, section 6 of the 1860 Act and *Lancashire and Yorkshire Railway* were the crucial material discussed. That material began with a provision (the Third Rule) which was incapable of being construed in an entirely satisfactory manner. It then advanced to a provision (section 6 of the 1860 Act) which was capable of two different constructions – and may well have been defectively drafted. It then advanced to a case whose wider implications remained uncertain. The ambit of the expanding charge to income tax under Schedule E was not a house built upon a rock.

B. Developments After 1864

In the years following 1842, Schedule E was not an important schedule in terms of its yield. In the year to 31 March 1869, net receipts amounted to some £521,000. Schedule E was ahead of Schedule B (£418,000), but behind Schedule C (£847,000), Schedule A (£3.1m) and Schedule D (£3.8m). Of total net receipts of £8.6m, Schedule E accounted for 6 per cent.[19]

---

[17] ibid, 97.
[18] ibid, 98.
[19] Inland Revenue, *Report of the Commissioners of Inland Revenue on the duties under their management for the years 1856 to 1869 inclusive* (C 82, 1870) 120.

As Table 1 demonstrates,[20] the relative importance of Schedule E gradually increased.

Table 1 Gross income brought under review for income tax purposes: 1893–94 to 1918–19 (selected years)

Year	Schedule D (£M)	Schedule E (£M)	Total (£M)	Schedule E (as % of total)
1893–94	356.6	52.6	673.7	7.8
1898–99	416.5	65.3	762.7	8.5
1903–04	502.4	86.1	902.8	9.5
1908–09	565.6	109.6	1,009.9	10.9
1913–14	670.6	145.6	1,167.2	12.5
1918–19	1,629.9	348.1	2,445.7	14.2
1920–21	2,386.1	596.3	3,477.1	17.1

One important component of this increase was the rise of limited liability companies. The ITA 1842 antedated the provision of incorporation by registration, as opposed to a special Act or charter (in 1844), and the introduction of limited liability (in 1855). A comprehensive statute relating to companies dated from 1862. The number of joint stock companies then rose gradually. There were 9,344 in 1885 and 62,762 in 1914.[21] Shortly before the Finance Act (FA) 1922 was enacted, the Inland Revenue estimated that about 750,000 individuals were assessed under Schedule E: 300,000 government employees; 100,000 employees of local authorities and corporations; 250,000 employees of companies, banks and suchlike; and 100,000 railway employees.[22]

The Inland Revenue's starting point, during the period from 1864 until after the First World War, continued to be that the words 'any office or employment of profit held under … any company' should be given their full meaning. *Lancashire and Yorkshire Railway* was accordingly viewed as a derogation from the general rule. The department, furthermore, had considerable success in administering Schedule E on this basis. Such legal authority as came into existence assisted the Inland Revenue as opposed to those who might wish to contest its

---

[20] Sources: for the years 1893–94 and 1898–99, Inland Revenue, *Forty-fifth Report of the Commissioners of His Majesty's Inland Revenue for the year ended 31st March 1902* (Cd 1216, 1902) 173; for years from 1903–04 to 1913–14, Royal Commission on the Income Tax, *Appendices and Index to the Minutes of Evidence* (HMSO, 1920) 20; for later years, Inland Revenue, *Seventy-first Report of the Commissioners of His Majesty's Inland Revenue for the year ended 31st March 1928* (Cmd 3176, 1928) 75.

[21] W Ashworth, *An Economic History of England 1870–1939* (London, Methuen, 1960) 95.

[22] 'Second Budget: Inland Revenue memoranda (Part 2)', The National Archives, T 171/120 (1915).

approach. In *Tennant v Smith*,[23] Lord Watson expressed the opinion that income arising from the taxpayer's employment as a bank agent was assessable under Schedule E where the bank employing the agent was a company.[24] The decision in that case, however, did not depend on such an opinion being held. Later, in *Berry v Farrow*,[25] the plaintiff, the manager of a limited company, was successful in an action for wrongful distress; and, in his judgment, Bankes J expressed the opinion that the authorities had been right in assessing the plaintiff under Schedule E and not under Schedule D.[26] In this case too, however, the Court could have reached its decision without reference to this opinion.

The Inland Revenue's approach also received support from those who wrote about income tax. One writer, in a study published in 1909, considered that the holders of 'any office or employment … under any company … whether corporate or not corporate' 'clearly include officers of limited liability companies, eg, directors, secretaries, chief accountants, bank managers and other superior employees'.[27] The first edition of Konstam's work on income tax law,[28] published in 1921, began its treatment of Schedule E by stating that:

> Schedule E provides for the taxation of the profits received in respect of public offices and employments of profit, including offices and employments held in the United Kingdom under a company or other corporation; the word 'public' does not signify that the office or employment 'has duties direct to the public'; it has indeed 'practically disappeared'.[29]

In the years immediately before 1922, expositions of the law and practice of income tax gave no indication that the scope of the charge under Schedule E was an area where the tectonic plates of income tax law were capable of shifting.

The situation was nevertheless far from ideal. Some employees were assessed to income tax under Schedule E and some under Schedule D – but there were difficulties both with the statute law and the case law relevant for making the distinction. The distinction between the two schedules also had practical implications. Schedule D was assessed on the average income during the three preceding years of assessment; Schedule E on the current year of assessment. The two different bases of assessment could – and did – give rise to different liabilities in any one year of assessment. It was also the case that the deductions allowable under Schedule E were more restricted than those allowable under

---

[23] *Tennant v Smith* [1892] AC 150, 3 TC 158.

[24] ibid, 159, 167.

[25] *Berry v Farrow* [1914] 1 KB 632.

[26] ibid, 637.

[27] TH Fry, *Income Tax: Its Return, Assessment, and Recovery* (London, Stevens & Sons, 1909) 58. Fry is described on the title page as a barrister-at-law of Gray's Inn.

[28] EM Konstam, *A Treatise on the Law of Income Tax* (London, Stevens & Sons, 1921).

[29] ibid, 227. At the end of the passage quoted, there is a footnote pointer '(aa)' to the judgment of Rowlatt J in *Bater* (above n 7) 234. There is a ready inference, from the use of the reference '(aa)', that this was a late addition to the text.

Schedule D. Under the law as it was applied, furthermore, there were anomalies. If a firm converted its business into a limited company, its officials ceased to be assessable under Schedule D and instead became assessable under Schedule E. Schedule E was also administered with a known practice under which the Inland Revenue acquiesced in the outcome if General Commissioners decided that subordinate employees of limited companies could be assessed under the three years' average appropriate for Schedule D and not on the earnings of the current year as required by Schedule E. This practice had no legal foundation and depended upon particular decisions taken by particular bodies of General Commissioners. Those bodies did not all make the same decision; and they could change the basis on which any decision was made.[30]

The Royal Commission on the Income Tax, which reported in 1920, recommended that all income from employments then assessable under Schedule D should be transferred to Schedule E. The Commission could see no sufficient reason for the continuance of the anomalous state of affairs then existing, and considered that both justice and commonsense demanded that employees of all kinds should be treated as nearly as possible on the same basis and according to the same rules.[31]

The First World War placed the administration of Schedule E under further short-term strains.[32] The threshold at which income tax was charged was lowered; and inflation worked to ensure that more individuals had earnings above that threshold. Among those affected was Mr WH Hall of 42 County Road, Swindon, a fourth-grade clerk in the Locomotive and Carriage Department of the GWR. For the 1917/18 year of assessment, Mr Hall had no liability to income tax on the three years' average basis applicable for Schedule D. But Mr Hall was considered to fall within Schedule E: and, on the current year basis, his income of £175 per annum gave rise to an income tax liability.[33]

---

[30] The file '"Three Years Average" cases', The National Archives, IR 40/2708 (1921–22) is concerned with the aftermath of a decision, taken by the Liverpool General Commissioners, late in 1921, that all individuals earning more than £500 per annum were employed in a responsible and not in a subordinate capacity – thus causing transfers from the three years' average to the current year basis. There were aggrieved individuals – and correspondence which also involved MPs, Inland Revenue officials and the Chancellor of the Exchequer.

[31] Report of the Royal Commission on the Income Tax (Cmd 615, 1920) 104, para 470.

[32] It has been stated that the years between 1914 and 1920 'saw the most significant re-ordering of wealth in recent English history. There was via inflation, taxation and the pressures of the wartime labour market a general redistribution of wealth downwards: all, more or less, gained at the expense of those immediately above them'. R McKibbin, Parties and People: England 1914–1951 (Oxford, Oxford University Press, 2010) 41.

[33] The details relating to Mr Hall have been taken from the following National Archives files: 'Finance Bill; report stage and third reading. Vol. III', The National Archives, T 171/210 (1922) and 'Reports of Solicitor upon Legal Business', The National Archives, RAIL 250/522 (1919–20), Solicitor's Report dated 3 February 1919. For the expression 'fourth grade clerk' see Bater (above n 7) 234.

II. THE COURSE OF THE LITIGATION

A. The Initial Stages

On 12 November 1917, Mr Hall wrote to HM Inspector of Taxes, Paddington District:

> I am much obliged for yours of the 7th instant, returned herewith, and beg leave to appeal against the assessment of my salary etc., and ask to be allowed to claim to be assessed on the three years' average.[34]

The first move in the litigation was accordingly taken by Mr Hall himself.[35] Section 6 of the 1860 Act, however, operated so that the assessment was made upon the GWR, and not upon Mr Hall; and, on 18 March 1918, the GWR's Chief Accountant wrote to the Clerk to the Special Commissioners stating that 'upon the request of Mr WH Hall' the GWR gave formal Notice of Appeal against his assessment to Income Tax for the year 1917–18 under Schedule E 'and on his behalf claim to be assessed under Schedule D'.[36]

The GWR's solicitor later reported that:

> The point raised is one of importance, and if decided in Hall's favour, would affect a large number of the Company's salaried staff. It not only involves the interpretation of the words 'offices and employments of profit held in or under any Railway Company' contained in section 6 [of the Income Tax Act 1860] ... but it also raises the question as to the true scope of Schedule E itself and of the Rules thereunder ...

> It is to be observed that both in Schedule E and in [the Third Rule] ... the public nature of the office or employment appears to be regarded as an essential element in assessments under that Schedule, and it may even be on a strict construction of the wording of the Schedule and the Rule none of the offices in a Railway Company's service properly falls within the category of 'public offices or employments'.

> However this may be, the question having been raised it was clearly incumbent upon the Company to take the steps necessary to obtain an authoritative decision upon the point. An appeal against Hall's assessment was accordingly lodged by the Company with the Special Commissioners.[37]

It is clear from these paragraphs that the GWR had already given careful thought to the course of action it was proposing to take and about how crucial aspects of the litigation would need to be approached. The company, for example, would clearly argue for the overall view and not the detailed view of the Third Rule. (It may readily be conjectured that counsel's advice had already been sought and given.) The most revealing passage, however, may perhaps be found in the final

---

[34] Treasury (above n 33).
[35] There was speculation, during the course of the litigation, that Mr Hall had played no independent role, but had been selected as a suitable test case by the GWR (see, eg, *Bater* (above n 7) 240–41). That speculation was wide of the mark.
[36] Treasury (above n 33).
[37] 'Reports of Solicitor' (above n 33), Solicitor's Report dated 3 February 1919.

paragraph quoted. The question having been raised, it was 'clearly incumbent' on the GWR 'to take the steps necessary to obtain an authoritative decision'. The protracted litigation that followed is explained by the obligation felt and assumed by the GWR to obtain a decision that was authoritative.

B. The Special Commissioners

The quest for that decision began with the hearing before the Special Commissioners on 2 January 1919.[38] It is recorded that the GWR's solicitor and chief accountant were both present;[39] so there is an obvious inference that the GWR treated the case as important. The sole question for determination, the Special Commissioners later recorded, was whether the GWR had rightly been assessed on behalf of Mr Hall under Schedule E of the Income Tax Acts. The Special Commissioners therefore made findings concerning Mr Hall's employment by the GWR: these included that Mr Hall had been employed by the GWR for more than 20 years and had an annual salary payable in instalments every 28 days. The GWR argued in favour of the overall view of the Third Rule; and that, even on the assumption that 'the principal officers of a railway company could be held to fall within the scope of Schedule E, the junior members of the staff holding no definite appointments in the service could not be so included'. The Crown contended that the GWR was a company or society within the meaning of the Third Rule and that Mr Hall held an office or employment of profit within the meaning of the Third Rule and the 1860 Act. Since the GWR was a railway company, section 6 of the 1860 Act was applicable, and required the assessment to be made on the GWR. The assessment was therefore rightly made – and should be upheld. The Special Commissioners decided the case in favour of the Crown, and recorded that: 'We, the Commissioners who heard the Appeal, were of opinion that the contentions put forward on behalf of the Crown should succeed, and we therefore confirmed the assessment'. Two views could be taken of the passage quoted. A first view was that the passage made findings of fact – and entitled the Crown to an easy victory in all subsequent litigation. The Inland Revenue took this view.[40] If that should be correct, the GWR had a further hurdle to overcome – a hurdle that was likely to prove insurmountable. The opposing view was that a clear distinction should be drawn between findings of fact (which could not be disturbed unless there was no basis

---

[38] The Case Stated recording the proceedings at the hearing before the Special Commissioners is printed at *Bater* (above n 7) 231–33.

[39] 'Reports of Solicitor' (above n 33), Solicitor's Report dated 3 February 1919. Neither in this report nor in the later Case Stated is it recorded whether Mr Hall was present or gave evidence, or who argued the case for the two contending parties.

[40] House of Lords Bundle for *Bater* 25, 'Points for Argument on behalf of the Respondent' (in the High Court [ie, before Rowlatt J]). A copy of this bundle is held in the library at Lincoln's Inn.

for the factual finding) and questions of law (which were matters for the appellate court). On this view, the passage from the Special Commissioners' decision blurred this distinction – and should be criticised.

The GWR's solicitor considered that it was

> difficult to see on what principle a distinction can be drawn between members of the weekly wages and salaried staffs and the other members of the salaried staff – at any rate so far as concerns those who hold only subordinate positions.[41]

The Special Commissioners were required to state a Case for the opinion of the High Court.[42]

C. The High Court (Rowlatt J)

The case was heard in the High Court by Rowlatt J on 2 June 1920. The GWR's solicitor later recorded that the company's case was based on two grounds.[43] The first ground was that employment in a railway company's service was not service in a *public* office or employment of profit within the meaning of the charge to Schedule E. Rowlatt J dismissed this argument. A public office or employment of profit within the meaning of the schedule did not mean an office or employment which had duties direct to the public: 'it seems to me … that the word "public" very nearly disappears from this definition'.[44] Rowlatt J, therefore, upheld the detailed view and not the overall view of the Third Rule.

The second ground on which the GWR's case was presented was that Mr Hall, a subordinate clerk, was not the holder of an office or employment falling within the ambit of the Third Rule. This argument led to a very famous passage in United Kingdom revenue law:

> Now it is argued, and to my mind argued most forcibly, that that shows that what those who use the language of the Act of 1842 meant, when they spoke of an office or employment, was an office or employment which was a subsisting, permanent, substantive position, which had an existence independent from the person who filled it, which went on and was filled in succession by successive holders; and if you merely had a man who was engaged on whatever terms, to do duties which were assigned to him, his employment to do those duties did not create an office to which those duties were attached. He merely was employed to do certain things and that is an end of it; and if there was no office or employment existing in the case as a thing, the so-called office or employment was merely an aggregate of the activities of the particular man for the time being. And I think myself that that is sound … [M]y own view is that the people in 1842 who used this language meant by an office a substantive thing that

---

[41] 'Reports of Solicitor' (above n 33), Solicitor's Report dated 3 February 1919.
[42] The Case Stated by the Special Commissioners was dated 31 October 1919.
[43] 'Reports of Solicitor' (above n 33), Solicitor's Report dated 6 June 1920.
[44] *Bater* (above n 7) 234.

existed apart from the holder. If I thought I was at liberty to take that view I should decide in favour of the Appellants.[45]

Rowlatt J then went on to hold, however, that he should not give effect to this view, because he thought that it was really contrary to what was proceeded upon in substance in *Lancashire and Yorkshire Railway*. As far as he could see, it was taken as common ground in that case that permanent officials of a clerical kind would be within Schedule E. Therefore, thinking that he was in substance following what was the authority, Rowlatt J dismissed the GWR's appeal.[46] It does not appear, however, that it was correct to view *Lancashire and Yorkshire Railway* as establishing that proposition.[47]

The GWR's solicitor, writing shortly after Rowlatt J's decision, recorded that counsel 'doubt the correctness of the judgment and think it ought to be put right by the Court of Appeal'.[48] The GWR accordingly appealed.

D. The Court of Appeal

In the Court of Appeal, the case was heard by the Master of the Rolls (Lord Sterndale) and Scrutton and Younger LJJ on 9 and 10 February 1921. The Court gave its judgment on the latter day.

The Court of Appeal also decided the case in favour of the Crown; however, the judgments delivered have attracted much less subsequent attention than those delivered by Rowlatt J or in the House of Lords.[49] This result follows from the Court of Appeal's acceptance of the Crown's argument that the Special Commissioners had made findings of fact. Scrutton LJ did 'not profess for a moment that this will be satisfactory to the parties who have come to this Court';[50] and the GWR's solicitor certainly considered the position unsatisfactory. The decision, in his view, was clearly wrong: 'the question involved was not one of fact but of the construction of the Act of Parliament'. The question affected a large number of clerks in the service of the GWR, of other railway companies, and of large corporations; and 'I am advised that the Company would succeed on appeal to the House of Lords'.[51]

The GWR then appealed to the House of Lords – having been advised that it would succeed in its appeal. The Inland Revenue (no doubt fortified by the

---

[45] ibid, 235.

[46] ibid.

[47] See text following n 18 above.

[48] 'Reports of Solicitor' (above n 33), Solicitor's Report dated 6 June 1920.

[49] Two substantial judgments were delivered in the Court of Appeal – by Lord Sterndale and Scrutton LJ. Younger LJ agreed with those two judgments.

[50] *Bater* (above no 7) 241.

[51] 'Reports of Solicitor upon Legal Business', The National Archives, RAIL 250/523 (1921), Solicitor's Report dated 7 March 1921.

judgments given in the Court of Appeal) proposed to argue that the appeal should be dismissed (among other reasons) because

> the Special Commissioners have found that the position of WH Hall in the service of the Appellant Company was an office or employment of profit within Schedule E of the Income Tax Act, 1853, and the provisions subsidiary thereto, and as the question in the particular circumstances of the case was one of fact and degree, and as there was evidence to support the finding, it is not open to review.[52]

E. The House of Lords

Bater was argued in the House of Lords on 23 and 24 February 1922. Judgment was reserved, and was delivered on 13 March 1922.

In the House of Lords, the GWR was finally victorious – and so obtained its 'authoritative decision'. Four of the five members of the House of Lords (Lord Atkinson, Lord Sumner, Lord Wrenbury and Lord Carson) gave judgment for the company; Lord Buckmaster dissented in favour of the Crown. Lord Buckmaster's speech is nevertheless of considerable interest: for he was prepared to uphold a combination of views not upheld by any other judge who heard the case. He supported the overall view of the Third Rule, but then went on to support the wider construction of section 6 of the 1860 Act. It was not contended, however, that *Lancashire and Yorkshire Railway* was wrongly decided, and Lord Buckmaster did not hesitate to accept it as an authority 'having regard to the subject matter of the dispute and the length of time that has elapsed during which the practice established has been obeyed'. He considered, however, that Mr Hall's employment had characteristics enabling it to be said that

> he is definitely in the employment of the Company on terms other than that of a weekly wage, and these are, I think, the distinctions that justify the Crown in their contention that the railway company is liable to be assessed directly, and not Mr Hall.

The majority in the House of Lords, however, dealt with the case in a very different manner. Of the majority, Lord Carson delivered a short concurring speech, but Lord Atkinson, Lord Sumner and Lord Wrenbury all gave full judgments – and all three decided the major issues arising in the case in the same way.

The majority were quite clear that the case raised a question of law, which had to be distinguished carefully from questions of fact. Lord Wrenbury was especially emphatic upon this point, and then launched an onslaught on the language in which the income tax legislation was expressed:

> My Lords, there is in this case much that is difficult, but one thing seems to me quite plain, and that is that the question here is not, as the Court of Appeal thought, a question of fact. It was for the Special Commissioners to find and state all the facts respecting the nature of the office or employment as to which the question arises.

---

[52] House of Lords Bundle for *Bater* (above n 40), 'Statement of the Case of the Respondent'.

It was not for the Court to question those facts in any way. But the question for the Court was whether, upon those facts, Mr Hall held an office or employment of profit *within the meaning of the Act*. That is a question of law. What does the Act mean? What is the true construction? It is impossible to escape deciding that question of law by saying that the Act is so slovenly and so unintelligible that it is impossible satisfactorily to ascertain and declare its meaning. If it were competent to a Court of Law to censure the Legislature, or if any useful purpose could be served by censuring the Legislatures of 1842 or 1853, no censure could be too strong, I think, for having expressed an Act, and that a taxing Act, in language so involved, so slovenly and so unintelligible as is the language of the Acts of 1842 and 1853. But there it is. A Court cannot say it means nothing and cannot be construed at all. The Court must, as best it can, arrive at some meaning of the language which bears upon the particular case before it for decision ... As a member of the Joint Committee of both Houses to which was referred the Consolidation Bill which is now the Income Tax Act 1918, I strove to find some way in which we could deal with the language of confusion and unintelligibility of the Acts to be consolidated. It was, however, impossible to do so. The Committee had only to consolidate and could not substitute plain words to express a plain meaning without going beyond the limits of consolidation. The Act of 1918 therefore reproduces the old language with all its faults and has done little more than improve matters a little by some rearrangement. If Parliament had the time, which it has not, the law of Income Tax, which now so vitally affects the subjects of the Realm, ought as speedily as possible to be expressed in a new Statute which should bear and express an intelligible meaning.[53]

The majority then went on to uphold the overall view of the Third Rule and the narrower construction of section 6 of the 1860 Act. They concluded by holding that Mr Hall's earnings were not assessable under Schedule E.

The opinions delivered in the House of Lords are capable of being correlated with the Law Lords' political opinions. Buckmaster had served as Solicitor-General in the Liberal government before the First World War; in 1929 he was to write a letter of support when Jowitt, who had been elected as a Liberal MP, took the office of Attorney General in the new Labour government.[54] On the other side, Carson had been a leading Conservative politician; and Atkinson had also served as a Conservative MP. Sumner's views, by the early 1920s, had become extremely conservative.[55] Details of Lord Wrenbury's party political allegiances are not readily available: but he was certainly no friend of the Inland Revenue. In April 1921, the *Times* published a long-reasoned opinion in the form of a letter to its editor, contesting the view of the Special Commissioners that the personal reliefs given for income tax were not available for supertax.[56]

---

[53] *Bater* (above n 7) 254–55.

[54] Buckmaster concluded that letter by stating 'My time is over – May you long be able to urge on the only cause that ever made the Liberal Party live – the cause of those who are beaten down & oppressed in the fierce race for wealth'. RFV Heuston, *Lives of the Lord Chancellors 1885–1940* (Oxford, Oxford University Press, 1964) 295.

[55] For Sumner, see A Lentin, *The last Political Law Lord: Lord Sumner 1859–1934* (Newcastle, Cambridge Scholars Publishing, 2008).

[56] This letter is also printed in *Kennard Davis v CIR* (1922) 8 TC 341, 344–46.

The view is nevertheless taken that, in *Bater*, this correlation is not a matter to which significance should be attached: for the political opinions of the members of the House of Lords are not in evidence in the speeches delivered in this case. It may nevertheless still be worth bearing in mind, however, that, at a time when the power, ability and willingness of central government to undertake redistributive measures was increasing, and at a time when class conflict could be prominent and deep, underlying attitudes towards these developments could perhaps manifest themselves in unexpected ways.

III. LEGISLATION IN THE FINANCE ACT 1922

The decision given by the House of Lords in *Bater* meant that the earnings of employees needed to be treated, for income tax purposes, in a manner differing greatly from existing well-established practice. The majority of the House of Lords, however, gave little guidance about the principles on which this brave new world should be governed. Lord Wrenbury, for example, considered it 'impossible to declare in general terms the true meaning' of the relevant statutory provisions 'so as to guide and control in the future a decision upon other facts'. A railway company might employ persons in such a manner that they held offices or employment falling within Schedule E. 'I do not attempt to say what they are. But I do say that this clerk is not among them'. Each case had to be determined on its facts 'and in every case the question will be whether upon the facts the office or employment is public within the meaning of the Act'.[57]

Against this background, it is not surprising to find that, on 20 March 1922, one week after the members of the House of Lords had delivered judgment, the Chairman and Deputy Chairman of the Board of Inland Revenue sent a memorandum to the Chancellor of the Exchequer (Sir Robert Horne).[58] An 'unexpected decision' of the House of Lords had made it necessary 'that we should bring to your notice a matter of urgency and importance which so affects the Income Tax machine as, in our opinion, to render early legislation almost inevitable'. The 'unexpected decision', which so affected the income tax machine, was, of course, the decision in *Bater*.

The memorandum recorded that the decision in *Bater* had placed the Inland Revenue in very great difficulties. The speeches delivered in the House of Lords

> have given little or no help in the direction of furnishing criteria which would enable the Commissioners of Income Tax and others concerned in the administration of the Income Tax Acts to decide whether particular persons and classes of persons do or do not fall within the scope of Schedule E.

---

[57] *Bater* (above no 7) 255, 256.

[58] 'Finance Bill 1922: vol 2 memoranda', The National Archives, IR 63/101 (1921–22) 155–64. 'Memorandum to Chancellor of the Exchequer on position of assessment to Income Tax of employments, arising out of position in Bater case', 20 March 1922.

... In the light of – or perhaps more accurately in the darkness following upon – the decision, ... it will be a matter of the greatest difficulty for any body of Income Tax Commissioners to decide with any degree of certainty which officers or employees of companies, ... public corporations, local authorities, etc. do in fact and in law hold public offices or employments of profit within the meaning of Schedule E. It would be useless in these circumstances to hope for any sort of uniformity in the decisions of the numerous separate and independent bodies of Income Tax Commissioners who are concerned.

Many appeal hearings could be expected. Employees whose average earnings exceeded their current earnings would seek to bring themselves within Schedule E; and employees whose current earnings exceeded their average earnings would seek to bring themselves within Schedule D – 'and the natural and proper instinct of the District Commissioners will to be give to each class of postulant as favourable a decision as possible'. The (understated) conclusion was that '[i]n the circumstances, in order to avoid serious confusion, we are bound to advise that steps should be taken in the coming Finance Bill to put matters upon a workable basis'.

The memorandum considered the possibility of legislation to restore the status quo – but advised against legislation with any such aim. As the law had previously been administered there had been a serious lack of uniformity in the income tax treatment of different classes of taxpayer, with some assessed on the three years' average and some on the current year basis. The law, furthermore, had not been properly enforced: for many subordinate employees of limited companies had been assessed on the three years' average appropriate to Schedule D 'a non-statutory concession which cannot be reconciled with any terms in Income Tax law'. This concession, 'which is as illogical as it is old', depended upon the actions of particular bodies of General Commissioners. Those actions were not identical, and gave rise to difficulties as regards the distinction between subordinate and responsible employment. Even before the decision of the House of Lords, therefore, 'the position was very unsatisfactory and was becoming increasingly embarrassing'.

The importance and impact of the decision in *Bater* may accordingly be gauged from the Inland Revenue's view that it was 'impossible to escape the conclusion, now that the House of Lords decision has rendered legislation inevitable, that the legislation should be of such a kind as to clear the whole matter up'. The right course of action was to adopt the recommendation of the Royal Commission on the Income Tax and to transfer to Schedule E all employments which were not already within the scope of that schedule 'so as to have one common basis of assessment for all employees, high or low, public or private, viz: the amount of the emoluments of the year of assessment'.

Matters moved forward accordingly; and there is evidence that the Inland Revenue was very keen that the proposed legislation should reach the statute book safely. The department's notes on one amendment put down for the committee stage of the Finance Bill recorded that 'it would ... leave untouched

the chaotic position as regards the assessment of very large numbers of employees which would, but for the provisions now before Parliament, result from the
decision recently given by the House of Lords' in *Bater*. 'The absolute necessity
to straighten out the tangle as regards the basis of Income Tax assessment in
the case of employees' had been fully explained in other papers prepared by the
department.[59]

The proposed legislation was duly enacted as section 18 of the FA 1922.
Subsection (1) of that section transferred to Schedule E the profits and gains
accruing to any person from an office, employment or pension which were previously chargeable under Schedule D (other than those with a foreign element).
Subsection (3) referred to Rule 7 of the Rules applicable to Schedule E (the desti-
nation in the ITA 1918 of the former section 6 of the ITA 1860) and provided
that that Rule 'shall apply to all offices and employments held under, and
pensions paid by, a railway company'. In this manner, the legislation relating to
the income tax treatment of the earnings of employees, which had been unclear
at the time of the litigation in *Lancashire and Yorkshire Railway* and of the litigation in *Bater*, was finally clarified.

IV. LATER DEVELOPMENTS

A work published in 1927 expressed the view that, following the enactment
of section 18 of the FA 1922, the decision in *Bater* 'is now only of academic
interest'.[60] This view, however, may be contested. The decision in *Bater* had
long-term implications for the detailed wording of the income tax legislation;
for the relative importance of Schedule E among the income tax schedules; and
for the change from the classification of the charge to income tax according to
a number of schedules to a classification according to the nature of the profit
or gain.

In the House of Lords, in *Bater*, Lord Atkinson approved a passage from the
judgment of Rowlatt J,[61] and that passage came to feature, very prominently,
in expositions of income tax law. In *Edwards v Clinch*,[62] Lord Wilberforce
mentioned 'the well known Rowlatt definition of office',[63] and went on to say
that this definition or statement

> was, I dare to say, bred into the bones of every practitioner in income tax matters, and
> more importantly, was known to the legislature, and its drafting agents, on the many
> occasions when revisions of the Schedules were made or considered.[64]

[59] 'Finance Bill 1922: Parliamentary Papers', The National Archives IR 86/102.
[60] RN Carter, *Murray & Carter's Guide to Income-Tax Practice*, 11th edn (London, Gee & Co,
1927) 53.
[61] *Bater* (above n 7) 246. For the passage in question see text before n 45 above.
[62] *Edwards v Clinch* (above n 6).
[63] ibid, 860.
[64] ibid.

The passage in question may be regarded as receiving the ultimate seal of approval in section 5(3) of the Income Tax (Earnings and Pensions) Act 2003, which provided that: 'In the employment income Parts "office" includes in particular any position which has an existence independent of the person who holds it and may be filled by successive holders'. This statutory guidance, which did not appear in previous legislation, may be traced back to the judgment of Rowlatt J in *Bater*.

The crucial importance of *Bater*, however, was that it precipitated a real-location of component parts of the income tax system; and this reallocation manifested itself in two different ways. As far as the income tax schedules were concerned, employments which were formerly charged to income tax under Schedule D were transferred to Schedule E; and the employments so transferred included those subject to the special arrangements for weekly wage earners.[65] The ambit of Schedule E accordingly expanded, while that of Schedule D contracted. The result was to increase the importance of Schedule E relative to the other income tax schedules; and, in time, as Table 2 demonstrates, to give Schedule E an unquestionable ascendancy among the income tax schedules.[66]

Table 2 Actual income of taxpayers estimated in accordance with the provisions of the Income Tax Acts: 1923–24 to 1958–59 (selected years)

Year	Schedule D (£M)	Schedule E (£M)	Total (£M)	Schedule E (as % of total)
1923–24	985	936	2,303	40.6
1928–29	1,065	995	2,494	39.9
1933–34	756	1,271	2,505	50.7
1938–39	1,071	1,757	3,341	52.6
1948–49	2,318	5,901	8,824	66.9
1953–54	3,141	8,495	12,190	69.7
1958–59	4,095	11,957	16,592	72.1

Bater, however, also played a role of the utmost importance in another realloca-tion of component parts of the income tax system. Following the enactment of section 18 of the FA 1922 (and leaving aside foreign income) all income

---

[65] s 18(2), FA 1922.

[66] Sources: for 1923–24 and 1928–29, *Seventy-fourth report of the Commissioners of His Majesty's Inland Revenue for the year ended 31st March 1931* (Cmd 4027, 1932) 76; for 1933–34, *Seventy-ninth report of the Commissioners of His Majesty's Inland Revenue for the year ended 31st March 1936* (Cmd 5297, 1937) 52; for 1938–39, *Ninety-first report of the Commissioners of His Majesty's Inland Revenue for the year ended 31st March 1948* (Cmd 7738, 1949) 25; for 1948–49 and 1953–54, *Ninety-eighth report of the Commissioners of Her Majesty's Inland Revenue for the year ended 31st March 1955* (Cmd 9667, 1956) 40; for 1958–59, *Report of the Commissioners of Her Majesty's Inland Revenue for the year ended 31st March 1964: Hundred and Seventh Report* (Cmnd 2572, 1965) 45.

from offices, employment and pensions was chargeable to income tax under Schedule E – whatever the collection mechanism. The immediate effect of the legislative changes made in the FA 1922 as a result of the decision in *Bater*, it is true, was to give the charge to income tax under Schedule E a composite character. Thus, in the consolidating ITA 1952, the Schedule E charge was set out in section 156. Paragraph 1 of Schedule E reproduced the original Schedule E charge, introduced in 1853; and paragraph 2 reproduced the charge on other offices and employments transferred from Schedule D in 1922. There was, however, a further restatement of the charge to income tax under Schedule E in the FA 1956;[67] and, at this point, the charge to income tax in respect of any office or employment came to depend, essentially, on the nature of the profit or gain and not on the collection mechanism.

At the end of the twentieth century, it was under Schedule E that employment income, pension income and social security income were charged to income tax. The Income Tax (Earnings and Pensions) Act 2003, which restated the income tax provisions previously falling within the ambit of Schedule E and was prepared by the Inland Revenue's Tax Law Rewrite project, was accordingly able to restate those provisions according to the nature of the profit or gain by imposing charges to income tax on employment income, pension income and social security income. References to Schedule E were omitted. Those references harked back to an earlier time in the history of income tax when the classification of income was by reference to the collection mechanism.

---

[67] s 10(1), FA 1956.

6

The Archer-Shee *Cases (1927)*
Trusts, Transparency and Source

MALCOLM GAMMIE

O N 30 JANUARY 1925, Mr Braithwaite and Mr Coke, Commissioners for
the Special Purposes of the Income Tax, met at York House in Kingsway
to hear an appeal by Lieutenant-Colonel Sir Martin Archer-Shee, CMG
DSO, previously (until 1923) Member of Parliament for Finsbury.[1] Sir Martin
was appealing assessments made on him by the Additional Commissioners of
Income Tax for the Division of St James for the two years ending 5 April 1925.
The assessments were in significant amounts for the time – estimated at £12,000
apiece.

Sir Martin was the son of Martin Archer-Shee and his wife Elizabeth, née
Pell of New York, and the great grandson of Sir Martin Archer-Shee, President of the Royal Academy of Arts from 1830 until his death in 1850.[2] The
wealth giving rise to the assessments, however, was not his but his wife's,[3]

---

[1] And so commenced a course of litigation that would end on 15 December 1930 after four hearings before the Commissioners, four in the High Court and three in the Court of Appeal, two of
which then went to the House of Lords. The *Archer-Shee* cases comprise *Archer-Shee v Baker* [1927]
AC 844, 11 TC 749 (*Baker*); *Archer-Shee v Baker (No 2)* (1928) 15 TC 1 (*Baker No 2*) and *Garland
v Archer-Shee* [1931] AC 212, 15 TC 693 (*Garland*). The Official and Tax Case reports differ slightly
in their language, to which attention will be drawn as appropriate. Otherwise, specific citations are
taken from the Official Report (save in the case of *Baker (No 2)* which is only reported in Tax Cases).
The chapter describes the course of this litigation and explains the House of Lords decisions in
Baker and *Garland* in the light of the charge to income tax at the time. It does not attempt to trace
the subsequent legal controversy or income tax history of those decisions.

[2] Sir Martin's half-brother was George Archer-Shee who, as a Royal Navy cadet, was accused
of theft but was successfully defended in the High Court by Sir Edward Carson and acquitted. His
case provides the basis for Terence Ratigan's play, *The Winslow Boy*. George was killed, aged 19, at
the first battle of Ypres on 31 October 1914 (See M De-la-Noy, 'Shee, George Archer- (1895–1914)',
literary prototype' in *Oxford Dictionary of National Biography* (Oxford, Oxford University Press,
2014)).

[3] A married woman was an 'incapacitated person', together with infants, lunatics, idiots and
insane persons (s 237, ITA 1918). Such persons, if incapable of making a return, were assessed and
charged in the name of their trustee, guardian, tutor, curator or committee having control of their

Lady Frances Archer-Shee, also née Pell. Lady Frances' parents were Alfred and Mary Pell. Alfred was the son of Alfred Shipley Pell and an earlier Elizabeth Pell. Mary Pell's sister, also named Frances, was the wife of John Pierpont Morgan. Alfred Shipley Pell, however, had evidently first been married to Eliza Pell. Eliza was the mother of the younger Elizabeth (Sir Martin's mother). Thus, it appears that Sir Martin and his wife, Frances, shared a common grandparent, Alfred Shipley Pell. His mother, Elizabeth, was the half-sister of her father, Alfred.

Alfred Pell died in 1901 and his wife, Mary Huntington Pell (as appears from the terms of the will, not Frances' mother),[4] died in 1904. Sir Martin and Frances married in 1905.[5] Under Alfred's will Frances had received certain land in New Brunswick and her father's yacht, the 'Pelican', to enjoy. Under the trust created by the will, however, she became entitled following Mary's death to the income of her father's residuary estate during her life. The trust was governed by New York law and the trust assets comprised foreign shares, foreign government securities and other foreign property.[6] In the years in issue, the trustee, a New York trust corporation, had credited the net income to her bank account in New York, while retaining sufficient to meet its expenses and US tax liabilities.[7]

Prior to the FA 1914, income from foreign possessions was only taxed to the extent that it was received in the United Kingdom (known as the 'remittance basis'). Section 5 of that Act, however, provided that income from securities, stock, shares or rents in any place out of the United Kingdom should be taxed as it arose and not as it was remitted to the United Kingdom.[8] The income of other

property. The rules of assessment, however, were substantially modified as regards married women. Rule 16 of the General Rules applicable to all Schedules provided that, 'a married woman acting as a sole trader, or being entitled to any property or profits to her separate use, shall be assessable and chargeable to tax as if she were sole and unmarried'. This was immediately qualified, however, by Proviso (1) which stated that, 'the profits of a married woman living with her husband shall be deemed the profits of the husband, and shall be assessed and charged in his name, and not in her name or the name of her trustee'.

[4] Lady Frances' mother (Mary Kirkland Tracey) may have died as early as 1882 when Frances was only four years old; see www.susandoreydesigns.com/genealogy/clirehugh/AncestryOfJohnPellArcher-Shee.pdf.

[5] Franklin D Roosevelt and Eleanor Roosevelt as well as the bride's uncle, JP Morgan, evidently attended the wedding at Pellwood, Highland Falls, NY; see above (n 5).

[6] Referred to hereafter as 'securities'. A list of the securities in question (so far as the trustee's investments were known to Sir Martin) can be found in *Baker (No 2)* (above n 1) 4–5.

[7] The evidence recorded in *Garland*, however, indicates that the trustees deducted administration expenses and a 1% commission but not US income tax. That was paid by Lady Archer-Shee or JP Morgan & Co (as the bank to which payments were made) on her behalf (see 15 TC 693, 708). It is unclear whether this only relates to the later years in dispute in *Garland* or also to the earlier years with which *Baker* was concerned.

[8] Schedule D Case IV charged tax 'in respect of income arising from securities out of the United Kingdom' and Case V charged tax 'in respect of income arising from possessions out of the United Kingdom'. In 1923/24 and 1924/25 all Case IV income was 'to be computed on the full amount thereof arising in the year of assessment, whether the income has been or will be received in the United Kingdom or not' (ITA 1918, sch 1, Rules applicable to Schedule D Case IV, rule 1 (DIV Rule 1)). Income 'arising from stocks, shares or rents in any place out of the United Kingdom shall be computed on the full amount thereof on an average of the three preceding years, as directed

foreign possessions, however, continued to be taxed on a remittance basis only. Accordingly, Mr Maugham KC argued on Sir Martin's behalf that Lady Frances' interest in her father's trust amounted to the right under New York law to have the trusts duly administered and that this was a foreign possession chargeable under Case V of Schedule D only on remittance.[9] The Special Commissioners disagreed. They decided that the income was Lady Frances' income and assessable on Sir Martin. They confirmed the assessments, subject to final determination of the precise figure of income.

I. THE INITIAL STAGES OF APPEAL

A. The High Court

On appeal to the High Court, Mr Justice Rowlatt did not disagree with the description that had been given of Lady Frances' rights as beneficiary. As he noted,[10] she did not own the securities and she was not entitled specifically to the income that arose to the trust from them. He acknowledged that her entitlement was to call upon the trustee, and, if necessary, to compel it, to administer the fund during her life so as to give her the income of the fund according to the terms of the trust.[11] Nevertheless, he accepted the Revenue's view that for income tax purposes, she did not need to own the securities in question; it sufficed that she in fact received the income of the trust fund. As it was put for the Revenue: 'she has the income from the stocks and shares *de facto*'.[12] He concluded:[13]

> It seems to me that I must adopt that latter view. Without in the least impugning the correctness of Mr Maugham's description of the position of the appellant's wife from a legal point of view, for the purposes of classifications in the Income Tax Act, 1918, I must adopt the view that she has income from the stocks and shares constituting the trust fund. I do not think I can possibly hold otherwise having regard to the decision in the House of Lords in the case of *Williams v Singer (No 2)*.[14]

in Case I, whether the income has been or will be received in the United Kingdom or not' (ITA 1918, sch 1, Rules applicable to Schedule D Case V, rule 1 (DV Rule 1)). Case V income other than stock, shares or rents, 'shall be computed on the full amount of the actual sums annually received in the United Kingdom from remittances payable in the United Kingdom' (ITA 1918, Rules applicable to Schedule D Case V, rule 2 (DV Rule 2)).

[9] ie, not being income arising from stocks, shares or rents and therefore within DV Rule 2.

[10] *Baker* (above n 1) [1927] 1 KB 109, 116; 11 TC 749, 753–54.

[11] Rowlatt J's view of the nature of Lady Archer-Shee's rights as a beneficiary under the trust was approved by Sargant LJ in the Court of Appeal: ibid, [1927] 1 KB 109, 128; 11 TC 749, 763.

[12] Or as the official report puts it, 'it is sufficient if she in fact receives the income from the stocks and shares constituting the trust fund', ibid, 116–17. As Lord Wrenbury would point out in the House of Lords, her receipt of the income was a matter of fact, but what mattered was her entitlement to be paid the income as a matter of law: ibid, [1927] AC 844, 865; 11 TC 749, 778–79.

[13] ibid, [1927] 1 KB 109, 117; 11 TC 749.

[14] *Williams v Singer (No 2)* [1920] 36 TLR 661, 7 TC 387; see below.

B. The Court of Appeal

Sir Martin duly appealed to the Court of Appeal, which found in his favour. Mr Maugham was not even called upon to reply to the Revenue's counsel. Lord Hanworth MR made much of the fact that what Lady Frances received from the trustee (and, in his view, all she was entitled to receive) was a net sum of money – which had 'lost its origin or parentage' in the securities – representing the balance remaining after payment of the trust expenses.[15] In contrast to Rowlatt J, who had followed the House of Lords decision in *Williams v Singer*, Lord Hanworth drew upon the House of Lords decision in *Lord Sudeley v AG*[16] to conclude that Lady Frances was only entitled to any payment once the trustee had ascertained the balance that should be paid to her.[17] She could not demand that the income be paid to her *in specie* and was only entitled to the balance of the income when ascertained. That balance could not be described as income from securities: it was instead income from a foreign possession, namely her rights under the New York trust.

II. A SUBTLE SHIFT IN EMPHASIS

A summary of the main argument advanced by the Revenue in the High Court and Court of Appeal can be found in the Law Reports, as follows:

> Where there is a trust fund composed of foreign stocks and shares someone must receive the interest and dividends arising therefrom. In the case of a trust there are only two persons who can receive them – namely, the trustee or the *cestui que trust*. If the trustees were resident in this country and the beneficiary resident abroad the trustees would not be chargeable with income tax in respect of dividends not remitted to this country: see *Williams v Singer*. The House of Lords there negatived the contention that the revenue authorities were not entitled to look beyond the legal ownership of the fund, and laid down the proposition that *the person to be charged with the tax is neither the trustee nor the beneficiary as such, but the person in actual receipt and control of the income which is sought to reach.* If the beneficiary receives the profits he is liable to be assessed upon them.[18]

---

[15] See *Baker* (above n 1) [1927] 1 KB 109, 120; 11 TC 749, 757. Lord Atkinson in the House of Lords professed himself unable to understand this part of Lord Hanworth's judgment. In particular, he did not see how it mattered that the trustee paid the dividend cheques (which were presumably in its name) into its bank account and retained part on account of its expenses. It was no different from paying the cheques into Lady Archer-Shee's account and leaving her to meet the expenses; see [1927] AC 844, 860–61; 11 TC 749, 775.

[16] *Lord Sudeley v AG* [1897] AC 11. Sargant LJ was also of the view that the general reasoning in *Sudeley* was 'precisely applicable'; *Baker* (above n 1) [1927] 1 KB 109, 128; 11 TC 749, 763. Viscount Sumner in the House of Lords thought that that this was correct ([1927] AC 844, 856; 11 TC 774, 771). Both Viscount Sumner and Lord Blanesburgh relied on *Sudeley* in their dissenting speeches. For further consideration of this case, see below.

[17] ibid, [1927] 1 KB 109, 121; 11 TC 774, 758.

[18] ibid, [1927] 1 KB 109, 114 (emphasis added). This extract is the argument put to Rowlatt J in the High Court and was effectively repeated in the Court of Appeal, see ibid, 118.

As appears, emphasis was laid on the fact that Lady Frances was the person in actual receipt of the income in question and this derives from the decision in *Williams v Singer*.[19] The income in that case was dividends on shares in the Singer Manufacturing Company of New Jersey. The shares were held by UK resident trustees, but the dividends were paid direct to the Princesse de Polignac, the income beneficiary under the trust, who was resident in France. The Singer dividends were credited direct to the beneficiary's bank account in New York. The Revenue nevertheless sought to assess the trustees in respect of the income on the basis that, as legal owners, they were the persons entitled to the dividends and therefore liable to be assessed in respect of them. If that argument had been successful, it would have had the effect of imposing UK income tax on the foreign income of a foreign beneficiary.[20]

The House of Lords had little difficulty in rejecting this proposition. As Viscount Cave put the matter:[21]

> My Lords, I think it clear that such a proposition cannot be maintained. It is contrary to the express words of Section 42 of the Income Tax Act, 1842, which provides that no trustees who shall have authorised the receipt of the profits arising from trust property by the person entitled thereto, and who shall have made a return of the name and residence of such person in manner required by the Act, shall be required to do any other act for the purpose of assessing such person.[22]

Nevertheless, the Income Tax Act 1842 (ITA 1842) explicitly recognised that a trustee could be assessed to tax and, in relation to foreign income, section 108 of the Act provided that a trustee in receipt of the same could be charged to tax on any profits or gains arising from foreign possessions or securities. Even apart from specific provision, Viscount Cave was

> not prepared to deny that there are many cases in which a trustee in receipt of trust income may be chargeable with the tax upon such income ... The fact is that, if the Income Tax Acts are examined, it will be found that the person charged with tax is neither the trustee nor the beneficiary as such, but *the person in actual receipt and control of the income which it is sought to reach.*[23]

It was these final words that found their way into the Revenue's argument in the High Court and Court of Appeal in *Baker*. Some care is necessary in this field, however, to distinguish two aspects of the matter, which become apparent from the more precise statement of the position in *Williams v Singer* by Lord Wrenbury. Lord Wrenbury (who was to deliver the main speech for the majority in *Baker*) noted that the ITA 1842 drew a distinction between

[19] *Williams v Singer and Others; Pool v Royal Exchange Assurance* [1921] 1 AC 65, 7 TC 387. For the interesting history of the *Singer* litigation, see D Parrot and JF Avery Jones, 'Seven Appeals and an Acquittal: The Singer Family and their Tax Cases' [2008] *BTR* 56.
[20] ibid, 71 (Viscount Cave).
[21] ibid, 411.
[22] s 76(1), Taxes Management Act 1970.
[23] *Williams v Singer* (above n 19) 72 (emphasis added).

two things, as he put it, 'the property chargeable is one thing, the person liable to be charged is another.'[24]

This appears from the charge to tax under Schedule D to the Income Tax Act 1918 (ITA 1918). The charge under paragraph 1(a)(i) fell upon the annual profits or gains arising to any resident person from any kind of property, whether situate in the United Kingdom or elsewhere. By contrast, under paragraph 1(a)(iii), the charge fell upon any property whatever in the United Kingdom, irrespective of the residence of the person to whom it arose. In other words, in the first case it was necessary to identify both the property and the person charged; in the second it was only necessary to identify the property.

The essential point is that in both cases the Act charges to tax income from particular property but, in the case of foreign property, only when it arises to a resident person. The income of foreign property (ie, foreign source income) is not charged to tax if it arises to a non-resident. Thus, a UK resident recipient of foreign income (such as a trustee) is not liable to tax if the income belongs to a non-resident beneficiary. In the second case, however, the person assessed to tax need not be the person entitled to the income because the income, being the income of UK property (ie, UK source income), is charged to tax in any event.

In the majority of cases, the person to whom income arises and the person who is assessable in respect of it will be one and the same. However, that need not necessarily be the case, particularly where trustees are involved. Thus, in *Williams v Singer*, the person to whom the income was treated as arising (the foreign beneficiary) was not the same as the person (the trustees) who could be said to be a person entitled (as the legal owner) to receive the same. But the charge to tax on foreign income required that the person to whom it arose should be resident in the United Kingdom. The ability to identify the trustee as a person legally entitled to receive the foreign income counted for nothing where the income itself was not charged to tax because it was the foreign income of a foreign beneficiary.

Equally, the fact that the non-resident trustee in *Baker* was in receipt of the foreign income did not mean that the income escaped the charge to UK income tax, if the person in fact entitled to it – the person to whom it arose for UK income tax purposes – was UK resident. As appears from the extract above, in the High Court and Court of Appeal, the Revenue's counsel appears to have emphasised who actually received and controlled the income. Rowlatt J may not have been misled but the Court of Appeal had responded that what Lady Frances received was not the securities' income in question – as had been the case for the Princesse de Polignac in *Williams v Singer* – but a distribution of income out of the trust funds by the US trustee net of its expenses and US tax. An argument based on 'receipt and control' therefore looked rather unpromising because it failed adequately to distinguish what income was charged to tax and who might be assessed to tax in respect of it.

---

[24] ibid, 71.

III. IN THE HOUSE OF LORDS

Accordingly, in the House of Lords, there was a subtle change of emphasis in the Revenue's argument. The Revenue's counsel focused instead on the nature of Lady Frances' *entitlement* to the income, and not just the fact of receipt, on the assumption (in the absence of evidence to the contrary) that New York law was the same as English law. This appears from the Revenue's written case and also from the summary in the Law Reports of Revenue counsel's argument.[25] The written case makes the point that the income belonged to Lady Frances as the person beneficially entitled to the income, as was the case in *Williams v Singer*. The fact that the income was legally vested in the trustee and initially received by it was therefore irrelevant, save to the extent that the trustee might as a result be assessable on behalf of the person beneficially entitled to the income. In this respect, it was said that Rowlatt J's reasoning by reference to *Williams v Singer* was entirely correct. In particular, as the Attorney General, Sir Douglas Hogg KC, evidently said for the Revenue in argument, reflecting Rowlatt J's view below,[26] '*A trust fund as such is not a source of income and is not chargeable to tax; the constituent elements of the fund must be looked at*'. In other words, what is charged to tax is the income from securities, provided – in the case of foreign securities – that the income belongs to a UK resident person.

Against that argument, Sir Martin's written case noted that since the ITA 1842, so far as foreign income was paid *in formâ specificâ* to a beneficiary in the United Kingdom, it was taxed as income from securities, usually at source through deduction by the paying agent. If, on the other hand, it was not paid *in formâ specificâ*, it represented income from a foreign possession. This, then, was what distinguished Lady Frances' case from the Princesse de Polignac's case. Income not paid *in formâ specificâ* would be included in a return of the net amount of income received in the UK from the trust estate. It was only treated as part of the beneficiary's income if the beneficiary was in possession of the specific income or able under the trust to require the trustee to transfer the securities to him or her. The point made in the written case and in oral argument was that Lady Frances' only right was to have the trusts duly administered according to the law of New York and, on that basis, she was only entitled under that law to receive such net income as she in fact received. She was not, and never

---

[25] *Baker* (above n 1) [1927] AC 844, 845. The pace at which the appeals progressed was remarkable by current standards: the case was stated by the Commissioners on 28 October 1925, heard by the High Court on 26 February and 1 March 1926, by the Court of Appeal on 19 and 20 May 1926 and by the House of Lords on 14, 15 and 17 February 1927, which gave its decision on 26 July 1927. The decision in *Swift v HMRC* [2010] UKFTT 88 (TC) (which concerned similar issues relating to a Delaware limited liability company) was given on 22 February 2010. The case was finally disposed of by the Supreme Court on 1 July 2015 (*Anson v HMRC* [2015] UKSC 44).

[26] 'Trustees, it seems to me, drop out for the purposes of discussing *the liability*', ie, the charge to tax in contrast to assessment; see *Baker* (above n 1) [1927] 1 KB 109, 118; 11 TC 744, 755 (emphasis added).

had been, entitled to call for the transfer of any securities or for payment of the income on any specific security comprised in the trust fund.

The House of Lords found for the Revenue by a bare majority. Lord Wrenbury (with whom Lord Atkinson and Lord Carson agreed) began by considering the scope of the charge to tax under Schedule D and noted that the question was whether the sums that Lady Archer-Shee received were income from a foreign possession. He continued:

> In this state of facts Lady Archer-Shee's interest under her father's will is beyond all question 'property'. The question for determination is what is the nature of that property ...?
>
> ... The will is an American will. The law of America is in an English Court question of fact. In the Case stated by the Commissioners there is no finding as to what is the American law ... The members of the Court of Appeal ... founded themselves upon the statement that there is paid over to Lady Archer-Shee's account only such part of the sums which the trustees have received from the funds as they considered to be income. My Lords, the question is not what the trustees have thought proper to hand over and have handed over (which is a question of fact) but what under the will Lady Archer-Shee *is entitled to* (which is a question of law) ... Under Mr Pell's will Lady Archer-Shee (if American law is the same as English law) is, in my opinion, as matter of construction of the will, *entitled in equity specifically during her life to the dividends upon the stocks.*[27]

> If the estate had not been fully administered I could well understand a contention that the right to whatever in administration might turn out to be the fund, the subject of this gift was a 'foreign possession', and fell under Case V, Rule 2. But that is not the case. I have to read the will and see what is Lady Archer-Shee's right of property in certain ascertained securities, stocks and shares now held by the trust company 'to the use of my said daughter'. It is, I think, if the law of America is the same as our law, *an equitable right in possession to receive during her life the proceeds of the shares and stocks of which she is tenant for life.* Her right is not to a balance sum, but to the dividends subject to deductions as above mentioned. Her right under the will is 'property' from which income is derived.[28]

For his part Lord Blanesburgh (dissenting) pointed out that Lady Archer-Shee had no interest in the corpus of the trust fund. Thus,

> the payments made to Lady Archer-Shee were payments of all that remained of a fund of miscellaneous income receipts after there had been paid or retained thereout

---

[27] ibid, [1927] AC 865–66 (emphasis added).

[28] It is this final sentence that creates a certain confusion. It suggests that the source of Lady Archer-Shee's income is her right under the will trust and not the underlying securities. A beneficiary's rights under the will trust, as a foreign possession within DV Rule 2 of Case V (above n 8), might be the source of the beneficiary's income but one that can then only lead to taxation on the remittance basis. Lady Archer-Shee's rights under the will trust, however, were what entitled her to the trust income and therefore rendered her husband liable to assessment on an arising basis by reference to the true source of the income charged to tax in that case: the underlying foreign securities.

sums deemed by the trustees to be sufficient to discharge the trust and other outgo-
ings that had first to be provided for. The payments represented, in other words, the
actual net residuary income available for the tenant for life ascertained and only
ascertained after payment or provision had been made of or for all prior claims
against the gross residuary receipts. The income the lady received was the net
income of a totality, not of particular items of property ... Lady Archer-Shee had
no right ... to demand more than she received or to demand any of it at any earlier
date than she received it ... until the moneys paid to her were actually paid over, she
had neither property in them nor right to receive them. The proper result of any
account taken would have shown ... that the liability of the trustees to pay, and in
the precise amounts, accrued only at the respective times at which the payments were
actually made.[29]

In their dissenting speeches, both Lord Blanesburgh and Viscount Sumner were
at pains to point out what they saw as the difficulties that would arise in apportioning the income of a fund in a case in which there was more than one life
tenant. The majority, however, were unconvinced.

IV. SUBSEQUENT CONTROVERSY

The nature of a beneficiary's interest under a trust is a controversial issue for
equity lawyers.[30] At law, a beneficiary's rights went unacknowledged and the
trustee was regarded as the sole owner of trust property. In equity, a beneficiary initially had rights *in personam* against the trustee, entitling him to
compel the proper administration of the trust according to its terms. Over
time, however, the influence of equity predominated to ensure that a beneficiary's rights were good against allcomers except the *bona fide* purchaser for
value of the legal estate/legal interest without notice of the trust and anyone
claiming the property through such a purchaser. It was this development that
led to equitable rights being characterised as akin to rights *in rem* or rights to
property.[31]

Snell's Equity offers an up-to-date view of a beneficiary's interest under a
trust:

[T]he beneficiary's interest does not give him beneficial rights directly enforceable
against the property itself. His beneficial rights derive from the trustee who owns the

---

[29] *Baker* (above n 1) [1927] AC 844, 873.

[30] For the debate whether the interest of a trust beneficiary is essentially a personal or a proprietary right, see FW Maitland, *Equity*, 2nd edn (Cambridge, Cambridge University Press, 1936)
chs 9, 11; AW Scott, 'The Nature of the Rights of the "Cestui que trust"' (1917) 17 *Columbia Law
Review* 269; HG Hanbury, 'The Field of Modern Equity' (1929) 45 *LQR* 199; and the other sources
cited in J McGhee (ed), *Snell's Equity*, 33rd edn (London, Sweet & Maxwell, 2017) ch 2, para 2-002,
fn 5.

[31] See, eg, G Thomas and A Hudson, *The Law of Trusts*, 2nd edn (Oxford, Oxford University
Press, 2010) ch 7: 'The Nature of a Beneficiary's Interest'.

property and they are primarily enforceable against him. But it does not follow that the beneficiary is no more than a creditor against the trustee with standing to enforce a chose in action against him. The beneficiary's right also has a proprietary character that entitles him to protect the property from wrongful interference by third parties. Any attempt to explain the beneficiary's interest solely as a personal right against the trustee or solely as a proprietorial interest enforceable against third parties fails to do justice to all the features of the interest. It does not lend itself to simplistic reduction into just one kind of right.[32]

For the editor of the *Law Quarterly Review* at the time, the House of Lords decision in *Baker* was close to heresy. In first reporting the House of Lords decision, he noted that, 'if there were ... a higher tribunal the counsel for the unsuccessful respondent in *Baker v Archer-Shee* ... could, with propriety, advise his client that a further appeal might prove successful'.[33] A subsequent contributor to the *LQR*, HG Hanbury, expressed his view more forcefully still, in explaining the significance of the distinction between rights *in personam* and rights *in rem* in following terms:

> A student beginning the study of equity cannot be better than to soak himself in the incomparable book written on the subject by Professor Maitland. That very learned author, even at the risk of monotony, pronounces and reiterates the root principle that equitable rights and interests are not *iura in rem*. They much resemble these, but the dividing line appears at once in the recollection of the bone fide purchaser for value of the legal estate. Of course the distinction is only necessary for the lawyer; the layman finds it naturally convenient enough to regard the *cestui que trust* as an absolute owner and to stigmatize as pedantic and, if the word may be used in the connexion, slightly 'priggish', the insistence of a lawyer, with Maitland, on the undoubted character of the *cestui que trust's* interest as a mere *ius in personam*. Now nobody relishes the imputation of 'priggishness', so the lawyer is ready enough to adopt lay phraseology, and to talk loosely of 'equitable ownership.' The utter chaos which would result, if it were really true, that equity regarded A as owner, while law so regarded B, he well knows, but in nine cases out of ten this looseness of language produces no ill effects. But unfortunately there always arises the periodical tenth case, where looseness of thinking may lead to a decision round which criticisms subsequently rage and will not be checked.[34]

Baker, according to Hanbury, was one of those periodical tenth cases.

---

[32] McGhee (above n 30) ch 2, para 2-002. See also DWM Waters, 'The Nature of the Trust Beneficiary's Interest' [1967] *Canadian Bar Review* 219; B Macfarlane and R Stevens, 'The Nature of Equitable Property' (2010) 4 *Journal of Equity* 1; T Cutts, 'The Nature of Equitable Property: A Functional Analysis' (2012) 6 *Journal of Equity* 44.

[33] AJ Goodhart (ed), 'Notes' (1928) XLIV *LQR* 8. The comment was based on an address given by Lord Justice Atkin to the Cambridge University Law Society in 1926, when he had noted that some 33% of appeals from the Court of Appeal to the House of Lords were successful and suggested that a similar proportion of appeals might be expected to succeed if there were an appeal from the House of Lords to some higher tribunal. The editor's comment was prescient in the light of the outcome of *Garland v Archer-Shee*.

[34] HG Hanbury, 'A Periodical Menace to Equitable Principles' (1928) XLIV *LQR* 468.

Hanbury shared the minority's view of the matter and concluded that, 'It is to be fervently hoped that the decision in *Baker v Archer-Shee* will be confined within narrow limits [of income tax law], and not allowed to upset well-established principles of equity'.[35]

He need not have been concerned but the controversy – or confusion – surrounding the *Baker* decision still has more recent echoes. In writing on *The Legal Nature of the Unit Trust*, Kam Fan Sin analysed *Baker* and noted that:

> Despite the number of post-*Baker* cases, there is still no consensus on the *ratio decidendi* of *Baker*. To those dissatisfied with *Baker's* doctrinal position, it is best to be considered as a case explicable of no more than a tax law principle, or to be applicable only when there is only one beneficiary. A broader interpretation is to see the life tenant in *Baker* as having a proprietary interest in the trust assets that generated the income paid into her account by the trustee.[36]

The simple answer to this is that *Baker* was illustrating an important principle of income tax law: that what the Act charges to tax is income and the income must have a source in terms of the property or activities from which the income is derived and by reference to which it is charged to tax. The person and the rights that he or she has in the income are important to the process of assessment. The confusion surrounding the case arises from the fact that the trust property is vested in trustees.

Thus, from the trust law perspective one might anticipate that income from foreign securities held in trust is *not* charged to tax where the securities are held by non-resident trustees and they are therefore entitled to the income as it arises or accrues. From the beneficiary's perspective they are only entitled to that income if their rights under the foreign trust entitle them to receive it: but in that case it might be thought that the source is not the underlying trust property but the foreign possession, ie, their rights under the foreign trust. On the other hand, from a UK income tax perspective, the income arising on the underlying foreign securities is charged to tax if an assessment can be raised on a UK resident person as the person entitled to the income. In other words, the fact of assessment on a UK resident person answers the question whether the foreign income is charged to tax.

The point here lies in the fact that, from a UK income tax perspective, the immediate entitlement of a life tenant to the income of a UK trust renders the trust transparent because it allows one to look to the underlying property of the trust for the purposes of assessment. That will also be true where foreign trust law is to the same effect. The effect is that the trust disappears as a source of the income in question. How did UK income tax law reach that result?

---

[35] ibid, 472.
[36] KF Sin, *The Legal Nature of the Unit Trust* (Oxford, Clarendon Press, 1997) ch 5, 276.

V. THE TRANSPARENT NATURE OF TRUST
INTERESTS FOR INCOME TAX[37]

A. Income Producing Property and Participatory Rights in Income

The ITA 1842 contained an implicit distinction between:

1) Property or activities that are 'income producing' – classified by Schedule and Case.
2) Rights (incorporeal property not within any Schedule or Case) representing an entitlement to income within 1).

What the Act charged to tax was the income from the property or activities within 1). The property or activities were 'the source' of the income they produced and served to identify the income that the Act charged to tax. Thus, what was charged to tax was the income from particular income producing property or activities within 1) and not a person's right to participate or share in that income within 2). This was a function of Addington's original scheme to collect income tax as close to the source as possible, ideally by way of deduction by the payer at the source where what was paid was immediately recognisable as taxable income, and otherwise by way of assessment on the person in whose hands the income first emerged. The Act was not necessarily concerned with whose income it was, in the sense of who ultimately had beneficial enjoyment of the income.[38]

It followed from this approach that certain species of incorporeal property were not regarded as a source of income within the Act; merely the right to participate in or enjoy income derived from particular income-producing sources. These participatory rights fell into three main categories: trust interests, partnership interests and company shares.[39] Most obviously, in the case of a partnership, the source was the partnership trade and it was the profits of the trade that the Act charged to tax. The partner's interest provided the basis for a partner's liability to assessment on what was charged under Schedule D. The partner's interest was not a separate source of income: it was merely the partner's entitlement to share in the underlying income generated by the partnership's

---

[37] For an extended analysis of the issues, see M Gammie, 'The Origins of Fiscal Transparency in UK Income Tax' in J Tiley (ed), *Studies in the History of Tax Law: Volume 4* (Oxford, Hart Publishing, 2010).

[38] Most obviously this was the case for interest, annuities and other annual payments where tax was charged on the income of the fund out of which such payments were made, and the person assessable in respect of that income was the owner of that fund (whether in his own right or as trustee) and the person obliged to pay the interest, annuity or other annual payment. Usually the payment was made under deduction of tax, with no separate assessment to income tax on the recipient and where the payment was made from a taxed fund, the payer was entitled to retain the income tax deducted to offset against his own liability on the taxed fund.

[39] A possible fourth category would be rights under a policy of life insurance.

activities and assets.[40] In contrast to the partnership case, a payment from an underlying fund of income-producing property – such as a trust fund – might itself be characterised as income in the form of an annuity or other annual payment. Nevertheless, the prior question was, who could properly be assessed on the income arising on the underlying property within the trust fund?

B. *Baker* Explained

This simple perspective of a charge to tax imposed on the income produced by particular property (the source) and the identification of the person who can be assessed in respect of it by reference to their receipt of or right to participate in the income, becomes potentially more complicated once it becomes necessary to identify the income charged to tax not solely by reference to its source (as in the case of UK property) but also by reference to the person entitled to it (as became the case for income from foreign property). The complication, however, is easily solved by reference to who can be assessed in respect of the income: if a UK resident can be assessed on the foreign income, the question answers itself.

Thus, from a UK income tax perspective, the straightforward question raised in *Baker* can be seen to be whether Lady Archer-Shee (through her husband) could be assessed on income from securities that was plainly the subject matter of charge on the basis that Sir Martin was a person properly assessed in respect of it as the person entitled (through his wife) to the income. This explains the change in emphasis in the Revenue's argument between the Court of Appeal and the House of Lords. The trustee, as a person in actual receipt of the foreign income and being non-resident, could not be assessed. Furthermore, the trustee received the income because it was the legal owner of the property from which the income arose. Lady Archer-Shee's entitlement to the income, however viewed, could only arise from a foreign possession (her rights as beneficiary under a US trust) and not directly from the securities. From a UK income tax perspective, however, what was opaque as a matter of charge – the income from securities held by the trustee – could still became transparent as a matter of assessment. The only question was whether she could be said to be entitled to the income from the underlying securities so as to sustain the assessment that had been made in respect of that income.

The question posed by the ITA 1918 was whether the person sought to be assessed was entitled to the income that was the subject matter of charge. The answer to that question is not necessarily supplied by analysing the nature of the person's entitlement to the *property* from which the income derives.

---

[40] See Vinelott J's description of the three stages of partnership computation and assessment in *MacKinlay v Arthur Young McClelland Moores & Co* [1986] 1 WLR 1468, 1474–75, approved by the House of Lords [1990] 2 AC 239, 249 (Lord Oliver).

The property (as the source of the income) identifies the income with a particular Schedule or Case. The Act identified income from foreign securities (as the source) with Schedule D Case IV and based on an English law analysis (in the absence of evidence of New York law), the question was whether Lady Archer-Shee's entitlement to that *income* supported the assessment, even though her entitlement only arose from her ability to call upon the trustee to account to her for the trust income and not from an analysis of her property right in the underlying securities.

At the heart of this distinction between the nature of Lady Archer-Shee's interest in the underlying property and her right to call upon the trustee to account to her for the trust income (or, in other words, to perform the trust), is the unresolved debate as to the nature of a beneficiary's interest in a trust: is it a right *in personam* or a right *in rem*? For income tax purposes, however, the distinction is irrelevant. The majority in the House of Lords was in essence deciding that the *in rem/in personam* debate amongst equity lawyers was unimportant for income tax purposes, even though it might be of a fundamental matter for probate, inheritance or other property tax purposes. Lady Archer-Shee could have an *in rem* interest in the trust assets or she could have an *in personam* right against the trustees; either way, it was her income. The importance of the underlying securities (whatever the nature of her interest (if any) in them) was to identify that income as something that the Act charged to tax for the purposes of assessment under a particular Schedule and Case; the importance of her rights under the foreign trust was to identify her entitlement to that income for the purposes of its assessment; her residence in the United Kingdom ensured that the income was indeed charged to tax.

VI. THE AFTERMATH OF *BAKER*

A. Evidence of New York Trust Law

Following its decision, the House of Lords reversed the decision of the Court of Appeal, set aside the decision of Rowlatt J and remitted the matter to the Special Commissioners to restate their case. They were ordered to set out details of the trust assets in question and, in particular, whether they fell within DIV Rule 1, DV Rule 1 or DV Rule 2, to determine the correct basis on which the income from the underlying investments was to be assessed.[41] Only those within DV Rule 2 would be taxed on a remittance basis.

---

[41] It appears from the second Court of Appeal hearing that until the House of Lords made this order, there had been an agreement between Sir Martin and the Commissioners that Sir Martin would be taxed under DIV Rule 1 on the sums actually paid to his wife in the years in question, ie, on the amount actually arising in the year of assessment, rather than, for example, on a three-year average applicable to income from stocks, shares or rents; see *Baker (No 2)* (above n 1) 8 (Lord Hanworth MR)

The Special Commissioners duly complied but, at the reconvened hearing, Sir Martin sought to produce evidence of New York law to the effect that all the income of Lady Frances from the trust fund should be treated as derived from possessions out of the United Kingdom.[42] This stratagem could not have been anticipated by the House of Lords but, nevertheless, had some justification in the order the House had made: if the aim was to identify the correct head of charge under Schedule D, why should Sir Martin not be entitled to produce evidence to show that it was in fact income within DV Rule 2 because that was the effect of New York law?

Messrs Braithwaite and Coke, however, were having none of it and confirmed the assessments based on the list of investments with which they had been provided. Rowlatt J likewise confirmed the assessments and suggested that Sir Martin should refer the matter to the House of Lords if he felt that the Commissioners had not done what they had been ordered to do. Sir Martin appealed to the Court of Appeal. His ground of appeal was that the Commissioners should have heard evidence of New York law because they could only determine accurately the Schedule and Case and Rule under which income on the investments was charged if they did so. Lord Justice Greer was prepared to admit the evidence but Lord Hanworth and Lord Justice Russell refused to do so. Their decision was given on 8 November 1928 and by that time fresh appeals in respect of later years were already underway, having been heard by the Special Commissioners on 27 July 1928 for the three years ending 5 April 1928: *Garland*[43] had started its journey to the House of Lords.

B. *Garland*

The Special Commissioners in *Garland* – Mr Braithwaite again, but now joined by Mr Jacob – heard evidence of New York law and concluded that the evidence showed

> that differences exist in several important respects between the English and American law of trusts, differences which, it seems very likely, would, if they had been before the Court, have been enough to turn Lord Wrenbury (who assumed there were no differences) and Lord Atkinson, over to the side of the Appellant in the previous appeal.[44]

and above n 8. It may be that this agreement was the reason why the Revenue accepted throughout that the amounts retained by the trustee for administration expenses should be allowed to be deducted. DIV Rule 1 and DV Rule 1 permitted a deduction for any foreign income tax paid in respect income charged on an arising basis (and see above n 8).

[42] *Baker (No 2)* (above n 1).

[43] *Garland* (above n 1).

[44] ibid, 700. The expert evidence was tendered by Sir Martin and was objected to by the inspector on the grounds that the matter was *res judicata*. This was accepted by the Commissioners but overruled by Rowlatt J who remitted the case to the Commissioners. No contrary evidence of New York law was tendered for the inspector and he unsuccessfully argued that the Commissioners were bound

Nevertheless, they initially determined the appeals in favour of the Revenue on the basis that the principle of *res judicata* prevented the matter being reopened. Following Lord Justice Greer's judgment in *Baker (No 2)*, however, the Revenue agreed to abandon its argument based on that principle and Rowlatt J directed the Special Commissioners to restate their case, dealing fully with the evidence of US trust law and removing any reference to *res judicata*. That done, the Special Commissioners concluded that Lady Frances' income was derived from the exercise by the trustee of its discretion and not from the underlying securities. And thus the case returned yet again to Rowlatt J.

This allowed him the opportunity to explain his decision in *Baker*:

> In [*Baker*] I did not think that this lady had any right to the specific investments or the specific dividends. What I thought was that when you come to construe and apply this particular part of the Income Tax Acts which classifies and distinguishes between income according as it arises from securities, stocks, shares, and rents or other property, you have got – I do not fail to notice the difficulties – to go back until you find something from which the income arose, the investment which bore the income, and see what that was; and that the fact that a trust was interposed, a trust which holds the principal and administers the income after it has been earned did not give you a source of income which came into this classification at all. That was my view.[45]

His reasoning encapsulates precisely what was in issue: whether, for the purposes of assessment, 'the source' of Lady Archer-Shee's income was (a) the securities from which the income derived or (b) her rights under the foreign trust. From an income tax perspective, the Act clearly treated securities as a source of income and charged income from the securities to tax in the hands of a UK resident person, but that Act did not so treat trust rights. Income might emerge from a trust as an annuity or annual payment or as income from a foreign possession, but that did not affect the charge on the underlying income of the securities or deny her entitlement to share in that income.

Rowlatt J seems to have thought that nobody in the earlier case had agreed with his view.[46] The Revenue's written case in the House of Lords in *Baker* does not bear that out: his view was said to be the correct view. And, indeed, far from disagreeing with Mr Justice Rowlatt, the majority of the Law Lords were

---

by the decisions in *Williams v Singer* (above n 19) and *Baker* (above n 1). It has been suggested that the evidence was in fact wrong (see JF Avery Jones et al, 'The Origins of Concepts and Expressions used in the OECD Model and their Adoption by States' [2006] *BTR* 695, 749, fn 354, citing AW Scott et al, *Scott on Trusts*, 4th edn (New York, Aspen Publishers, 1998) vol 2, 400. The citation, however, does not appear to provide a clear answer on the point. It deals with the nature of the beneficiary's interest as a matter of New York trust law in the 'subject matter of the trust'. The question is whether that refers to the property or the income it generates.

[45] *Garland* (above n 1) 710–11.

[46] See ibid, 711: 'That was my view. I do not think anybody agreed with it'. That is correct to the extent that his decision was based on the fact of Lady Frances' receipt of the income and recognises that the House of Lords set aside his decision. His analysis in *Baker* of *Williams v Singer* can, however, be seen to be essentially correct and was supported by the House of Lords.

essentially adopting his view of the matter once allowance is made for the subtle shift in the Revenue's argument to lay more emphasis on Lady Archer-Shee's entitlement to the income rather than her actual receipt of it. In *Garland*, Rowlatt J upheld the Special Commissioners' decision in favour of Sir Martin. The Revenue, however, appealed and the Court of Appeal (Greer LJ dissenting) allowed its appeal on the basis that the evidence of New York law did not suggest that Lady Frances' rights differed sufficiently from those assumed to exist under English law as the basis of the House of Lords decision in *Baker*.[47] The seeds of future potential confusion were already taking root.

The House of Lords duly reversed the Court of Appeal again. Lord Tomlin explained why:

> The evidence upon American law adduced before the Commissioners in the present case contains statements to the effect that the whole estate in law and in equity in the trust funds is vested in the trustees and that the words of the trust give to the Appellant's wife merely the right to resort to a Court of equity to compel the trustees to discharge the task imposed upon them which was to apply the money which they receive as a net income from the trust to her use, that they have, within the limits of reasonable and conscientious behaviour, an absolute discretion as to the application of the income for her benefit, that if they decided to apply the money for her benefit instead of paying it over they must exercise the power to do so reasonably, and that she had no right to any specific dividends or interest at all.[48]

And so ended, on 15 December 1930, Sir Martin's journey through the courts on account of Lady Frances' trust income.[49]

VII. EXPLAINING *ARCHER-SHEE*

A. The Transparent Nature of Trust Rights

What is obvious is that the decisions in the *Archer-Shee* cases did not depend upon Lady Archer-Shee's ownership or interest in the trust securities. She did not hold legal title to them and her right under the will trust was a right to share in the income of the trust fund. It was not a right to any of the trust assets from which the income was derived. The fact that the majority of the Law Lords in *Baker* was prepared to support the assessment was based on their analysis (applying English law principles to the New York trust) of her entitlement to the income of the trust fund, and the proposition that the character of that

---

[47] See in particular ibid, 715–16 (Lord Hanworth MR) and 722 (Lawrence LJ).

[48] ibid, [1931] AC 212, 222; 15 TC 693, 735. Lord Tomlin concluded in the light of this that Lady Frances had no property interest in the income arising from the securities but only a chose in action available against the trustees. That goes to her ability to compel the trustees to pay over the income and, therefore, found the basis of an assessment of the income in her hands.

[49] The decision in *Garland* was, however, reversed by s 19, FA 1940.

income was unaffected by the interposition of the trustees between the property ('the source') from which the income was derived and the person who, ultimately, was entitled to enjoy that income and therefore could be assessed in respect of it. In other words, Lady Archer-Shee's rights under the foreign trust entitled her to the income of the trust but her rights as beneficiary were not the source of the income.

At every stage of the case everyone assumed that Lady Archer-Shee's interest under the trust was a foreign possession, so that Sir Martin was liable to assessment to the extent that she remitted trust payments to the UK. In that respect, an interest in a foreign trust or company has always been recognised as a potential source of income within the scope of charge to tax under Schedule D Case V. A comparable interest of a beneficiary under a UK trust, however, is not identified with any particular Schedule or Case. Income arising to a UK trust would ordinarily have been received net of tax deducted at the source or taxed by assessment on the trustees if received gross. A beneficiary could be assessed on the trust's income if they were in receipt of or entitled to it but that would be by reference to the underlying trust property (the source) from which the income derived. Otherwise, a distribution by trustees of trust funds to a beneficiary might amount to a charge on the trust fund, such as an annuity or other annual payment, and paid net of tax.

The trustee in *Archer-Shee* was not UK resident and could not be assessed (being outside the jurisdiction and able to object that it was a foreign person in receipt of foreign income). Lady Archer-Shee as a resident person could, however, be assessed (through her husband), provided that what was assessed was income from the source specified in the assessment. Sir Martin was therefore liable to assessment on the income from foreign securities (whether remitted to the UK or not), provided his wife was entitled to the income from that source. As the net income had been paid to Lady Archer-Shee by the trustee, Sir Martin could not deny that she had received the income in question (hence the initial emphasis of the Revenue's case) but, of course, the reason why the trustee *had* paid the income to her was because she was entitled to it under the trust.

Sir Martin's case, therefore, rested upon the proposition that the nature of his wife's rights as beneficiary under the trust affected the character of what she had received. That depended, however, on his showing that his wife received the income, not as a matter of entitlement pursuant to her interest under the trust, but as a result of the trustee's decision to exercise some discretion or power to pay her the income. In other words, there needed to be some intervention by the trustee pursuant to the trust to prevent the income being treated as hers as it arose. Admissible evidence to that effect was only produced in respect of the later years covered by *Garland*.[50] In *Baker*, the majority of the Law Lords treated the trust as transparent on the basis that Lady Archer-Shee's rights as beneficiary

---

[50] *Garland* (above n 1).

(however viewed in equity) entitled her to the income of the underlying trust fund. From an English law perspective, her right to the income as beneficiary did not represent a separate source of income but provided the basis for assessment. What was charged and assessed on Sir Martin was the income from the real source – the foreign securities held in trust – rather than from her right to be paid the income as a matter of New York trust law.

B. Lord Sudeley's Case

The other case that pervades the *Archer-Shee* decisions is *Lord Sudeley and Others v AG*.[51] The Court of Appeal in *Baker* and the dissenting minority (Viscount Sumner and Lord Blanesburgh) in the House of Lords relied on *Lord Sudeley*. The headnote of that case is as follows:

> A testator, who died domiciled in England, by his will after bequeathing legacies gave the residue of his real and personal estate to his executors in trust for his wife for life, and by a codicil gave one-fourth of his 'said residuary real and personal estate' to his wife absolutely. His will was proved in England by his executors domiciled in England. His estate included mortgages on real property in New Zealand. His wife afterwards died and her will was proved in England. At her death her husband's estate had not been fully administered, the clear residue had not been ascertained, and no appropriation had been made of the New Zealand mortgages or of any securities to particular shares of the ultimate residue:
>
> *Held*, that the right of the wife's executors was, not to one-fourth or any part of the mortgages in specie, but to require her husband's executors to administer his personal estate and to receive from them one-fourth part of the clear residue, that this was an English asset of the wife's estate, and that probate duty was therefore payable under her will upon one-fourth part of the value of the New Zealand mortgages.

As this indicates, *Lord Sudeley* concerned probate duty and, therefore, raised the question of the nature and *situs* of particular property for the purposes of that tax. The same principles do not apply for income tax purposes.[52] The point appears in Lord Halsbury's speech in *Lord Sudeley*:

> In a certain sense a person may have a claim; a person may be entitled to this, that, and the other; but the whole controversy turns upon the character of the particular thing to which the legatee is entitled. With reference to a great many things, it would be quite true to say that she had an interest in these New Zealand mortgages – that she had a claim on them: in a loose and general way of speaking, nobody would deny that that was a fair statement. But the moment you come to give a definite effect

---

[51] *Lord Sudeley* (above n 16).

[52] For further analysis of this point, see M Gammie, 'The Relationship of *Situs* and Source Rules for Tax Purposes' in J Tiley (ed), *Studies in the History of Tax Law: Volume 6* (Oxford, Hart Publishing, 2013).

to the particular thing to which she becomes entitled under this will, you must use strict language, and see what it is that the person is entitled to; because upon that in this case depends the solution of the question. It is idle to use such phrases as your Lordships have heard, ... that this was what the person was 'entitled to'– that she had an 'interest' in this estate. All those phrases are perfectly true in a general way of speaking, but are not applicable to the particular discussion before your Lordships, unless you establish as the starting-point the proposition that the thing that the legatee was entitled to was the actual mortgage itself, so that the New Zealand mortgage – the foreign asset – was the thing that was to be administered. When one looks at it accurately, that is an entire mistake.[53]

In the case of a tax imposed on property, or a transaction involving property, such as estate or probate duty or stamp duty, the essential statutory question is, what is the nature of the property on which the tax falls? And where the tax falls on the property at a particular moment in time (such as on death or on the execution of a particular instrument), the nature of that property – as domestic or foreign property – depends upon a strict analysis of the property right involved at that time (in the absence of specific statutory provision adopting other rules).

The same is not necessarily true for income tax because the tax is not dealing with the property as such but with the flow of income that it generates. The property identifies the income with the Schedule or Case under which the income is charged but the statutory question in assessing that income to tax is not, simply, what is the nature of a person's right to the underlying property? The questions are: is this income? Whose income is it? On whom can tax be charged by deduction at source or assessment? And, to the extent that it is important to know whether the income is domestic or foreign income, the relevant statutory question is not, where is the property in question situated,[54] but what is the true source of this income?

The difficulty that *Lord Sudeley* illustrated was whether a beneficiary under a trust must show that they have a right *in rem* over the trust assets or a right *in personam* against the trustee. That is a distinction that mattered for property taxes, which are concerned to identify interests in property, but which did not matter for income tax purposes because the tax was merely concerned to identify who could be assessed in respect of the income charged to tax under the Act by reference to particular property (the source).

The issue in *Lord Sudeley* is relevant in an income tax context because a residuary beneficiary is not entitled to the income of an estate in the course of

---

[53] *Lord Sudeley* (above n 16).

[54] A question that, in the case of property taxes, is likely to be answered by the rules of private international law. Those rules do not, however, apply to determine whether the source of income is UK or foreign, see Gammie, 'The Relationship of *Situs* and Source Rules for Tax Purposes' (above n 52).

administration: the executors stand between the source and the beneficiary. Only once the share of residue is ascertained by transfer, assent or on appropriation, is the way free to assess the beneficiary.[55] This, however, is a particular application of the point that income tax in its original conception looks for a source (in the sense of identifying the property from which the income is derived and by reference to which it is charged to tax) rather than just a right (such as an interest in a trust, partnership or company) to participate in an underlying fund. A residuary beneficiary's interest is effectively in the aggregate fund represented by the deceased's estate. Residuary beneficiaries have no entitlement to any specific item of income within the estate that would make them liable for assessment or entitle them to claim exemption in respect of it.

VIII. CONCLUSION

The *Archer-Shee* cases began with an emphasis on the fact that Lady Archer-Shee was in receipt of the trust income but, following a change in emphasis, *Baker* was resolved by reference to her entitlement to that income based on the assumption that New York trust law replicated English trust law. In its conception, the income tax regarded an English law trust as transparent, in the sense that trust rights entitling the beneficiary to the trust income allowed the beneficiary to be assessed in respect of that income. The assessment, however, had to be by reference to the underlying trust property from which the income derived given the fundamental importance of 'source' in charging tax: income was charged to tax by reference to its derivation from particular income producing property or activities. An interest under a trust is not itself income-producing property and therefore not a source of income in that sense.[56] An immediate entitlement to participate or share in that income provided the foundation for assessment rather than charge. Thus, the charge to tax was by reference to particular property, but assessment was by reference to receipt or entitlement to income.

These principles were subject to the qualification in the case of income derived from foreign property that the person entitled to the income had to be

---

[55] See, eg, *R v Income Tax Special Commissioners ex parte Dr Barnado's Homes* [1921] 2 AC 1, 7 TC 646; *Marie Celeste Samaritan Society v IRC* (1926) 11 TC 226, 43 TLR 23; *Corbett v IRC* [1938] 1 KB 567, 21 TC 449.

[56] Unsurprisingly, judicial language in subsequent case law has often failed to observe the distinction drawn in this analysis between the source, in terms of the property or activity from which the income is immediately derived, and the right to participate in that income under a trust. This is because (as *Baker* illustrates) the nature of the participatory trust right may be such as to support an immediate assessment by reference to the underlying property of the trust. Where it is not of that nature, however, (as *Garland* illustrates), it may still be such as to support a later assessment when income emerges from the trust, either on the basis that the trust interest is a foreign possession and the payment from the trust is foreign income, or because the payment amounts to a charge on the trust fund in the form of an annual payment or annuity or is otherwise within a head of charge as income.

a UK resident for the income to be charged. The source of Lady Archer-Shee's income, in the sense of what identified the income as charged to tax under the Act, was the foreign securities by reference to which the assessment was raised. The sole issue for determination was whether Sir Martin Archer-Shee could be assessed in respect of that income on the basis that his wife, as a UK resident, was entitled to the income under the terms of the trust. From an English law perspective in *Baker*, she was entitled and he could be assessed but, from a New York law perspective in *Garland*, where the evidence showed that the trustee's discretion intervened, she was not entitled and he could not be assessed.

7

Commissioners of Inland Revenue v Crossman *(1936)* Keeping it in the Family

ANN MUMFORD*

WHITECHAPEL ROAD IS a part of the main thoroughfare leading east from the City of London. Bombing and planners notwithstanding, it contains many buildings of historical interest. One is the Blind Beggar, a pub that owes its name to of the legend of Henry de Montfort, who was blinded at the Battle of Evesham (1265),[1] then fell upon hard times, and became a symbol for Bethnal Green. Inns have been on the site of the Blind Beggar at least since the seventeenth century. It is notorious as the scene of the killing by Ronald Kray of someone who insulted him.[2] The Albion Brewery was constructed in 1808 next to the Blind Beggar.[3] By 1826 it was in the ownership of John Mann: Robert Crossman and Thomas Paulin joined him as partners in 1846. Initially they brewed porter, but tastes changed from the 1860s towards lighter, sparkling beers – hence, Mann, Crossman & Paulin adapted to the changing tastes and the brewery thrived[4] into the 1950s.[5] Various changes were

---

* For substantial assistance in the research for this chapter, I am enormously indebted to John Pearce, Catharine Macmillan, Peter Alldridge and the editors of this volume.

[1] Things could have been worse for Henry. The severed head of his father, Simon, the loser of Evesham, was sent to his widow. Other branches of the de Montfort family survived, and in the early seventeenth century, with their name anglicised to Mumford, some members migrated to North America.

[2] *R v Kray et al* [1969] EWCA Crim J0722-1; [1970] 1 QB 125. See also R Kray, *Our Story: London's Most Notorious Gangsters, in Their Own Words* (London, Pan Macmillan, 2015) 74.

[3] H Janes, *Albion Brewery, 1808–1958: The Story of Mann, Crossman & Paulin Ltd* (London, Harley Publishing Company, 1958).

[4] 'The Company is a very prosperous one and had been paying a dividend at the rate of 45 per cent annually for some years'. *CIR v Crossman; CIR v Mann* [1937] AC 26, 37 (Viscount Hailsham LC), '[C]ompany's exceeding prosperity' 44 (Lord Blanesburgh).

[5] R Porter, *London: A Social History* (Cambridge, MA, Harvard University Press, 1998) 327.

made to the structure of the partnership[6] and then the company was incorporated in 1901,[7] as were many family brewery businesses around that time.[8]

I. THE *MANN* AND *CROSSMAN* ESTATES

The brewing industry in London was still very important until the 1960s.[9] Major breweries were still almost all family businesses,[10] and the shares were enormously valuable.[11] Between 1885 and 1985, four Manns, two Crossmans and a Paulin were masters of the Worshipful Company of Brewers.[12] The Mann and Crossman families had landed estates, respectively in Thelveton, outside Diss in Norfolk where the Manns lived in Thelveton Hall and the Paulins in the Manor House, and Great Bromley, outside Colchester in Essex, and where the Crossmans lived in Great Bromley Hall. Percy Crossman was Essex Master of Hounds of the Essex and Suffolk Hunt from 1921 until 1925.

In the 1930s the 'family business' paradigm remained a major feature in the organisation of companies of all sizes, even the largest. Various mechanisms were deployed to maintain the 'family business' structure. In particular, appointment and promotion practices had to be afforded preferential status to jobs to people in particular categories – 'the family' – and restrictions upon the sale of shares (usually rights of pre-emption) also had to be put in place. In the case of the Mann, Crossman & Paulin shares, the critical term was clause 34 in the articles of association,[13] by which rigorous restrictions were imposed upon the transfer of shares. It enabled a male holder to transfer his shares or appoint them by will to sons or brothers, or sons of sons, or of brothers, subject to the transferees or appointees attaining the age of 25 years and being in other respects duly qualified in the opinion of the directors; subject to that, it gave the other holders of ordinary shares a right of pre-emption over the shares of living members and an option to purchase the shares of deceased members in each case at a price equal to the par value of the shares, plus a proportion of the reserve fund, undivided profits and accruing profits of the company; finally, it granted a general power to

---

[6] Some are detailed in *Crossman v R* (1886) 18 QBD 256.

[7] *Crossman* (above n 4) 27.

[8] TR Gourvish and RG Wilson, 'Profitability in the Brewing Industry, 1885–1914' (1985) 27 *Business History* 146.

[9] The standard histories are P Mathias *The Brewing Industry in England 1700–1830* (Cambridge, Cambridge University Press, 1959) and TR Gourvish and RG Wilson, *The British Brewing Industry 1830–1980* (Cambridge, Cambridge University Press, 1994). The decline of the London breweries is dealt with in Gourvish and Wilson, ch 11, 'Merger Mania'.

[10] See the Appendix to D Gutzke, 'The Social Status of Landed Brewers in Britain since 1840' (1984) 17 *Social History/Histoire Sociale* 93.

[11] And this was not the first litigation as to the tax implications of succession in the family: *Crossman v R* (above n 6).

[12] www.brewershall.co.uk/the-company.

[13] Set out in full in the judgment of Viscount Hailsham LC, *Crossman* (above n 4) 32–36.

the directors, for whose exercise reasons need not be given, to refuse the registration of any transfer where they were of opinion that a proposed transferee was not a desirable person to be admitted to membership.

Put simply, if the shares were to be sold, then: (1) the holder would have been bound to give notice in writing to the company of their intention to sell; (2) such notice would have constituted the company their agent for the sale of the shares; and (3) the company would be required to sell them to a member of the company holding ordinary shares at a price determined in accordance with clause 34. The price determined by reference to clause 34 would be favourable to the purchaser, and the shares would be kept in the family. This provision was discriminatory on the basis of gender and might, if operated today, give rise to an action by female members of the family for the enforced replacement of the terms denoting male gender with terms indicating either or none.[14] The discrimination in respect of the holder of the power was noted by Lord Blanesburgh,[15] not as being objectionable, but as speaking to an argument about the nature of the share and its valuation. The discrimination so far as concerns beneficiaries was not remarked upon.

The *Crossman* case, which concerned estate duty, remains important for inheritance taxation today. Sales in the open market, for the purposes of valuation for inheritance taxation,[16] in some instances, will be conducted on a hypothetical basis. If the property in question is incapable of being sold on the open market, then that fact will be disregarded for inheritance tax purposes. This is the continuing legacy of *Crossman*, which values the property as if it had been sold immediately before the date of death. The *Crossman* principle is enduring,[17] and most recently was cited in the litigation concerning the administration of Lehman Brothers International.[18]

II. THE ESTATE DUTY LITIGATION

Legacy Duty (first instituted in 1796)[19] was payable on personal or moveable property (including leaseholds, up until 1853). Succession Duty was payable on

---

[14] s 142, Equality Act 2010.

[15] *Crossman* (above n 4) 45–46. He was gazetted 'Blanesburgh' (Anon, 'Sir Robert Younger's Title' *The Times* (17 November 1923)) and this spelling will be used throughout, even though 'Blanesborough' appears in the *Law Reports*.

[16] s 160, Inheritance Tax Act 1984: 'Market value: Except as otherwise provided by this Act, the value at any time of any property shall for the purposes of this Act be the price which the property might reasonably be expected to fetch if sold in the open market at that time; but that price shall not be assumed to be reduced on the ground that the whole property is to be placed on the market at one and the same time'.

[17] And, indeed, is a reiteration of a principle first developed in *Re Aschrott, Clifton v Strauss* [1927] 1 Ch 313, concerning the 'enemy property' of a German national during the First World War.

[18] *Re Lehman Brothers International (Europe) (In Administration)* [2016] EWHC 2417 (Ch), [2017] 2 All ER (Comm) 275.

[19] Legacy Duty Act 1796 (48 Geo 3 c 52).

realty, settled personalty, and leaseholds. Its imposition in 1853[20] by William Gladstone was partly an attempt to equalise the taxes on realty and personalty, which were considered to have unfairly penalised personalty, and partly an attempt to avoid reliance on income tax as a source of revenue.[21] The single Estate Duty was put in place by Harcourt's 1894 Finance Act. The Duty was payable on all estates of £100 or more. It was paid out of the estate, before distribution, rather than by the beneficiaries. It was a graduated tax, with larger estates paying proportionately much more than smaller ones.[22] By 1930, the sums raised by the Treasury had become very significant.[23] The estates in *Crossman* were large enough to bring them into what then was the highest (40 per cent) band.[24]

Percy Crossman died on 17 August 1929. He was at that time the registered holder of 1,000 ordinary shares in the company. By his will, he had disposed of all these shares in favour of relatives under the provisions of article 34, sub-clause 2, and these persons became the registered holders of these shares. Sir William Paulin died on 26 February 1931. At the time of his death, he was the registered holder of 1,600 ordinary shares in the Company. By his will, Sir William Paulin gave 500 of these shares to each of his two daughters, who became registered holders of these shares. The remaining 600 shares formed part of his residuary estate, and on 14 May 1931, his executors served a transfer notice in respect of those 600 shares on the Company, in accordance with the provisions of sub-clause 14 of article 34. The price fixed under the provisions of sub-clause 14a of article 34 was £209 13s 8d, and Sir William Paulin's executors accordingly sold and transferred these 600 shares to other members of the Company at that price. The price fixed in accordance with article 34, sub-clause 14a, in the case of Percy Crossman would have been £221 4s 5d.

The charge to Estate Duty was upon the 'principal value' of the property.[25] Under section 5(7):

> The principal value of any property shall be estimated to be the price which, in the opinion of the Commissioners, such property would fetch if sold in the open market at the time of the death of the deceased.

The issue upon which the litigation turned was as to the valuation for the purposes of Estate Duty of the shares in the company in the hypothetical sale on the 'open market'. *Crossman*, thus, did not address: controlling shares;[26]

---

[20] Succession Duty Act 1853 (16 & 17 Vict c 51).

[21] L Hoskins et al, 'The Death Duties in Britain, 1859–1930: Evidence from the Annual Reports of the Commissioners of the Inland Revenue', History of Wealth Working Paper 1, available at historyofwealth.files.wordpress.com/2013/06/working-paper-1.pdf, 8; and for the complications of the changes see, ibid, 9–12.

[22] ss 1 and 17, FA 1894.

[23] Hoskins et al (above n 21) 2, figure 1.

[24] ibid, 29.

[25] s 1, FA 1894.

[26] B Sutherland, 'The Valuation for Tax Purposes of Controlling Holdings of Unquoted Shares' [1996] *BTR* 397.

preference shares (which are quoted) or the timing of the hypothetical sale;[27] the relationship between sections 1 and 2 of the 1894 Act;[28] the nature of the market;[29] or, whether members of the hypothetical market should have ascribed to them confidential information.[30]

The Commissioners notified the executors, by letter dated 6 January 1933, of their decision to the effect that the value of the 1,600 ordinary shares for the purposes of the estate duty payable on the death of the deceased was £475 per share. A petition[31] was taken by the taxpayers to Finlay J.[32] This raised issues of fact and of law. Expert evidence was offered by Lord Plender[33] as to the value of the shares under the various hypotheses. The evidence of a Mr Hely Hutchinson[34] contemplated a particular trust company, having particular advantages for a purchase of such shares by reason of its allied companies or subsidiaries. The argument that a trust company might have been prepared to pay more than any other investor seems to have been based on the idea that it would not make provision for Estate Duty. Finlay J, upon the evidence which had been adduced before him, held that a trust company would not, and could not, have been in the market, because the directors would have refused to register such a purchaser. Finlay J did set the value of a share at the higher figure of £395, if a trust company were to be considered as a possible purchaser. That evidence was dismissed by Lord Hanworth MR as being too particular, and not fitting in well with an 'open market',[35] and thus was disregarded explicitly in the House of Lords by Viscount Hailsham LC and Lord Blanesburgh.[36]

There were three major possibilities as to which of the valuations should be adopted as the 'principal value' for Estate Duty purposes.[37] First, there was the view attributed[38] to Palles CB in the lower court in Ireland[39] to the effect that:

> We must exclude the consideration of such provisions in the articles of association as would prevent a purchaser at a sale from becoming a member of the company, registered as such in respect of the shares purchased by him at such a supposed sale.

[27] *Buccleuch (Duke) v IRC* [1967] 1 AC 506.

[28] There is a suggestion in the speech of Viscount Hailsham LC that the outcome in *Crossman* is dictated by the statement of Lord MacNaghten in *Cowley v IRC* [1899] AC 198, 210–11 who said they were mutually exclusive, and that in the event of a clash then s 1 would prevail, In *Public Trustee v IRC (Re Arnholz)* [1960] AC 398 Viscount Simonds LC expressed the contrary view.

[29] *In re Holt* [1953] 1 WLR 1488.

[30] *Lynall v IRC* [1972] AC 680.

[31] Under s 10, FA 1894.

[32] *Mann, Crossman & Paulin Ltd v Compton* [1947] 1 All ER 742, 28 TC 410. Finlay J's judgment is available at (1933) 12 *Annotated Tax Cases* 586.

[33] A very distinguished accountant: See ME Murphy, 'Lord Plender: A Vignette of an Accountant and His Times, 1861–1948' (1953) 27 *Bulletin of the Business Historical Society* 1.

[34] It is unclear from the report whether this was John Michael Henry Hely-Hutchinson, later Seventh Earl of Donoughmore (1902–81).

[35] *Re Paulin; Re Crossman* [1935] 1 KB 26, 48.

[36] *Crossman* (above n 4) 48, 60.

[37] Identified by Slesser LJ in *Re Crossman* (above n 35) 49–50.

[38] Lord Blanesburgh was at some pains to show that this was not Palles CB's view.

[39] *AG for Ireland v Jameson* [1905] 2 IR 218.

That is, to disregard both the restrictions imposed upon the hypothetical purchaser, and also the restrictions upon that purchaser regarded as a vendor, when he is the register. On this account, the valuation would have been very high. It was estimated by Lord Roche (on the basis of the income they produced) that a share in such a company as this, with an unrestricted right of transfer, would probably be worth at least twice as much as the £355 fixed by Finlay J.[40] Second was the view that the 'principal value' of the shares ought to be estimated on the terms that the purchaser should be entitled to be registered as holder of the shares, but should take them subject to the restrictions imposed by the articles on the alienation by him of the shares. This was the position taken by the Court of Appeal in Ireland (Lord Ashbourne, Chancellor; and FitzGibbon, Walker and Holmes LJJ) in *Jameson*, best expressed in a much-quoted passage from Holmes LJ as follows:

> The defendants ... contend that the only sale possible is a sale at which the highest price would be [the pre-emption price], and that this ought to be estimated value. My objection is that this estimate is not based on a sale in open market as required by the Act. Being unable to accept either solution, I go back to my own, which is in strict accordance with the language of the section.[41]

On this account the figure of £355 was reached. Third was the opinion of the majority in the King's Bench Division in *Ireland* (Kenny and Boyd JJ) that, in estimating the value, the special provisions in the articles of association must be taken into account, both as regards the rights of a purchaser and as regards the rights of alienation by that purchaser when he is upon the register. On this view the lower values, based upon the pre-emption price (£210 &c) were correct. This view was that contended for by the executors.

Finlay J held that the precedent of the Irish Court of Appeal in *Attorney-General for Ireland v Jameson*[42] governed,[43] and that the shares were to be treated as if sold in the open market on the terms that the purchaser should be entitled to be registered as holder of the shares, but should take and hold them subject to the articles of association, *including* the articles relating to the alienation and transfer of the shares of the company. The value accorded to them, on the evidence of Lord Plender, was therefore the higher one (around £350 each). The Court of Appeal[44] (Slesser and Romer LJJ, Lord Hanworth MR dissenting) overruled, holding that every ordinary share of the company must be regarded

---

[40] 'At the prescribed price the shares show a return of about 20 per cent per annum and even at the price adopted by the learned judge of about 12½ per cent *per annum*' (*Crossman* (above n 4) 75 (Lord Roche).

[41] Approved by Lord Reid in *Lynall* (above n 30) 693.

[42] [1905] 2 IR 218 unanimously overruling the majority decision of the Irish Court of King's Bench reported in [1904] 2 IR 644. *Jameson*, a whiskey case, was followed in *Crossman*. A whiskey with a beer chaser is called a boilermaker.

[43] Technically it was only of persuasive authority, but by a highly regarded court on the same legislation.

[44] *Re Crossman* (above n 35).

as containing as a necessary incident the obligation (when it was being sold) to offer it through the agency of the company to the shareholders at the price set by the relevant article.

The House of Lords (Viscount Hailsham LC, Lord Blanesburgh and Lord Roche, Lord Russell of Killowen and Lord Macmillan dissenting), held that the value of the shares for the purpose of estate duty was to be estimated at the price they would fetch if sold in the open market, on the terms that the purchaser should be entitled to be registered and to be regarded as the holder of the shares, and should take and hold them subject to the provisions of the articles of association, including those relating to the alienation and transfer of shares in the company. The principal value of the shares was fixed at £355.

III. REASONS

Read from this distance in time, the speeches in the House of Lords are not particularly pellucid, but several types of reasons may be discerned. First, a great deal of attention was given to the precedent of *Jameson*.[45] It was not binding upon any of the English courts, but, at that time, an English court of first instance was expected to follow the Court of Appeal in Ireland. So far as concerns the Court of Appeal and House of Lords, the judgments in *Jameson* clearly were only persuasive, but, since *Crossman* was, in essence, a re-litigation of the issues in *Jameson*, in which all the main issues had been fully explored, it provided almost all of the ammunition needed for both sides.

Second, emphasis was given to the consideration that the construction of the statute ensures that the property in respect of which estate duty is levied shall include all that property which passes on the death of the deceased and not merely such part of that property as could be disposed of in open market.[46] Third, the analytical method advocated by counsel would attribute one quality and character (and one value) to the shares held by women, and another to the shares held by men.[47] Fourth, in the Court of Appeal, Lord Hanworth argued that the language of the Finance Act conveyed the idea that all property passing from a deceased person should contribute its quota to the necessities of the state which had nurtured and preserved it.[48] Finally, the possibility of using a decision to the contrary is raised by Lord Roche[49] as a consequentialist mechanism for

---

[45] A radical suggestion by counsel for the taxpayers (Wilfrid Greene KC and David Ll Jenkins, both subsequently very distinguished judges), 'that the principle of accepting a decision when there is antiquity of decision does not apply to taxing cases. Each subject is entitled to have his liability to tax considered afresh' (ibid, 37–38) was not taken up.

[46] *Crossman* (above n 4) 42 (Viscount Hailsham LC).

[47] ibid, 45–46 (Lord Blanesburgh).

[48] ibid, 42.

[49] ibid, 71–72.

adopting the higher value.[50] He did not wish, however, to put in place financial incentives to structure the arrangement such that the Duty gathered, artificially to be reduced.

The dissentient Lords, Lord Russell of Killowen and Lord Macmillan, expressed very firmly the position that it was wrong to charge duty on a sum that the decedents never had,[51] and could never have had.[52] They added that it is inconsistent to ignore one set of constraints in the company's constitution when imagining the notional sale, but not others: 'I do not know, my Lords, why, on the principle there invoked, the pre-emption rights should have been so carefully safeguarded and the directors' veto on any transfer should have been so completely ignored'.[53]

IV. WHAT EXACTLY DID *CROSSMAN* DECIDE?

Viscount Hailsham LC's speech concluded: 'in my opinion the judgment of the learned judge ought to be restored, the order of the Court of Appeal should be discharged … [&c]'.[54] Lord Blanesburgh said: 'on the whole case I am in complete agreement with the motion just made by the Lord Chancellor'.[55] Finally, Lord Roche's speech ended: 'My Lords, for these reasons I am for allowing the appeals so far as the restoration of the judgments of Finlay J is asked for but not further'.[56] It is consequently surprising that the order of the House of Lords was

> that the cause be remitted back to the King's Bench Division of the High Court of Justice to do therein as shall be just and consistent with this judgment. The same order, mutatis mutandis, was made in Sir Edward Mann's case.[57]

---

[50] Lord Roche's reasoning was expressly favoured by Lord Donovan in *Lynall* (above n 30) 704.

[51] 'I cannot bring myself to believe that these shares if sold in the open market would fetch a price of over 300l. each, yet that is what the House is about to decide … It may be unfortunate for the Revenue that the Legislature has chosen a method of measuring value for estate duty purposes which may not in the present instance yield the real value of these shares. But that is not your Lordships' concern' (*Crossman* (above n 4) 68–70).

[52] 'How can any higher price be, in the Commissioners' opinion, the price which the shares would fetch at the hypothetical sale envisaged by s 7, sub-s 5? What justification is there for saying that the shares to be sold at the hypothetical sale are to be free from the rights of pre-emption; that they are in other words to be hypothetical shares? I can find none in the language used. The sub-section is perfectly general in its terms, dealing with "any property" and therefore covering all property which passes on the death; and the Commissioners have to form an opinion as to the highest price which a person in the "open market" would be prepared to pay for the particular property under consideration. That I conceive is the price which "such property would fetch"' (ibid, 69, Lord Macmillan).

[53] ibid, 71–72 (Lord Macmillan).

[54] ibid, 43.

[55] ibid, 63.

[56] ibid, 75.

[57] *House of Lords Journal* (27 March 1936).

At that time, the civil jurisdiction of the House of Lords was the (fairly) wide one conferred by the Appellate Jurisdiction Act 1876.[58] On the face of it, it seems that the House made a different order from that for which the majority voted. Why did the House not simply order the restoration of Finlay J's original order (or, why was that not implied by the overruling of the Court of Appeal's decision)? – or, impose its own valuation at the same figures? Additionally, and since the taxing provision actually required the Commissioners to form an opinion, why did the House not direct the Commissioners to take the decision again? The Parliamentary Archive file on the case contains nothing more than the texts of the judgments, so sheds no light.

Crossman held that the 'principal value' of the shares was the price which would be realised in the open market at the date of valuation on the assumption that a purchaser would be registered as a holder of the shares subject to the same restrictions. This is now referred to as the 'Crossman Principle'.[59] The 1991 case of Baird's Executors[60] held that this principle should be interpreted broadly, and not simply as relevant to the transfer of shares.[61] The principle, for example, does not operate only when shares are capable of being sold – it is broader than that.[62] There are restrictions, however – for example, the principle would not apply where the buyer eventually holds interests or rights which differ completely from those held by the seller – say, where the seller relinquished a protected life interest.[63]

A. *Crossman* as one of the 'Estate Duty Cases' Considered in *Gray* (1994) and *Grays Timber Products* (2010)

Crossman is sometimes referred to as one of the 'estate duty cases', in unison with *Ellesmere v IRC*,[64] and *Duke of Buccleuch v IRC*,[65] all of which tend to be cited as authority for the principle that, if it is beneficial to divide property and sell it in parts, as opposed to as a whole, then such a sale can be presumed, even where impractical.[66] This 'combined principle' was considered in the context

---

[58] s 4, Appellate Jurisdiction Act 1876: 'Every appeal shall be brought by way of petition to the House of Lords, praying that the matter of the order or judgment appealed against may be reviewed before Her Majesty the Queen in her Court of Parliament, in order that the said Court may determine what of right, and according to the law and custom of this realm, ought to be done in the subject-matter of such appeal'.

[59] Valuation Office Agency (VOA) Inheritance Tax Manual, available at manuals.voa.gov.uk/corporate/publications/manuals/inheritancetaxmanual/pnotes/b-iht-man-pn1.html.

[60] *Baird's Executors* [1991] SLT (Lands Tr) 9.

[61] S Eden, 'The Mystical Art of Valuing Agricultural Tenancies' [1991] *BTR* 181, 184.

[62] ibid.

[63] ibid.

[64] *Ellesmere v IRC* [1918] 2 KB 735.

[65] *Buccleuch* (above n 27).

[66] R Adams, 'Gray v IRC: Unnatural Units of Property' [1995] *BTR* 338, 339.

of a valuation of agricultural land for Capital Transfer Tax (CTT) in the 1994 case of *Gray (surviving executor of Lady Fox deceased).*[67] *Crossman*, here, was applied as authority that, when valuing property, it is appropriate to assume that (at the point of valuation) it was capable of being sold in the open market, even if, in fact, the conditions that then adhered would have rendered this impossible.[68] The *Duke of Buccleuch* case was applied here as authority that it was appropriate to assess the property in this way *as it actually existed*, even if, were this a real sale, it could be assumed that the owner may have attempted some improvements to the property to enhance the sale price.[69] Thus, the court in *Gray* held that, for the assessment of CTT and in accordance with the 'Crossman Principle', the restrictions imposed by a partnership deed must be taken into account for the purposes of valuation.[70]

Fifteen years later, the case of *Grays Timber Products* (2010) returned to this interpretation of *Crossman*, specifically on the subject of a 'subscription agreement' (which directs that a certain number of shares should be sold, at a pre-agreed price) which had been contracted by the managing director of Grays Timber Products, Mr Gibson. Mr Gibson subscribed for shares in the parent company on the condition that, in the event of a takeover, the amount of consideration to which he otherwise would be entitled would increase.[71] After the takeover, HMRC assessed Grays Timber Products to income tax and national insurance contributions for Mr Gibson, taking into account the increased amount of consideration (per ITEPA, chapter 3, part 7). The question arose of whether the shares had been sold at market value, or greater than market value, given the condition which promised increased consideration. In particular, the court considered whether, if the special consideration were to be taken into account, then, what its value should be.[72]

ITEPA 2003, part 7, chapter 3D imposes income tax on any amount of employment-related income securities which exceeds the market value of shares. The court focused particular attention on the 'homely metaphor' that a buyer of shares should 'stand in the shoes' of the seller, so as to be able to determine

---

[67] *Gray v IRC* [1994] STC 360.

[68] VOA (above n 59) 'Practice Note 1: Appendix F: Inland Revenue Commissioners v Gray (Executor of Lady Fox Deceased) (1994)', available at manuals.voa.gov.uk/corporate/publications/Manuals/InheritanceTaxManual/pnotes/g-iht-man-pn1-appf.html.

[69] ibid.

[70] In *Gray* (above n 67), Hoffmann LJ explained: '[a]s between themselves, partners are not entitled individually to exercise proprietary rights over any of the partnership assets ... As regards the outside world, however, the partnership deed is irrelevant. The partners are collectively entitled to each and every asset of the partnership, in which each of them therefore has an undivided share. It is this outside view which identifies the nature of the property falling to be valued for the purpose of Capital Transfer Tax, although in accordance with the Crossman principle the restrictions imposed by the partnership deed must be taken into account in assessing its value (see *Burdett-Coutts v IRC* [1960] 1 WLR 1027)'.

[71] ibid, 361.

[72] ibid.

the market value of the shares.[73] The metaphor, however, has its limits. It is not meant to imply that the seller should pretend to be the buyer in every way. There will be specific rights, for example, that are specific to the seller, and that should be taken into account. The important questions, thus, are which rights, and how should they be taken into account.[74]

The court considered whether, when determining which rights should be taken into account when determining the value of a share, it should categorise those rights as either 'intrinsic' or 'extrinsic'. The answer was neither; rather, it was necessary to determine whether or not a right 'runs' with a share, such that its benefit is experienced by the buyer after purchase. In reaching this holding, Lord Walker (at paragraph 27) referred to Lord Blanesburgh's reliance, in *Crossman*, on what he described as the 'classic' definition in *Borland's Trustee v Steel Bros & Co Ltd*.[75] In *Borland's*, a share was defined as an instrument, which, while still 'one indivisible piece of property',[76] nonetheless represented a variety of different obligations from all of the shareholders.[77] This was described by Lord Macmillan in *Crossman* as 'an entirely conventional creation', and a 'creature of the Companies Act'.[78] The key task in these cases, Lord Walker argued in *Gray's*, was to consider the articles of association, and whether any special rights accrued to the shares of Mr Gibson, upon disposal.[79]

B. *Crossman* and Company Law

The 'man on the street' may be perplexed by this holding, and perhaps might suggest that, as Mr Gibson was contractually guaranteed £1,451,172 for the disposal of his shares under the subscription agreement, then that must be the 'market value' of the shares.[80] How else was this figure reached, other than – given a lack of family or other personal connection between Mr Gibson and *Grays Timber Products* – by virtue of the market? Sections 272–73 of the Taxation of Chargeable Gains Act, however, require one to enter 'a dim world peopled by the spirits of fictitious or unborn sales'.[81] The point is that the position and individualities of actual people are irrelevant, as '[c]ase law has decided that parties to this sale are hypothetical, anonymous and willing'.[82] The seller, similarly, under this principle, is, although anonymous, a 'prudent man of business'.[83]

---

[73] *Grays Timber Products v HMRC* [2010] UKSC 4, para 41.
[74] ibid.
[75] *Borland's Trustee v Steel Bros & Co Ltd* [1901] 1 Ch 279, 288.
[76] *Crossman* (above n 4) 51.
[77] *Grays Timber Products* (above n 73) para 27.
[78] *Crossman* (above n 4) 69.
[79] ibid.
[80] D Bowes, 'Timber!' [2010] 165 *Taxation* 18.
[81] *Holt* (above n 29).
[82] Bowes (above n 80).
[83] *Gray* (above n 67).

Morse argued that there is a 'fundamental difficulty with this hypothetical market', as unquoted shares also will be governed by a company's articles, and subject to restrictions. [84] These shares could not be sold freely without adhering to the conditions of these restrictions, under 'basic company law rules'.[85] The answer to this problem, Morse explains, was provided by the 'stand in the shoes' principle of *Crossman*, such that the sale occurs free of the restrictions, but the buyer later is bound by them.[86] Lord Macmillan's 'entirely conventional ... creature of the Companies Act' would appear, when considered within the context of the holding in *Grays Timber*, to cause some difficulties in the context of company law. For example, in company law, a right may be classified as 'intrinsic' even if it is not 'assignable'.[87] Additionally, from a company law perspective, Morse emphasises that the important issue in *Grays Timber* was not whether the rights could be transferred to an actual or theoretical buyer, but, rather, whether the holder of the shares had rights which could be protected in company law.[88]

V. WAS THERE A JUDICIAL POLITICS TO *CROSSMAN*?

Out of the nine judges to hear the *Crossman* case there was a 5:4 split. That is, it was incontestably a 'hard case' on which opinions on both sides might quite legitimately be entertained. One might ask whether the judges' conclusions were affected by their political or personal views. Four of the judges had previously been Members of Parliament, and a fifth, Finlay J, was the son of a liberal Lord Chancellor. If political persuasion were the determining criterion, one might assume that persons of the Left would hold for the higher value (and that which attracts the higher duty), and persons of the Right, the lower. To the contrary, the judge with the closest links to advocates of redistribution of property was Slesser LJ, a former Labour MP and a distributist,[89] who went for the lower value and Hailsham, a Conservative, adopted a higher one. Personal interest does not seem to have affected Lord Blanesburgh, who before being ennobled was Robert Younger, scion of the Younger[90] and McEwan brewing families.[91]

---

[84] G Morse, 'Grays Timber Products Ltd v Revenue and Customs Commissioners: Valuing Employee Shares with Non-Assignable Rights' [2010] *BTR* 210.

[85] ibid.

[86] ibid.

[87] Morse (above n 84) 213.

[88] ibid.

[89] When in Parliament, he had advanced the position of the Distributist League, which was associated with Chesterton and Belloc and other Catholics who did not want to be identified as socialists. See H Slesser, 'The Failure of Distributism' (1975) 1 *The Chesterton Review* 51.

[90] That is George Younger & Co of Alloa, not William Younger & Co of Edinburgh. George Younger had incorporated in 1897, on very much the same sorts of terms as Mann, Crossman & Paulin & Co.

[91] Lord Macmillan and R Stevens, 'Younger, Robert, Baron Blanesburgh (1861–1946), judge' in *Oxford Dictionary of National Biography* (Oxford, Oxford University Press, 2004): 'The ample means which he enjoyed enabled Younger to gratify his generous instincts by many benefactions'.

No suggestions of impropriety seem to have been made, although Lord Blanesburgh's involvement might fall foul of modern rules on judicial conduct.[92]

The table which follows indicates the political allegiances of each of the judges (where public); and, whether they opted for a higher, or lower, valuation for the purposes of tax.

Table 1 Judges' Politics

Higher		Lower	
William Finlay	Liberal		
Hanworth (Ernest Pollock)	Liberal	Slesser	Labour
		(Mark) Romer	
Hailsham (Douglas Hogg)	Conservative	(FX) Russell of Killowen	
Blanesburgh[93]		Macmillan	Conservative[94]
Roche	Conservative		

By 1971, when the *Lynall* case came before the House of Lords,[95] counsel for the Revenue (Jeremiah Harman QC and Leonard Hoffmann) did feel obliged to make clear that their brief was not to extract the largest sum possible from the taxpayer, but was to endeavour to establish a rational principle applicable to all cases of a similar nature.[96] No such caution needed to be exercised at the time of *Crossman*. It does not seem to have been suggested by anyone that this case should be considered in the politicised contexts of either avoidance, or the taxation of inherited wealth.

VI. MOTIVE? *CROSSMAN* IN THE CONTEXT OF CHILDREN, FAMILY AND AVOIDANCE

Viewed from 2017, it is tempting to describe the imposition of pre-emption rights or of any other restrictions upon sale, which have the effect of lowering the value of assets for the purposes of estate duty, as avoidance mechanisms.

---

[92] Judiciary of England and Wales, *Guide to Judicial Conduct* (March 2013): 'Impartiality 3.8 If a judge, or to the knowledge of the judge, a member of the judge's family (family as defined below in the Bangalore principles) has any significant financial interest in the outcome of the case that will plainly disqualify'.

[93] 'Politically, he had the cross bench mind, just as judicially he had the dissenting mind'. Anon, 'Lord Blanesburgh: An Appreciation' *The Times* (27 August 1946). When he died in 1946 Lord Blanesburgh left £337,980 (National Archive), including shares in Scottish Brewers and George Younger which were valued on *Crossman* principles.

[94] He had served as Lord Advocate in a Labour administration short of lawyer MPs.

[95] *Lynall* (above n 30).

[96] ibid, 686.

At no stage in the argument before any of the courts involved was that argument raised. The case was decided by the House of Lords in the period immediately after the decision in the *Duke of Westminster's* case.[97] There is no reference in *Crossman* to that case,[98] or to general issues about the construction of tax statutes. Furthermore, the only reference to the consequentialist argument was in the speech of Lord Roche: 'if we permit the lower valuation to be the operative one, that will put in place incentives for shareholders in these sorts of concerns artificially to depreciate the shares by imposing very severe restrictions upon their sale'.[99] That is, *Crossman* is almost wholly a valuation case, not an avoidance case.

Avoidance devices generated to deal with Estate Duty[100] were well known during its day; and, indeed, until 1957 someone with a short expectation of life could avoid Estate Duty simply by giving away a short-dated gilt which was about to be redeemed (he had only to survive the redemption date). Until 1958 a life tenant with a short expectation of life could avoid the duty by purchasing the reversion (so depleting his free estate without making a gift). The motive behind the development of these devices will be presumed to fall within the category of 'avoidance', but it is important to remember that such motives are likely to evolve over time, and especially as expectations of the family change.

The motives behind bequests are considered 'crucial' by the economists and sociologists who study inheritance.[101] The reason for this is that identification of motives will enable economists, in particular, to decide how different incentives will impact upon decisions to direct the division of wealth after death.[102] These decisions are considered to be crucial, as '[i]nheritance has enormous effects upon social inequality'.[103] This situation is complicated by the fact that these

---

[97] *CIR v Duke of Westminster* [1936] AC 1.

[98] Which had not then taken on the significance later ascribed it.

[99] *Crossman* (above n 4) 72.

[100] And see R Walker, 'Reflections on the Finance Act 1894' [1994] *BTR* 368.

[101] M Kohli, 'Intergenerational Transfers and Inheritance: A Comparative View' in M Silverstein (ed), *Intergenerational Relations Across Time and Place: Annual Review of Gerontology and Geriatrics: Annual Review of Gerontology and Geriatrics* (New York, Springer, 2004) 266, 268.

[102] ibid.

[103] T Warren, 'Moving Beyond the Gender Wealth Gap: On Gender, Class, Ethnicity, and Wealth inequalities in the United Kingdom' (2006) 12 *Feminist Economics* 195, 199. An additional issue is that the continuation of this duty of care through inheritance may be based on gendered assumptions. See B Cass and D Brennan, 'Taxing Women: The Politics of Gender in the Tax/Transfer System' (2003) 1 *eJournal of Tax Research* 37, 38: 'Women, like men, pay income tax as individuals; but when it comes to tax and transfer arrangements for women with partners and women as mothers with dependent children, gendered circumstances enter the system of eligibility and entitlement'. Studies have suggested that societies which use primogeniture to distribute wealth suffer more inequality than those which divide wealth equally between the sexes. PL Menchik, 'Primogeniture, Equal Sharing, and the US Distribution of Wealth' (1980) 94 *Quarterly Journal of Economics* 299, 299. But *cf* AS Binder, 'A Model of Inherited Wealth' (1973) 87 *Quarterly Journal of Economics* 608, 609: 'While the popular wisdom probably overstates the quantitative importance of inheritance

decisions still are made, typically, within the context of relationships that are the subject of enormous state persuasion as to behaviour – for example, parents are encouraged to take care of their children[104] – during the time of *Crossman*, and now. Brown suggests that '[i]t is, in short, illogical to abolish completely the inheritance of wealth unless we also abolish the family and make all children wards of the state'.[105]

In the US, the case of *Perkins*[106] dismissed, definitively, a claim that an inheritance tax violated the equal protection clause of the Fourteenth Amendment of the US Constitution.[107] This case is worth considering in the context of *Crossman*, because many of the responses to Estate Duty, CTT and Inheritance Tax discourse presently were formed from the academic response to this case.[108] The *Harvard Law Review* suggested at the time of the case that the Fourteenth Amendment, equal protection claim against an inheritance tax was clearly a desperate move, the litigants having 'despaired' of convincing the court that an inheritance tax deprived citizens of property without due process of the law. This case provides an interesting analysis of the common law background to inheritance taxation. As Brown J explained,

> [b]y the common law, as it stood in the reign of Henry the Second, a man's goods were to be divided into three equal parts, of which one went to his heirs or lineal descendants, another to his wife, and a third was at his own disposal; or, if he died without a wife, he might then dispose of one moiety, and the other went to his children; and so, e converso, if he had no children, the wife was entitled to one moiety, and he might bequeath the other; but, if he died without either wife or issue, the whole was at his own disposal.[109]

---

of nonhuman wealth, it is true that the distribution of inheritances is terribly unequal and, as such, is a contributor to the total inequality in incomes'. Families which do not discriminate on the basis of sex still may foster inequality with their intergenerational bequests – say, for example, where parents attempt to provide for one child, who may be perceived as disadvantaged, at the expense of another; or where parents fear to 'spoil' children with wealth they have not earned – and thus impact upon the 'social mobility' of their descendants for generations to come. N Tomes, 'The Family, Inheritance, and the Intergenerational Transmission of Inequality' (1981) 89 *Journal of Political Economy* 928, 929.

[104] This is discussed throughout DN Lye, 'Adult Child–Parent Relationships' (1996) 22 *Annual Review of Sociology* 79.

[105] HG Brown, 'Criteria for a Rational Tax System' (1961) 20 *American Journal of Economics and Sociology* 443, 445–46.

[106] *United States v Perkins* 163 US 625 (1898) (McKenna J).

[107] This was an odd case, as the decedent had bequeathed the entirety of his estate to the federal, US government. The State of New York imposed an inheritance tax on this bequest. The issue, thus, was 'whether personal property bequeathed by will to the United States is subject to an inheritance tax under the laws of New York', ibid, 625.

[108] This is part of what Epp describes as the transnational 'rights revolution' which occurred throughout the twentieth century. See generally CR Epp, *The Rights Revolution: Lawyers, Activists, and Supreme Courts in Comparative Perspective* (Chicago, IL, University of Chicago Press, 1998).

[109] 2 Bl Comm 492, cited at *Perkins* (above n 106) 627.

Indeed, disposing of an estate by testament was made possible only by the Statute of Wills, introduced under Henry VIII.[110] Even then, the right was restricted by the conditions listed above, ie, the tripartite division of the estate.[111] These restrictions were eradicated in England, and never existed in the US.[112] Yet an inheritance tax is still, in theory, a tax on a right of a decedent, as opposed to the receipts of the beneficiaries. In this strict sense, the burden of the tax does not fall upon those who will benefit from it.[113] The *Crossman* holding falls in line with this approach of the natural right in children, and shares no resemblance to the approach during the time of Henry II.

VII. CONTEMPORARY REACTION TO *IRC v CROSSMAN*

Analyses of the right of children to receive their parents' property were in short supply amidst the contemporary reaction to *Crossman*. A short note on Crossman appeared in the *Modern Law Review* over the initials AG,[114] which also had (immediately following) one dealing with *Whelan v Leney* [1936] AC 393, in which the House of Lords had held that no Schedule D income had accrued to a brewer because the Schedules were mutually exclusive. The juxtaposition suggested that the tax system was operating to favour brewers and the then system of tied houses.

After the Court of Appeal decision, the *Law Times*[115] approved of the view of Lord Hanworth MR:

> [I]t does seem, if we may respectfully say so, more reasonable and more convenient to value shares of the kind in question as though a purchaser would be entitled to be on the register and obliged to hold upon all the terms of the articles.

The *Law Times*, while noting the House of Lords decision, did not comment upon it.[116]

VIII. JUDICIAL RECEPTION OF *CROSSMAN*

As mentioned above, *Crossman* came to be viewed as one of the 'estate duty cases', and both within that category and independently, it has continued to be followed in Supreme Court cases until this day. Its fame perhaps was secured by

---

[110] ibid, 627.
[111] ibid.
[112] ibid.
[113] ibid.
[114] AG, 'Inland Revenue v Mann; Same v Crossman' (1937) 1 *MLR* 82.
[115] Anon, 'Estate Duty: Valuation of Shares with Restricted Right of Transfer' (1934) 178 *Law Times* 83.
[116] Anon, 'Estate Duty: Valuation of Shares with Restricted Right of Transfer' (1936) 81 *Law Times* 301.

the House of Lords in *Buccleuch*,[117] in which Lord Guest cited it as authority for the following:

> It is irrelevant in arriving at the value to consider what would have been the circumstances attending an actual sale. It is not necessary to assume an actual sale; a hypothetical market must be assumed for all the items of property at the date of death. The impossibility of putting the property on the market at the time of death or of actually realising the open market price is irrelevant. In other words, you do not have to assume that the property had actually to be sold; the assumption is that it sold at the moment of death.

The later decision in *Lynall v IRC*[118] was decided at a time when the House of Lords was working through the consequences of the 1966 *Practice Statement* on *Precedent*.[119] There had at that time been no explicit overruling by reference to the *Practice Statement*.[120] The Statement had emphasised 'the danger of disturbing retrospectively the basis on which contracts, settlement of property, and fiscal arrangements have been entered into and the especial need for certainty as to the criminal law', so it would have been unexpected for the first overruling to be a tax case.

Lord Reid forestalled argument on the appropriateness of overruling[121] by indicating during argument[122] that the House was not at that time disposed to overrule *Crossman*. Lord Morris said that, even if they had thought *Crossman* to be wrong, there were important features militating against overruling it. They were the long-standing of the decision;[123] its having been acted upon many times; and, the fact that Parliament could have intervened, and had not.[124] Yet the House also agreed with *Crossman*. Lord Reid said:

> I support the view of the majority on the ground that section 7(5) is merely machinery for estimating value, that it will not work if section 7(5) is read literally, that it must be made to work, and that the only way of doing that is the way adopted in Crossman's case.[125]

---

[117] *Buccleuch* (above n 27). Although decided on 20 December 1966, no reference seems to have been made to the possibility of overruling *Crossman*, by reference to the recently made (26 July 1966) *Practice Statement (Judicial Precedent)* [1966] 1 WLR 1234. Since the decision related more to the extent of the 'Crossman principle', it was not necessary directly to confront it.

[118] *Lynall* (above n 30), on *appeal* from Plowman J ([1969] 1 Ch 421) and the CA ([1970] Ch 138).

[119] Above n 117.

[120] The first two were *The Johanna Oldendorf* [1974] AC 179, overruling *The Aello* [1960] 1 Lloyds Rep 623 and *Miliangos v Frank* [1976] AC 443, overruling *Re Havana United Railways* [1961] AC 1007. The first overruling in a tax case was *Vestey v IRC* [1980] AC 1148, overruling *Congreve v IRC* [1948] 1 All ER 948.

[121] AA Paterson, 'Lord Reid;s unnoticed Legacy – A Jurisprudence of Overruling' (1981) 1 *OJLS* 375, JW Harris, 'Towards Principles of Overruling – When Should a Final Court of Appeal Second Guess?' (1990) 10 *OJLS* 135. See now *Knauer v Ministry of Justice* [2016] UKSC 9; [2016] AC 908 ('changed legal landscape' test) and *Willers v Joyce* [2016] UKSC 44.

[122] *Lynall* (above n 30) 691.

[123] Compare *R v Shivpuri* [1987] AC 1 overruling *Anderton v Ryan* [1985] AC 560 after a year.

[124] *Lynall* (above n 30) 696.

[125] ibid, 693–94. 'The Act of 1894 could have provided – but it did not – that the value should be the highest price that could reasonably have been expected to be realised on a sale of the property at

Lord Donovan said that, 'So far from being shown to be wrong, I think the two decisions quoted have emerged from the further examination to which they have been subjected with enhanced authority'.[126] The House of Lords in *Lynall* held that, in the open market postulated by section 7(5) of the Finance Act (FA) 1894, only that information which was in the public domain could be assumed to be available to hypothetical purchasers of shares. Because this was contrary to the long-standing practice which had been applied in the valuation of unquoted shares, section 51 of the FA 1973, was enacted. Upon the abolition of Estate Duty, a virtually identical valuation rule was introduced for the purposes of the capital gains tax in section 44(1) of the FA 1965, re-enacted as section 272(1) of the Taxation of Chargeable Gains Act 1992. On the introduction of CTT, the same valuation rule was prescribed by section 38(1) of the FA 1975, re-enacted as section 160 of the Inheritance Tax Act 1984.[127]

IX. WHAT HAPPENED AFTER ESTATE DUTY?

The change from estate duty to CTT involved a shift in the essential nature of the tax, given the incorporation of an element of gift taxation. This change, however, was in response to the perceived inefficiencies of Estate Duty, which had been too easy to avoid. So the intention was not exactly to tax gifts, but to devise legislation means for ensuring that, upon death, a tax was levied. The gift element, therefore, was in some ways a targeted anti-avoidance rule.[128]

CTT encountered several distinct challenges in its operation. One issue arose in the context of valuing unquoted shares, which was necessary for practically any transfer or transaction, and in a family company, like the one in *Crossman*, particularly.[129] An additional issue concerned whether a power to accumulate denies the possibility of there being an interest in possession.[130] The essential charging provisions were found in sections 19–24 of the FA 1975, with special provisions for settled property in Schedule 5 of that Act. The significant provisions included section 19(1), which taxed the 'value transferred' by a 'chargeable transfer'.[131] The key concept was a 'transfer of value', which, as defined in

the time of the death. If that had been the test then the respondents would succeed, subject to one matter which I need not stop to consider. But the framers of the Act limited the inquiry to one type of sale – sale in the open market – and we are not entitled to rewrite the Act. It is quite easily workable as it stands' 695 (Lord Reid).

[126] ibid, 702 (Lord Donovan).

[127] Sutherland (above n 26) 397.

[128] Indeed, when the CTT was announced to Parliament, it was presented in this way. Mr Healy said, by way of introduction: 'I intend to take measures to close the loopholes which prevent the estate duty from performing the role assigned to it' HC Deb 26 March 1974, vol 871, cols 313–14.

[129] *Sessional Papers, vol 37*, HC 917, 1555 (HM Stationery Office, 1974).

[130] RM Walters, Finance Act 1978: taxation changes/prepared for the Society of Company and Commercial Accountants (Society of Company and Commercial Accountants, 1978) para 5.3.

[131] R Dymond, RK Johns and RR Greenfield (eds), *Dymond's Capital Transfer Tax: A Companion Volume to the Fifteenth Edition of Dymond's Death Duties* (London, Oyez Publishing, 1977) 9.

section 20(2), led to the value of an estate immediately after the disposition being less than it would be but for the disposition. The amount by which it is less (including the amount of the tax payable if it comes out of the transferror's estate) is the value transferred by the transfer, and was liable to CTT.

Excluded property was defined under section 24(1) and was not covered by the tax.[132] It largely dealt with trusts, and property abroad, and was exempted from the charge through a curious amount of legal wrangling.[133] Distinctly *not* excluded from the charge was the family company, a clear target of the CTT. Sherring suggested that the most important reference to close and unquoted companies in the legislation was found in section 20(4) of the FA 1975, where

> having stated that a disposition on arm's length terms with no donative intent is not a transfer of value, the legislation goes on to say that this does not apply to a sale of shares or debentures which are not quoted, unless it is shown that the sale was at a price freely negotiated or at a price which free negotiations might have been expected to produce.[134]

X. A FINAL NOTE ON 'FAMILY VALUES'

Viewed from 2017, we might entertain doubts about attempts to keep things 'in the family'. It was, at the times under consideration, entirely normal for the time.

Consider the following:

1. William Finlay, the first instance judge, had in 1905 been appointed (four years after his call) to the lucrative role of junior counsel to the Board of Inland Revenue. At that time the appointment was in the gift of the Attorney General who happened to be Robert Finlay, later the first Viscount Finlay, his father.[135] Again his elevation to the bench, while his father was still judicially active,[136] the *DNB* reports some raised eyebrows, but no real censure.

---

[132] ibid, 15.

[133] ibid, 17: '"[e]xcluded property" therefore occupies a somewhat curious position. It is technically part of the estate while the owner of it is alive, but not such a part that its transfer out of the estate (or, if it is settled property in which he has an interest in possession, the transfer or termination of such interest) can be a transfer of value by him, and it magically disappears from the estate immediately before his death and so likewise cannot be chargeable with Capital Transfer Tax on his death'.

[134] ibid, 16–17, where Dymond continues: '[t]he words "freely negotiated" are the most important. During the debates on the 1975 Act, it was made clear that this phrase meant that one should temporarily ignore the restrictions which the Articles of a private company place on any transfer. This is the same position which we had for estate duty. Once one accepts the idea of an open market value, one accepts the idea that there are no restrictions on the hypothetical sale which one has to imagine in order to discover the open market value'.

[135] GR Rubin, 'Finlay, Robert Bannatyne, first Viscount Finlay (1842–1929), Lord Chancellor' in *Oxford Dictionary of National Biography* (Oxford, Oxford University Press, 2004).

[136] RFV Heuston, *Lives of the Lord Chancellors 1885–1940* (Oxford, Oxford University Press, 1964) 332.

2.   When Romer LJ became a Lord of Appeal, there was some mention of the fact that the person making the appointment was his brother-in-law, Viscount Maugham.[137]

3.   The Crossman family only ever employed one firm of solicitors – variously called Crossman, Crossman and Prichard; Shum, Crossman, Crossman, and Prichard; Shum, Crossman and Keith; and Shum, Crossman and Block. The lawyer and brewer Crossmans were related.[138] There are now rules about lawyers acting for family members, and while none of them would have been infringed by these involvements, they would be considered unusual. A public company would be obliged by its corporate governance arrangements to go out to tender for its legal services.

4.   In the Court of Appeal, *Lynall*[139] was argued by Jeremiah Harman QC before a bench including his father, Harman LJ.

Few if any of these events would be permitted nowadays. They are all more objectionable than the efforts of the Manns, Crossmans and Paulins to keep the property in the family. It was, ultimately, their company.

XI. CONCLUDING

In 1959, Mann, Crossman & Paulin merged with Watney Combe Reid to form Watney Mann.[140] In 1960 it fought off a takeover bid from Charles Clore, benefactor of the Institute of Advanced Legal Studies. In the 1970s the brewery produced 'Watney's Red Barrel', a very successful pasteurised keg beer that was a target of the Campaign for Real Ale, and of 'Monty Python's Flying Circus'.[141] The Albion brewery was sold to Grand Metropolitan in 1972 and closed in 1979. After lying empty for several years, in the 1990s, the Grade II listed frontage was converted into flats and offices, and a supermarket was constructed to the rear of the site. Part of the site is currently being used as a work site for the Elizabeth Line, whose Whitechapel station will open shortly. Mann's Brown Ale is now brewed in Burton.

---

[137] RFV Heuston, rev R Stevens, 'Romer, Mark Lemon, Baron Romer (1866–1944) in *Oxford Dictionary of National Biography* (Oxford, Oxford University Press, 2004).
[138] H Janes, *The Red Barrel: A History of Watney Mann* (London, John Murray, 1963) 80.
[139] *Lynall* (CA) (above n 118).
[140] Janes, *The Red Barrel* (above n 138) 203.
[141] *Monty Python*, 'The Travel Agent sketch', available at www.montypython.net/scripts/travagent-long.php.

8

Edwards v Bairstow and Harrison *(1955)*

Fact Finding and the Power of the Courts

ANNE FAIRPO

*E*DWARDS V BAIRSTOW *and Harrison*[1] is one of those cases that every law student learns at an early stage in their career. It is principally cited as the authority for the proposition that the findings of fact of a first instance tribunal cannot be reviewed by a higher court unless, in the obiter statement of Viscount Simonds, that tribunal 'acted without any evidence or upon a view of the facts which could not reasonably be entertained'. The case is also cited as a leading case on the question of what amounts to a trade.

This chapter examines the case in the context of the evolution of the law as to the powers of higher courts to examine the decisions of lower courts, particularly the Tribunals, Courts and Enforcement Act 2007 and judicial commentary from the Supreme Court in recent cases. It argues that *Edwards v Bairstow* was not proposing a new principle but, rather, correcting a tendency of the High Court and Court of Appeal to interpret too strictly a long-standing principle. In that context, what may appear to be changes in judicial practice in more recent years can be argued to be an extension of the position of the House of Lords in this case: that findings of fact should be respected, but that the threshold for review of those findings need not be considered to be almost insurmountable.

I. BACKGROUND

The story is well known: the respondents, Harold Bairstow and Fred Harrison acquired the cotton and merino wool spinning plant of a mill in Yorkshire

[1] *Edwards v Bairstow* (1955) 36 TC 207.

in 1946.[2] Harrison, who worked for a spinning firm, had found the plant for sale but had no money to buy it; Bairstow, a director of a leather manufacturing company, had the money. Harrison therefore introduced the prospect to Bairstow, who agreed to acquire the plant. The expectation was that it would sell quickly to a single buyer, but this plan did not quite come to fruition.

The anticipated buyer, the International Export Company, failed to get a necessary import licence for China for the entire plant and so only purchased the botany spinning section, for which they had obtained an import licence, in November 1946.

The rest of the plant ended up taking two more years to sell, in various lots. Although the arrangements took rather longer than anticipated, the net result was a reasonable return on the funds employed. The purchase price paid to acquire the plant in 1946 was £12,000 0s 0d. The net profit on the transaction when all was finally disposed of in March 1949 was £18,225 11s 3d (approximately £580,000 in 2017 terms).

At some stage during the unexpectedly protracted sale process Bairstow had taken the view that he was entitled to all the profits from the enterprise, presumably because he had provided all the money for the acquisition of the plant. He considered that the profits were outside the scope of tax, as the proceeds of an investment, and completed his tax return on that basis.[3]

Eventually, the Inland Revenue took an interest and came to the opposite view: that these profits were subject to income tax and assessed Bairstow accordingly to £10,326 for the year ended 5 April 1947 and £5,000 for the year ended 5 April 1948.

Harrison's involvement in the profits – and the tax – came later, although little detail is given in the extant documentation. One presumes there was some sort of argument on the point which, in the end, resulted in the profits being shared 50:50 – and the tax bill also being shared 50:50. It was common ground that the assessment was treated as being made in their joint names by the time the matter came to a hearing.

II. PROGRESSION THROUGH THE COURTS

The case had an unpromising start. It opened on 14 October 1949, at a meeting of the General Commissioners, in Halifax. In the case stated, the General

---

[2] Although referred to the case as 'Whitworth Mill' there is no record of a mill by that name in Luddenden Foot, and research indicates that the mill in question seems to have been Coopers House Mill, owned at the relevant time by Whitworth & Co. As a point of trivia: the House of Lords refers to the plant as being a 'cotton' spinning plant – but the first sale, to the International Export Company, is of the 'botany' spinning section of the plant. 'Botany' is another term for merino wool, not a type of cotton. The *Yorkshire Textile Directory* for 1930/31 (the closest year available) shows Whitworth & Co as manufacturers of both cotton and wool textiles.

[3] Capital Gains Tax would not trouble investors for another couple of decades, being introduced in 1965.

Commissioners set out the background, the contentions for the respondents and the contentions for the Crown. They then concluded that 'this was an isolated case and not taxable'. No further explanation was given other than to say that the Commissioners had considered the facts and evidence submitted to them. From a distance of more than 60 years this seems a surprisingly short decision: the style of decisions has changed substantially between the Commissioners then and the First-tier Tribunal now.[4]

The case proceeded to the High Court when the Crown appealed the decision. The case apparently took some diversions somewhere along the way as the appeal was not heard until April 1953, some three-and-a-half years after it had been heard by the General Commissioners. No explanation was given for the delay.

Upjohn, J looked at the case stated and considered that he did 'not quite know what was in their minds' when he was considering the findings of the Commissioners. He noted that the Commissioners, having identified that this was an isolated case, should have continued to consider whether it was an adventure in the nature of trade, and that '[t]he fact that the transaction was isolated is a relevant consideration to be taken into account, but it has not been suggested that it is decisive or conclusive of the matter'. The case should, therefore be remitted back to the General Commissioners for them to consider the matter on the basis of the correct test.

However, before the case was remitted, a Scottish question arose. The Crown had submitted that recent Scottish decisions meant that the judge should consider that the question of whether an adventure in the nature of trade had arisen should be considered to be a question of law, or a mixed question of fact and law, rather than a question of fact so that the judge could (and should) come to a conclusion upon that matter rather than remit the case back to the General Commissioners.

Upjohn J did not agree and noted that the Court of Appeal, in *Cooper v Stubbs*[5] had held that 'a finding as to whether a trade is or is not being carried on as a finding fact which is binding on the Court'. Instead, he chose to follow *Leeming v Jones*, which he considered had also found that this was a question of fact alone. He therefore remitted the case back to the General Commissioners on the basis that they had not given a definite answer to the question whether the transaction was an adventure in the nature of trade and asked them to 'consider and answer the question: Aye or no, was this transaction an adventure in the nature of trade?'

---

[4] The First-tier Tribunal does produce short and summary decisions but these are not published and cannot form the basis of an appeal as written. A party will have to request a full decision in order to appeal that decision so that any discussion of the First-tier decision in higher courts will be in reference to the full decision.

[5] *Cooper v Stubbs* (1925) 10 TC 29.

Upjohn J also directed that the General Commissioners should hear further argument on the question as to whether or not this was an adventure in the nature of trade before stating a Supplemental Case.

The General Commissioners duly produced a Supplemental Case dated 30 October 1953. Their decision stated simply that:

> After hearing legal argument on behalf of the Appellant, Her Majesty's Inspector of Taxes, and the Respondents, and after further consideration, we, the Commissioners, decided as follows: We find that the transaction, the subject matter of this Case, was not an adventure in the nature of trade.

No indication was given as to what legal argument was put forward by the Appellant and Respondents. No explanation was given for the finding.

The case returned to the High Court on appeal on 17 February 1954, where Wynne-Parry J took the view that:

> It is perfectly clear from the original Case that the Commissioners went into the facts with very considerable care ... and no Judge is entitled to refuse to recognise the force of their decision merely because he can perhaps fasten upon one or more points with which he might not find himself in agreement.

He took the view that it was 'quite impossible to say that the decision of the Commissioners in this case, reviewed as a matter of fact, was so perverse that it cannot stand'.

Wynne-Parry J's view that it 'appears from the Supplemental Case that they must again have considered the facts' is not really supported by the brevity of the Supplemental Case. The Crown took the case on to the Court of Appeal.

Having started rather slowly, with the years-long gap between the first General Commissioners hearing and the first High Court hearing, the case gathered pace. The Court of Appeal heard the Crown's appeal in May 1954, a scant three months after the second High Court hearing. The appeal was heard by the Master of the Rolls (Sir Raymond Evershed) and Jenkins and Hodson JJ.

The Court of Appeal dismissed the appeal, finding that it was 'quite clear that there is not, upon the face of the Case Stated, any such clear and material (or indeed any) misdirection in law which would entitle the Appellant successfully to impugn the relevant finding'.

The Court did, however, decide to follow the case into the Scottish question that had been opened up at the first appearance in the High Court, with the Master of the Rolls noting that

> there is nothing in the two Scottish cases which supports the view that the decisions of the English Court of Appeal were decided per incuriam or otherwise in such circumstances as would entitle this Court now to decline to follow them.

The Crown asked for leave 'to get this divergence solved in the House of Lords'. The Master of the Rolls noted that the possibility of a 'divergence created by a certain independence of spirit north of the Tweed' made it desirable to have such possible divergence resolved and agreed to allow the appeal to the House of Lords, on the basis that the Crown should pay the Appellants' costs of such an appeal.

He also noted that the result of such appeal may be that the Appellants 'have to pay the tax. But you will have had all this learning without any costs'. The rather dry short response from the Appellants' lawyer suggests that he wasn't wholly impressed: 'Years after the transaction'.

Overall, this was a relatively unremarkable passage through the lower courts – to those used to more modern cases, the most striking points is the brevity of the General Commissioners' Supplemental Case – and certainly, heading on to the House of Lords, the main question in the minds of the judiciary seemed to be simply that 'something needed to be done' about the direction that the law seemed to be taking in Scotland. The House of Lords did not entirely agree.

A year or so later, in late June 1955, the matter came before the House of Lords, heard by Viscount Simonds and Lord Radcliffe, Lord Tucker and Lord Somervell of Harrow. Detailed opinions were provided by Viscount Simonds and Lord Radcliffe: both took broadly the same position, with Lord Radcliffe providing rather more detail for his reasoning.

Viscount Simonds set out the background to the case and then immediately took issue with the approach of both the Court of Appeal and High Court, stating that 'having read and re-read [the facts] with every desire to support the determination if it can reasonably be supported, I find myself quite unable to do so'.[6] Lord Radcliffe's comments were a little less blunt, but nevertheless come to the same point: 'I can see only one true and reasonable conclusion. The profit from the set of operations that comprised the purchase and sales of the spinning plant was the profit of an adventure in the nature of trade'.

The House of Lords decision focused on three elements. First, as the higher courts can only intervene in errors of law, was the question as to whether something is an adventure in the nature of a trade a question of fact (following earlier English cases), a question of law or a mixed question of fact and law (following recent Scottish cases)? Secondly, in the light of that question, to what extent could the higher courts intervene in the decisions of the court of first instance? Thirdly, albeit briefly, what was an adventure in the nature of trade?

Throughout, it is notable that neither Viscount Simonds nor Lord Radcliffe appeared to consider that they were saying anything new: indeed, Lord Radcliffe stated that he 'should not, myself, have through that the principles which govern a case of this sort offered much scope for controversy at this date'.[7]

---

[6] *Edwards v Bairstow* (above n 1) 224.
[7] ibid, 228.

III. QUESTIONS OF FACT AND QUESTIONS OF LAW

'When I use a word,' Humpty Dumpty said, in a rather scornful tone, 'it means just what I choose it to mean – neither more nor less.'

'The question is,' said Alice, 'whether you can make words mean so many different things.'

'The question is,' said Humpty Dumpty, 'which is to be master – that's all.'[8]

The Lords agreed that an appeal can only be heard on an error of law; that point has been established in English law for centuries. Although Viscount Simmonds did not expressly say as much, it is clearly implied in his approach and reasoning. Lord Radcliffe clearly stated that 'if a determination cannot be shown to be erroneous in point of law, the Statute does not admit of its being upset by the Court on appeal'.[9]

Lord Radcliffe noted that '[n]or do I think that there can be any real divergence of opinion as to what constitutes error of law for this purpose', the purpose being the ability of a higher court to overturn a decision of the lower courts. Radcliffe further commented that the 'only difficulty that I see arises from the fact that in some cases judges have not been at pains to distinguish in their judgments what are the conditions which make the particular question before them no more than a question of fact'.[10] That difficulty, however, is the point around which this entire case revolves.

The issue, as set out by both Viscount Simmonds and Lord Radcliffe, was to determine whether the decision of the General Commissioners as to whether this was an adventure in the nature of a trade was a matter of law, which was appealable, or whether it was a matter of fact which was not appealable.

The Court of Appeal had previously held in *Cooper v Stubbs*[11] that a finding as to whether a trade is or is not being carried on is a finding of fact, such that the decision of the General Commissioners was binding upon the court. Although the overall decision as to the assessment in that case was unanimous, the judges disagreed as to whether they could disturb the findings of the Commissioners.

Pollock MR noted that 'the basis on which the Commissioners have placed their decision is not sound in law and therefore is capable of being reviewed'. Warrington LJ noted, in contrast, that 'I do not think that this is a case in which it can be said that there was no evidence upon which the Commissioners could arrive at that conclusion'. Atkins LJ took the same view, stating that 'there is no tribunal more competent to deal with that question of fact than the Special Commissioners … if the Commissioners come to a conclusion of fact

[8] L Carroll, *Through the Looking Glass* (London, Macmillan, 1872).
[9] *Edwards v Bairstow* (above n 1) 228.
[10] ibid.
[11] *Cooper v Stubbs* (above n 5).

without having applied any wrong principle, then their decision is final upon the matter'.

The Court of Appeal in *Cooper v Stubbs* was obviously in agreement as to the test to be applied to determine whether they could disturb the decision of the Commissioners but differed in their conclusion as to whether that test was satisfied.

The House of Lords, in the subsequent case of *Leeming v Jones*, accepted that position without examining it.[12]

The 'divergence created by a certain independence of spirit north of the Tweed' referred to by the Master of the Rolls in *Edwards v Bairstow* was troubling precisely because it appeared that the Scottish courts were potentially taking a different approach, as the Scottish cases referred to in the appeal to the High Court[13] could have been (and, in the lower courts, were) read as indicating that the question of whether there is an adventure in the nature of a trade should be regarded as a question of law, or at least a mixed question of fact and law,[14] and that as such the Court of Session had found that the decision of the Commissioners was not binding on the higher courts.

The Court of Appeal's concerns that Scotland was heading off in a different legal direction were not shared by Lord Radcliffe. He confirmed that

> it is a question of law what meaning is to be given to the words ... 'adventure or concern in the nature of trade' ... The only thing that I would deprecate is too much abbreviation in stating the question, as by asserting that it is simply a question of fact whether or not a trade exists. It is not simply a question of fact.

Lord Radcliffe clearly did not consider that he was saying anything particularly new, noting that he was 'only saying what was said by' judges in a number of other cases, including *Cooper v Stubbs*, although with respect to the ultimate decision in that case he notes '*sed victa Catoni*'[15] indicating that he agreed with the principle set out by Warrington and Atkins LJ although perhaps not with their conclusions as to the application of that principle.

Looking at the Scottish decisions, Lord Radcliffe noted that the same principle is being applied 'though sometimes in somewhat different words'[16] and quoted Lord Normand in *Fraser* with approval:

> Where it is competent for a tribunal to make findings in fact which are excluded from review, the Appeal Court has always jurisdiction to intervene if it appears either

---

[12] *Leeming v Jones* (1930) 15 TC 333; the appeal to the House of Lords was with regard to an alternative assessment under a different case, so that there was no requirement for the Lords to scrutinise the point.

[13] *CIR v Fraser* (1942) 24 TC 498; *CIR v Toll Property Co Ltd* (1952) 34 TC 13; *CIR v Reinhold* (1953) 34 TC 389.

[14] See Lord Russell's comment in *Reinhold* (above n 13) 395.

[15] *Edwards v Bairstow* (above n 1) 229 – referring to Lucan, *Pharsalia*, I.128: 'Victrix causa deis placuit sed Victa Catoni' – 'The victorious cause pleased the gods, but the vanquished [cause pleased] Cato'.

[16] *Edwards v Bairstow* (above n 1) 229.

that the tribunal has misunderstood the statutory language ... or that the tribunal has made a finding for which there is no evidence or which is inconsistent with the evidence and contradictory of it.[17]

Viscount Simonds agreed, noting that

> where all the admitted or found facts point one way and the inference is the other way ... it is easy either to say that the Commissioners have made a wrong inference of fact because they have misdirected themselves in law or to take a short cut and say that they have made a wrong inference of law, and I venture to doubt whether there is more than this in the divergence between the two jurisdictions which has so much agitated the Revenue authorities.[18]

In short, the lower courts' concerns as to the direction being taken by the Scottish courts (effectively, the entire basis of the permission to appeal in *Edwards v Bairstow*) were not shared by the House of Lords, which took the view that Scottish law had not headed off in any strange direction, on this point at least.

Lord Radcliffe concluded that it

> may be that the facts found are such that no person acting judicially and properly instructed as to the relevant law could have come to the determination under appeal. [The Court] has no option but to assume that there has been some misconception of the law ... So there, too, there has been error in point of law.

The courts had previously tried to determine exactly what form such an error in law might take but Lord Radcliffe sidestepped the question, noting that he did not think that it made much difference whether

> this state of affairs is described as one in which there is no evidence to support the determination or as one in which the evidence is inconsistent with and contradictory of the determination or as one in which the true and only reasonable conclusion contradicts the determination.

He preferred the latter interpretation since 'in cases such as these many of the facts are likely to be neutral in themselves and only to take their colour from the combination of circumstances in which they are found to occur'.[19]

Although Lord Radcliffe's opinion is the one most often quoted, Viscount Simonds came to the same conclusion, albeit in somewhat fewer words:

> [T]o say that a transaction is or is not an adventure in the nature of trade is to say that it has or has not the characteristics which distinguish such an adventure. But it is a question of law not of fact what are those characteristics.[20]

---

[17] ibid, 299, quoting *Fraser* (above n 13) 501.
[18] ibid, 227.
[19] ibid, 230.
[20] ibid, 226.

IV. PRIMACY OF THE FACT-FINDING COURT

It is, arguably, curious that *Edwards v Bairstow* continues to be quoted as the authority for the view that findings of fact by the court of first instance are not to be disturbed unless no court could reasonably come to that conclusion,[21] given that the Lords themselves rather seemed to take that principle for granted as one of long-standing origin. As set out above, there is no indication that they considered that they were saying anything new – quite the opposite, with the decision largely taking the view that 'of course this is how it works'.

However, a review of preceding cases suggests that perhaps that the caveat to the principle, that the conclusion or finding had to be reasonably arrived at, was becoming overlooked.

In 1921, Lord Sterndale had noted that 'if the Commissioners come to a conclusion of fact *without having applied any wrong principle*, then their decision is final upon the matter'[22] (emphasis added). In 1925, as mentioned above, the Court of Appeal in *Cooper v Stubbs* noted in various forms that 'if [the Commissioners] have rightly directed themselves in law their decision cannot be interfered with' and Atkins LJ approved of Lord Sterndale's words. However, again as previously discussed, although all three judges in *Cooper v Stubbs* agreed with the principle, only one of the judges (Pollock MR) felt able to say that the Commissioners had applied any wrong principle.

By 1933, in *Townsend v Grundy*[23] Finlay J in the High Court noted that

in *Cooper v Stubbs* … Mr. Justice Rowlatt and the Master of the Rolls appear to have thought that it might be got rid of, I suppose, on the basis of there being no evidence, but the majority of the Court of Appeal thought otherwise. That being so, it is unnecessary for me to deal further with that point.

As the Crown had chosen not to challenge the finding in *Townsend v Grundy*, the High Court did not actually consider whether they could challenge the finding, but the judge seemed to be taking the Court of Appeal's decision in *Cooper v Stubbs* as meaning that a finding of fact by the Commissioners could only be disturbed where there is no evidence *at all* to support it.

---

[21] See, eg, *Samarkand Film Partnership No 3 and others* [2017] EWCA Civ 77, para 59 quoting with approval *Eclipse Film Partners (No 35) LLP v HMRC* [2015] EWCA Civ 95, para 113: 'It follows that the conclusion of the tribunal of fact … can only be successfully challenged as a matter of law if the tribunal made an error of principle or if the only reasonable conclusion on the primary facts found is inconsistent with the tribunal's conclusion'. See also *Oak Tree Motor Homes Ltd* [2017] UKUT 27 (TCC), para 26: 'Findings of fact by the FTT cannot normally be challenged because they are not matters of law unless the facts found are such that no person acting judicially and properly instructed as to the relevant law could have come to the determination under appeal which is an error of law'.

[22] *Currie v CIR* [1921] 2 KB 332, (1921) 12 TC 245.

[23] *Townsend v Grundy* (1933) 18 TC 140.

Moving on to 1942, this hardening of the position continued in the High Court in *Hesketh Estates*[24] where Wrottesley J noted that

> if there is evidence in this case on which the Commissioners could find what they did find, then it is not for me to weigh the pros and cons in order to see whether in my judgment the scales at the end of the weighing turn in one direction or the other.

Whilst that was consistent with the principle in general, the question of whether it was *reasonable* for the Commissioners to find as they did was noted but not considered. Instead, the question under consideration again seemed to be the stricter question of whether there was any evidence at all, with the judge noting that 'I find myself quite unable to say that there is no material upon which the Commissioners could find as they did find'. Although the decision of the Commissioners upon that material might have been reasonable, the judge did not touch upon the question of whether or not it was so reasonable.

This arguable narrowing of their own powers by the higher courts appears to have led to the position in the High Court and Court of Appeal in *Edwards v Bairstow* on which Lord Radcliffe commented that

> the English Courts have been led to be rather over-ready to treat these questions as 'pure questions of fact' ... there is no reason to ... invite the Courts to impose any exceptional restraints upon themselves because they are dealing with cases that arise out of facts found by Commissioners. [The] duty [of the higher courts] is no more than to examine those facts with a decent respect for the tribunal appealed from, and, if they think that the only reasonable conclusion on the facts found is inconsistent with the determination come to, to say so without more ado.

In other words, the House of Lords decision could be regarded as indicating that the High Court and the Court of Appeal should have had the courage of their convictions and not simply considered themselves bound by the General Commissioners' decision without further question, where the Commissioners' decision was not a sustainable one.

To the extent that this case is a landmark case this is, in my view, the key point: the House of Lords reminding the lower courts that findings of the court of first instance are to be respected but not revered. Where the finding is not one which can be reasonably made, that is an error of law open to appeal in the same way as any clear misstatement of the law in the decision.

V. THAT WAS THEN; WHAT NOW?

The question of the extent to which an error of fact can be regarded as an error of law has, in more recent years, been raised in the context of administrative law and in changes in the courts and tribunals themselves.

---

[24] *Hesketh Estates v Craddock* (1942) 25 TC 1.

In administrative law, the court had long been very reluctant to permit judicial review on the basis of errors of fact and had taken the view that questions of fact were to be decided solely by the relevant public body. This approach seemed to be contrary to that in *Edwards v Bairstow* and persisted long after the House of Lords decision had criticised the Court of Appeal and the High Court for not properly considering the Commissioners' analysis of the facts.

Administrative law, particularly in the context of judicial review, starts from the principle that the institutional capacity of the original decision maker should be respected and has been dominated by the concept of unreasonableness established by Lord Greene MR in *Wednesbury*[25] in 1948 that the courts should only interfere where a decision is so unreasonable that no reasonable authority could ever come to it.

Although that principle is echoed in the House of Lords decision in *Edwards v Bairstow*, the *Wednesbury* principle was interpreted as requiring extreme behaviour. This arguably brought administrative law into the same position as that of the lower courts criticised by the House of Lords in *Edwards v Bairstow*. Attempts were made to reformulate the *Wednesbury* principle in relation to errors of fact but the courts were slow to accept that an error of fact could be grounds for review, given that it appeared to involve the court in assessing the merits of the decision in an area of law where the court's role in relation to judicial review was considered to be purely supervisory. Nevertheless, judicial review applies only where there is no other remedy available. To refuse to allow *any* review of errors of fact would be contrary to justice.

It was not until the case of *R v Secretary of State for the Home Department ex parte Khawaja*[26] that matters began to change, when Lord Bridge held that the court was able to consider whether the evidence justified the conclusion reached by the Secretary of State and was not simply limited to seeing whether there was any evidence at all for the conclusion: in effect, taking a similar view to that confirmed some three decades earlier in *Edwards v Bairstow*.

This was eventually established clearly in 2004 in *E v Secretary of State for the Home Department*[27] when Carnwath LJ concluded that an error of fact could form a ground of review in a judicial review of a decision from the Immigration Appeal Tribunal bringing administrative law into accord with the approach of the courts in other areas of law (including *Edwards v Bairstow*), albeit with very specific requirements as to what would be required for an error of fact to amount to a ground for review.

A few years later, in 2009, the General and Special Commissioners of Income Tax were replaced by the Tax Chamber of the First-tier Tribunal and the Tax and Chancery Chamber of the Upper Tribunal, under the Tribunals, Courts and Enforcement Act 2007 (TCEA 2007). That Act gives a number of powers to

---

[25] *Associated Provincial Picture Houses v Wednesbury Corporation* [1948] 1 KB 223.
[26] *R v Secretary of State for the Home Department ex parte Khawaja* [1982] 1 WLR 625.
[27] *E v Secretary of State for the Home Department* [2004] EWCA Civ 49.

the tribunals and other courts, including a power to the Upper Tribunal under section 12(4) of TCEA 2007 to make 'such findings of fact as it considers appropriate' where the Upper Tribunal sets aside a First-tier Tribunal decision and remakes the decision. Section 14(4) gives the same power to the Court of Appeal when remaking an Upper Tribunal decision.

At first glance, this power to making findings of fact would suggest that TCEA 2007 bulldozes the principle confirmed in *Edwards v Bairstow*, that findings of fact by the General and Special Commissioners are to be respected (but not revered) unless unreasonably arrived at, albeit with a less extreme interpretation of 'unreasonable' than that taken by administrative law.

However, a little more exploration makes it clear that the bulldozer has not been unleashed: section 11 permits an appeal from the First-tier Tribunal to the Upper Tribunal on a point of law only, and section 13 permits an appeal from the Upper Tribunal to the Court of Appeal on the same basis only (in each case continuing the centuries-old principle of English law that an error of law is required for an appeal). The point is reinforced in sections 12 and 14, each of which operate only where the Upper Tribunal or Court of Appeal (as relevant) have found that there was an error of law.

The fact-finding powers in section 12(4) and section 14(4) therefore only operate where an error has been made on a point of law by the lower court. The powers are not a blanket invitation to the appellate courts to re-find facts, but they do permit facts to be found by the appellate courts, and in this they seem to broaden the scope of the appellate court: previously, as indicated in *Edwards v Bairstow* itself, where an appellate court found that there had been an error of law, the case was sent back to the lower court;[28] the courts did not specifically have power to remake findings of fact. There has, however, been little use of this power in the Tax Tribunal at least. It is more usual for matters to be sent back to the First Tier Tribunal for a re-hearing where there has been an error in law; this seems to be a practical point in that, unless it is clear on the face of the decision before the hearing that there has been an error in law, the Upper Tribunal hearing is unlikely to be in a position to investigate the facts. The evidence and arguments presented will be focused on the decision being appealed and not arranged to facilitate what would be, in effect, a re-hearing.

There is some question whether the powers given by TCEA 2007 extend even further than that: Carnwath LJ in *Pendragon*[29] considered the appellate powers given by TCEA 2007 and noted that:

> Having found errors of approach in the consideration by the First-tier Tribunal, it was appropriate for [the Upper Tribunal] to exercise their power to remake the decision, making such factual and legal judgments as were necessary for the purpose …

---

[28] eg, Rowlatt J in *Edwards v Bairstow* sent the case back to the General Commissioners on the first appeal, on the basis that they had used the wrong test in law to determine whether the amounts were taxable.

[29] *HMRC v Pendragon plc & Ors* [2015] UKSC 37, para 50.

Although no doubt paying respect to the factual findings of the First-tier Tribunal, they were not bound by them.

So far, not so different from *Edwards v Bairstow* (given the new specific power to remake the decision given by sections 12 and 14). The principle echoes Lord Radcliffe's comment in *Edwards v Bairstow* that

> [the] duty [of the higher courts] is no more than to examine [the facts found by the lower court] with a decent respect for the tribunal appealed from, and, if they think that the only reasonable conclusion on the facts found is inconsistent with the determination come to, to say so without more ado.

However, matters may begin to diverge from *Edwards v Bairstow* if TCEA 2007 is in future interpreted in line with Lord Carnwath's further comment in *Pendragon* that, following Lord Hoffmann in *Lawson v Serco*,[30] the evaluation of primary facts to decide whether a question of law is a question of fact or a question of law would depend 'upon whether as a matter of policy one thinks that it is a decision which an appellate body with jurisdiction limited to errors of law should be able to review'.

This is not the only occasion on which Lord Carnwath has made this point: in *R (Jones) v First Tier Tribunal*[31] together with Lord Hope he quoted Lord Hoffmann again and notes that in establishing the tribunal system under TCEA 2007, it 'was hoped that the Upper Tribunal might be permitted to interpret "points of law" flexibly to include other points of principle or even factual judgment of general relevance to the specialised area in question'.[32]

Lord Carnwath's comments have been interpreted[33] as expanding the appellate jurisdiction of the Upper Tribunal, suggesting that the Upper Tribunal is no longer limited by *Edwards v Bairstow* when considering the First-tier Tribunal's evaluation of primary facts.

It is questionable whether the decisions of Lord Carnwath in *Pendragon* and Lord Hoffman in *Lawson v Serco* can be interpreted in quite so expansive a manner as such commentators suggest. Lord Hoffmann was considering the argument that the Employment Tribunal's evaluation of primary facts was in itself a finding of fact which the Employment Appeal Tribunal had no jurisdiction to disturb and he goes on to state that it is a question of law whether a statutory provision is met on given facts but that it is also 'a question of degree on which the decision of the [lower court] is entitled to considerable respect'. He notes, as quoted by Lord Carnwath, that

> whether one characterises this as a question of fact depends ... upon whether as a matter of policy one thinks that it is a decision which an appellate body with jurisdiction limited to errors of law should be able to review.

[30] *Lawson v Serco* [2006] UKHL 3.
[31] *R (Jones) v First Tier Tribunal* [2013] UKSC 19.
[32] ibid, para 43.
[33] See, eg, J Brinsmead-Stockham, 'Analysis – Tax appeals: What is the "Point of Law"?' (26 September 2015) 1278 *Tax Journal* 14; JF Avery Jones, 'A New Approach to Tax Disputes' (1 November 2015) *Tax Adviser*.

Lord Hoffmann appears to be echoing the decision of Lord Radcliffe in *Edwards v Bairstow* in his assertion that what is a trade is a question of law, but that there is a question of degree as to whether a particular set of facts amounts to a trade. If the evaluation of those facts leads to a conclusion which could not be reasonably reached, that evaluation could be regarded as an appealable error of law. Although Lord Carnwath described Lord Hoffmann's decision as a 'flexible approach' it is obviously not a new approach to the point.

Where, however, TCEA 2007 may go beyond *Edwards v Bairstow* is this: once the Upper Tribunal has concluded that there has been an error in law and remade the decision, Lord Carnwath's interpretation of TCEA 2007 is that the Court of Appeal's role on a further appeal is only to consider 'the merits of the Upper Tribunal's reasoning in its own terms, rather than by reference to their evaluation of the First Tier's decision'.[34]

If the Upper Tribunal's 'evaluation of the First-tier's decision' which is not to be considered in this context extends to an evaluation of whether there has been an error of law enabling the Upper Tribunal to remake the decision, this could arguably bulldoze through the principle in *Edwards v Bairstow* at the First-tier Tribunal level. If that evaluation is to be disregarded entirely there would appear to be no check on the ability of the Upper Tribunal to substitute its own preferred interpretation of facts for those of the First-tier Tribunal even where the First-tier Tribunal's evaluation is not unreasonable.

Although a logical conclusion from his words, it does seem that this is not quite what Lord Carnwath intended, as he also noted that there must be an error of law before the Upper Tribunal has jurisdiction to remake the decision, and the focus of his comments were on the Court of Appeal's assessment of the remade decision and, it could be said, not on any consideration of the Upper Tribunal's assessment as to whether there had been an error in law.

The Court of Appeal has recently made it clear that it considers that it is required to take into account both the First-tier Tribunal and Upper Tribunal decisions when considering an appeal: in *Criminal Injuries Compensation Authority v Hutton*[35] the Court of Appeal overturned a decision of the Upper Tribunal which had found the First-tier Tribunal's decision to be legally flawed. In the Court of Appeal, Gross LJ made it clear that the Court of Appeal, as a generalist court, should act with restraint when considering the decisions of the specialist tribunals but when

> determining whether a question was one of 'fact' or 'law', this Court should have regard to context … ('pragmatism', 'expediency' or 'policy', per *Jones*), so as to ensure both that decisions of tribunals of fact are given proper weight and to provide scope for specialist appellate tribunals to shape the development of law and practice in their field.

---

[34] *Pendragon* (above n 29) para 51.
[35] *Criminal Injuries Compensation Authority v Hutton* [2016] EWCA Civ 1305.

In *Hutton*, Gross LJ also took the view that although it might on occasion be appropriate for the Upper Tribunal to take a broad view of what amounts to a question of law, it should not do so where the circumstances of the case do not clearly require it to 'shape the development of law and practice' in a particular area. This is, of course, as equally pragmatic an approach as that in *Jones*, and still treats questions of fact and law as flexible where there are good reasons for the Upper Tribunal to undertake such shaping. In *Hutton*, the Court of Appeal concluded that there were no such good reasons.

Back in the area of tax, the Upper Tribunal considered Lord Carnwath's comments a short while later[36] and took the view that his analysis was that

> the proper approach of the Upper Tribunal to challenges to findings of fact made by the First-tier depended on the stage at which those challenges were being considered ... However, once an error of law has been established – whether on the application of the *Edwards v Bairstow* test or because of some other kind of error of law – it is important to recognise the power of the Upper Tribunal under s12 of the Tribunals, Courts and Enforcement Act 2007 to re-make the decision of the FTT and, in doing so, to make appropriate findings of fact.[37]

Lord Carnwath's comments can certainly be interpreted as being consistent with a two-stage approach, as noted above, although the comments were not quite as specifically stated as the Upper Tribunal describes.

As a result, the Upper Tribunal concluded that they 'consider that challenges to issues of pure finding of fact by the First-tier Tribunal can only succeed on the familiar basis set out by the House of Lords in *Edwards v Bairstow*' and

> The proper approach thus remains ... that for a question of law to arise in the circumstances, the appellant must first identify the finding which is challenged; secondly, show that it is significant in relation to the conclusion; thirdly, identify the evidence, if any, which was relevant to that finding; and, fourthly, show that that finding, on the basis of that evidence, was one which the tribunal was not entitled to make. What is not permitted ... is a roving selection of evidence coupled with a general assertion that the tribunal's conclusion was against the weight of the evidence and was therefore wrong.

Lord Carnwath's comments were again raised at the Upper Tribunal in *Eclipse 35*,[38] where it was submitted, taking Lord Carnwath's comments in support, that 'the Upper Tribunal ... should now apply a more expansive approach to what qualifies as a question of law than was laid down by the House of Lords in *Edwards v Bairstow*'.[39] Tax scheme cases such as *Eclipse 35* have revived the question of what amounts to a trade, as such cases tend to consider the question of the extent to which losses are available for offset, and so have brought *Edwards v Bairstow* back into consideration in decisions in a new context.

---

[36] *Massey & Anor (t/a Hilden Park Partnership)* [2015] UKUT 405.
[37] ibid, para 83.
[38] *Eclipse Film Partners (No 35) LLP v HMRC* [2013] UKUT 0639.
[39] ibid, para 42.

The Upper Tribunal did not follow this submission in *Eclipse 35*, on the basis that 'No clear policy-based reason to justify departure from the conventional approach has been made out on this appeal'.[40] However, the Upper Tribunal did note that

> some issues of evaluative judgment in tax cases may be found to lend themselves to a more intrusive policy-based classification as questions of law (amenable to appeal) rather than as questions of fact [where the Upper Tribunal is] making a contribution to the coherent development and consistent application of the law applicable in its specialist field by doing so.[41]

In this case, the Upper Tribunal seems to be taking a similar view to that which the Court of Appeal took later in *Hutton*, noting that there may in some cases be good reasons for the Upper Tribunal to take a flexible approach as to whether there is an error in law – but that this was not one such case.

The Upper Tribunal also noted that

> that in the tax field such cases are likely to be unusual … A particularly clear policy-based reason would need to be shown to justify the Upper Tribunal departing on any particular issue from well-established principles of classification of questions of fact and questions of law in the tax field.

However, perhaps with an eye to resource and other constraints, the Upper Tribunal further pointed out that

> broadening the ambit of the classes of case which are regarded as involving appeal on a point of law would extend the business which the Upper Tribunal would have to conduct, which would be detrimental to its overall ability to cope with the business coming to it without delay [and so] the Upper Tribunal should not be overly ready to change the conventional approach in the tax field by reference to *R (Jones) v First-tier Tribunal*, and should only do so where strong reasons to justify such a change are made out.[42]

The Court of Appeal in *Eclipse 35*[43] did not chose to take on the submission in detail or to elaborate on this. The decision in that case noted only that

> the conclusion of the tribunal of fact as to whether the activity is or is not a trade can only be successfully challenged as a matter of law if the tribunal made an error of principle or if the only reasonable conclusion on the primary facts found is inconsistent with the tribunal's conclusion. These propositions are well established in the case law: *Edwards v Bairstow*.[44]

---

[40] ibid, para 46.
[41] ibid, para 43.
[42] ibid, para 44.
[43] *Eclipse Film Partners (No 35) LLP v HMRC* [2015] EWCA Civ 95; the subsequent Supreme Court decision in *Eclipse Film Partners (No 35) LLP v HMRC* [2016] UKSC 24 is limited to a question of the power of the First-tier Tribunal to make an order for costs and so does not venture into this territory at all.
[44] *Eclipse 35* (CA, above n 43) para 113.

Lord Carnwath's views were considered in more detail recently by the Upper Tribunal in *Rasul*[45] which nevertheless held that they 'can find nothing in Lord Carnwath's judgment suggesting that the Upper Tribunal should be free to interfere with the FTT's findings of primary facts except on the basis described in [*Edwards v Bairstow*]'.

Accordingly, the Upper Tribunal does not yet appear to be entirely seizing the view that Lord Carnwath intended that it should be free to reinterpret evaluations of fact by the First-tier Tribunal even where the conclusions are not unreasonable: the principle for which *Edwards v Bairstow* is primarily known seems to remain largely intact. Where it may, perhaps, be stretched a little in future is in the context of avoidance cases: in *Eclipse 35*, the Upper Tribunal declined the opportunity to 'take a more expansive approach' but did not reject the concept out of hand.

VI. NATURE OF TRADE

The decision in *Edwards v Bairstow* makes very little reference to what is, or is not, in an 'adventure in the nature of trade', with the House of Lords principally noting that it was strikingly obvious that a trade existed.

Viscount Simonds states that 'I do not find in the careful and indeed exhaustive statement of facts any item which points to the transaction not being an adventure in the nature of trade. Everything pointed the other way'.[46]

Lord Radcliffe in his turn added a bit more detail, referring to a similar decision in *Leeming v Jones* and stating that

> I am bound to say, with all respect to the judgments under appeal, that I can see only one true and reasonable conclusion. The profit from the set of operations that comprised the purchase and sales of the spinning plant was the profit of an adventure in the nature of trade.[47]

Even in *Leeming v Jones* Viscount Dunedin had said that

> this case is a striking example of the class of appeal in Income Tax cases, which on a recent occasion I felt bound to deprecate. There is no new question of law involved in it, merely the application of old principles to the particular facts.[48]

It should be noted that HMRC's Business Income Manual cites *Edwards v Bairstow* as authority for the proposition that 'the breaking down of assets into smaller lots to facilitate a sale may be a pointer to a trading motive'.[49] Although

---

[45] *Rasul v HMRC* [2017] UKUT 357 (TCC), [2017] STC 2261.
[46] *Edwards v Bairstow* (above n 1) 226.
[47] ibid, 231.
[48] *Leeming v Jones* (above n 12) 358.
[49] HMRC, 'Meaning of trade: badges of trade: modification of the asset' in *Business Income Manual*, BIM20275, available at www.gov.uk/hmrc-internal-manuals/business-income-manual/bim20275.

this obviously occurred in the facts, the authority for the point might be better found in *Leeming v Jones*, as Lord Thankerton there said that 'a transaction may be treated as of the nature of trade where, although there may have been only one initial purchase there has been a series of sub-sales of an ordinary market nature'.[50]

Nevertheless, even with the earlier cases, it is *Edwards v Bairstow* that has made its way into the collective legal consciousness: recently, the First-tier Tribunal in *Gill*[51] quoted *Wannell v Rothwell*[52] which stated that

> in general a substantial degree of organisation (a very imprecise term, especially across the whole range of trading activities) is neither a necessary not a sufficient condition for carrying on a trade (for the first limb see the observations of Lord Radcliffe in *Edwards v Bairstow*).

VII. CONCLUSION

Edwards v Bairstow appears to be a 'landmark' case by virtue of being the right case at the right time, rather than because it sets out any particularly new principles. In terms of the original dispute, whether the sale of the plant was an adventure in the nature of trade, the decision merely follows earlier cases, particularly *Leeming v Jones*, with no additional commentary; indeed, the Lords appeared to find it obvious that the activity amounted to a trade.

The most notable feature of the case is that the Lords hauled back an apparently increasing tendency of the lower appellate courts in the previous decades to treat as sacrosanct the findings of fact of the court of first instance. That point is now primarily what this case is known for; although it is occasionally mentioned in the context of what is a trade, the overwhelming majority of the citations of the case in legal databases such as BAILII are references to the question as to when and whether the evaluation of facts of a tribunal can be challenged in a higher court.

Most recently, the case has been revived in discussions as to the underlying purpose of the Upper Tribunal as a result of the TCEA 2007, particularly influenced by Lord Carnwath. Comments in decisions, both by Lord Carnwath and by others, suggest that TCEA 2007 allows the Upper Tribunal to take a wider view of what is a question of law when evaluating whether the Upper Tribunal has jurisdiction to remake a decision of the First-tier Tribunal. The basis for these comments is the view that under TCEA 2007 'an important function of the Upper Tribunal is to develop structured guidance on the use of expressions which are central to the scheme, and so as to reduce the risk of inconsistent

---

[50] *Leeming v Jones* (above n 12) 364.
[51] *Gill v HMRC* [2017] UKFTT 597.
[52] *Wannell v Rothwell* [1996] STC 450.

results by different panels at the First-tier level' and that, as such, '"law" for this purpose being widely interpreted to include issues of general principle affecting the jurisdiction in question'.[53]

Commentators, as noted above, have argued that TCEA 2007 has therefore allowed for a widening of the *Edwards v Bairstow* principle. It is, however, questionable whether such a widening is really a new consequence of TCEA 2007 itself or is instead an ongoing judicial evolution as, even in administrative law, the extent to which facts can be reviewed has expanded. There is nothing specific in TCEA 2007 to support the widening as a new concept; the White Paper which preceded TCEA 2007 does refer to the role of 'the appellate tier in achieving consistency in the application of the law'[54] but does not particularly set out to establish a broadening of the *Edwards v Bairstow* principle.

Judicial evolution may be at point in an article in 2009 in which Lord Carnwath noted that 'if expediency and the competency of the tribunal are relevant, the dividing line between law and fact may vary at each stage'.[55] He considered that an expert appellate tribunal is 'peculiarly fitted to determine, or provide guidance, on categorisation issues [and] should be permitted to venture more freely into the "grey area" separating fact from law, than an ordinary court' and that 'expediency requires that, where Parliament has established such a specialist appellate tribunal in a particular field, its expertise should be used to best effect, to shape and direct the development of law and practice in that field'.

Further, in 2013, Lord Carnwath also noted that

> In 19 years as a judge of administrative law cases I cannot remember ever deciding a case by simply asking myself whether an administrative decision was 'beyond the range of reasonable responses' ... My approach I suspect has been much closer to the characteristically pragmatic approach suggested by Lord Donaldson in 1988: 'the ultimate question would, as always, be whether something had gone wrong of a nature and degree which required the intervention of the court and, if so, what form that intervention should take'. If the answer appears to be yes, then one looks for a legal hook to hang it on. And if there is none suitable, one may need to adapt one.[56]

Arguably, Lord Carnwath's comments in cases such as *Pendragon* are, therefore, not so much occasioned by TCEA 2007 but instead indicate that TCEA 2007 was a legal hook on which to hang a long-standing 'pragmatic approach' which he had taken in earlier cases such as the administrative law case of *E*. This pragmatic approach was not new to Lord Carnwath: Lord Denning to the House

---

[53] See above, in *Pendragon* (above n 29) and *R (Jones) v First Tier Tribunal* (above n 31).

[54] Department for Constitutional Affairs, *Transforming Public Services: Complaints, Redress and Tribunals* (July 2004), available at webarchive.nationalarchives.gov.uk/+/http:/www.dca.gov.uk/pubs/adminjust/transformfull.pdf, para 7.20.

[55] R Carnwath, 'Tribunal Justice, A New Start' [2009] *PL* 48, 63–64.

[56] R Carnwath, 'From Judicial Outrage to Sliding Scales – Where Next for Wednesbury?' ALBA Annual Lecture (12 November 2013), available at www.supremecourt.uk/docs/speech-131112-lord-carnwath.pdf.

of Lords in *Griffiths*[57] set out the same point in rather fewer words, saying simply 'Here is a question of law, if your Lordships please to treat it as such'.

Indeed, it is perhaps arguable that this is precisely what the House of Lords did in *Edwards v Bairstow*: the opinions of both Lord Radcliffe and Viscount Simonds could be summarised by the pragmatic 'it's obviously a trade, we need to intervene' – although they perhaps didn't need to look too far for the legal hook on which to hang their intervention.

---

[57] *Griffiths (Inspector of Taxes) v JP Harrison (Watford) Ltd* (1962) 40 TC 281, 300.

9

Odeon Associated Theatres Ltd v Jones (HM Inspector of Taxes) *(1971)*

A Delphic Pronouncement and a Fundamental Tension

JUDITH FREEDMAN*

I. INTRODUCTION

O DEON THEATRES V *Jones (Odeon)*[1] is frequently cited as setting out the relationship between legal decision-making and accounting evidence on the definition of taxable profits. Like many oft-cited cases, the actual decision may be less important than the repeated dictum. One particular phrase caught hold of the tax community's imagination. Pennycuick V-C explained that, although the court would listen to the evidence of accountants, it was for the court to make the final decision when ascertaining the true profit of the taxpayer.

> At the end of the day the Court must determine what is the correct principle of commercial accountancy to be applied. Having done so, it will ascertain the true profit of the trade according to that principle, and the profit so ascertained is the subject of taxation.[2]

This quote comes from the High Court decision, later upheld by the Court of Appeal. It has been selectively cited to suit both sides of the debate.

* The author thanks the anonymous referees, the editors, Alexander Kanischev and Jane O'Hare for their assistance and comments. The usual disclaimers apply.

[1] *Odeon Associated Theatres Ltd v Jones (HM Inspector of Taxes)* (1971) 48 TC 257 (HC and CA).

[2] ibid, Pennycuick V-C, 273. Sir John Pennycuick became Vice-Chancellor during the course of this case. A new judicial post of Vice-Chancellor (its last holder having been that of 1882) was created by the Administration of Justice Act 1970, which came into effect on 1 October 1971.

Like many deceptively clear summaries of the state of the law, Pennycuick V-C's famous 'few words by way of explanation' in the *Odeon* case have turned out to contain deep and unanswered questions, buried beneath the apparent simplicity of his phraseology.[3] The Vice-Chancellor put his finger on a tension that remains unresolved and is unlikely ever to be resolved while we use profit as the basis for business taxation.[4] The fact that the UK Office of Tax Simplification is continuing to explore the relationship between financial reporting and taxable profits now shows both the significance of the issue and the difficulties involved.[5]

It is no coincidence that *Odeon* was first heard in 1969, the year in which the first UK Accounting Standards Steering Committee was set up. The decision marks a stage in the 'uneasy relationship between accounting and law'.[6] As Napier and Noke explain, 'the problems of variability and subjectivity in accounting measures'[7] had been exacerbated by a boom in takeovers and mergers in the 1960s and the increasing emphasis on financial reporting as a tool to be used by investment analysts led to moves towards establishing agreed, published accounting standards. Initially, standardisation of accounting principles seemed to offer technical and certain answers, but it was not long before this was seen to be over-complacent.

It is now clearly recognised in much academic accounting literature that accounting standards can be value-laden and contentious. The concept of profit is seen in this writing as a chosen construction of reality.[8] In making judgements about what is to be included and how, the accounting profession is making policy decisions and prioritising the objectives it has decided upon for financial accounting. These may or may not be the same objectives as those being considered by a court in a tax or company law case, given that the objectives in such cases may differ from those of financial accounting.

---

[3] A similar supposedly simple description of the state of the law that buries much scope for dissension can be found, eg, in the case of *Collector of Stamp Revenue v Arrowtown Assets Ltd* [2004] 1 HKLRD 77. Intended as a descriptive summary it was developed into a dictum that is the starting point for every discussion of the judicial approach to tax avoidance in the UK and yet which tells us very little and gives the courts scope to decide either way in many cases.

[4] There are arguments for moving to other bases for taxation, such as sales, but this chapter will not explore these further as they are outside the scope of a discussion of the landmark case.

[5] Office of Tax Simplification, *Simplification of the Corporation Tax Computation* (July 2017) and see discussion below.

[6] C Napier and C Noke, 'Accounting and Law: An Historical Overview of an Uneasy Relationship' in M Bromwich and A Hopwood, *Accounting and the Law* (London, Prentice Hall and ICAEW, 1992).

[7] ibid, 42.

[8] G Morgan, 'Accounting as Reality Construction: Towards a New Epistemology for Accounting Practice' (1988) 13 *Accounting, Organizations and Society* 477; M Gill, *Accountant's Truth: Knowledge and Ethics in the Financial World* (Oxford, Oxford University Press, 2009). One only needs to consider issues like transfer pricing to appreciate that there are sometimes no correct answers on profit definition, only judgements within a range. But this runs much deeper and covers decisions such as whether to use fair value accounting: see the discussion in P Miller and M Power, 'Accounting, Organizing, and Economizing: Connecting Accounting Research and Organization Theory' (2013) 7 *The Academy of Management Annals* 557, 590.

The objectives of financial accounting can be said to be to inform a range of stakeholders (albeit that the standards are aimed primarily at shareholders, prospective shareholders and creditors);[9] to bring information quickly to market; to measure economic strength and performance; and to focus on decision usefulness, relevance and therefore materiality.[10]

The objectives of tax law are different. Tax rules need to bring information to revenue authorities that is reliable, precise and results in reasonably definite answers. Tax authorities prefer one figure, not a range of figures or a note in the accounts qualifying a figure.[11] All taxpayers need to be taxed in a standard way; it should not be a matter of judgement, if at all possible, and for this reason materiality is not usually a relevant consideration. Some areas of tax law are firmly based on a realisation principle, for example, capital gains tax. Accruals accounting systems move away from this, but how much it is wise to do so for tax purposes is a central question. Volatility is even more of a problem for taxation than it is for financial accounting more generally because, once paid out, tax can be difficult to recover or may have been borne by the wrong group of people or in the wrong year for certain reliefs. Like rules on distributions under company law, tax systems may lean further towards prudence than financial accounting for this reason.[12] Tax computation rules also very often seek to provide incentives or to deter certain behaviour. Further, they may be designed to serve public policy – for example, restrictions on the ability to deduct fines or entertainment expenses. Tax rules may also need to deal with complex avoidance issues that interact with other areas of law.[13]

In the light of these differences, it seems that the courts will never relinquish complete control of the basis for legal decisions about taxation, and it is doubtful if they should do so. Even if the accounting concept is the starting point for legal decisions about taxation, the final legal decision needs to take account of factual context, any relevant legislation and underlying legal principles from other areas of law such as contract or property law and generally the objectives of the law in the case in question. Whether this qualification includes taking into account unlegislated tax law principles is the question that remains

[9] International Accounting Standards Board, 'Conceptual Framework for Financial Reporting 2018', available at www.iasplus.com/en-gb/standards/other/framework; some would argue against this investor primacy, but they have not prevailed so far.

[10] G Whittington, 'Tax Policy and Accounting Standards' [1995] *BTR* 452; J Freedman, 'Financial and Tax Accounting: Transparency and "Truth"' in W Schön (ed), *Tax and Corporate Governance* (Berlin, Springer Science, 2008).

[11] Of course, there are exceptions, such as transfer pricing rules, and other rules that rely on valuation, and these tend to lead to much difficulty. Generally, tax rules need to give a definite answer, eg, on timing or what is or is not eligible for a relief, rather than giving a choice of approach as an accounting standard may do.

[12] J Freedman, 'The Role of Realisation: Accounting, Company Law and Taxation' in International Fiscal Association Congress Seminar Series 21B, *The Influence of Corporate Law and Accounting Principles in Determining Taxable Income* (Alphen aan den Rijn, Kluwer Law International, 1997).

[13] See Freedman, 'Financial and Tax Accounting' (above n 10) for an elaboration of these differences.

unanswered. The citation above[14] might suggest that is does, but *Odeon* read as a whole suggests not. Current thinking suggests that unlegislated tax principles are non-existent, but they have a habit of creeping back into the discourse when this is least expected. There is a central tension encapsulated in the *Odeon* decision that remains a puzzle today.

The line in the sand between a factual issue, to be decided purely on the basis of accounting evidence, and one that involves a point of law for the courts, is an important one from a constitutional and regulatory point of view. Whether Pennycuick V-C knew it or not, he was contributing to the drawing of that line, but in a way that would create much discussion further down the line. As shall be discussed below, the legislature in 1998 explicitly declined to change that balance where there is no specific detailed statutory intervention.[15] This leaves open questions such as that discussed in *Odeon* around the divide between capital and income, where there may be accounting evidence taken on board as a question of fact, but that are ultimately often treated as involving a question of law in a mixed matrix of law and fact, with the assertion of a legal point being brought in very much as a policy instrument by the judges.[16] These questions raise the larger question of whether principles of law external to accounting that govern the definition of profit exist and, if so, where they might come from. Arguably, as discussed below, in *Odeon*, Pennycuick V-C both accepts the existence of such principles and denies their existence, ensuring a continuing debate.

Following this introduction, the chapter discusses the decision in *Odeon* in more detail in part II. Part III considers in what context *Odeon* might be regarded as a 'landmark' case, looking at the cases in that period on the capital/income divide and on revenue recognition. Part IV considers the attempt to embed the relationship between tax law and accounting in statute in 1998. Part V discusses some post-1998 case law in so far as it highlights the unresolved tensions so clearly seen in the *Odeon* case itself. Part VI concludes.

II. CAPITAL AND REVENUE; ACCOUNTANTS AND THE COURTS

Odeon Associated Theatres Ltd 'carried on the trade of proprietors of cinematograph film theatres'.[17] This was a time at which 'film theatres' were expanding rapidly. Odeon was a major cinema circuit in the UK, a position it had achieved both by building new theatres and by buying existing theatres. Odeon cinema theatres were something close to a national institution. The case stated notes

---

[14] Text to n 2 above.

[15] Finance Act 1998, s 42, now rewritten as ITTOIA 2005, s 25; CTA 2009, s 46.

[16] HH Monroe, *Intolerable Inquisition? Reflections on the Law of Tax* (London, Stevens & Sons, 1981) 75; J Laws, 'Law and Fact' [1999] *BTR* 159; J Freedman, 'Aligning Taxable Profits and Accounting Profits: Accounting Standards, Legislators and Judges' (2004) 2 *eJournal of Tax Research* 71.

[17] Head note to *Odeon Associated Theatres Ltd* (above n 1).

that the Odeon group, by this time controlled by Lord Rank, had a policy 'aimed at protecting the British film industry from control and domination by United States film companies'.[18] This required well-maintained film theatres; a major feature of Odeon cinemas was their Art Deco buildings and their plush interiors, making them 'not only simply somewhere to watch films, but somewhere to experience them'.[19] During the war period and until the early 1950s, there were considerable restrictions on building works, meaning that the only way Odeon could expand was by buying theatres and theatre-owning companies.[20] For the same reason, many repairs that would normally have been done year on year were deferred. The taxpayer company acquired theatres from third parties and through inter-group acquisitions during the post-war period and then commenced a catch up with deferred repairs. Paragraph 6 of the case stated notes that during the war, when negotiations for the acquisition of the theatres were taking place, the taxpayer company's representative was aware that building restrictions were likely to continue in force for some time and so did not pay as much attention to a theatre's state of repair as might otherwise have been the case.[21] For the most part, the deficiencies were not of a nature requiring immediate remedy.[22] Once the building restrictions were lifted, the repairs were undertaken. Naturally enough, Odeon wanted to deduct the cost of these repairs from profits. This was before the introduction of Capital Gains Tax and so the only way to make a claim was for revenue expenses. The question seemed to boil down to the distinction between capital and revenue expenditure.

At the best of times, the distinction between capital and revenue in computing taxable profits is, as Templeman J pointed out in *Tucker v Granada*,[23]

> an intellectual minefield in which principles are elusive … analogies are treacherous … precedents appear to be vague signposts pointing in different directions and the direction finder is said to be judicial common sense. The practice of judicial common sense is difficult in revenue cases.[24]

---

[18] *Odeon Associated Theatres Ltd* (above n 1) 260; R Davenport-Hines, 'Rank, (Joseph) Arthur, Baron Rank (1888–1972)', available at doi.org/10.1093/ref:odnb/31585.

[19] *Epsom and Ewell History Explorer* 'The 1937 Odeon Cinema', available at epsomandewell historyexplorer.org.uk/Odeon1937.html; 'Our Cinemas', available at www.dcm.co.uk/our-cinema-partners. The Odeon cinemas were not unique in this – many cinemas at that time were built in grand style: see *Cinema Treasures*, 'Odeon Marble Arch', available at cinematreasures.org/theaters/12786, describing the Roman Style used in that cinema before it was taken over by Odeon in 1945.

[20] *Odeon Associated Theatres Ltd* (above n 1) 269.

[21] ibid, 261.

[22] Associated British Cinemas (ABC) operated the Marble Arch cinema until early January 1945. Odeon Theatres then took control and refurbished it, but before they could reopen, the Regal Cinema suffered damage from one of the last flying bombs to hit London and it remained closed until September 1945 when it reopened as the Odeon Marble Arch; *Cinema Treasures* (above n 19). It would seem that bomb damage could be repaired despite the restrictions. The 1945/46 accounts were not the subject of this appeal.

[23] *Tucker v Granada Motorway Services Ltd* [1977] 1 WLR (Ch) 1411, 1412.

[24] ibid, as cited by Lord Edmund-Davies on appeal to the House of Lords [1979] 1 WLR 683, 691.

The key question is whether that judicial common sense has become in any way a set of legal principles as a result of the doctrine of precedent. Judges have some sense of what the distinction is. They take criteria from previous cases. But are these legal principles? Some of the ideas repeated in the cases come from outdated or disputed ideas of economists – concepts that have moved on, but the judges have not kept up. For example, the 'hallowed distinction between the fruit of a tree and the tree itself'[25] arises from agrarian economies[26] and the eighteenth-century economist Adam Smith.[27] It was applied in trust law to decide on allocation between beneficiaries. But this concept prevented the courts from defining capital gains as income or from allowing depreciation to be deducted: an early example of the tension between commercial accounts and tax law. As Daunton puts it: 'The income tax simply did not take account of the employment of capital in the estimation of profit and did not allow for investment in newer, more expensive and productive plant'.[28] It required legislation to put it right.[29]

In the *Odeon* tax litigation, the additional complication was that there was a judicial decision in *Law Shipping v IRC*[30] that had been assumed for many years to be binding, deciding that expenditure on deferred repairs was capital in nature, where deferred repairs were taken over from a vendor. The Commissioners did feel bound by the *Law Shipping* decision, but in the High Court Pennycuick V-C distinguished *Odeon* from *Law Shipping* on the facts (whilst not rejecting the reasoning in the *Law Shipping* case, thus leaving it intact). The High Court decision of Pennycuick V-C was upheld by the Court of Appeal.[31]

At one level, then, *Odeon* is a heavily fact-based case on a simple question around the distinction between capital and revenue. It is frequently cited alongside *Law Shipping* to illustrate a dividing line between expenditure on

---

[25] As it is described by Arden LJ in *John Lewis Properties Plc v CIR* [2002] EWCA Civ 1869, [6]; [2003] Ch. 513.

[26] M Daunton, *Trusting Leviathan: The Politics of Taxation in Britain, 1799–1914* (Cambridge, Cambridge University Press, 2001) 206.

[27] A Smith, *An Inquiry into the Nature and Causes of the Wealth of Nations* (first published 1776; London, Penguin Classics, 1999), notably cited by Viscount Haldane in *John Smith & Son v Moore* [1921] 12 TC 266, 282: 'My Lords, it is not necessary to draw an exact line of demarcation between fixed and circulating capital. Since Adam Smith drew the distinction in the second book of his *Wealth of Nations*, which appears in the chapter on the division of stock, a distinction which has since become classical, economists have never been able to define much more precisely what the line of demarcation is. Adam Smith described fixed capital as what the owner turns to profit by keeping it in his own possession, circulating capital as what he makes profit of by parting with it and letting it change masters'.

[28] Daunton (above n 26) 209.

[29] Capital allowances are currently deductible under a special legislative scheme in the UK, although see n 90 below on the activities of the Office of Tax Simplification.

[30] *Law Shipping Co Ltd v IRC* [1924] SC 74; 12 TC 621.

[31] The case took a long time to get to court. The years under appeal were 1946–47 to 1955–56, and the case did not get to the Special Commissioners until 1969 and to the Court of Appeal in 1971: a total of 25 years. There was no comment on this delay in the case.

repairs and improvements (the former being revenue expenditure and the latter, capital).[32] If property can be used without undertaking the repairs, if the price paid is not affected and if the repairs are carried out only after a long period of time after the purchase, it can be shown that the expenditure was of an income not a capital nature, and so deductible by the purchaser.

Such a fact-driven case might not, in itself, be worthy of note in a book of landmark cases. However, the initially apparently cogent comments of Pennycuick V-C on the relationship between 'ordinary principles of commercial accountancy' elevated the case beyond this. Whilst one frequently repeated sentence has been cited above, Pennycuick's words are worth setting out in full:

> I ought to say a few words by way of explanation of the time-honoured expression 'ordinary principles of commercial accountancy'. The concern of the Court in this connection is to ascertain the true profit of the taxpayer. That and nothing else, apart from express statutory adjustments, is the subject of taxation in respect of a trade. In so ascertaining the true profit of a trade the Court applies the correct principles of the prevailing system of commercial accountancy. I use the word 'correct' deliberately. In order to ascertain what are the correct principles it has recourse to the evidence of accountants. That evidence is conclusive on the practice of accountants in the sense of the principles on which accountants act in practice. That is a question of pure fact, but the Court itself has to make a final decision as to whether that practice corresponds to the correct principles of commercial accountancy. No doubt in the vast proportion of cases the Court will agree with the accountants, but it will not necessarily do so. Again, there may be a divergency of view between the accountants, or there may be alternative principles, none of which can be said to be incorrect, or, of course, there may be no accountancy evidence at all. The cases illustrate these various points. At the end of the day the Court must determine what is the correct principle of commercial accountancy to be applied. Having done so, it will ascertain the true profit of the trade according to that principle, and the profit so ascertained is the subject of taxation. The expression 'ordinary principles of commercial accountancy' is, as I understand it, employed to denote what is involved in this composite process.[33]

These words explain a process of weighing accounting evidence as a question of fact, but they have a problematic circular quality. The facts must be measured up against 'correct principles'. These correct principles must come from the evidence of the accountants, which informs the court as to the principles on which accountants act in practice. However, the court itself has to make a final decision as to whether the practice of accountants corresponds with the correct

---

[32] Most textbooks refer to the cases side by side, eg, A Fairpo and D Salter, *Revenue Law Principles and Practice*, 35th edn (London, Bloomsbury Professional, 2017) paras 10.142 and 12.43; G Loutzenhiser, *Tiley's Revenue Law*, 8th edn (Oxford, Hart Publishing, 2016) para 22.4.3.8. Further, they are often noted in 'tips' for practitioners: see, eg, J Bailey, 'Landlords! Is Your Buy to Let a "Cinema" or a "Ship"? – Repairs Before the First Letting' *Tax Insider* (July, 2010); HMRC, 'Capital/revenue divide: tangible assets: asset bought in a defective condition', Business Income Manual BIM35450.

[33] *Odeon Associated Theatres Ltd* (above n 1) 273.

principles of commercial accountancy. Taken on its own, as it often is, this quotation suggest that in theory the court could hear evidence from accountants and all accountants could agree on practice, yet the court could still decide that this was not correct. The subsequent words within this passage qualify this. The court will only have a role if there is diverging accountancy evidence, or none at all, or if accountants would permit more than one treatment. In 2018 there will almost always be an applicable accounting standard, issued by an appropriate body and agreed by experts, so it would be very rare indeed to find no evidence at all.[34] However, given that one difference between accounting standards and tax legislation is that the former frequently leave room for judgement and do not dictate one single treatment, this leaves open considerable scope for the courts. But if the court does have this scope, where is the evidence to come from if not from accountants? What is the role of the case law cited? If the accounting standard in question refers to a distinction like the one between capital and income, does that override commercial accounting, or is it more accurate to say that the legal principles and interpretations are, in such a case, assumed to be part of correct commercial accounting principles?

If one turns to the paragraph of Pennycuick V-C's judgment immediately preceding the one set out above (which is so often cited out of context) we see that the judge made it quite clear that he did not consider that there were principles to be applied that were 'divorced from the principles of commercial accountancy':

> Mr Watson, who appeared for the Crown, contended that there is a third and distinct requirement, namely that the profit of the trade must be ascertained for the purpose of income tax. It was not clear to me (I do not suppose that is Mr Watson's fault) precisely what standard the Court should adopt, apart from that of the ordinary principles of commercial accountancy, in arriving at the profit of a trade for the purpose of income tax. Mr Watson used the word 'logic'. If by that he intended no more than to say that one must apply the correct principles of commercial accountancy, I agree with that, as I will explain in a moment. I think, however, he intended to go beyond that and meant that the Court must ascertain the profit of a trade on some theoretical basis divorced from the principles of commercial accountancy. If that is what is intended, I am unable to accept the contention, which I believe to be entirely novel.[35]

But then how was the Court to come to the decision set out in the process described by Pennycuick V-C in his famous proposition that 'At the end of the day the Court must determine what is the correct principle of commercial accountancy to be applied'? If 'logic' is not the answer, then the Court has to use some process to decide between two conflicting propositions.

---

[34] In the UK the relevant accounting standards will be International Accounting Standards Board (IASB) standards, known as International Financial Reporting Standards (IFRS), or UK accounting standards set by the Financial Reporting Council (which took over from the Accounting Standards Board) (ASB). Which standards are used depends on the size and nature of the company.

[35] *Odeon Associated Theatres Ltd* (above n 1) 274.

One answer to this question is, as suggested above, that if an accounting standard refers to a distinctly legal question such as when beneficial ownership passed, for example, the courts have a basis on which to intervene. In such a case, there is a legal element to the correct principle of commercial accountancy.[36] But that might be misleading too. There are occasions when such concepts are quite properly interpreted by accountants with more regard to substance than to form, and this may raise a question for the courts about whether they are to insist on the stricter legal interpretation. And where the issue is whether something is capital or revenue, we go around in a circle. Is that a question of law, and if so, how is accounting practice relevant at all?

In fact, Pennycuick V-C in the High Court and then all the members of the Court of Appeal, followed the accounting evidence, but all of them reiterated that it was for the Court itself to make a final decision as to where a given practice corresponds to the correct principles of commercial accountancy. As we shall see later in this chapter,[37] Pennycuick V-C was not averse to the idea that there might be overriding legal principles and therefore, to make sense of his somewhat Delphic statement, one has to assume that he believed that the decision of the courts about what are 'correct accounting principles', whilst not having a 'theoretical basis divorced from the principles of commercial accountancy' could and should have input from decided case law as well as statute.

Salmon LJ, perhaps the Court of Appeal judge who was most persuaded by accounting practice, commented that the courts 'will follow the established principles of sound commercial accounting unless they conflict with the law as laid down in any Statute' and that 'no help can be derived from the Statute in deciding the question of what is capital expenditure', but he does then proceed to discuss the case of *Law Shipping* in detail, distinguishing it with care, which suggests that, had he not been able to distinguish it, the case law might have been relevant.[38] It seems that this reference to law laid down by statute encompasses case law in that any legislation referring to capital and income is to be construed in accordance with the decided cases, which are thus brought into the qualification by statute. In this way, a considerable body of case law is rendered relevant, should the judges feel so inclined.

Buckley LJ was clear that the question of whether a payment was capital or income was a question of law, citing Lord Reid in *Strick v Regent Oil Co Ltd*[39] to this effect and stating:

> In answering that question of law it is right that the Court should pay regard to the ordinary principles of commercial accounting so far as applicable. Accountants are,

---

[36] See, eg, *Peter Merchant Ltd v Stedeford (H M Inspector of Taxes)* 30 TC 496 (CA) (Tucker LJ) 510: 'If, on analysis, it appears that the opinion expressed by the chartered accountant is based upon an erroneous interpretation of the obligations under this contract, of course the whole value of his evidence goes, and equally any finding of the Commissioners based thereon disappear'.

[37] See the discussion of *Willingale* (below n 71).

[38] *Odeon Associated Theatres Ltd* (above n 1) 283.

[39] *Regent Oil Co Ltd v Strick (Inspector of Taxes)* [1966] AC 295, 313 (HL).

after all, the persons best qualified by training and practical experience to suggest answers to the many difficult problems that can arise in this field. Nevertheless, the question remains ultimately a question of law.[40]

Whilst seeming to hand much power over taxation to the accountancy profession with one hand, each of the judges to varying degrees held onto it with the other. As will be shown in the ensuing sections of this chapter, even now, despite legislation on the topic, thousands of pages of accounting standards that have been subject to intensive consultation and rigorous adoption processes, and much further case law, significant questions remain about the relationship between accounting evidence (a question of pure fact) and the determination of the correct principles of commercial accountancy (a matter of law for the court). And the seeds of those questions can be found in the *Odeon* case.

III. A LANDMARK CASE?

A. Capital and Income

The *Odeon* decision was recognised as being something more than a case about the capital/revenue divide immediately it was decided, by no less an authority than GSA Wheatcroft. Writing in the *British Tax Review* very soon after *Odeon* was finally decided, Wheatcroft pointed out that sound accountancy principles change, but asked whether it is possible that *the law* as to what is capital and what is income expenditure for tax purposes can change from one decade to another because sound accountancy principles change?[41] As usual, Wheatcroft got right to the heart of the matter.

In his own characteristically forthright way, Lord Denning, in the case of *Heather v PE Consulting Group*,[42] had no doubts at all. He commented that:

> The commissioners were entitled to give weight to that evidence of Mr Bailey, but the judge went further … He seems to have thought that, as a result of the decision of this court in *Odeon Associated Theatres Ltd v Jones (Inspector of Taxes)* the evidence of accountants should be treated as conclusive and that all the commissioners or the court would have to do would be to evaluate their evidence. And counsel for the taxpayer company submitted to us that the *Odeon* case had upgraded the evidence of accountants so that the commissioners and the courts were bound by their evidence to a greater degree than they had been in the past. I cannot agree with that for a moment. It seems to me that that case does not add to or detract from the value of accountancy evidence. The courts have always been assisted greatly by the evidence of accountants. Their practice should be given due weight; but the courts have never regarded themselves as being bound by it. It would be wrong to do so. The question of what is capital and what is revenue is a question of law for the courts.

---

[40] *Odeon Associated Theatres Ltd* (above n 1) 299.
[41] GSA Wheatcroft, 'The Law Shipping Rule Eroded' [1972] *BTR* 51.
[42] *Heather (Inspector of Taxes) v PE Consulting Group Ltd* [1973] Ch 189 (CA).

They are not to be deflected from their true course by the evidence of accountants, however eminent.[43]

Lest this be thought purely the reaction of a judge who liked to be different, Lord Justice Orr also expressed his views in *Heather* in the same vein. His thoughts are particularly relevant as he had been on the bench in *Odeon* too. He stated that:

> The main issue in the *Odeon* case was whether it was governed by the earlier decision in *Law Shipping Co Ltd v Inland Revenue Comrs*, and this court found a number of differences between the two cases of which only one was that accountancy evidence had been called in the *Odeon* case but not in the *Law Shipping* case. Nothing in any of the judgments in the *Odeon* case throws any doubt on the proposition, which was common ground in this appeal and is supported by a long line of authority, that the question whether an expenditure is for tax purposes on revenue or on capital account is ultimately a question of law. Accountancy evidence may be helpful in a case of this kind insofar as it discloses in what manner accountants dealt in practice with a particular item; but it is for the court to decide whether what is done in practice is in accordance with sound accountancy practices; and, further, what is in other respects properly done in practice may not, for the reasons given by Lord Greene MR in *Associated Portland Cement Manufacturers Ltd v Inland Revenue Comrs* ([1946] 1 All ER 68 at 70) accurately reflect the difference between income and capital expenditure for the purposes of income tax.[44]

Does this indicate that, far from being a landmark case, the *Odeon* case made no difference at all? Certainly, in cases where the courts could find a legal point to make they often continued to do so. The question of whether expenditure or a receipt is capital or income is absolutely within that category. Judges have been deciding that issue for centuries, in cases involving trusts amongst other things, and they are hardly likely to turn it over entirely to accountants. When they state that commercial accounting practice is subject only to statute law, these judges mean to include statute that requires them to use the case law authorities to distinguish capital and income.

A different view was expressed by Mary Arden LJ (dissenting) in *John Lewis Properties*:

> The approach which the court must adopt is one of practical and business reality. Thus, Dixon J in *Hallstroms Pty Ltd v Federal Commissioner of Taxation* [1946] 72 CLR 634, 648 in a passage cited by Lord Nolan when giving the advice of the Privy Council in *CIR v Wattie* [1999] 1 WLR 873, [1998] STC 1160 held that the answer to the question whether expenditure is of a capital or revenue nature–
>
> > 'depends on what the expenditure is calculated to effect from a practical and business point of view, rather than upon the juristic classification of the legal rights, if any, secured or exhausted in the process'.[45]

[43] ibid, 217.
[44] ibid, 224.
[45] *John Lewis Properties Plc* (above n 25) [13].

Odeon was not cited in that case and the accounting point was not argued, somewhat to Lady Justice Arden's disappointment.[46] The other Court of Appeal judges took a much more legally based approach and cited precedents and analysed the facts extensively.

A more recent example of a very legal approach is the decision of the First-tier Tribunal in *Ingenious Games LLP and others v HMRC (Ingenious Games)*.[47] This supplemental case in the *Ingenious* series is a real turn of the knife for the investors in that scheme, since it means many of them will have to pay tax greater than their investment if this decision stands.[48] The *Odeon* case was not cited, but the tribunal judges decided, although not without 'misgivings and reluctance',[49] that

> sums which we regarded as properly deductible for *GAAP [Generally Accepted Accounting Principles]* purposes as provisions for the impairment of the rights under the relevant agreements were not deductible in computing taxable profits as a result of section 33 ITTOIA (or its predecessor section 74(1) ICTA) on the basis that they were capital or of a capital nature.[50]

In paragraphs headed 'Absurdity or unfairness'[51] they recognised that to a practising accountant 'the idea that profit should be struck without taking account of the depreciation of capital assets is absurd'. Nevertheless they decided, following Lord Reid in *Regent Oil Co Ltd v Strick*[52] that this was the result of the statutory provision, now in section 33 of the Income Tax (Trading and Other Income) Act 2005 (ITTOIA), that no deduction is allowed for items of a capital nature.

This is an excellent example of the capital/revenue decision being held to override GAAP by the courts. The argument is that the modification to GAAP is the result of statute, but in practice what is relied upon is case law. Harking back to Wheatcroft's *British Tax Review* comment, cited at the beginning of this section of this chapter, the tribunal judges stated: 'We see no warrant for reading the words of the statute differently because accounting practice has changed'.[53] They add that the very fact that there are specific reliefs for research and development and intellectual property rights 'indicates that the meaning of "capital" in the prohibition in section 33 remains as it was understood more than half a century ago'. But the words of the statute simply refer to 'capital', which could be thought of after *Odeon* as having a meaning that is, at least partially,

---

[46] ibid, [3].
[47] *Ingenious Games LLP and others v HMRC* [2017] UKFTT 0429 (TC).
[48] STEP Newsletter, 'Ingenious Media clients face unenviable choice', 5 June 2017, available at www.step.org/news/ingenious-media-clients-face-unenviable-choice.
[49] *Ingenious Games LLP* (above n 47) [88].
[50] ibid, [1].
[51] ibid [19]–[23].
[52] *Regent Oil Co Ltd* (above n 39).
[53] *Ingenious Games LLP* (above n 47) [22].

derived from accounting practice. So again we are taken around in the circle of Pennycuick V-C's comments.

It remains to be seen whether this decision of the First-tier Tribunal in *Ingenious Games* will survive the appeals process in this long-lasting saga, but the fact that this case was argued on the basis of many very old cases makes it clear that it would be premature to suggest that accounting evidence will now be always in the ascendancy as some suggested was the case following the *Odeon* decision.

B. Revenue Recognition

When we move away from the capital/income distinction to other issues, and in particular timing of revenue and expense recognition, we do see more inclination to subordinate legal reasoning and precedent to accounting practice, especially when that is set out in an agreed and published standard. Sir Thomas Bingham MR in *Gallagher v Jones*[54] decided in favour of following an accounting standard,[55] after citing the *Odeon* case. The Master of the Rolls in *Gallagher* commented that he quoted from *Odeon* 'at length because it seems to me to define with great clarity the task on which the court is engaged and the way in which it should set about it'.[56] In fact it led him to give a judgment which echoed those in *Odeon*, both by asserting the importance of commercial accounting but also by reserving the final word to the courts in certain circumstances, leaving much scope for future argument on the point, just as *Odeon* had done. Lord Bingham's summary has been frequently cited as giving accounting standards primacy. He stated that:

> The authorities do not persuade me that there is any rule of law such as that for which the taxpayers contend and the judge found. Indeed, given the plain language of the legislation, I find it hard to understand how any judge-made rule could override the application of a generally accepted rule of commercial accountancy which (a) applied to the situation in question, (b) was not one of two or more rules applicable to the situation in question and (c) was not shown to be inconsistent with the true facts or otherwise inapt to determine the true profits or losses of the business. I need not pursue this speculation, however, since I do not understand it to be challenged that the principles embodied in the Statements of Standard Accounting Practice Nos 2 and 21 meet these three conditions and I find no judge-made rule which could require these principles to be displaced.[57]

---

[54] *Gallagher v Jones (Inspector of Taxes), Threlfall v Jones (Inspector of Taxes)* [1994] Ch 107; [1993] STC 537.

[55] Financial Reporting Council, 'Statement of Standard Accounting Practice 21 on accounting for leases and hire purchase contracts (SSAP 21)' (1984), now superseded by Financial Reporting Standard 102 (2015).

[56] *Gallagher* (above n 54) 133.

[57] ibid, 134.

The interesting thing about these three conditions is that they could have been argued to have been unmet in this case, as this author has argued previously.[58] The court could have found a let out here had it wanted to, but the taxpayers did not bring any accountancy evidence at all. Rather they relied upon there being a legal principle that 'For the purposes of the computation of trading profits for income tax purposes expenditure falls in the period in respect of which it is incurred'.[59]

The facts in *Gallagher* were that the taxpayers wanted to deduct for tax purposes a large upfront payment for long leases of some narrowboats. The parties had agreed that the payments under the relevant agreements were revenue, not capital,[60] an issue which could have been disputed had either party felt so inclined and might have formed part of the discussion of the applicability of the accounting standard for tax purposes. In practice that aspect of the accounting standard was not explored. The Inland Revenue, as it then was, had just published a statement of practice, SP3/91, which purported to follow SSAP 21, and there was no appetite from the taxpayer community to unsettle this agreement.[61] This was not least because of the acceptance by the Inland Revenue that rental payments on long leases were revenue, whereas SSAP 21 treated a proportion of the rentals as a capital repayment. There was a clash between the treatment in SAAP 21 and the legal analysis, but this was not pursued in *Gallagher* and this was quite deliberate. For the purposes of the case it was accepted by the taxpayer that SSAP 21 represented correct commercial accounting but argued that there was an overriding principle of tax law that gave a different result. This presented the court with a stark choice. The court rejected the notion that there was an overriding legal principle though they analysed the case law, but did not analyse the accounting standard in detail. The judges of the Court of Appeal did not consider they were changing the law by applying the accounting standard to determine at what time expenditure was deductible for tax purposes and they cited various cases, including *Odeon*, to support that point.[62] However they distinguished the case of *Regent Oil Co Ltd v Strick*[63] on the grounds that it was about the distinction between capital and income, an issue 'not before the court' in *Gallagher*. Since the parties had agreed that the payments in *Gallagher* were revenue payments, the court did not address this point, nor did they appear to appreciate that this agreed 'common ground' was not in accordance with the accounting standard they purported to be applying.

---

[58] See J Freedman, 'Ordinary Principles of Commercial Accounting – Clear Guidance or a Mystery Tour?' [1993] *BTR* 468 for a more detailed analysis of this case.

[59] *Gallagher* (above n 54) 113: argument as put by Rex Bretten QC and Robert Grierson for the taxpayer.

[60] ibid, 121.

[61] Lyon, 'Gallagher v Jones: The Revenue Loses by a Length' *Asset Finance and Leasing Digest* (April 1993) 14 (note on Ch D decision).

[62] They also placed reliance on, inter alia, *Sun Insurance Office v Clark (Surveyor of Taxes)* [1912] AC 443 and *Symons (Inspector of Taxes) v Weeks* [1983] STC 195.

[63] *Regent Oil Co Ltd* (above n 39).

It was also not questioned that the taxpayers were not limited companies and so, arguably, did not have to apply the accountings standards. That was an important point to the Inland Revenue, which was keen to bring professionals into line with other businesses, as explained in the next part of this chapter. This was a case where the court chose to relinquish the upper hand, but could have claimed it by focusing on the legal analysis in the standard that part of the rentals were of a capital nature. This was not the way the case was argued by the parties but the decision in *Gallagher* was not an inevitable consequence of the *Odeon* decision and nor is it such an outright rejection of the application of judicial principles as at first appears.

IV. CODIFYING THE RULE?

In the Finance (No 2) Act 1998 the government decided to withdraw the cash basis for those carrying on a profession or vocation, 'in order to level the playing field for all businesses and correct an anomaly for which there is no justification'.[64] At the same time, the Tax Law Rewrite Group was working on the trading income of individuals and they had proposed making explicit in the statute that accounting profit was the starting point for computing taxable trading profit. This was designed to encompass the law as it had evolved up to and including the decision in *Gallagher*, itself so dependent on *Odeon*. There did seem to be a view that the case law had become more accepting of the idea that accounting standards should be followed even though, in reality, neither *Odeon* nor *Gallagher* intended to change the pre-existing law on this point. The proposals attracted a large number of responses. At this point,[65] ministers decided that the withdrawal of the cash basis took priority over the rewrite of existing law and they chose to insert a clause about the use of accounting practice that was devised with the cash basis withdrawal in mind, rather than the one consulted on as part of the Rewrite process.

The resulting clause, which became section 42 Finance Act 1998, required that 'the profits of a trade, profession or vocation must be computed on an accounting basis which gives a true and fair view, subject to any adjustment required or authorised by law in computing profits for those purposes'. The reference to 'true and fair view' was used because the Inland Revenue was concerned that if it referred to generally accepted accounting practice (GAAP), GAAP for professionals might turn out to be different from GAAP for other businesses. However,

---

[64] Inland Revenue Press Release, 22 December 1997, cited in D Hole, 'Withdrawal of the Cash Basis – sections 42 to 46 and Schedules 6 and 7' [1998] *BTR* 405. Professionals were benefiting from the cash basis, which gave them considerable cash flow advantages. Just five years later, cash accounting was reintroduced for small unincorporated businesses in lengthy legislation with many restrictions by FA 2013 ss 17–18 and sch 4.

[65] Hole, ibid.

in 2002 they did amend the provision to refer to GAAP and this is how it reads now in its amended versions.[66]

In terms of the relationship of this provision with *Odeon*, the most interesting aspect is the qualification 'subject to any adjustment required or authorised by law'. This could have read 'subject to any adjustment required or authorised by statute' but it did not state this. The reference to 'law' was intended to be wider and to preserve pre-existing case law. The Explanatory Memorandum to clause 42 is explicit:

> 4. Although the Clause applies to all taxpayers carrying on a trade, profession or vocation the Government's view is that it does not effect any change in the law on the computation of profits of traders.
>
> 5. The computation of profits for tax purposes remains subject to adjustments permitted or required by tax law, for example, adjustments to ensure that neither a profit nor a loss is anticipated.[67]

The example given of an adjustment in the Memorandum is derived from the case law, for example *Ostime (Inspector of Taxes) v Duple Motor Bodies Ltd* (Lord Reid): 'It is a cardinal principle that profit shall not be taxed until realised',[68] and *BSC Footwear Ltd v Ridgeway*, again from Lord Reid, who dissented, but not on the principles:

> The application of the principles of commercial accounting is, however, subject to one well established though non-statutory principle. Neither profit nor loss may be anticipated ... But it is admitted that this matter is not governed by any rigid rule of law. It depends on general principles which have been elaborated by the courts for the purpose of ensuring that so far as practicable profits shall be attributed to the year in which they were truly earned.[69]

Moreover, as Macdonald has pointed out,[70] Sir John Pennycuick himself (by now in the Court of Appeal), soon after the *Odeon* case, was prepared to accept an 'overriding principle of tax law' that profits must not be anticipated, despite having rejected the idea of a 'third test' in *Odeon*.[71] It seems that these overriding principles were themselves derived from accounting evidence that these judges had heard, but then absorbed into tax law. Perhaps

---

[66] Now see ITTOIA 2005, s 25; ITTOIA 2005, s 5 (profits); CTA 2009, s 46 (corporations).

[67] Explanatory Note to Finance (No 2) Bill 1998 cl 42: Computation of Profits of Trade, profession or Vocation.

[68] *Ostime (Inspector of Taxes) v Duple Motor Bodies Ltd* [1961] 1 WLR 739; (1961) 39 TC 537 (HL) 569–70.

[69] *BSC Footwear Ltd v Ridgway* [1972] AC 544; (1972) 47 TC 495 (HL).

[70] G Macdonald, 'HMRC v William Grant & Sons Distillers Ltd and Small (Inspector of Taxes) v Mars UK Ltd: Accountancy Practice and the Computation of Profit' [2007] *BTR* 366.

[71] *Willingale v International Commercial Bank Ltd* [1977] Ch 78 (CA), decision affirmed by the House of Lords in *Willingale (Inspector of Taxes) v International Commercial Bank Ltd* [1978] AC 834; 52 TC 242. See the discussion on the 'third test' in text to n 35 of this chapter.

Sir John Pennycuick therefore did not see this as inconsistent with his ruling in *Odeon*. In *Willingale v International Commercial Bank Ltd* he stated:

> Counsel for the Crown rested his contention on the well-established rule that the profit of a trade must be ascertained in accordance with the principles of commercial accountancy. For an application of the principle see *Odeon Associated Theatres Ltd v Jones (Inspector of Taxes)*. But it is likewise well established that the principles of commercial accountancy must yield not only to statutory provisions, in particular the prohibition of specified deductions, but also to obey overriding principles of tax law: see the explicit statement of Lord Reid in *BSC Footwear Ltd v Ridgway* [1971] 2 All ER 534 at 536, [1972] AC 544 at 552, 47 Tax Cas 495 at 524, 525 in relation to the anticipation of profit.[72]

The only way to reconcile this with Pennycuick's own views expressed in *Odeon* is to assume that he sees these principles of tax law not as 'a theoretical basis divorced from the principles of commercial accountancy'[73] but as part of what goes into the court's decision about what are 'correct principles' of commercial accountancy. In *Willingale* he also points out that to tax profit earned but not realised in the sense that a legal right to income has arisen could render a trader insolvent.[74] He seems to believe that no correct rule of accountancy could have this result; this is not external logic but what should be an accounting rule. The problem is that modern accounting has deviated some way from this concept of realisation. What Sir John Pennycuick would have made of this we can only guess.

It seems unlikely that a court would now assert a principle of prudence or non-anticipation of profits or losses in the face of developed accounting standards that deviate from them or, at least, have different interpretations of these concepts.[75] Subsequent cases have been clear that this is not required.[76] But it is conceivable that there could be a choice of treatment left to the person making up the accounts, and the possibility is retained by the legislation and the explanatory memorandum that the courts could then look to these principles. Like *Odeon*, the legislation leaves options open.

---

[72] *Willingale*, ibid (CA) 97.

[73] As discussed in part II of this chapter.

[74] *Willingale* (above n 71 (CA)) 98 and see discussion in J Freedman, 'Profit and Prophets – Law and Accountancy Practice on the Timing of Receipts' (Part II) [1987] *BTR* 104, 114.

[75] See now Financial Reporting Council, 'Financial Reporting Standard 102' (above n 55). Prudence is now referred to in FRS 102, para 2.9; on revenue recognition see appendix to section 23: 'The following examples focus on particular aspects of a transaction and are not a comprehensive discussion of all the relevant factors that might influence the recognition of revenue. The examples generally assume that the amount of revenue can be measured reliably, it is probable that the economic benefits will flow to the entity and the costs incurred or to be incurred can be measured reliably'. The examples that follow show a mixture of examination of legal rights and economic substance. This maintains a role for law but the extent of it is unclear. See also Appendix III, Note on legal requirements, which refers to realisation in a legal context.

[76] *Symons v Weeks* (above n 62) discussed in detail in Freedman, 'Profit and Prophets' (above n 74); *Herbert Smith v Honour* [1999] STC 173 (Ch).

V. *ODEON* POST 1998: UNRESOLVED TENSIONS

HMRC v William Grant & Sons and Small v Mars UK Limited (Mars)[77] were cases that had caused the lower courts considerable difficulties and on which there was much comment before they were finally decided by the House of Lords.[78] The issue was around valuation of stock and

> the question was how much depreciation on assets used in production should be added back in the tax computation where part of it is 'capitalised' in stock: the gross amount written off the assets, or the net amount after charging part of it to stock.[79]

To most accountants the answer was obvious. It should only be the net amount that was added back, because part of the depreciation was to be carried forward as part of the value of the stock. This deferred tax payment and so was the position taken by the taxpayers and opposed by HMRC. To some lawyers this is more problematic. As the Court of Appeal explained in the *Mars* case,[80] depreciation has a separate code governing it – the capital allowances legislation. Capital elements should be excluded from the income calculation altogether and cannot be turned into part of the income calculation because of changing accounting practices. However, the House of Lords held that generally agreed accounting principles did just that and should be followed.

Lord Hoffmann cut through many of the points raised by following the accounting evidence presented by the taxpayers. Purporting to rely on *Odeon* to settle this issue, he stated that:

> Submissions that accounts must comply with fundamental principles of accounting additional to the best practice of accountants as embodied in the accounting standards have been made in other cases. But they have always been rejected. In *Odeon Associated Theatres Ltd v Jones* (1971) 48 TC 257 Sir John Pennycuick VC (at p 275) described the argument as 'entirely novel'.[81]

Whatever the rights and wrongs of the final decision in this case, it is doubtful whether this quotation can bear the weight that Lord Hoffmann placed on it.[82] However, Sir John Pennycuick was not averse to looking at decided case

---

[77] *HMRC (Respondents) v William Grant & Sons Distillers Limited (Appellants) (Scotland) Small (Her Majesty's Inspector of Taxes) (Respondent) v Mars UK Limited (Appellants)* (Conjoined Appeals) [2007] UKHL 15; 78 TC 442.

[78] For a small selection see Macdonald (above n 70); M Parry-Wingfield, 'Deprecation in Stock: Where Next?' [2007] *Tax Journal* 13; D Goldberg, '*Mars and Secan:* There Illusion and Here Truth; The Computation of Profit' (2008) 7 *GITC Review* 1; J Snape, *The Political Economy of Corporation Tax: The Political Economy of Corporation Tax* (Oxford, Hart Publishing, 2011) 93–96.

[79] Parry-Wingfield, ibid.

[80] *Mars* (above n 77).

[81] ibid, [15].

[82] Lord Hoffmann was very much inclined to accept accounting standards, having been co-author with Dame Mary Arden on seminal opinions on the overriding nature of accounting standards in relation to the meaning of the 'true and fair' concept in company accounts: see www.frc.org.uk/accountants/accounting-and-reporting-policy/true-and-fair-concept.

law on what makes correct commercial accounting, as shown by the examination of *Willingale*, above.[83] He was certainly not saying that accounting standards should be followed without question. That is why the court was to have the final say. Had he been around, he would have been likely to have been very interested in the interplay between section 74(1)(f) of the Income and Corporation Taxes Act 1988, which provided that in computing profits for tax purposes, no sum shall be deducted in respect of 'any sum employed or intended to be employed as capital in … the trade', and the relevant accounting standards.

Mars[84] was a case where the House of Lords could have overridden accounting practice had they wanted to. Given that the issue concerned the interaction between a statutory regime and accounting standards, it would have been easy to declare that this was an issue governed by statute, as was done in the *Ingenious* case discussed above.[85] Other recent cases have also shown the willingness of the courts to impose their views about the correct interpretation of accounting standards in a tax context.[86] It is hard not to conclude that the *Odeon* formulation gives the courts considerable scope to decide whether to intervene or not in decisions about what amounts to correct commercial accounting in tax cases, with the courts being prepared to interpret published accounting standards themselves in conjunction with the relevant statutes and contrary to the evidence of the 'Big Four' accountants.

VI. CONCLUSION

These comments mark a staging post in the long-standing engagement between accountants and the courts over who should have the final say over what amounts to taxable profit in the UK. John Snape argues that the decision of the House of Lords in *Mars* was a case of the House of Lords judges avoiding superimposing their own will on that of Parliament.[87] We might question, however, what came closer to the will of Parliament: substituting accounting standards for a statutory provision construed by the judiciary may not be seen that way by all. One major objection to permitting supremacy of accounting standards for tax purposes in the UK, and even more so elsewhere, is the argument that this involves loss of sovereignty.[88]

---

[83] *Willingale* (above n 71).

[84] *Mars* (above n 77).

[85] *Ingenious Games LLP* (above n 47).

[86] *Greene King plc v Revenue and Customs Commissioners* [2016] EWCA Civ 782; [2017] STC 615); *Ball UK Holdings Ltd v HMRC* [2017] UKFTT 457 (TC).

[87] Snape (above n 78).

[88] Freedman, 'Financial and Tax Accounting' (above n 10); and see the way in which the EU's Common Consolidated Corporate Tax Base has moved away from reliance on international financial reporting standards, as discussed in that chapter, partly in response to concerns about handing over control of the tax base to accounting standard setters. See also Snape (above n 78) 56, 60.

The debate over the interaction between tax and accounting standards around profit definition will continue as long as we rely on profits for tax purposes. No country now has total alignment, although some refer more than others to accountings standards. The Office of Tax Simplification recently suggested that UK taxation should follow financial accounts more closely than at present.[89] The signs are that this will not be followed up by the government,[90] but it is an issue that returns frequently. Even if action were to be taken in this direction, however, the courts would continue to show an interest in questions about the final determination of what should be in the financial accounts for tax purposes.

The interaction of these two very different systems – tax law and accounting – will always require one system to have the ultimate say over the other, since they can never be fully integrated, and finality is required. It will be the courts that will be required to adjudicate in cases of doubt and this will mean that judges will retain the upper hand, despite the increasing formality and extensive nature of consultation on accounting standards. But the legal system is conceptually unprepared for the demands of accounting – a very different system.[91] King and Thornhill explain the problem in systems theory terms as follows:

> Systems are unable to communicate directly with one another, for each system uses different criteria of validity, different forms of authority and different codes for deriving meaning from and assessing the value of information. Put in its simplest terms, they see things differently and there is no possibility of one system being able to internalise the world-view of another. All that it is able to achieve is an internalisation according to its own 'way of seeing' of what it understands from the communications of the other system.[92]

Pennycuick V-C in *Odeon* would not have recognised this comment and would have considered the issue to be somewhat simpler than the theorists suggest. He was a very pragmatic judge. But in his famous comments from *Odeon*, that have been taken up so enthusiastically because they are seen as 'defining with great clarity the task on which the court is engaged and the way in which it should

---

[89] Office of Tax Simplification (above n 5).

[90] See the letter from the Chancellor, Philip Hammond MP, dated 14 August 2017, addressed to Angela Knight and Paul Morton, Office of Tax Simplification, available at www.gov.uk/government/uploads/system/uploads/attachment_data/file/640563/CX_letter_corporation_tax_August_2017.pdf. Also see now Office of Tax Simplification, *Accounting Depreciation or Capital Allowances?* (June 2018).

[91] G Teubner, 'How the Law Thinks: Toward a Constructivist Epistemology of Law', (1989) 23 Law and Society Review, 727, cited in P Miller and M Power, 'Accounting, Law and Economic Calculation' in M Bromwich and A Hopwood, Accounting and the Law (London, Prentice Hall, 1992) 236. Miller and Power themselves argue that Teubner underestimates the significance of the shift created by the 'recent intensification of economic calculation in ... accounting'. They argue that accounting and law can be both competing and interdependent, 251.

[92] M King and C Thornhill, *Niklas Luhmann's Theory of Politics and Law* (Basingstoke, Palgrave Macmillan, 2003) 27 cited and discussed in Freedman, 'Aligning Taxable Profits and Accounting Profits' (above n 16); Miller and Power, ibid, 236.

set about it',[93] he actually produced a set of ground rules that reflects very well the difficulties of engagement described by the theorists. Accountants rule in their world but at some point, although maybe not often, the courts will assert their own world view of 'correct commercial accounting'. Whilst influenced by accountants, this is also derived from an evolving set of internal legal principles that themselves relate back to statutory interpretation and understanding of legal concepts. There is no 'third set' of external tax principles but there is a legal view of correct principles of commercial accountancy.

It seems unlikely that the choice taken by the courts on whether to intervene will appear rational to accountants in every case but the two worlds will develop in parallel with occasional interactions because they are two different systems, with different objectives, although often coalescing around taxation. Possibly unwittingly, the *Odeon* case expressed this tension perfectly.

---

[93] Bingham in *Gallagher* (above n 54).

10

WT Ramsay v Commissioners of Inland Revenue *(1981)*

Ancient Values, Modern Problems

JOHN SNAPE

I. 'FROM MEADOW TO MAYFAIR'*

WT RAMSAY LTD, a Lincolnshire family's farming company, had bought a corporation-tax avoidance scheme, though the family did not understand how it worked: Denis Rawling, who possibly did understand, had bought a similar one for CGT.[1] In *Ramsay*, the idea

> was to create out of a neutral situation two assets one of which would decrease in value for the benefit of the other. The decreasing asset ['the first loan'] would be sold, so as to create the desired loss; the increasing asset ['the second loan'] would be sold, yielding a gain which it was hoped would be exempt from tax.[2]

In *Rawling*, the idea was 'to split a reversion [under a settlement] into two parts so that one would be disposed of at a profit' but would be exempt 'and the other would be disposed of at a loss but could be covered by the exception. Thus there would be an allowable loss but a non-chargeable gain'.[3] Each scheme was

---

*Each of the section headings, except the first, is a quotation given in the subsequent text. The first is the name of a 1931 orchestral suite by Eric Coates (1886–1957). I would like to thank the following for their comments: Dominic de Cogan, Victor Baker, John Pearce (who emphasised Millett's role to me), Philip Ridd and other participants in the workshop held at Warwick Law School on 6 October 2017. The writer has also benefited from a conversation with Philip Ridgway in February 2018. 'The views here expressed', as a one-time lecturer at the University of Birmingham said, 'are my own responsibility' (see J Tiley, 'The Rescue Principle' (1967) 30 *MLR* 25, 45, fn 82).

[1] eg, R Walker, 'Ramsay 25 Years On: Some Reflections on Tax Avoidance' [2004] *LQR* 412; J Tiley, 'Tax Avoidance Jurisprudence as Normal Law' [2004] *BTR* 304; E Simpson, 'The Ramsay Principle: A Curious Incident of Judicial Reticence?' [2004] *BTR* 358; J Freedman, 'Interpreting Tax Statutes: Tax Avoidance and the Intention of Parliament' [2007] *LQR* 53; G Aaronson, QC, 'The Swing of the Pendulum: Tax Avoidance in Modern Times' *Tax Journal* (30 September 2016) 6.

[2] *Ramsay* [1982] AC 300, 321G.

[3] ibid, 330E.

designed to wipe out chargeable gains realised by Rawling and WT Ramsay Ltd. Neither scheme had the desired effect. The judicial committee of the House of Lords held, unanimously, that each scheme contained a specific technical flaw. Generally, though, the schemes as a whole were fiscal nullities, creating neither loss nor gain.

The judicial committee's decision, in both cases, was handed down on 12 March 1981.[4] The *Ramsay* scheme had been implemented in February and March 1973.[5] The facts of *Rawling* had taken place two years afterwards. Each one had been designed by tax advisers whose business it was to market, sell and implement tax avoidance schemes.[6] All the client had to do 'was to say how much tax he wanted to avoid' and to pay the advisers' fee.[7] In *Ramsay*, the designer of the scheme ('the exempt-debt scheme'), was a Mayfair chartered accountant, one Roy Tucker, of Roy Tucker and Company. Tucker, a small, thin, bespectacled man, with improbably long hair, was once described as 'a walking compendium of the taxes acts'.[8] 'An ingenious deviser of tax avoidance schemes'[9] was how Graham Aaronson QC described him in 2016. Tucker worked with Jerrold Moser, a West End solicitor, and partner in a law firm, called Slowes, and Moser it was who drafted the documentation.[10] The requisite banking facilities were provided by Slater, Walker, a finance company headed by the well-known financier, Jim Slater (1929–2015). In *Rawling*'s case, the scheme's designer and drafter was another solicitor, one John Memery, with a company called Thun as banker. It is not discussed further here, frankly, because the issues that it raised were almost identical and *Ramsay* was more colourful. Although Tucker later moved into mass-marketing avoidance schemes, back in 1973 the advertising was relatively low key. Dovercliff Consultants Ltd, also in Mayfair, publicised the exempt-debt scheme, on Tucker's behalf, among non-specialist professionals.[11] It cost WT Ramsay Ltd, who heard about it from their estate agent, £14,000.[12] The different provenance of the *Rawling* scheme illustrates the fact that, prominent though Tucker was, he was far from alone in his particular line of business.

This chapter analyses and interprets the two cases in their historical context.[13] This is, in part, a matter of people and events, in part a history of ideas. Ideas

---

[4] ibid, 300C.

[5] M Gillard, *In the Name of Charity: The Rossminster Affair* (London, Chatto & Windus, 1987) 39–40.

[6] ibid, 32.

[7] AG Davies, 'The Tax Raiders: In the Name of Charity *Review Article*' [1988] *BTR* 311.

[8] Gillard (above n 5) 46.

[9] Aaronson (above n 1) 7.

[10] *Moser v Cotton and Others*, CA, unreported (July 31, 1990); see the discussion in Gillard (above n 5) 32, 277.

[11] Gillard (above n 5) 32.

[12] To put this in perspective, a three-bedroom semi-detached house at the time cost about £10,000 (see N Tweedie and P Day, '1973: A Year of Conflict and Scandal' *Daily Telegraph* (1 January 2004), available at www.telegraph.co.uk/news/uknews/1450672/1973-a-year-of-conflict-and-scandal.html).

[13] See also N Tutt, *The History of Tax Avoidance* (London, Wisedene, 1989, originally published as *The Tax Raiders: The Rossminster Affair* (London, Financial Training, 1985)). References below are to the former. See Davies (above n 7).

are foremost in section III, which discusses arguments about tax policy and large-scale tax avoidance in the 1970s. How these ideas related to contemporary judicial approaches, especially in *Ramsay*, and how practising professionals realised or resisted them, are discussed in the fourth and fifth sections. The sixth considers *Ramsay*'s short-term legacy. Putting aside recent readings, and focusing instead on the cases in context, is a way of countering over-ambitious claims sometimes made for them. The chapter begins, though, by opening a window on a wide panorama.

II. 'NOT PLAYING CRICKET ON THE VILLAGE GREEN'

The UK, when the *Ramsay* decision was handed down, was changing from the highly centralised and introspective, unitary, state that it had been in the 1970s, to something more familiar. The tax system was controversial, both because of perceptions about widespread tax avoidance and tax evasion, and because changes to tax law introduced by the Labour governments of the 1960s and 1970s had yet to gain wide acceptance. There was also much political violence and, in one part of the UK, great bloodshed.

With devolved administrations, and largely open borders, the UK can today almost be thought of as a federal state, nurturing a large and open economy, but the transformation had only just begun in spring 1981. '[E]ver more stringent curbs on local authority expenditure, especially on high-spending Labour-controlled metropolitan authorities'[14] were being imposed by HM Government and, despite the growth in Scottish and Welsh nationalism,[15] both Scotland and Wales were being firmly governed from London. Exchange controls had been abolished in 1979, four decades after their introduction,[16] though in spring 1981, when *Ramsay* was decided, their proposed reintroduction was still seriously advocated on the Left.[17]

Controversies over the tax system centred on its relative ineffectiveness and manipulability, and on the sweeping reforms, both to the tax base and to tax rates. For the Left, the problems with the system were evidenced by media

---

[14] B Harrison, *Finding a Role? The United Kingdom, 1970–1990* (Oxford, Clarendon Press, 2010) 465.

[15] ibid, 461. 'Inside every fat and bloated local authority, there is a slim one struggling to get out', said Thatcher's close friend, Nicholas Ridley, MP, in 1988 (quoted, ibid, 467). Ridley eventually presided over the poll tax failure of 1990 (ibid, 469). 'Ridley's memoirs, which were ... published two years before his death ... show a reckless delight in antagonizing opponents, however impotent they might have been' (G Robb, *The Debateable Land: The Lost World Between Scotland and England* (London, Picador, 2018) 17).

[16] D Kynaston, 'The Long Life and Slow Death of Exchange Controls' (2000) 2 *Journal of International Financial Markets* 37, cited in B Harrison, *Finding a Role? The United Kingdom, 1970–1990* (Oxford, Clarendon Press, 2010) 8.

[17] Harrison, *Finding a Role?* (above n 14) 532.

investigations into tax avoidance, and by perceptions of widespread tax evasion. Evasion, no less than avoidance, was indeed a problem. In 1979, the Inland Revenue chairman, Sir William Pile (1919–97), put 'undeclared income' at about 7.5 per cent of gross national product.[18] High levels of 'large unrecorded transactions' were requiring high denomination banknotes, available in unprecedented numbers.[19] Even Pile admitted that he had to pay cash to get work done around his house.[20] For the right, by contrast, the system's unacceptability was characterised by a combination of high tax rates, an enhanced tax base (including, since 1965, chargeable gains), sterling devaluation in 1967, high inflation and (pre-1979) restrictions on capital movements.[21] In addition, the 1970s saw statutory incomes policies that restricted wage increases and dividend receipts.[22] Many of the controversies arose from the work of a Labour Treasury headed by Denis Healey (1917–2015),[23] but Anthony Barber (1920–2005), Conservative Chancellor of the Exchequer from 1970 to 1974, had either retained previous Labour initiatives or introduced similar new ones. The years to 1979 were the era of 'corporatism' in government: interventionism, forbearance and dialogue between trades unions and employers.[24]

A focus of political conflict, of an 'ethno-nationalist' kind, was Northern Ireland, but there was also industrial unrest in Great Britain.[25] It was not simply that 'The Troubles' occasioned terrible bloodshed, especially after 'Bloody Sunday' in 1972: they hampered policy development generally. 'The Barnett formula' of 1978[26] had one objective of allocating public revenue to a part of the UK lacking fully representative institutions. On the mainland, there was much industrial unrest and both legal – and illegal – 'industrial action'. There was 'the battle of Saltley' coke depot,[27] in the 1972 miners' strike, at which 'the young Arthur Scargill [born 1938] won his spurs'.[28] There was the 1977–78 'battle of Grunwick',[29] a photo-processing plant in Willesden. Both involved violent clashes on a large scale. Such political violence was closely related to, though

---

[18] ibid, 324.

[19] ibid.

[20] Gillard (above n 5) 9.

[21] ibid, 8, 293; R Douglas, *Taxation in Britain Since 1660* (Basingstoke, Macmillan, 1999) ch 13.

[22] Harrison, *Finding a Role?* (above n 14) 290; D Healey, *The Time of My Life* (London, Michael Joseph, 1989) 394. Lonrho Group's avoidance of incomes policy restrictions though the making of payments via the Cayman Islands were famously described by Edward Heath as 'the unpleasant and unacceptable face of capitalism' (quoted in B Harrison, *Finding a Role? The United Kingdom, 1970–1990* (Oxford, Clarendon Press, 2010) 324).

[23] Quoting Hector Berlioz, Healey said that being Chancellor in a Labour government was as bad as 'being Finance Minister in a Republic' (Healey (above n 22) 372–73; J Barnett, *Inside the Treasury* (London, André Deutsch, 1982) 54).

[24] Harrison, *Finding a Role?* (above n 14) 288.

[25] D Sandbrook, *State of Emergency: The Way We Were: Britain, 1970–1974* (London, Allen Lane, 2010) ch 3.

[26] Harrison, *Finding a Role?* (above n 14) 459–60.

[27] Sandbrook, *State of Emergency* (above n 25) 121–33.

[28] F Mount, 'A Time to Moan and Weep' *Spectator* (2 October 2010) 34.

[29] D Sandbrook, *Seasons in the Sun: The Battle for Britain, 1974–1979* (London, Allen Lane, 2012) 599–618. But see J Dromey and G Taylor, *Grunwick: The Workers' Story*, 2nd edn (London, Lawrence & Wishart, 2016).

entirely distinct from, the widespread tax avoidance and tax evasion. Michael Gillard alleges that Tucker's tax avoidance schemes often involved keeping cash offshore or transferring it offshore in such a way as to avoid exchange controls.[30] In this sense, there is a certain equivalence between industrial action, seen as the withholding of labour, and offshore tax avoidance, viewed as the withholding of capital.[31] Each involves withdrawing from the market the holder's most valuable asset. For the poor man, it is his labour, for the rich man, the property rights in his assets. In the context of the 1970s, tax avoidance is a kind of guerrilla action: if a Labour government cannot collect the tax, it cannot carry out the policies that wealthy tax avoiders so deplore. Furthermore, by manipulating tax rules on charities, tax avoiders can further their own – as opposed to a Labour politician's – idea of the common good.[32] By parity of reasoning, industrial action is also designed to prevent Conservative governments from carrying out their policies. 'We were in a class war ... We were not playing cricket on the village green like they did in '26' (said Scargill of the miners' strike). 'We were out to defeat [Sir Edward] Heath [1916–2005] and Heath's policies because we were fighting a government'.[33] Both extremes seemed necessary, and inevitable, because of the 1970s corporatist consensus in Parliament.[34]

III. 'NOW MUCH MORE A VIRTUE'

The impulse to transform this troubled corporatist state was fiercely contested. Economic arguments concentrated on reducing inflation and, as regards taxation, debate focused on tax reduction and the evils of tax avoidance. Political ideologies were starkly opposed to each other, the contrasts between them further chilled by the 'Cold War' background.

The impulse for state transformation came, in part, from the USA, though it was fiercely resisted. Two small-state thinkers had pre-eminence among certain Conservative politicians. Of these, the more important, by far, was Friedrich von Hayek (1899–1992).[35] The other, frequently cited, but seemingly less

---

[30] Gillard (above n 5) 163, 166 (the Ellerman job). A Slater Walker Bermudan subsidiary apparently 'dropped out of' the capital income plan because of concerns about Treasury consents; and ICTA 1970, s 482 (Gillard (above n 5) 2).

[31] Certain anti-avoidance measures have been designed to prevent the withholding of investment capital, notably the old close-company apportionment.

[32] Charities involved in Tucker's schemes had, by definition, non-political main motives (Gillard (above n 5) 24, 28 (but see ibid, 30, and *Sotnick v CIR* [1993] WLR 266)). Roy Tucker's involvement with the actor George Murcell and the St George's Elizabethan Theatre, Tufnell Park, beginning in early 1974, was of that kind (Gillard (above n 5) ch 8). Possibly, too, was Tucker's involvement in the Don Boyd films, including 'East of Elephant Rock' (1978), 'Scum' (1979) and 'Sweet William' (1980) (ibid, 152, 157).

[33] Sandbrook, *State of Emergency* (above n 25) 120.

[34] Harrison, *Finding a Role?* (above n 14) 292, 303, 309.

[35] B Harrison, 'Mrs Thatcher and the Intellectuals' (1994) 5 *Twentieth Century British History* 206, 212; K Tribe, 'Liberalism and Neoliberalism in Britain, 1930–1980' in P Mirowski and D Plehwe, *The Road from Mont Pèlerin: The Making of the Neoliberal Thought Collective* (Cambridge, MA, Harvard University Press, 2009) 68.

significant, was the monetarist economist, Milton Friedman (1912–2006).[36] Both men's ideas, on cutting back the state and freeing the economy from political interference, were vigorously promoted, from the mid-1970s onwards, by the Conservative MPs, Sir Keith Joseph (1918–94), Geoffrey Howe (1926–2015)[37] and Margaret Thatcher (1925–2013):[38] 'Joseph articulated ideas, Howe formulated policies, and Mrs Thatcher was the essential conduit from one to the other'.[39] Joseph's success owed much to his involvement, from 1964 onwards, with the Institute of Economic Affairs (IEA) and to his foundation, in 1974, of the Centre for Policy Studies, together with Thatcher and the libertarian polemicist, Sir Alfred Sherman (1919–2006). Significantly, Hayek emphasised the *economic* importance of 'the rule of law'.[40] These think-tank links, between philosophers and politicians, constituted a crucible of right-wing UK 'neoliberal' thought. Monetarist ideas, meanwhile, were vigorously challenged by two Cambridge economists, Frank Hahn (1925–2013) and Robert Neild (born 1924), who coordinated a March 1981 letter to *The Times*, signed by 364 academic economists, and demanding monetarist policies' rejection.[41]

Arguments for tax reduction, and around tax avoidance, accompanied ones about the size of the state and what subjects owed both to government and to one another. Lowering high tax rates and abolishing the taxation of chargeable gains were long-standing philosophical tropes. Throughout the 1970s, Joseph relentlessly pushed the idea that the burden of taxation was too great.[42] '[W]e are', he said, 'over-governed, over-spent, over-taxed, over-borrowed and over-manned'.[43] Long standing, too, were philosophical arguments about tax avoidance, which tended to divide predictably along partisan lines. The point of departure, or conflict, as the case warranted, was the Hayekian conception of the rule of law. Its economic emphasis stressed law's role in providing a structure for markets. With the rule of law, wrote Hayek,

> government in all its actions is bound by rules fixed and announced beforehand – rules which make it possible to foresee with fair certainty how the authority will use its coercive powers in given circumstances and to plan one's individual affairs on the basis of this knowledge.[44]

[36] C Moore, *Margaret Thatcher: The Authorized Biography: Volume One: Not for Turning* (London, Allen Lane, 2013) 576.

[37] D Willetts, 'Quiet Hero of Thatcherism who became its nemesis' *Financial Times* (12 October 2015) 2.

[38] Harrison, *Finding a Role?* (above n 14) 315.

[39] H Young, *One of Us: A Biography of Margaret Thatcher*, 3rd edn (London, Pan, 1993) 107, quoted in Harrison, *Finding a Role?* (above n 14) 313.

[40] AA Shenfield, 'Hayek on Law' in N Barry (ed), *Limited Government, Individual Liberty and the Rule of Law* (Cheltenham, Edward Elgar, 1998) 33, 41.

[41] Harrison, *Finding a Role?* (above n 14) 325.

[42] G Howe and K Joseph et al, *The Right Approach to the Economy* (Conservative Central Office, 1977) ch 3.

[43] Quoted in Harrison, *Finding a Role?* (above n 14) 312.

[44] FA von Hayek, *The Road to Serfdom* [1944] (London, Routledge, 1997) 75–76, quoted in S Humphreys, *Theatre of the Rule of Law: Transnational Legal Intervention in Theory and Practice* (Cambridge, Cambridge University Press, 2010) 79–80 (also, ibid, 78–80).

Alongside the philosophy were technical arguments about how the creative tax adviser could manipulate the tax rules with which he, or she, was presented.[45] Tucker discreetly took a lead here. His repertoire of devices was relatively simple to conceptualise, though extremely difficult to implement, and exploited structural features of each tax. With capital gains tax (CGT), or corporation tax on chargeable gains, it relied on allowable losses as having the same constituent elements as chargeable gains, and on the netting-off of one against the other for each tax year. Typically, the client would have a realised, or anticipated, chargeable gain, and the object of the scheme was to generate an allowable loss to set against the gain. This was the aim in *Ramsay* itself. WT Ramsay, via its director, Robert Ramsay, a farmer,[46] wished to use the exempt-debt scheme to wipe out an already realised chargeable gain.[47] With income tax, schemes relied on the fact that most relevant provisions (especially relating to interest costs) required *payment*. With surtax (approximately 1972–77), schemes proposed 'to turn income into capital' ('the capital income plan').[48] More generally, it was sought to accumulate income in tax-exempt charities. Later, there was an attempt to 'use ... commodity "straddles" ... to generate on one side artificial losses ... and on the other matching profits which ... could ... be realised offshore' ('the commodity-carry scheme').[49] All of these techniques were tried, especially between 1973 and 1977, by Tucker and by the newly founded Rossminster group, a sort of tax-avoidance Behemoth, crucially having its own bank and publicity machinery.

The rival ideologies of the 1970s were shaped by the wider context of the Cold War. United Kingdom clashes over the role of the state and the morality of tax avoidance illustrated much wider-ranging ideological difference and the rise of colonial nationalisms. In the USA, in 1974, Robert Nozick (1938–2002) had set up a moral equivalence between the '[t]axation of earnings from labor' and 'forced labor':[50] 1973 had seen Augusto Pinochet's coup in Chile; 1979 had witnessed Soviet expansion into Afghanistan; and, in 1981, HM Government's defence cutbacks were being watched intently by an Argentinian *junta* intent on retaking the Falkland Islands.[51] Pinochet's Chile became a 'showcase' for in-practice neoliberalism, the Soviet Union for its radical antithesis, though the UK easily paid for the 1982 Falklands War out of public revenue generated by

---

[45] Avoidance did not feature strongly before 1964 except for estate duty (see A Johnston, *The Inland Revenue* (London, Allen & Unwin, 1965) 53, 151–52). But see, too, J Turing, *Nothing Certain But Tax* (London, Hodder & Stoughton, 1966) ch 12; PF Vineberg, QC, 'The Ethics of Tax Planning' [1969] BTR 31; O Stanley, *Taxology* (London, Weidenfeld & Nicolson, 1972).

[46] Tutt (above n 13) 96.

[47] Gillard (above n 5) 32.

[48] ibid, 23 (subsequently closed in FA 1977).

[49] Gillard (above n 5) 183.

[50] R Nozick, *Anarchy, State, and Utopia* (New York, BasicBooks, 1974) 169.

[51] Harrison, *Finding a Role?* (above n 14) 40.

the corporatist state just described.[52] The imaginative pull of 1970s tax avoidance schemes, as well as the motivations of purchasers, such as WT Ramsay Ltd, has to be understood in the light of these sharply divergent ideologies. Today, the taxation of chargeable gains is a given; back then it was highly conflictual. It was no accident that so many of Tucker's schemes, notably *Ramsay* itself, involved chargeable gains taxation. Taxing chargeable gains had been a flagship policy of the first, and most radical, Labour government of Harold Wilson (1916–95).[53] Tax was indeed so conflictual that, in a 1968 lecture published by the IEA, the lawyer and political economist, Arthur Shenfield (1909–90), concluded with the startling claim that,

> though it can be in some respects a vice, tax avoidance is now much more a virtue. In our semi-totalitarian democracy the tax avoider renders us all two services. He upholds the Rule of Law, and he undermines policies of confiscation.[54]

Evolving neoliberal ideas, namely, that taxes should not be designed for redistribution, that the benefit principle, not ability to pay, should rule, and that tax rates were too high, were all motors of Shenfield's claim. In assaults on corporatist tax policies, these ideas also prized personal autonomy and contractual nexuses between persons: the term 'taxpayer', popularly disused since Victorian times, gained 'new prominence in public discussion', as too did 'the customer', to denote the subject in private/public relations.[55]

IV. 'USING THE LAW TO DEFEAT THE LAW'

Throughout the decades just surveyed, the judiciary tended to embody a conservatism unsympathetic to socialist reaction and warily supportive of the developing neoliberalism, or, as it came to be called, 'Thatcherism'. In *Ramsay*, evidently, the 'Law Lords' sought to distance themselves from Hayekian partisanship, while paradoxically and prospectively augmenting HM Government's taxing capacity in a new and evolving free-market political order. Tax advisers, and clients such as WT Ramsay Ltd, pioneered the new ideological disposition and paid the price.

Significantly, senior judges resisted the 'Keynesian enclaves'[56] that had formed in the left-wing metropolitan authorities. The judicial committee held unlawful, for example, the Greater London Council's attempt to cut London

---

[52] ibid, 42.

[53] This may have set the tone for later retribution (eg, the refusal of an Arts Council grant to Wilson's beloved D'Oyly Carte Opera Company in 1982 (B Pimlott, *Harold Wilson* (London, William Collins, 2016) 731)).

[54] AA Shenfield, *The Political Economy of Tax Avoidance* (London, IEA, 1968) 35.

[55] Harrison, *Finding a Role?* (above n 14) 312.

[56] ibid, 465.

Transport fares and to impose a supplementary rate to pay for it.[57] There was, however, a dearth of cases in which, after Thatcher's 1979 general election victory, the courts struck down a *government* initiative. The senior Law Lord, Lord Wilberforce (1907–2003), was important early in this process and the oldest judge on the *Ramsay* panel.[58] Ascetic, wizened, inscrutable, profoundly learned,[59] Wilberforce nevertheless had, in RFV Heuston's words, 'a touch of steel under the donnish exterior'.[60] Sometime a brigadier in the Royal Artillery, his temperament nonetheless had a sensitive and compassionate side.[61] He had a lifelong devotion to his forebear, William Wilberforce (1759–1833).[62] Few today can conceive how intellectual, closed and traditional, the Chancery Bar would have been of which, since 1932, Wilberforce had been a member.[63] His conservatism was in a much more traditional mode than that of Joseph and Howe.[64] When Wilberforce handed down his speech in *Ramsay*, he had been a Law Lord for 17 years. Behind him, in 1971, lay his generous pay recommendation for striking electrical workers.[65] Then, imprudently, '[a]t the very least, Wilberforce had proved that strikes worked'.[66] So, by March 1981, he was not inclined to make similar mistakes, and he knew that times were changing. Lord Fraser (1911–89), Lord Russell (1908–86), Lord Roskill (1911–96) and Lord Bridge (1917–2007), followed him in rejecting the exempt-debt scheme. They were adjudicating on an old scheme but with an eye on the tax base of a new political order.

The judiciary had long stuck to an older view of the interpretation of tax legislation. Cases before *Ramsay*, including those involving Wilberforce,[67] tended to go against the Revenue.[68] Judges below the level of the judicial committee were

---

[57] *R v Greater London Council, ex parte Bromley LBC* (1981) 125 Solicitors' Journal 809.

[58] RO Wilberforce in S Wilberforce (ed), *Reflections on My Life* (Croydon, Privately Published, 2003) 84, 189.

[59] P Neill, 'Wilberforce, Richard Orme, Baron Wilberforce (1907–2003)' in *Oxford Dictionary of National Biography* (Oxford, Oxford University Press, 2007); online edn, January 2009, available at www.oxforddnb.com.pugwash.lib.warwick.ac.uk/view/article/89469.

[60] 'Obituary (RFV Heuston)' *Independent* (19 February 2003).

[61] Wilberforce (above n 58) 94. See his diary comment after, as a young man, attending a performance of Bach's 'St Matthew Passion', with one Phyllida Pumphrey ('the extremely pretty wife and grass-widow of a friend in the Sudan Civil Service'): 'when it was over I sat for several minutes with tears streaming and unable to speak' (ibid, 92–94).

[62] Who believed firmly in meeting his tax obligations, even in acts of 'superogation', 'in preservation of the Constitution' (see W Hague, *William Wilberforce: The Life of the Great Anti-Slave Trade Campaigner* (London, HarperPress, 2007) 284).

[63] See, eg, J Hackney, 'The Politics of the Chancery' [1981] *CLP* 114.

[64] Gillard (above n 5) 173.

[65] Sandbrook, *State of Emergency* (above n 25) 78–79.

[66] ibid, 79.

[67] *CIR v Herdman* [1969] 1 WLR 323; *CIR v Europa Oil (NZ) Ltd* [1971] AC 760, PC; *Ransom v Higgs* [1974] 1 WLR 1594; *Floor v Davis (HM Inspector of Taxes)* [1980] AC 695; *CIR v Plummer* [1980] AC 896; *Vestey v CIR* [1980] AC 1148 (see P Knightley, *The Rise and Fall of the House of Vestey* (London, Warner Books, 1993) 139). Interestingly, *CIR v Garvin* [1981] WLR 793 followed *Ramsay*, though the taxpayer succeeded.

[68] But see *Chinn v Hochstrasser (HM Inspector of Taxes)* [1981] 2 WLR 14, sub nom *Chinn v Collins*.

bound to apply *CIR v Duke of Westminster*.[69] Provided, as required by Lord Clyde, in *Ayrshire Pullman Motor Services & Ritchie v CIR*,[70] a tax avoidance scheme was an 'honest' one, then the form of the transaction, rather than its substance, was what mattered. Law Lords themselves tended to accept the claim of the Hayekian rule of law. Lord Simon of Glaisdale (1911–2006), a former Conservative law officer and Financial Secretary to the Treasury (1958–59), took this line in November 1974, in *Ransom (HM Inspector of Taxes) v Higgs*.[71] It was certainly wrong, he said, that the 'cunningly advised taxpayer' could escape his fair share of tax by using a scheme. But this was, in effect, the lesser of two evils. The alternative would be to subvert the rule of law.[72] Again, when Leviathan struck, and Rossminster's offices in Hanover Square were raided, pursuant to warrants issued by the Common Serjeant (with Pile's approval), in July 1979, the ensuing judicial review saw the Master of the Rolls, Lord Denning, following a related path on the methods used. Likening the warrants to eighteenth-century general warrants, Denning commented that, although

> those who defraud the revenue ... should be found out and brought to justice ... the means which are adopted ... should ... not be such as to offend against the personal freedom, the privacy and the elemental rights of property.[73]

There are similar examples from this time,[74] emphasising property rights and the rule of law, including *Ramsay* itself at first instance.[75] Such views were not, however, shared by all senior judges, a shift away from the uncompromising 'upholding' of 'property rights' having already begun.[76] This was apparent from both Viscount Dilhorne (1905–80) and Lord Diplock (1907–85), in *CIR v Plummer*,[77] dissenting from the majority in holding Tucker's capital income

---

[69] *CIR v Duke of Westminster* [1936] AC 1; R Stevens, *The English Judges: Their Role in the Changing Constitution* (Oxford, Hart Publishing, 2005) 29; A Likhovski, 'Tax Law and Public Opinion: Explaining *IRC v Duke of Westminster*' in J Tiley (ed), *Studies in the History of Tax Law: Volume 2* (Oxford, Hart Publishing, 2007) 183.

[70] *Ayrshire Pullman Motor Services & Ritchie v CIR* (1929) 14 TC 754.

[71] *Ransom (HM Inspector of Taxes) v Higgs* [1974] STC 539.

[72] ibid, 1616H–1617B. Lord Simon feared that, to do otherwise, the judges would incur 'the censure of history', as had the judges in the *Case of Ship-Money* (1637) 3 St Tr 826 (see [1974] 1 WLR 1594, 1617B–C). The effect of successful tax avoidance on the burden borne by other taxpayers was highlighted by Robert Ramsay's mother: 'My mother was ... against [the purchase of the scheme] ... as she thought it was wrong to engage in such a scheme which was unfair on other taxpayers' (quoted in Gillard (above n 5) 39). But see Shenfield, *The Political Economy of Tax Avoidance* (above n 54) 22–24.

[73] *CIR and Another v Rossminster Ltd and Others* [1980] AC 952, 976G–H. See A Seldon, AR Ilersic, DR Myddelton et al, *Tax Avoision* (IEA, 1979) 36, fn 8, 97 (thanks to Philip Ridgway for drawing this book to my attention).

[74] eg, *Vestey v CIR* [1979] 3 WLR 915 (Walton J); *CIR v Plummer* [1979] Ch 63 (Buckley LJ).

[75] *WT Ramsay Ltd v CIR* [1978] 1 WLR 1313 (Goulding J).

[76] Harrison, *Finding a Role?* (above n 14) 470.

[77] *CIR v Plummer* [1980] AC 896; D Stopforth, 'Getting Tough on Avoidance – Blocking Reverse Annuities' [2005] *BTR* 557.

plan ineffective.[78] Ronald Plummer, Tucker's fellow chartered accountant, and the founder of Rossminster, was Tucker's main associate and had himself bought that scheme. In *Plummer*, Dilhorne described the capital income plan as 'an ingenious, complicated and well thought out scheme … to avoid the payment of tax by those who participated and to raid the Treasury using the technicalities of revenue law as the necessary weapon'.[79] Wilberforce, who had himself identified tax as an idiosyncratic area,[80] administered Denning a magisterial rebuke, in reinstating the warrants, when *Rossminster* reached the judicial committee that October.[81] Emphasising the importance of advancing 'the democratic process' over rights of property, Wilberforce stated that the 'complexity of "tax frauds" and the different persons who may be involved' meant that it would be 'impracticable' to require the Revenue to 'particularise the alleged offence(s)'.[82]

The attitudes of advisers and clients were as Hayekian as those of certain judges. When Healey introduced the Finance Bill provisions eventually relied on in *Rossminster* to the House of Commons, in 1976, he envisaged 'that the powers … [would] be used at the most in only a handful of the most serious cases'; even so, Howe, for the opposition, announced that they were 'absolutely opposed by the Conservative Party'.[83] Tucker's and Rossminster's clients typified those who fell the wrong side of the governing ideologies in the 1960s and 1970s. They had innate respect for the rule of law, possibly because, as relatively well-off people, they had much to lose from its subversion. The Ramsays, Lincolnshire yeomen of Scottish ancestry,[84] were, in this sense, typical. WT Ramsay Ltd was one of 20 or 30 of Tucker's clients that bought the exempt-debt scheme.[85] By 1973, agriculture was seeing significant change.[86] The tax consequences that the exempt-debt scheme sought to avoid would not have occurred in a previous generation. 'We wanted to be able to roll over the cash from the farm for the future rather than pay so much of it in tax', explained Robert Ramsay to Gillard, 'I was fighting for my own, it had nothing to do with morality, it was simply a matter of pounds, shillings and pence'.[87] Ramsays' advisers, in general, had similar views. Tucker, who devised the exempt-debt scheme, was only one of several like-minded individuals. Plummer ('prematurely grey and clinically precise')[88] opined that '[p]eople can get carried away with moral questions. Once you start going down

---

[78] [1980] AC 896, 913G–925C.
[79] ibid, 913G-914A. Note, though, that both Diplock and Dilhorne (but not Wilberforce) were in *Newstead (HM Inspector of Taxes) v Frost* [1980] 1 WLR 135, a notable taxpayer victory.
[80] Lord Wilberforce, 'Law and Economics: Presidential Address' (Holdsworth Club, 1966) 14–18.
[81] [1980] AC 952.
[82] [1980] AC 952, 999E–F.
[83] Quoted in T Bingham, *Tax Evasion: The Law and the Practice* (London, Alexander Howden, 1980) 1. But see Gillard (above n 5) 237.
[84] Tutt (above n 13) 321.
[85] Gillard (above n 5) 39.
[86] Harrison, *Finding a Role?* (above n 14) 57–58.
[87] Quoted in Gillard (above n 5) 39.
[88] ibid, 16.

the moral route, there is no end to it'.[89] Nicholas Pilbrow, another accountant, and Dovercliff's managing director, seems to have agreed (he reportedly gave 'odds at worst 60:40, beforehand', that the judicial committee would pronounce in Ramsay's favour).[90] Finally, of course, there was Slater ('arch-exponent ... of financially driven business deals'),[91] who prudently claimed not to understand Tucker's schemes.[92] That said, it would be possible to mischaracterise the narrowness of their vision. Interviewed much later, Peter Rees QC (1926–2008) (not involved with *Ramsay* but often instructed by Tucker) said: 'As a QC you're just asked about the law. The questions are always very carefully phrased. You're not asked if it's good to do it or if it's in the public interest or moral'.[93] In the words of someone familiar with the Rossminster story,

> they were all fairly right-wing people. They took the view that it was a bit of a moral crusade – especially after the Labour Party raised the tax rates to 83 per cent and 98 per cent [this was in the 1974 Budget]. They saw themselves as using the law to defeat the law.[94]

When, several months after the *Ramsay* scheme had been implemented, Tucker and Plummer (but not Slater) founded Rossminster, they drew in others with similar views, most notably Desmond Miller QC, a leading tax silk.[95] These advisers' views found expression in a broadly Hayekian understanding of the rule of law. Ironically, it might be said that they had a rather touching faith, as suggested by their view of the world, in Hayek's conception. They were at pains to point out, following Lord Clyde, that their schemes were 'honest' and legal.[96] Miller, chairman of Rossminster, though not involved in *Ramsay*, while deeply concerned whether something was 'illegal', was inclined to dismiss wider concerns about tax avoidance as 'Boy Scout morality'.[97] If that was the case, some were at the very edge of legality from the outset, as also those that did not go according to plan. They relied conspicuously on a cloak of secrecy[98] – clearly what angered certain judges, such as Dilhorne[99] – because 'you cannot

---

[89] Quoted in Tutt (above n 13) 108.

[90] Gillard (above n 5) 258.

[91] 'Obituary (R Cowe)' *The Guardian* (22 November 2015).

[92] Gillard (above n 5) 42.

[93] Quoted ibid, 178. Even Wilberforce, as a QC, took this line (ironically) (Gillard (above n 5) 258).

[94] Quoted in Gillard (above n 5) 45. Rossminster was a (small) Conservative Party donor (ibid, 75, 88, 168, 171). In cases of illegality, such as that involving Lord Marples (1907–78) in 1975, 'not even Tucker and Plummer were able to help' (ibid, 130).

[95] Gillard (above n 5) 43.

[96] ibid, 44. And see Lord Brightman in *Furniss (HM Inspector of Taxes) v Dawson* [1984] 1 AC 474, 518G.

[97] Quoted in Gillard (above n 5) 44. Also, ibid, 81. A common 'mild insult' in the 1970s. '"It sounds like a Boy Scout code", was Austin Mitchell's response when Callaghan explained how he expected ministers to handle civil servants: "what is wrong with the Boy Scouts?" was the rejoinder' (Harrison, *Finding a Role?* (above n 14) 247).

[98] Gillard (above n 5) 46, 87 (use of the adverb 'optically').

[99] Dilhorne had wanted to extradite Slater with Tarling in April 1978 (Gillard (above n 5) 255; J Slater, *Return to Go: My Autobiography* (London, Weidenfeld & Nicolson, 1977) chs 18 and 19).

get patent protection for a tax avoidance scheme'.[100] The confidence the advisers had in the legality of their schemes is revealed in a letter from Pilbrow to clients including WT Ramsay Ltd: 'The scheme is a pure tax avoidance scheme', it read, 'and has no commercial justification insofar as there is no prospect of [the client] making a profit; indeed he is certain to make a loss representing the cost of undertaking the scheme'.[101] It might be said, indeed, that tax avoidance (as distinct from evasion) *necessarily* implies an impulse to legality. They failed seriously to countenance the possibility of retrospective legislation, presumably for the same reason. How much less they must have expected judicial interference. Shenfield had acknowledged, in his 1968 lecture, that the ambivalent morality of tax avoidance 'leaves it in a precarious half-world in which its lawfulness is always at risk'.[102] When retrospective legislation was used against the 'commodity-carry scheme' in the Finance Act 1978, it wrecked Tucker's business model[103] as surely as *Ramsay* was later to do. Plummer and Tucker, as if in illustration of this point, began proceedings against the Revenue in 1985.[104] Denning, too, who had evidently sympathised with Tucker in the main *Rossminster* case, had changed his tune when, in May 1980, the Revenue unsuccessfully sought to have Tucker committed for contempt,[105] expressing his deep disapproval both of Tucker's failure to swear an affidavit and of the destruction by his secretary, Lynette Binks, of five *Financial Times* desk diaries covering the years from 1974 to 1977. On the Hobbesian, and Hayekian, view of laws, whatever is not clearly banned is permitted, since laws are 'as hedges are set, not to stop travellers, but to keep them in their way'.[106] But such an exaltation of legality was not, by itself, a sufficient apology to the sharpest critics of such schemes and those who used them, critics including politicians on the Left.[107]

V. 'NOT A TAX ON ARITHMETICAL DIFFERENCES'

It was the task of the judiciary, Wilberforce no less than other judges, to stabilise the seemingly irreconcilable claims of the policy of a new government and a particular vision of the rule of law. He did so, in *Ramsay*, by attempting to transcend political division and to reach back to ancient ideas of equity, characteristic of the exercise of the Chancery jurisdiction. Other judges, lacking Wilberforce's intellectual formation, complemented his approach but for different reasons.[108]

---

[100] Davies (above n 7) 312.

[101] [1982] AC 300, 323A, 328A–B; also Gillard (above n 5) 39.

[102] Shenfield, *The Political Economy of Tax Avoidance* (above n 54) 7.

[103] Gillard (above n 5) 192.

[104] ibid, 278 ('we will have Roy Tucker's balls', the writ averred, in 'sixty pages of detail', ibid).

[105] *In the Matter of An Application by Rossminster Ltd and Others* (1980) 22 May, unreported.

[106] T Hobbes, *Leviathan* [1651], M Oakeshott (ed) (Oxford, Basil Blackwell, 1955) 227.

[107] Notably, at the time, Jeff (now Lord) Rooker (Tutt (above n 13) 311–12).

[108] When Templeman died in 2014, obituary writers were quick to allege that, as a Chancery barrister, he had had an estate duty-avoidance practice (above n 45).

In considering the judiciary's role in stabilising seemingly irreconcilable claims, it is necessary to note the constitutional position of Her Majesty's judges. '[T]he Crown's relationship with the courts', as Lord Woolf said, 'does not depend on coercion'.[109] Wilberforce, like all judges, had sworn both an oath of allegiance to the Queen and an oath to do right after the laws and usages of the realm. To a soldier, such oaths have peculiar sanctity, and the closeness of HM judges to the Crown was axiomatic in the 1980s. Reflecting on his 1971–74 presidency of the ill-starred National Industrial Relations Court (NIRC), Sir John Donaldson (1920–2005) told JAG Griffith that 'I regard all judicial activity as "political" since I consider the judiciary to be an independent arm of government with a small "g". Perhaps an independent arm of the machinery of governance might be a better description'.[110] Wilberforce's Chancery background, and his learning, had a considerable significance here. Equity, the historical Chancery jurisdiction, is administered on the Crown's behalf and has prerogatival origins.[111]

The modes of equity are both ancient and modern.[112] The Aristotelian *epieikeia* is 'just, but not what is legally just: it is a rectification of legal justice'.[113] The Hobbesian 'equity' gives the duty of administering equity to the sovereign.[114] Its association with the Crown is what gives equity, like tax, its public law character. The fact that, through repeated exercise, its methods apparently resemble those of the common law, masks four effects. First, that equity is different from the common law. Secondly, that the difference finds expression in its declining to be applied in a formulaic fashion. Thirdly that, when it is not invoked, it leaves common law property rights undisturbed.[115] Fourthly, that it does not need to be specifically invoked in order to be deployed. So viewed, equity would simply not allow a tax statute to be used in the way that WT Ramsay Ltd's advisers had argued. Judges, like politicians, must 'trim', 'as guardians of public law'.[116] They must recognise 'the necessity of others facing in a different direction' and

---

[109] *M v Home Office* [1994] 1 AC 377, 425D (see A Tomkins, *Public Law* (Oxford, Oxford University Press, 2003) 54).

[110] Quoted in M Spencer and J Spencer, 'The Judge as "Political Advisor": Behind the Scenes at the National Industrial Relations Court' (2006) 33 *Journal of Law and Society* 199, 209.

[111] I Williams, 'Developing a Prerogative Theory for the Authority of the Chancery: The French Connection' in M Godfrey (ed), *Law and Authority in British Legal History, 1200–1900* (Cambridge, Cambridge University Press, 2016) 33, 36.

[112] CK Allen, *Law in the Making*, 7th edn (Oxford, Clarendon Press, 1964) ch 5.

[113] Aristotle, *The Nicomachean Ethics*, JAK Thomson, H Tredennick and J Barnes (eds and trans) (London, Penguin, 2004) 139, 140; SR Letwin, *On the History of the Idea of Law*, NB Reynolds (ed) (Cambridge, Cambridge University Press, 2005) 34–37; G Watt, *Equity Stirring: The Story of Justice Beyond Law* (Oxford, Hart Publishing, 2009) 26.

[114] Hobbes (above n 106) ch 26; P Zagorin, *Hobbes and the Law of Nature* (Princeton, NJ, Princeton University Press, 2009) 92–95, esp 94; T Poole, 'Hobbes on Law and Prerogative' in D Dyzenhaus and T Poole (eds), *Hobbes and the Law* (Cambridge, Cambridge University Press, 2012) 90–96.

[115] J Hackney, *Understanding Equity and Trusts* (London, Fontana Press, 1987) 24–25.

[116] M Loughlin, *The Idea of Public Law* (Oxford, Oxford University Press, 2003) 152.

dispose their 'weight so as to keep the ship upon an even keel'.[117] So *Ramsay* was not so much a matter of statutory interpretation as of the uses to which statute was put.[118] Whether the second loan was a debt on a security,[119] which had to be negated, if the scheme was to work, was a question of interpretation. Whether it was permissible to look not only at that question, but at the effect of the scheme as a whole, was a matter of judicial prudence, designed to ascertain what the statute was being used to achieve and whether this objective was permissible. *Ramsay* was about creating an allowable loss without a corresponding chargeable gain, at no cost to WT Ramsay Ltd except the adviser's fee.[120] What Tucker was guilty of was a category error – the sin of presumption. He had mistaken a prudential rule about the preservation and welfare of the state for a rule of arithmetic. That is why Wilberforce says that chargeable gains taxation 'was created to operate in the real world, not that of make-belief' and 'is not a tax on arithmetical differences':[121]

> To say that a loss (or gain) which appears to arise at one stage in an indivisible process, and which is intended to be and is cancelled out by a later stage, so that at the end of what was bought as, and planned as, a single continuous operation, there is not such a loss (or gain) as the legislation is dealing with, *is in my opinion well and indeed essentially within the judicial function* (emphasis added).[122]

The category error also explains why Robert Venables QC denies that '[t]he rule in *Ramsay* is ... a rule of construction at all, in any normal sense of the word'.[123] Tax-avoidance advisers could not therefore expect judges to interpret and apply statutory provisions as though engaged in a 'box-ticking' exercise.[124] What Wilberforce had devised was an equitable judicial intervention comparable to the 'executive equity' that had long been part of the tax system.[125] The consequence of Tucker's category error was that, as things turned out, a tax liability had arisen. There was no evasion in *Ramsay* itself because the tax due, if the appeal failed, had already been paid.[126] Complicit in the error were tax

---

[117] ibid, quoting M Oakeshott, *The Politics of Faith and the Politics of Scepticism*, T Fuller (ed) (New Haven, CT, Yale University Press, 1996) 123.

[118] See SE Thorne, 'The Equity of a Statute and *Heydon's Case*' (1936–37) 31 *Illinois Law Review* 202; J Tiley, 'An Academic Perspective on the Ramsay/Dawson Doctrine' in J Dyson (ed), *Recent Tax Problems: Current Legal Problems* (London, Stevens, 1985) 19, 24.

[119] [1982] AC 300, 329H.

[120] ibid, 322F.

[121] ibid, 326D–E.

[122] ibid.

[123] R Venables, QC, 'Tax Avoidance – A Practitioner's Viewpoint' in A Shipwright (ed), *Tax Avoidance and the Law: Sham, Fraud or Mitigation?* (Oxford, Key Haven Publications, 1997) 25, 49.

[124] Watt (above n 113) 240.

[125] C Stebbings, 'The Equity of the Executive: Fairness in Tax Law in Nineteenth-Century England' in M Godfrey (ed), *Law and Authority in British Legal History, 1200–1900* (Cambridge, Cambridge University Press, 2016) 258; commentary thereon by Avery Jones (ibid, 288).

[126] Gillard (above n 5) 258. There were to be three test cases and *Ramsay* was slotted in to replace a case involving a taxpayer who had died (ibid).

counsel and their preparedness to put clients in a 'twilight zone'. No or minimal disclosure, together with a seal of confidence, were the only two protections that they relied on. To mitigate this edgy situation, the marketing material for the exempt-debt scheme included counsel's opinion 'attesting to its likely success' and a promise to litigate if necessary.[127] The tax Bar did not seem to object to this use of privileged documents.[128] They may have felt fortified by the fact that, in 1973, the Revenue was heavily decentralised and its local officers unlikely to spot trends.[129] All reckoned without Wilberforce's equitable intervention. Judges cannot decide on tax policy. They do, however, have a keen sense of political order, Wilberforce perhaps more than most. By March 1981, having read and seen the media investigations into Tucker's post-*Ramsay* activities,[130] he would have known of people queuing in North Audley Street and St George Street,[131] to buy tax schemes. He would have known something, too, of the 'Sark Lark',[132] whereby Tucker's contacts in the Channel Islands were falling over themselves to administer Rossminster's offshore companies.[133] In their own way, these various activities would have seemed to Wilberforce like a strike or picket line. 'I felt that it was wrong that these schemes should be sold widely',[134] he told Gillard. More than that, Rossminster had become Behemoth to Leviathan. Wilberforce would have had no wish to see this disorder carried through into the government elected in 1979. He would have known that this approach was not flawless but thought it was better than the alternative.

Although not certain, it nonetheless seems likely that Wilberforce saw his intervention in *Ramsay* in this light, whether or not other judges did. He took the opportunity that, in reliance on American cases including *Gregory v Helvering*,[135] Peter Millett QC, leading for the Crown, had presented to him.[136]

---

[127] Gillard (above n 5) 36. Gillard lists the main barristers involved as George Graham, QC, Michael Wheeler, QC (on the company law side) and Andrew Park, 'a then leading junior barrister ... who was to become a familiar name in the legal opinions that accompanied Tucker sales packages' (ibid, but see A Park, 'Tax Law in and after the Wheatcroft Era' [1997] *BTR* 371, 378). *Ramsay* itself was argued at all levels by the same counsel, DC Potter, QC, and David Milne.

[128] Gillard (above n 5) 36.

[129] ibid, 37.

[130] Wilberforce had been reading 'knowledgeable articles by financial journalists' (quoted by Gillard (above n 5) 260).

[131] Gillard (above n 5) 59.

[132] ibid, 53–56, 122–24.

[133] These factors were not present in *CIR v Garvin* [1981] 1 WLR 793. The decision in this case followed that in *Ramsay* but no mention was made of the latter in *Garvin*. The scheme in *Garvin* had been designed by Godfrey Bradman, 'a well-known practitioner in this business' (see [1981] 1 WLR 793, 795H).

[134] Quoted in Gillard (above n 5) 262.

[135] *Gregory v Helvering* (1935) 55 S Ct 266; A Likhovski, 'The Story of *Gregory*: How Are Tax Avoidance Case Decided?' in SA Bank and KJ Stark (eds), *Business Tax Stories* (New York, Foundation Press, 2005) 89.

[136] P Millett, 'A New Approach to Tax Avoidance Schemes' (1982) 98 *LQR* 209; P Millett, *As in Memory Long* (London, Wildy, Simmonds & Hill Publishing, 2015) 116–18.

On the one hand, there would have been no wisdom in blindly following the American example. On the other, *Gregory v Helvering*, etc, had hardly wrecked the world's largest economy. Presumably, the other *Ramsay* Law Lords were thinking the same. Legislative manipulation such as *Ramsay* involved has existential potential in relation to taxes. Since it might make them optional, it might subtract an essential ingredient of the very tax concept, namely, compulsoriness. The significance of this point is perhaps felt, not by tax avoiders themselves, but by other taxpayers. Of other judges, the most notable was Lord Templeman.[137] For Templeman, all tax avoidance schemes involved a 'trick and a pretence'.[138] He would ridicule tax avoiders by using a theatrical metaphor. In the Court of Appeal, in *Ramsay*, Templeman LJ highlighted the fact that the client's only expenditure was hiring the 'actors' of the drama.[139] 'The object of the performance is to create the illusion that something has happened', he said, 'that Hamlet has been killed and that Bottom did don an ass's head so that tax advantages can be claimed as if something had happened'.[140] His rhetoric was consistent with that of Labour politicians, who characterised such schemes as 'improper and mischievous'. By *Ramsay*, though, even some conservative judges shared Templeman's views, without troubling themselves overmuch at its contrast with Wilberforce. The Court of Appeal in *Cairns v MacDiarmid (HM Inspector of Taxes)*,[141] which straightforwardly applied *Ramsay*, was led by the Thatcherite Donaldson. By then, Labour had fallen and, crucially, the Conservatives were in office. It is tempting to think that, one reason why *Cairns* straightforwardly applies *Ramsay*, is that it had become necessary to ensure that the new conservative vision of the tax system had a chance of working.[142]

VI. 'A SIGNIFICANT CHANGE IN THE APPROACH'

With time, it has become possible to see Wilberforce's contribution to twentieth-century jurisprudence in delicate colours and to appreciate the subtlety of his interventions. There had to be something to attract Wilberforce to the 'American argument'.[143] *Ramsay* did not resolve the controversies of

---

[137] See *Black Nominees v Nicol* [1975] STC 372 (the Julie Christie case); *Chinn v Hochstrasser (HM Inspector of Taxes)* [1979] Ch 447 (reversed on appeal, above n 68); *Sotnick v CIR* (above n 32).

[138] Templeman became known either as 'Citizen Sid' (presumably, after 'Citizen Smith' (Sandbrook, *Seasons in the Sun* (above n 29) 306) or, in a reference to the punk rock band, the Sex Pistols, as 'Sid Vicious'). See Templeman (above n 123) 1.

[139] [1979] 1 WLR 974, 979D-E.

[140] ibid, 979E.

[141] *Cairns v MacDiarmid (HM Inspector of Taxes)* [1983] STC 178.

[142] Howe and Joseph (above n 42).

[143] According to a person present throughout the HL argument in *Ramsay*, the mention of *Gregory v Helvering* was greeted by Lord Wilberforce with 'Ah, this is your American argument, Mr Millett'. Both that person and another present throughout attribute to Wilberforce the quality of seeming to fall asleep during the legal argument of a case, only to awake having apparently followed the argument exactly.

the 1970s over the nature and purpose of the tax system, but it did close down a particular type of tax avoidance. Here, it is suggested, given the sacrifice of principle involved, and though it looked back, that *Ramsay*'s main significance was prospective.[144]

Wilberforce was certainly an elliptical character, so he was unlikely to clarify his own motives. *McPhail and Others v Doulton and Others*[145] and *Anns and Others v Merton LBC*[146] provide two famous examples out of his 460-plus speeches as a Law Lord.[147] *McPhail* was about property rights. *Anns* was about policy and the limits of private law. *Ramsay*, too, was about property rights. As with all judicial innovation in property cases, *Ramsay* recharacterised all similar transactions entered into on or after the date on which the transaction took place.[148] Freedom to act as a property-holder had retrospectively turned out to be no freedom at all. *Ramsay*, as a Law Society committee pointed out, flatly contradicted the judicial committee's 1966 Practice Statement, which recognised the problems of 'disturbing retrospectively the basis on which contracts, settlements of property and fiscal arrangements have been entered into'.[149] Wilberforce and the other Law Lords could have struck at any time, but they struck in 1981 and they did so, for maximum effect, against a very early Tucker scheme. All since *Ramsay*, since March 1973, would fall. *Ramsay*, in these terms, is the soul of prudence. If *Ramsay* was a judicial wrong turning, then it was because it was an attack on constitutionally protected property rights. Respect for property rights, like the binding nature of contracts, is a form of morality, though argumentatively unpopular on the Left. The status of the acts-in-the-law that WT Ramsay Ltd had engaged in, far from being clear, had been uncertain all along. Comments on Wilberforce's personal inscrutability are commonplace,[150] so it is hard to be categorical as to his motives. Maybe, by the time of *Ramsay*, he had been convinced by Dilhorne, though the latter had died in September 1980.[151] Dilhorne's posthumous reputation suffered at the hands of Lord Devlin[152]

---

[144] JD Heydon, 'Equity and Statute' in M Godfrey (ed), *Law and Authority in British Legal History, 1200–1900* (Cambridge, Cambridge University Press, 2016) 237.

[145] *McPhail and Others v Doulton and Others* [1971] AC 424.

[146] *Anns and Others v Merton LBC* [1978] AC 728.

[147] Neill (above n 59).

[148] Gillard (above n 5) 191.

[149] *Practice Statement (Judicial Precedent)* [1966] 1 WLR 1234G–H, quoted in Special Committee of Tax Law Consultative Bodies, *Tax Law After Furniss v Dawson* (London, Law Society of England and Wales, 1988) 36.

[150] Before the judgment in *Ramsay*, even Charles Potter, QC, WT Ramsay Ltd's counsel, thought 'the hearing had gone well' (Gillard (above n 5) 258).

[151] Dilhorne differed from Wilberforce in his conclusion in *Floor v Davis* [1980] AC 695 (above n 67). Earlier, he had found for the Crown in *CIR v Mills* [1975] AC 38, involving Hayley Mills. See L Baum, *Ideology in the Supreme Court* (Prince, NJ, Princeton University Press, 2017) 18–30, on the importance of 'group affect' in the context of the US Supreme Court.

[152] See P Devlin, *Easing the Passing: The Trial of Dr John Bodkin Adams* (London, Faber & Faber, 1986).

but Wilberforce evidently held him in high regard, praising Dilhorne privately 'for an unintellectual but instinctive understanding of values higher than his own'.[153] Maybe, too, as some thought, the Lord Chancellor, Lord Hailsham[154] (who evidently esteemed Wilberforce) had intervened.[155] However it may be, by striking down a 1970s tax scheme, Wilberforce instantiated a new approach to taxes in a system that would come to favour the attitudes of Tucker and his clients.

Arguments about what *Ramsay* amounted to embodied earlier disputes about the purpose and the nature of the tax system. It was in part the inequalities of the 1960s and 1970s[156] that had prompted the steeply progressive tax rates and broader tax base. Thatcher's general election victory in May 1979 occasioned the immediate abolition of the Royal Commission on the Distribution of Income and Wealth.[157] This was shortly followed by the dismantling of steeply progressive income tax rates, the 1979 removal of exchange controls having necessitated it. Wilberforce's prudential intervention in *Ramsay* seems to fit within this general context. Some said *Ramsay* was a substantive constitutional doctrine. In *CIR v Burmah Oil Co Ltd*,[158] Diplock warned taxpayers of the change: '[i]t would be disingenuous to suggest ... that *Ramsay*'s case did not mark a significant change in the approach adopted by this House'.[159] In *Furniss (HM Inspector of Taxes) v Dawson*,[160] Lord Roskill claimed that *Ramsay* had killed off the *Duke of Westminster*, but this sat ill with Wilberforce's express endorsement of the latter. In *Furniss*, Lord Brightman (1911–2006) reformulated the *Ramsay* approach, deflecting attention from its central idea, and attempting to give its scope Hayekian certainty:[161]

> First [he said], there must be a pre-ordained series of transactions; or, if one likes, one single composite transaction ... Secondly, there must be steps inserted which have no commercial (business) purpose apart from the avoidance of a liability to tax – not 'no business effect'. If those two ingredients exist, the inserted steps are to be disregarded for fiscal purposes.[162]

---

[153] Wilberforce (above n 58) 105.

[154] 1907–2001. Hailsham, deeply and paternalistically conservative, was a fierce opponent of the reform of the legal profession. When he 'was outvoted in a cabinet committee on the monopolies of barristers and solicitors he banged his walking sticks on the table and stormed out' (Harrison, *Finding a Role?* (above n 14) 150.

[155] Gillard (above n 5) 262. It is interesting that Lord Hailsham subsequently cited Lord Wilberforce's speech in Ramsay as an example of Wilberforce's classical formation. Hailsham thought there was something about it, not of Aristotle, but of the Achilles paradox of Zeno of Elea (see Lord Hailsham, 'Richard Wilberforce: A Man for All Seasons' in M Bos and I Brownlie, *Liber Amicorum for Lord Wilberforce* (Oxford, Clarendon Press, 1987) 3, 9).

[156] ibid, 134–35.

[157] Harrison, *Finding a Role?* (above n 14) 133.

[158] *CIR v Burham Oil Co Ltd* [1982] SC (HL) 114.

[159] ibid, 124.

[160] [1984] 1 AC 474.

[161] Douglas (above n 21) ch 14.

[162] [1984] 1 AC 474, 527D-E.

Brightman had been Thatcher's pupil master[163] and, with Donaldson, one of only three NIRC judges. With the change of government in 1979, with the 1980s seeing the expansion of financial journalism, and with the range of 'products' sold by banks expanding to include tax avoidance products,[164] the need for *Ramsay* was still present, though its rationale had subtly and paradoxically changed, in a political settlement that prized property rights above all else and had prioritised tax reform.[165]

For all these reasons, other judges might have misinterpreted Wilberforce's approach. The view that *Ramsay* was a substantive constitutional doctrine that, exceptionally, allowed judges to interfere in matters of taxation, held sway for a surprisingly long time.[166] The view that *Ramsay* embodied only an approach to statutory interpretation has produced differing schools of thought. One school has emphasised Wilberforce's endorsement of *Duke of Westminster*.[167] Another, as in *Barclays Mercantile Business Finance v Mawson (HM Inspector of Taxes)*,[168] has emphasised the need for purposive construction.[169] A third has reached back, somewhat clumsily, to Wilberforce's equitable inspiration. First *UBS AG v Revenue and Customs Commissioners*,[170] then the *Rangers* case, imply that *Ramsay* is not really about statutory interpretation at all.[171] It is not about 'the equity of the statute', a common law approach that refers, not to the equitable jurisdiction, but to strongly purposive construction.[172] Wilberforce

---

[163] Moore (above n 36) 128.

[164] Harrison, *Finding a Role?* (above n 14) 343.

[165] M Daunton, 'Creating a Dynamic Society: The Tax Reforms of the Thatcher Government' in M Buggeln, M Daunton and A Nützenadel (eds), *The Political Economy of Public Finance: Taxation, State Spending and Debt since the 1970s* (Cambridge, Cambridge University Press, 2017) 32.

[166] Though it might, or might not, work in the Revenue's favour: see *Craven (HM Inspector of Taxes) v White* (1988) 62 TC 1; *Fitzwilliam (Countess) and Others v CIR* [1993] STC 502; *Shepherd (HM Inspector of Taxes) v Lyntress Ltd* (1989) 62 TC 495; *Ensign Tankers (Leasing) Ltd v Stokes (Inspector of Taxes)* [1992] 1 AC 655; *R v CIR, ex parte Matrix-Securities Ltd* (1994) 66 TC 587. For a clear outline, albeit from the perspective of 1996, see P Ridgway, *Lecture Notes: Revenue Law* (Abingdon, Routledge-Cavendish, 1996) ch 2. Templeman was the chief architect of this 'fiscal nullity' doctrine (see also A Fairpo and D Salter, *Revenue Law: Principles and Practice*, 35th edn (London, Bloomsbury Professional, 2017) para [2.34]).

[167] Including Peter Millett (see *Ramsay* [1982] AC 300, 316H; P Millett, 'Artificial Tax Avoidance: The English and American Approach' [1986] *BTR* 327, 329–30).

[168] *Barclays Mercantile Business Finance v Mawson (HM Inspector of Taxes)* [2004] UKHL 51; (2004) 75 TC 446.

[169] Consistent with the themes of this chapter, there may be something in the thought that, in the eighteenth and nineteenth centuries, judges with a Whig/liberal/Conservative background (Ellenborough, Esher, etc) tended to favour literal construction, while Tories (eg, Mansfield, Garrow, Tenterden, etc) favoured the purposive. There are exceptions, though (eg, Halsbury) and it would therefore be wrong to push this too far.

[170] *UBS AG v Revenue and Customs Commissioners* [2016] 1 WLR 1005; D de Cogan, 'Defining Tax Avoidance: Flirting with Chaos, Again' [2016] *CLJ* 474.

[171] *RFC 2012 plc (in liquidation) (formerly The Rangers Football Club plc) v Advocate General for Scotland* [2017] UKSC 45; [2017] 1 WLR 2767.

[172] R Ekins, *The Nature of Legislative Intent* (Oxford, Oxford University Press, 2012) 275–84; Allen (above n 112) 451–56; Williams (above n 111) 34, fn 2.

anyway rules this out early in his analysis.[173] Instead, *Ramsay* underplays interpretative extremes and steers a path between them that relies not on interpretative technique but on proscribing the use of a taxing statute for inequitable dealing. Tax avoidance is, by definition, not in the public interest or the national interest,[174] because HM Government has already spelt out, for the time being, and in the legislation itself, what that interest is.

VII. CONCLUDING: 'THEORETICAL, NOT LIBERAL'

Ramsay's landmark significance is to be assessed relative to ideas of state and government in the early 1980s, to the judiciary's role as a political institution and to the views of a precociously intellectual judge. The conflictual context of *Ramsay*, and its historical situation at the beginning of an era of radically different tax policy, is significant. Few, if any, have really appreciated the approach that Wilberforce took, and we should not be afraid to reassess it.

The political divisions that provided the context for *Ramsay* were, in the end, softened, though not to the tax avoiders' advantage. The technical knowledge of the 1970s tax advisers was not matched by wisdom about human nature. Tucker, like Plummer, evidently believed passionately in human autonomy,[175] and thus that clients went into his schemes with open eyes. Their fate, after *Ramsay*, was, in some respects, not unlike the strikers they seemed to resemble. They were not surging in clashes with police, with Tucker and Plummer directing operations from a rooftop,[176] but their intent was real enough. Tucker's clients were showing how greatly they disagreed with the way in which public revenue was raised and applied. '[We] provide a necessary service for the taxpayer', Tucker told a *Guardian* journalist in 1976. '[W]e act as a safety valve against evasion … and emigration. We've stopped many very wealthy people leaving the country. The government believes in redeploying wealth and we think too much wealth is concentrated in the government'.[177] Compare this with Scargill's declaration of defiance quoted above. Taxation is such that those who take one view of its nature and purpose will never, *under any circumstances*, agree with those who take another. Tax avoidance will never go away because the loathing of taxes imposed by those of one ideology by those of another is elemental. An important argument against sophisticated tax avoidance is that its techniques are available only to the wealthy and cunning. But this argument only holds

---

[173] [1982] AC 300, 323C.

[174] J Snape, *The Political Economy of Corporation Tax: Theory, Values and Law Reform* (Oxford, Hart Publishing, 2011) 118–25.

[175] Gillard outlines Plummer's later charitable and ethical preoccupations (Gillard (above n 5) 285).

[176] Sandbrook, *State of Emergency* (above n 25) 123.

[177] Quoted in Gillard (above n 5) 81–82.

for people who think that taxation should be based on ability to pay and is essentially non-reciprocal. For those who think that tax should be based on benefit, and that it is essentially contractual, the very premise on which that anti-avoidance argument is based is wrong. People bargain for tax benefits in the same way as for any other good. Even the non-transparency of the tax-avoidance market is no worse than the opaqueness of any other. Like Scargill and the metropolitan authorities, though in a different sphere, WT Ramsay Ltd's advisers were principled (though misguided) activists. As with Scargill and New Labour, their efforts were forgotten as soon as their views began to take political form in Thatcher's neoliberal order.

For their part, rather than studying Wilberforce in context, lawyers have mapped onto his approach, expectations of their own, perhaps missing what it really is. They have failed to perceive him disposing his meagre weight to keep the ship of state on an even keel. Wilberforce's own description of himself as 'a theoretical judge, not a liberal judge'[178] provides a terse explanation of what was really going on in this landmark case. When the judgment in *Ramsay* was handed down, I was at school in Blackburn, Lancashire, as ignorant of Lincolnshire's rural fastness as the bright lights of the West End. Experiencing life in Lancashire under the Thatcher government, I saw something of the misery that free market Thatcherite ideas brought to that part of the world. So I am no Thatcherite. But I am a lawyer. And, thinking as lawyers do, I believe that law, and the mere possibility that legal argument might save one's skin, should be taken seriously. With *Ramsay*, you never know.

---

[178] ibid, 258.

11

CIR v National Federation of Self-Employed and Small Businesses *(1981)*

All Grievances Converging on Tax Law

DOMINIC DE COGAN*

T HE HOUSE OF Lords case involving the National Federation of Self-Employed and Small Businesses (NFSE) is familiar to most English lawyers from our days of studying standing rules as part of administrative law or public law courses. Yet the most cursory overview of the litigation history of the NFSE reveals riches well beyond what I had myself expected. David Kelly, the National Spokesman of the NFSE between 1975 and 1976, was imprisoned in Armley Gaol in Leeds over a £43 debt for Class 4 National Insurance Contributions (NICs).[1] In *Martin v O'Sullivan*[2] a NFSE member challenged the validity of the NIC legislation on the 'remarkable'[3] and predictably unsuccessful ground that MPs had become salaried employees of the Crown and were thereby disqualified from

* My understanding of the events in Fleet Street has been assisted enormously by Alan Walker, a casual for the *Sunday Times* in the late 1970s and now an employee of Christ's College Cambridge; by Philip Ridd, a solicitor for the Revenue in the NFSE case; and by the efforts of Kate Faulkner at the Squire Law Library in procuring television footage from 1978. Thanks also to supporters of the Centre for Public Law, the Tax Administration Research Centre and the tax stream of the Society of Legal Scholars as well as to John Snape and David Collison for helpful comments on earlier drafts. Any errors and controversial opinions are my own responsibility.

[1] M Bettsworth, *The Growth of a Business Pressure Group: Federation of Small Businesses 1974–1999* (NFSE, 1999) 55.

[2] *Martin v O'Sullivan* [1984] STC 258; Bettsworth, ibid, 67.

[3] *Martin v O'Sullivan*, ibid, 259 (Stephenson LJ); *cf British Railways Board v Pickin* [1974] AC 765.

representing the public in Parliament. The claim that NICs discriminated against small businesses was brought to the European Commission of Human Rights in a series of cases in the name of the NFSE (*NFSE v The UK*)[4] and of the chairman of its National Insurance committee (*Juby v The UK*).[5] In *C&E v Corbitt*[6] it was argued that customs officials were applying officiously exacting standards of record-keeping on a coin merchant who purchased most of his stock from private sellers and therefore wished to apply the VAT margin scheme. The contentions of the NFSE member involved were upheld by a majority of the Court of Appeal, helped by a characteristically lyrical judgment of Lord Denning MR, but this was overturned by a 4:1 majority of the House of Lords despite some demonstrations of sympathy for the taxpayer.

This brief summary of disputes involving the NFSE, which excludes at least two unreported cases,[7] demonstrates a few important points. First, the NFSE was litigious, in some instances proceeding in its own name (eg, *NFSE v The UK*), in others providing support to officers (eg, *Martin v O'Sullivan*, *Juby v The UK*) and members (eg, *C&E v Corbitt*). Second, the NFSE was persistent in the face of continual disappointment in the courts, suggesting that litigation formed part of a wider strategy rather than an end in itself. Third, most of the cases involved taxation. Fourth, there is a sense of profound amateurism and even enthusiasm from the cases and associated materials, combined with a sustained anger at the treatment of the 'small man' by government, unions and large business representatives. A more general observation is that the large and sophisticated literature dealing with *CIR v NFSE* places little emphasis on the rather colourful history of the early years of the NFSE, let alone the wider context of the Fleet Street dispute itself. The focus is instead on the legal questions of standing to apply for judicial review[8] and the scope of Revenue powers.[9] The background to the case is generally overlooked, with the important exceptions of the extended discussions by Harlow

---

[4] *NFSE v The UK* App no 7995/77 (Commission Decision, 11 July 1978); Bettsworth (above n 1) 89.

[5] *Juby v The UK* App No 9793/82 (Commission Decision, 13 March 1984); *Juby v The UK* App no 11254/84 (Commission Decision, 10 December 1984); *Juby v The UK* App no 11592/85 (Commission Decision, 16 July 1987); Bettsworth (above n 1) 131. Note that only the last of these decisions is reported even on the ECHR case law database, hudoc.echr.coe.int.

[6] *Customs and Excise v JH Corbitt (Numismatists)* [1979] STC 504; Bettsworth (above n 1) 90.

[7] Two sickness benefit cases are mentioned in Bettsworth (above n 1) 87.

[8] eg, D Feldman, 'Public Interest Litigation and Constitutional Theory in Comparative Perspective' (1992) 55 *MLR* 44; P Cane, 'Statutes, Standing and Representation' [1990] *PL* 307; J Miles, 'Standing under the Human Rights Act 1998' [2000] *CLJ* 133; M Elliott and J Varuhas, *Administrative Law: Text and Materials*, 5th edn (Oxford, Oxford University Press, 2016) 549–74.

[9] eg, S Daly, 'The Life and Times of ESCs: A Defence?' in P Harris and D de Cogan (eds), *Studies in the History of Tax Law: Volume 8* (Oxford, Hart Publishing, 2017); J Alder, 'The Legality of Extra-Statutory Concessions' (1980) 1 *NLJ* 180; T Bowler, 'HMRC's Discretion: the Application of the Ultra Vires Rule and the Legitimate Expectation Doctrine', TLRC Discussion Paper no 10 (London, IFS, 2014), available at www.ifs.org.uk/uploads/publications/TLRC/TLRC_DP_10.pdf.

and Rawlings,[10] King and Nugent,[11] Bennett[12] and of course the NFSE's biographer Bettsworth.[13]

The aim of the present chapter is to build on this latter literature in order to address the connected questions of why the NFSE chose to litigate in response to the tax treatment applied to Fleet Street casual workers, and how this choice relates to the ongoing legal significance of the decision of the House of Lords. These questions are less straightforward than they seem. As noted below, the case is rather curious in not fitting neatly within the NFSE's evergreen tax campaigns. It is also difficult to find a 'smoking gun' that explains the decision to litigate.[14] Not for the first time in this series of books, a close examination of the factual context also encourages a reassessment of what it means to describe *CIR v NFSE* as a 'landmark case'. The decision undoubtedly represented a softening of the response of the House of Lords to attempts in the 1970s to channel various political and social grievances into the courts.[15] Nevertheless, less was decided on the facts than might be imagined. Indeed, it might be said that the decision was conveniently ambiguous, leaving threads of reasoning to be developed by future courts but avoiding immediate commitment to any conception of the law of standing in particular.[16] In this sense that *CIR v NFSE* was both a landmark and a holding position, there are interesting parallels with other politically charged tax cases of approximately the same era, including *WT Ramsay v CIR*[17] on avoidance and *R v CIR ex p Rossminster* on administration.[18]

These arguments are unpacked in the remaining parts of this chapter. Parts I–III describe a Venn Diagram of concerns facing the NFSE, comprising grievances relating to corporatism in government, the organisational needs of the nascent Federation and grievances relating to taxation respectively. Part IV explains the Fleet Street dispute and situates it at the centre of the Venn diagram, and part V examines how an understanding of the NFSE as a young and aggressive organisation using litigation broadly as a means of attracting new members alters our understanding of the significance of *CIR v NFSE*. Part VI concludes

---

[10] C Harlow and R Rawlings, *Pressure Through Law* (Abingdon, Routledge, 1992).

[11] R King and N Nugent (eds), *Respectable Rebels* (London, Hodder & Stoughton, 1979).

[12] R J Bennett, *Local Business Voice* (Oxford, Oxford University Press, 2011).

[13] Bettsworth (above n 1).

[14] Compare *NFSE v The UK* (above n 4), where the decision to proceed was made by vote at the NFSE's conference: see King and Nugent (above n 11) 65.

[15] The Denning Court of Appeal was of course a different matter: see *AG (McWhirter) v IBA* [1973] QB 629; *R v Greater London Council, ex parte Blackburn* [1976] 3 All ER 184; *Gouriet v Union of Post Office Workers* [1977] QB 729. On the more restrictive approach taken by Lord Denning towards social security claimants, see T Prosser, *Test Cases for the Poor* (London, CPAG, 1983) 30–32; JAG Griffith, *The Politics of the Judiciary* (London, Fontana, 1977) 177.

[16] Refer to text following n 111 below.

[17] *WT Ramsay v CIR* [1982] AC 300.

[18] *R v CIR ex parte Rossminster* [1980] AC 952.

by suggesting that the case formed part of a wider juridification of political grievances relating to taxation in the late 1970s and early 1980s that has already been observed by Loughlin amongst others.[19]

I. CORPORATISM

The essence of the complaint against corporatism was that key conditions of doing business were regulated by tripartite negotiations between government, trades union leadership and 'insider' business organisations such as the Confederation of British Industry (CBI). This was considered to neglect the interests of those not naturally represented under such a system, principally the self-employed and small businesses,[20] but perhaps also shop-floor union officials dissatisfied with the deals being struck by their national representatives.[21] At the heart of the problem was the inherent difficulty in representing small businesspeople as a whole, from childminders to barristers to car mechanics. In the words of the Bolton Committee in 1971,

> small businessmen are often fiercely independent, very reluctant to join in group activities and also heavily overworked, so that even if they have the inclination for such activities it is very hard to find time for them. The consequence is that the sector is so weakly and diversely represented that it cannot bring effective pressure to bear on Government.[22]

Moreover, the bodies that might have been considered natural champions of small businesses were for various reasons not always ideally placed to help. The CBI was an insider to the tripartite system more closely associated with large business,[23] in spite of its establishment of a Small Firms Council.[24] The Conservative Party was assumed to receive the electoral loyalty of most small businesspeople[25] and certainly contained some elements sympathetic to the sector.[26] However, this masks sustained hostility both to the general direction of the Heath government and to the impact of its policies on small businesses.

---

[19] M Loughlin, *Legality and Locality* (Oxford, Oxford University Press, 1996) ch 7.

[20] J McHugh 'The Self-Employed and the Small Independent Entrepreneur' in R King and N Nugent (eds), *Respectable Rebels* (London, Hodder & Stoughton, 1979); Bennett (above n 12) 37; J Bolton, *Report of the Committee of Inquiry on Small Firms* (Cmnd 4811, 1971–72) ch 9.

[21] Refer to text at n 77 below.

[22] Bolton (above n 20) 93.

[23] Bennett (above n 12) 37; McHugh (above n 20) 48–49; Bettsworth (above n 1) 50.

[24] Bolton (above n 20) 93.

[25] ibid.

[26] The most notable example was Teresa Gorman, briefly a NFSE member but soon founder of the more overtly ideological Alliance of Small Firms and Self-Employed People. She was an independent (anti-Heath) candidate in the October 1974 general election but was subsequently a Conservative MP: E Pearce, 'Teresa Gorman obituary' *The Guardian* (28 August 2015).

Bettsworth reports David Kelly[27] as complaining variously about VAT, local government reorganisation, the abolition of resale price maintenance and the UK's entry into the Common Market.[28] The Chambers of Commerce, Chambers of Trade and their national equivalents really did represent small businesses but had been weakened by tripartism,[29] legal restrictions[30] and a restrained attitude towards political activism that left a vacuum ready to be filled by new and more aggressive competitor organisations.

The specific grievances of small businesspeople were extremely disparate, as the reference to David Kelly demonstrates. However, a few important themes can be identified with a common underlying message that the entire system was felt to be rigged against those unrepresented by corporatism. The first set of grievances concerned the disproportionate impact upon small enterprises of certain restrictions on doing business, principally employment legislation but also requirements relating to training, industrial safety and so forth.[31] Second, there was a widespread belief that trades unions benefited not only from certain legal immunities but also official tolerance in circumstances where individuals could expect no such leeway.[32] Third, there was an acute defensiveness in response to 'monstrous' suggestions that small businesses were especially prone to fraud, especially when made by left-of-centre political operatives such as Frank Field of the Child Poverty Action Group (CPAG).[33] The point was not precisely that Field was wrong, but again that entrepreneurs were being unfairly treated relative to trades unions in a political and economic system in which they were not effectively represented.[34] Fourth, the self-employed were ineligible for certain state benefits that were provided to employees as a matter of course, as detailed in the early NFSE publication with the memorable title of *Twenty Diabolical Injustices*.[35] Fifth, tax rules and administrative practices were thought to be applied to the sector in a particularly officious manner; a full discussion of this matter is postponed to part III below.

---

[27] See n 1 above.

[28] Bettsworth (above n 1) 56.

[29] Bennett (above n 12) 40.

[30] eg, the National Chambers of Trade (NCT) refused to endorse a VAT 'strike' in part because, not being a trade union, it had no protection against a charge of conspiracy: Bettsworth (above n 1) 52.

[31] Bolton (above n 20) 80.

[32] This grievance was taken up with enthusiasm by the National Association for Freedom (NAFF): Harlow and Rawlings (above n 10) 146. See also n 30 above; M Pirie, *Think Tank: The Story of the Adam Smith Institute* (London Biteback Publications, 2012) ch 1. For a review of the law, see A Denning, *The Closing Chapter* (London, Butterworths, 1983) Section 6.

[33] Bettsworth (above n 1) 69. See also F Field, M Meacher and C Pond, *To Him Who Hath: A Study of Poverty and Taxation* (Harmondsworth, Penguin, 1977) 162–63.

[34] Interestingly, similar arguments are voiced by shop-floor trades unionists in BBC, 'Panorama: The Battle for Printing House Square' (20 November 1978), available at genome.ch.bbc.co.uk/99c53c86410b4c83b70a6e95da093fc7.

[35] Bettsworth (above n 1) 39.

II. ORGANISATIONAL NEEDS OF THE NFSE

It has been observed above that the underrepresentation of entrepreneurs by the CBI, Conservatives and Chambers of Trade and Commerce left a vacuum ready to be filled by competitor organisations. The NFSE was founded in Lytham St Anne's in Lancashire in 1974 as one such new entrant. With the benefit of hindsight, it is unremarkable that the NFSE survived and now operates as an insider body under the name of Federation of Small Businesses.[36] At the time, however, the NFSE's success was far from guaranteed. It faced stiff competition from similar bodies such as the National Association for the Self-Employed (NASE) and Teresa Gorman's Alliance of Small Firms and Self-Employed People (ASP)[37] as well as inevitable attempts by the older bodies to protect their position.[38] It also experienced what might be described as overtrading, with the organisation's leaders and accounting systems equally unable to cope with the burgeoning workload.[39] Perhaps as a result of these teething difficulties, the NFSE was to experience both a high turnover of leadership and a stubborn ceiling on membership at a small fraction of the overall population of small businesspeople.[40]

These tensions came to be reflected in a protracted struggle within the NFSE between what might be termed the professionals and the radicals. The former wished to take up the Bolton Committee's challenge of establishing an insider group for small businesses, adding a fourth side to the tripartite system of corporatist bargaining. They were particularly worried about the threat of the NFSE being associated with 'extremism'.[41] It is not always entirely clear what was intended by this term,[42] but a practical consequence was a deliberate distancing from the National Association for Freedom (NAFF), a group then associated with the conservative Right but adopting 'freedom of the individual' views that might now be associated with libertarianism.[43] The radicals within the NFSE, by

---

[36] On the process by which this happened, see further G Jordan and C Halpin, 'Cultivating Small Business Influence in the UK: The Federation of Small Businesses' Journey from Outsider to Insider' (2003) 3 *Journal of Public Affairs* 313.

[37] The rivalry with NASE seems to have concerned the level of subscription fees; with ASP, ideology: see King and Nugent (above n 11) 54.

[38] ibid, 71.

[39] See, eg, Bettsworth (above n 1) 33–36 on the troubles caused by the disorganised accounting practices of the NFSE in its early days.

[40] King and Nugent (above n 11) 67–68.

[41] Bettsworth (above n 1) 75.

[42] For instance, modern apprehensions towards Enoch Powell were not universally shared within the NFSE; indeed, disappointment was voiced at his lukewarm stance towards the organisation: ibid, 56, 90. There was also a sense at one point that the NFSE might resemble Poujadism in France: King and Nugent (above n 11) 52.

[43] See N Nugent, 'The National Association for Freedom' in R King and N Nugent (eds), *Respectable Rebels* (London, Hodder & Stoughton, 1979); King and Nugent (above n 11); Bettsworth (above n 1) 53.

contrast, favoured a deliberately confrontational approach towards campaigning. As McHugh writes:

> In an era increasingly dominated by 'big' business, interventionist government and powerful trade unionism, the small independent entrepreneur, the typical representative of the petits-bourgeois has [been marginalised]. The emergence of various groups over the past few years purporting to represent the small entrepreneur and the self-employed in an aggressive, radical fashion can be seen as a reaction to these forces.[44]

This element within the NFSE had no hesitation in taking inspiration from the tactics of NAFF, and in particular the repeated use of litigation as a means of generating publicity and increasing membership.[45] Bettsworth reports memorably that *NFSE v The UK* was attended by 'huge media publicity' but that, in the words of the NFSE's magazine 'First Voice', 'considerable publicity was lost through the untimely death of Elvis Presley'.[46] Some of the early campaigns were notably childish and included paying tax on concrete slabs and factory-soiled knickers;[47] these ludicrous antics may well have been inspired by AP Herbert's fictional case of *Board of Inland Revenue v Haddock*, in which a taxpayer was said to have written a cheque in favour of the tax authorities on the side of a cow.[48] David Kelly's visit to prison in Leeds over a £43 NIC debt has already been noted.

This was all good fun, but the central problem remained as identified by the Bolton Committee in 1971.[49] The small business sector was highly diverse and its members often fiercely independent, weakening the opportunities for effective representation within a corporatist system. The NFSE's often rather playful antics did not address this problem, but its focus on taxation did.

III. TAX GRIEVANCES

The NFSE seems to have been fond of lists, and in particular lists of demands and grievances.[50] From the outset these lists were dominated by a small group of recurring tax issues. The most prominent of all was the levying of 8 per cent NICs on the self-employed individuals without offering state benefits of an equivalent value to those received by employees.[51] Another predictable frustration

---

[44] King and Nugent (above n 11) 46.

[45] Harlow and Rawlings (above n 10) 145–46. The Child Poverty Action Group (CPAG) pursued very similar tactics and may also have been an inspiration, although it is difficult to find a direct acknowledgement of this: see Prosser (above n 15).

[46] Bettsworth (above n 1) 79.

[47] ibid, 70.

[48] AP Herbert, *More Misleading Cases in the Common Law* (London, Methuen & Co, 1930). Thanks to John Snape for drawing my attention to this.

[49] See above, n 22.

[50] See, eg, n 35 above.

[51] *NFSE v The UK* (above n 4); *Juby v The UK* (above n 5).

concerned the means by which taxes were administered, and in particular the ways in which tax officials sought to prevent evasion in the small business sector. The photocard known as the 714 certificate allowed self-employed building contractors to receive payment without deduction of income tax.[52] Besides the usual resistance to identification cards, it was alleged that the Revenue had engaged in an abuse of power by withholding certificates from taxpayers involved in previous irregularities.[53] More generally, the NFSE complained about tax authority power to inspect books and premises; one of its most useful and successful early publications has the suitably menacing title of *An Inspector at the Door*.[54] The *Corbitt* case[55] was important to the NFSE because it combined these administrative concerns with a more general dissatisfaction with the introduction of VAT by Heath's government in 1973.[56] Bettsworth notes revealingly that 'Despite the defeat over the *Corbitt* case, the Federation still had its teeth sunk deep into the VAT men'.[57] This language is striking but seems well judged; the whole point was for the small person to seek symbolic confrontations with overbearing officialdom. Importantly in view of later developments, the inequities of the rating system also made frequent appearances on the NFSE's lists.[58]

In line with the tax payments on concrete slabs, many of the specific grievances were rather petty in nature, but the NFSE's point was that these epitomised deeper inequities especially when compared with the tax treatment of unionised workers or large businesses. This comes across very strongly from the NFSE's affidavit in *CIR v NFSE*, in which extreme examples of official pettifogging against the self-employed and small businesses are contrasted with the alleged blanket forgiveness of tax evasion by union members.[59] The other piece of relevant context is that with income tax marginal rates of up to 98 per cent in the mid-1970s, taxation was a matter of wide concern to the public and – crucially – to the whole range of the NFSE's members and non-members. This role of taxation as a point of common interest to the otherwise heterogenous small business sector explains more than anything else the obsession of the NFSE with fiscal campaigns.[60]

---

[52] A Seely, 'Taxation in the construction industry', Standard Note: SN814, House of Commons Library, 20 May 2011, available at researchbriefings.files.parliament.uk/documents/SN00814/SN00814.pdf.

[53] King and Nugent (above n 11) 63. Conservative Party support for the scheme was met with dismay by the NFSE: see Bettsworth (above n 1) 53.

[54] NFSE, *An Inspector at the Door* (Adam Smith Institute and NFSE, 1979).

[55] *C&E v Corbitt* (above n 6).

[56] Bennett (above n 12) 41–42; in particular, the NFSE complained that the VAT turned business people into unpaid tax collectors: see King and Nugent (above n 11) 51.

[57] Bettsworth (above n 1) 109.

[58] See text at n 122 below.

[59] See text at n 100 below.

[60] Bettsworth (above n 1) 100. As John Snape pointed out in conversation, this is a curious variant on the role that taxation can play in cementing allegiances within a state.

These campaigns included not only litigation but what was thought to be the 'first tax strike of recent memory'[61] whereby Class 4 NICs were paid not to the tax authorities but into a special fund pending negotiations on the NFSE's demands. This strike attracted notice[62] but only 2 per cent of members participated and in 1982, only a few years later, a rate strike was rejected by the NFSE's conference in what was seen as a mark of the organisation's increasing maturity.[63] Even more interesting than the campaigning history of the NFSE is an item conspicuous by its absence, which is any sustained reference to the problems in Fleet Street before the submission of the application for judicial review in April 1979.[64] The industrial unrest at the newspapers was deep-seated[65] and would certainly have been in the public consciousness, but did not form one of the NFSE's evergreen campaigns and had not previously appeared in its famous lists of grievances prior to 1979.

IV. THE FLEET STREET DISPUTE

In order to understand the background to *CIR v NFSE* it is worth outlining in brief the background to the newspaper dispute. The first point to note is that many of the problems in Fleet Street were not new, and indeed can be found in the minutes of evidence to the Royal Commission on the Press of 1961–62.[66] At the heart of the problem lay a deeply unhealthy system of staffing newspaper production that persisted because there were advantages both for newspaper managers and union members. On the one hand, management gained access to a 'labour force the size of which could be related easily to the economic circumstances of individual newspapers' which comprised not only 'regular casuals' (employees who worked less than full-time) but 'casual casuals' (individuals who did not work on a regular basis for an employer).[67] On the other hand, unions wished 'to protect employment in the industry from outside incursion, to maximise (and at least retain) their individual claims on jobs within the industry, and, especially latterly, to ensure that job opportunities were fairly distributed among their own members'.[68] Wages were generous and could be supplemented further, particularly for those who secured Saturday evening shifts;

---

[61] ibid, 45–46.

[62] King and Nugent (above n 11) 51.

[63] Bettsworth (above n 1) 55, 134.

[64] There is admittedly scope for additional work to be performed on this question by reference to the NFSE's internal documents.

[65] See, eg, Baron Shawcross, *Royal Commission on the Press* (Cmnd 1811, 1961–62).

[66] See, eg, the evidence of the NATSOPA union in Baron Shawcross, *Royal Commission on the Press, Minutes of Oral Evidence, Volume II* (Cmnd 1812-1, 1961–62) 150–71.

[67] Baron McGregor, *Royal Commission on the Press, Industrial Relations in the National Newspaper Industry, a Report by ACAS* (Cmnd 6680, 1976–77) paras 78 and 80, which also notes the ambiguities in these terms.

[68] ibid, para 80.

in consequence, many print workers preferred to work on a casual basis in Fleet Street than in permanent positions elsewhere.[69]

These considerations help to explain the failure of attempts to reduce or eliminate the use of casual workers in the newspaper industry.[70] Nevertheless, the problems of the system were severe. In an immediate sense, casuals could be placed in an extremely precarious position, sometimes travelling to a 'calls office' at their own expense and waiting for hours without any guarantee of work.[71] Part of the reason for this situation was that recruitment was controlled by union chapels,[72] in large part independently of the national leadership of the unions.[73] This control in particular extended to the exact procedure by which a casual would go to work, and as is well known, the keeping of relevant records.[74] The conduct of chapels would have varied widely, but there were persistent allegations of malpractice under the umbrella term 'Spanish practices'.[75] These included overmanning including the use of 'ghost workers', or in other words dead or non-existent individuals whose wages would be divided amongst the living workers.[76] A slightly less serious suggestion was that threats by chapels to engage in unofficial strike action led to ad hoc pay concessions with the newspapers, ironically bypassing the corporatist system so disliked by the NFSE.[77] Whoever was to blame, the outcome was poor and declining productivity combined with a resistance to the technological innovations that might have reversed the trend.[78]

Things came to a head at the *Times* and *Sunday Times*. The immediate trigger seems to have been the support of the Thomson Organisation, the then proprietors, for the government's pay restraint policy.[79] This had pushed the titles to the bottom of the pay league,[80] with consequences as described by

[69] ibid, paras 86, 97, 105 and 119.

[70] ibid, paras 108, 123 and 124.

[71] ibid, para 115. The priority given to 'red toppers', or older and more experienced 'time-served craftsmen' was understandable in view of poor pension provision, but further disadvantaged younger workers: ibid, paras 94, 100, 102 and 103.

[72] These were a long-established means of union organisation within individual newspaper offices: ibid, ch 8.

[73] This was again a persistent issue: see Shawcross, *Royal Commission on the Press, Minutes of Oral Evidence* (above n 66) 152.

[74] McGregor (above n 67) para 111. Note, therefore, that the challenge for tax officials in getting hold of intelligible employment information was exponentially more difficult than if the unions had held the relevant records centrally.

[75] NJ Wilkinson, *Secrecy and the Media* (London, Routledge, 2009) 350.

[76] The allegation is denied in heartfelt manner in the 'Panorama' programme (above n 34) and it seems likely that many chapels did not engage in such behaviour. The ACAS report notes rather half-heartedly that they have been 'assured … that it is difficult for an individual to improperly obtain and use a union authorisation to undertake casual work': McGregor (above n 67) para 122.

[77] J Grigg, *The History of the Times: the Thomson Years 1966–1981* (London, Times Books, 1993) 451–52.

[78] This was also a persistent issue: see, eg, Shawcross, *Royal Commission on the Press, Minutes of Oral Evidence* (above n 66) 164; Wilkinson (above n 75); ibid, 453.

[79] Grigg (above n 77) 451, who also reports the possibility that Thomson was seeking to protect its other business interests, and in particular a contract to fly British troops to and from Germany.

[80] ibid, 452.

Grigg: 'Throughout 1977 the papers had been suffering the effects of unofficial industrial action on an unprecedented scale. The group as a whole had lost 7,337,000 copies, £1,136,000 in profit, and £911,000 in advertisement revenue during the year'.[81] The only escape route acceptable to the government was to improve productivity. This in practice meant reducing overmanning and bringing newly purchased machines into use, and was blocked by the NGA union whose members were already nervous about the impact of new technology on their livelihoods.[82] Ultimately, management threatened to suspend production if no agreement were reached,[83] and this threat was carried out with effect from 1 December 1978.

It was in this febrile atmosphere that the BBC, on 20 November 1978, aired an episode of 'Panorama' entitled 'The Battle of Printing House Square: Behind The Times'.[84] It was not the first coverage of the press disputes during 1978,[85] but contains the following critical passage:

> What the euphemism 'old Spanish customs' really conceals is corruption. We've learnt that the Inland Revenue has just completed an investigation into ninety thousand casual call slips in Fleet Street. It found that the vast majority of names and addresses were entirely fictitious and it estimates that at least a million pounds in income tax is being lost each year. Some men apparently even use blatantly false names like Sir Gordon Richards of Tattenham Corner, Sir Max Aitken or William Shakespeare … Union leaders privately confirm that this happens but they allege that some middle managers also receive kickbacks from the system.

Such activity would normally be curtailed by the normal operation of the PAYE system, depending perhaps on the precise employment status of a worker. Unfortunately, as pointed out in the NFSE's affidavit in *CIR v NFSE*, the Fleet Street printing industry was one of a very few instances in which PAYE was disapplied, along with Smithfield meat porters and farm workers at harvest time.[86] In a curious passage in the affidavit of JAP Hoadley, Principal Inspector of Taxes, it was claimed variously that PAYE was disapplied in a number of situations; that the NFSE was mistaken in citing Smithfield meat porters, who were Schedule D taxpayers and therefore ineligible for PAYE anyway; and that the treatment of Fleet Street casuals was 'near unique'.[87] A less tortuous explanation might be

---

[81] ibid, 450.

[82] ibid, 453.

[83] ibid, 455.

[84] *BBC*, 'Panorama' (above n 34).

[85] See, eg, *BBC*, 'Revolution at the Mirror' (24 January 1978), genome.ch.bbc.co.uk/2283e970a559 4dc69a757161f271e2c3.

[86] Parliamentary Archives, HL/PO/JO/10/11/2057/42, Appendix 5: Affidavit of LF Payne, para 7 (this is the book commonly known as the 'bound volume'). The authority cited for the disapplication was Regulation 50 of the Income Tax (Employments) Regulations 1973, dealing with situations where the Inland Revenue was of the opinion that the normal operation of PAYE was impractical: see HC Deb 20 March 1979, vol 964, col 565-9W, (Robert Sheldon, Labour).

[87] Parliamentary Archives (above n 86) Appendix 9: Affidavit of JAP Hoadley (Principal Inspector of Taxes) para 12.

that an industry in which 'the degree of production control exercised at the workplace by [union] chapels has few, if any, equal in Britain'[88] was provided with a tax regime strikingly different from the '714 certificate'[89] in order to allay threats of unofficial strike action.[90]

In any case, things started to move quickly in March of the subsequent year. On 4 March 1979, the Inland Revenue put in place a new enforcement system and in return agreed not to investigate co-operative casual workers for suspected historic evasion.[91] The first part of this exchange became apparent very quickly. On 5 March 1979 *The Guardian* noted that

> [a] number of newspapers in Fleet Street faced production difficulties last night when new regulations affecting the tax position of casual employees came into force. Worst hit was the Sun where a number of casual staff failed to report for work and more than half the print order – two million copies – was lost.[92]

On the following day the same newspaper apologised on its front page for distribution difficulties.[93] On the evening of 7 March 1979, a different spin emerged, as explained by Terence Higgins MP: 'a report late last night on television, and in the press today, [stated] that casual workers in Fleet Street who are members of trade unions are to be given a tax amnesty'.[94] On 8 March 1979, *The Guardian* ran the headline 'Print workers offered tax amnesty' and explained that the policy had been announced 'after negotiations with the unions concerned'.[95] Accusations of trades union impropriety were made immediately. Again, Terence Higgins MP:

> [A] letter has been sent by the Society of Graphical and Allied Trades to its members ... One paragraph reads: 'What we are saying to [a casual worker] is that if there is a general acceptance of new procedures and if he co-operates fully with the Revenue, we' – that is, SOGAT – 'will release him from most of the liabilities which the Revenue could demand'.
>
> ... no one can argue that it is right that a trade union should be able to negotiate individual tax returns on behalf of its members. This seems to be wholly unreasonable.[96]

---

[88] McGregor (above n 67) para 13.

[89] See n 52 above.

[90] This is one reading of Hoadley's affidavit (above n 87) para 10, although it is contradicted at para 9. There are parallels with the arguments of the NFSE cited with apparent sympathy by Lord Denning MR: *CIR v NFSE* [1980] QB 407, 423.

[91] See HC Deb 22 March 1979, vol 964, col 701W (Robert Sheldon, Labour).

[92] Anon, 'Fleet Street hit' *The Guardian* (5 March 1979) 22. *The Guardian* has been used because of the quality and availability of its archives; for obvious reasons there was no *Times* coverage.

[93] Anon, 'The Guardian' *The Guardian* (6 March 1979) 1.

[94] HC Deb 08 March 1979, vol 963, cols 1502–04 (Terence Higgins, Conservative).

[95] Anon, 'Print workers offered tax amnesty' *The Guardian* (8 March 1979) 28. The Financial Secretary to the Treasury admitted that there had been 'discussions' with the print unions, but claimed that the offer to casuals 'was not negotiated with a union' and also stated that 'ministers were informed about, but not involved in, the discussions': Sheldon (above n 86).

[96] Higgins (above n 94).

Soon afterwards, the treatment of Fleet Street casuals started to be contrasted in Parliament with that of self-employed workers and small businesses. A prominent contributor to this particular debate was David Mitchell MP, Chairman of the Conservative Party's Small Business Bureau that had been established by Margaret Thatcher in 1976:[97]

> Mr David Mitchell asked the Chancellor of the Exchequer whether he will accord the same treatment in respect of tax found unpaid for past years on proprietors of small firms, subject to the Inland Revenue's special in-depth investigations, as is now being accorded to casual workers on Fleet Street newspapers; and if not give reasons for his decision.[98]

On the day after Mitchell's intervention, the Vice-President of the NFSE, Leonard Payne, prepared an affidavit that will be examined in more detail shortly. On 22 March the NFSE applied *ex parte* for leave to apply for judicial review of the Revenue's conduct, which was granted on the following day.[99]

This explains neatly why the tax treatment of the Fleet Street casuals was not prominent in the NFSE's earlier tax campaigns; only three weeks elapsed between the exposure of the arrangements in the national press and the commencement of proceedings. Nevertheless, it is not difficult to see why it was such an ideal case for the NFSE. Bearing in mind that the disapplication of PAYE itself appeared generous,[100] Payne's affidavit contrasted the compounded lenience of the 4 March settlement with a whole catalogue of enforcement woes supposedly suffered by NFSE members.[101] In Case 1, a £6,000 tax dispute ended in divorce; in Case 3, a taxpayer was questioned about the price of a coat; in Case 4, the taxpayer received treatment for stress over a £300 dispute; in Case 6, the Revenue threatened to inspect the taxpayer's accounts back to 1953; Cases 7 and 12 ended in suicide over beer wastage treatment and a crooked accountant respectively; and in Case 10 the taxpayer was asked for a breakdown of weekly food costs.[102] The sense of grievance and unfair treatment underlying these examples was encapsulated exactly by Lord Denning:

> News of the amnesty was given in the newspapers and on the television. Many were shocked by it. Especially some self-employed and small shopkeepers – good men and true who pay their taxes. They asked themselves: 'Why should these "Fleet Street casuals" – who have defrauded the revenue – be given this preferential treatment?

---

[97] J Langdon, 'Sir David Mitchell obituary' *The Guardian* (2 September 2014); Anon, 'Sir David Mitchell obituary' *The Telegraph* (31 August 2014).

[98] HC Deb 19 March 1979, vol 964, cols 441–44W (David Mitchell, Conservative).

[99] *CIR v NFSE* [1982] AC 617, 655; J Andrews, 'Fleet Street tax amnesty faces High Court challenge' *The Guardian* (23 March 1979) 2.

[100] The comparison with 714 certificates is understandably raised in Payne (above n 86) para 14.

[101] Bear in mind that the examples were described by Sir William Pile, Chairman of the Board of Inland Revenue as 'contentious'. Parliamentary Archives (above n 85), Appendix 7: Affadavit of WD Pile (Chairman of the Board of Inland Revenue).

[102] Payne (above n 86) para 12.

Why should they be let off when any one of us (if he did any such thing) would have been pursued to the uttermost farthing?'[103]

Moreover, the behaviour of the Revenue with respect to the Fleet Street casuals spoke to each part of the Venn diagram of priorities for the NFSE, as discussed in parts I–III of this chapter above. The lenience of the legal and administrative treatment of unionised workers was inconceivable for self-employed workers and small businesses who were outside tripartism.[104] The publicity needs of the NFSE were well served by widespread press coverage of the dispute, by memorable false names such as 'Mickey Mouse' and perhaps by the sensational nature of some of the cases of over-zealous enforcement against NFSE members listed in Payne's affidavit. Finally, unionised workers had been evading tax in a high-tax environment associated with a union-influenced Labour government. The NFSE's decision to litigate may have been hasty and opportunistic, but what an opportunity.

V. THE DECISIONS

As mentioned previously, there is a large and sophisticated body of legal scholarship that analyses the decision of the House of Lords in *CIR v NFSE* in particular.[105] The objective in this chapter is not to emulate this literature directly but rather to highlight certain ways in which the factual context sheds further light on the case. The first is that the NFSE was at the time a new and rather aggressive protest group at the conservative fringes, which engaged in litigation more as a means of furthering political aims and increasing membership than necessarily to win. Bettsworth explains, revealingly, that the adverse decision of the House of Lords in *CIR v NFSE* was received not merely as a disappointment but as confirmation of the unequal treatment of union workers relative to NFSE members.[106] That is, essentially the same as the NFSE's reaction to their victory in the Court of Appeal. Win or lose, the case could be used to support the Federation's previous assertions.

The second and more involved point is that the courts were equivocal in the face of this irruption of political campaigning into the courts, despite the recent experience of cases like *AG (McWhirter) v IBA*,[107] *R v Greater London Council ex parte Blackburn*[108] and *Gouriet v Union of Post Office Workers*.[109] The legal issues were identified as being, first, the scope of the Revenue's powers

---

[103] *NFSE* (CA) (above n 90) 419. These views need not be accepted uncritically: see n 15 above.

[104] This point is only partly weakened by the observation that union chapels did not always act in accordance with the wishes of their national leadership.

[105] See nn 8 and 9 above.

[106] Bettsworth (above n 1) 130.

[107] *McWhirter* (above n 15).

[108] *Blackburn* (above n 15).

[109] *Gouriet v Union of Post Office Workers* [1978] AC 435.

and duties, and second, the NFSE's standing to complain about the Revenue's conduct. Yet the decisions of the judges on these points varied widely. In the Divisional Court, the application was dismissed peremptorily for lack of standing. Widgery J thought it unnecessary to decide whether the agreement was within the Revenue's power; Griffiths J did not even mention the matter. A majority of the Court of Appeal, consisting of Lord Denning MR and Ackner LJ, overruled the lower court on the question of standing. The substantive unlawfulness of the Fleet Street arrangement would have to be proven by the NFSE in subsequent proceedings, but could be assumed for the purposes of establishing standing.[110] Lawton LJ, dissenting, took a similar approach to the Divisional Court.

The House of Lords, as is well known, took a different direction. Instead of overlooking or assuming the question of whether the Revenue had exceeded its powers, it was decided explicitly that no such excess had taken place. In doctrinal terms this was highly significant. It involved a much more serious examination of the Revenue's statutory powers of 'care and management'[111] than any court had previously carried out, and a recognition that these powers conferred 'a wide managerial discretion as to the best means of obtaining for the national exchequer from the taxes committed to their charge'.[112] This would have been sufficient to dispose of the application. The interest and complexity of the litigation lies in how the judges arrived at this conclusion and how they rationalised the question of standing. The members of the House of Lords agreed unanimously that the question of standing was not absolutely separable from the merits and circumstances of the application. They also agreed that the introduction of the 'sufficient interest' test for standing in Rule 53 of the Rules of the Supreme Court in 1977 prevented the Revenue from unqualified reliance on older precedents that had established more technical rules for standing, the consequences of which depended on the particular remedy sought by the applicant.

The most conventional approach was adopted by Lord Fraser, who essentially endorsed the emphasis of the Divisional Court and Lawton LJ on the NFSE's lack of standing but added significantly that a group like the NFSE might have standing in the event of 'exceptionally grave or widespread illegality'.[113] Lord Wilberforce and Lord Roskill made similar pronouncements on the scope of standing, stating respectively that it might be granted in a 'case of sufficient gravity' and 'a most extreme case'.[114] However, they were much more clearly

---

[110] This may have rested on a concession by the Revenue to this effect: see *NFSE* (CA) (above n 90) 424. This entertainingly allowed Lord Denning to claim that his decision accorded with that of the House of Lords: see Denning (above n 32) 218.

[111] Then contained in s 1 of the Taxes Management Act 1970.

[112] *NFSE* (HL) (above n 99) 636 (Lord Diplock).

[113] ibid, 647. This is problematic given Lord Fraser's assertion that standing 'is a separate, and logically prior, question which has to be answered affirmatively before any question on the merits arises'. Matters are further confused by Lord Fraser's express agreement with the reasoning of Lord Wilberforce and Lord Roskill, both of whom reject this logical priority: see ibid, 630, 645, 656.

[114] ibid, 633, 662.

influenced than Lord Fraser by their view that the Revenue had no case to answer on the merits. This logic was taken even further by Lord Scarman, who observed that too narrow an approach to standing would leave the courts powerless to address administrative unlawfulness. He would therefore have granted standing to a body such as the NFSE not only in extreme circumstances but in any 'case ... which merited investigation and examination by the court'.[115] The most radical position of all was taken by Lord Diplock, who preferred not to rest his decision on 'outdated technical rules of locus standi' at all, but instead squarely on the absence of a tenable case against the Revenue.[116]

The reader is referred elsewhere for a deeper review of these richly textured judgments.[117] For present purposes, the important point is that the courts adopted a strikingly circuitous route to telling a still rather marginal political pressure group to get lost. Especially noteworthy is Lord Scarman's description of standing requirements as a means of requiring applicants 'to show ... a prima facie case' and thereby to protect the court from 'busybodies, cranks and other mischief-makers'.[118] In contrast to Lord Denning, Lord Scarman neglected to exclude the NFSE from this description, and indeed rather suggested the contrary by his decision that no prima facie case had been established.[119] It is no particular affront to the NFSE to prefer Lord Scarman's interpretation. Indeed, it has already been seen that troublemaking was a deliberate selling-point of the NFSE,[120] and that litigation was only one way of furthering its political objectives along with lobbying, protests and writing cheques on knickers. Why, then, was it so difficult for the higher courts to reject the Federation's claim?

One answer to this question is to be found in Lord Denning MR's statement that the Revenue had conceded the unlawfulness of the Fleet Street arrangements for the purposes of standing. It is not clear whether a concession was indeed made,[121] but it allowed Lord Denning to shift the focus from the question 'ought the NFSE to be heard?' to 'ought an admittedly unlawful act of the Revenue to remain unchallenged?'

This would seem a much more favourable formulation from the NFSE's perspective,[122] so it is curious that much of the detailed argument concerned the recent decision of the House of Lords in *Arsenal v Ende*[123] that a ratepayer had standing to challenge the valuation of the famous football club. That case

---

[115] ibid, 655.

[116] ibid, 644.

[117] See n 8 above.

[118] *NFSE* (HL) (above n 99) 653.

[119] ibid, 654; *cf NFSE* (CA) (above n 90) 425.

[120] Accepting always that the organisation had its moderate elements.

[121] *NFSE* (HL) (above n 99) 661 (Lord Roskill).

[122] It also tapped into certain philosophical anxieties as to whether judicial review should focus on protecting private interests or on preventing public wrongs: see further J Varuhas, 'The Public Interest Conception of Public Law' in J Bell, M Elliott, J Varuhas and P Murray (eds), *Public Law Adjudication in Common Law Systems* (Oxford, Hart Publishing, 2016).

[123] *Arsenal v Ende* [1979] AC 1.

depended on the correct interpretation of the term 'person … aggrieved' in the General Rate Act 1967, but also contained *dicta* to the effect that the applicant's status as a taxpayer would not have been sufficient. In particular, a decrease in the valuation of one property might increase the rates burden on others; moreover, this would be visible from the rating lists.[124] This in turn seemed to support the Revenue's contention in *CIR v NFSE* that rating law promotes 'fairness and uniformity between ratepayers'[125] and hence that ratepayers have an interest in each other's assessments that is absent from the income tax with its duties of confidentiality. The problem is that rating valuation involves judgement, whereas NFSE was making the *more* straightforward request that the Revenue apply the tax legislation faithfully to the Fleet Street workers. Besides, if the NFSE could not petition the court for uniform enforcement of the law, who else could? On this view, *Arsenal* added nothing to a more general argument for restricted standing, and it is unsurprising that the Court of Appeal majority as well as Lord Diplock and Lord Scarman considered the rates–tax distinction too technical on which to base their decisions.[126]

A more convincing answer is that Lord Denning's long impatience with the restrictive rules of standing[127] was brought back into focus by the increased use of litigation for political purposes by groups such as the NFSE. Politically motivated litigation was neither new[128] nor confined to the right wing of the political spectrum.[129] However, it is tolerably clear that the decision of the NFSE to make frequent recourse to the courts, semi-independently of its chances of winning, was something of a novelty amongst small business advocates at the time of the Federation's establishment in the mid-1970s. Some of the cases supported by the NFSE were conventional enough. Others, such as *CIR v NFSE*, confronted judges with the politics of taxation in an unaccustomed manner. David Williams noted in a well-known article in 1979 that extra-statutory tax concessions were not straightforward to challenge despite Walton J's emphatic disapproval of them two years previously.[130] It is clear that the NFSE had hit a nerve; that their means of challenge in *CIR v NFSE* was not precisely recognised by existing precedent but also that the apparent impunity of the Revenue had been subject to repeated and recent criticism.[131]

Even on the assumption that Revenue concessions ought to be circumscribed, though, it is possible to understand the ambivalence of judges in 1979 towards

---

[124] *NFSE* (CA) (above n 90) 426–27 (Lawton LJ).

[125] *NFSE* (HL) (above n 99) 622.

[126] *NFSE* (CA) (above n 90) 433; *NFSE* (HL) (above n 99) 640, 652.

[127] See Denning (above n 32) 214; *McWhirter* (above n 15).

[128] See generally Harlow and Rawlings (above n 10).

[129] A well-known left-of-centre organisation with an active litigation strategy was the CPAG: see Prosser (above n 15). As seen previously, relations between the CPAG and NFSE were not always cordial: see n 33, above.

[130] D Williams, 'Extra-Statutory Concessions' [1979] *BTR* 137; *cf* Alder (above n 9).

[131] See also *Vestey v CIR* [1979] Ch 177, 197.

the extension of judicial control over the tax authorities at the instance of a political campaigning group. Admittedly the tax position of the Fleet Street casuals seemed strikingly indulgent – even disgraceful in some lights – but if the NFSE were granted standing to challenge it, what other actions of the Revenue might be vulnerable? Nothing about the NFSE suggests that the organisation would have been restrained in its next campaign, or circumspect about the genuine needs of the administration. Would the Revenue have changed its behaviour in order to stave off challenge, and could this affect tax collection? Might it become easier for interested parties to impugn historic tax assessments, despite the bemused rapidity with which *Martin v O'Sullivan*[132] was dismissed at all levels? The decision facing the courts in *CIR v NFSE* was not just about making unionised workers pay their dues; it involved a potential juridification of tax administration with cascading consequences.[133]

In this light, it was rather a stroke of luck for the judges of the House of Lords that they considered the substance of the NFSE's complaint so manifestly untenable. This allowed them an opportunity to ruminate on the difficult questions of standing raised by Lord Denning's unorthodox decisions, the juridification of political problems and the new judicial review procedures in RSC o 53, without causing too much damage too quickly. More generally, the decision of the House of Lords shows a cautious attitude to legal change, with all five judges ultimately prepared to award standing to relax the standing rules in a suitable case, Lord Diplock and Lord Scarman on a more adventurous basis than the others. It is well documented elsewhere that these latter judgments in particular had a deep influence on the subsequent development of the law.[134] Not that this would have been much comfort to the NFSE, which witnessed an entire industry being exempted from PAYE for unconvincing reasons and then forgiven for widespread and wholly predictable evasion, whilst their own members were being threatened with imprisonment over pounds and pence. If this was not a sufficiently serious case for standing to be granted, they might have asked, what on earth was.

VI. THE WIDER TAX CONTEXT

In this chapter *CIR v NFSE* has been presented as an example of the irruption of the ever bitterer politics of the late 1970s into the courts, with this particular case being litigated because taxation was a common concern of the NFSE's

---

[132] *Martin v O'Sullivan* (above n 2).

[133] The language of juridification is taken from Loughlin (above n 19) ch 7. An interesting parallel is the increased activity of the courts at the turn of the twentieth century at the instance of taxpayers, which Stebbings interprets as a response to the hollowing out of the old system of local lay Commissioners: see C Stebbings, *The Victorian Taxpayer and the Law: A Study in Constitutional Conflict* (Cambridge, Cambridge University Press, 2009) ch 4.

[134] See Elliott and Varuhas (above n 8) 549–55.

target membership and because the Fleet Street dispute happened to be making headlines at the time. The judgments of the House of Lords, in turn, involved a simple decision that the Revenue's behaviour was within its statutory powers, but with inconclusive and arguably *obiter* discussions of questions of interest group standing. At the same time, the behaviour of all parties involved – the NFSE, the Revenue, the casuals, the unions, the newspaper proprietors and the courts – seems deeply opportunistic but also reflective of deeper political and legal currents.

Again, the juridification of tax politics is one of the most striking of these currents. Most famous of all is the slew of litigation that followed from the activities of the Rossminster group, founded in 1973 and notable for devising and mass-marketing highly artificial tax avoidance schemes. No evidence has been found by the present author of any co-operation between Rossminster and the NFSE even though small businesspeople formed a key market for the former's schemes.[135] Indeed the Federation's wounded reaction to accusations of tax 'dodging' against small businesses and its cautious interactions with other right-of-centre groups suggests that formal links were likely to be avoided. Yet the claim in *R v CIR ex parte Rossminster*,[136] that the Revenue had exceeded its powers in searching and removing documents from Rossminster's premises, accorded with long-held concerns of the NFSE on heavy-handed tax adminis-tration. There are also parallels with the demand in *CIR v NFSE* that the courts clarify and enforce the statutory limits on Revenue powers.[137]

More significantly still, the leading case on the substance of Rossminster's schemes, *WT Ramsay v CIR*,[138] contains elements familiar from previous sections of this chapter. Whatever the individual motives of the directors of WT Ramsay Limited and of Denis Rawling, the political tensions and high tax rates of the 1970s undoubtedly formed a key element of Rossminster's appeal. It seemed possible to save money and at the same time to register a political protest.[139] As is well known, this would be done by finding ways in which certain tax provisions could have more benign consequences for taxpayers than previ-ously surmised (ie, loopholes). Should the courts, faced with these politically motivated schemes in which taxpayers sought to apply familiar tax legislation out of context, apply the strict law in favour of those taxpayers, or find a way

---

[135] N Tutt, *The History of Tax Avoidance* (London, Wisedean, 1989) 62.

[136] *Rossminster* (above n 18).

[137] A further coincidence is the publication of the powerful editorial, 'A Leaky Umbrella' *The Times* (18 December 1979) 13, soon after the resumption of publication in November 1979. This echoed the NFSE's views on tax administration and criticised the adverse decision of the House of Lords in *ex parte Rossminster* as an example of the 'leaky umbrella' of judicial protection of the 'the liberty of the subject'.

[138] *Ramsay* (above n 17).

[139] Tutt (above n 135) 312. For similar phenomena in Australia, including a discussion of the notori-ous 'bottom of the harbour' schemes, see T Boucher, *Blatant, Artificial and Contrived: Tax Schemes of the 70s and 80s* (ATO, 2010).

of making a common-sense decision in favour of the Revenue? As with the Fleet Street dispute, *Ramsay* required a clear decision on the facts but also intersected with much wider questions of interpretation, fairness, politics and tax design.

The House of Lords engaged with these underlying considerations in the course of its decision for the Revenue, but was no more able to resolve them than the courts in *CIR v NFSE* resolved the status of pressure groups in judicial review proceedings.[140] In each case the House of Lords grappled with important and long-running tensions in the law, but reached a holding position rather than a final answer. Furthermore, the channelling of political anger into the courts had a corresponding effect in making the law less clear-cut. Before 1979, there might have been something to say for the idea of taxation law as a black-letter backwater in which statutory rules could be expected to operate mechanically; *Ramsay* and *CIR v NFSE* have made such a position untenable.[141]

The parallel between these two cases might be dismissed as a coincidence, but the most thoroughly studied example of tax-driven juridification has not even been touched upon in detail in this chapter. This is the jurisprudence arising from the efforts of left-wing councils to avoid the controls that Mrs Thatcher placed upon local authority spending and tax-raising.[142] The details are discussed in Martin Loughlin's magisterial account of the relationship between local and central government, *Legality and Locality*,[143] but the relevant point for present purposes is very familiar. The behaviour of activists, on this occasion typically on the opposite side of the spectrum from the NFSE, was forcing the courts to consider unfamiliar and rather charged questions, which in turn had to give clear answers in individual cases without promising too quick a resolution of complex and controversial underlying problems.

If anything, the most striking feature of the local government finance cases is the irresolution of the government response.[144] The printing unions no longer operate a closed shop, newspaper workers are governed by PAYE like everyone else and new technology has been introduced (to an extent that scarcely could have been imagined in 1979). In relation to *WT Ramsay v CIR*, there has been a concerted effort to close down mass-market schemes of the Rossminster type, although avoidance in general has hardly been eradicated. Local government

---

[140] Indeed, *UBS v HMRC* [2016] UKSC 13 may have reopened aspects of *Ramsay* that had previously been thought resolved: see D de Cogan, 'Defining Tax Avoidance: Flirting with Chaos, Again' [2016] *CLJ* 474. Refer also to John Snape: J Snape, '*WT Ramsay Ltd v Inland Revenue Commissioners; Eilbeck (HM Inspector of Taxes) v Rawling)*, ch 10, section VI entitled 'A Significant Change in the Approach' in this volume.

[141] There is no shortage of commentators willing to argue that taxation *should* take such a form, which is a different matter.

[142] The legal legacy of this episode in history has been very wide indeed: see, eg, *Westdeutsche Landesbank v Islington LBC* [1996] AC 669.

[143] Loughlin (above n 19).

[144] This is perhaps less excusable than a similar hesitancy on the part of judges, the primarily responsibility of whom is to reach reasoned decisions in concrete cases.

finance, by contrast, contributed to the downfall of Mrs Thatcher and remains in an unstable and unsatisfactory state.[145]

It is inherent in Loughlin's argument that the pressure placed on the courts by those who channel essentially political grievances through the law can have lasting effects even after it has abated. This is clearly the case for the local government finance system, which was scarcely recognisable in 1992 from the system a decade previously when left-wing councils were testing the limits of their entitlements under the law. It is equally the case for *WT Ramsay v CIR* and *CIR v NFSE*, which presaged clarifications in the treatment of tax avoidance, the standing rules and the powers of tax authorities that now form part of a basic understanding of the respective areas of law. It is in this sense that landmark status can intelligibly be given to the Fleet Street case, which on the face of things boils down to the rather unexciting confirmation that the Revenue correctly understood the ambit of its own powers.

An interesting comparison here can be made with the *UK Uncut* case.[146] This case, which concerned a compliance arrangement concluded between HMRC and Goldman Sachs shortly after the financial crash of 2007, contained many of the same elements as *CIR v NFSE*. It took place in straitened fiscal circumstances, engaged with concerns that powerful organisations were receiving preferential tax treatments and provided the young organisation UK Uncut with a rallying point. The key difference from *CIR v NFSE* is that neither the lawfulness of the settlement nor UK Uncut's standing to challenge troubled the judge for too long. The settlement was lawful and counsel for the Revenue did not even press the standing point, being content to accept the logic of Lord Scarman's judgment in the earlier case.[147] In sum, *CIR v NFSE* and *UK Uncut* arose from two of the most rancorous episodes in recent UK tax history, but only the former became a permanent point of reference for legal change. The sophistication, complexity and occasional lyricism of the judgments can hardly have harmed the status of this fascinating case as a repository of ideas for legal change. At least in this sense its reputation as a landmark is richly deserved.

---

[145] See, eg, J Mirrlees et al (eds), *Tax by Design: The Mirrlees Review* (Oxford, Oxford University Press, 2010) ch 16.

[146] *R (UK Uncut Legal Action) v HMRC* [2013] EWHC 1283 (Admin), [2013] STC 2357. It is also noteworthy that UK Uncut has not become a repeat litigant in the manner of the NFSE or CPAG and seems not to be particularly active as at the time of writing.

[147] ibid, para 68.

12

Conservative and Unionist Central Office v Burrell *(1981)*

A Case of Hidden Significance

VICTOR BAKER

A S A SERVING officer of HM Revenue and Customs[1] the author's first task is to make clear that, although *Conservative and Unionist Central Office v Burrell*[2] (referred to here as *Conservative Central Office*) involves a political party, it is nothing to do with tax avoidance, real or perceived, but turned on whether investment income of the central office of a political party was within the charge to corporation tax. If not, it would have been liable to income tax, either by deduction at source, or by assessment of the party officials as 'persons receiving or entitled to the income'. The issue only became material with increasing divergence between income tax and corporation tax rates.

The interest of *Conservative Central Office* lies rather in the light it casts on the status and significance of unincorporated associations, and the issues that arise in relation to this little studied class of entities within the corporation tax charge.[3] Unincorporated associations are mainly seen as vehicles for clubs and societies, and it is true that they are most often encountered in this area. But a review of the history of unincorporated associations demonstrates that it is easy to misunderstand their nature. And the increasing importance of institutions[4] which come into being under foreign law jurisdictions may lead to a revival in

---

[1] Writing in a personal capacity. The views expressed are not necessarily those of the Commissioners for HM Revenue and Customs (HMRC).

[2] *Conservative and Unionist Central Office v Burrell* [1982] 1 WLR 522; 55 TC 671.

[3] The general definition of 'company' for the purposes of the Corporation Tax Acts (CTA company) is at s 1121 CTA 2010, and includes any body corporate or unincorporated association, but not a partnership.

[4] 'Institution' is used where appropriate to avoid difficulties with partnerships as 'entities'.

the importance of unincorporated associations when undertaking an analysis of how the institution is to be classified for the purposes of UK taxation.[5]

I. THE *CENTRAL OFFICE* CASE

The Conservative and Unionist Central Office was distinct from both the National Union, a federation of constituency associations, and from the parliamentary party. It provided central services to the party and was funded both by direct donations and from voluntary quota contributions from the constituency associations. The Central Office was under the direct control of the party chairman, who was appointed by the party leader. The party leader was appointed by a series of ballots of Conservative MPs, leading to a candidate 'presented for election to the Party Meeting'.[6]

A. The Special Commissioners

The Special Commissioners held that the Conservative Party was an unincorporated association whose members comprised the members of the constituency associations and the parliamentary party, and that this broader unincorporated association was liable to corporation tax on its investment income.

B. The High Court

Vinelott J held that the Special Commissioners' conclusion was not tenable based on the primary facts found. In particular, rules governing the selection of the party leader were one essential element of the contract which the Commissioners had found to exist, but Central Office works under the direction of the party leader. Further, before 1965, there had been no evident rules, yet the wider unincorporated association the Commissioners had identified had not been re-established at that time. Moreover, it was unclear who had

---

[5] Applying the principle from, eg, *CL Dreyfus v CIR* (1929) 14 TC 560 that, when dealing with foreign institutions, their domestic constitutive law established as a question of fact is examined against the relevant UK tax law.

[6] This approach was developed in 1965; before then the leader of the party emerged from what were called 'the usual processes of consultation'. The last leader who emerged under that approach was the Fourteenth Earl of Home, who became Sir Alec Douglas-Home, and subsequently Lord Home of the Hirsel. Mr Edward Heath was the first leader appointed under the new procedures. As Vinelott J said, 'the process of consultation ha[d] never been, and ... probably could not be, recorded in any body of rules'.

established the 'usual processes', which seemingly had emerged from the mists of time.

The Conservative Party as a political movement comprised many parts (some of which were unincorporated associations) that worked together towards a common end, but links were functional rather than constitutional. Vinelott J also found that, rather than members' contributions adding to the funds of an unincorporated association, each contributor enters into a contract with the treasurer who undertakes to use the subscription for the association's purposes. It was not necessary to create a trust to hold funds (a legal impossibility in this situation as a trust for non-charitable purposes).

C. The Court of Appeal

The Court of Appeal, upholding Vinelott J's decision to allow Central Office's appeal, took a slightly different tack. Lawton LJ could find nothing which links contractually and directly members of the local constituency associations and the Conservative members of the House of Commons, still less members of the House of Lords. There were no mutual understandings between all the members, no mutual rights and obligations and no rules governing control where it evidently lay, in the hands of the party leader. Nor was it possible to say when the putative unincorporated association was formed.

Brightman LJ dealt with the issue of the legal relationship between a contributor to Central Office funds and the recipient of them. As there was, in fact, no unincorporated association including Central Office, the principle in *Re Recher's Will Trusts*,[7] that the contributions take effect as an accretion to funds which are the subject of an inter-member contract, could not apply. Brightman LJ analysed the issue in terms of mandates given by the contributors to the Central Office treasurer to add the contributions to Central Office funds, permitting them to be used for Conservative Party purposes as directed by its leader. It was not necessary to invent a wider party unincorporated association which was not otherwise supported by the facts.

Lawton LJ's analysis largely reflects six characteristics of unincorporated associations identified by counsel for the Appellant in argument before the Special Commissioners: (i) membership; (ii) contract *inter se*; (iii) constitution; (iv) adherence of assets; (v) continuity; and (vi) formation, but as a preliminary he 'inferred' a widely quoted definition of unincorporated associations.

The issues raised will be considered against historical background and a review of types of institution.

---

[7] *Re Recher's Will Trusts* [1972] Ch 526.

II. HISTORICAL BACKGROUND: CORPORATE INCOME TAX
AND ITS SUBJECTS OF CHARGE

William Pitt's Act of 1799,[8] which introduced income tax,[9] charged the sources of income of a 'Company, Fraternity or Society of Persons (whether Corporate or not Corporate)'. Addington's Act of 1803, which included the familiar Schedules of charge, A to E, addressed the sources of income of 'all Bodies Politick, Corporate or Collegiate, Companies, Fraternities or Societies of Persons, whether Corporate or not Corporate'.[10] So the concept of a charge on *unincorporated* companies was well established.

It is significant that partnerships, as we now understand them, were separate subjects of charge upon the trade carried on:

> [T]he Computation of Duty arising in respect of any Trade or Manufacture carried on by two or more Persons jointly, shall be made and stated jointly, and in one Sum, separately and distinctly from any other Duty chargeable on the same Persons.[11]

Unincorporated companies of later Georgian times were chiefly 'deed of settlement companies' formed as an early example of a nimble approach to regulation. The 'Bubble Act' of 1720[12] forbade the formation of joint-stock companies with transferrable shares:

> All undertakings ... presuming to act as a corporate body ... raising ... transferrable stock ... transferring ... shares in such stock ..., either by Act of Parliament or any charter from the Crown, ... and acting under any charter ... for raising a capital stock ... not intended ... by such charter ... and all acting ... under any obsolete charter ... for ever be deemed illegal and void.[13]

---

[8] Income Tax 1799 (39 Geo III c 22).

[9] Although purists will point out that there was an income tax, as a kind of alternative minimum tax, in the 'triple assessment' 1798 Income Tax Act (38 Geo III c 16).

[10] Income Tax Act 1803 (43 Geo III c 122) s LXXXVIII. The 'Chamberlain or other Officer acting as Treasurer, Auditor or Receiver' was responsible.

[11] ibid, s XCV. This demonstrates the focus of UK tax law on source of income, here the trade carried on in partnership. Income tax is a tax on income, and from 1803, where possible, it was collected by deduction from the payer. The partnership charge is on the trade, and not on the partnership as an institution. See JF Avery Jones, 'The Sources of Addington's Income Tax' in P Harris and D de Cogan (eds), *Studies in the History of Tax Law: Volume 7* (Oxford, Hart Publishing, 2015) 7. John Avery Jones concludes that the land tax and Adam Smith's *The Wealth of Nations* were major factors influencing Addington's developments of Pitt's tax.

[12] 6 Geo I c 18; the Act's full title included 'restraining several extravagant and unwarrantable Practices', but in spite of its familiar non-statutory title the Act was largely about marine insurance and borrowing money on the security of ships' hulls ('bottomry'). Nor was it specifically directed at the famous South Sea Bubble, which describes the speculative collapse in value of South Sea Company shares. In fact, the South Sea Company initially promoted the Act and continued to operate, having restructured, for many years after 1720. It seems the Act was later applied to check speculative mania when industrialisation took off in the early nineteenth century, but was repealed in 1825 as largely ineffective.

[13] R Harris, 'The Bubble Act: Its Passage and Its Effects on Business Organization' (1994) 54 *Journal of Economic History* 610.

Evidently the early tax law recognised the unincorporated status of many commercial companies, and this recognition continues to be reflected in modern tax law. In historical terms, at least, there is no reason why an unincorporated body should not have trading or business objects, or carry on significant commercial activities.

Income tax was repealed following the end of the Napoleonic wars, in 1816, but was reintroduced by Sir Robert Peel in 1842, as opinion started to move in favour of free trade, which led to the removal of more than 700 import and export duties whose revenue needed replacing. The Income Tax Act 1842 (the 1842 Act)[14] closely resembled the 'Addington Act' of 1803 as developed further in 1805 and 1806, including Schedules A to E, with additional administrative material. The charge on 'bodies of persons', as they came to be called,[15] is at section 40 of the 1842 Act, and the rule for applying the charge to any trade etc carried on by two or more persons jointly is the third rule applying to Cases I and II of Schedule D in section 100.

The 1842 Act, which is the wellspring of modern tax law, *predated* the Act[16] which introduced incorporation by registration by two years; and what we would now call a partnership (the trade etc carried on by two or more persons in common for profit) was distinguished from incorporated and unincorporated companies: even though companies were regarded as a 'branch of the law of partnerships';[17] the word 'partnership' was used more widely than in the trading partnership context we now recognise.

The substance of the 1842 Act has been carried through successive amendments, additions and consolidations but its approach can still be detected in modern tax law. Particular milestones were Gladstone's Act of 1853,[18] and the consolidations of 1918, 1952, 1970 and 1988. Even now the system is 'schedular', although Schedules A to E disappeared with the Tax Law Rewrite project, which also split the income tax and corporation tax into separate acts; corporation tax in its original Finance Act (FA) 1965 form sat on top of the income tax system, which enabled the length of the new corporation tax to be restricted.[19] As time passed, the corporation tax system increasingly diverged from income tax (for instance, the special codes for loan relationships, derivative contracts and intangible fixed assets) and this was in part the justification for the separation of

---

[14] 5 & 6 Vict, c 35.

[15] Below n 34.

[16] Joint Stock Companies Act 1844 (7 & 8 Vict, c 110).

[17] Lord Lindley first published in 1860 *A Treatise on the Law of Partnership*, including its application to companies. Later editions became *A Treatise on the Law of Companies, Considered as a Branch of the Law of Partnerships* (London, Sweet & Maxwell, 1902). In terms of company law, the incorporated company was not firmly established as a person distinct from its members until the House of Lords seminal decision in *Salomon v A Salomon & Co Ltd* [1897] AC 22.

[18] Income Tax Act 1853 (16 & 17 Vict, c 34). Notoriously introduced by the longest continuous Budget speech in history (4 hours, 45 minutes).

[19] FA 1965 introduced two new taxes – corporation tax and capital gains tax – but is much shorter than modern less ambitious Finance Acts.

income tax and corporation tax; but not everyone thinks this is a good idea,[20] and it also supports the complaints of those who equate length with complexity.

Until the 1965 introduction of corporation tax the system for charging income tax on bodies of persons was recognisably that of the 1803/06 and 1842 Acts. Distributed profits were taxed by deduction, and undistributed profits were subject to what one of the draughtsmen of FA 1965, Sir Anthony Stainton, called 'representative assessment' on the company. The company retained the income tax deducted from distributions made, leading to what is now called economic single taxation of profits. Introducing a separate corporation tax firmly established the company as a taxpayer distinct from – and moved away from the concept of a company as a body of – its members. This prepared the ground for economic double taxation of distributed profits, taxing both members and company.[21]

Nevertheless, it took the parliamentary draughtsman of the 1965 company distribution provisions[22] to point out to his instructing official that the position had fundamentally changed: the company was now a source of dividends and distributions, and that a new charging provision for them was certainly needed.[23]

III. UNINCORPORATED ASSOCIATIONS

The Explanatory Notes to the Tax Law Rewrite 'Bill 5' that became the Corporation Tax Act (CTA) 2009[24] quote Lawton LJ's judgment in *Conservative Central Office* and observe that the HMRC view differs, both on the question of whether the tie between the members needs to be legally enforceable and on whether an unincorporated association may have trading or business objectives and carry on significant commercial activities. The Notes also refer to the

---

[20] See P Harris, *Corporate Tax Law: Structure, Policy and Practice* (Cambridge, Cambridge University Press, 2013) 78.

[21] Economic double taxation did not last long. The Conservative opposition in the later 1960s promised to repeal the corporation tax, but in the event the FA 1973 retained the procedure introduced in 1965 of accounting for tax on distributions to the Exchequer on Form CT61 (now as a dividend-equalisation tax called 'advance corporation tax' or ACT) and imputed this company-paid tax to the ultimate shareholder through a tax credit. Advance corporation tax was set off against corporation tax to restore the principle of economic single taxation, thus re-creating much of the effect of the pre-corporation tax system in an elegant if complex manner.

[22] John Fiennes.

[23] Fiennes suggested using the then vacant Schedule A, available because the FA 1963 had repealed the annual value-based Schedule A and replaced it with income-based Case VIII of Schedule D. Schedule F was, however, chosen and Schedule A, taxing rents was restored by the consolidation act, the Income and Corporation Taxes Act 1970 (ICTA 1970) (see FA 1965 drafting papers, *The National Archives*, Public Record Office, file IR40/16688).

[24] Corporation Tax Bill (as introduced 4 December 2008), Explanatory Notes, Volume 4, Annex 1, 'Minor Changes in the Law', Change 2.

distinction drawn by Hoffmann J[25] between a partnership, whose partners are individually entitled to some proportion of profits, and an association, whose members are not individually entitled to share in any profits which might arise from its activities but whose entitlement is governed by prescribed rules.

The HMRC manuals at CTM41305[26] describe the CTA company definition as bringing within its scope unincorporated organisations of all kinds that have some recognisable existence and suggest that an unincorporated association: (i) is not a legal entity; (ii) is an organisation of persons with an identifiable membership (possibly changing); (iii) has a membership bound together for a common purpose by an identifiable constitution or rules (which may be written or oral); (iv) has a form of association not recognised in law as being something else (incorporated body or partnership); and (v) must have an existence distinct from those persons who would be regarded as its members. The paragraph also concludes that the tie between the persons need not be a legally enforceable contract.[27]

The guidance observes that whether an institution is an unincorporated association is a question of fact and will depend upon a consideration of all the relevant circumstances. It cannot be determined simply by looking at what the institution calls itself or the form of its rules. And there is no reason why an unincorporated body should not have trading or business objects or carry on significant commercial activities.

Conservative Central Office is referred to at CTM41325, but without considering Lawton LJ's judgment in detail. An internal Inland Revenue memorandum recorded that there were several examples of unincorporated entities that plainly were not partnerships (the business was not carried on by persons in common) and that any suggestion based on Lawton LJ's judgment that a commercial body could not be an unincorporated association 'could not be supported'.[28] It is commercial factors that influence the choice of institution and incorporation is strongly favoured, but sometimes incorporated companies, or groups

---

[25] In *Blackpool Marton Rotary Club v Martin* (1988) 62 TC 686.

[26] This guidance in substance originated in June 2003.

[27] This is based on *General Assembly of the Free Church of Scotland v Overtoun* [1904] AC 515, 643, but on the other hand in *The Caledonian Employees' Benevolent Society* [1928] SC 633, 635 the Lord President took the view that the absence of any consensual contract was a bar to the claim that the Society was an unincorporated association. Lawton LJ in *Conservative Central Office* (above n 2) observed that agreements conferring rights and obligations must be justiciable, so the approach may depend on context, with a Christian organisation treated differently from one where rights and obligations are commercially significant.

[28] Joint ventures or syndicates may be organised as unincorporated associations, and historic examples include the (London) Stock Exchange, which operated under a deed of settlement without member limited liability until the 'Big Bang' reforms of 1986. In Pablo Pebrer's *Resources of the British Empire*, quoted in its anonymous review in (1833) 10 *The Eclectic Review: Third Series* 22, 36, it is observed that, 'it is by this means, by "the deed of settlement", and by its "regulations and bye-laws", that the Stock Exchange has become a more politic, exclusive, and corporate body, than the Bank of England, without incurring the expense of a charter, or the odium of possessing one'.

and consortia are not commercially appropriate. Lawton LJ's analysis is broadly descriptive and pragmatic rather than definitive.

Lawton LJ had signalled clearly that his observation was *obiter*; he 'inferred' the status of an unincorporated association,[29] and the decision of the Court of Appeal was not dependent on restricting the scope of the business of unincorporated associations. Moreover, the 'not for business purposes' qualification does not appear in the cases cited before the Special Commissioners, *Re Tackrah*[30] and *Macaulay v O'Donnell*.[31]

The CTA company definition originated as section 46(5)(a), FA 1965, which reads: '"company" means, subject to sections 66 and 67 of this Act',[32] 'any body corporate or unincorporated association, but does not include a partnership'. The Note on Clause relating to clause 42(4) of the Bill as introduced, which became section 46(5) of the 1965 Act, reads:

> A company means any body corporate or unincorporated association but not a partnership. Thus apart from companies as the term is ordinarily understood, ie, bodies which are bodies corporate under the Companies Act 1948 or any other statute or charter, the clause brings within the scope of the corporation tax unincorporated associations of all kinds which have some recognisable existence distinct from their members. To avoid doubt, partnerships are specifically excluded from the definition.

The term 'body of persons' continued to be part of The Tax Acts.[33] In 1965, when corporation tax was introduced, it was found at section 526(1) of the Income Tax Act (ITA) 1952 then in force, and was carried forward to the ICTA 1970 consolidation as section 526(5). It is still found in the Corporation Tax Acts: for example, at section 1119 CTA 2010 as 'meaning any body politic, corporate or collegiate and any company, fraternity, fellowship and society of persons whether corporate or not corporate'. The phrase 'body of persons' was introduced by ITA 1918,[34] but the substance of it (see section II) has been used with variations since Pitt's 1799 Act.[35]

---

[29] This has not prevented Lawton LJ's words being treated by distinguished commentators as possessing definition status: see, eg, JF Avery Jones, 'Bodies of Persons' [1991] *BTR* 453, 465, where the view is taken that a body carrying on business must be a registered company or a partnership. There are numerous other examples.

[30] *Re Tackrah* [1939] 2 All ER 4.

[31] *Macaulay v O'Donnell* [1943] Ch 435n.

[32] Which deal with local authorities and unit trusts.

[33] Interpretation Act 1978, sch 1, defines The Tax Acts as The Income Tax Acts and The Corporation Tax Acts.

[34] s 237.

[35] For a comprehensive review of the phrase, and its use in the Tax Acts, see Avery Jones, 'Bodies of Persons' (above n 29). Avery Jones notes that the Interpretation Act 1978 defines 'person' as including any body of persons corporate or uncorporate and impliedly gives a more general meaning to the expression by including anything that may be described as a body of persons, whether or not incorporated, and may include a partnership (*CCE v Glassborow* [1974] STC 142). It is therefore necessary to distinguish between Interpretation Act and Tax Acts bodies of persons. Avery Jones concludes that context requires that the Tax Acts definition should not be used to determine the

At one time there was uncertainty over whether in some cases a body of trustees might be considered an unincorporated association. However, the fiduciary responsibilities of trustees are inconsistent with the characteristics of an unincorporated association. Even if, which is doubtful, one could regard trustees as an association, this would be the result of, and incidental to, their compliance with duties as trustees; quite apart from the fact that section 6(1) CTA 2009 would prevent a corporation tax charge on profits accruing in a fiduciary or representative capacity.

Issues relating to unincorporated associations were reviewed quite recently in *Hanchett-Stamford v A-G and Others*.[36] This case addressed the difficult question of how unincorporated associations hold property, the applicability of charity law to them and dissolution when membership declines. *Hanchett-Stamford* concerned an association, originally founded as 'The Performing and Captive Animals Defence League' in 1914. It originally had a written constitution, but this was mislaid; it was originally managed by an executive committee but later on by a director appointed. Subsequently Mr Hanchett-Stamford took de facto control and acquired as 'trustee', along with a Mr Hervey, a substantial property. The association also had a portfolio of stocks and shares. It went into decline and when Mr Hanchett-Stamford died in 2006, he and Mrs Hanchett-Stamford were found to have been the only members. At that time the aim was to transfer the assets to the Born Free Foundation, and Lewison J had to decide: (i) whether the League was a charity; and (ii), if not, how the assets should be dealt with. He decided that the League was not a charity but an unincorporated association, and the assets devolved absolutely to the last surviving member, Mrs Hanchett-Stamford, although she argued the property was held on charitable trust.

The interest in the present context lies first in the application of the 'contract-holding theory' of ownership by unincorporated associations, which is that their assets are held nominally by association officers on trust for the membership who hold equitable title under a form of joint tenancy, with members contracting with each other *inter se*, implicitly to the effect that: (i) an individual member undertakes not to sever and claim his equitable share; and (ii) in the event of death or resignation, the equitable interest remains unserved and devolves to the remaining members, so the association continues until, in accordance with its rules, the members decide to wind-up the association and distribute its assets. The contrast with *Conservative Central Office* is that its funds were given at the ultimate control and disposal of the party leader, which Brightman LJ interpreted as a mandate. Secondly, Lewison J addressed the question of what happens where in time the association collapses into a single individual. He decided that the association ceases to exist and, relying on the principle above, the survivor takes the property.

meaning of the phrase in any of the various places where it appears, and that the definition of bodies of persons and references to it in the Tax Acts should now be regarded as defunct.

[36] *Hanchett-Stamford v A-G and Others* [2008] EWHC 330 (Ch); [2009] Ch 173.

In coming to the latter conclusion, the judge followed the judgment of Walton J in *Re Bucks Constabulary Widows and Orphans Fund Friendly Society (No 2)*[37] in one respect but differed from it in another, agreeing that an unincorporated association ends when reduced to its last member, because if members' rights are founded in contract there must be a contracting party; but differing on the application of *bona vacantia*. Lewison J considered that the assets of an unincorporated association belong to the members subject to the implied contract terms, quoting Pennycuick J in *Abbatt v Treasury Solicitor*[38] in the context of a members' club. He considered there was an implied term that an individual member cannot obtain the realisation of assets and their distribution, 'so long as the club functions. But once the club ceases to function the reason for this disappears and the right of existing members must I think crystallise for once and for all'.[39]

The essence of the 1965 company definition, for the purposes of corporation tax, is that it is comprehensive as to bodies, both incorporated and unincorporated, and excludes partnerships 'to avoid doubt'. To understand the definition fully it is therefore necessary to consider also in some detail the concepts of partnership and body corporate. In particular, the definition assumes that a partnership can be readily identified, to be discussed next.

IV. PARTNERSHIPS

There is a fundamental difference between the concepts of partnership under English common law and under continental civil law, and this has created significant problems in the realm of 'entity classification'. Broadly speaking, an English law partnership observes the 'aggregate' principle, and is the business relationship itself. There is no entity. Civil law partnerships, on the other hand, observe the 'entity' principle. This makes identifying legal personality as a comparative characteristic on the courts' view of entity classification[40] tricky for two reasons. First, there is no common understanding of what legal personality means, and, secondly, using this criterion uncomfortably imports a civil law analytical approach into a common law system.

[37] *Re Bucks Constabulary Widows and Orphans Fund Friendly Society (No 2)* [1979] 1 WLR 937.
[38] *Abbatt v Treasury Solicitor* [1969] 1 WLR 561.
[39] See the full discussion of *Hanchett-Stamford* in J Brown, 'Unincorporated Associations: Property Holding, Charitable Purposes and Dissolution' (2009) 21 *Denning Law Journal* 107.
[40] In *Memec v CIR* (1998) STC 754, which concerned the entity classification of a German silent partnership or *stille Gesellschaft* (French equivalent *société en participation*), it was stated that 'what ... we have to do is to consider the characteristics of an English or Scots partnership which make it transparent and then to see to what extent those characteristics are shared or not by the silent partnership in order to determine whether the silent partnership should be treated for corporation tax purposes in the same way'. Characteristics identified by reference to the *Memec* case make up five of the six listed by HMRC in its guidance manual at INTM180010 on entity classification, and are largely built around the concept of 'legal personality', including who carries on the business and owns the assets.

Scots law partnerships (due to the influence of Roman law) and the US (revised) Uniform Partnership Act (UPA) or Revised Uniform Partnership Act (RUPA)[41] general partnerships (by policy choice) are hybrid, and in both cases it is the partners and not the partnership that carry on the business even though business assets are held by a 'legal person'. It is not clear that identifying 'legal personality' flowing from the entity principle as distinct from a more clearly established feature, such as strong entity protection by partitioning of assets,[42] solves the classification problem the courts have sought to address.

A. Historical Origin of Partnerships

Civil law partnerships originated in Roman times in most ancient form as a relationship created among brothers for the purposes of holding assets inherited from their father which they could not divide, the *consortium ercto non cito*. It was not concerned with business, and to this day in France there is a distinction between *sociétés civiles* and *sociétés commerciales*.[43] The *societas* came later along with the concept of management of an activity and created a difficult split between the 'firm' as an entity holding assets which can only be transmitted with partners' agreement (*affectio societatis*), and the business managed by the partners (*intuitu personae*, looking to the persons). This dichotomy can be seen reflected in the Official Comments on RUPA (1997). That for section 202 argues that the partners are co-owners of the business[44] where ownership is the power of ultimate control, but on the other hand section 201 declares the partnership to be an entity distinct from its partners, the US having decided in 1994 to 'embrace the entity theory', in the words of the section 201 Comment.

B. Scots Partnerships

'In Scotland a firm is a legal person distinct from the persons of whom it is composed'.[45] Yet a Scots partnership, along with an English partnership, is

---

[41] Strictly speaking, it is the UPA, but UPA (1914) reflects the common law aggregate principle. RUPA is customarily used to mean any UPA with the major revisions published in 1994, when the switch to the entity principle took place. But there is a succession of RUPAs, or strictly, UPAs, with a date suffix such as RUPA (1997), the version most often quoted. An interesting observation from 1914, in the context of discussions on the then new UPA, is 'one of the crying evils of the times is the vast legislative output of statutes each year' (see S Williston, 'Uniform Partnership Act with Some Remarks on Other Uniform Commercial Laws' (1914–15) 63 *U Pa L Rev* 196, 203).

[42] This is discussed at section IV.D.

[43] And the further sui generis complication of *sociétés civiles commerciales*.

[44] Described as 'a series of acts directed to an end'.

[45] s 4(2), Partnership Act 1890 (PA 1890). PA 1890 was one of three important codifications of the common law in late Victorian times, drafted by Sir Frederick Pollock. The others were the Bills of Exchange Act 1882 and the Sale of Goods Act 1893.

'the relation which subsists between persons carrying on a business with a view to profit'.[46] Hence the conclusion that an English or Scots partnership is a relationship between persons, rather than an entity; yet the 'firm', meaning the partners collectively, is a separate 'legal entity' in Scotland, though perhaps not one that is complete but rather one that serves a representative function.

In a Trade Descriptions Act case, the Fife and Kinross Sheriff Court in *Douglas v Phoenix Motors*[47] found that a Scots partnership, being a collection of individuals recognised as a separate legal entity is, as such, a body corporate. The point is considered further below, but it is generally accepted that a Scots partnership has no perpetual succession[48] and although, in principle, a firm's separate personality should permit title to its property to be taken in the name of the firm alone, the lack of continuity means this approach is impractical. There is not the necessary permanence to retain the required relationship under the Scots land tenure system, so the practice is for current partners to act as trustees for themselves and their successors. This is antithetical to the principle of the body corporate, as is the fact that Scots partnerships are not formed by authority.

On the other hand, the legal personality is sufficiently developed for one Scots partnership to be a member of another,[49] and in a Scots partnership the partners are agents of the partnership which is the principal. The firm has primary responsibility for debts and obligations incurred through the agency of its partners, and the partners' liability is subsidiary, in effect as guarantor,[50] but ultimately they are liable *singuli in solidum*. There is nothing to prevent Scots partnership A suing Scots partnership B with some common members. The possession of legal personality by Scots partnerships has been described as a 'convenience'.[51]

C. Foreign Partnerships

There are two especially difficult issues with foreign partnerships. First, dealing with a different jurisdiction and gaining an effective and accurate factual

[46] s 1(1), PA 1890.

[47] *Douglas v Phoenix Motors* 1970 SLT 57.

[48] Law Commission and Scottish Law Commission, *Partnership Law: A Joint Consultation Paper* (Law Com No 159 and Scottish Law Com No 111, 2003) para 2.10, where it is said that there is 'serious doubt' about the continuity of the Scots partnership. D Keenan and J Bisacre, in *Smith and Keenan's Company Law*, 13th edn (Harlow, Pearson, 2005) 593 are more certain.

[49] *Major v Brodie* [1998] STC 491, in which it was decided that the Partnership A as a member of Partnership B was carrying on its (farming) business, notwithstanding the legal personality of Partnership B. This is consistent with the ownership of assets standing in contrast to the ownership of the business.

[50] *Mair v Wood* [1948] SC 83, 86 (Lord President Cooper).

[51] The Mercantile Law Amendment Commission of 1855 expressed the opinion that the principle of legal personality of the firm is 'a very convenient and useful one' and recommended its introduction into the law of England and Ireland. After more than 160 years, it has still not been put into effect.

understanding of its system, and secondly, deciding how the constitutive juris-diction's rules are to be applied for the purposes of the other jurisdiction's tax legislation. A paper of 2002[52] of some 33 pages examines the problems in detail and makes proposals for reducing them.

For convenience, the paper divides civil law partnerships into what it calls the 'formal' *société de personnes* and the 'informal' *société de capitaux* whose existence is not necessarily apparent to third parties. Referring back to the Latin origin, the *société de personnes* as *intuitu personae*, looking to the persons, has a *contractual* legal nature stronger than the *société de capitaux* as *intuitu pecuniae* (or *materiae*), looking to the capital (money or assets).

It is generally possible to assign *sociétés* of different types to one or other category, but the distinction is theoretical and difficult to apply strictly in prac-tice. It is clear the *société anonyme* (SA) and *société en commandite par actions* (SCA) are *sociétés de capitaux*, and that *sociétés en nom collectif* (SNC) and *sociétés en commandite simple* (SCS) are *sociétés de personnes*, but the *société à responsabilité limitée* (SARL) is not so easy to classify in this way, though it is usually taken to be most similar to an English private company and thus *société de capitaux*.

Looking at the 'informal' versus 'formal' classification, it seems odd that the *société anonyme*, the vehicle for public companies, as a *société de capitaux* might be bracketed with 'informal partnerships'. This suggests that the 'formality' of the partnership if that is linked with 'legal personality' may not be an effective classification tool. The distinction based on looking to the persons in contrast to looking to the capital may be sounder.

The 2002 paper suggests that 'a Scots partnership is categorised as a corporation as there is no intermediate category into which it can be put and accordingly it has to be excluded from the tax definition of company'. The question of body corporacy is discussed at section VI. However, a Scots partnership is not a body corporate[53] in tax law. Partnerships (including Scots partnerships) are excluded from the tax definition of company, which includes both incorporated and unincorporated bodies, because they have always been taxed as partnerships in the modern sense, not because they are corporations or 'bodies of persons' that needed an operative rather than clarifying exclusion.

Formation by registration is not decisive: a French SNC,[54] as a 'formal partnership', acquires its 'legal personality' in French law on registration, but

---

[52] JF Avery Jones et al, 'Characterization of Other States' Partnerships for Income Tax' (2002) 56 *Bulletin for International Fiscal Documentation* 288; [2002] *BTR* 375.

[53] Or corporation. English law does not distinguish.

[54] The SNC is 'a partnership the members of which are all *commerçants* who are jointly and sever-ally liable for the debts and obligations of the partnership' (Code de commerce Article L.221-1). It is generally regarded as the closest institution under French law to an English general partnership yet on the facts found (including that the SNC has 'legal personality' in France) the court in *CL Dreyfus* (above n 5) held the SNC to be opaque, a decision which has not been followed in practice – see HMRC's archived *International Tax Handbook* ITH1673. Frank Wooldridge in 'The General

UK limited partnerships without legal personality in English law must also be registered.[55]

D. Entity Protection

Commercial law theory in the US[56] has developed the concept of 'entity protection', or 'affirmative asset partitioning'. This is the reverse of the 'member protection', usually known as limited liability. The latter protects the personal assets of members against recovery by entity creditors; the former protects entity assets against recovery by creditors of their members. UK partnership assets enjoy limited protection.[57]

The US state of Wyoming developed the limited liability company (LLC) in 1977,[58] designed to support transparent federal tax treatment similar to a partnership while affording the strong entity asset partitioning which is a keystone of the corporate form. Limited liability companies are described as 'uncorporates' by experts and often confused with corporations by those less expert, known in the US as 'corporification'.

In a civil law partnership, liability is in general on the partnership first, followed by liability on the partners jointly and severally.[59] Applying the principles of distinguishing (i) between partnerships *intuitu personae* and *intuitu pecuniae*, and (ii) between institutions with strong entity protection and those

---

Partnership Under French Law' (2009) 77 *Amicus Curiae* 29, notes that, although endowed with legal personality, the SNC is transparent 'in certain respects', notably the possibility of an order for judicial liquidation. In any case, there is authority for the proposition that the fact that a partnership as 'firm' is a separate legal entity in Scotland, but not so in England, should not affect the incidence of taxation: *R v City of London General Commissioners ex p Gibbs* [1942] AC 402 and *Special Commissioners v Pemsel* [1891] AC 531. It is not clear why the position should be different for civil law partnerships.

[55] s 5, Limited Partnerships Act 1907 (LPA 1907).

[56] See, eg, H Hansmann and R Kraakman 'Organizational Law Asset Partitioning' (2000) 44 *European Economic Review* 807.

[57] s 23, PA 1890 introduced a method of making a partner's share in partnership assets available to the creditors of a partner, but a judgment against a single partner, as distinct from the firm, cannot be enforced against the firm's assets as there is a distinction between the liability of a single partner, enforceable against his share, and the liability of the firm itself, enforceable against its assets. Nevertheless, the share of an individual partner may be the subject of a charging order and ancillary receivership on the application of a judgment creditor of the individual partner. Other partners may redeem or acquire the share involuntarily charged or may dissolve the partnership (see M Blackett-Ord and S Haren, *Partnership Law* (Haywards Heath, Bloomsbury Professional, 2015) 182).

[58] Apparently based on the German Gesellschaft mit beschränkter Haftung, or GmbH (see JAM McCahery and EPM Vermeulen, *Topics in Corporate Finance: Understanding (Un)incorporated Business Forms* (Amsterdam Center for Corporate Finance, 2005) 18.

[59] In a silent partnership under civil law (see section IV.C) a partner binds only himself to a third party. In other partnerships, the partners may be equally liable, or in some cases jointly and severally liable. The practice varies.

without, may be a more effective approach to entity classification than relying on 'legal personality'.

The second of six HMRC foreign entity classification criteria listed in guidance at INTM180010 considers whether the entity issues share capital, or something analogous to it. This does not directly originate in the *Memec* case mentioned at section IV and is arguably circular. An entity which is truly opaque and asset-partitioned must create interests for its members broadly equivalent to company shares or joint stock, since the members will not jointly or in common own the business or its assets.

Whether the entity *issues* an instrument of some kind may be less important than the nature of the interest created, in a partitioned entity or in a business and over its assets. Other criteria identified in the *Memec* case are interrelated: entity protection follows from asset partitioning, which would also mean the entity owns and employs the entity assets in carrying on the business without qualification and is responsible for its debts. A further issue is member ownership of profits as they arise and with ability to remove correlative assets absent a distribution process.

V. JOINT VENTURES

The term 'joint venture' is loosely used to denote a commercial relationship between parties rather than indicating any specific legal structure. Such relationships may be formed as partnerships, incorporated companies or consortia, for example. But sometimes they may be unincorporated associations.[60] If the joint venture is not constituted as an incorporated company or a consortium of companies, it will not be a partnership unless the business is carried on in common with a view to profit. Sometimes a 'no partnership' declaration is made, but that would only be determinative in case of doubt and provided the declaration did not contradict the facts.

Even if the parties undertake joint and several liability for each other's obligations to third parties, there will not be a partnership relationship if the contracting parties carry on their respective parts of the joint venture project independently, and no profit is shared at the joint venture level. The arrangement may, for example, involve entitlement to profit from the parts of the joint venture and the sharing of residual profits, supervised by a joint executive committee. Depending on the precise relationships under the contractual arrangements, that would amount to an unincorporated association.

---

[60] See, eg, *Spree Engineering and Testing Ltd v O'Rourke Civil and Structural Engineering Ltd* [1999] EWHC QB 272.

VI. BODIES CORPORATE

The term 'body corporate' has no clearly defined meaning in UK law, nor has 'corporation'.[61] It is not defined in the Tax Acts or in the Interpretation Act. The concept has been extensively reviewed in the context of whether a foreign state is a body corporate.[62] Grant in 1850[63] defined a corporation as:

> A continuous entity: endowed at its creation with capacity for endless duration; residing in the grantees of it and their successors, its acts being determined by the will of the majority of the existing body of its grantees or their successors at any given time, acting within the limits imposed by the constitution of their body politic, such will being signified to strangers by writing under a common seal; having a name, and under such name a capacity for taking, holding or enjoying all kinds of property, a qualified right of disposing of its possessions, and also a capacity for taking, holding and enjoying, but inalienably, liberties, franchises, exemptions and privileges, together with the right and obligation of suing and being sued only under such name.[64]

The grant of status is important in distinguishing a body corporate from an institution with legal capacity, such as a Scots partnership. It is noted at section IV.B that a Sheriff Court described a Scots partnership as a body corporate. But a Scots partnership is formed (and not registered) and it is not granted the privilege of incorporation.[65] Legal personality is essentially a functional characteristic, criticised from the US perspective as a tautology[66] and those

---

[61] The US Internal Revenue Code defines a 'corporation' as including 'associations, joint-stock companies and insurance companies'. The Check-the-Box regulations now define a partnership as for tax purposes as 'a business entity which is not a corporation … and that has at least two members'. This is quite different from the English law concept of a partnership.

[62] G Montagu, 'Is a Foreign State a Body Corporate?' [2001] *BTR* 421.

[63] J Grant, *A Practical Treatise on the Law of Corporations in General, As Well Aggregate as Sole* (London, Butterworths, 1850) 4.

[64] In the *Case of Sutton's Hospital* (1612) 77 ER 960, Sir Edward Coke said: 'And it is great reason that an hospital, &c in expectancy or intendment, or nomination, should be sufficient to support the name of an incorporation when the corporation itself is only *in abstracto*, and rests only in intendment and consideration of the law; for a corporation aggregate of many is invisible, immortal, and rests only in intendment and consideration of the law; and therefore in 39 H. 6. 13. b. 14. a dean and chapter cannot have predecessor nor successor, 21 E. 4. 27. (72.) a & 30 E. 3. 15. They cannot commit treason, nor be outlawed, nor excommunicate, for they have no souls, neither can they appear in person, but by attorney 33 H. 8. Br. Fealty. A corporation aggregate of many cannot do fealty, for an invisible body can neither be in person, nor swear, Plow. Com. 213, and The Lord Berkley's case 245, it is not subject to imbecilities, death of the natural body, and divers other cases'. This is somewhat obscure in terms of modern understanding, although it was quoted by Lord Templeman in *Hazell v Hammersmith and Fulham LBC* [1992] 2 AC 1.

[65] s 13 of the Transparency of Lobbying, Non-Party Campaigning and Trade Union Administration Act 2014 distinguishes between bodies corporate and Scots partnerships for the purposes of the Act. It also uses the phrase 'a partnership constituted under the law of Scotland', rather than 'in Scotland' as found at s 4(2) PA 1890, a clearer formulation.

[66] K Blanchard, 'Entity Classification: The Significance of Legal Personality' *Business Entities* (March/April 2016) 4. This author has difficulty with the English common law concept of the partnership as the business relationship between the partners, free of any dimension of personality and

definitions which describe bodies corporate as 'artificial legal persons' miss an important dimension.

The characteristics identified in the 1850 definition are: (i) grant of the incorporation privilege by authority; (ii) continuity, or perpetual succession; (iii) a constitution covering management of the body's affairs; (iv) external relations conducted under name and seal; (v) ability to hold and, subject to its constitution, dispose of property of all kinds; (vi) possessing full legal capacity; and (vii) the right and obligation of suing and being sued in its name. These characteristics may be compared with those applied by the US Internal Revenue Service before the Check-the-Box system.[67] These so-called *Kintner* rules[68] looked for a preponderance of 'corporate characteristics': (i) continuity of life; (ii) centralisation of management; (iii) limited liability; and (iv) free transferability of interests. It was the difficulty of satisfactorily applying these which led to Check-the-Box.[69]

Limited liability for all owners and strong entity asset protection while securing flow-through or transparent taxation are what led to the development of LLCs in the United States. The closest development under UK law is the LLP formed under the Limited Liability Partnerships Act 2000,[70] which is by statute a body corporate,[71] although for most *tax* purposes it is treated as a partnership.[72] The tax status under UK tax law of an LLC formed under state laws in the US is complex.[73] Limited liability has never been a 'corporate characteristic' in UK law, however. Unlimited companies incorporated under the Companies Acts continue to be formed, because of their restricted reporting requirements.

---

not simply a contract. England (*sic*) is described as unique in that 'it does not have clear classification rules for either domestic or foreign entities' (ibid, 14). The decision in *CRC v Anson* [2015] UKSC 44; [2015] STC 1777 is rationalised either on the basis of a rejection of legal personality as an aid to entity classification, or as reflecting a mistaken reading of Delaware law. It is US federal tax law that provides for the recognition of profits, not Delaware 'corporate' law, and the latter does not specifically provide that the entity's income belongs to its members 'as it arises' (ibid, 16).

[67] Introduced 1 January 1997.

[68] Taken from *United States v Kintner* 216 F 2d 418, 422 (9th Cir 1954). These factors owe their origin to *Morrissey v Commissioner* 296 US 344 (1935). The 1935 case identified six factors determining whether an entity was to be taxed as a corporation under the Internal Revenue Code, the two additional factors being 'associates', presumably meaning at least two members, and business profit motive.

[69] In proposing the Check-the-Box classification regulations, the Treasury Department observed that '[o]ne consequence of the increased flexibility under local law in forming a partnership or other unincorporated business organisation is that taxpayers generally can achieve partnership tax classification for a non-publicly traded organisation that, in all meaningful respects, is virtually indistinguishable from a corporation' (Internal Revenue Service, US Treasury, 26 CFR Part 301 (PS–43–95), *Simplification of Entity Classification Rules* 61: 93 *Federal Register* (10 May 1996) 21989, 21990, available at www.gpo.gov/fdsys/pkg/FR-1996-05-13/pdf/96-11780.pdf.

[70] Not to be confused with the United States LLP, which is a partnership with limited liability more similar to the UK limited partnership formed under LPA 1907.

[71] s 1(2).

[72] ss 10–13.

[73] See *CRC v Anson* (above n 66).

In terms of classical theory there are two schools of thought in the approach to bodies corporate, the 'fiction' and 'real entity' theories. The fiction theory considers the legal person with no substantial reality, no mind and no will, existing only in legal theory. This appears to originate in the canon law of the Roman Catholic Church to deal with persons who cannot be held sinful, dating back to the thirteenth century or earlier.[74] It applied to ecclesiastical bodies that were 'but a name and incorporeal *res* which could not be punished because *nomina sunt juris et non personarum*: they have neither a mind nor a body'.

The real entity theory, which seems to originate from a German realist philosophy school of the nineteenth century, and in particular from Otto von Gierke,[75] sees corporate personality as not merely juristic but as a fact of society with a nature, the function of law being to recognise it.

There are also two theories of origin of the corporation or body corporate, 'concession' and 'contract'. The concession theory is essentially that adopted in the discussion above, the idea that the legal rights and obligations derive from authority of the state, the concept of granting corporate existence, whether by the Sovereign (Royal Charter), Parliament (private Act) or statutory registration (Companies Act company). But it seems not necessarily to follow that because State A explicitly grants corporate status for its purposes that State B will have to follow if it considers that important criteria are lacking.

The contract theory on the other hand holds that corporations are associations formed by shareholders, and this supports an approach which looks rather at what the terms of the relationship actually lead to on the factual matrix created, viewed from the perspective not of the constituting State A but applying the principles recognised by State B.

These theories have current resonance and go to the question, for example, of whether an LLC (a 'creature of contract' and by US regulations declared not to be a corporation) should be regarded as a body corporate under UK law.[76] On the concession theory, viewed from the US perspective, evidently not. The US Treasury regulations provide that the term 'corporation' includes a business entity organised under a federal or state statute if the statute describes or refers

---

[74] Bodies corporate are earlier – the Weavers' guild was chartered in 1155. In addition, a corporate body could arise at common law by 'customary prescription', under which the flexibility of the common law was able to infer the existence of lost Royal Charters in order to recognise the existence of certain time-honoured corporations: *Fulwood's Case* (1590) 76 ER 1031; *Byrd v Wilford* (1592) 78 ER 717. This seems to be an application of the concept of 'time whereof the memory of man runneth not to the contrary'.

[75] O von Gierke, *Die Genossenschaftstheorie und die deutsche Rechtsprechung* (Frantfurt, Weidmann, 1887).

[76] Not so much a creature of contract, however, that the LLC entity itself is not a party to the LLC agreement: Delaware Limited Liability Company Act, § 18-101(7): 'A limited liability company is not required to execute its limited liability company agreement. A limited liability company is bound by its limited liability company agreement whether or not the limited liability company executes the limited liability company agreement'. In *CRC v Anson* (above n 66), however, Lord Reed thought that, based on the facts found by the tribunal, the LLC was not a party to the agreement: [2015] UKSC 44 [119].

to the entity as a corporation, and LLCs are 'uncorporates'. But this approach is designed to support the US Check-the-Box system, which is not a feature of UK tax law.

On the contract theory the LLC would seem to have most or all of the necessary corporacy characteristics,[77] including formation by state authority, and the question whether the local laws which deny status as a corporation for US tax reasons should affect UK tax law definitions which focus specifically on bodies corporate[78] is moot, and may at some stage need to be clarified by the courts. If not a body corporate, an LLC may be an unincorporated association. There is also the reciprocal issue where State A declares the status of, say, a limited liability partnership to be that of a body corporate yet from State B's perspective certain fundamental characteristics of body corporacy are lacking. It is not obvious that State B is obliged to follow the declaration for its own tax purposes.[79]

VII. UNITED KINGDOM COMPANY LAW

UK company law provides some pointers in relation to bodies corporate, partnerships and legal persons for its own purposes:

1. A partnership may be regarded as a legal person under the law by which it is governed.[80]
2. 'Undertaking' means a body corporate or partnership, or an unincorporated association carrying on a trade or business, with or without a view to profit.[81]
3. 'Body corporate' and 'corporation' include a body incorporated outside the UK, but do not include a corporation sole or a partnership that is not regarded as a body corporate under its governing law, whether or not it is a legal person. 'Firm' means any entity, whether or not a legal person, including a body corporate, corporation sole, partnership or other unincorporated association, but not an individual.[82]
4. 'Partnership' for the purposes of Part 41 (business names) includes both general partnerships within PA 1890 and limited partnerships registered

---

[77] There is a question over perpetual succession.

[78] As distinct from the CTA company definition, which in any case includes unincorporated associations.

[79] See G Montagu, 'Anson and Entity Classification Revisited in the Light of Brexit: Can an LLC Constitute a "Body Corporate"?' [2016] *BTR* 466.

[80] s 1152(4), Companies Act 2006 (CA 2006).

[81] s 1161, CA 2006. This is plainly inconsistent with Lawton LJ's 'inference'.

[82] s 1173(1) CA 2006. Company law therefore appears to regard a partnership as a subset of unincorporated association (see also ss 1123(4) and 1258(4), CA 2006), but in tax law the phrase 'unincorporated association' is invariably used in contrast to 'partnership', as in *Conservative Central Office*, and as in the CTA company definition.

under LPA 1907, and a firm or entity of similar character formed under the law of a country or territory outside the United Kingdom.[83]

5. 'Partnership or other person' is used in the context of appointing auditors, but a partnership constituted under the law of England and Wales, or Northern Ireland, is not a legal person, and this may apply to other countries or territories.[84]

Examples of corporations sole, which may be formed by customary prescription[85] or by statute, are the Crown and certain ministers of the Crown; and under ecclesiastical law in the Church of England, a vicar of a parish, and a diocesan bishop which stand independently of the natural person who may occupy the offices from time to time. Certain public officials are also corporations sole.[86]

The act of incorporation does not therefore necessarily mean the making of an aggregate of natural persons into a body. Until fairly recently there had to be two corporators, but section 7(1), Companies Act 2006, provides that a company is formed by *one* or more persons subscribing their names to a memorandum.[87] And the act of incorporation is applied to the union of the 'body politic' and 'body natural' in the person of the sovereign. Queen Elizabeth I said in her accession speech of 1558, 'I am but one bodye naturallye considered though by … [God's] permission a bodye politique to governe'.[88] This was the incorporation of the sovereign as a corporation sole, at a time when the divine right of kings and queens was accepted, and illustrates the idea of incorporation as granted or conferred by authority, in this case divine authority. Also, in the 1561 *Case of the Duchy of Lancaster*:

> So that he [namely, the King] has a body natural adorned and invested with the estate and dignity royal, and he has not a body natural distinct and divided by itself from the office and dignity royal, but a body natural and a body politic together indivisible, and these two bodies are incorporated in one person and make one body and not divers, that is, the body corporate in the body natural et e contra the body natural in the body corporate. So that the body natural by the conjunction of the body politic to

---

[83] s 1208, CA 2006.

[84] s 1216, CA 2006. By implication, a Scots partnership is recognised as a legal person.

[85] Above n 74.

[86] See J Snape, 'Corporate Income Tax Subjects in the United Kingdom' in D Gutmann (ed), *Corporate Income Tax Subjects* (IBFD, 2016) 535. In this context HMRC does regard a body corporate as including a corporation sole, in contrast to the company law rule. This may be inferred from s 987A, CTA 2010. It exempts chief constables and the Commissioner of the Metropolitan Police from corporation tax, and would not be needed were those corporations sole not considered bodies corporate.

[87] This followed a recommendation at para 9.2 of The Company Law Review Steering Group, *Modern Company Law For a Competitive Economy Final Report*, 2 vols (Department of Trade and Industry, 2001) vol 1, which led to the addition of a new subsection 1(3A) to the Companies Act 1985. The Review was launched in March 1998 by the Department of Trade and Industry.

[88] The National Archives, 'Elizabeth's First Speech', available at www.nationalarchives.gov.uk/education/resources/elizabeth-monarchy/elizabeths-first-speech.

it (which body politic contains the office, government and majesty royal) is magnified and by the said consolidation hath in it the body politic.[89]

Incorporation has an ancient heritage, and remains a difficult and diffuse concept that is not congruent with 'legal personality'.

VIII. CONCLUSION

This chapter has ranged widely beyond the immediate issues of unincorporated associations raised by *Conservative Central Office*, challenged its oft-quoted definition and reviewed the institutions, corporate and unincorporate, included in the Corporation Tax company definition and the partnerships excluded from it. The analysis addresses a number of difficult and still developing areas, including that of foreign entity classification, and considers whether the courts may need to develop further the law in this area.

The variety of approaches and conclusions reflected in *Conservative Central Office* illustrate the need both to find the primary facts clearly and to draw the appropriate secondary factual conclusions from them. And this comes before applying the relevant legal principles. The difficulty of this task is reflected in various entity classification cases that have reached the courts.

---

[89] E Plowden, *The Commentaries, or Reports* (first published 1548–79; London, Brooke, 1816) 212a.

13

Mallalieu v Drummond *(1983)*
Allowable Deductions, Inadmissible Arguments

GEOFFREY MORSE

I T IS AXIOMATIC that tax law is constantly changing and expanding on an annual basis. But within that legislative leviathan there are some core provisions which have remained unaltered for nearly two hundred years, being transposed directly from one legislative consolidation to another, even surviving intact through the recent tax rewrite process.[1] One such provision sets out the well-known general rule as to what expenses are allowable as a deduction from the taxable receipts of a trade, profession or vocation in order to establish the 'full amount of the profits'[2] which is then chargeable to income tax.

The current manifestation of this rule can be found in section 34(1) of the Income Tax (Trading and Other Income) Act 2005:[3]

'In calculating the profits of a trade,[4] no deduction is allowed for –

(a) Expenses not incurred wholly and exclusively for the purposes of the trade'.[5]

Following that general rule, the section then lists several specific items of expenditure which are also disallowed as deductions. The section therefore has

---

[1] The income tax legislation was 'rewritten' into three Acts following the Tax Law Rewrite Project of the 1990s. Their reports can be found at webarchives.nationalarchives.gov.uk/20140109143644/http://www.hmrc.gov.uk/rewrite.

[2] Income Tax (Trading and Other Income) Act 2005, s 7(1).

[3] Hereafter ITTOIA 2005, one of the rewrite Acts.

[4] This includes professions and vocations – see ITTOIA 2005, s 6(3).

[5] This is qualified by s 34(2) which provides that: 'If an expense is incurred for more than one purpose, this section does not prohibit a deduction for any identifiable part or identifiable proportion of the expense which is incurred wholly and exclusively for the purposes of the trade'. But this does not allow an apportionment where there is a dual purpose for the expenditure. It applies only if the expenditure can be clearly dissected into business and non-business parts, each having a single purpose. As such it had no role to play in *Mallalieu v Drummond*.

two unusual characteristics: first that there is a detailed list as well as a general rule, and second, that they are all expressed in the negative. To discover what is generally allowed therefore requires turning the double negative into a positive. Both these characteristics can be traced back to the Income Tax Act 1799,[6] which introduced the concept of a list of specific prohibited items of expenditure. There was, however, at that stage no general rule about wholly and exclusively, etc.[7] That first appeared in the Income Tax Act 1805 and again in the Income Tax Act 1842,[8] which reintroduced income tax to the nation after it had been discontinued following the end of the Napoleonic wars. That Act also retained both the use of the negative and the list approach. The wording of 'wholly and exclusively for the purposes of the trade' has remained unchanged ever since.

There are therefore three key words: 'wholly', 'exclusively' and 'purposes', which are clearly thought to be so important that they cannot be altered. 'Wholly' has a dictionary meaning[9] of: 'exclusively, solely, only'. 'Exclusive' has a dictionary meaning of: 'to the exclusion of', and 'purpose' a dictionary meaning of: 'the reason for which something is done; the result or effect intended'. As we shall see that last definition has played a key role in the interpretation of section 34(1) and was central to the issue before the courts, and which came to a head in *Mallalieu v Drummond*,[10] the subject of this chapter. The specific issue in that case concerned what precisely is meant by 'exclusively for the purposes of the trade' in the context of expenditure which although it has a business purpose is also an everyday living or private expense; that is one which the taxpayer would have had to expend in any event to live a normal life.[11] Such expenses would include such items as clothing, food, accommodation etc. In what circumstances, therefore, could a taxpayer claim such expenditure as being exclusively

---

[6] 'An Act to repeal the duties imposed by an Act made in the last session of Parliament ... and to make more efficient provision for the like purpose by granting certain Duties upon Income in lieu of the said duties'. This raised necessary funds for the Napoleonic wars. Trading income was taxed under the 'Fifteenth Case' and it first used the concept of the full amount of the profits, which were to be calculated as 'no less than the fair and just average for one year of the profits or gains of such trade'.

[7] The Income Tax Act 1803 introduced the concept of Schedule D Cases I and II which applied to the taxation of a trade, profession or vocation until ITTOIA 2005, but it did not introduce the wholly and exclusively rule.

[8] In the First Rule applying to both Cases I and II of Schedule D. This specific restriction appeared amongst a list of other specific restrictions rather than being prioritised as it is today.

[9] These definitions are taken from the *Shorter Oxford English Dictionary*.

[10] *Mallalieu v Drummond* [1983] 2 AC 861; [1983] STC 665 (HL), reversing [1983] 1 WLR 251; [1983] STC 124 (CA), which had upheld [1981] 1 WLR 908, [1981] STC 391. In all this is one of those cases where four judges found for the Revenue (who won) and five for the taxpayer (who lost), but HL judges, like away goals, effectively count double. It should be added, however, that the General Commissioners also found for the Revenue.

[11] The concept of 'wholly' had apparently been relegated to a question of quantum before then because of a concession in a case: *Bentleys, Stokes and Lowless v Beeson* [1952] 2 All ER 82, 85. There is some doubt as to whether that should have been given but either way, given its dictionary meaning, it would seem to have little effect on the issues in *Mallalieu v Drummond*.

for the purposes of the trade? Should the tax system in effect subsidise such everyday living expenses even if incurred in a business context?[12]

I. INITIAL SUBJECTIVITY SOLUTION: CONSCIOUS PURPOSE WITH INCIDENTAL EFFECT

The initial solution was promulgated by Romer LJ, a very experienced tax judge, in the case of *Bentleys, Stokes and Lowless v Beeson*.[13] That case revolved around business lunches given by a firm of solicitors to clients.[14] The Court of Appeal, upholding Roxburgh J, made the very important decision that the test was essentially a subjective one, so that if the taxpayer's sole purpose was a business one (discussing clients' business at a convenient time) the fact that the expenditure might have an incidental private effect (eating) did not disallow the claim for a deduction. To revert to the dictionary for a moment, the purpose was thus the taxpayer's subjective intended effect and if that was solely a business purpose that was the end of the matter. The problem was then apparently further solved by the decision that to discern that subjective intention was an evidential question and one therefore of fact.[15]

The problem did not, however, go away. Subjectivity is a difficult concept to discern in practice and there were many cases as to what the taxpayer's subjective purpose really was. Ultimately it would have to be tested in a case where the facts were such that the Revenue had to object to a claim for expenses because of the potential fallout for the whole of the self-employed tax system.[16] That case proved to be the seminal[17] case of *Mallalieu v Drummond*.

Miss Ann Mallalieu (as she then was) was a practising barrister with a mixed criminal and personal injury practice.[18] She was seeking to deduct sums she had spent in the specimen tax year (1977–78) on the replacement and laundry of clothes[19] which were specifically needed for her to comply with the Bar rules as

---

[12] The issue also arose in the context of allowable expenditure for employee tax, which uses the same words, albeit with the additional requirement of necessity.

[13] [1952] 2 All ER 82 (CA). See D Stopforth, 'Restricting Tax Relief on Business Entertaining and Gifts: 1948–1965' in J Tiley (ed) *Studies in the History of Tax Law: Volume 5* (Oxford, Hart Publishing, 2011).

[14] It was both the cost of the clients' meals and those of the partners which were the subject of the dispute.

[15] So that if on the evidence there are two intended effects, business and personal, the claim will fail. See, eg, *Prince v Mapp* [1970] 1 All ER 519.

[16] It would also have consequences for the employee taxation system as well since the words 'wholly and exclusively' are used as one of the limitations on allowable expenditure there as well (below n 22).

[17] As so described by Lord Oliver in *MacKinlay v Arthur Young McClelland Moores & Co* [1990] 2 AC 239, [1989] STC 898 (HL).

[18] Baroness Mallalieu, as she is now, was also the first female president of the Cambridge Union in 1967.

[19] The initial expenditure would have been of a capital nature and so disallowed on that basis.

to the appropriate dress whilst she was appearing in court.[20] The point, however, was these were everyday clothes – there was no real dispute as to her wig and gown.[21] Could everyday clothes ever be worn purely for a business purpose, even subjectively? If they could then 'Pandora's Box' might well be open and claims for allowable deductions flow in. The Revenue felt that they had to take a stand. Previous cases had generally disallowed such ordinary clothes worn for business or indeed employment purposes[22] as a deductible expense.[23]

The case first came before the General Commissioners and not the professional Special Commissioners.[24] The Commissioners found for the Revenue and disallowed her claim. As required under the procedure at the time, on a request by the taxpayer, they then stated a case for the High Court. That case stated sets out the relatively straightforward findings of fact which were not disputed thereafter. As ever it was the interaction of those facts and the law which occupied the courts all the way up to the House of Lords: so therefore, first, to the facts as found.[25]

The clothes in question were necessary for the taxpayer to comply with the rules for barristers' dress in court but they were also standard everyday clothes available from Marks & Spencer Ltd.[26] The significant point was that they were black. That was significant because the taxpayer considered that black did not suit her colouring[27] and preferred clothes that were less formal and more stylish and colourful. Thus, she would only wear the black clothes[28] whilst in court, in chambers,[29] travelling to and from work and on other occasions when 'she did

---

[20] The Notes for Guidance on this matter issued by the Bar Council were enforced by the judiciary and it was found as a fact that it would have been impossible for her to have carried out her practice without complying with them.

[21] Or indeed as to expenditure on her specialised collars which was originally disputed but then dropped from the case.

[22] The expenses rules for employee taxation also require that the expenditure be wholly and exclusively in the performance of the duties of the employment: ITEPA 2003, s 336. They must also be necessary.

[23] See, eg, *Hillyer v Leeke* [1976] STC 490; *Woodcock v CIR* [1977] STC 405; and *Ward v Dunn* [1979] STC 178.

[24] In fact, the particular General Commissioners (for the division of the Inner Temple) were mainly legally qualified, although not necessarily in tax law but described as experienced by Slade J [1981] STC 391, 403h. Usually appeals to the General Commissioners were taken on disputes as to facts rather than the law, which presumably is what the case was thought to involve; ie, what was her subjective intention.

[25] The case stated is set out at [1983] STC 391, 394g onwards.

[26] There was a written statement from the executive head of design of that company that that was the case and that such clothes had to have a broad popular appeal for retail purposes. The items were tights, shoes, suits, dresses and shirts.

[27] Although, the description of the taxpayer by the Commissioners as an 'attractive blonde barrister' shows the age in which the decision was made (1980), the fact that she was blonde was her expressed reason for her dislike of black and so germane to the findings made; ie, as to the validity of her evidence.

[28] Although she did wear black shoes on other occasions, the ones in the claim were low heeled whereas she wore high-heeled shoes on other occasions.

[29] Her practice was such that she could be called to appear in court at short notice and so wore the black clothes even if she did not have a conference that day.

not find it necessary or desirable to change'. Going from chambers to a social event she would change clothes. The other finding was that she had plenty of other clothes that conformed to her natural taste.

In summary, the Commissioners distilled the facts thus:

> We consider that the evidence shows that when she bought the clothes she bought them to wear in court and that she would not have bought them but for the exigencies of her profession. She had no intention of wearing them except when in court or in chambers or in the other circumstances mentioned ... above.[30]

But they were not specialised clothes in the sense that a wig or gown would be. They could easily be worn as everyday wear and indeed were by many people. Nevertheless, given the taxpayer's clear 'intention', was the expenditure wholly and exclusively for the purposes of her profession?

The Commissioners, albeit noting the possibility of a sole purpose giving rise to dual effects, both deliberate and incidental as in *Bentleys, Stokes and Lowless v Beeson*,[31] without going into any general principles and apparently accepting that the test was subjective, distinguished instead between the taxpayer's sole 'motive' (professional exigencies) and her dual 'purpose' (professional, and warmth and being properly clothed). Thus, she had two purposes, only one of which was for the profession, and so the claim failed.[32] 'Motive' has a dictionary meaning of: 'a factor or circumstance inducing a person to act in a certain way', or 'an inward prompting or impulse'.[33] Remember that the dictionary definition of 'purpose' is: 'the reason for which something is done; the result or effect intended'. It is therefore possible linguistically to separate them since purpose, unlike motive, refers to the effect as well as the impulse. So, was the separation of motive and purpose the answer to the problem?

The taxpayer duly appealed to the High Court and the case was heard by Slade J in 1981.[34] He reversed the decision of the Commissioners and found for the taxpayer. The question it was agreed was a subjective one; there was no apparent attempt to argue to the contrary. But there was a significant almost unnoticed shift in his approach to that of the Commissioners. The judge took the view that what was in issue was not the distinction between motive and purpose but the distinction between the purpose and the incidental effects of the expenditure. Motive thus becomes subsumed into purpose rather than into

---

[30] [1981] STC 391, 395h.

[31] [1952] 2 All ER 82 (CA).

[32] [1981] STC 391, 396c. The Commissioners also alluded to the fact that whether the expenditure was necessary or not did not affect the issue either way – that is not a condition of business unlike employee expenditure, where it is an additional requirement (see ITEPA 2003, s 336). That poses additional problems, compare, eg, the cases of *HMRC v Decadt* [2007] EWHC 1659 (Ch); [2008] STC 1103 and *HMRC v Banerjee* [2010] EWCA 61 (Ch); [2010] STC 2318. The latter case also raised the wholly and exclusive question as to where a payment required by the employment also advanced the taxpayer's career prospects.

[33] From the *Shorter Oxford Dictionary*.

[34] [1981] 1WLR 908; [1981] STC 391.

effect. Thus, a single motive/purpose could have two effects and still satisfy the test, whereas under the Commissioners' formulation a single motive could have two purposes and thus fail.

But the judge was alive to the difficulties raised by such a subjective test, both as to the veracity of many taxpayers' evidence[35] and the amount of inference needed on the part of the Commissioners to ascertain the motive/purposes from that evidence.[36] Although he regarded the Commissioners' decision that the taxpayer had a dual purpose as essentially a finding of fact[37] he regarded it as an inference (wrongly) drawn from the facts.[38] At all relevant times 'the preservation of warmth and decency' did not enter her mind; she had an ample wardrobe of clothes[39] and so only wore the black clothes for professional purposes. The Commissioners had confused purpose and incidental effect. In effect, however, they had simply made a different distinction: motive *versus* purpose rather than motive *versus* effect.

Their error, on Slade J's analysis, therefore was to conflate purpose and effect. The real distinction, according to the judge, was that the Commissioners had assumed that feeding, clothing or accommodating oneself must always give rise to both a dual effect and a dual purpose. He justified this criticism by the Commissioners' use of the decision in *Bentleys, Stokes and Lowless v Beeson*.[40] The Commissioners had only considered that case from the point of view of the clients' lunches – feeding a customer as part of a business deal was an incidental effect. But the court had also allowed the costs of the partners' lunches so that feeding oneself could also be an incidental effect. A fortiori so could clothing oneself if the circumstances so dictated.[41]

Having thus rephrased the possibilities, Slade J himself having accepted the facts as found, applied what might be termed the 'pure' subjective test – what from the evidence was in the taxpayer's mind at the date the expenditure was incurred? The answer was that she was solely seeking to fulfil the requirements of her profession, so that it was expenditure wholly and decisively for the

---

[35] '[T]he fact that the clothes in question were perfectly suitable for wearing on social occasions and, on the evidence, were from time to time worn by her outside the strict course of her profession, though she would not ordinarily have chosen to do so. Factors such as these would, I conceive, be very relevant when any tribunal of fact ... had to ascertain the true intentions of the taxpayer at the date of purchase. In particular, they would be relevant in determining whether they could accept a taxpayer's evidence that she bought the clothes solely because of the requirements of her profession' [1981] STC 391, 406j.

[36] See [1981] STC 391, 400g.

[37] And so only reversible if the law was then misapplied to the facts or there was no evidence to support that finding: in *Bentleys, Stokes and Lowless v Beeson* [1952] 2 All ER 82, 86 (Romer LJ).

[38] Whereas in the light of his analysis of the test that finding was that there were two effects.

[39] This seems to be dangerously close to bringing necessity into play as a factor. If she had only possessed the black clothes, then she must have worn them at all times and the current dispute would not have arisen (above n 28).

[40] [1952] 2 All 82.

[41] See [1981] STC 391, 405g.

purposes of the profession. The benefits of warmth and decency were purely incidental to the carrying on of her profession.[42]

In effect, therefore Slade J's decision was that a single motive/purpose could have two effects even if one of those effects would inevitably satisfy an everyday expense of existence. That does seem to be the natural conclusion from *Bentleys, Stokes and Lowless v Beeson*.[43] But the important word there is of course 'could'. The judge was aware of this: 'Everything must depend on the available evidence as to the purpose of the particular taxpayer in effecting a particular purchase'.[44] As the judge further stated this is an inevitable consequence of applying a purely subjective test – it resolves itself into a question of evidence and so each case must be decided on that basis. It leads to uncertainty and a welter of apparently random decisions.[45] In the world of VAT the application of a purely subjective test as to whether food was supplied for the purpose of being hot or for some other purpose (such as freshness) led to countless contradictory tribunal decisions and led to a change in the law, initially by reference to the principle of fiscal neutrality, and then by a change to Schedule 8 of the Value Added Tax Act 1994 so as to impose an objective test.[46]

Thus, the issue in *Mallalieu v Drummond* was now left to evidential analysis in all but the most obvious cases and that if the evidence was such then everyday expenses could well be allowed. The Revenue did indeed regard this as unsatisfactory, on the Pandora's Box principle, and appealed to the Court of Appeal.

The Court of Appeal upheld the decision of Slade J in favour of the taxpayer.[47] Their decision, again without any challenge as to the subjective nature of the test, essentially reiterated the point that one could have a single purpose/motive which had two effects, which had in their view happened in the case. Both Sir John Donaldson MR and Kerr LJ used the analogy of aiming at one bird or two. If the taxpayer aimed at two (professional and personal) then she could not recover the costs, but if she aimed at one and fortuitously hit two then that was allowable.[48] They rejected the Revenue's argument that in all such cases where the business expenditure would also fulfil a basic human need there must *a fortiori* be a dual purpose. The obvious hole in that argument was that no such items could ever be claimed, such as heating an office or the provision

---

[42] ibid, 406h.

[43] [1952] 2 All 82.

[44] [1981] STC 391, 407b.

[45] 'This, however, seems to me the inevitable result of the wording of [s 34(1) of ITTOIA 2005] coupled with the principle … that in applying the subsection the purpose of any expenditure must be determined subjectively. This principle inevitably makes the application of any "rules of thumb" much more difficult, save where the purpose of the relevant expenditure is obvious (for example, the purchase by a practising barrister of a wig and gown)', [1981] STC 391, 407d.

[46] See *Sub One Ltd v HMRC* [2014] EWCA Civ 773; [2014] STC 2508. There were over 1,200 appeals pending from Sub One franchisees to the Upper Tribunal on this one issue at the time.

[47] [1983] 1 WLR 252; [1983] STC 124.

[48] [1983] STC 124, 129f and 132a. Sir Sebag Shaw delivered only a short concurring judgment.

of specialist clothing, as both would also fulfil the ordinary needs of keeping warm and decency respectively.[49] Since both are allowed then that cannot be the test. The problem, as ever, for the Revenue was how to counter the claim in the present case without going down the total prohibition route, which they have never attempted to date.

Lord Donaldson MR followed Slade J's purpose/motive *versus* effect analysis and rejected the Commissioners' motive *versus* purpose/effect approach. Distinguishing between motive and purpose did not accord with the decision in *Bentleys, Stokes and Lowless v Beeson*.[50] It followed that the question was whether on the facts as found by the Commissioners, the taxpayer had one or two motives/purposes, given that there were clearly two effects.[51] In the opinion of the Court there was only one answer on the facts as found – the taxpayer's sole purpose (motive) in incurring the expenditure was a professional purpose. Any other benefit was purely incidental.[52] In addition to the facts that she had ample clothing without the black clothes, and that she wore them only whilst carrying out her profession and had to have them for that purpose, the critical finding was that 'the preservation of warmth and decency was not a consideration which crossed her mind when she bought the disputed items'. The only reasonable conclusion therefore to be drawn from those facts was that her sole purpose was a professional one.[53]

There remained the problem of dealing with the previous decisions to the contrary as to ordinary clothing expenses.[54] For Sir John Donaldson MR there was a clear factual distinction, which seems, however, somewhat unconvincing. In the present case, the taxpayer had ample clothing apart from the black clothes whereas the earlier decisions were,

> all consistent with a state of fact in which the taxpayers had indeed sufficient clothes for this purpose [warmth etc] but only if those used at work were included. Accordingly, on this supposition, they had to buy the work-clothes for warmth and decency and whilst their purpose was to acquire clothes suitable for work this was not the sole purpose.[55]

Apart from this being a supposition, it seems to import consideration of necessity into the argument which at best can only have an effect of the findings

---

[49] 'Beyond recalling the argument, I do not think it is necessary to take the matter further since either it would involve embarking on an entirely different case, or, still worse, it might inspire the Revenue to start disallowing the cost of renting and heating chambers', ([1983] STC 124, 129c).

[50] [1952] 2 All ER 82. See also *Robinson v Scott Bader Co Ltd* [1980] STC 241, 249 (Walton J).

[51] Much of both judgments was taken up with the issue as to whether the court could interfere with the Commissioners' conclusions from the facts as found under the well-known principles laid down by the HL in *Edwards v Bairstow and Harrison* [1956] AC 14 (see ch 8, this volume). This can be done if that conclusion was inconsistent with the facts.

[52] [1983] STC 124, 129h and 132b.

[53] ibid, 129h and 132b.

[54] *Hillyer v Leeke*; *Woodcock v CIR*; and *Ward v Dunn* (above n 23).

[55] [1983] STC 124, 128j.

as to motive. Kerr LJ took a more pragmatic approach by treating the issue as one of the reasonable conclusion which could be made from the primary findings of fact. In the previous cases the findings of fact had led to the dual-purpose conclusion, 'or at any rate the taxpayer did not succeed in establishing the contrary'.[56]

The Court of Appeal were careful, as Slade J had been, to stress that in their opinion in many such cases the facts would point to a dual purpose so that only where the findings were such that only a single purpose could be divined would a claim for ordinary clothing etc be upheld. The result was that by using the purpose/motive *versus* effects dichotomy coupled with the purely subjective test, everything resolved itself back into the evidence leading to the primary findings of fact and the reasonable conclusion to be drawn therefrom. By not reverting to either the total prohibition solution of never allowing any clothing expenses etc or challenging the subjective nature of the test, the Revenue had what appeared to be a real problem. The ruling might be taken to allow anyone who could show that they only bought specific items of everyday clothing purely for business use, would never wear them except for work[57] and who had plenty of other clothes, to put in a claim. Pandora's Box remained at least partially open if the taxpayer could marshal his or her facts correctly.[58]

II. SUBJECTIVE PURPOSE(S) NOW TO BE OBJECTIVELY CONSTRUED

So, the Revenue appealed to the House of Lords.[59] One clue as to the argument to be pursued came in the Court of Appeal. Counsel for the Crown, Peter Millett QC, submitted there that whatever a taxpayer may identify as the primary purpose of the expenditure on everyday clothes, his or her secondary purpose must be to keep warm and to be decently dressed, or at least that would be a possible conclusion of fact. That argument had been dismissed by Sir John Donaldson as being one which was 'remarkably less subjective'.[60] It could also be seen that this new point was once again apparently reverting to

---

[56] ibid, 131c.

[57] It might be wondered, however, how many such items there might be in practice. No one, eg, appears to have asked what Miss Mallalieu might have worn at a funeral or memorial service. In a leader of 16 December 1982, *The Times* made a similar point. The paper also pointed out the resulting apparent distinction between those who had sufficient alternative clothing and those who had not.

[58] It would seem to be enough on one reading if one simply reserves the clothes for work purposes only.

[59] [1983] 2 AC 861, [1983] STC 665. Counsel for both sides remained the same: Peter Millett QC (later Lord Millett) for the Crown and Andrew Park QC (later Park J) for the taxpayer. Millett QC also led for the Crown in *Ramsay (WT) Ltd v CIR* [1982] AC 300 (see ch 10, this volume), before becoming a judge and later a Law Lord. Park QC also became a judge hearing many tax cases. It was a heavyweight contest indeed.

[60] [1983] STC 124, 128f.

the motive/effect *versus* purpose approach rather than the subjective motive/ purpose *versus* effect used by Slade J and the Court of Appeal. Nevertheless, that was to be at the centre of the decision in the House of Lords which was heard within six months of the Court of Appeal decision.

Their Lordships, by a majority of four to one, reversed the decisions of Slade J and the Court of Appeal and restored that of the Commissioners. Lord Brightman gave the only reasoned speech for the majority,[61] Lord Elwyn Jones dissented. That dissent was based squarely on the reasoning of Slade J and the Court of Appeal that the findings of fact led inevitably to the conclusion that the taxpayer's only subjective purpose was to carry on her profession. In doing so he therefore also accepted that her actual purpose and motive were distinct from their effects and that subjective motive meant what the taxpayer, credibly, could be said to have intended.

Lord Brightman did not dissent from the basic proposition that a taxpayer may have a single objective which is different from the effects, so that there can be exclusivity of purpose even if one of the effects gives the taxpayer a personal advantage.[62] Subjectivity of intention[63] rather than objectivity of effect remained in place. The appeal was therefore, in his words, concerned with the distinction between object and effect. He presumably omitted any reference at this stage to purpose deliberately, so that the taxpayer's purpose could influence both.[64] Lord Brightman also made the point that the wording 'for the purposes of the trade' in the section was not the same as for the purposes of the taxpayer,[65] as Sir John Donaldson MR had said in the Court of Appeal.[66] Apart from a rather academic thrust at the Master of the Rolls it is hard to see what force there is in the point. As Lord Brightman, himself, pointed out the purposes of the taxpayer are fundamental to the application of the criteria. It is the purposes of the taxpayer to fulfil the dictates of the trade which go to the heart of the matter. All Sir John Donaldson was guilty of at most was of paraphrasing.

---

[61] Lord Diplock, Lord Keith and Lord Roskill endorsed both his decision and reasoning. This was Lord Brightman's first major decision in the HL on tax matters. He later played a significant role in the decision in *Furniss v Dawson* [1984] AC 474, [1984] STC 153. Lord Keith went on to give the main speech in *Craven v White* [1989] AC 398.

[62] Curiously Lord Brightman does not refer to *Bentleys, Stokes and Lowless v Beeson* as authority for this. That case is generally regarded as being the one where that distinction was made, as discussed by each of the lower tribunals. Nevertheless, he clearly accepted the principle. He illustrated the proposition by reference to a well-known but rather esoteric example of a medical consultant attending a patient in the South of France and claiming his air fare. If his only object was to attend his patient and a week on the Riviera was not a reason for his journey, then the expense would be deductible: [1983] STC 665, 669f. That naturally takes us back to the evidence.

[63] 'Intention' is used in this chapter in its non-technical sense rather than its specific legal meaning, eg, in criminal law.

[64] The *Shorter Oxford Dictionary* interestingly defines 'object' in this context as 'the end to which effort is directed: a thing sought, or aimed at; a purpose, an end, an aim'.

[65] [1983] STC 665, 669a.

[66] [1981] STC 124, 127.

Before turning to Lord Brightman's analysis of the object/effect distinction it is very important to see where he was coming from. He rejected the lower courts' insistence that their decision was based on the particular facts of the case and thus had a limited effect. It was in no way exceptional. In his view the fact that the taxpayer was blonde and so did not wear black clothes except for her professional purposes did not make the case special, as Andrew Park QC, counsel for Miss Mallalieu, apparently conceded. Brunette barristers, or any members of the Bar, who might well have appropriate clothes which they could wear either in court or otherwise, would equally be able to claim if they set aside particular clothes for professional use only.[67] He also rejected the idea that the taxpayer would not be able to practise her profession without black clothes as being at all relevant. The degree of sanction (other professions might only lose goodwill or their clients) and necessity played no part in the test. There could also be no difference between barristers and any other self-employed person in applying the test.

Lord Brightman therefore characterised the issue before the Court as:

[I]f the argument for the taxpayer is right, it will be open to every self-employed person to set against his gross income the cost of the upkeep of a complete wardrobe of clothes, so long as he reserves such clothes strictly for use only at work, or when proceeding to and from work.[68]

All that of course ignores the fact that it would always depend on the evidence and the credibility of the taxpayer. It also introduces an air of factual unreality.[69] The facts of the taxpayer's colouring and the sanction involved clearly affected the Commissioners' acceptance of the evidence as to her motivation. If the test is subjective, and that was never openly disputed, then that will always be the central issue. But, having generalised the issue, raising again the Pandora's Box scenario, it is not surprising that his Lordship found a way to deny the claim. The question was how.

Lord Brightman's solution was to re-examine what he referred to as the 'so-called' subjective approach to the application of the section.[70] Slade J had concentrated on what was in the taxpayer's conscious mind when spending the money[71] and according to the accepted evidence she had no conscious thoughts of warmth and decency. His decision was therefore a foregone conclusion.

---

[67] 'Any distinction between different barristers according to their colouring would be "absurd"': [1983] STC 665, 672c.

[68] ibid, 672h.

[69] Lord Brightman's inclusion of underwear as being potentially subject to the same test shows a degree of unreality in his approach. Was he considering a female professional who should wear white blouses for work but only otherwise only wears black underwear which would show through (this was the 1980s) and so needs white underwear for work only?

[70] Again, it is relevant that he made no reference to the words of Romer LJ and Roxburgh J in *Bentley, Stokes and Lowless v Beeson* at this point.

[71] See [1981] STC 391, 399, 400 and 406.

The Court of Appeal[72] had taken the same approach. Anything outside her consciousness was an incidental advantage. Lord Brightman expressly rejected that consciousness approach:

> I reject the notion that the object of a taxpayer is inevitably limited to the particular conscious motive in mind at the moment of expenditure. Of course, the motive of which the taxpayer is conscious is of vital significance, but it is not inevitable the only object which the commissioners are entitled to find to exist. In my opinion the commissioners were not only entitled to reach the conclusion that the taxpayer's object was both to serve the purposes of her profession and also to serve her personal purposes, but I myself would have found it impossible to reach any other conclusion.[73]

The taxpayer's evidence as to her motives was downgraded by his Lordship to 'of course what she was thinking of' and as a 'natural way that anyone incurring such expenditure would think and speak'.[74] The difference between Lord Brightman and the courts below is, in essence, that the lower courts accepted the single purpose on the evidence from the facts as found (whilst being aware of that being unlikely in most ordinary expense cases) whereas Lord Brightman in effect regarded the issue as being a mixed question of law and fact such as spelt out by a majority of the House of Lords in *Fitzpatrick v CIR*,[75] albeit he phrased that as being a matter of fact and degree.

Lord Brightman reinforced this approach by quoting from the decision of Goulding J in *Hillyer v Leek*,[76] the case distinguished, not altogether convincingly, by the Court of Appeal earlier.[77] In *Hillyer*, which was an employment tax case, the judge made a clear distinction between clothing worn of a special character dictated by the occupation (allowable) and ordinary civilian clothing of a standard required for the occupation (not allowable as the personal element was not an incidental effect).[78] It must be remembered that for employment tax purposes there is the additional requirement of 'necessary' which may explain the use of the word 'dictated'. Lord Brightman also took on the problem of specialised clothing, often referred to as the uniform cases. Those were a matter of fact and degree. If the taxpayer could not work without a particular design of clothing, then the Commissioners could in fact find an exclusively professional purpose. The examples he gave were a nurse's uniform and a waiter's 'tails', the latter again putting the case squarely in its time and place.

---

[72] And Lord Elwyn Jones dissenting in the House of Lords.
[73] [1983] STC 665, 673b. Although the Commissioners did indeed find that there were two objectives there is a disjunct in the case stated between that conclusion and the facts that they found from the evidence.
[74] ibid, 673a.
[75] *Fitzpatrick v CIR* [1994] 1 WLR 306, [1994] STC 237.
[76] [1976] STC 490.
[77] Above n 55 *et seq*.
[78] [1976] STC 490, 492–93.

Lord Brightman had therefore closed the lid on the idea that everyday cloth-ing, and, by analogy, other everyday personal expenditure, was an allowable expense subsidised by the tax system. He had put his finger in the dyke. But had he left the dyke in a watertight condition? To begin with, what did Lord Brightman do as a result of his interpretation of the subjective test as includ-ing subconscious motives, to the motive/purpose/effect dichotomy which was central to the case? The taxpayer's motive/purpose (or object) is still to be distin-guished from its effects so that a single purpose could still have a dual effect (one or more of which would then be incidental). But now, if there are two effects, professional and personal, that could lead back to a dual purpose, one conscious and one unconscious. So, one begins not with purpose but effect. Unconscious motives may be divined despite the expressed, and credible, evidence of the taxpayer. Second guessing can be an unscientific activity. But it is still, on the face of it, a subjective test of motive and not an objective test of effect.

Subjectivity, however, is a difficult concept once one goes beyond the expressed and credible evidence. Does the new approach amount to little more than, to quote a memorable phrase from the past,[79] 'he would [say that], wouldn't he?'[80] If one is now starting with looking at the effects of the expenditure and then reading those back into motive(s) then just how subjective is that? If the effects are X and Y and the taxpayer's credible evidence is that she only intended X, to say that she must also have intended Y, substitutes the court's view of the taxpay-er's motives for her own. It is in fact using an objective factor, Y, to determine the subjective intent. In other words, it separates conscious motives from subjective intent. Although it stops short of saying that the taxpayer was being economical with the truth it is clearly second guessing her evidence, which it must be remem-bered has been accepted by the fact-finding tribunal. The subjective/objective distinction becomes blurred – the test as formulated by Lord Brightman is in effect, what would the reasonable taxpayer have intended in this situation. It is not all clear that that was the test as formulated by Romer LJ and Roxburgh J in *Bentleys, Stokes and Lowless v Beeson*,[81] which Lord Brightman of course omit-ted any reference to in his speech.

This subjective/objective dilemma is not confined to income tax. There is a close parallel in the world of VAT where a supply of goods or services is made in return for non-cash consideration. That must be given a monetary equivalent so that VAT can be charged upon it.[82] The question is how that cash value to

---

[79] To those of a certain generation.

[80] During the fall-out from the Profumo scandal in 1963, Mandy Rice-Davies, at the trial of Stephen Ward, is reported to have said that when she was told that one of the main characters had denied her allegations as to the events during house parties at Cliveden (see E Knowles (ed), *Oxford Dictionary of Quotations*, 7th edn (Oxford, Oxford University Press, 2009) 660).

[81] [1952] 2 All ER 82 (CA).

[82] 'If the supply is for a consideration not consisting or not wholly consisting of money, its value shall be taken to be such an amount in money as, with the addition of the VAT chargeable, is equiva-lent to the consideration': VATA 1994, s 19(3).

be attributed to the non-cash consideration is to be measured. The jurisprudence of the European Court of Justice (as it was then titled) on this point[83] was considered and applied by the House of Lords in *Lex Services Ltd v CEC*.[84] The test is: 'such consideration is a subjective value since the basis of assessment for the provision of services is the consideration actually received and not a value assessed according to objective criteria'.[85] But subjective in that context means 'the value which the parties have themselves recognised in the course of their dealings and have in that way attributed to goods or services which amount to non-monetary consideration'.[86] This is not a purely subjective test as it requires the courts to look at what the parties by their agreement or course of dealings *must* have attributed the amount to be which is not necessarily what was in their thoughts.

This has been applied many times,[87] and one example will suffice. In *CEC v Westmorland Motorway Services Ltd*,[88] it was well known that a coach driver who brought a coach with at least 20 passengers and stopped for at least 30 minutes at the company's motorway service station[89] would be given, amongst other things, a free meal from the usual menu. The Court of Appeal found the consideration for the supply of that meal was the normal retail price and not the, lower, cost of providing it. That was the value the parties must have attributed to it. What the coach driver would have thought was the saving he made. VAT must be certain and a purely subjective test (the actual thoughts of the parties as opposed to the inference from the facts) would cause a great deal of uncertainty. The test is therefore in fact objective as applying the reasonable coach driver approach rather than any idiosyncrasies of an individual even if credible.

III. APPLYING THE SUBJECTIVE/OBJECTIVE TEST

So, there is nothing inherently novel in the idea of applying the objective/subjective test to discern the purposes of a taxpayer expending money in connection with a trade or profession. It should, as in VAT, encourage certainty and a level playing field for taxpayers. The reality following Lord Brightman's formulation

---

[83] See, eg, Judgment of 5 February 1980, *Staatssecretaris van Financien v Cooperatieve Aardappelenbewaarplaats GA*, C-154/80, EU.C.1981.38 and cases there cited.

[84] *Lex Services Ltd v CEC* [2003] UKHL 67; [2004] STC 11.

[85] [2004] STC 11, [17] (Lord Walker), quoting C-154/80, EU.C.1981.38, para 13.

[86] ibid, [19].

[87] See, eg, Judgment of 23 November 1988, *Naturally Yours Cosmetics Ltd v CEC*, C-230/87, EU.C:1988:508 and *Rosgill Group Ltd v CEC* [1997] STC 811 (CA). Only if it is impossible to extract a value from the course of dealing etc will an objective (cost) amount be used: see Judgment of 2 June 1994, *Empire Stores Ltd v CEC*, C-33/93, EU.C:1994:225.

[88] *CEC v Westmorland Motorway Services Ltd* [1998] STC 431 (CA).

[89] The service station in question is in fact in a very scenic part of the country (Cumbria) and has often received awards for its facilities, including an excellent local farm shop.

in *Mallalieu v Drummond*, however, has not proved to be quite so straightforward. There is a fundamental problem with that formulation. Take the 'uniform cases' as an example, with Lord Brightman's example of a nurse and her nursing uniform which must also clearly have two effects or consequences: one of fulfilling the needs of the profession and one of warmth and decency. Surely that nurse must also have the subconscious motive of the latter even if his/her conscious motive is the former. Why would Miss Mallalieu's subconscious motive count as a double purpose but the nurse's as an incidental effect? One difference of course is that nurses' uniforms are not everyday clothing whereas clothes from Marks & Spencer usually are. But why does that make a difference as to wholly and exclusively for the purposes of the profession? Necessity plays no part in that evaluation. So is the real distinction that most people could have worn the everyday clothes both for professional and personal purposes whereas the nurse's uniform is confined to the former. In effect is the real answer that warmth and decency in the latter case is an incidental effect simply because, having asked the correct question, it is, and that is a question of inference from the facts. As Lord Brightman said it is a question of fact and degree – a value judgement.

Given the need in double effect cases to distinguish between conscious and subconscious purposes and between subconscious purposes and incidental effects, it is not surprising that the courts have had since *Mallalieu v Drummond* to apply Lord Brightman's test to a variety of situations. In *MacKinlay v Arthur Young McClelland Moores & Co*,[90] the relocation costs paid by the partnership to two partners who moved to a new house because of moving offices within the firm were disallowed as having a double purpose: relocation for work and establishing a comfortable private home. Lord Oliver, who gave the only substantive speech, simply applied Lord Brightman's test – the latter must have been a purpose.[91]

More significantly, the Brightman test was also applied by the House of Lords in *McKnight v Sheppard*,[92] but in a way which produced a different result. The taxpayer was a stockbroker who incurred legal expenses in defending himself against breaches of the Stock Exchange Rules and who now claimed them as an allowable expense. The Revenue refused the claim partly on the basis that there was a double purpose – professional (to preserve his business) and personal (to preserve his reputation).[93] Lord Hoffmann who gave the only substantive speech decided that the personal aspect was only an incidental effect so that

[90] [1990] 2 AC 239, [1989] STC 898 (HL).

[91] The real problem in the case was that the earlier courts had concentrated on the motives of the partners paying the money and not on those of the partner receiving it. Partnership is not a legal entity so that the taxpayers were in fact paying themselves. It was therefore a 'much clearer and easier case than Mallalieu', [1989] STC 898, 906b.

[92] *McKnight v Sheppard* [1999] 1 WLR 1333, [1999] STC 669 (HL).

[93] They also argued, unsuccessfully, that such expenditure was not for the purposes of the trade at all. The fine he paid was, however, disallowed on policy grounds.

the sole purpose of the expenditure was professional.[94] But there was a slight twist to his analysis of the motive/effect distinction. The Special Commissioner had expressly found that despite the taxpayer saying that he did not care about his personal reputation, he did not accept that the taxpayer was unconcerned about the advantages of a successful defence for his personal relationship. But he still found that the sole object of the expenditure was professional, and Lord Hoffmann could see no inconsistency between the two.[95]

As a result, it is now possible for the taxpayer to have two conscious motives – professional and personal – which have two effects – professional and personal – but for the personal motive to be downgraded so that the personal effect becomes an incidental effect. Miss Mallalieu's accepted evidence was that she had no consideration of warmth and decency so that that had to be added on as a subconscious motive/purpose. In *McKnight*, the taxpayer's express denial of the secondary purpose was doubted, but nevertheless it was not added on as a dual purpose. The result is that preserving warmth and decency was found to be a dual purpose even though it genuinely never crossed the taxpayer's mind, whereas preservation of personal reputation was not a dual purpose even though it did cross the taxpayer's mind. Not a great deal of certainty there perhaps.

Lord Hoffmann in *McKnight* made no reference on that point to the Court of Appeal decision in *Vodafone Cellular Ltd v Shaw*, some two years earlier,[96] where Millett LJ (as he then was) sought to rephrase the subjective/objective issue.[97] Having summarised the propositions to be derived from *Mallalieu v Drummond* and *MacKinlay v Arthur Young McClelland Moores & Co*,[98] he added an additional one of his own:

> The question does not involve an inquiry of the taxpayer whether he consciously intended to obtain a trade or personal advantage by the payment. The primary inquiry is to ascertain what was the particular object of the taxpayer in making the payment. Once that is ascertained, its characterisation as a trade or private purpose is in my opinion a matter for the commissioners, not for the taxpayer.[99]

That re-emphasises the objective nature of the issue and it is instructive that when the Lord Justice went on to analyse *Mallalieu v Drummond*, he said that the primary question was not whether Miss Mallalieu intended one or two

---

[94] He likened the case to Lord Brightman's consultant who travelled to the Riviera purely to treat his patient.

[95] [1999] STC 669, 673f. Returning to the consultant analogy, Lord Hoffmann thought that it would be unlikely that the consultant would not have thought about 'sitting on the terrace with his friend and a bottle of Côtes de Provence', yet it would still have been allowed.

[96] *Vodafone Cellular Ltd v Shaw* [1997] STC 734 (CA).

[97] It should be noted that this was not a case involving everyday personal expenditure but a commercial transaction. Millett LJ had been counsel for the Crown in *Mallalieu*.

[98] These included the fact that there must be an enquiry into the taxpayer's intentions at the time, that there could be a single purpose with an incidental effect and that there is a distinction between subjective intentions and conscious motives.

[99] [1997] STC 734, 742j.

things but rather whether *it* was intended to achieve those two things. In what sense is 'it' subjective in that context?

Interestingly in *Vodafone Cellular Ltd v Shaw*, the Special Commissioners[100] had found that the company had had a dual purpose in making a payment because the directors had also sought to benefit its two trading subsidiaries.[101] They decided that the directors must have had in mind the fact that the payment would benefit the two subsidiaries more than the company itself.[102] The Court of Appeal reversed their decision on this point.[103] The Commissioners had confused benefit (effect) with purpose and had failed to ask what was the object the directors were seeking to achieve. They had only asked which company the directors were intending to benefit. The answer to that was clear, the purpose was to benefit the trading position of the whole group and the consequential ending of the group's arrangements for compensation was simply an incidental effect.[104] If one reads Millett LJ's additional proposition in that context it does of course explain the objectivity he required. The facts are a long way from *Mallalieu v Drummond*.

IV. OBJECTIVE TEST OF FACT AND LAW: FRAMING THE QUESTION

So, what is *Mallalieu v Drummond*'s legacy? It has clearly had the effect of limiting claims for trading expenses where the expenditure is on what can be regarded as satisfying everyday human needs. The reliance of the judge and the Court of Appeal on the specific factual elements and the accepted veracity of the taxpayer to limit potential claims was at best a rusty weapon. The issue as identified in the House of Lords, had it been decided the other way, would have surely opened the floodgates, leading to an endless series of claims based on conscious motives. These motives would all have had to be decided by the fact-finding body, now the First Instance Tribunal, as to whether the taxpayer's claim that there was no thought of Y but only of X could be believed.[105] There would have had to have been statutory intervention after over two hundred years. Instead, the hallowed wording of the section remains unchanged.[106]

To achieve that result, however, the House of Lords abrogated any idea that the issue was purely subjective (that is, as to what the taxpayer's conscious

---

[100] Upheld by Jacob J (see *Vodafone Cellular Ltd v Shaw* [1995] STC 353).

[101] The payment was made to relieve the three companies from the consequences of an unfavourable trading contract to purchase technology which was now redundant. The case was also fought on the issue as to whether that payment was one of income or capital.

[102] They would have had to reimburse the company if the trading contract had not been cancelled.

[103] Hirst LJ and Sir John Balcombe simply agreed with Millett LJ's judgment.

[104] [1997] STC 734, 745a.

[105] Or they could have thought that the taxpayer did consider Y but it was still only an incidental effect as the Special Commissioners so found in *McKnight v Sheppard* (above n 92).

[106] There have been some additions covering some specific everyday expenses, particularly business entertaining expense now prohibited, in the main, by s 45, ITTIOA 2005.

motives were). As Millett LJ opined in *Vodafone*, it was what 'its' (that is, spending the money's) object was. It is now for the Tribunal to decide that from the primary facts as they find them, unless of course that decision cannot be supported on those facts. The basic propositions from *Bentleys, Stokes and Lowless* remain, however. Purpose and effect are still to be distinguished, and a single purpose with an incidental effect is possible. The problem remains, however, especially in the case of everyday living expenses, as to why some private consequences are objects or purposes whilst others are incidental effects. If one looks at HMRC's website for example it tells you that you can potentially claim for: uniforms, protective clothing needed for work and costumes for actors and entertainers but not for ordinary clothing even if worn at work.[107]

In the fields of accommodation and meals, which might be regarded as the other major everyday human requirements, the application of the *Mallalieu* principle has produced another pragmatic rather than logical solution.[108] Apparently, the cost of accommodation and meals at the annual conference of a firm is deductible as a business expense, the obvious personal effects being incidental,[109] whereas meals on their own, even on a business trip have a dual purpose.[110] The situation regarding accommodation was discussed recently by the Upper Tribunal in *HMRC v Healy*,[111] where the taxpayer rented a flat in London for the duration of a musical in which he had a part. His home was in Manchester. Having reviewed the case law,[112] the Tribunal considered that whether the expenditure had a dual purpose was a matter of 'looking into the taxpayer's mind' and applying the 'dual purpose test'. They phrased the test as:

> Whether in all the circumstances of the case, the sole purpose for renting the flat was in order to carry on his profession of an actor. In order to determine that issue [the Tribunal] needed to consider whether the effect of his taking the flat, namely of providing him with the warmth, shelter and comfort that we all need was merely incidental to that purpose or was a shared purpose.[113]

On the case being remitted to the First Instance Tribunal, their answer was that because the flat had three bedrooms, part of the intention of renting it was to provide a family home rather than a *pied a terre*.[114] The taxpayer's intentions were therefore ultimately determined by counting the number of bedrooms.

---

[107] Gov UK, *Expenses if you're self-employed*, available at www.gov.uk/expenses-if-youre-self-employed/clothing.

[108] The same question arises about travelling expenses for the self-employed as, unlike employee taxation, there is no separate provision for them (see, eg, *Samadian v HMRC* [2014] STC 763, [2014] UKUT 0013 (TCC)).

[109] *Watkis v Ashford Sparkes & Harwood* [1985] 1 WLR 994, [1985] STC 451.

[110] *Caillebotte v Quinn* [1975] 1 WLR 731, [1975] STC 265.

[111] *HMRC v Healy* [2013] UKUT 0337 (TCC).

[112] See especially *Hanlin v HMRC* [2011] UKFTT 213 (TC).

[113] [2013] UKUT 0337, para 69.

[114] *HMRC v Healy* [2015] UKFTT 4425 (TC).

That is clearly using objective criteria to ascertain a subjective intent by the pragmatic use of facts.

That case is a prime example of the two important consequences of the *Mallalieu* decision which have stood the test of time. First, that the question as to whether an 'everyday' expense has been incurred wholly and exclusively for the purposes of the trade, although subjective in nature, is to be answered by reference to an objective dissection of the taxpayer's purpose(s) of the expenditure. It is not limited to conscious motives. The second is that that issue is then resolved into a question of fact after asking the question – was there one purpose with two effects or two purposes with two effects? It follows that so long as the First Instance Tribunal asks itself that question correctly its decision will stand unless it fails to identify the salient facts in reaching its decision.[115] Of course there will always be apparent anomalies as to why a particular effect is incidental as opposed to being a shared purpose, but the law and practice since *Mallalieu* have developed pragmatic guidelines to assist in this process. Some types of expenditure are regarded as obviously dual purpose (everyday clothing), others seem to indicate a presumption of a single purpose (uniforms). So, in typical common law fashion the system works even though some of the distinctions are difficult to justify logically.

Above all, the decision in *Mallalieu* prevented the system from potentially being blown wide open. It did this in a very British way, with a clever sleight of hand by continuing to promulgate the subjective test of fact whilst turning it into what was, in reality, an objective one of fact and law, camouflaged as an issue of fact. Its solution was one which tribunals could work with.[116] It also meant that the 1805 wording could continue to work even in a very different age, not just for everyday expenses but across the whole range.

---

[115] For an example of a misreading of what constituted the taxpayer's trade and so whether the expenditure was wholly and exclusively for the purposes of its trade, see *HMRC v McLaren Racing Ltd* [2014] UKUT 0269 (TCC); [2014] STC 2417.

[116] For just one recent example see *The Crown and Cushion Hotel (Chipping Norton) Ltd v HMRC* [2016] UKFTT 0765 (TCC) as to whether sporting sponsorship was allowable. See the judge's statement that 'the effect of the statutory provision is well known' and her summary of that effect at paras 113 *et seq*.

14

Zim Properties Ltd v Proctor *(1985)*
Compromise of Action, Compensation and CGT

DAVID SALTER

ZIM PROPERTIES LTD *v Proctor*[1] is one of a number of cases[2] decided in the late 1970s/early 1980s which are concerned with aspects of the 'new' capital gains tax which had been introduced in the Finance Act 1965 (FA 1965).[3] The early judicial probing in these cases focused, principally, on the interpretation of several (interlocking) provisions in the FA 1965, namely sections 19(1) and 22(1)–(3) and, more particularly, with the meaning to be attributed to operative words such as 'asset'[4] and the parameters of phrases such as 'capital sum derived from an asset'.[5]

In 1978 in his judgment in *Aberdeen Construction Group Ltd v CIR*,[6] Lord Wilberforce offered general guidance on the approach to the judicial interpretation of the relatively novel provisions in FA 1965. His Lordship acknowledged that FA 1965 was necessarily *complicated* and that its detailed provisions should be considered with care. Nevertheless, a guiding principle for any interpretation of FA 1965 was that its purpose is to tax capital gains and to allow for capital losses, each of which should be determined by applying normal business

---

[1] *Zim Properties Ltd v Proctor* (1985) 58 TC 371.
[2] See, eg, *O'Brien v Benson's Hosiery (Holdings) Ltd* [1980] AC 562; *Marren v Ingles* [1980] 1 WLR 983; *Davenport v Chilver* [1983] STC 426; and *Drummond v Austin* [1984] STC 321.
[3] For the background to the introduction of capital gains tax in the UK, see D Stopforth, 'The Birth of Capital Gains Tax – The Official View' [2005] *BTR* 584. See also A Seely, 'Capital Gains Tax: Background History', House of Commons Library, SN860 (2 June 2010).
[4] See RS Evans, '"Assets" for Capital Gains Tax Purposes' (1988) 138 *NLJ* 275.
[5] These provisions have been reproduced in subsequent consolidations of UK capital gains tax in the Capital Gains Tax Act 1979 (CGTA 1979) and the Taxation of Chargeable Gains Act 1992 (TCGA 1992), and can now be found, respectively, in ss 1(1), 21(1)–(2) and 22(1)–(3), TCGA 1992. See P Sparkes, 'The Derivation of Capital Sums' [1987] *BTR* 323.
[6] *Aberdeen Construction Group Ltd v CIR* [1978] AC 885.

principles. In this respect, courts should be wary of accepting interpretative results which were paradoxical and contrary to business sense. In short and more generally, his Lordship declared 'the capital gains tax is a tax upon gains: it is not a tax upon arithmetical differences'.[7]

This chapter focuses, initially, on the judgment of Warner J in *Zim Properties* noting, in particular and in light of the above guidance, his approach to the interpretation of the statutory provisions in FA 1965 which were relevant to the determination of that case. Consideration is then given to the reaction from commentators, decisions in several subsequent cases and, as will be seen, significantly from, initially, the Inland Revenue and, latterly, HMRC. The chapter concludes with some reflections.

At the time it was decided, it might have been reasonable to expect that this High Court decision would not have retained any greater degree of prominence than other decisions of similar ilk which were similarly concerned with early interpretation of the capital gains tax provisions in FA 1965. However, as this chapter shows, *Zim Properties*, notwithstanding that it was far from universally welcomed, has, possibly due in part to the reaction to it by the Inland Revenue (now HMRC), enjoyed longevity and a lasting influence that warrants its designation as a landmark case in revenue law.

I. *ZIM PROPERTIES*

Zim Properties concerned a right of action by a company, Zim Properties Ltd (the taxpayer company) against its solicitors, for damages in negligence arising from advice given by the solicitors relating to a sale of certain properties by Zim Properties Ltd which fell through. A capital sum was received by the company by way of compromise of that action. The question for determination in the High Court (Warner J) was whether that capital sum was derived from the right of action itself or the properties, the aborted 'sale' of which had given rise to the right of action.

The Special Commissioners, who found the issues in the case 'elusive and difficult', rejected the taxpayer company's contentions, first, that the capital sum was 'derived' from the properties (the consequence of which was that it could not make a deduction of the acquisition costs of those properties in computing any liability to capital gains tax on the capital sum) and, secondly, that no tax was payable because there was no asset from which the capital sum was derived; a right to compensation for loss is not an 'asset' for capital gains tax purposes.

---

[7] ibid, 893. See also the subsequent reiteration by Lord Wilberforce that capital gains tax is not a tax on arithmetical differences and his declaration that it 'was created to operate in the real world, not the world of make-belief' in *Ramsay (WT) Ltd v CIR* [1982] AC 300, 326.

The Special Commissioners rejected the taxpayer company's contentions. They determined that (1) the taxpayer company's right of action against its solicitors was a chose in action that fell within the definition of 'asset' in section 22(1) FA 1965; (2) the capital sum was derived from that right within the meaning of the general words of section 22(3) of FA 1965 and that payment of that sum constituted a part disposal of that right; (3) for the purpose of computing the amount of the chargeable gain, the taxpayer company's right arose when the contract was entered into, ie, 12 July 1973 and it had been acquired 'otherwise than by way of a bargain made at arm's length' within the meaning of section 22(4) FA 1965. Therefore, it was deemed to have been acquired for a consideration equal to its market value at that date.

Both parties appealed against the Special Commissioners' findings. In the High Court, counsel for the taxpayer company reiterated the above contentions whilst the Crown cross appealed that section 22(4) FA 1965 had no application in computing the taxpayer company's chargeable gain because there had been no 'acquisition' by the taxpayer company of the right to sue its solicitors.

After summarising the facts, Warner J considered the contentions of the parties. With regard to the taxpayer company's primary contention that the capital sum was derived from the properties, Warner J identified the statutory provisions that were directly relevant to that contention, namely section 19(1) and section 22(1), (2) and (3) of FA 1965. Section 19(1) was the general charging provision. It provided that: 'Tax shall be charged in accordance with this Act in respect of capital gains, that is to say chargeable capital gains computed in accordance with this Act and accruing to a person on the disposal of assets'. The above provisions of section 22 were set out in Warner J's judgment as follows:

(1) *All forms of property shall be assets* for the provisions of this Part of the Act, whether situated in the United Kingdom or not, including – (a) options, debts and incorporeal property generally, and (b) any currency other than sterling, and (c) any form of property created by the person disposing of it, or otherwise coming to be owned without being acquired.

(2) For the purposes of this Part of this Act – (a) *references to a disposal of an asset include*, except where the context otherwise requires, references to a *part disposal of an asset*, and (b) there is a part disposal of an asset where an interest or right in or over the asset is created by the disposal, as well as where it subsists before the disposal, and, generally, there is a part disposal of an asset where, on a person making a disposal, any description of property derived from the asset remains undisposed of.

(3) Subject to subsection (6) of this section, and to the exceptions in this Part of this Act, *there is* for the purposes of this Part of this Act *a disposal of assets by their owner where any capital sum is derived from assets notwithstanding that no asset is acquired by the person paying the capital sum*, and this subsection applies in particular to – (a) capital sums received by way of compensation for any kind of damage or injury to assets, or for the loss, destruction or dissipation of assets or for any depreciation or risk of depreciation of an asset, (b) capital sums received under a policy of

insurance of the risk of any kind of damage or injury to, or the loss or depreciation of, assets, (c) capital sums received in return for forfeiture or surrender of rights, or for refraining from exercising rights, and (d) capital sums received as consideration for use or exploitation of assets.[8]

The taxpayer's company's primary contention involved, initially, a rejection of the Special Commissioners' finding that the capital sum was derived from the company's right of action against the solicitors; a finding that was supported by counsel for the Crown before Warner J. In this respect, it was argued on behalf of the taxpayer company that, in this case, the company's 'right of action' was 'no more than a claim which might or might not succeed'. This was not a form of property and, therefore, could not be an asset for capital gains tax purposes. Counsel for the Crown submitted that either the right of action was a form of property or, if it was not a form of property, it was, nevertheless, an 'asset' for capital gains tax purposes.[9] Warner J found in favour of the Crown. He said:

> I have, after considerable hesitation, come to the conclusion that counsel for the Crown is entitled to succeed on that point. He is entitled to do so, I think ... on the strength of the decision of the House of Lords in O'Brien v Benson's Hosiery (Holdings) Ltd. True the contractual rights that were held to constitute an asset for capital gains tax purposes were undisputed. They were not a mere claim. But that formed no part of the ratio decidendi of the case. The ratio decidendi was that those rights were an asset for capital gains tax purposes because they were something that could be turned to account.[10]

As indicated in the above extract, Warner J relied on the reasoning of House of Lords in *O'Brien*[11] in support of the position that the words of section 22(1) of FA 1965 did not require that an 'asset' for capital gains tax purposes should necessarily consist of some form of property. Warner J suggested that this position might have been reached by the House of Lords in one of two ways. First, it was possible to take the view that section 22(1) was not intended to provide an exhaustive definition of 'assets', but to enact that it included all forms of property which would mean that 'assets' was a wider concept than 'property' and that it included any right that could be turned to account. Alternatively, in agreeing with the approach adopted by Fox J and restoring his decision at first instance, their Lordships may have decided that, as did Fox J, the word 'property' was not a precise term and that, therefore, its meaning might vary depending on the context.[12] Walton J concluded that whichever of these ways

---

[8] *Zim Properties* (above n 1) 386–87 (emphasis added).

[9] In support of his submission, counsel for the Crown opined that it would be undesirable to reach a conclusion that would make it necessary in a later similar case for the Commissioners to decide whether a civil action which had been compromised would or would not have succeeded.

[10] *Zim Properties* (above n 1) 387–88.

[11] *O'Brien v Benson's Hosiery (Holdings) Ltd* (1979) 53 TC 241.

[12] In this respect, Warner J also referred to *Trendtex Trading Corporation v Credit Suisse* [1980] 3 All ER 721 in which Oliver LJ used the phrases 'right of property' and 'property rights' in relation to

represented the position taken by the House of Lords in *O'Brien*, it would be inconsistent with that decision

> to hold that a right to bring an action to seek to enforce a claim that was not frivolous or vexatious, which right could be turned to account by negotiating a capital sum, could not be an 'asset' within the meaning of that term in the capital gains tax legislation.[13]

Having decided that a right of action may constitute an asset for capital gains tax purposes, Warner J returned to and rejected the taxpayer company's primary contention that the capital sum was derived from the properties and that receipt of the capital sum should be treated as a part disposal of those properties.[14] Apropos the first limb of this contention, Warner J considered, as he put it, the 'reality of the matter' which involved looking for 'the real (rather than the immediate) source of the capital sum'.[15] This was an approach, which as will be seen, commended itself to judges in subsequent cases and involves determining whether it is possible in a given case to identify a right of action as the 'real' source of a capital sum from any property to which it relates. In *Zim Properties*, Warner J was not persuaded that the capital sum was derived from the properties which were 'unaffected and unimpaired' by the aborted contract. Further, this was not a case in which the capital sum could be attributed, simply, to a right to compensation for loss which, as suggested by counsel for the taxpayer company, was not an 'asset' for capital gains tax purposes and in respect of which, therefore, no liability to capital gains tax could arise, ie, this was a pure capital gain.[16] In this regard, Warner J stated that he had no difficulty in accepting that not every right to a payment is an 'asset' for capital gains tax purposes, for example, the right of a seller of property to the payment of the price where the property itself is the 'asset'. This was indicative of the fact that the interpretation of capital gains legislation requires 'the exercise of common sense, rather than just the brute application of verbal formulae'.[17]

Warner J decided that 'the reality of the matter' dictated that the capital sum received by the taxpayer company was derived from the right of action which was the relevant asset for capital gains tax purposes. Consequently, the

---

the right to litigate and did so regardless of whether litigation undertaken in pursuance of that right would succeed.

[13] *Zim Properties* (above n 1) 390.

[14] Counsel for the taxpayer company submitted that the capital sum was derived from the properties under ss 22(2) and 22(3), FA 1965 and that the receipt of capital sum should be regarded as a part disposal of those properties by virtue of either the 'general words' in s 22(3) or, alternatively, in accordance with either s 22(3)(a) or section 22(3)(c), FA 1965.

[15] *Zim Properties* (above n 1) 391.

[16] This finding which discounted the taxpayer company's secondary contention, namely that, in the event of a determination that the capital sum was not derived from the properties, there was no 'asset' from which the capital sum was derived.

[17] *Zim Properties* (above n 1) 392.

arguments presented on behalf of the taxpayer company in support of the primary contention, which were predicated, broadly, on the proposition that the capital sum was derived from the properties, could not succeed. In reality, the right of action was the 'real' source of the capital sum. A necessary corollary of this outcome was that the second limb of the taxpayer's main contention that the capital sum could be treated as arising from a part disposal of the properties was also unsuccessful.

One further consequence of this decision and one which, as will be seen, has attracted some criticism was that the capital sum was treated as a chargeable gain for capital gains tax purposes without any deduction for acquisition expenditure incurred in relation to the properties (nor did it allow for the availability of reliefs which might be used to shelter the gain).

Finally, and in furtherance of the finding that the capital sum was derived from the right of action, Warner J decided that the taxpayer company acquired this right at the time when the aborted contract of sale was entered into. This acquisition was 'not by way of a bargain made at arm's length', and so under section 22(4) of FA 1965 the taxpayer company should be deemed to have acquired that right for a consideration equal to its market value. In computing the amount of the liability to tax in respect of the capital sum the market value of the taxpayer company's right of action at the time of its acquisition should be deducted.

In the light of these findings, the appeal and cross-appeal were dismissed.

As indicated above, it is possible to view *Zim Properties* as simply an example of purposive judicial interpretation conducted, as advocated by the House of Lords in *Aberdeen Construction*,[18] in accordance with normal business principles. If so, there is little, arguably, to distinguish it from the other early and exploratory decisions relating to the interpretation of FA 1965 which have been alluded to in this chapter.[19] However, as will be seen, its significance is not so confined and lies, initially, in Warner J's perception of what, in the absence of an all-embracing definition of 'asset' in FA 1965,[20] might, generically and then more specifically in relation to rights of action, constitute an 'asset' for capital gains tax purposes. In the former respect, it has been seen that Warner J purported to follow the reasoning of the House of Lords in *O'Brien*[21] with the consequence that he felt that 'asset' might either be regarded as a wider concept than property or, more narrowly, fall within the compass of property in appropriate circumstances. However, his disavowal of the various authorities relating to the concept of a chose in action, which had been cited by counsel for the Crown to establish whether a right of action might be treated as an 'asset', suggests that Warner J

---

[18] *Aberdeen Construction* (above n 6).
[19] See above n 2.
[20] A position which, of course, has not been altered by subsequent capital gains tax legislation.
[21] *O'Brien* (above n 11).

was more inclined to the view that provided a right of action could be 'turned to account' that would be sufficient for it to constitute an 'asset' (even though the right of action in *Zim Properties* could not be directly equated to the contractual rights in *O'Brien*).

The decision in *Zim Properties* has been variously described by commentators. John Walters has referred to the decision as 'extraordinary',[22] whilst David Southern QC (*Southern*) in a recent paper presented to the Chancery Bar Association and Revenue Bar Association stated that, in his opinion, the law had taken a wrong turn in *Zim Properties*. He also felt that it was 'inconvenient' pointing out, first, that a right of action generally has no base cost with the result that the whole amount of compensation is liable to capital gain tax, secondly, that the identification of the source of the capital sum is problematic where there is an underlying asset (ie, the properties in *Zim Properties*) and finally, the underlying asset may be exempt whereas the right of action will always be a chargeable asset.[23]

Zim Properties has also been considered, judicially, in the three cases included in the next part of this chapter. Whilst it may be the case that references in these cases to *Zim Properties* are somewhat oblique there is no retraction from the position adopted by Warner J as to the generic meaning of 'asset' for capital gains tax purposes and its compatibility or otherwise with 'property', or questioning of the ratio decidendi in *Zim Properties*, namely that a right of action to enforce a claim, which is not frivolous or vexatious and that may be turned to account by negotiating a compromise yielding a capital sum, may constitute an 'asset'. This is important especially within the context of the introduction by the Inland Revenue in 1988, three years after *Zim Properties*, of Extra Statutory Concession ESC D33,[24] which, inter alia, it has been suggested by Southern, in effect, 'overrules' *Zim Properties*;[25] a matter to which further attention will be given in the final substantive part of this chapter.

II. POST-*ZIM PROPERTIES* CASES

As intimated above, the cases examined in this part of the chapter, namely *Pennine Raceway Ltd v Kirklees Metropolitan Council (No 2)*,[26] *Weston v HMRC*[27]

---

[22] J Walters, 'Taxation of Damages, Costs and Interest (3)' (2003) II(2) *GITC Review* 75.

[23] D Southern, 'Changes to the taxation of compensation (ESC D33)', Chancery Bar Association/ Revenue Bar Association (25 March 2015), available at www.chba.org.uk/for-members/library/all-london-seminars/2015-seminars/changes-to-the-taxation-of-compensation-esc-d33, 5–6, 8.

[24] Inland Revenue, 'Capital Gains Tax on Compensation and Damages; Zim Properties Ltd – Compensation and Damages', ESC D33, available at webarchive.nationalarchives.gov. uk/20140604074002/http://www.hmrc.gov.uk//news/extra-statutory-concession-d33-changes. htm#8.

[25] Southern (above n 23) 6.

[26] *Pennine Raceway Ltd v Kirklees Metropolitan Council (No 2)* [1989] STC 122 (CA).

[27] *Weston v HMRC* [2014] UKFTT TC03152.

and *Hardy v HMRC*[28] are concerned with instances where a taxpayer had received a capital sum or incurred a capital loss and where the court or tribunal sought, inter alia, to identify, within the context of capital gains tax, the source from which that capital sum or capital loss was derived. To use the phraseology employed by Warner J in *Zim Properties* the court or tribunal was required to seek out the 'real' source of the capital sum or capital loss. Similarly, as in *Zim Properties*, it was conceivable, as will be seen, that in each case the respective capital sums or capital losses might be regarded as derived from a right of action to which the taxpayers were entitled and which, correspondingly, fell within the meaning of 'asset' for capital gains tax purposes.

Thus, in *Pennine Raceway*, the pertinent question was whether a compensation payment was attributable to a statutory right of action or to the asset in respect of which the compensation was payable. In this case, Pennine Racing Ltd (the company) had been granted a licence, which accorded with an existing planning permission, to conduct drag racing on a disused airfield. Kirklees Metropolitan Council (the council) decided to revoke that permission. A subsequent application for a new planning permission was refused, ultimately, by the Secretary of State. Thereafter, the company sought compensation under section 164(1) of the Town and Country Planning Act 1971 (TCPA 1971) for loss of profits incurred as a result of the revocation of the initial planning permission.[29] The Lands Tribunal awarded compensation to the company on the basis of loss of profits from which it deducted tax in order 'to reflect the corporation income tax which would have been payable by the company if those profits had in fact been earned in the relevant years'. The Lands Tribunal added that the compensation was not intended to be a capital payment, but if it was so regarded it was not derived from an asset (the licence) nor paid as compensation for any damage or injury to an asset within the meaning of section 20(1)(a) of the Capital Gains Tax Act 1979 (CGTA 1979).[30]

In the light of this finding, the company assumed that there would be no liability to tax on the compensation which it received and did not appeal. In due course, the Inland Revenue informed the company that the compensation was liable to capital gains tax on the compensation payment. In view of the prospect of double taxation to which this gave rise, the company appealed against the Lands Tribunal decision and argued, inter alia, that as the compensation was taxable (whether as income or as a chargeable gain) it should have been paid by

---

[28] *Hardy v HMRC* [2016] UKUT 0332 (TCC).

[29] More specifically, s 164(1), TCPA 1971 provides, inter alia, that where planning permission is revoked or modified and, on a claim to the local planning authority, it is shown that a person interested in land has sustained loss or damage which is directly attributable to that revocation or modification the local planning authority shall pay that person compensation for that loss or damage.

[30] See now s 22(1)(a), TCGA 1992.

the council without any deduction. The council submitted that it was clear that the compensation, whether it was classified as income or capital, would not be taxed in the hands of the company and that the Lands Tribunal had been correct to make the deduction (although some adjustment of the actual figures might be necessary) and award a net sum. Moreover, however, the compensation was calculated by the Lands Tribunal, must be treated as capital in the hands of the company and, as such, was not subject to capital gains tax as it did not constitute a capital sum derived from an asset (the licence) within the meaning of section 20(1)(a) of CGTA 1979; it was compensation derived from the statutory right to compensation given by section 164(1) of TCPA 1971.

In allowing the appeal, the Court of Appeal found, without deciding whether the compensation was properly taxable as income or capital, that the council should pay the compensation gross as it would be taxable in the hands of the company. In making this finding, the members of the Court of Appeal (Croom-Johnson, Ralph Gibson and Stuart-Smith LLJ) indicated that if the compensation was to be regarded as a capital sum[31] it was necessary in the words of Warner J in *Zim Properties* to look 'for the real (rather than the immediate) source of the capital sum'.[32] In this respect, the fact that a right to sue for compensation arose under a statutory provision, namely section 164 of TCPA 1971, did not prevent the compensation awarded from being a capital sum derived from an asset within the meaning of section 20(1) of CGTA 1979. In the words of Croom-Johnson LJ:

> In my view, the authorities cited by counsel for the council [*Davis (Inspector of Taxes) v Powell; Drummond (Inspector of Taxes) v Brown* and *Davenport (Inspector of Taxes) v Chilver*] do not support a general proposition that compensation awarded by statute is outside s 20 of the Capital Gains Tax Act 1979. One must look in each case to see whether the capital sum is derived from the asset or something else.[33]

In this case, the Court of Appeal took the view that the pertinent asset was the licence to operate drag racing and not the statutory right of action against the council for revoking the planning permission. As an asset, the licence depreciated in value when the planning permission was revoked to the extent that it had become worthless. Hence, the asset had sustained loss or damage for which the company was entitled to compensation. For the purposes of section 20(1) CGTA 1979, it was a capital sum derived from that asset. In the leading judgment, Croom-Johnson LJ explained the rationale for the Court of Appeal's decision. He stated that the company had an asset, namely the licence, and that it had depreciated in value when the planning permission was revoked.

---

[31] It was accepted by the company and the council that if the compensation was for loss of profits it would also be taxable in the hands of the company.

[32] See *Pennine Raceway* (above 26) 130 (Croom-Johnson LJ); 133 (Ralph Gibson LJ); and 137 (Stuart-Smith LJ).

[33] ibid, 130.

Such depreciation entitled the company to a capital sum by way of compensation (a right to compensation that was given by TCPA 1971), because the licence had sustained loss or damage which was directly attributable to the revocation of the planning permission. For capital gains tax purposes, the capital sum (compensation) was 'derived' from the asset.

Further, as Stuart-Smith LJ observed, the fact that the right to compensation is statutory as opposed to one that arises at common law does not prevent the capital sum being derived from the asset. The capital sum was derived from the depreciation of the licence. The revocation of the planning permission turned the licence into 'a totally emasculated creature compared with what it was before; indeed although the licence continued alive it could be likened to someone in permanent coma'.[34]

It is clear that the Court of Appeal acknowledged the existence of the statutory right of action and contemplated the possibility, as had been mooted by the council, that the compensation paid to the taxpayer could have been attributed to that right of action. Nevertheless, it found that, on the facts, the compensation was paid to cover the depreciation in the value of the licence (the underlying asset) which had arisen as a result of the revocation of the planning permission. Consequently, the licence, not the statutory right of action, was the real source of the compensation and, further, the depreciation in the value of the licence might be contrasted with the 'unaffected and unimpaired' properties in *Zim Properties*.

In the subsequent case of *Weston*,[35] Mr Weston invested £1,000,000 in a non-negotiable Certificate of Deposit (the CD) issued to him by the Stanford International Bank Limited (SIB) in June 2006. The CD provided that 'unless otherwise stated, all amounts specified are in US Dollars or an equivalent amount if deposits are made in currency other than US Dollars'. The CD with accrued interest was due to mature in June 2009. In April 2009, SIB went into liquidation and was the subject of a complaint by the US Securities and Exchange Commission which alleged fraud. Subsequently, Mr Weston made a claim in the liquidation of SIB which was accepted by the liquidators. It became apparent that any distribution to depositors with SIB was likely to be '10 pence in the pound'. Consequently, Mr Weston made a negligible value claim in his tax return for the tax year 2008/09 (amounting to 90 per cent of his initial deposit and the outstanding interest due under the CD which was unpaid) to the effect that his claim against SIB had become of negligible value whilst owned by him. He sought to use some of the loss to which the negligible claim gave rise against chargeable capital gains arising in the tax year 2008/09 and to carry forward unused losses arising in respect of the negligible value claim to be set off against chargeable capital gains arising in the subsequent tax year, 2009/10.

---

[34] ibid, 137.
[35] *Weston* (above n 27).

In 2012, HMRC issued closure notices which disallowed the capital losses which had been claimed by Mr Weston by way of the negligible value claim in the above tax years.

Mr Weston appealed to the First-tier Tribunal against these closure notices.

The issues for determination by the First-tier Tribunal were whether, first, Mr Weston's investment represented by the CD constituted a chargeable asset for capital gains tax purposes, and secondly, if so, whether that asset became of negligible value within the meaning of section 24 TCGA 1992 at the time when Mr Weston's claim for capital loss relief was made in the tax year 2008/09.[36]

It was submitted on behalf of Mr Weston that the asset which he held was either a dollar asset (comprising either foreign currency or a foreign currency bank account) or, alternatively (which is pertinent to this chapter), a right of action against SIB either acquired for the cost of that asset or derived from that asset; the right of action was a chargeable asset for capital gains tax purposes which had become of negligible value in 2008/09. The former stance was supported by the evidence that SIB's monetary assets were denominated in US dollars, ie, its financial statements were drawn up in US dollars and by the acceptance by the liquidators of SIB of Mr Weston's claim expressed in US dollars which showed the reality of Mr Weston's asset as a dollar asset. As to the alternative submission, namely that Mr Weston's asset was a right of action against SIB, it was contended that the CD was an instrument of fraud and that, in reality, Mr Weston's asset was the right to sue SIB for the misappropriation of his funds. In this respect, the base cost of this asset was what he paid for it, ie, £1,000,000 and the deemed disposal proceeds the 'negligible value' (meaning virtually worthless or having no market value) supporting the negligible value claim. It was suggested that this satisfied normal business principles and was in accordance with the decision in *Zim Properties*.

HMRC submitted that the asset held by Mr Weston was not a dollar asset. It was a debt denominated in sterling. Such a debt was not an asset for capital gains tax purposes and so no chargeable gain (or allowable loss) could accrue to Mr Weston (the original creditor) on the disposal of that debt. On redemption of the CD, the amount that Mr Weston was entitled to expect to receive was £1,000,000 together with accrued interest, not the sterling equivalent of an amount expressed in US dollars. Further, if, as submitted on behalf of Mr Weston, the asset held by Mr Weston was a dollar asset it did not become of negligible value in 2008/2009. The phrase 'negligible value' meant 'next to nothing' – this did not cover an expectation of a dividend of 10 pence in the pound. HMRC acknowledged that Mr Weston might have a chargeable asset in the form of a right of action against SIB for the misappropriation of his funds,

---

[36] The pertinent provisions of s 24, TCGA 1992, namely sub-sections (1)(a) and (1)(b) provide that a negligible value claim may be made by the owner of an asset if the asset has become of negligible value while owned by the owner.

but submitted that its acquisition cost would be nil as it was not acquired in consideration for the sum given for the CD but by accretion, ie, as a consequence of Mr Weston's acquisition of the CD and SIB's subsequent alleged misappropriation of his funds.

The First-tier Tribunal determined that the CD was a sterling deposit made with SIB. This transaction set up the relationship of debtor (SIB) and creditor (Mr Weston) between the parties. Mr Weston's subsequent claim based on the CD was a sterling claim against SIB, albeit one that could be satisfied by an equivalent payment in US dollars. The asset acquired by Mr Weston was not currency other than sterling and was a debt in relation to which Mr Weston was and remained the original creditor and SIB the debtor. Accordingly, the CD was not a chargeable asset for capital gains tax purposes and no chargeable gain or allowable loss could arise on its disposal.

As to the related question of whether Mr Weston was entitled to the capital loss relief claimed by reason of his right of action against SIB for non-performance by SIB of its obligations under the CD, the First-tier Tribunal found that although Mr Weston had a right of action against SIB, which was acquired when he made the investment in the CD, that right was not a separate asset for capital gains tax purposes. It was merely one of the rights which Mr Weston held by virtue of holding the CD, and it was a right that was akin to the right of a seller of property to the payment of the price. Moreover, it would be 'very difficult or impossible' to apportion the consideration paid by Mr Weston for the CD between the rights making up the beneficial ownership of the CD. The full consideration was given for the CD.

Consequently, neither the CD nor Mr Weston's right of action against SIB was a relevant asset for capital gains tax purposes and, in view of this, the First-tier Tribunal dismissed the appeal. This outcome obviated the need for the First-tier Tribunal to consider whether the CD became of negligible value in the tax year 2008/2009.[37]

Within the context of this chapter, the critical finding was that whilst Mr Weston had acquired a right of action it had no 'independent' existence for capital gains tax purposes, but, rather, it was subsumed within the bundle of rights to which he was entitled as the holder of the CD which, itself, did not qualify, for the reasons given by the First-tier Tribunal, as an 'asset' for capital gains tax purposes. As a consequence, he did not qualify for the capital loss relief which he had claimed.

---

[37] Nevertheless, the First-tier Tribunal opined that the CD had a negligible value within the meaning of s 24, TCGA 1992 because it would have been impossible for Mr Weston to realise anything more than a negligible consideration if he had disposed of the CD in the open market to a willing purchaser. This did not, however, mean that the capital loss relief sought by Mr Weston should be allowed. In keeping with the First-tier Tribunal's finding that the CD was not a chargeable asset for capital gains tax purposes, it followed, as the First-tier Tribunal had stated earlier in its decision, that no loss arising in respect thereof could be regarded as an allowable loss (see *Weston* (above n 27) paras 53–60).

Consequently, whilst the taxpayer was entitled to a right of action it was not regarded as an independent asset for capital gains tax purposes, but was simply a constituent element of the CD.

Recently, in *Hardy*,[38] Mr Hardy appealed to the Upper Tribunal following a decision of the First-tier Tribunal to uphold a closure notice issued by HMRC which disallowed a claim by Mr Hardy for capital loss relief in respect of the deposits on the purchase of two properties which were forfeited when he was unable to complete the contracts. The appeal to the Upper Tribunal related to the closure notice that applied in respect of one only of the two forfeited deposits which had been considered by the First-tier Tribunal.

Before the Upper Tribunal, the facts were not in dispute. Mr Hardy and his wife entered into the pertinent contract with St James Group Ltd (the vendor) on 7 May 2008 to purchase a leasehold property in Roehampton. A deposit comprising 10 per cent of the purchase price was paid. This sum was to be credited against the purchase price on completion. The date for completion was 22 May 2009. On that date, Mr Hardy and his wife were unable to raise sufficient funds to complete, because they had been unable to sell two properties which they owned jointly; sales which had been intended to part fund the purchase. The vendor served a completion notice on Mr Hardy and his wife on 27 May 2009. Mr Hardy and his wife were unable to complete. Accordingly, on 12 June 2009, the vendor rescinded the contract and forfeited the deposit. Subsequently, Mr Hardy and his wife disposed of the two properties the proceeds of which they had planned to use to fund the aborted purchase(s). Each of these sales gave rise to a capital gain.

In 2012, Mr Hardy filed a self-assessment tax return for the tax year 2009/10. In that return, he declared the above-mentioned gains (even though the properties had been in the names of himself and his wife) and sought to set off the losses arising from the forfeiture of the deposits against those capital gains. HMRC disallowed his claim to those capital losses.

As intimated above, the First-tier Tribunal, on appeal, dismissed Mr Hardy's appeal against the closure notices in which HMRC disallowed his claim for the capital losses. In so doing, it rejected Mr Hardy's argument that on entering into the contracts to purchase the two properties he acquired the beneficial ownership of those properties, and that, consequently, when the vendor rescinded the contracts he had disposed of that asset and suffered losses commensurate with the forfeited deposits. The First-tier Tribunal stated, inter alia, that the exchange of contracts did not signify the acquisition of assets by Mr Hardy because the intended transactions did not take place, and the rescission of those contracts did not amount to a disposal of assets on which either a gain or a loss could be realised.

[38] *Hardy* (above n 28).

In the course of its determination, the Upper Tribunal considered three questions: (i) did Mr Hardy acquire an asset?; (ii) did Mr Hardy dispose of an asset?; and (iii) did Mr Hardy incur an allowable loss?

In these respects, it was contended on behalf of Mr Hardy that when he entered into the contract he had acquired valuable rights. These rights constituted an asset and when the vendor rescinded the contract those rights were extinguished. This was a disposal which resulted in a loss corresponding to the forfeited deposit. In turn, this was an allowable loss for capital gains tax purposes. HMRC denied that Mr Hardy had acquired an asset. If, however, he was regarded as having acquired an asset he had not disposed of it. Finally, if he was regarded as having disposed of an asset, the loss incurred through the forfeiture of the deposit did not amount to an allowable loss.

Before embarking on its consideration of the three questions, the Upper Tribunal reiterated the principle enunciated by Lord Wilberforce in *Aberdeen Construction*[39] that cases relating to capital gains tax should be decided in accordance with normal business principles, and added that whilst Mr Hardy had suffered a loss it did not follow that it was an allowable loss under the TCGA 1992. It was necessary to ascertain whether the legislative conditions for an allowable loss had been satisfied.

As to the first question (and the one which is germane for this chapter), the Upper Tribunal acknowledged that, in the light of the decision in *O'Brien*, contractual rights are capable of being an asset. In this case, Mr Hardy acquired the right, subject to compliance with his own obligations, to compel performance of the vendor's obligations under the contract, notably specific performance of the obligation to convey the legal title to the property to him. This was a valuable right, but the Upper Tribunal found that Mr Hardy did not acquire an asset for capital gains tax purposes when he entered into the contract because when a seller and a buyer enter into a contract for the sale of land, the seller does not dispose of an asset and the buyer does not acquire an asset. The asset, which is the land, is disposed of by the seller and acquired by the buyer when completion takes place. If the buyer fails to complete, there is no disposal or acquisition of the asset.

It followed that Mr Hardy did not acquire an asset for capital gains tax purposes when he entered into the contract. Therefore, he had no asset to dispose of when the contract was rescinded. In effect, the deposit had not been paid for the acquisition of the contractual rights under the contract but as a part-payment of the purchase price of the property. This conclusion was sufficient for the appeal to be dismissed and for Mr Hardy's claim for capital loss relief to be denied. It also meant that the Upper Tribunal did not need to resolve the second and third questions.[40]

---

[39] *Aberdeen Construction* (above n 6).
[40] Nevertheless, the Upper Tribunal considered that, first, if Mr Hardy's rights under the contract had constituted an asset, the loss of the right to enforce performance of the contract, resulting in the

In short, the Upper Tribunal concluded that whilst the right to compel specific performance of a contract for the sale of land was a valuable right, its exercise by a buyer was contingent upon the buyer being able to comply with his own obligations under the contract which was not the position in this case. Further, the pertinent asset for capital gains tax purposes in such cases is the land which is the subject matter of the contract – the right to sue for specific performance which arises at the time of contract is not an 'asset' for capital gains tax purposes.

In conclusion, these cases illustrate that not *every* right of action will constitute an 'asset' for capital gains tax purposes, and that rights of action are often subsumed in a bundle of rights in property which is regarded as the 'asset' for capital gains tax purposes. Equally, however, they do not question the generic nature of 'asset' as explored by Warner J in *Zim Properties* nor that on the facts of that case, a right of action could be regarded, notwithstanding the existence of an underlying asset, namely the properties, as an 'asset'.

III. THE INTRODUCTION OF ESC D33

ESC D33 was introduced by the Inland Revenue with effect from 19 December 1988 following, and albeit some time subsequent to, the High Court decision in *Zim Properties*.[41]

For the purposes of this chapter, it has two principal operative paragraphs, namely paragraphs 9 and 11. Paragraph 9 provides:

9. Underlying assets

Where the right of action arises by reason of the total or partial loss or destruction of or damage to a form of property which is an asset for capital gains tax purposes, or because the claimant suffered some loss or disadvantage in connection with such a form of property, any gain or loss on the disposal of the right of action may by concession be computed as if the compensation derived from that asset, and not from the right of action. As a result a proportion of the cost of the asset, determined in accordance with normal part-disposal rules, and indexation allowance, may be deducted in computing the gain. For example if the compensation is paid by an estate agent because his negligence led to the sale of a building falling through, an appropriate part of the cost of the building may be deducted in computing any gain on the disposal of the right of action.

---

forfeiture of the deposit, did not amount to a disposal, and, secondly, if the contractual rights were an asset and had been disposed of, the deposit was not an allowable loss because it had not been paid wholly or mainly for the acquisition of the contractual rights but as a part payment of the purchase price of the property (see paras 44–52); for a commentary on the case, see, K Gordon, 'Return of the Naïve' (December 2016) *Tax Adviser* 44.

[41] Inland Revenue Press Release (19 December 1988), available at [1988] *Simon's Tax Intelligence* 865. See, generally, G Richards, 'Revenue Concession on Zim' (1989) 86 *LSG* 28 (19 April 1989); and C Greene and C Maddalena, 'Zim Reversed by Concession' (1989) 103 *Accountancy* 51–52.

> The gain may be computed by reference to the original cost of the underlying asset, with time-apportionment if appropriate if the asset was acquired before 6 April 1965, or by reference to its market value on 6 April 1965. For disposals on or after 6 April 1988, the gain may be computed in appropriate cases by reference to the value of the asset on 31 March 1982.

This paragraph covered and continues to cover the position where there is an 'underlying asset' which subsists in conjunction with the right of action, for example, the properties in *Zim Properties*. In such a case, an award of damages or a capital sum derived from a settlement of a right of action is assessed by concession to capital gains tax by reference to the 'underlying asset'. Consequently, in cases akin to *Zim Properties*, the 'gain' or 'loss' is calculated by reference to the acquisition cost and proposed sale price of 'the form of property' rather than by reference to the right of action itself.

Paragraph 11 deals with cases where there is no 'underlying asset' which could be used to calculate the amount of tax due on an award of damages or capital sum derived from a settlement, ie, a right of action that is acquired 'in connection with some matter which does not involve a form of property that is an asset for capital gains tax purposes'. In the latter regard, paragraph 11 provided, initially, that awards of damages or settlement sums which involved no underlying asset, for example for the provision of negligent tax advice, were exempt from capital gains tax or corporation tax (as the case may be). However, with effect from 27 January 2014[42], this provision was amended so that any gain accruing on the disposal of the right of action is exempt from tax only up to a limit of £500,000 'for any compensation awarded in a single set of proceedings'.[43]

It is implicit in each of these paragraphs that a right of action may constitute an 'asset' for capital gains tax purposes. However, under paragraph 9, the underlying asset, not the right of action, is treated as the source of the capital sum or compensation, to use the term employed in paragraph 9, with the result that any statutory reliefs and exemptions germane to the underlying asset may be applied in computing any gain or loss for capital gains tax purposes. Consequently, the concession lies, principally, in the benefit which this conveys to the taxpayer, one which would not be available if *Zim Properties* was followed;[44] whilst the exemption granted under paragraph 11 (with or without the cap) relates to the gain rather than to the 'asset', ie, the right of action.

It should be added in passing and without more that ESC D33 in its latter two substantive paragraphs, namely paragraphs 12 and 13, dwells on two further

---

[42] See HMRC, '*D33* Extra Statutory Concession D33 (Capital Gains Tax on compensation and damages) is changing' (27 January 2014), available at webarchive.nationalarchives.gov.uk/20140109 143644/http://www.hmrc.gov.uk/news/extra-statutory-concession-d33-changes.htm.

[43] The amended paragraph 11 also provides that any awards of compensation above the £500,000 threshold will be reviewed on a case-by-case basis 'to ensure that they remain within the Commissioners' collection and management powers'.

[44] See Southern's reference to the 'inconvenient' outcome in *Zim Properties* (above n 23).

matters relating to the capital gains tax treatment of compensation or damages, the latter of which is specifically referable to the decision in *Zim Properties*. Paragraph 12, which is headed 'Personal Compensation or damages' and which influenced the thinking behind paragraph 11, extends by way of concession the exemption from capital gains tax provided for by section 51(2) TCGA 1992 in respect of sums obtained by way of compensation or damages for any wrong or injury suffered by an individual as individual or in his profession or vocation. Paragraph 13 purports to cover through the grant of an exemption certain payments in the form of an indemnity or warranty which could otherwise attract capital gains tax through the application of *Zim Properties*. It provides that '[t]he principle in Zim Properties Ltd is not regarded as applicable to payments made by the vendor to the purchaser under a warranty or indemnity included as one of the terms of a contract of purchase and sale'. The situation envisaged by paragraph 13 is evidenced, commonly, in arrangements that are made between a vendor and purchaser in relation to the sale of shares in a private company. Such arrangements may be executed through a tax deed whereby, inter alia, provision is made through an indemnity or warranty to protect the purchaser against unforeseen or, otherwise, unprovided for tax liabilities that may arise in relation to the transaction. In the absence of paragraph 13, a payment made by a vendor to a purchaser under such an indemnity or warranty could be treated as consideration for the disposal of a contingent right to receive payment under that indemnity or warranty and, hence, in accordance with *Zim Properties*, be liable to capital gains tax. Paragraph 13 treats the payment as a reduction in the amount of consideration paid by the purchaser with a commensurate adjustment in the purchaser's base cost and in the proceeds received by the vendor for the shares.[45]

On a more general level of inquiry, whilst it is beyond the scope of this chapter to engage in a wider discourse about the legitimacy, or otherwise, of extra-statutory concessions per se,[46] it is instructive to view, in particular, paragraphs 9 and 11 of ESC D33, initially, within the context of the following statement that has accompanied HMRC's current list of concessions for some time (the list was last updated on 6 April 2016):

> An Extra-Statutory Concession is a relaxation which gives taxpayers a reduction in tax liability to which they would not be entitled under the strict letter of the law. Most concessions are made to deal with what are, on the whole, minor or transitory anomalies under the legislation and to meet cases of hardship at the margins of the

---

[45] For the taxation of the proceeds of insurance policies to cover tax risk, see, eg, D Wilson, 'Insuring M & A Tax Risk (2016) 1319 *Tax Journal* 12 (29 July 2016); and G Miles, 'The Taxation of Pay-outs under Buy-side Warranty and Indemnity Insurance Policies' (2016) 1334 *Tax Journal* 12 (2 December 2016).

[46] In this respect, see, eg, D Williams, 'Extra-Statutory Concessions' [1979] *BTR* 137; M Gammie, 'Extra-Statutory Concessions' [1980] *BTR* 308; J Alder, 'The Legality of Extra-Statutory Concessions' (1980) 1 *NLJ* 180; and E Troup, 'Unacceptable Discretion: Countering Tax Avoidance and Preserving the Rights of the Individual' (1992) 13(4) *Fiscal Studies* 128.

code where a statutory remedy would be difficult to devise or would run to a length out of proportion to the intrinsic importance of the matter.[47]

This statement shows the relatively narrow confines within which extra-statutory concessions should operate and it also indicates, latterly, that the application, or otherwise, of a concession may be influenced, further, by any special circumstances, for example, where there is an attempt to use a concession for tax avoidance purposes. However, there is no reference in the statement to the constitutional proprieties that HMRC should follow in making a concession. A reminder of these proprieties was offered by Lord Hoffmann in *R (Wilkinson) v CIR*.[48] In this respect, his Lordship alluded to the statutory duty of the Commissioners under the Inland Revenue Regulation Act 1890 to 'collect and cause to be collected every part of inland revenue' and to section 1 of the Taxes Management Act 1970, which, according to Lord Diplock in *CIR v National Federation of Self-Employed and Small Businesses*,[49] gave them a wide managerial discretion in determining the best means of collecting the taxes for which they are responsible.

Further, Lord Hoffmann opined that the Commissioners in exercise of this discretion could formulate policy within the interstices of tax legislation, deal pragmatically with minor or transitory anomalies and with cases of hardship at the margins or cases in which a statutory rule is difficult to formulate or where its enactment could take up a disproportionate amount of parliamentary time. However, it was not permissible to construe the discretion so widely as to enable the Commissioners to concede, by extra-statutory concession and on grounds other than the pragmatic collection of tax, an allowance which Parliament could have granted, but, nevertheless, did not grant.

It is equally clear that the executive (here in the guise of HMRC) cannot through the purported exercise of its managerial discretion set aside a court or tribunal decision. The principle underlying this position was reiterated in relation to ministerial powers, recently, in a non-tax case by Lord Neuberger in *R (Evans) v AG*.[50] His Lordship stated that it was a basic principle that a court or tribunal decision, subject to being overruled by a higher court or statute, is binding between the parties and cannot be ignored or set aside by the executive however cogent or strongly held the executive's reasons for disagreeing with that decision may be.

In fact, *Wilkinson*[51] prompted HMRC to undertake a review of all its extra-statutory concessions, including ESC D33. The first manifestation of the review of ESC D33 was the introduction in January 2014 of the £500,000 cap on the

---

[47] HMRC, 'Extra-Statutory Concessions: ex-Inland Revenue', available at www.hmrc.gov.uk/specialist/esc.pdf.

[48] *R (Wilkinson) v CIR* [2006] STC 270.

[49] *CIR v National Federation of Self-Employed and Small Businesses* [1982] AC 617, 636.

[50] *R (Evans) v AG* [2015] UKSC 21.

[51] *Wilkinson* (above n 48).

exemption in paragraph 11 ostensibly because there was concern that the initial unlimited exemption might be outside HMRC's discretionary powers of collection and management.[52] Evidence of a more wide-ranging review appeared, subsequently, in a Consultation Document entitled *Legislating Extra Statutory Concession D33* which was published on 31 July 2014.[53]

The coverage of paragraph 9 falls within a section encompassing paragraphs 8–10 and headed 'Treatment where there is an underlying asset'. It is concluded in this section, somewhat disingenuously and without more, that it is 'inaccurate to say that paragraphs 9 [and 10] are a concession when they reflect the position in law as it stands after decided cases'.[54] Those decided cases would appear to be *Zim Properties* and *Pennine Raceway*[55] both of which are referred to in this section. It is hard to see how *Zim Properties* can be reconciled with this statement. Nor is it a conclusion, which, with the benefit of hindsight, it can be said is necessarily supported by either *Weston*[56] or *Hardy*.[57]

The treatment of paragraph 11 is more fulsome, not least because the Consultation Document proposed and sought views on a further change to its operation, namely that there should be an absolute limit of £1 million exemption, rather than £500,000, for capital sums/compensation derived from a right of action where there is no underlying asset with any amount above £1 million chargeable to capital gains tax or corporation tax as the case may be. There were several reasons for this proposed change: it was not practical to legislate the amended paragraph 11 as there was insufficient certainty for a person receiving compensation over £500,000; the introduction of an absolute limit of £1,000,000 avoided adding complexity to the tax code and provided certainty of treatment to the recipient of compensation; and courts would be aware that any compensation awarded in excess of £1,000,000 would be subject to tax.

In this regard, consultees were asked to respond to two questions, namely, Question 1: Is £1,000,000 the right level of exemption? If not, what would be a more appropriate amount and why? Question 2: Are you aware of any cases which would be taxable under the proposed changes which would result in hardship? A six-week consultation period was specified as ESC D33 was regarded by HMRC as a long-standing concession with which professionals were familiar – a clear departure from the standard 12-week period prescribed as a default by HM Government.[58]

---

[52] For a stinging criticism of this move, see McKie & Co, 'Ensuring the Fair Administration of the Tax System' (2014) XVII *Rudge Revenue Review* 7.

[53] HMRC, *Legislating Extra Statutory Concession D33* (July 2014), available at www.gov.uk/ government/consultations/legislating-extra-statutory-concession-d33. See F Kaye and M Hodgson, 'The Taxman Cometh' (2014) 164 *NLJ* 31 (31 October 2014), and P Howard, 'HMRC's consultation on legislating ESC D33', (2014) 1228 *Tax Journal* 8 (29 August 2014).

[54] HMRC (above n 53) 12.

[55] *Pennine Raceway* (above n 26).

[56] *Weston* (above n 27).

[57] *Hardy* (above n 28).

[58] HM Government, Consultation Principles, available at assets.publishing.service.gov.uk/govern-ment/uploads/system/uploads/attachment_data/file/691383/Consultation_Principles__1_.pdf.

A Summary of Responses to the Consultation Document was published in November 2015 (*Summary*).[59] For the purposes of this chapter, the *Summary* shows that none of the respondents agreed with the proposal that a £1,000,000 exemption for compensation derived from a right of action should be introduced with amounts in excess of this figure being subject to capital gains tax/corporation tax. Most suggested that any such limit would, to a degree, be arbitrary and some disagreed with the principle of taxing compensation and damages. Further, some respondents raised the question of whether the proposed discretionary treatment in the Consultation Document exceeded HMRC's discretionary powers, but indicated that, in any event, Parliament should legislate with a view to replicating the unlimited concession which applied before January 2014. As to the possibility of hardship if the proposed changes were introduced, a number of respondents opined that 'because (in their view) any tax charge on compensation would be unfair, hardship (or at least injustice) was likely in many cases'. HMRC also addressed the fundamental concern expressed by some respondents about the principle of taxing compensation, albeit generally (and through two illustrative examples) and, ultimately, inconclusively in terms of any course of action that might follow.

This concern was based on the ground that compensation payments merely put parties back in the position they would have been in but for the negligent action, and that, consequently, it was wrong to tax claims for compensation/damages for any amount. Whilst accepting the basic tenet of the concern that compensation or damages claims are intended to put a party making the claim back in the position that party would have been in if it were not for the negligent action, HMRC rejected the mooted consequence that it was appropriate or right, therefore, to exempt all payments that might be regarded as damages or compensation from capital gains tax. Nevertheless, HMRC acknowledged that as many respondents had raised points about this issue and other aspects of ESC D33 it was important prior to determining the next course of action to discuss the issues raised in more detail with respondents to ensure that concerns which had been expressed were fully understood – whatever the outcome of this mooted detailed discussion of the issues between HMRC and the pertinent respondents it would appear that the presumed search for some degree of consensus on the key issues continues.

IV. SOME CONCLUDING REFLECTIONS

Although *Zim Properties* was decided over 30 years ago the 'elusive and difficult' issues with which it was concerned and others to which it gave rise continue

---

[59] HMRC, 'Legislating Extra Statutory Concession D33: Summary of Responses' (November 2015), available at assets.publishing.service.gov.uk/government/uploads/system/uploads/attachment_data/file/473989/Legislating_Extra_Statutory_Concession_D33_summary_of_responses.pdf.

to be matters of reflection, especially, as seen in the Consultation Document, for HMRC.

Within the province of that reflection, it might be asked, first, whether the meaning of 'asset' for capital gains tax purposes is commensurate with 'property' (however that may be defined); secondly, whilst it is accepted, post-*Zim Properties*, that a right of action may, in appropriate circumstances, constitute an 'asset' how likely, in view of the decisions in *Pennine Raceway*,[60] *Weston*[61] and *Hardy*,[62] is it that a court will find that a right of action is sufficiently 'independent to constitute an "asset"' from which a capital sum may be derived; thirdly, what prompted the Inland Revenue's apparent *volte face* in 1988 when it introduced paragraph 9 of ESC D33 (disregarding the later rationalisation in the Consultation Document that paragraph 9 is simply reflective of decided cases), and, in terms of *vires*, to what extent is paragraph 9 a legitimate exercise of administrative discretion? More broadly in relation to compensation/capital sums paid in respect of rights of action where there is no underlying asset, clearly doubts remain about the legitimacy of taxing such sums at all and, consequently, about the manner in which such sums are taxed under paragraph 11.

Zim Properties is a case, like many others, which was concerned with judicial interpretation of discrete statutory provisions, but, as this chapter has shown, its consequences – many of which it would seem were unforeseen – endure. Indeed, in retrospect, some might feel that the Inland Revenue would have been best advised to have heeded the following words of Avery Jones in an article in 1988:

> It might put the Revenue in a difficult position to accept that their winning argument [in *Zim Properties*] was wrong; could they not find another taxpayer willing to litigate the matter again and merely announce that meanwhile they will not be following *Zim* in practice.[63]

---

[60] *Pennine Raceway* (above n 26).
[61] *Weston* (above n 27).
[62] *Hardy* (above n 28).
[63] JF Avery Jones, 'Further Thoughts on Zim' [1988] *BTR* 29, 32.

15

The Commerzbank Litigation (1990)
UK Law, Tax Treaty Law
and EU Law

PHILIP BAKER

T HE COMMERZBANK LITIGATION comprises three reported cases all
involving aspects of the same dispute between the German bank
Commerzbank AG and the Inland Revenue.[1] The first decision is that
of Mummery J in the Chancery Division in February 1990, and contains what
has become the classic starting point for any discussion of the approach to the
interpretation of double taxation conventions in the United Kingdom.[2] The
second case is a decision of Nolan LJ and Henry J in the High Court in respect
of a judicial review application in April 1991, and concerns the approach to
non-discrimination in the United Kingdom.[3] Finally, the third decision is a judgment of the European Court of Justice (ECJ) of 13 July 1993 on a reference for
a preliminary ruling from the High Court, which concerns the application of
European law to a tax measure which discriminates on grounds of residence.[4]
The Commerzbank litigation merits selection as one of the leading cases in UK
tax law, primarily because of its summary of the approach to the interpretation
of double taxation conventions, but also because of its discussion of discrimination on grounds of residence in UK and EU law.

---

[1] There are surprisingly few articles that discuss simply the Commerzbank litigation. There are
notes on the cases in the *British Tax Review*: JDB Oliver, 'Withholding Tax and Tax Credits, with
some Reflections on Union Texas' [1991] *BTR* 245 and D Sandler, 'Commerzbank – Fast Track to
Harmonisation?' [1993] *BTR* 517. Aside from that, the case is discussed in virtually all articles or
chapters in books about the approach to tax treaty interpretation in the UK, as well as in discussions
of EU law and direct taxation.

[2] *CIR v Commerzbank AG* [1990] STC 285, 63 TC 218.

[3] *R v CIR ex parte Commerzbank AG* [1991] STC 271, 68 TC 252.

[4] Judgment of 13 July 1993, *R v CIR ex parte Commerzbank AG*, C-330/91, EU:C:1993:303;
[1993] STC 605. The STC report includes the report of the Juge Rapporteur at [1993] STC 607–13.

I. BACKGROUND AND HISTORY OF THE LITIGATION

The background facts to the litigation are very simple. During 1973 Commerzbank AG, a German bank, established a branch in the United Kingdom.[5] It began making loans to US corporations, on which it received interest. The interest formed part of the profits of the UK branch, and was subject to corporation tax as such. However, the branch sought exemption from UK tax under article XV of the UK–United States double taxation convention of 16 April 1945, as amended by the Supplementary Protocol of 17 March 1966 (which inserted article XV), which provided as follows:

> Article XV
>
> Dividends and interest paid by a corporation of one Contracting Party shall be exempt from tax by the other Contracting Party except where the recipient is a citizen, resident, or corporation of that other Contracting Party. This exemption shall not apply if the corporation paying such dividend or interest is a resident of the other Contracting Party.

Commerzbank's argument was disarmingly simple: the interest it received was 'interest paid by a corporation of [the United States]', the bank was not a 'citizen, resident, or corporation of [the United Kingdom]', and the 'corporation paying such ... interest' was not a resident of [the United Kingdom]. Consequently, the interest was exempt from tax by [the United Kingdom]. The argument was based on a pure, straightforward, literal interpretation of the words of the convention. The words of the article were not in a standard form that one might have expected if the convention had been based on the OECD Model.[6]

Commerzbank's claim for exemption related to the four years ended 31 December 1973 through to 31 December 1976. It was not until 7 January 1985, however, that the Inland Revenue formally refused the claim for exemption. Commerzbank claimed both a repayment of the corporation tax that the branch had paid on the interest (which amounted to £4,222,234), as well as repayment supplement (the equivalent of interest on the repayment – which amounted to £5,199,258 by the time the judicial review commenced). The Inland Revenue denied both the exemption under the convention and the claim for repayment supplement. The specific issue relating to repayment supplement – which figures more directly in the later stages of the litigation – was that section 48(2) of the Finance (No 2) Act 1975 (which provided for repayment supplement) applied

---

[5] There is nothing particularly significant in the establishment of a branch rather than a subsidiary. Most banks establish branches where they can since then the branch is not subject in the country where it operates to the same capital adequacy requirements to which a subsidiary would be subject. There is nothing to suggest in any way that the choice of the form of a branch was made for any reasons other than the usual commercial ones, or that the tax treatment of interest highlighted in this case was anything other than a consequence of that normal, commercial decision.

[6] OECD, *Model Tax Convention on Income and on Capital*. The version applicable at the time of the protocol in 1966 would have been the 1963 Draft of the Model.

only to residents of the UK. The bank was not a resident of the UK, only having a branch in the UK, and so was not entitled on the face of the legislation.

Commerzbank's claim for exemption and repayment of the tax plus repayment supplement was first heard by a Special Commissioner, Mr Everett, on 11 November 1987.[7] The Special Commissioner was asked to assume jurisdiction over the question of the bank's entitlement to repayment supplement, but declined to do so because no claim to repayment supplement had yet been made and refused, there was no appeal machinery in relation to repayment supplement, and it appeared to the Special Commissioner that, if the bank should succeed and be denied repayment supplement, its remedy would be to issue proceedings for recovery of the amount. The remainder of his decision focused, consequently, on the interpretation and application of article XV of the double taxation convention.

It was common ground between the parties that on a straightforward, literal construction of article XV, the bank was entitled to the exemption and to repayment of the tax.[8] The argument of the Inland Revenue (put forward by Mr WJ Durrans of the Solicitor's Office) was that, notwithstanding the clear words of the article, there was an implied limitation that benefits under the double taxation convention were not to be conferred on persons who were not citizens or residents of either the UK or the US. The bank was a resident of Germany, and so not entitled to access the benefits of the UK–US convention.

The Special Commissioner approached the matter by asking first if there was any ambiguity in the language of article XV, and whether the courts were permitted to have regard to any *travaux préparatoires* which would lead to a different conclusion from the literal interpretation. Sadly for the Revenue's argument, nothing could be produced by way of *travaux préparatoires*. The Special Commissioner concluded that there was no presumption against benefiting third parties (that is, resident or citizens of third states) under a treaty. The Inland Revenue was unable to produce any evidence that there was a general principle applicable to double taxation conventions that branches of non-resident corporations were unable to take the advantage of the benefits of a treaty concluded by the state in which they were situated.[9] By a decision of 30 November 1987, the Special Commissioner accepted Commerzbank's claim for exemption under the tax treaty, but rejected the claim for repayment supplement. Both parties requested a case stated: the bank against the refusal to consider the repayment supplement claim, and the Revenue against the decision in favour of exemption for the bank.

---

[7] *CIR v Commerzbank* (above n 2) 286 j.

[8] ibid, between f and g.

[9] One might regard this as a general problem of the application of tax treaties to permanent establishments (branches or agencies) situated in a contracting state. The PE is not a resident of its host state, even though for some tax purposes it is treated as if it were a local enterprise. One might contrast this position under international tax law with the position under EU law – see Judgment of 21 September 1999, *Compagnie de Saint-Gobain*, C-307/97, EU:C:1999:438.

It should be mentioned that, two days before the hearing of the Commerz-bank application, a similar claim under the same article of the UK–US convention had also been made by the Banco Do Brasil SA, which was similarly rejected by the Special Commissioner and a case stated signed on 15 August 1988.[10] The two cases, raising the same point, went to the Chancery Division together (but the focus of this chapter is on the Commerzbank litigation, which included also the two other proceedings).[11]

The appeal by way of case stated was heard by Mummery J on 17 to 19 January 1990. At the time, he had been a judge of the Chancery Division for less than a year. It appears that he had never previously decided a case involving a double taxation convention, and it is not even clear if he had ever seen a double taxation convention previously.[12] In some respects, therefore, it is remarkable that his decision has become the accepted starting point for any discussion of the approach to tax treaty interpretation in the UK. He issued his decision only three weeks after the hearing, on 9 February 1990. He decided in favour of the bank on the exemption under article XV. (His judgment does not deal at all with repayment supplement, so it appears that the bank had abandoned its appeal against the Special Commissioner's decision on this issue and had decided by this stage that separate proceedings would be necessary in respect of that issue.) No appeal was brought against Mummery J's decision, and it is assumed that, sometime after the judgment, HMRC repaid £4,222,234 to the bank by way of corporation tax which had been wrongly paid.

That concluded the claim for exemption and repayment of the corporation tax, but it left the issue of repayment supplement.

Separate proceedings were brought in the Queen's Bench Division by way of judicial review of the Inland Revenue's refusal to pay repayment supplement. The case was heard by Nolan LJ (who wrote the judgment) and Henry J on 26 to 28 February 1991. On 12 April 1991 they issued a judgment conclud-ing that the bank's claim for repayment supplement in accordance with UK law or the non-discrimination article of the UK–Germany double taxation convention failed.[13] However, they referred a single question for a preliminary ruling to the ECJ.[14] That question asked whether the failure of UK law to grant

---

[10] Which suggests that the possibility for branches of foreign banks in the UK to make a claim for exemption on interest derived from the US was relatively well known to the advisers to foreign banks, and not simply to Commerzbank.

[11] Commerzbank was represented before the Special Commissioners by Stephen Oliver QC, while Banco Do Brasil was represented by Stewart Bates QC; the Inland Revenue was represented by Mr WJ Durrans of the Solicitor's Office in both hearings.

[12] Though it is clear that Sir John Mummery had some experience with revenue matters. He had been instructed by the Inland Revenue in a number of tax cases while in practice as a barrister. So far as one can tell from the reported cases, none of those matters had involved tax treaties.

[13] Note: the non-discrimination claim was based on the UK–Germany treaty (Commerzbank being a national and resident of Germany), and not under the UK–US convention under which the exemption was claimed.

[14] This was not the first reference to the ECJ in a direct tax case from the UK (that honour belongs to *R v HM Treasury and CIR ex parte Daily Mail and General Trust plc*: Judgment of 27 September 1988, C-81/87, EU:C:1988:456), but it does appear to be the second.

repayment supplement to non-residents constituted a restriction of the freedom of establishment and indirect discrimination on grounds of nationality, contrary to what were then articles 5, 7, 52 and 58 of the EEC Treaty.

There was a hearing before the ECJ on 20 January 1993.[15] The opinion of Advocate General Darmon was issued on 17 March 1993, advising the Court that it should answer the question in favour of the bank. The Opinion concluded that the freedom of establishment precluded legislation which limited the payment of repayment supplement only to resident companies and refused it for non-resident companies.

On 13 July 1993 the ECJ issued its judgment in favour of the bank, confirming that the freedom of establishment prevented legislation from granting repayment supplement only to companies resident in the United Kingdom. The Court was made up of seven judges including the UK judge, David Edward.

A note at the end of the Tax Cases report of the litigation records that a consent order was issued in the Queen's Bench Division dated 31 March 1995 declaring that the Inland Revenue was not entitled to apply the requirement of UK residence as a condition for eligibility for repayment supplement, and that Commerzbank was entitled to repayment supplement accordingly.[16]

By way of summary, therefore, it took some 22 years (assuming that the dispute stretched back to the first year of operation of the branch in the UK) for Commerzbank to obtain repayment of the tax (to the tune of a little over £4 million.) and repayment supplement (to an amount of a little over £5 million), and four full hearings to do so: before the Special Commissioners, the Chancery Division, the Queen's Bench Division, and finally the European Court of Justice.

The remainder of this chapter focuses on the three main issues in the litigation: the UK approach to the interpretation of double taxation conventions (the decision of Mummery J); the domestic approach to non-discrimination (the decision written by Nolan LJ); and the European Union law approach to discrimination on grounds of residence (the judgment of the ECJ).

II. THE UK APPROACH TO TAX TREATY INTERPRETATION: THE DECISION OF MUMMERY J

The part of the decision of Mummery J which is most frequently quoted in subsequent cases is his six-bullet-point summary of the approach to interpretation, which merits being quoted in full as follows:[17]

> (1) It is necessary to look first for a clear meaning of the words used in the relevant article of the convention, bearing in mind that 'consideration of the purpose

---

[15] Commerzbank was now represented by Gerald Barling QC and David Anderson, and the UK government by Alan Moses QC and Derrick Wyatt.

[16] *R v CIR ex parte Commerzbank* (above n 3) 68 TC 252, 278.

[17] *CIR v Commerzbank* (above n 2) 297.

of an enactment is always a legitimate part of the process of interpretation': per Lord Wilberforce (at 272) and Lord Scarman (at 294).[18] A strictly literal approach to interpretation is not appropriate in construing legislation which gives effect to or incorporates an international treaty: per Lord Fraser (at 285) and Lord Scarman (at 290). A literal interpretation may be obviously inconsistent with the purposes of the particular article or of the treaty as a whole. If the provisions of a particular article are ambiguous, it may be possible to resolve that ambiguity by giving a purposive construction to the convention looking at it as a whole by reference to its language as set out in the relevant United Kingdom legislative instrument: per Lord Diplock (at 279).

(2) The process of interpretation should take account of the fact that–

'The language of an international convention has not been chosen by an English parliamentary draftsman. It is neither couched in the conventional English legislative idiom nor designed to be construed exclusively by English judges. It is addressed to a much wider and more varied judicial audience than is an Act of Parliament which deals with purely domestic law. It should be interpreted, as Lord Wilberforce put it in *James Buchanan & Co. Ltd v. Babco Forwarding & Shipping (UK) Limited*, [[1978] AC 141 at 152], 'unconstrained by technical rules of English law, or by English legal precedent, but on broad principles of general acceptance': per Lord Diplock (at 281–82) and Lord Scarman (at 293).

(3) Among those principles is the general principle of international law, now embodied in art 31(1) of the Vienna Convention on the Law of Treaties, that 'a treaty should be interpreted in good faith and in accordance with the ordinary meaning to be given to the terms of the treaty in their context and in the light of its object and purpose'. A similar principle is expressed in slightly different terms in McNair's The Law of Treaties (1961) p 365, where it is stated that the task of applying or construing or interpreting a treaty is 'the duty of giving effect to the expressed intention of the parties, that is, their intention as expressed in the words used by them in the light of the surrounding circumstances'. It is also stated in that work (p 366) that references to the primary necessity of giving effect to 'the plain terms' of a treaty or construing words according to their 'general and ordinary meaning' or their 'natural signification' are to be a starting point or prima facie guide and 'cannot be allowed to obstruct the essential quest in the application of treaties, namely the search for the real intention of the contracting parties in using the language employed by them'.

(4) If the adoption of this approach to the article leaves the meaning of the relevant provision unclear or ambiguous or leads to a result which is manifestly absurd or unreasonable recourse may be had to 'supplementary means of interpretation' including travaux préparatoires: per Lord Diplock (at 282) referring to art 32 of the Vienna Convention, which came into force after the conclusion of this double taxation convention, but codified an already existing principle of public international law. See also Lord Fraser (at 287) and Lord Scarman (at 294).

---

[18] These are references to the speeches in the House of Lords in *Fothergill v Monarch Airlines Ltd* [1981] AC 251 on which Mummery J drew heavily for his approach to treaty interpretation in general.

(5) Subsequent commentaries on a convention or treaty have persuasive value only, depending on the cogency of their reasoning. Similarly, decisions of foreign courts on the interpretation of a convention or treaty text depend for their authority on the reputation and status of the court in question: per Lord Diplock (at 283–84) and per Lord Scarman (at 295).

(6) Aids to the interpretation of a treaty such as travaux préparatoires, international case law and the writings of jurists are not a substitute for study of the terms of the convention. Their use is discretionary, not mandatory, depending, for example, on the relevance of such material and the weight to be attached to it: per Lord Scarman' (at 294).

Commerzbank was not the first reported case to consider the application or interpretation of tax treaties in the UK.[19] However, it was the first case to treat the issue of tax treaty interpretation as a distinct topic for discussion, and the first to attempt to summarise the approach to the interpretation of double taxation conventions in bullet points. It is this formulation of a summary of the correct approach which has made it so easy for subsequent judges in subsequent cases to quote from this judgment. It is not possible to determine whether the summary was developed from submissions by counsel[20] or by the judge himself.

The six-point summary has been cited with approval by judges at various levels in subsequent cases,[21] and has become the classical starting point for any discussion of tax treaty interpretation in the UK. In many respects this illustrates what one might refer to as 'tax treaty interpretation meets the doctrine of *stare decisis*'. It is a process one can observe in a number of common law countries: a judgment is issued (not necessarily of the highest court) in which a judge summarises the approach to tax treaty interpretation. That summary is then quoted with approval by later courts, including higher courts, and eventually receives the approval of the highest court in that jurisdiction. The doctrine of precedent then coalesces around that summary, and, to a certain extent, ossifies that approach, which, by definition, is an approach unique to that particular jurisdiction.[22]

---

[19] In fact, four earlier cases involving tax treaties were cited in Commerzbank: *Avery Jones v CIR* [1976] STC 290; *CIR v Exxon Corp* [1982] STC 356; *Lord Strathalmond v CIR* [1972] 1 WLR 1511; and *Sun Life Assurance Company of Canada v Pearson* [1986] STC 335.

[20] Before Mummery J the Revenue was represented by Alan Moses, and Commerzbank by Stephen Oliver QC and David Ewart, and Banco Do Brasil by Graham Aaronson QC. Any one of these gentlemen would have been capable of formulating the approach to interpretation in a series of bullet points. However, the judgment does not record that the judge was basing his summary on submissions of counsel.

[21] This includes the First-tier Tribunal in *FCE Bank Plc v Revenue & Customs* [2010] UKFTT 136 (TC), and *Felixstowe Dock & Railway Company Ltd v Revenue & Customs* [2011] UKFTT 838 (TC); the Court of Appeal in *HMRC v UBS AG* [2007] EWCA Civ 119, and *Ben Nevis (Holdings) Ltd v HMRC* [2013] EWCA Civ 578; and most recently the decision has been referred to in the Supreme Court in *Anson v Revenue & Customs* [2015] UKSC 44.

[22] One can see the same process at work in Canada, for example, around the decision of the Supreme Court in *R v Crown Forest Industries* (1995) DTC 5389, and in Australia around the decision in *McDermott Industries v CoT* (2005) 7 ITLR 800.

This process raises a number of issues of significance, which can be illustrated by *Commerzbank* and Mummery J's judgment. First, how to ensure that the approach adopted in each country and formalised through the doctrine of precedent is broadly the same as in other countries? Secondly, what to do if the summary is 'wrong', in the sense that it does not reflect an international consensus on the approach to the interpretation of double taxation conventions? Both these issues can be illustrated by Mummery J's summary of the approach to tax treaty interpretation.

First, the summary is not comprehensive. The most significant omission is any discussion of the role of the Commentaries to the OECD Model[23] as an aid to interpretation. These Commentaries are, in most cases, one of the first items anyone would turn to as an aid to interpretation. It is not entirely surprising, however, that Mummery J's summary does not make any reference to the Commentaries. The 1945 UK–US double taxation convention pre-dated and was, therefore, not based on the OECD Model. The OECD Model contained no provision equivalent to article XV of that convention, and, most significantly, the 1945 convention did not contain a provision equivalent to article 1 of the OECD Model, which states: 'Persons Covered: This Convention shall apply to persons who are residents of one or both of the Contracting States'.[24] The Commentaries did not feature as part of the issue in the Chancery Division.[25] Mummery J's summary does not, therefore, provide any guidance on the use of the Commentaries, including particularly the question of the use of subsequent Commentaries. It has been left to later cases to elaborate on this point.[26]

To be clear on the issue, the reference in Mummery J's summary at paragraph (5) to 'subsequent commentaries' is a reference to works written by academic commentators and not to official commentaries such as the Commentaries to the OECD Model. This becomes clear if one looks back at the paragraphs in the decision of the House of Lords in *Fothergill v Monarch Airlines Ltd*[27] which are cited by Mummery J as the basis for each of his six points in the summary. It would be an obvious error for anyone to think that Mummery J was making any reference whatsoever to subsequent Commentaries to the OECD Model.

---

[23] OECD, *Model Tax Convention on Income and on Capital* (the current version is that adopted in November 2017).

[24] One can entirely understand the position of the Inland Revenue as proceeding on the assumption that *all* double taxation conventions have an implied limitation equivalent to article 1 of the OECD Model; the decision of Mummery J reflects the fact that no such wording was found in the UK–US 1945 convention, and there was inadequate evidence to suggest that this reflected a general principle. Perhaps one might say that it was only by the 1960s, and the adoption of the OECD Draft of the Model, that this came to be recognised as a general principle applicable to all tax treaties. By the time the case was argued in 1987, this had become a general principle, but not in respect of a convention originally concluded in 1945.

[25] Before the Special Commissioners, the Revenue had cited from the Commentaries in support of the argument that there was an implied limitation that only residents of one of the two states could take a benefit from the treaty: no reference to this appears in the Chancery Division judgment.

[26] See, in particular, *Smallwood v HMRC* (2008) 10 ITLR 574.

[27] *Fothergill* (above n 18).

The second issue that arises (and in many respects the more interesting issue) is where summaries of this kind on the approach to treaty interpretation contain items that may be seen to be inaccurate in part, or simply wrong. In one sense, the judge presenting the summary cannot be inaccurate or wrong; the judge sets out his or her summary, and subsequent cases adopt that summary. However, what he or she explains in the summary may conflict with the views expressed in other countries, or possibly with the international consensus on the approach to interpretation, if one assumes that such consensus exists.[28] This can be illustrated by two points in Mummery J's judgment.

It is very hard to take issue with any of the six points in Mummery J's summary. However, outside that summary there are two other issues relating to treaty interpretation in the case with which one might justifiably take issue.

First, the Inland Revenue relied in argument on a joint statement issued by the US Internal Revenue Service and the Inland Revenue in 1977. This reflected a competent authority agreement and completely supported the Inland Revenue's position in the case.[29] As to the competent authority agreement, Mummery J says this:

> I should add, however, that this joint statement has no authority in the English courts. It expresses the official view of the Revenue authorities of the two countries. That view may be right or wrong. Although article XXA authorises the competent authorities to communicate with each other directly to implement the provisions of the convention and 'to assure its consistent interpretation and application' it does not confer any binding or authoritative effect on the views or statements of the competent authorities in the English courts.

The issue of the status of the competent authority agreement merited, perhaps, a more detailed and nuanced treatment. As Mummery J explains, the convention itself provided for competent authority agreements and, as such, any agreement reached merited more than a relatively abrupt dismissal.[30] It may be correct that the final arbiter on the meaning of the convention would be the English court, but the competent authority agreement might well be a matter to

---

[28] The existence of such a consensus is a contentious issue in itself (if one examines, for example, the widely divergent views on the legal status of the OECD Commentaries and particularly subsequent changes to the Commentaries). One may assume, however, that there are certain points that are non-contentious and widely accepted – this would include, for example, the applicability of the approach to treaty interpretation outlined in the Vienna Convention on the Law of Treaties 1969.

[29] This issue is dealt with at *CIR v Commerzbank* (above n 2) 301j–302d, and the competent authority agreement is quoted at the top of p 302.

[30] The provision in the 1945 UK–US convention was Art XXVIA(2) which provides: 'The competent authorities of the Contracting Parties may communicate with each other directly to implement the provisions of the present Convention and to assure its consistent interpretation and application'. This is perhaps not quite as clear a statement of authority to enter into binding interpretations as Art 25(3) of the OECD Model which provides: 'The competent authorities of the Contracting States shall endeavour to resolve by mutual agreement any difficulties or doubts arising as to the interpretation or application of the Convention'.

take into account, for example under article 31 of the Vienna Convention on the Law of Treaties.

The issue has been visited subsequently in the *Ben Nevis* litigation.[31] The Court of Appeal there reached a different conclusion on the significance of a competent authority agreement, referring to article 31 of the Vienna Convention and implying (wrongly, perhaps) that Mummery J had taken a different view because the provisions of the Vienna Convention had not been considered in respect to the status of the competent authority agreement.[32] If one looks at Mummery J's summary, however, there is explicit reference to the Vienna Convention (at paragraphs 3 and 4), so he was clearly aware of the provisions of the Vienna Convention. One might conclude that the issue of the status of competent authority agreements remains to be resolved by the Supreme Court in the UK.

The second point on which one might take issue with the judgment of Mummery J concerns the treatment of decisions of foreign courts. A decision of the US Court of Claims was cited by the Inland Revenue, *The Great West Life Assurance Company v United States*[33] which, while considering the US–Canada convention and a slightly different scenario, nevertheless discussed the rationale behind a provision similar to article XV of the UK–US convention. This discussion of the rationale supported the argument presented by the Inland Revenue. Nevertheless, Mummery J concluded that the decision was of little assistance, partly because the US Court had been heavily influenced in its decision by statements issued by the US Department of State and the US Treasury.

It will often be the case that courts in other countries have relied on material, or have adopted an approach, which would not have been relied upon or taken in the United Kingdom. Nevertheless, the principle of common interpretation would suggest that these foreign authorities are at least given consideration and treated as potentially persuasive authorities. It would, perhaps, be going too far to blame Mummery J for the dearth of cases in the United Kingdom where foreign judgments have been cited on the interpretation of equivalent provisions in the UK's treaties. Nevertheless, a more accommodating approach to foreign case law might have done more to further the principle of common interpretation.

Mummery J's decision is, of course, that of a judge sitting in the High Court. As one can see from the issue of competent authority agreements, higher courts are able to depart from or add to the approach taken by Mummery J. The issues raised by the doctrine of precedent formalising and rigidifying an erroneous approach to treaty interpretation are much greater where the decisions are those of the highest court in a country.

---

[31] *Ben Nevis* (above n 21).
[32] ibid, para 39.
[33] *The Great West Life Assurance Company v United States* 678 F 2d 180 (1982), (1982) 49 AFTR 2D, 82-1316.

Overall, one may say that Mummery J's six-point summary provided a good starting point for the development of an approach to the interpretation of tax treaties in the United Kingdom. The significance is proved by the number of subsequent cases in which the summary has been cited with approval.[34]

Before leaving Mummery J's judgment, one final point might be made. Despite the reference in point 1 of the summary to a purposive approach to interpretation, and the explicit rejection of a strictly literal approach, as well as references to article 31(1) of the Vienna Convention and the 'object and purpose' of the convention, in the final analysis the decision accepts a purely literal approach to the interpretation of article XV. As explained above, the Inland Revenue had accepted that on a literal interpretation the bank was entitled to the exemption. The task of the Revenue was to displace that by showing that the object and purpose led to a different conclusion. One may say that the Revenue simply failed to discharge that burden. Alternatively, one may say that, faced with little evidence that the purpose of article XV was not to grant an exemption in the circumstances, the judgment did, in the final analysis, revert to a strict, literal approach. Despite lip service paid in the six-point summary to a purposive approach to the interpretation of tax treaties, Mummery J ultimately reverts to the literal approach to interpretation, which was common in the interpretation of tax legislation at that time. This is a point which is returned to at the end of this chapter.

III. NON-DISCRIMINATION UNDER UK LAW AND THE UK–GERMANY DOUBLE TAXATION CONVENTION: THE DECISION OF NOLAN LJ

As explained above, the Inland Revenue did not appeal the decision of Mummery J, and paid the corporation tax back to the bank. That, however, left the issue of repayment supplement, and specifically the fact that under UK legislation it was available only to residents and not to non-residents such as the bank. The issue of discrimination on grounds of residence was, therefore, taken up in an application for judicial review of the Revenue's refusal to pay repayment supplement, heard by Nolan LJ and Henry J. The judgment was given by Nolan LJ.

Several arguments were advanced on behalf of the bank in support of its claim for repayment supplement.

First, the bank argued that, since it was paying corporation tax assessed on it in the same manner as a resident company, it should be treated as a resident company for the purposes of repayment supplement. This relied heavily on section 78 of the Taxes Management Act 1970 which provided that non-residents would be assessed to corporation tax 'in like manner and to the like amount' as a resident person. On that point, however, Nolan LJ concluded that

---

[34] See n 21 above.

too much weight was being placed on section 78. The bank was a non-resident company with a UK branch, and section 48(2) of the Finance (No 2) Act 1975 only provided for repayment supplement to be paid to residents.

Secondly, the bank relied upon the non-discrimination article in the UK–Germany double taxation convention of 1967. It cited both article XX(1), which dealt with discrimination on grounds of nationality, and also article XX(3) which provided that 'The taxation on a permanent establishment ... shall not be less favourably levied ... than the taxation levied on enterprises of that other territory carrying on the same activities'.

On the non-discrimination article, Nolan LJ first concluded that the refusal to extend repayment supplement constituted more burdensome taxation on the bank than was imposed on a UK-resident. However, there were three more general arguments which prevented the bank from relying on the non-discrimination article.

The first of these, and perhaps the most significant element of the decision on this point by the High Court, was that double taxation conventions are given effect in UK domestic law by what was then section 788(3) of the Income and Corporation Taxes Act 1988. That paragraph provides that double taxation conventions are to have effect in domestic law for a number of purposes specified in the subsection. None of those purposes referred to or covered repayment supplement. This was, therefore, a classic example – and perhaps the first instance identified by the UK courts – of 'tax treaty under-ride' by the United Kingdom. That is, the provision in the Taxes Act giving effect to the double taxation convention did not give full effect to the convention and, in particular, did not give effect to the non-discrimination article with regard to repayment supplement.

While the term 'treaty under-ride' is not used, and was not in fact invented until many years later, this is a clear identification of an example of treaty under-ride. In principle, the failure to extend repayment supplement to permanent establishments of German residents might well have contravened at least article XX(3) of the UK–Germany convention.[35] However, the contravention of the convention rested only at the level of public international law. The United Kingdom is a dualist country, and international treaties need to be given effect in domestic legislation in order to create rights on persons that can be enforced by them. The essence of treaty under-ride is that the United Kingdom, while undertaking the international obligation vis-a-vis the foreign country, has not given full effect in domestic law so that a person cannot rely upon breach of the convention to bring a claim and obtain relief. This remains the position today, and the Commerzbank litigation appears to be the first recorded example of a

---

[35] There is an argument that, if the non-discrimination article had been given effect in domestic law, the bank would still have failed because, if compared with a UK-resident company, such a company would not have been entitled to the exemption under the UK–US convention in the first place. I am grateful to Dr Avery Jones for this comment on the issue of the correct comparator.

judgment in the United Kingdom in the tax context identifying a case of treaty under-ride.

The second ground which prevented the bank from relying on the non-discrimination article, at least in terms of article XX(1), was that this paragraph prohibited discrimination on grounds of nationality. However, the refusal to grant repayment supplement was based upon the non-resident status of the bank, and not its German nationality. A UK-incorporated bank (incorporation being the equivalent of nationality for a company) which was resident in Germany for tax purposes[36] would equally have been refused repayment supplement. Unlike the European Court (as can be seen below), the High Court could not consider whether discrimination on grounds of residence amounted to indirect discrimination on grounds of nationality. Article XX(1) explicitly targeted only discrimination on grounds of nationality and not on grounds of residence. The German bank could not, therefore, argue that it had been discriminated against on grounds of nationality.

The final difficulty in relying upon the non-discrimination article raised the same issue as that raised by the application of European Union law: in determining whether there had been discrimination, should a broad or a narrow view be taken of the factual circumstances that led to the alleged discrimination? This was one of the points that the Queen's Bench Division decided should be left to the European Court.

Having rejected the claim to repayment supplement either under UK domestic law or under the non-discrimination article of the UK–Germany double taxation convention, Nolan LJ concluded that it was appropriate to refer the issue of application of European law to the ECJ. The issues raised concerned both discrimination under the general prohibition of discrimination of nationality, and also the application of the freedom of establishment. These issues were not *acte claire*, were necessary for the final determination of the claim to repayment supplement, and were appropriate for referral to the ECJ.

It is perhaps rather easy to regard the judgment of Nolan LJ as being of primary importance because it paved the way for the reference to the European Court. However, the judgment has significance in its own right. In particular, it is a clear example of treaty under-ride in the United Kingdom, an issue which has not been resolved to the present day.

IV. NON-DISCRIMINATION UNDER EU LAW: THE DECISION OF THE EUROPEAN COURT OF JUSTICE

There were essentially two issues before the ECJ which were raised by the single question referred by the High Court.

---

[36] Because its central management and control was in Germany, which was the sole test of residence at the time that the issue arose.

First, whether in determining if there was discrimination or an infringement of the freedom of establishment, should a broad view of the factual circumstances be taken, or a narrow view? The argument for the United Kingdom government was that a broad view should be taken: had Commerzbank been a UK-resident bank, it would not have been entitled to the exemption from tax under article XV of the UK–US treaty. It was only because it was *not resident* in the UK that it could take advantage of that exemption. Factoring this element in, Commerzbank was treated no worse overall than a UK-resident company in similar circumstances; to the contrary, it was treated better in that it was entitled to exemption and repayment of the tax, even if it was not entitled to the repayment supplement. By contrast, on a narrow view, Commerzbank – as a German resident – having become entitled to a repayment of tax was denied repayment supplement, while a UK-resident company being entitled to a tax repayment (for whatever reason) was entitled to the supplement. This raised very neatly the general question whether in determining the question of discrimination one should look broadly at the issue or take a narrower approach.

The second issue is an even more general question. The prohibition on discrimination in what was then articles 5 and 7 of the EC Treaty[37] prohibited discrimination on grounds of nationality. Similarly, the freedom of establishment in articles 52 and 58 of the Treaty[38] referred not to a resident but (in this case) to a company having its seat in a Member State. The condition attached to repayment supplement, which prevented Commerzbank from claiming it, was, by contrast, a condition attaching to residence. As a very general question, which had not at that time been resolved by the European Court, could discrimination on grounds of residence be equated to, or be an indirect form of, discrimination on grounds of nationality?

This latter point is, of course, of general importance. Tax systems often apply different rules to residents and non-residents, and less commonly apply different rules on grounds of nationality. If the prohibition of nationality discrimination in the EC Treaty also encompassed rules that discriminated on grounds of residence, then the impact on the direct tax systems of the Member States would be far more significant. Since the principles of international taxation, in accordance with the doctrine of territoriality, generally accept that a resident and a non-resident are not in a comparable position, an approach taken by European law that generally prohibited discrimination on grounds of residence (subject, of course, to justification and proportionality) would mean that, in the direct tax field, EU tax law and the general principles of international taxation would begin to diverge along different paths. On this second general issue, therefore, the decision of the ECJ would have far-reaching consequences.

---

[37] Now Arts 18 and 20 of the Treaty on the Functioning of the European Union (2007).
[38] Now Arts 49 and 54 of the Treaty on the Functioning of the European Union.

The Advocate General, Darmon, advised the Court to determine both issues in favour of Commerzbank. On the issue of broad or narrow approach, a narrow approach should be taken. Once a German company became entitled to repayment of tax, it would breach the freedom of establishment if it was denied repayment supplement while a UK-resident company was entitled to that supplement. It was not appropriate to go further and consider the reasons why the tax was repayable: the simple, and narrow, comparator was between a UK-resident company entitled to a repayment of tax and a German company entitled to a repayment of tax. To refuse the repayment supplement infringed the freedom of establishment exercised by the German company when it formed a branch in the United Kingdom.

On the second issue, the Advocate General asked whether discrimination on grounds of residence can be analysed as indirect discrimination on grounds of nationality.[39] He concluded that a residence condition may constitute disguised discrimination on grounds of nationality in as much as, in practice, such a condition principally affects nationals of other Member States. Put quite simply, resident persons were likely to have the nationality of the state of residence, while non-residents were more likely to have the nationality of another Member State. This applied equally to residence as a connecting factor for tax purposes.

Having examined the UK test of central management and control, the Advocate General stated that the criteria of residence and nationality overlapped to a large extent. The Advocate General seemed well aware of the potentially far-reaching implications of the view he was expressing. Nevertheless, a condition based upon residence in a Member State could, very clearly, result in an unjustifiable difference of treatment which interfered with the enjoyment of the freedom of establishment of companies having their seat in another Member State.

The ECJ dealt with the entire issue in a remarkably concise fashion. The entire decision on the right of establishment is contained in eight paragraphs which may be quoted in full.

The right of establishment

13. As the Court held in its judgment in Case C-270/83 *Commission v France* [1986] ECR 273, at paragraph 18, the freedom of establishment which Article 52 grants to nationals of a Member State, and which entails the right for them to take up and pursue activities as self-employed persons under the conditions laid down for its own nationals by the law of the Member State where such establishment is effected, includes, pursuant to Article 58 of the EEC Treaty, the right of companies or firms formed in accordance with the law of a Member State and having their registered office, central administration or principal place of business within the Community to pursue their activities in the Member State concerned through a branch or agency.

---

[39] See paras 28–53 of the Advocate General's Opinion: AG's Opinion of 17 March 1993, *R v CIR ex parte Commerzbank AG*, C-330/91, EU:C:1993:101.

With regard to companies, it should be noted in this context that it is their seat in the abovementioned sense that serves as the connecting factor within the legal system of a particular State, like nationality in the case of natural persons. In the same judgment the Court held that acceptance of the proposition that the Member State in which a company seeks to establish itself may freely apply to it different treatment solely by reason of the fact that its seat is situated in another Member State would deprive the provision of all meaning.

14. Moreover, it follows from the Court's judgment in Case 152/73 *Sotgiu v Deutsche Bundespost* [1974] ECR 153 (at paragraph 11) that the rules regarding equality of treatment forbid not only overt discrimination by reason of nationality or, in the case of a company, its seat, but all covert forms of discrimination which, by the application of other criteria of differentiation, lead in fact to the same result.

15. Although it applies independently of a company's seat, the use of the criterion of fiscal residence within national territory for the purpose of granting repayment supplement on overpaid tax is liable to work more particularly to the disadvantage of companies having their seat in other Member States. Indeed, it is most often those companies which are resident for tax purposes outside the territory of the Member State in question.

16. In order to justify the national provision at issue in the main proceedings, the United Kingdom Government argues that, far from suffering discrimination under the United Kingdom tax rules, non-resident companies which are in Commerzbank's situation enjoy privileged treatment. They are exempt from tax normally payable by resident companies. In those circumstances, there is no discrimination with respect to repayment supplement: resident companies and non-resident companies are treated differently because, for the purposes of corporation tax, they are in different situations.

17. That argument cannot be upheld.

18. A national provision such as the one in question entails unequal treatment. Where a non-resident company is deprived of the right to repayment supplement on overpaid tax to which resident companies are always entitled, it is placed at a disadvantage by comparison with the latter.

19. The fact that the exemption from tax which gave rise to the refund was available only to non-resident companies cannot justify a rule of a general nature withholding the benefit. That rule is therefore discriminatory.

20. It follows from those considerations that the reply to be given to the national court is that Articles 52 and 58 of the Treaty prevent the legislation of a Member State from granting repayment supplement on overpaid tax to companies which are resident for tax purposes in that State whilst refusing the supplement to companies which are resident for tax purposes in another Member State. The fact that the latter would not have been exempt from tax if they had been resident in that State is of no relevance in that regard.

On the second question of discrimination on grounds of residence, paragraph [15] quoted above concludes the issue by stating that 'the use of the criterion of fiscal residence within national territory for the purpose of granting repayment supplement on overpaid tax is liable to work more particularly to the disadvantage of companies having their seat in other Member States'. This approach, which can be traced back to the *Avoir Fiscal* case,[40] set EC direct tax law on a path where it was certain to diverge from the general approach taken in international taxation. International taxation is based on a principle of territoriality that residents and non-residents are not in a comparable position with respect to the imposition of taxes; by contrast, this case confirmed that under EU law a difference in treatment on grounds of residence might well be seen as an indirect restriction of freedoms based on nationality.

On the first issue identified above, as to whether one should take a broad or a narrow approach, the ECJ clearly adopted the narrow approach. At paragraphs 16–19 quoted above, the Court considered that the only comparison was between the resident company entitled to a tax repayment and a non-resident company entitled to a tax repayment. To deny repayment supplement to the UK branch of the non-resident company interfered with the freedom of establishment.

The *Commerzbank* case is, of course, not the only decision of the ECJ to conclude that discrimination on grounds of fiscal residence might involve discrimination on grounds of nationality or infringe one of the fundamental freedoms. However, particularly having regard to the opinion of Advocate General Darmon, it is the earliest case where the distinction between fiscal residence and nationality is most clearly discussed, and the view taken that a difference of treatment on grounds of fiscal residence might involve indirect discrimination on grounds of nationality. In that respect, it represents one of the fundamental steps in the development of European Union tax law.

As explained above, when the judgment of the ECJ was reported back to the High Court in London, the litigation concluded by a consent order under which it was ordered and declared that the Inland Revenue was not entitled to apply a requirement of UK residence to deny repayment supplement to Commerzbank, and Commerzbank was entitled to the repayment supplement accordingly. In effect, the Inland Revenue accepted that the condition of residence in the UK for entitlement to repayment supplement had to be disapplied to give effect to the directly applicable EU law rights of Commerzbank.

V. CONCLUDING COMMENTS

The Commerzbank litigation justifies its inclusion in a compilation of leading cases on UK taxation on several grounds: it contains the now standard summary of the approach to tax treaty interpretation; it contains a discussion

---

[40] Judgment of 28 January 1986, *Commission v France*, C-270/83, EU:C:1986:37 – see para [13] quoted above.

of non-discrimination under tax treaties and, in particular, an example of treaty under-ride; and it is one of the ECJ cases that most clearly concluded that discrimination on grounds of residence could be regarded as indirect discrimination on grounds of nationality and be challenged as an infringement of the freedom of establishment or the general prohibition of nationality under the EC Treaties.

All that being said, it is reasonable to conclude by asking whether the case was rightly decided at the outset. It is difficult not to have a degree of sympathy with the position of the Inland Revenue from the beginning. Anyone steeped in double taxation convention practice would automatically assume that provisions in a double taxation convention are intended to apply only to persons who are residents of one or both of the two countries that are parties to the convention. The UK–US convention should, in principle, apply only to persons who are resident in the US or the UK. A German bank should, in principle, have never been entitled to access the benefits of that convention. Conventions based upon the OECD Model state this explicitly in article 1; the fundamental approach of the Inland Revenue (rejected by Mummery J) was to seek to imply that principle into an earlier convention of 1945 which did not have the explicit wording of article 1 of the Model. Had Mummery J perhaps been more steeped in the principles of international taxation, he might have had less difficulty in recognising such an implied, general principle.

Even if one were unwilling to imply that as a general limitation, an examination of the object and purpose of article XV might well have led to the conclusion that the purpose was to deal with a particular issue related to the deemed US source rule for interest paid by a foreign corporation.[41] A claim for exemption by the UK branch of a German bank was never within the object and purpose of the article.

The UK branch of Commerzbank enjoyed an exemption from tax which, one may assume, was never within the contemplation of the negotiators of the UK–US double taxation convention of 1945 (or the supplementary protocol of 1966):[42] the branch enjoyed an unintended windfall, and got both repayment of tax and repayment supplement as well.

All that being said, the litigation forms the canvas for the development of some fundamental principles which go well beyond the particular circumstances: these include the approach to the interpretation of double taxation conventions, and the application of EU tax law to provisions discriminating on grounds of residence. Litigation is like armed conflict: once begun, one can never predict

---

[41] That explanation for the purpose of the article comes from the joint statement of the revenue authorities and from *Great West Life* (above n 33) which Mummery J was averse to following.

[42] The enactment of a specific provision on losses of branches in receipt of exempt interest in s 50(1), FA 1976 suggests that the possible ramifications of Art XV were seen relatively early. I am indebted to Dr Avery Jones for pointing out this provision.

the outcome or its consequences. When Commerzbank was advised that it might make a claim for exemption and repayment supplement, only the most far-sighted of legal advisers might have appreciated that this would give rise to a leading case on treaty interpretation and on the application of EU law in the direct tax context. That, however, is where the case ended up, and the Commerzbank litigation deserves its place in a collection of leading cases on UK taxation for those reasons.

16

Pepper v Hart and Others *(1992)* The Case of the Misunderstood Minister

PHILIP RIDD

I. INTRODUCTION

'**H**ANSARD ADMISSIBLE – Law Lords' U-turn' – so might a headline have run following the decision of the House of Lords given on 26 November 1992 in *Pepper v Hart*.[1] More precisely, the conclusion was that, on an issue of statutory construction, reference to statements made in the course of the passage of the legislation through Parliament, as recorded in Hansard, may, without contravention of Article 9 of the Bill of Rights 1689, be admitted in evidence provided that certain conditions are satisfied: those conditions are that (a) the legislation concerned is ambiguous or obscure or leads to an absurdity; (b) the material relied upon consists of one or more statements by a minister or other promoter of the bill, together, if necessary, with such other parliamentary material as is necessary to understand such statements and their effect; and (c) the statements relied upon are clear.[2] This conclusion was reached by a majority of six to one at a second hearing, no reference to Hansard having been made at the first hearing. It led to a decision in favour of the taxpayers concerned. Lord Mackay of Clashfern LC disagreed on the Hansard issue but, by different reasoning, agreed with the decision. The case is a landmark in that a long-standing rule was abandoned and it provoked controversy on an industrial scale. It may be unique in that it gives rise to a respectable argument that the reasoning of as many as 12 judges, in fact all who considered the case, was off beam.

It may be helpful to give an overview of the response which will be given to the main questions which arise. It was open to the House of Lords to reach

---

[1] *Pepper v Hart* [1993] AC 593.
[2] ibid, 640.

the Hansard ruling because it was a self-denying judge-made ruling and it lacked justification in the modern era of purposive interpretation of legislation already buttressed by consideration of many extraneous sources which might cast light. There was also a need for confirmation that purposive interpretation applied as much to tax legislation as to other legislation, there being no logical reason otherwise. *Pepper v Hart* was not, however, a suitable vehicle in which to make the Hansard change because, on a close examination, it will be found that the Law Lords misunderstood what they read in Hansard and misconstrued the statutory provision concerned. But, before proceeding, it is necessary for the writer to declare an interest. At the time of *Pepper v Hart* he was a member of the office of the Solicitor of Inland Revenue at Principal Assistant Solicitor level, the level immediately below that of the Solicitor, and did in fact attend throughout both hearings in the House of Lords. This may suggest the possibility of bias, or at any rate an appearance of bias, so it is worth making it clear straightaway that in the writer's view the taxpayers concerned rightly won the case.

II. THE CONTEXT

The facts and the issue in *Pepper v Hart* were straightforward. Derek Pepper, an Inspector of Taxes, raised assessments to income tax for the year 1983–84, 1984–85 and 1985–86 on 10 taxpayers (of whom Mr John Thornton Hart was one) who were members of the staff of Malvern College. During the years concerned children of theirs were educated at the school under an arrangement by which the parents paid one-fifth of the standard school fees; the school was not bound, contractually or otherwise, to make this concession available to a member of staff; the school was not full, though it did have sufficient full fee-paying pupils to reach its budget break-even point.[3] The benefit of the arrangement was within the scope of the charge to income tax under Schedule E. The bone of contention was the monetary amount to be attributed to the benefit. The statutory provisions which governed that amount were the Finance Act 1976 sections 61 and 63. The parties differed as to the meaning and application of section 63.

Section 61 provided that the amount should be 'the cash equivalent of the benefit', as determined under section 63 which, as relevant, read:

> (1) The cash equivalent of any benefit chargeable to tax under section 61 above is an amount equal to the cost of the benefit, less so much (if any) of it as is made good by the employee to those providing the benefit. (2) ... the cost of a benefit is the amount of any expense incurred in or in connection with its provision, and ... includes a proper proportion of any expense relating partly to the benefit and partly to other matters.

---

[3] The full facts may be found in the Case Stated at 65 TC 421, 424–33.

The taxpayers' case was based on the marginal method of calculation, ie, the cost to the employer was to be measured by reference to the additional expenses attributable to the taking in of the taxpayers' children – extra food and laundry costs, for example. The Revenue advocated the average method of calculation, ie, take the expenses of running the school and divide by the total number of pupils to ascertain a figure for each pupil. The difference between the approaches was, therefore, that under the taxpayers' method the general costs of running the school were attributed to the full-paying pupils only, whereas under the Revenue's method those expenses were attributed to all the pupils. That basis would give rise to a charge to tax, but the taxpayers' basis produced a figure lower than the (one-fifth) fees payable, so that there would be no charge to tax.

III. THE PROCEEDINGS SHORT OF THE HOUSE OF LORDS SECOND HEARING

To set the scene it is unnecessary to describe the earlier course of the proceedings in any detail. The taxpayers' appeals against the assessments were first heard by the Special Commissioners, sitting by a single Commissioner, Mr THK Everett, and were successful. The Revenue's appeal against that decision was heard by Mr Justice Vinelott. The judge considered that section 63(2) (which, he thought, the Special Commissioner had overlooked) justified the Revenue's case. The Court of Appeal (Slade, Nicholls, Farquharson LJJ) upheld the High Court decision.

The first hearing in the House of Lords took place on 4 November 1991 before Lord Bridge of Harwich, Lord Emslie, Lord Griffiths, Lord Oliver of Aylmerton and Lord Browne-Wilkinson. While the Revenue were called on, the taxpayers' submissions had not gone down at all well. Lord Emslie was silent. The only remark made by Lord Griffiths was that whenever he travelled by plane he had to walk past the first class or business class seats which seemed all to be occupied by airline employees on 'freebies'. The other three Law Lords, Lord Bridge in the lead, intervened with comments which were firmly antipathetic to the taxpayers' submissions. The writer's personal diary for that day has the entry 'the signs are 5-0 up'. A decision before the Christmas break was a realistic possibility, failing which January. A mysterious silence followed. On 27 February 1992 a letter arrived, stating that the House of Lords would rehear the case and would consider whether to relax the Hansard exclusionary rule. That extraordinary news would have been less extraordinary if the taxpayers' case had had even a moderately decent run at the first hearing. While several rumours became current, there seems never to have been any clear explanation as to how the decision to rehear came about. Among the possibilities is that one of the Law Lords noticed a brief mention towards the end of Mr Justice Vinelott's decision of 'observations made by the Chief Secretary to the Treasury in the course of the debate on the Finance Bill in Committee'[4] and researched to see what those observations were.

IV. THE BACKGROUND HISTORY

The rule, that statements made in the course of the passage of legislation through Parliament, as recorded in Hansard, were not admissible in evidence on issues of statutory construction – 'the exclusionary rule' – stood for over 200 years. Its chronological development is set out in a scholarly analysis in *Bennion on Statutory Interpretation*.[5] It has to be said that it is a history which does not reflect great credit on the judiciary. The earliest statement of the exclusionary rule was in *Millar v Taylor*[6] but it was broken by the judges in the very same case.[7] There followed several cases in which the exclusionary rule was reiterated but no reasons were given to justify it. On a few occasions the rule was broken.[8] It will be no surprise that Lord Denning MR went his own sweet way, applying the rule,[9] sidestepping it,[10] or brazenly defying it.[11] Some judges wavered and vaguely floated the idea of an exception where parliamentary material would decisively dispose of an issue.[12] Notwithstanding those expressions of doubt, the exclusionary rule was strongly affirmed in the House of Lords in 1975,[13] 1978[14] and 1982.[15] Yet, as early as 1992, the exclusionary rule fell from grace. It is a somewhat sorry tale.

For present purposes the reasons for the exclusionary rule must be ascertained from a potted history. At the outset it was remarked that what happened to a bill in one House of Parliament would not be known in the other House.[16] Next, the rule was said to reflect rule that parol evidence was not admissible to construe a record.[17] Another criterion was untrustworthiness.[18] Reliance was

---

[4] [1990] 1 WLR 204, 211.

[5] O Jones, *Bennion on Statutory Interpretation*, 6th edn (London, Butterworths, 2013) 602–16.

[6] *Millar v Taylor* (1769) 4 Burr 2303.

[7] ibid, 2333.

[8] *In re Mew and Thorne* (1862) 31 LJ Bcy 87; *Hebbert v Purchas* (1871) LR 3 PC 605; *Edwards v Attorney-General for Canada* [1930] AC 124.

[9] *Escoigne Properties Ltd v IRC* [1958] AC 549.

[10] *R v Local Commissioner for Administration for the North and East Area of England, Ex parte Bradford Metropolitan City Council* [1979] QB 287, 311–12, and *R v Secretary of State for the Environment, Ex parte Norwich City Council* [1982] QB 808, 824.

[11] *R v Greater London Council ex parte Blackburn* [1976] 1 WLR 550, 556.

[12] Notably, Lord Reid in *Warner v Metropolitan Police Commissioner* [1969] 2 AC 256, 279, and Lord Simon of Glaisdale in *McMillan v Crouch* [1972] 1 WLR 1102, 1119.

[13] *Black-Clawson International Ltd v Papierwerke Waldhof-Aschaffenburg AG* [1975] AC 591.

[14] *Davis v Johnson* [1979] AC 264.

[15] *Hadmor Productions Ltd v Hamilton* [1983] 1 AC 191.

[16] *Millar* (above n 6) 2332.

[17] *Shrewsbury (Earl of) v Scott* (1859) 6 CBNS 1, 213.

[18] *R v West Riding of Yorkshire County Council* [1906] 2 KB 676, 716.

placed on practical reasons – time, expense and difficulty of access.[19] Sometimes an admixture of reasons of principle and of practicality was given.[20] Another justification was the danger that judges would be distracted from concentrating on the statutory language.[21] Yet another reason was the unreliability of responses given in the cut and thrust of debate.[22] And another was the uncertainty of knowing to what extent a speaker's view was shared by others.[23]

Taken as a whole, this reasoning does not have the benefit of consistency and clarity. The justifications for the exclusionary rule resort variously to principle and practicality. At this stage comment on those justifications will generally be reserved, but it is important to note two negative points. One is that there is no reference to any statute, not even the Bill of Rights 1689, so the exclusionary rule must be regarded as judge-made. The other is that there is no rejection of the proposition that the object of statutory interpretation is to ascertain and give effect to the intention of Parliament. It is true that there is qualification in that in the *Black-Clawson* case Lord Reid said:

> We often say that we are looking for the intention of Parliament, but that is not quite accurate. We are seeking the meaning of the words which Parliament used. We are seeking not what Parliament meant but the true meaning of what they said.[24]

The judges have steered clear of the oft-advanced argument that it is logically impossible to attribute an intention to an institution such as Parliament.

In passing it is worth noticing that, in expressing his concurrence with the exclusionary rule, Lord Halsbury LC warned against making 'an *a priori* presumption that an Act did not mean what it said'.[25]

V. THE ARGUMENT

Alongside counsel for the parties, and properly attired in wig and gown, was Mr John Griffiths of the Incorporated Society for Law Reporting for England and Wales. Mr Griffiths reported cases in the House of Lords for many years. It is to him that we are indebted for the thorough record of argument.[26] It runs to some 8,500 words, so it is necessary to encapsulate it brutally.

Anthony Lester QC[27] was leading counsel for the taxpayers at the second hearing in the House of Lords.[28] The record of his opening argument shows

---

[19] *Beswick v Beswick* [1968] AC 58, 74.
[20] *Black-Clawson* (above n 13) 629–30, 638.
[21] *Davis* (above n 14) 337.
[22] ibid, 350.
[23] *Ealing London Borough Council v Race Relations Board* [1972] AC 342, 361.
[24] *Black-Clawson* (above n 13) 614.
[25] *Herron v Rathmines and Rathgar Improvement Commissioners* [1892] AC 498, 502.
[26] *Pepper v Hart* (above n 1) 597–612.
[27] Now Lord Lester of Herne Hill QC.
[28] Mr Lester had not been instructed at earlier stages of the case.

that, as was to be expected, he duly introduced the exclusionary rule by reference to all the main cases. The essence of the argument in favour of modification of the rule appears in two sentences as follows:

> It is irrational for the courts to maintain an absolute rule depriving themselves of access to potential relevant evidence or information for [the] purpose [of statutory interpretation] … Where a statutory provision has been enacted following an authoritative ministerial statement as to the understanding by the Executive of its meaning and effect, such a statement may provide important evidence about the object and purpose of the provision and the intention of Parliament in agreeing to its enactment, and may create reasonable expectations among Members of Parliament and those affected by the legislation.[29]

The argument examined the position in several countries other than the United Kingdom, and it was by reference to a report of the New Zealand Law Commission[30] that it was submitted that the exclusionary rule was not justifiable. The core of the argument was that the dangers and difficulties of resorting to Hansard were outweighed by the advantages of doing so.

The Attorney General, Sir Nicholas Lyell QC,[31] presented the argument in relation to the exclusionary rule, but left Alan Moses QC[32] to present the argument on the tax issue.[33] The record of the argument in relation to the exclusionary rule is, it must be said, somewhat diffuse and repetitive. Most of the arguments were to the effect that a change would be undesirable and would in any event be better left to Parliament, and reference was, of course, made to the concerns raised in previous cases as already mentioned above. The only new point lay in the submission that the exclusionary rule accorded with Article 9 of the Bill of Rights in that reference to Hansard could involve 'questioning' the debates and proceedings in the House of Commons (and the Lords) contrary to Article 9, as

> analysis in the courts, both in argument and by way of decision, of what was said in the course of proceedings in Parliament, can easily lead to questioning whether the explanation of the application of an intended Act of Parliament reveals an imperfect understanding of the words used or of the particular situation in question.[34]

A weakness in the argument is evident in the words 'can easily lead' because, equally easily, courts could refer to Hansard with proper respect, and the Bill of Rights argument therefore did not seem to suggest an absolute bar but merely joined other arguments which submitted that a change would be undesirable.

---

[29] *Pepper v Hart* (above n 1) 600.

[30] New Zealand Law Commission, *A New Interpretation Act: To Avoid Prolixity and Tautology* (NZ Law Com No 17, 1990).

[31] Later Lord Lyell of Markyate.

[32] Later Moses LJ.

[33] The Attorney General had not appeared at earlier stages of the case, but Mr Moses had.

[34] *Pepper v Hart* (above n 1) 607.

It may be mentioned that the second hearing was a most unusual one. Hearings nowadays in the Supreme Court do not in their nature differ essentially from the hearings of old in one of the committee rooms of the House of Lords in that they consist of lively debate between the judges and counsel. Six days were set aside for the second hearing of *Pepper v Hart*, but it was evident from the outset that, if Anthony Lester QC was to be able to deploy the vast array of material on which he wished to rely, interactive debate needed to be curtailed – indeed, breakneck speed was necessary. Thus, the arguments were scarcely tested by debate. Moreover, the Hansard point was so dominant that little attention was paid to the task of construing the statutory provision in issue.

VI. THE QUIET REVOLUTION

Aside from Hansard, though crucial to the Hansard argument, there is an important point which is seldom mentioned in commentary on the case. It was the first occasion on which the House of Lords recognised that purposive interpretation had superseded literal interpretation in relation to tax cases. That imprimatur is to be found in the speeches of Lord Griffiths and of Lord Browne-Wilkinson.[35] The change may have been inevitable as tax legislation could not sensibly have been equiparated with criminal legislation, but it is surprising that it was made without any protest beforehand, and it is yet more surprising that it has almost been ignored subsequently.[36]

VII. THE FATE OF THE EXCLUSIONARY RULE

As previously mentioned, Lord Mackay LC disagreed that the exclusionary rule should be modified. The leading speech in favour of modification was given by Lord Browne-Wilkinson. The other five Law Lords expressly agreed with him, and Lord Bridge, Lord Griffiths and Lord Oliver also delivered speeches. Lord Browne-Wilkinson's speech runs to some 13,500 words. Once again, the task of analysis must be brutally curtailed.

In the decisive section of the speech Lord Browne-Wilkinson noted that there was a modern case in which the court had looked at parliamentary debates as an aid to construction. This was *Pickstone v Freemans Plc*[37] which concerned

---

[35] ibid, 617 and 635 respectively.

[36] In *CIR v McGuckian* [1997] 1 WLR 991, 999 Lord Steyn said that tax law had 'remained remarkably resistant to the new non-formalist methods of interpretation' and that tax law had been 'by and large left behind as some island of literal interpretation'. He went on to say that 'a breakthrough was made in *Ramsay (WT) Ltd v CIR* [1982] AC 300', but that case, unlike *Pepper v Hart*, contained no express endorsement of purposive interpretation and it may be argued – and will be argued elsewhere – that the modern notion that *Ramsay* franked purposive interpretation involves what may politely be called creative remodelling.

[37] *Pickstone v Freemans Plc* [1989] AC 66.

a statutory instrument relating to equal pay. Lord Browne-Wilkinson commented that the case 'represents a major inroad on the exclusionary rule'.[38] Incidentally, Lord Mackay noted that the propriety of looking at the parliamentary debates was not questioned by anyone involved in that case.[39] After outlining the history of the exclusionary rule Lord Browne-Wilkinson explained the difficulties which confronted the courts when grappling with ambiguous statutory wording and asked the questions:

> Why … should the courts blind themselves to a clear indication of what Parliament intended in using those [ambiguous] words? The court cannot attach a meaning to words which they cannot bear, but if the words are capable of bearing more than one meaning why should not Parliament's intention be enforced rather than thwarted?[40]

He then derived support from other factors; the use of White Papers and official reports; the 'logically indistinguishable'[41] decision in *Pickstone v Freemans Plc*, doubts expressed by Lord Reid[42] and, extra-judicially, by Lord Wilberforce;[43] textbook references; and judicial evasion of the rule.

Lord Browne-Wilkinson then turned to the Attorney General's arguments, starting with those based on practicalities. First, he considered that difficulties of access to parliamentary material were overstated. Secondly, lawyers' and judges' lack of familiarity with parliamentary proceedings was not thought overwhelming. Thirdly, the increase in court time was considered insignificant provided that limits on the modification of the rule were adhered to, and cost orders could be made against those who improperly sought to introduce parliamentary material. Fourthly, while it was accepted that legal advisers would be bound to research parliamentary material and would often discover nothing useful, the attendant cost should not be overestimated.

Having dismissed the arguments based on practicalities, Lord Browne-Wilkinson turned to the Bill of Rights and observed that the Attorney General's argument would result in there being no freedom to refer anywhere, not just in the courts, to what was said in Parliament. Article 9 was considered only to protect Members of Parliament from 'any penalty, civil or criminal for what they said'.[44] It was then pointed out that Hansard had frequently been used in court proceedings involving issues other than statutory interpretation. Lord Browne-Wilkinson then turned to the objection that use of parliamentary material in construing legislation would confuse the roles of Parliament as the maker of law and the courts as the interpreter, but again the use of White Papers

---

[38] *Pepper v Hart* (above n 1) 631.

[39] ibid, 615.

[40] ibid, 635.

[41] ibid.

[42] In *Black-Clawson* (above n 13) 613–15 and in *Warner* (above n 12).

[43] Attorney-General's Department, *Symposium on Statutory Interpretation* (Australian Government Publishing Service, 1983).

[44] *Pepper v Hart* (above n 1) 638.

and official reports was given to support the conclusion that no constitutional impropriety would be involved. Finally, in dealing with the rights and privileges of Parliament, Lord Browne-Wilkinson prayed in aid what he had said about the Bill of Rights.

Thus, the conclusion was reached that the exclusionary rule should be modified on the terms previously described.

It is not necessary to say much about the supporting speeches. Lord Griffiths' speech included the question 'Why then cut ourselves off from the one source in which may be found an authoritative statement of the intention with which the legislation is placed before Parliament?'[45] Lord Oliver confessed that he was a 'somewhat reluctant convert'[46] and considered that it was necessary to be 'very cautious in opening the door to the reception of material not readily or ordinarily accessible to the citizen whose rights and duties are to be affected by the words in which the legislature has elected to express its will'.[47]

Lord Mackay's objection to modifying the exclusionary rule was based entirely on the practicalities, especially the resulting increase in the costs of litigation.[48] It is a telling limitation. It seems impossible to quarrel with Lord Browne-Wilkinson's disposal of the argument based on the Bill of Rights: it is a killer point that, if the Revenue's argument were correct, Hansard could never be referred to anywhere.[49] So, it was open in law for the Hansard ruling to be reached. Moreover, the Hansard ruling was well-nigh inevitable, given that the courts had already gone far down the road of admitting extraneous material as aids, and given that purposive construction drove wide enquiry.

It is submitted, however, that there is no great significance in the three conditions for admissibility which were laid down. Unless the legislation concerned is ambiguous or obscure or leads to an absurdity, the plain meaning will be adopted, so reference to Hansard would achieve nothing. It is inconceivable that anything said by someone other than the minister or other promoter of the bill would be of assistance. Moreover, statements which lacked clarity would be no help. Thus, the conditions are no more than a recognition of the circumstances in which reference to Hansard would serve a useful purpose. In so far as the exclusionary rule may be said to have been modified, rather than abrogated, it now exists only to exclude material which, if considered, would fail to cast any light. Moreover, the continued existence of that rule is redundant in point of practice, because the written material of any party who wishes to rely on Hansard material will include an assertion that the conditions for admissibility are satisfied and will

---

[45] ibid, 617.

[46] ibid, 619.

[47] ibid, 620.

[48] ibid, 615.

[49] As to Art 9 of the Bill of Rights more generally, and discussion of the copious material on the subject, see Joint Committee on Parliamentary Privilege, *Parliamentary Privilege (first report)* (1998–99, HL 43-1, HC 214-I), available at publications.parliament.uk/pa/jt199899/jtselect/jtpriv/43/4302.htm.

then go on to expound the material in question, and it is virtually certain that the judge(s) will read the material before coming to any decision that, technically, it is not admissible. The allegedly strict conditions are a snare and delusion, but this does not impinge on the soundness of the Hansard ruling.

VIII. RESOLUTION OF THE CASE

In his speech Lord Browne-Wilkinson dealt thoroughly with the parliamentary history. What happened, put shortly, was that in 1976, when there was an overhaul of the taxation of benefits in kind, the government put forward a different rule for putting a monetary figure on a benefit in kind but, under pressure, gave way on the proposed change and reverted to the position under the predecessor legislation (Finance Act 1948). Various questions were put to the Financial Secretary to the Treasury, Robert Sheldon MP. As to airline travel and railwaymen, he spoke of the cost of benefits as 'very little', possibly even a 'negative cost' and confirmed that 'We are reverting to the present practice'. As to service industries generally he said that ' the costs to the employer … could be much less than the arm's length cost to the outside person taking advantage of such a service'. As to a mariner's spouse having a free passage on a ship he stated that only the nominal charge for food would give rise to a tax charge. Finally, the position of the education of teachers' children at reduced fees was raised and the answer given was that the cost to the employer would be 'very small indeed'.[50] There could not be a scintilla of doubt that the Financial Secretary was envisaging application of the marginal method of calculation in the examples put to him, and the Revenue did not suggest otherwise in argument.

The conditions for admission of Hansard material were considered to be satisfied. As to condition (a) Lord Browne-Wilkinson's view was that the words 'expense incurred in or in connection with' were ambiguous as between marginal cost and average cost.[51] Lord Griffiths and Lord Oliver expressly shared that view.[52] Lord Browne-Wilkinson thought that it was right to attribute to Parliament as a whole the intention identified by the Financial Secretary.[53] Condition (b) was plainly satisfied. As to condition (c) Lord Browne-Wilkinson found that the Minister's repeated assurances were quite inconsistent with tax being charged on anything but the additional or marginal costs basis,[54] and others agreed.[55]

---

[50] *Pepper v Hart* (above n 1) 625–30 for the full examination of the relevant parliamentary history.

[51] ibid, 640–41. This conclusion should, it is suggested, be held firmly in the reader's mind because in due course it will be argued that it was unsound and, furthermore, it was based on a misrepresentation of the Revenue's argument.

[52] *Pepper v Hart* (above n 1) 618 and 620–21.

[53] ibid, 642.

[54] ibid, 641.

[55] ibid, 616–17, 621.

IX. A PAUSE FOR BREATH

A moment will be taken to stand back and speculate on how all this might strike the non-lawyer commentator, whether on a Clapham omnibus or standing by officiously. The view taken might well be that it was all plain sailing; that judges plainly have no business to disregard any source which may help them to accomplish their duties; and that assurances given, on advice from Revenue officials, by a minister should obviously be honoured. The outcome might have provoked a cheer that the Revenue, granted an inch, had been prevented from taking an ell. Disfavour might be expressed that it took four court hearings, involving 12 judges, to achieve confirmation that the Special Commissioners had reached the right result. It might be looked at askance that citizens who had an almost undeniable grievance that the Revenue were misbehaving could not go to law without risking the heavy bill of costs which would result if the courts somehow found the grievance insusceptible of remedy. It is, however, all too easy to raise questions which go beyond the proper scope of this chapter, so our train must not be let loose on sidetracks.

X. THE CASE OF THE MISSING CONSTRUCTION

This section deals principally with the question whether the majority of the Law Lords accurately understood what they read in Hansard, or whether they misunderstood what they read in Hansard and misconstrued the statutory provision concerned. The heading to this section sounds like the title of a work from the 'Golden Age of Detective Fiction',[56] but the excuse for it lies in its accuracy. Two commentators, the late Francis Bennion QC and the writer, have put forward the view that in *Pepper v Hart* the House of Lords misunderstood the statutory provisions, that the constructions put forward by the parties should both have been rejected, and that a third construction was the correct one.[57] But, as to the detail of that third construction, there is a difference between the two views put forward.

The missing construction is that there is no ambiguity or obscurity in the statutory wording and the foundation for it is that, unlike the constructions put forward by the parties, it enables the provision to be applied sensibly in any of the wide range of circumstances in which employee benefits may arise. To make all this good, it is necessary to demonstrate the soundness of four

---

[56] Several books by Christopher Bush have titles beginning 'The Case of', as also do many of Erle Stanley Gardner's books.

[57] Apart from the book already referred to, *Bennion on Statutory Interpretation*, 6th edn (above n 5), and other sources, Francis Bennion's views are best found at [2007] *PL* 1. In the most recent edition of the book, D Bailey and L Norbury, *Bennion on Statutory* Interpretation, 7th edn (London, Lexis Nexis, 2017), Francis Bennion's views have not been repeated. The writer's view is to be found at P Ridd, 'Verdict by Misadventure' *Tax Journal* (16 July 2007) 18.

propositions, viz (i) that the taxpayers' construction, as adopted by the House of Lords, was flawed; (ii) that the Revenue's construction, as adopted by the lower courts, was flawed; (iii) that the missing construction is a viable interpretation of the provision; and (iv) that the missing construction is consistent with what the Financial Secretary said.

As to (i) the fundamental proposition is that benefits will arise in a wide range of circumstances, including external benefits, that is to say, benefits unconnected with the employer's business.[58] The statutory provision, if it is to be effective, must be construed to enable its application across the range. Restrictive interpretations would fail to meet that need. If the benefit is something which the employer has purchased, the cost will be the employer's outlay and the marginal method will be incapable of application because, there having been no cost in the first place, there is no extra element of cost. In the Court of Appeal Nicholls LJ used the example of maintenance of a swimming pool made available to employees to show that the statutory provision could not be sensibly interpreted to refer to marginal cost.[59] The Law Lords failed to deal with this point: indeed, the speeches paid no attention whatever to the reasoning in the courts below. It does, however, deal a mortal blow to the Law Lords' conclusion that that the words 'expense incurred in or in connection with' were ambiguous as between marginal cost and average cost, because, quite simply, it fails to cope with circumstances in which neither marginal nor average cost would be capable of application.

In this connection it is to be noted that the headnote to the *Appeal Cases* report[60] confines the decision to the correct construction of the statutory provisions in relation to in-house benefits. That limitation is beyond criticism because the speeches in the House of Lords did not address the question of how to measure the cost of external benefits. As the marginal method is incapable of application to external benefits, it follows that the statutory provisions must also encompass some other method or methods of calculation. But there can be one rule for in-house benefits and another rule for external benefits only if the statutory provisions draw a distinction between those different types of benefit. On the face of it they do not draw any such distinction. To make sense of the Law Lords' decision it is, therefore, necessary, to say that such a distinction must be inferred. But there is no hint of this in the speeches. As it was only 'cost', and not 'benefit', which was conceived to be ambiguous, the analysis in the speeches was defective in failing to address the whole of the problem.

---

[58] *Pepper v Hart* (above n 1) 622, referring to the differentiation drawn by Nicholls LJ at [1991] Ch 203, 210.

[59] [1991] Ch 203, 211. In argument Revenue counsel had mentioned an undertaking which provided a facility which was not provided to customers (eg, chiropody for shop assistants in a supermarket) to demonstrate circumstances in which the marginal costs approach could not be applied (ibid, 208).

[60] *Pepper v Hart* (above n 1) 594.

In any event the Law Lords were barking up a non-existent tree when declaring that the words 'expense incurred in or in connection with' were ambiguous as between marginal cost and average cost. That choice did not arise. The Revenue's reliance was not on those words but on 'proper proportion' as justifying the average method; it would have been absurd to suggest that 'expense incurred in or in connection with' encompassed not only actual costs but also hypothetical amounts derived from an averaging process. What the Revenue argued was that 'expense incurred in or in connection with' were plain words which denoted all the expenses which related to the benefit, and that those words should not somehow be construed to be limited to marginal expense.

As to (ii) it is a curious thing that the average cost approach was not tested for soundness in the courts below: once the marginal cost approach had been rejected, it seems to have been assumed without question that taking a rateable proportion of the whole expenses of running the school would follow. It was not noted that some circumstances may involve disparity of value. This may, whatever the position in relation to Malvern College, be tested in the educational context. It might be inapposite to consider school pupils as alike in relation to the costs of educating pupils. That would be obvious in the case of a school which had both boarding and day pupils, as a boarding pupil is, self-evidently, a more expensive proposition than a day pupil. Furthermore, a school may incur distinct costs because of special needs or requirements on the part of some pupils. Examples of special needs might be disabilities such as blindness or deafness (whole or partial); as to special requirements, it is not unusual for expert musicians to have to be drafted in to teach particular instruments. Specialised costs, say of teaching a pupil to play the contra-bassoon, are referable to that pupil and should be attributed to that pupil alone. In terms of statutory interpretation, the point here is that 'proper proportion' does not mean 'average' or 'rateable' proportion, and in any instance what may be found to be the proper proportion will depend on the particular circumstances of the case.

As to (iii) it has already been suggested that the words 'the amount of any expense incurred in or in connection with [the] provision [of the benefit]' were plain words which denoted all the expenses which related to the benefit. Moreover, there would appear to be no justification for departing from the plain meaning of the words. There might be issues of fact as to whether any particular item of expense satisfied the 'incurred in or in connection with' test; for example, depreciation was the subject of a difference between the accountants who gave evidence before the Special Commissioner,[61] but the possibilities of factual disputes do not bear on the meaning of the statutory words. Equally 'proper proportion' are words which plainly denote fair and reasonable apportionment.

As to (iv) it is submitted that the missing construction is entirely consistent with what the Financial Secretary said in Parliament. He was answering

---

[61] See *Pepper v Hart* (1992) 65 TC 421, 429–30.

questions about the application of the statutory provisions. In giving clear answers, he did not say anything to the effect that the meaning of the provisions was such that they necessarily led to the results described. The Law Lords inferred that he must have given his answers on the basis that 'cost' meant marginal cost. That inference is, at best, unsafe, because the Minister's answers are equally consistent with the missing construction; there is nothing implausible in the possibility that his advisers were telling him that the Revenue's practice under the new provision would be the same as that under the 1948 predecessor, namely to apply the marginal cost method in the situations being put to him.[62] Indeed it is difficult to imagine what other advice might have been offered; the advice cannot have been that the new provision was to be understood as referring to marginal cost because the advisers, unless afflicted with a sudden attack of oversight, will have been aware of the wide variety of circumstances in which the marginal cost method would have been incapable of application. If a choice had to be made between the inference drawn by the Law Lords and the inference that the missing construction underlay the Minister's remarks, it is the latter inference which has the hallmarks of conviction. The cardinal point is, though, that, while what the Minister said about outcomes is plain, he was not clear about the basis on which those outcomes would be reached, and condition (c), as laid down by Lord Browne-Wilkinson, was not met if, as has been argued, the missing construction was at least a possible construction, even if not, as the writer believes, the correct construction.[63]

For these reasons it is submitted that section 63(2) was not ambiguous but meant exactly what it said, namely that all expenses incurred in relation to the benefit were to be brought into account and, if the account then proved to cover matters other than the benefit, a fair apportionment was to be made in accordance with the circumstances of the particular case.

An incidental reference should be made to Slade LJ's drawing attention to 'the short and sparsely drafted section 63(2)'.[64] It was a fair comment, but the explanation for the sparsity is surely that Parliament chose a short general rule because, otherwise, it would have been necessary to lay out a set of detailed rules applicable to the wide variety of circumstances in which benefits arise. In the absence of detailed rules, the governing principle is that every case must be resolved in accordance with its particular circumstances.

---

[62] Note, however, that the previous practice was described as one of 'compromise or fudge and muddle' in which the Revenue 'had acquiesced'; so said Alan Moses QC in a handout (of which the writer has a copy) for a conference held in April 1994 at Balliol College, Oxford.

[63] It should be noted that in *R v Secretary of State for the Environment, Transport and the Regions, Ex parte Spath Holme Ltd* [2001] 2 AC 349, 392 Lord Bingham of Cornhill disagreed with Francis Bennion's view but he did not go into the matter deeply and the remark that '[t]he minister gave what was no doubt taken to be a reliable statement on the meaning of [the cost of a benefit]' is not sustainable as the minister in fact said nothing about the meaning of the provision as opposed to its application.

[64] [1991] Ch 203, 215.

It is an odd thing that the missing construction was never spotted in the courts. It is, of course, all too easy to be mesmerised into thinking that one or other of the parties to a case must be right. But it is commonplace that judges, especially the Law Lords, look at cases in a wide-ranging way, conscious that statutory provisions will be applicable not just to the instant case but also to other circumstances, possibly similar, but also possibly quite different. Moreover, it was noted that employee benefits arise in all manner of circumstances.[65] Yet the speeches in the House of Lords clung tenaciously to the arguments put forward by counsel and seem tacitly to have assumed that a decision in favour of the construction advanced by the taxpayers would not have any adverse effects so far as the integrity of the statutory provisions was concerned.

This section also needs to deal with the question whether Lord Mackay's reasoning was sound. He concluded that it was 'a reasonable construction of the statutory provisions'[66] that they adopted the marginal cost method, so it cannot be said that he spotted and adopted the missing construction.

As already mentioned, Francis Bennion also took the view, albeit not on precisely the same basis as the writer, that the statutory provisions were neither ambiguous nor obscure and had been misunderstood by all concerned in the case. His analysis differs materially from the writer's in only one respect. His view was that the statutory provisions required the cost to be determined by the Revenue by use of its judgment.[67] The problem with this is that, like the arguments in the case, it has no foundation in the words of the statute, or elsewhere.[68] This point is no mere quibble. In the event of a dispute an aggrieved taxpayer would, if Francis Bennion were right, have to establish that the Revenue's judgment was wholly unreasonable, whereas on the writer's approach the appeal Commissioners would be free to substitute whatever result they considered as the more appropriate one in the circumstances.

If the Law Lords had not fallen into error, but had adopted the missing construction, they would have had to face the choice between restoring the Special Commissioners' decision or remitting the case. It is suggested that examination of the Case Stated shows that a remitter would have been unnecessary. It is not apparent from the Case Stated that Mr Everett misunderstood the statutory provisions; it has to be accepted that it is not altogether clear exactly how he did construe the provisions, but it is plain that Mr Everett preferred the approach of the accountant who advanced the marginal cost basis[69] and rejected the Revenue's view because it seemed to 'ignore the commercial realities of the situation'.[70] On a fair reading of the reasons given by Mr Everett for his decision,

---

[65] *Pepper v Hart* (above n 1) 622.
[66] ibid, 613.
[67] *Bennion on Statutory Interpretation*, 6th edn (above n 5) 584–90.
[68] For an example of a statutory provision which confers a power of judgment on the Revenue, consider FA 1965, sch 6, para 21(4).
[69] (1992) 65 TC 421, 432.
[70] ibid, 430.

it seems undeniable that he considered the marginal cost as the cost most fitting in the circumstances; and that view is not out of keeping with section 63(2) either because 'the amount of any expense incurred in or in connection with [the] provision [of the benefit]' is, in the circumstances, the marginal cost, or, if regard is to be had in the first instance to all of the school's running costs, because the 'proper proportion' is, in the circumstances, the marginal cost. Both of those views on detailed application lead to the same result and accord with the governing principle that the cost is to accord with the circumstances of the case. It follows that the Special Commissioners' decision in favour of the taxpayers should have been restored.

If, as has been suggested, *Pepper v Hart* was not a suitable vehicle in which to consider the exclusionary rule, was there another suitable vehicle at the time? As it happens, there was. *R v Warwickshire County Council, ex parte Johnson*[71] concerned a prosecution under the Consumer Protection Act 1987 of an employee for his refusal to honour a promise about the price of goods. In the House of Lords debate on the Consumer Protection Bill the Minister explained that the wording of the Bill was, deliberately, such that employees would not be liable to prosecution. That statement plainly met the conditions laid down by Lord Browne-Wilkinson. In particular, the statement, unlike the parliamentary material in *Pepper v Hart*, specifically addressed the meaning of the proposed statutory wording.

An earlier opportunity arose in *Leedale v Lewis*,[72] which sponsored the concerns of Lord Wilberforce mentioned previously.[73] In that case the House of Lords, upholding the courts below, construed section 42(2) Finance Act 1965 in a way contrary to a ministerial assurance. Concerns were expressed at the time,[74] and remedial legislation was passed,[75] but it is evident that the case lingered in the folk memory.

XI. AFTERMATH

The Hansard ruling has survived, and it has not been questioned in litigation over the last several years. It has been expressly adopted and applied in several cases.[76] But there was, initially, debate on an impressive scale and doubts were expressed even in House of Lords speeches.[77] One Law Lord went beyond

---

[71] *R v Warwickshire County Council, Ex parte Johnson* [1993] AC 583.
[72] *Leedale v Lewis* [1982] 1 WLR 1319.
[73] Above n 43.
[74] See JF Avery Jones, 'The Leedale Affair' [1983] *BTR* 70 and HW Wiggins, 'Leedale v Lewis – Revenue Law-Making' [1983] *LSG* 461.
[75] FA 1981, s 80.
[76] eg, *Stubbings v Webb* [1993] AC 498; *Chief Adjudication Officer v Foster* [1993] AC 754; and *AE Beckett & Sons (Lyndons) Ltd v Midlands Electricity plc* [2001] 1 WLR 281.
[77] See *Robinson v Secretary of State for Northern Ireland* [2002] UKHL 32; [2002] NI 90, para 40 (Lord Hoffmann); para 65 (Lord Hobhouse of Woodborough). Lord Millett expressed his concerns extra-judicially (see Lord Millett, 'Construing Statutes' (1999) *SLR* 107).

what might be described as inconsequential obiter grumbling, and this was Lord Steyn. At first he raised his concerns in a lecture.[78] His paramount concern lay in the passage:

> Given that the ministerial explanation is *ex hypothesi* clear on the very point of construction, *Pepper v Hart* treats qualifying ministerial statements as canonical. It treats them as a source of law. It is in constitutional terms a retrograde step: it enables the executive to make law ... What is constitutionally unacceptable is to treat the intentions of the government as revealed in debates as reflecting the will of Parliament.[79]

In a response, Professor Stefan Vogenauer sought to demonstrate that, if the speeches were read as a whole, and isolated passages were not taken out of context, the Law Lords had not equated ministerial statements with the intention of Parliament.[80] The problem with that explanation is that, while ministerial statements were, as a general proposition, categorised as no more than a guide or aid, they were completely decisive in *Pepper v Hart*; without the Hansard material the taxpayers' case was doomed to ignominious failure; with that material an imminent 4-1 loss became a 6-0 win (plus Lord Mackay on other grounds).

Lord Steyn's concern cannot, therefore, be entirely dismissed, though it should perhaps be watered down to a warning that Hansard material should be treated with great caution to ensure that ministerial assurances do not become a source of law. That need for caution was subsequently stressed by Lord Nicholls of Birkenhead in the *Spath Holme* case as follows:

> If, however, the statements are clear, and were made by a minister or other promoter of the Bill, they qualify as an external aid. In such a case the statements are a factor the court will take into account in construing legislation which is ambiguous or obscure or productive of absurdity. They are then as much part of the background to the legislation as, say, Government white papers. They are part of the legislative background, but they are no more than this. This cannot be emphasised too strongly. Government statements, however they are made and however explicit they may be, cannot control the meaning of an Act of Parliament. As with other extraneous material, it is for the court, when determining what was the intention of Parliament in using the words in question, to decide how much importance, or weight, if any, should be attached to a Government statement. The weight will depend on all the circumstances. For instance, the statement might conflict with the principle of interpretation that penal legislation is to be construed strictly.[81]

The proposition that that caution was not exercised in *Pepper v Hart* itself finds support in a lecture given by Lord Phillips of Worth Matravers.[82] Lord Phillips made the general point that, once counsel seek to refer to Hansard references,

---

[78] J Steyn, '*Pepper v Hart*; A Re-examination' (2001) 21 *OJLS* 59.
[79] ibid, 68.
[80] S Vogenauer, 'A Retreat from *Pepper v Hart*? A Reply to Lord Steyn' (2005) 25 *OJLS* 629, 661–65.
[81] *Spath Holme* (above n 63) 399.
[82] Lord Philips of Worth Matravers, 'The First Lord Alexander of Weedon Lecture', available at www.supremecourt.uk./docs/speech_100419.pdf.

courts can hardly refuse to look at it and added: 'Once admitted they sometimes led the court to conclude that a statute was ambiguous where, otherwise, no ambiguity might have been found'.[83] That statement was not immediately fortified by examples, but later on Lord Phillips referred to Lord Nicholls' warnings that 'the courts must be careful not to treat the ministerial or other statement as indicative of the objective intention of Parliament. Nor should the courts give a ministerial statement, whether made inside or outside Parliament, determinative weight',[84] upon which Lord Phillips commented: 'Both of these were, I suggest, precisely what the House had done in *Pepper v Hart*'.[85]

Much the same point was made in an address given by Lord Dyson[86] who said

> [*Pepper v Hart*] has been subject to great scrutiny and criticism and, I think, the general view now is that the majority opinions were seriously flawed not least because they mistakenly equated the intention of government spokesmen in the House of Commons with the intention of Parliament.[87]

Incidentally, Lord Dyson also commented on Lord Griffiths' view, that the linguistic argument produced an unfair and absurd result which could not have been intended by Parliament, saying:

> But surely it did not produce an absurd result. And it was not inherently unfair. It would not have been unfair if nothing had been said during the course of the passage of the Bill through Parliament. It was only unfair because of what the Finance Secretary had said in committee.[88]

The need for caution is reinforced by the point that ministers are often replying to points of which they have not had advance notice: in the popular phrase they are 'caught on the hop'. The Attorney General made this point in argument in the case by observing that the context was 'words spoken by the Financial Secretary to the Treasury in Committee between 10.30 p.m. and midnight in exceptionally difficult circumstances'.[89] He subsequently hammered home this point, saying that the Minister was 'describing the effects of pre-existing legislation as interpreted in practice'[90] and observing: 'What [the House of Lords in *Pepper v Hart*] sought to do was to distil profound truths from the muddled picture that was necessarily conveyed to an embattled Minister in a very short space of time'.[91]

---

[83] ibid, para 10.
[84] *Wilson v First County Trust Ltd (No 2)* [2003] UKHL 40; [2004] 1 AC 816, [66].
[85] Lord Phillips (above n 82) para 15.
[86] J Dyson, 'The Shifting Sands of Statutory Interpretation', available at www.statute lawsociety. co.uk/wp-content/uploads/2014/01/Sir_John_Dyson.pdf.
[87] ibid, 14–15.
[88] ibid, 17.
[89] *Pepper v Hart* (above n 1) 604.
[90] N Lyell, '*Pepper v Hart*: The Government Perspective' (1994) 15 *Stat LR* 1.
[91] ibid, 5.

In his lecture Lord Steyn observed that an argument, that a statute is to be interpreted in accordance with a considered explanation given by a minister promoting the bill, looks like an estoppel argument, but he conceded that that was not how the reasoning in *Pepper v Hart* was formulated.[92] Lord Steyn went on to use judicial speeches to suggest that *Pepper v Hart* should be confined to being authority for the proposition that a categorical assurance given by the government in debates as to the meaning of the legislation may preclude the government vis-a-vis an individual from contending to the contrary.[93] Lord Hope of Craighead also took a similar line.[94] Sir Philip Sales took issue because the 'proposed distinction does not find any basis in *Pepper v Hart* itself' and he went on to address major conceptual difficulties for what he characterised as Lord Steyn's 'legitimate expectation thesis'.[95]

The fundamental problem with the estoppel argument is that it trespasses into the realm of fantasy. The ultimate issue in *Pepper v Hart* was whether or not the assessments raised by the Inspector of Taxes were justified in terms of the interpretation and application of the statutory provisions concerned. It was never suggested that the assessments had been improperly raised and pursued. If that had been an issue, then it is not one which could have been raised on an appeal against tax assessments; it would have been a logically prior issue as to the validity of the assessments, not as to their correctness as a matter of tax law. As is recognised by the references, in the various discussions of the estoppel argument, to legitimate expectation and abuse of power, it would have been a classic judicial review argument. It is as plain as day that at the second hearing in the House of Lords the main issue was whether Hansard might be admissible to assist resolution of an issue of statutory construction and there was no deviation into an enquiry as to whether the assessments had been properly raised. The estoppel argument therefore involves more than just an imaginative reconstruction of the Law Lords' speeches: it involves a transposition of the proceedings from what they were to what they were not. The estoppel argument may fairly be said to be too clever for its own good. The Law Lords accepted the opportunity to fashion a fork and ex post facto analysis to the effect that they fashioned a spade[96] is no more than fanciful.

The notion of confining the Hansard ruling seems to have died a quiet death so far as the judges are concerned, but it is still mentioned in *Bennion on Statutory Interpretation*.[97] That mention concludes a lengthy examination in which

---

[92] Steyn (above n 78) 67.

[93] *McDonnell v Congregation of Christian Brothers Trustees* [2003] UKHL 63; [2004] 1 AC 1101, 1116–17. See also *R (Westminster City Council) v National Asylum Support Service* [2002] UKHL 38; [2002] 1 WLR 2956, [6].

[94] *R v A (No 2)* [2002] 1 AC 45, [81] (referring also to his speech in *Spath Holme* (above n 63) 407–08).

[95] P Sales, '*Pepper v Hart*: A Footnote to Professor Vogenauer's Reply to Lord Steyn' (2006) 26 *OJLS* 585, 587 and 589–92.

[96] To adapt Lord Templeman's remark in *Street v Mountford* [1985] AC 809, 819.

[97] *Bennion on Statutory* Interpretation, 6th edn (above n 5) 590.

it is advanced that executive estoppel 'is a matter not of statutory interpretation of the resulting Act but of its future administration'.[98]

What is needed, however, is a clear examination of whether there is scope for a doctrine of executive estoppel distinct from the Hansard ruling. If a ministerial assurance accords with the plain meaning of the statutory provision concerned, or with a meaning which attracts judicial favour, then statutory interpretation is the means to resolution of dispute. But let it be supposed that a case arises in which a ministerial assurance is found to be wholly inconsistent with all possible meanings of the statutory wording. In such a situation it might be argued, in an action for judicial review, that there is a legitimate expectation that the executive should nevertheless honour the assurance. In various public law cases (some involving the Revenue, and some not), the courts have developed the concept of abuse of power.[99] There appears to be a strong case for saying that a government department abuses its power if it seeks to take any action in direct conflict with a statement made by one of its ministers in Parliament. It is to be acknowledged that there are powerful arguments to the contrary, as put by Sir Philip Sales[100] and in obiter dicta.[101] Unfortunately it is beyond the scope of this chapter to delve into the extensive case law on judicial review. The topic of legitimate expectation, considered in relation to the substance of a decision, as opposed to procedural matters, is a large one, as demonstrated by the fact that it occupies 11 pages of *Supperstone, Goudie and Walker: Judicial Review*.[102] All that can be said here is that the case law does not seem to rule out the argument advanced, and that one case[103] appears to afford a useful foundation for it.

The survival of the *Hansard* ruling is testified by its coverage in *Halsbury's Laws of England*.[104] Interestingly Halsbury goes on to assert that the exclusionary rule is also subject to an exception under the inherent jurisdiction of the court, as the court is master of its own procedure;[105] this seems a strangely circular proposition as the exclusionary rule was judge-made, and seems to amount to the courts having an untrammelled choice whether or not to admit Hansard material.

A final point on the aftermath is that *Pepper v Hart* preceded the general availability of the internet which renders access to research material so much easier than in days of yore. Moreover, for those sufficiently old-fashioned to read books, the notes *in Current Law Statutes Annotated* now carry a section headed 'Pepper v Hart'.

---

[98] ibid, 588.

[99] See, in particular, *R v CIR, ex parte Preston* (1985) AC 835.

[100] Sales (above n 93) 589–92.

[101] See *R v DPP, ex parte Kebilene* [2000] 2 AC 326, 339 and 347; and *Thoburn v Sunderland City Council* [2002] EWHC 195 (Admin); [2003] QB 151, 192.

[102] M Supperstone, P Walker, J Goudie and H Fenwick (eds), *Judicial Review*, 5th edn (LexisNexis UK, 2014) 243–53.

[103] *R v North and East Devon Health Authority, Ex parte Coughlan* [2001] QB 213.

[104] Supperstone et al (above n 102) para 1122.

[105] ibid, para 1124.

XII. CONCLUSION

During the writer's career as a government lawyer (1971–2005) there were two major developments in domestic law with which he had some association. They were the coming into prominence of judicial review and of the purposive interpretation of statutes. Of the several major cases with which the writer was privileged to be involved, if in relatively minor roles, *Pepper v Hart* was the most extraordinary. It provoked comment on an industrial scale and it is a matter of regret that much of that comment has, perforce, not been able to be considered in this chapter. The controversy has now largely died down, though not entirely.[106] As law librarians testify, vast amounts of researches into Hansard are done these days, and it may well be that a crock of gold is very seldom found. As, largely due to the good offices of Lord Steyn and Lord Nicholls, judges are aware of the need to treat Hansard material with caution, the Hansard ruling is no more than an addition to the judicial toolkit, if an expensive one and rarely of use. As indicated, it would be a grand thing if a judicial review came along in which it could be tested whether a ministerial assurance may, at least ordinarily, give rise to a legitimate expectation. It would also be grand if, by that or some other means, an opportunity arose for the decision in *Pepper v Hart* to be upheld on a proper footing.

A final comment is this. *Pepper v Hart* is an object lesson in the advisability of heeding the wise words of Lord Halsbury LC about avoiding an a priori presumption that an Act does not mean what it says[107] – to which there might usefully be added 'neither more nor less'.

---

[106] Apart from *Bennion on Statutory Interpretation*, 6th edn (above n 5), Supperstone et al (above n 102) still registers concerns (ibid, para 20.1.2).

[107] *Herron* (above n 25).

17

R v Secretary of State for Foreign and Commonwealth Affairs, ex parte World Development Movement *(1994)*

Financial Prudence, Interfering Busybodies

ABIMBOLA A OLOWOFOYEKU

O LIVER WENDELL HOLMES Jr once stated that taxes are what we pay for civilised society.[1] Assuming the truth of this statement, one might well wonder which 'civilised society' is one's tax paying for. The questions to what use is tax revenue being put, and, is such use appropriate, are of antiquity. The power of the state to tax its citizens and/or residents is undoubted. So is the power of the state to tax activities – even the ones that it cannot prevent.[2] Reliance on divine laws and masonic symbolism to reject such power is doomed to failure.[3] Complaints against the use for certain purposes of tax revenues are similarly doomed, if the intent is to impugn the tax itself.[4] However, complaints are sometimes tenable – perhaps more so when the civilised society that one's tax is paying for is in another country. This calls to mind 'the largest cash sum ever provided for a single scheme under the Overseas Development Administration's Aid and Trade Provision'[5] – the outcome of a decision of HM Government to provide aid to fund the construction of a hydroelectric power station on the Pergau river in Malaysia's Kelantan state. In *R v Secretary of*

---

[1] *Compania General de Tabacos de Filipinas v Collector of Internal Revenue* 275 US 87, 100 (1927).
[2] See Holmes J in *Compania*, ibid.
[3] *Lloyd v Taylor* (1970) 46 TC 539.
[4] *Cheney v Conn* [1968] 1 WLR 242.
[5] National Audit Office, *Pergau Hydro-Electric Project* (HC 1992–93, 908) para 1.

State for Foreign Affairs, ex parte World Development Movement Ltd[6] (*Pergau Dam*) the Divisional Court held that the government's decision was unlawful, causing the government considerable embarrassment and diplomatic and international trade difficulties.

The complainant, the World Development Movement (WDM) was a pressure group dedicated to improving the quantity and quality of British aid to other countries.[7] The WDM had nothing to do with the construction project or the relevant aid provision. In essence, it could possibly be seen as a 'busybody in other people's affairs'. For its challenge to be entertained – and upheld – by the court, raises questions that will be familiar to public lawyers. It is one thing to claim to be interested *qua* taxpayer or ratepayer in how public revenues are spent. But what was the interest of the WDM in the matter? What makes any such interest legitimate? Is the manner wherein tax revenues are deployed an appropriate subject for judicial determinations? On what basis can a political decision to grant overseas aid from central funds be considered 'unlawful'? The immediate aftermath of the case raised controversies (not canvassed in the case) relating to the tying of aid to trade, alleged corruption, and alleged racial slurs, resulting in damaged trade relations, and the subsequent refocusing of aid on poverty alleviation. These will be examined in this discussion, which will hopefully demonstrate how truly a landmark is *Pergau Dam*.

I. TWO PRIME MINISTERS

Mrs Margaret Thatcher was the (Conservative) UK Prime Minister. Dr Mahathir Mohamed was the Malaysian Prime Minister. Malaysia was in a state of rapid growth, and was experiencing a 'very rapid rise in demand for electricity and the need to expand generating capacity'.[8] Malaysia's increasing economic clout was not something that the UK could afford to ignore. Thus, 'strenuous efforts were made by British companies, and by Mrs Thatcher and her ministers on their behalf, to take advantage of Malaysia's booming economy and ambitions for a modernised defence force'.[9] Unsurprisingly, Dr Mahathir wished to diversify Malaysia's energy resources. He also 'wanted a major project for backward Kelantan state'.[10] Building a hydroelectric dam on the Pergau river

---

[6] *R v Secretary of State for Foreign Affairs, ex parte World Development Movement Ltd* [1995] 1 WLR 386; [1995] 1 All ER 611 (Pergau Dam).

[7] The WDM is now called 'Global Justice Now' (see www.globaljustice.org.uk/about-us). In its incarnation as 'Global Justice Now', it describes itself as 'a democratic social justice organisation working as part of a global movement to challenge the powerful and create a more just and equal world'.

[8] T Lankester, *The Politics and Economics of Britain's Foreign Aid* (Abingdon, Routledge, 2013) 23, 51.

[9] ibid, 25.

[10] ibid, 139.

would achieve both objectives. So, Dr Mahathir wanted the dam, 'and wanted it badly'.[11] If this could be done with British aid, so much the better. For free trade enthusiast Mrs Thatcher, interest in overseas aid apparently revolved around securing benefits for British exporters, winning and keeping friends and dealing with humanitarian crises.[12] Crucially,

> [t]he idea that poor countries had a moral right to aid and the rich had a moral duty to provide it was foreign to her. Mrs Thatcher believed that 'charity begins at home'; and at least as far as British tax-payers' money was concerned, it should pretty much end at home.[13]

Prudential deployment of taxpayer revenues was thus important to Mrs Thatcher, and, if providing overseas aid could help secure contracts for British companies, that could well secure the desired value for money. The setting for a great drama was thus complete.

II. MONEY TROUBLES

The Pergau river had been identified as a potential site for the construction of a hydroelectric power station and was considered a priority site by Malaysia's Electricity Authority. The World Bank's 1987 power sector report on Malaysia had recorded the Pergau river as a possible site for a 211 megawatt hydroelectric power station, but had concluded that Malaysia should concentrate entirely on gas-fired electricity generation until the turn of the century.[14] In late 1988, a British consortium, having informed the Department for Trade & Industry (DTI) of its interest in the Pergau dam site and that it would be seeking an 'aid and trade provision' (ATP) in relation to the site, submitted an application to the Overseas Development Agency (ODA) for an ATP. Indicative costs of £315 million were subsequently revised to £316 million, with a UK content of £195 million. Following a verbal report from the short appraisal mission sent to Malaysia,[15] Mrs Thatcher made a verbal offer to Dr Mahathir of ATP support for the Pergau Dam project, of up to £68.25 million, conditional on a full economic appraisal. The appraisal mission subsequently reported that the project's economic viability was, at the consortium's price of £316 million, 'marginal'. The consortium's budgetary estimate was later increased to £397 million – considered by an ODA economist to have now moved the project's

---

[11] ibid, 48.
[12] ibid, 33.
[13] ibid.
[14] National Audit Office (above n 5) para 8.
[15] ibid, para 14. The Public Accounts Committee (PAC) of the House of Commons considered this appraisal to be 'superficial and inadequate' (HM Treasury, 'Treasury Minute on the seventeenth to twenty-first reports from the Committee of Public Accounts' (Cm 2602, 1993–94), para 1).

viability from 'marginal' to 'uneconomic'. Nevertheless, a formal written notice of HM Government's offer was sent to the Malaysian government. HM Government faced a dilemma of four options, thus described by Sir Tim Lankester, Permanent Secretary in the ODA,

> (i) a formal offer of £397m, which was inconceivable on the economic view which had been taken; (ii) withdrawing the offer, which was politically impossible; (iii) confirming an offer at £316m, which was not tenable in view of the price rise; and (iv) making an offer based on £316m, but with an indication of willingness to discuss the possibility of further assistance.[16]

The fourth option was chosen. The ODA, after further economic appraisals, considered the project to be 'a very bad buy', which would not be an economic proposition until 2005 at the earliest,[17] that gas turbines would be cheaper, and that it would cost Malaysians £100 million more for their electricity over 35 years than the cheaper alternatives. At this point, the Permanent Secretary considered the project to be 'unequivocally a bad one in economic terms'. A further ODA economic appraisal priced the project at £417 million, which would require ATP funding of £108 million. The Permanent Secretary eventually advised against implementation of the project, requesting a specific ministerial direction if there was to be expenditure on the project.[18] Apparently, the Accounting Officer took the view that the project was 'an abuse of the aid programme in the terms that this is an uneconomic project' and that 'it was not a sound development project'.[19] The Foreign Secretary (Douglas Hurd) nevertheless approved ATP support for the project, taking the view that withdrawal of the UK's offer would adversely affect the UK's credibility, and gave the required specific directive to the Permanent Secretary.[20] The Malaysian and UK governments subsequently signed a financial agreement for ATP support for the Pergau project. Work on the project began in July 1991, and by 31 March 1993, the ODA had spent £9.953 million on the project from their ATP.[21] The cost of the project to the UK would eventually rise to £234 million.

The ODA's response to the 'surprise' of the Public Accounts Committee (PAC) as to 'why no attempt was made to establish the reasons why the client was so keen to continue with the project, when alternatives were apparently available'[22] was that they were 'well aware that the Malaysian Government was pursuing a policy of fuel diversification and wished to diversify further into

---

[16] See *Pergau Dam* (above n 6) 391 (Rose LJ).

[17] Lankester (above n 8) 129.

[18] The PAC considered that this request was 'right and in accordance with his responsibilities' (HM Treasury (above n 15) para 9).

[19] *Pergau Dam* (above n 6) 392 (Rose LJ).

[20] National Audit Office (above n 5) para 56.

[21] ibid, para 44.

[22] HM Treasury (above n 15) para 10.

hydro-electricity'. According to the ODA, Malaysia already had 'considerable experience with such sources and, having had severe teething problems with gas turbines in previous years, took the view that hydroelectric sources were a more reliable option, particularly for coping with peak loads'.[23]

The WDM sought judicial review of the decisions to grant ATP funding and to continue payments to the project. The relevant statutory provision was the Overseas Development and Cooperation Act (ODCA) 1980 which provided in section 1(1) that:

> The Secretary of State shall have power, for the purpose of promoting the development or maintaining the economy of a country or territory outside the United Kingdom, or the welfare of its people, to furnish any person or body with assistance, whether financial, technical or of any other nature.

It was held by the Divisional Court (Rose LJ and Scott Baker J) that the WDM had standing to bring the application and that the Secretary of State's decision to fund the project was not a lawful exercise of his powers under the Act.

While rightly described as 'a true high-water mark of judicial creativity prior to the HRA',[24] *Pergau Dam* was, in one sense, a straightforward judicial review case, engaging several issues that arise in such proceedings. WDM's standing was a major issue. The time limits imposed on applications for judicial review were engaged, although to a lesser extent. Availability of discovery in judicial review proceedings also arose as a minor point. The judgment itself turned on the correct construction of a statutory power – the meaning and scope of the power to grant overseas development aid. Questions of improper purposes and appropriate remedies also arose. However, underpinning the whole edifice were the notions of prudence[25] and value for money in the disposition of public revenues.

On time limits, the Court's view was that 'the general importance of the matter may itself be a reason for resolving the substantive issues, even where there has been delay'.[26] It was held that there was good reason for extending time, and that the delay in the case provided no basis in itself for refusing relief.[27] On the issue of discovery, Rose LJ noted[28] that 'general discovery is not available', and an application for discovery 'will be refused if discovery is not

---

[23] ibid, para 11.

[24] R Rawlings, 'Modelling Judicial Review' (2008) 61 *CLP* 95, 101.

[25] In this chapter, 'prudence' is used to refer to *financial* prudence, rather than *political* prudence (on which, see J Snape, *The Political Economy of Corporation Tax: Theory, Values and Law Reform* (Oxford, Hart Publishing, 2011)) 25–36.

[26] *Pergau Dam* (above n 6) 402 (Rose LJ).

[27] ibid, 403, Rose LJ. The Court's approach in this respect seems to have been endorsed in *Hardy v Pembrokeshire CC* [2006] EWCA Civ 240, [2006] Env LR 28. See generally, A Samuels, 'Permission for Judicial Review Out of Time: An Overview' (2002) 7 *Judicial Review* 216.

[28] *Pergau Dam* (above n 6) 396 (followed in *Re Quark Fishing Ltd (Disclosure)* [2001] EWHC Admin 920).

necessary for disposing of the case fairly'. Discovery was refused as not being necessary for fair disposition of the case. The Court's decisions on propriety of purpose and standing are far more controversial, and will now be scrutinised.

III. THE ECONOMICS OF PURPOSE

It is a basic principle of administrative law that statutory powers conferred for one purpose may not be exercised for other purposes. Thus, in *R v Somerset CC ex parte Fewings*[29] the council could not use a statutory power to manage land 'for the benefit, improvement or development of their area' to ban deer hunting on its lands, on the basis that hunting was 'cruel'. The principles relating to improper purposes apply with no less rigour to public revenues. So, in *Sydney Municipal Council v Campbell*,[30] a statutory power to acquire land required for widening, enlarging or extending public ways could not be used to acquire land to secure profits from projected increases in the value of the land. While it may be thought that the council was being prudent and entrepreneurial in seeking to enhance its revenues by sound investments, this was not the purpose of the statutory power. A similar attempt at unauthorised prudence was rejected in *Congreve v Home Office*,[31] where the Home Secretary was prevented from using his licensing powers to revoke TV licences renewed early so as to make up a shortfall in licence fees.

Propriety of purpose was the main point raised by the WDM in respect of the legality of the decision of the Secretary of State in *Pergau Dam*. According to the WDM, the purpose of the powers conferred by section 1(1) ODCA 1980 was to promote development, and the test was whether the Secretary of State decided to provide financial assistance to the Malaysian government for the purpose of promoting development. If aid was to be granted, projects had to be 'sound development projects'. The evidence demonstrated that the Secretary of State's decision was made in reliance upon 'irrelevant facts and matters and in defiance of relevant considerations and advice', particularly the view that the project was not 'sound economic development'.[32] The Secretary of State however claimed to have considered throughout the decision-making process that he was dealing with a 'development project' – one 'whose purpose was to help Malaysia to carry out its plans for addressing its energy needs and thus promote the country's economic development'. He confirmed that he 'was aware that formal offers of financial support had already been made – and renewed – to the Malaysian Government, which clearly regarded this project as a key element

---

[29] *R v Somerset CC ex parte Fewings* [1995] 1 WLR 1037.
[30] *Sydney Municipal Council v Campbell* [1925] AC 338.
[31] *Congreve v Home Office* [1976] 1 QB 629 (CA).
[32] *Pergau Dam* (above n 6) 399 (Rose LJ).

of their programme for addressing their substantial power requirements'. He thus 'took the view that the withdrawal of the offer to provide assistance would affect the United Kingdom's credibility as a reliable friend and trading partner and have adverse and far-reaching consequences for our political and commercial relations with Malaysia'.[33]

That the Secretary of State was entitled to take account of wider political and economic considerations was common ground between the parties, provided that there was a sufficient substantive power within the statute. Rose LJ accepted that 'that the *weight* of competing factors'[34] was a matter for the Secretary of State, once there was a purpose within the statute. However, it was for the courts to 'determine whether, on the evidence before the court, the particular conduct was, or was not, within the statutory purpose'. Arguments as to the dam's 'undoubted benefit' in meeting the need for electricity were stated to '[beg] the question of whether there was a need for energy generated at substantially greater cost than by any other means', and the Malaysian government's determination to go ahead with the scheme did not advance the argument, since it was just 'a necessary prerequisite for the granting of any overseas aid'.[35] According to Rose LJ, where the contemplated development is, on the evidence,

> so economically unsound that there is no economic argument in favour of the case, it is not … possible to draw any material distinction between questions of propriety and regularity on the one hand and questions of economy and efficiency of public expenditure on the other.

Rose LJ accepted that the Secretary of State was, 'generally speaking, fully entitled' to take account of the relevant political, economic, commercial and diplomatic issues – as long as there was a 'development purpose' within the Act.[36] However, no such purpose within the statute existed at the relevant time, and thus the decision of the Secretary of State was 'unlawful'. Scott Baker J also concluded that 'there was nothing in aid terms to justify the use of public money for the Pergau project'.[37]

Although courts have sometimes intervened in local government revenue dispositions on behalf of ratepayers,[38] the court's intervention in the manner wherein central government used public revenues was surprising. Prosser describes it as a 'suggestion of greater judicial activism'.[39] The focus on 'sound' in the

---

[33] ibid, 398–99 (Rose LJ).
[34] ibid (emphasis supplied).
[35] ibid, 402.
[36] ibid.
[37] ibid, 403.
[38] See, eg, *Bromley London Borough Council v GLC* [1983] 1 AC 768; *Prescott v Birmingham Corp* [1955] Ch 210; *Roberts v Hopwood* [1925] AC 578. On the differences between ratepayers and taxpayers, see Lord Wilberforce in *CIR v National Federation of Self-Employed and Small Businesses* [1982] AC 617, 632–33.
[39] T Prosser, *The Economic Constitution* (Oxford, Oxford University Press, 2014) 115.

context of 'economic development' was momentous, enabling the court to make a somewhat far-fetched connection between the statutory words and a requirement for what essentially is a prudential management by central government of taxpayers' money. Counsel for the Secretary of State had rightly highlighted that the word 'sound' was not in the statute. The response of Rose LJ that 'if Parliament had intended to confer a power to disburse money for unsound developmental purposes, it could have been expected to say so expressly'[40] is, with respect, unconvincing. It can equally be argued that, 'if Parliament had intended to impose a constraint of prudence on the grant of aid for developmental purposes, it could have been expected to say so expressly'. This constraint is simply a judicial gloss, and economics was probably no consideration in the conferment of the statutory power. However, Rose LJ felt 'comforted' in his approach by 'the way in which the successive ministers, guidelines, Governments and White Papers … have, over the years and without exception, construed the power as relating to economically sound development'.[41] But this comfort was arguably misplaced. The court was deciding a question of law on the correct interpretation of a statute, rather than a question on government policy. Interestingly, Lankester observed that at the core of the Pergau affair was the 'divergence of actual policy from officially stated policy'.[42] But politicians having always taken a particular line as a matter of government policy has no bearing on what a statute means. It is doubtful that the court could have found such comfort, had 'successive ministers, guidelines, Governments and White Papers over the years and without exception' taken the line that the power could be used to support rebellions against authoritarian regimes. Had it been so desired, ministers could have sought amending legislation to put their stated policy on a statutory basis.

Interestingly, New Labour's International Development Act (IDA) 2002, which replaced the ODCA 1980, addressed this issue specifically. Section 1(1) IDA 2002 empowers the Secretary of State to provide 'development assistance', which section 1(2) defines, inter alia, as assistance provided for the purpose of 'furthering sustainable development'. Crucially, 'sustainable development' is defined in section 1(3) to include 'any development that is, in the opinion of the Secretary of State, *prudent* having regard to the likelihood of its generating lasting benefits for the population of the country or countries in relation to which it is provided'.[43] It is likely, or, at least, possible, that inclusion of 'prudent' in section 1(3) is a direct consequence of *Pergau Dam*, which would support the view that prudence is a new requirement imposed by *Pergau Dam* itself. It may well be that a requirement for prudence or sound economics is appropriate when dealing with how governments spend taxpayers' money. Harden et al have stated

---

[40] *Pergau Dam* (above n 6) 402.
[41] ibid.
[42] Lankester (above n 8) 5.
[43] Emphasis added.

that 'The *Pergau Dam* case makes clear that legality and value for money cannot be treated as entirely separate matters' and that the '*Pergau* principle requires spending to pass a threshold value for money test as a condition of legality'.[44] However, matters such as 'value for money' are arguably political, for which governments are accountable to Parliament and the electorate.

The impact of requirement for 'soundness' on propriety of purpose was also significant. Because the Pergau project was economically unsound, the decision to fund it was 'not for a development purpose'. Consequently, any other factor that the Secretary of State may have been entitled to consider in addition to a development purpose could not rightly have been triggered. The court's decision on improper purposes may possibly be supported on the narrow view that a power to grant aid provision for development purposes cannot be used to avoid embarrassment to the government. The difficulty with supporting *Pergau Dam* on this basis is that there was, in the minds of all concerned, both in the UK and Malaysia, a clear 'development purpose' – construction of a hydroelectric power plant to meet an existing need for extra electricity. What converted the project into a non-development purpose in the view of the court was the economics of using a dam. Had the ATP funding been granted for gas turbines instead of a dam, no one would have supposed that it was not for a development purpose. Thus, simple economics converted a purpose into a non-purpose. For a court to take this approach, and via a gloss on the statutory language, is problematic, especially seeing that the question whether the project was indeed a 'bad buy' was contentious. For example, Dr Mahathir said that it was 'stupid' to so describe it. For Malaysia, it was an 'excellent buy', because they were receiving a grant of £234 million.[45] One could be forgiven for asking: 'must the question whether aid is for a development purpose be evaluated from the perspective of the donor or the donee?' The perspectives may well differ. A further question is whether this is an appropriate subject of judicial determinations.

Whether a statutory power is exercised for a particular purpose is a question of fact.[46] In both *Fewings* and *Campbell*, the evidence showed clearly that the relevant decision-makers did not advert their minds to the terms of the statutory powers that they were purporting to exercise. In *Pergau Dam*, the Secretary of State and all involved in advising him clearly did that. In both *Fewings* and *Campbell*, there was only one purpose, which was not the permitted purpose. In *Pergau Dam*, it seems that there may have been more than one purpose. Clearly, the Secretary of State had wanted to the avoid the embarrassment to the government that would arise from resiling from a clear undertaking given by a UK prime minister to a foreign prime minister, and it is clear that statutory powers

---

[44] I Harden, 'Value for Money and Administrative Law' [1996] *PL* 661, 680.

[45] See Lankester (above n 8) 120.

[46] Lord Loreburn in *Clanricarde (Marquess) v Congested Districts Board* (1914) 79 JP 481; Duff J in *Sydney Municipal Council* (above n 30) 343.

cannot be exercised simply for the purpose of avoiding embarrassment to the government.[47] But it would be difficult to cast *Pergau Dam* in this light. The Secretary of State's decision was the last in a long saga. Decisions to support the Pergau project had been taken long before the issue of embarrassment arose. The project was designed to fulfil a specific development need. The only problems related to the escalating costs of that project, and the feeling that there were cheaper ways of fulfilling the development need. The conclusion that the dam was uneconomic did not remove the need for electricity. Neither did the greater short-term cost effectiveness of gas turbines. It is significant that the focus of the economic arguments was short-term. A dam is likely to be more enduring than gas turbines, and a more long-term view (for example, 100 years) may render the case for one more attractive or more 'sound' in economic terms. So also may environmental sustainability. Indeed, the ODA, in response to a comment by the PAC, indicated its view that 'The proposed aid was for a valid development project which would produce much needed peak time power in an environmentally friendly and sustainable way'.[48] This is just another way of saying that there are possible concerns other than short-term economic viability. This surely must be a matter for the Secretary of State. As Sumption noted in his FA Mann Lecture 2011:

> The practical effect was to transfer to the court the discretionary powers of the Secretary of State on a matter of policy and the task of assessing the project's merits. As it happens, Parliament's view about the merits of the Foreign Secretary's decision was different. It subsequently approved without demur a supplementary estimate in an appropriation bill, which reallocated the available funds so as to allow the payments to Malaysia to be made anyway, along with payments for two other projects which were thought to be open to the same objections.[49]

Sumption considered that the decisions of the courts on the abuse of discretionary powers are often based 'on a judgment about *what it is thought right for Parliament to wish to do*',[50] that such judgments are political, 'dealing with matters (namely the merits of policy decisions) which in a democracy are the proper function of Parliament and of ministers answerable to Parliament and the electorate'.[51] There is much force in these observations. Harlow also highlighted the 'striking' character of *Pergau Dam*, 'because the department, through its Permanent Secretary, was accountable through the audit process to the PAC, while the minister was responsible to the House of Commons, where the matter was pursued actively'.[52] Furthermore, for an exercise of power for one purpose

---

[47] See, eg, *Padfield v Minister of Agriculture, Fisheries and Food* [1968] AC 997.
[48] HM Treasury (above n 15) para 12.
[49] J Sumption, 'Judicial and Political Decision-making: The Uncertain Boundary' (2011) 16 *Judicial Review* 301, 306.
[50] ibid, 307 (emphasis added).
[51] ibid.
[52] C Harlow, 'Public Law and Popular Justice' (2002) 65 *MLR* 1, 5.

to also permit another purpose to be achieved, is not necessarily fatal.[53] *R (UK Uncut Legal Action) v HMRC*[54] for example shows that, while avoidance of embarrassment is irrelevant, the court may sometimes excuse it – even in a case of public revenues foregone. The *Pergau* court arguably went too far.

IV. BUSYBODY OR NOT?

The court's decision on standing concretised a trend towards liberalisation of the standing rules. The following analysis explains how and why. It was noted earlier that the WDM had nothing to do with the Pergau project. So how could they possibly have standing? Section 31(3) of the Supreme Court Act[55] 1981 and Order 53 rule 3(7) of the Rules of the Supreme Court provide that the High Court 'shall not grant leave' to make an application for judicial review unless the Court 'considers that the applicant has a sufficient interest in the matter to which the application relates'. The phrase 'sufficient interest' was selected 'as one which could sufficiently embrace all classes of those who might apply, and yet permit sufficient flexibility in any particular case to determine whether or not "sufficient interest" was in fact shown'.[56] In *R v Liverpool Corporation, ex parte Liverpool Taxi Fleet Operators' Association*[57] Lord Denning MR said in respect of the requirement that a 'person aggrieved' could apply for certain prerogative orders that the term included a 'person whose interests may be prejudicially affected by what is taking place'. He also noted that the term 'does not include a mere busybody who is interfering in things which do not concern him; but it includes any person who has a genuine grievance because something has been done or may be done which affects him'.

The difficulty in standing cases is how to distinguish between a 'mere busybody' and someone with a 'genuine grievance'. Clearly, '[n]ot every member of the public can complain of every breach of statutory duty by a person empowered to come to a decision by that statute',[58] and, '[m]erely to assert that one has an interest does not give one an interest'.[59] If an applicant 'has no interest whatsoever', then the application for leave will be refused.[60] To 'have no interest

---

[53] See, eg, *Westminster Corporation v London and North West Railway Co* [1905] AC 426.

[54] *R (UK Uncut Legal Action) v HMRC* [2013] EWHC 1283 (Admin), [2013] STC 2357.

[55] Now restyled the Senior Courts Act 1981.

[56] Lord Roskill in *National Federation* (above n 38) 658.

[57] *R v Liverpool Corporation, ex parte Liverpool Taxi Fleet Operators' Association* [1972] 2 QB 299, 309.

[58] Schiemann J in *R v Secretary of State for the Environment, ex parte Rose Theatre Trust Co* [1990] 1 QB 504, 520. See also Dove J in *Wylde v Waverley BC* [2017] EWHC 466 (Admin) para 20; Lord Reed JSC in *Walton v Scottish Ministers* [2012] UKSC 44, [2013] 1 CMLR 28, para 94.

[59] Schiemann J in *Rose Theatre* (above n 58) 520.

[60] Sir John Donaldson MR in *R v Monopolies and Mergers Commission, ex p Argyll Group plc* [1986] 1 WLR 763, 773.

whatsoever', was later taken by Sedley J in *R v Somerset CC Ex parte Dixon*[61] as meaning 'to interfere in something with which one has no legitimate concern at all'. The threshold at the leave stage is set 'only at the height necessary to prevent abuse'.[62] In other cases, 'the question of sufficient interest cannot … be considered in the abstract, or as an isolated point: it must be taken together with the legal and factual context. The rule requires sufficient interest in the matter to which the application relates'.[63] In other words, 'the question of locus is considered in the context of the issues raised'.[64] This means that if the application 'appears to be otherwise arguable and there is no other discretionary bar', leave to apply will be granted. The test of interest or standing will then 'be re-applied as a matter of discretion on the hearing of the substantive application'.[65]

Even where the applicant can show an interest, 'mere interest alone in the matter in issue or the decision in question is not enough'.[66] The strength of the applicant's interest is one of the factors to be weighed in the balance,[67] and that interest must be 'sufficient'. In *Arsenal Football Club Ltd v Smith (Valuation Officer)*[68] for example, Lord Wilberforce held that, although the applicant was a taxpayer, his 'interest' was, in respect of his proposal for an alteration in the valuation list as regards Arsenal's hereditament, 'too remote'. These principles are clear enough – but where does one draw the lines of demarcation? The issue is compounded where the claimant for standing is an association of persons, a public interest or pressure group, etc, such as the WDM.[69] *National Federation* decided that one taxpayer usually has no sufficient interest to ask the court to investigate the tax affairs of another taxpayer.[70] This has implications for a body representing a group of applicants. According to Lord Wilberforce, 'an aggregate of individuals each of whom has no interest cannot of itself have an interest'.[71] A similar approach can be seen in *Rose Theatre*[72] where two of Schiemann J's 'propositions', which he felt were 'not inconsistent' with *National Federation*, were:

> The fact that some thousands of people join together and assert that they have an
> interest does not create an interest if the individuals did not have an interest … The

---

[61] *R v Somerset CC Ex parte Dixon* [1998] Env LR 111, 116–17.

[62] ibid.

[63] Lord Wilberforce in *National Federation* (above n 38) 630.

[64] *Ex parte Dixon* (above n 61) 115.

[65] Sir John Donaldson MR in *Argyll Group* (above n 60) 773.

[66] Dove J in *Wylde v Waverley* (above n 58) [20].

[67] Sir John Donaldson MR in *Argyll Group* (above n 60) 773.

[68] *Arsenal Football Club Ltd v Smith (Valuation Officer)* [1979] AC 1, 14.

[69] See generally, N Pleming, 'The Contribution of Public Interest Litigation to the Jurisprudence of JR' (1998) 3 *Judicial Review* 63.

[70] Note that a taxpayer can sometimes have standing in respect of the Revenue's treatment of other taxpayers – when complaining not *qua* taxpayer but *qua* competitor. See *R v Attorney-General Ex p ICI Plc* [1987] 1 CMLR 72.

[71] *National Federation* (above n 38) 633.

[72] *Rose Theatre* (above n 58).

fact that those without an interest incorporate themselves and give the company in its memorandum power to pursue a particular object does not give the company an interest.[73]

So, if no individual has standing, neither does a group of individuals. This naturally raises questions (addressed in *Pergau Dam*) as to situations wherein nobody would have a sufficient interest, resulting in unlawful governmental actions being unchallengeable. While Schiemann J recognised the force of counsel's concerns about this in *Rose Theatre*, his response was:

> The answer to it is that the law does not see it as the function of the courts to be there for every individual who is interested in having the legality of an administrative action litigated. Parliament could have given such a wide right of access to the court but it has not done so.[74]

Rose Theatre is not without its critics. Otton J declined to follow it in *R v Inspectorate of Pollution and another, ex parte Greenpeace Ltd (No 2)*.[75] Sedley J in *Ex Parte Dixon*[76] also declined to follow parts of it. *Pergau Dam* was highly influential to Sedley J's approach, for he emphasised[77] that it affirmed a 'strong line of modern authority', and restored a 'powerful line of older authority' on standing. While not dissenting 'from any of the eight numbered propositions set out by Schiemann J', Sedley J disagreed with (as not being 'universally true')[78] the proposition of Schiemann J that the court will decide whether statute gives the complainant 'expressly or impliedly a greater right or expectation than any other citizen of this country to have [the challenged] decision taken lawfully'. According to Sedley J:

> [T]he courts have always been alive to the fact that a person or organisation with no particular stake in the issue or the outcome may, without in any sense being a mere meddler, wish and be well placed to call the attention of the court to an apparent misuse of public power. If an arguable case of such misuse can be made out on an application for leave, the court's only concern is to ensure that it is not being done for an ill motive. It is if, on a substantive hearing, the abuse of power is made out that everything relevant to the applicant's standing will be weighed up, whether with regard to the grant or simply to the form of relief.[79]

So the answer to the question 'is a public interest litigant a mere busybody?' seems to be that 'it depends'. In the *Greenpeace* case Greenpeace was held to have standing to apply for judicial review of a governmental decision to grant variations of authorisations to discharge radioactive waste from British Nuclear

---

[73] ibid, 520.
[74] ibid, 522.
[75] *R v Inspectorate of Pollution and another, ex parte Greenpeace Ltd (No 2)* [1994] 4 All ER 329.
[76] *Ex parte Dixon* (above n 61) 117.
[77] ibid, 121.
[78] ibid, 118.
[79] ibid, 121.

Fuel's Sellafield site in Cumbria. In Otton J's view, Greenpeace was not a 'mere' or 'meddlesome' busybody, but was 'eminently respectable and responsible and its genuine interest in the issues raised is sufficient for it to be granted locus standi'.[80] Otton J referred to Lord Roskill's approval in *National Federation*,[81] of the view that whether an applicant has sufficient interest is a mixed question of fact and law. Thus, Otton J said that it 'must not be assumed that Greenpeace (or any other interest group) will automatically be afforded standing in any subsequent application for judicial review in whatever field it (and its members) may have an interest'. The issue must be 'considered on a case by case basis at the leave stage and if the threshold is crossed again at the substantive hearing as a matter of discretion'.[82] He had this consideration in mind in declining to follow Schiemann J in *Rose Theatre*. While Greenpeace was thus permitted to bring the application on behalf of its members, its application was denied on the merits.

In *R v HM Treasury, ex Parte Smedley*[83] the applicant, in his capacity as a taxpayer and elector, had standing to challenge the Treasury's expressed intention to pay the EU a sum in excess of £121.5 million out of the Consolidated Fund, seeking authorisation from Parliament via an Order in Council, rather than via statute. Slade LJ had little doubt 'that Mr. Smedley, if only in his capacity as a taxpayer, has sufficient locus standi to raise this question by way of an application for judicial review'.[84] Nevertheless, his application failed on the merits. Finally, in *R v Secretary of State for Foreign and Commonwealth Affairs, ex p Rees-Mogg*,[85] a member of the House of Lords with a keen interest in constitutional issues, had standing to challenge the decision of the Foreign Secretary to ratify the Maastricht Treaty. Again, he lost on the merits.

In the last three cases the applications were denied on the merits, raising the question why the applicants had standing to bring the applications in the first place. Were the courts just being 'nosy', or was there something deeper at play? As has been indicated, the Divisional Court also held in *Pergau Dam* that the WDM had the required standing. While Rose LJ accepted[86] that standing goes to jurisdiction, he also held that 'the merits of the challenge are an important, if not dominant, factor when considering standing'.[87] He referred with approval to Wade's view that 'the real question is whether the applicant can show some substantial default or abuse, and not whether his personal rights or interests are

---

[80] *Greenpeace* (above n 75) 351.
[81] *National Federation* (above n 38) 659. Compare Lord Wilberforce (at 631), Lord Scarman (at 653).
[82] *Greenpeace* (above n 75) 351.
[83] *R v HM Treasury, ex Parte Smedley* [1985] QB 657.
[84] ibid.
[85] *R v Secretary of State for Foreign and Commonwealth Affairs, ex p Rees-Mogg* [1994] QB 552.
[86] *Pergau Dam* (above n 6) 395.
[87] ibid.

involved'. There were also a number of 'factors of significance' in the case: the importance of 'vindicating the rule of law'; the importance of the issue raised; the likely absence of any other responsible challenger; the nature of the breach of duty against which relief is sought; and the prominent role of the applicants in giving advice, guidance and assistance with regard to aid.

With respect to the last factor, Rose LJ considered arguments relating to the nature and role of the WDM.[88] It was 'a non-partisan pressure group', with an 'associated charity which receives financial support from all the main United Kingdom development charities, the churches, the European Community and a range of other trusts'. Its council had cross-political party membership, including one MP from each of the three main political parties. It had 200 local groups whose supporters actively campaigned 'through letter writing, lobbying and other democratic means to improve the quantity and quality of British aid to other countries'. Among other things, it was also involved in making written and oral submissions to select committees in both Houses of Parliament, had official consultative status with UNESCO, promoted international conferences and brought together development groups with the OECD. Finally:

> Its supporters have a direct interest in ensuring that funds furnished by the United Kingdom are used for genuine purposes, and it seeks to ensure that disbursement of aid budgets is made where that aid is most needed. It seeks, by this application, to represent the interests of people in developing countries who might benefit from funds which otherwise might go elsewhere.[89]

The last statement is interesting on account of the question posed earlier as to which civilised society is one's tax paying for. One might wonder why a UK court should permit anyone to represent the interests of an amorphous group of 'people in developing countries'. This may well encourage 'busybodies'. The rest of the excerpt is equally contestable. Why should a pressure group have standing regarding how HM Government spends public revenues? Who determines where 'aid is most needed'? Ministers? Courts? The WDM? Why should the WDM have any legitimate interest in this decision? Does it have a similar interest in other central government spending decisions? If not, what is different about this case? These important questions require addressing.

The WDM's argument was that, if they had no standing, nobody would ensure that powers under the Act are exercised lawfully. Rose LJ felt that all the relevant factors indicated that the WDM had a sufficient interest. In his view, if the Divisional Court in *Ex Parte Rees-Mogg*

> was able to accept that the applicant in that case had standing in the light of his 'sincere concerns for constitutional issues', a fortiori, it seems … that the present applicants, with the national and international expertise and interest in promoting

---

[88] ibid, 392–93.
[89] ibid, 393.

and protecting aid to underdeveloped nations, should have standing in the present application.[90]

With respect, this does not necessarily follow. The issue of standing does not seem to have been contested in *Rees-Mogg*, and Lord Rees-Mogg was a member of the House of Lords. It is not clear that the Court would have been so sanguine had Lord Rees-Mogg just been a random 'man on the Clapham omnibus'.

Nevertheless, the broad approach to standing seems well established now, thanks in part to *Pergau Dam*.[91] For example, *Pergau Dam* was referred to with apparent approval by the Court of Appeal in *R (Corner House Research) v Secretary of State for Trade and Industry*[92] and was followed in *Re McBride's Application for Judicial Review*[93] where Kerr J[94] specifically adopted the reasoning in *Pergau Dam*. Sedley J's endorsement of *Pergau Dam* in *Ex Parte Dixon* has already been noted.[95] In *Walton v Scottish Ministers*[96] Lord Reed said that it will be necessary in many contexts 'for a person to demonstrate some particular interest in order to demonstrate that he is not a mere busybody'. However,

> there may also be cases in which any individual, simply as a citizen, will have sufficient interest to bring a public authority's violation of the law to the attention of the court, without having to demonstrate any greater impact upon himself than upon other members of the public.[97]

Notwithstanding general acceptance, the broad approach espoused in *Pergau Dam* is problematic.[98] The WDM was neither a taxpayer nor a ratepayer. But should the inclusion of MPs from the three main political parties in its council be significant? Rightly, nothing much was made of this in the judgment. Neither it nor its UK supporters could possibly be affected by a decision to grant overseas aid out of moneys already allocated for overseas aid. This distinguishes it from *Rees-Mogg* and *Greenpeace*. That government ministers may have acted inappropriately should arguably have no impact on standing. That nobody else would otherwise have standing should have no impact on whether one has standing. It would simply mean that there is a situation that is not covered

---

[90] ibid, 396.

[91] See, eg, *R (Kides) v South Cambridgeshire District Council* [2002] EWCA Civ 1370, [2002] All ER (D) 114 (Oct); *R (Hammerton) v London Underground* [2002] EWHC 2307 (Admin), [2002] All ER (D) 141 (Nov).

[92] *R (Corner House Research) v Secretary of State for Trade and Industry* [2005] EWCA Civ 192, [2005] 1 WLR 2600.

[93] *Re McBride's Application for Judicial Review* [1999] NI 299.

[94] ibid, 311.

[95] *Ex parte Dixon* (above n 61) 121.

[96] *Walton* (above n 58) para 94.

[97] ibid.

[98] Contrast A Tomkins, 'Judges Dam(n) the Government' (1996–97) 7 *Kings College Law Journal* 91; A Cygan, 'Protecting the Interests of Civil Society in Community Decision-Making: The Limits of Article 230 EC' (2003) 52 *ICLQ* 995.

by statute. This is nothing new, and, if considered a problem, the solution is amending legislation. The desire to 'vindicate the rule of law' by permitting egregious governmental action to be brought to the attention of the courts is laudable. However, excessive widening of the standing rules may not be the answer. The words of Schiemann J in *Rose Theatre* are pertinent.[99] The irony is that, in attempting to uphold the rule of law by relaxing the standing rules, the courts may be in danger of achieving the opposite. Lord Simon of Glaisdale rightly noted in *Ransom v Higgs* that 'for the courts to try and stretch the law to meet hard cases ... is not merely to make bad law but to run the risk of subverting the rule of law itself'.[100]

If the WDM had standing, so did everyone else in the country. This follows logically. But it cannot be right that everybody in the country has standing to challenge governmental action that affects nobody in the country. The difficulties with the *Pergau Dam* approach appear from *Merger Action Group v Secretary of State for Business, Enterprise and Regulatory Reform*[101] where the Competition Appeal Tribunal decided that the applicants had standing, despite taking the view that their claim to standing was borderline, that they had adduced no real evidence of their standing other than to assert that they have a generalised consumer interest in UK banking, that they had 'certainly failed to establish any specific concern that differentiates them from the general body of consumers of banking services', and that their challenge to the lawfulness of the decision had 'no legal merit'.[102] Yet the Tribunal felt that the circumstances of the case were 'wholly exceptional', and 'particularly in view of the specific interest and strong feeling' which was aroused in Scotland.[103] According to the Tribunal:

> We considered whether the fact that the application has, on examination, no legal merit should tip the balance the other way. We would certainly not wish to encourage unmeritorious and last minute applications of this kind. In the end, and with some hesitation, we have come to the conclusion that the wholly exceptional factors to which we have referred are decisive.[104]

Harlow rightly pointed out that the test applied in *Pergau Dam*, 'like the *Federation* case, noticeably shifts the centre of attention from the applicant to the merits of the cause (in technical terminology, from standing to justiciability)'.[105] Thus the decision was no longer really about sufficiency of interest, but about something else. This feels like 'mission creep'. *Merger Action Group* seems to have gone beyond even this. If Wade's view (approved by Rose LJ in

---

[99] Above n 74 and text.
[100] *Ransom v Higgs* [1974] 1 WLR 1594, 1617.
[101] *Merger Action Group v Secretary of State for Business, Enterprise and Regulatory Reform* [2008] CAT 36, 2009 SLT 10.
[102] ibid, paras 45–46.
[103] ibid, para 47.
[104] ibid, para 48.
[105] Harlow (above n 52) 6.

Pergau Dam) that 'the real question is whether the applicant can show some substantial default or abuse' is correct, then standing should have been denied. But, here, Scottish 'strong feelings' seemed to have played a significant role, thus embracing considerations additional to 'the applicant' and 'justiciability' mentioned by Harlow.

V. POLITICAL AND DIPLOMATIC DRAMAS

Interestingly, one of the most important issues relating to *Pergau Dam* did not feature in the court case. This is the tying of overseas aid to trade – specifically, arms deals. Unsurprisingly, this issue was picked up outside the confines of the court case. As one commentator put it:

> Essentially, Pergau dam was about the British government's engagement in an aid-for-arms deal with the government of Malaysia, with the agreement that 20 percent of an arms sale from Britain to Malaysia be spent on the construction of a dam to provide electricity.[106]

Lustgarten referred to the 'great damage' that was done to 'the integrity of our overseas aid programme, and of the procedures for scrutiny of financial propriety within a major department of government'.[107] He sought to explain why the government had 'so relentlessly insist[ed] on proceeding with a project whose cost had risen in a short period more than 25% over the original estimate'. The explanation was that:

> Underpinning the whole tawdry episode was the fact that arms sales had been part of the original deal, as both sides fully understood. But no one in government was prepared to admit this so-called 'linkage' publicly, nor were they willing to forego the benefits. Hence they resorted to presenting to the public what is immediately recognisable to those who followed the Scott Inquiry as 'half the picture' – in accordance with the view of a former ambassador who insisted in his testimony that 'half a picture can be accurate'.[108]

While some have referred to allegations of corruption in Malaysia (discussed below), the UK corruption angle has been thus described:

> In Britain, the 'arms for aid' issue, also known as the Pergau Dam affair, surfaced in 1994 involving giving monetary aid to developing countries by Britain in return for arms deals. It also revealed the undisclosed fact that the Conservative Government

---

[106] E Seyedsayamdost, 'Development as End of Poverty: Reform or Reinvention?' (2015) 21 *Global Governance* 515, 528–29.

[107] L Lustgarten, 'The Arms Trade and the Constitution: Beyond the Scott Report' (1998) 61 *MLR* 499, 507.

[108] ibid (internal citation omitted).

had allocated business deals to British companies, namely Balfour Beatty and Cementation, which contributed heavily to the Conservative Party funds.[109]

The connection of defence contracts to the Pergau project came early, with a 'Protocol on Malaysia Defence Procurement Programme' (paving the way for a Memorandum of Understanding on defence sales of £1 billion) being signed in March 1988 by the UK Defence Secretary and his Malaysian counterpart.[110] There was apparently 'a willingness on the part of the UK government to consider the possibility of providing aid for civil projects as part of the deal'.[111] As the Pergau dam saga developed, the link between the project and defence sales was more strongly made in the interactions between Mrs Thatcher and Dr Mahathir.[112] Unsurprisingly, there was much to say in Parliament about the matter. The linkage of aid to arms sales was a particular point of trouble. It was still being referred to in Parliament as late as 2012, with Chris Leslie saying that the Pergau affair 'involved a too-close relationship between the aid being given to a foreign country and the trade that was taking place, particularly in relation to arms exports'.[113] It is not difficult to imagine the tone of the contributions from the government and opposition benches. I will restrict my coverage of parliamentary debates to the House of Lords on 17 November 1994,[114] in the wake of the decision of the Divisional Court. Baroness Blackstone described as 'entirely unacceptable' the situation wherein 'scarce funding set aside for aid and development purposes [was] used, as happened in the case of the Pergau dam, to lubricate arms deals'.[115] Lord Cledwyn of Penrhos claimed that 'the Pergau dam affair' was 'a classic example of how foreign affairs should not be conducted'.[116] In his view, 'Such unscrupulous manipulation of the aid budget was … a disgrace'.[117] The Bishop of Worcester made a plea that aid be kept strictly separate from arms deals, and requested confirmation as to whether 'that particular deal ended in a 400 per cent. payback in defence contracts', since a Foreign Office spokesman 'was reported as saying that we give aid and sell arms but there is no connection between the two'.[118]

In what seemed like a classic case of denial, Lord Henley, Parliamentary Under-Secretary of State at the Ministry of Defence, said:

> [T]here is quite simply no link between aid projects and defence contracts in Indonesia, Jordan, Oman or in any other markets which noble Lords care to mention.

---

[109] YK Teh, 'The Future Fraud and Corruption Scenario in Developing and Developed Countries' (1997) 5 *Journal of Financial Crime* 58, 59.

[110] Lankester (above n 8) 54.

[111] ibid.

[112] ibid, 72–73.

[113] HC Deb 15 October 2012, vol 551, cols 85–86.

[114] HL Deb 17 November 1994, vol 559, cols 26–140.

[115] ibid, col 34.

[116] ibid, col 48.

[117] ibid, col 49.

[118] ibid, col 56.

Allegations of that sort are quite simply untrue. They are based on spurious correlations between provisions of aid and arms sales. I totally reject the allegations ... on this issue that our aid projects are linked in any way to arms sales.[119]

For her part, Baroness Chalker, Minister of State at the Foreign and Commonwealth Office said in respect of the judgment:

The Foreign Secretary and I stand by the evidence which we gave to the Select Committee. The Select Committee inquiry went wider than the court judgment. It examined the events of 1988 and the political and commercial background. The court did none of that. The court was not asked to enter, and did not enter, into the question of arms sales. I understand that the judgment has nothing to say on that point.[120]

It is not clear what point Baroness Chalker was making in noting that the Court did not go into the political and commercial background and did not enter into the question of arm sales. More interesting was her statement that:

The Pergau project is now 75 per cent complete and involves over 200 British companies. The judgment does not affect this Government's contractual obligations towards the banks financing the project. What it would mean ... is that the project should not henceforth be financed from funds voted under the Overseas Development and Cooperation Act 1980.[121]

While the last statement might delight those interested mainly in the overseas aid budget being used for 'legitimate' purposes, its implication is that, far from securing that taxpayers' money is used in a financially prudent manner, all that would happen is that the government would fund the Pergau project from other funds, the cost to the taxpayer remaining the same. Thus, prudential management of overseas aid funds does not necessarily equate to such management of general public revenues.

Another fallout of *Pergau Dam* related to damaged relations with Malaysia. Negative coverage from the British press, in particular, apparently unsubstantiated allegations of bribery in the *Sunday Times* in February 1994 against Dr Mahathir 'infuriated' Dr Mahathir.[122] The furore ultimately resulted in a 'sweeping trade ban on Britain',[123] which took the form of Malaysia's 'boycott of British companies for new public sector contracts'.[124] A February 1994 official statement from the Malaysian Finance Minister demonstrated the feelings of outrage. The statement read: 'The British media may have their own political agenda but we detest their patronising attitude and innuendoes that

---

[119] ibid, col 136.
[120] ibid, col 29.
[121] ibid, col 30.
[122] Lankester (above n 8) 119, 139.
[123] See, eg, R Williams, 'Pergau Dam Affair: "Sweeteners" row sparked trade ban' *The Independent* (7 September 1994).
[124] Lankester (above n 8) 120.

the government of developing countries, particularly a Muslim-led nation like Malaysia, are incompetent and their leaders corrupt'.[125] The minister thought that the allegations were 'racially motivated and that the British press in general implied that doing business with "brown Muslims" inevitably involved bribery'.[126] British–Malaysia relations suffered a setback, and British exporters were apparently 'furious', with some urging the government to intervene with *The Sunday Times* to ask them to retract.[127] Fortunately, the trade boycott was lifted in November 1994 after some mediation.[128]

VI. WHITHER OVERSEAS AID?

Lankester noted that the Pergau saga 'had a lasting effect on all who were concerned with British aid policy'[129] and became 'a turning point when British aid moved away from being so closely geared to British commercial interests and moved towards becoming today possibly the most highly respected amongst all donors with a much strengthened focus on poverty alleviation'.[130] The Divisional Court's judgment naturally led to government review of overseas aid. Baroness Chalker announced in the House of Lords that

> we have asked our officials to review carefully all the projects and activities they fund to see whether there are any others approved under our previous understanding of the Overseas Development and Cooperation Act 1980 which may also fall outside the interpretation of the Act given for the first time last week.[131]

Lankester referred to beneficial impact on aid from the lessons learnt from Pergau, to 'international moves to reduce the tying of aid', and to 'the election of a Labour government in 1997 with a mandate to increase the aid budget and strengthen aid effectiveness'.[132] These factors combined to 'bring about changes in British aid policy that gave greater weight to development and poverty alleviation and in due course all but eliminated the commercial influence in aid decisions'.[133] With respect to the aforesaid 'international moves', Member States of the OECD had adopted in December 1991, the 'Helsinki rules on tied aid credits aimed at limiting the use of concessional financing for projects that should be able to support commercial financing (ie, those which

---

[125] ibid.
[126] ibid.
[127] ibid.
[128] ibid, 121.
[129] ibid, 4.
[130] ibid, 141.
[131] HL Deb 17 November 1994, vol 559, col 30.
[132] Lankester (above n 8) 4.
[133] ibid.

are "commercially viable")'.[134] The OECD's Development Assistance Committee further recommended in May 2001 that aid to the least developed countries be untied.[135] With respect to the new 1997 Labour administration, the new Labour minister for overseas development, Clare Short, presided over a renamed Department for International Development. It seems that one of her first acts was to abolish ATP.[136] But her tenure also witnessed a substantial increase in the aid budget. One development under her leadership was the IDA 2002, which has been referred to earlier. The new focus on poverty reduction was firmly declared in section 1(1) – 'The Secretary of State may provide any person or body with development assistance if he is satisfied that the provision of the assistance is likely to contribute to a reduction in poverty'. This represented a major shift in the UK's aid legislation, and may well constitute the enduring legacy of *Pergau Dam*. The shift in focus is welcome, as is the enshrinement in statute of a requirement for 'prudence' in aid provision. But does any of this strengthen the hands of the courts in their scrutiny of the disbursement of taxpayer revenues? Some commentators think not. McAuslan thus reflected on the IDA 2002:

> The extent of the discretion conferred upon the Secretary of State may be seen by a closer examination of section 1 of the Act. Development assistance may be provided if the Secretary of State *is satisfied* that its provision *is likely to contribute to a reduction in poverty*. That is a subjective test. The Act does however go on to elaborate what development assistance means which might be thought to operate to limit the Secretary of State's discretion. Development assistance means 'assistance provided for furthering sustainable development'. 'Sustainable development' in turn *includes* 'any development that is, *in the opinion of the Secretary of State*, prudent having regard to the likelihood of its generating lasting benefits for the population of the country or countries to which it is provided'. Like a dam? A nuclear power station? A state-of-the-art air traffic control system? A striking new building to house a country's Supreme Court? If all that has to be shown is the reasonableness of the Secretary of State's opinion that such development is 'prudent' having regard to the 'likelihood' of its generating lasting benefits to the population, then the draftsman will have gone a long way to overcome the *Pergau Dam* case.[137]

Thus, did Parliament reassert itself to unravel *Pergau Dam*'s intrusion into matters of government policy.

Given the controversial nature of the Divisional Court's decision, the embarrassment that it caused the government, and the subsequent reassertion of itself

---

[134] See OECD, *Arrangement on Officially Supported Export Credits: Ex Ante Guidance for Tied Aid. 2005 Revision* (OECD, 2005) 2. See generally KP Rosefsky, 'Tied Aid Credits and the New OECD Agreement' (1993) 14 *U Pa L Rev* 437.

[135] See OECD, *Policy Brief: Untying Aid to the Least Developed Countries* (OECD, 2001) 1. See also OECD, *The Paris Declaration on Aid Effectiveness* (OECD, 2005).

[136] Lankester (above n 8) 20.

[137] P McAuslan, 'The International Development Act, 2002: Benign Imperialism or a Missed Opportunity?' (2003) 66 *MLR* 563, 583.

by Parliament, the question is why did the government not appeal? There are difficulties with the Divisional Court's decisions and reasoning on the main issues in the case. While the broad approach to standing is settled, it was arguably taken too far in *Pergau Dam*. But it is likely that an appeal on standing would have failed. Illegality is quite different however. It is this writer's view that the Divisional Court's decision was wrong, and that there would have been a reasonable chance of a successful appeal. Perhaps parliamentary action was considered more predictable and prudent than appealing.

VII. CONCLUSION

R v Secretary of State for Foreign Affairs, ex parte World Development Movement Ltd is truly a landmark case. Its lasting impact, mostly controversial, and mostly possibly undesirable, can be thus summarised. It extended the broad approach to standing, such that one can apparently have standing to protect the interests of indeterminate persons in foreign lands. It represented increased judicial interventionism in the deployment of public revenues, postulating that the disposition of tax revenues by central government is an appropriate matter for judicial determination. It expanded the concept of improper purpose, via a gloss on statutory powers, to require financial prudence in the management of central government revenues. The outcome of all this was that a pressure group with a tenuous claim to standing succeeded in derailing targeted central government spending. Finally, it resulted in the deprecation of tying aid to trade, and in overseas aid being focused on poverty reduction.

18

Barclays Mercantile Business Finance v Mawson *(2004)*

Living with Uncertainty

JOHN VELLA*

I. INTRODUCTION

T AX AVOIDANCE ROUSES strong emotions. To many it is emblematic of the ills of an economic and political system rigged in favour of the rich and characterised by greed and unfairness. In recent years, the public's ire was stoked again and again by revelations of the tax practices of wealthy individuals and prominent businesses.[1] Although tax avoidance may have never been higher on the public and political agenda, the problem is long standing. Courts struggled in formulating their approach to tax avoidance over many years, and the authorities have sought to address the issue with layer upon layer of anti-avoidance measures. The UK now boasts a veritable arsenal. Some measures – such as specific anti-avoidance rules, targeted anti-avoidance rules, and a General Anti-Abuse Rule (GAAR) – are essentially additional statutory hurdles that tax arrangements must overcome to succeed. They re-draw the boundary between arrangements that work and those that do not. Other measures, such as disclosure rules, codes of conduct, a requirement to publish tax strategies and to prepare country-by-country reports, procurement rules, and cooperative

---

*I would like to thank John Snape, Dominic de Cogan and the anonymous referees for helpful suggestions and comments. Over the years, I have been very fortunate in being able to discuss the broad issues covered in this chapter with Judith Freedman and John Tiley. I am very grateful for this.

[1] Unfortunately, practices ranging from outright evasion to the use of tax incentives in the manner intended by Parliament are often conflated in public and political debates under the heading of 'tax avoidance'. For the author's views on the meaning of 'tax avoidance' see the report commissioned by the National Audit Office, by MP Devereux, J Freedman and J Vella, *Tax Avoidance* (Oxford University Centre for Business Taxation, 2012), available at www.sbs.ox.ac.uk/sites/default/files/Business_Taxation/Docs/Publications/Reports/TA_3_12_12.pdf.

compliance programmes, have multiple aims. They include increasing transparency, addressing informational asymmetries between taxpayers and the revenue authority, and allowing the revenue authority to allocate resources according to risk. Expressly or implicitly, these measures also have the aim of changing tax planning behaviour by inducing taxpayers to maintain some distance from the boundary. This regulatory strategy chimes with popular campaigns to shame taxpayers into changing behaviour which is considered too aggressive or leads to less than a 'fair share' of tax being paid.

Barclays Mercantile Business Finance Limited v Mawson (BMBF)[2] is a landmark tax case for a number of reasons. Avoidance remains one of the most important policy issues in taxation and one of its most intellectually challenging.[3] *BMBF* brought much needed clarity on the approach courts are to adopt when faced with avoidance, and – despite the masses of anti-avoidance legislation now in force – this remains a critical test in determining whether a transaction is effective. *BMBF* reaffirmed that the courts' approach is based on purposive interpretation. However, a careful examination of the case also reveals the difficulties and uncertainty this entails; issues that unsurprisingly resurfaced in later cases and partly explain the proliferation of anti-avoidance measures since then, including the GAAR. In particular, *BMBF* illustrates the interpretative space purposive interpretation affords the judiciary. This might allow broader considerations – including the prevailing public and political mood on avoidance – to come into play. It is useful to keep this in mind when studying *BMBF* and the relevant case law preceding and following it.

BMBF also informs the debate on the merits of regulatory strategies that seek to keep taxpayers away from the boundary between transactions that work and those that do not. The transaction in *BMBF* might have been classified by some as 'unacceptable' or 'aggressive' avoidance that the authorities ought to discourage taxpayers from attempting. Clearly Her Majesty's Revenue and Customs (HMRC) believed that the taxpayer should not have undertaken the transaction. However, the House of Lords found that the transaction worked at law, thus bringing into sharp focus the rule of law issues surrounding these regulatory strategies. On the other hand, even if not related to *BMBF* per se, in later years the Barclays group – of which the taxpayer formed part – acknowledged that it had been too aggressive in some of its tax planning behaviour and vowed

---

[2] *Barclays Mercantile Business Finance Limited v Mawson* (BMBF) [2004] UKHL 51, [2005] STC 1.
[3] Note the considerable number of articles written by Law Lords on tax avoidance. See, eg: P Millett, 'A New Approach to Tax Avoidance Schemes' (1982) 98 *LQR* 209; P Millett, 'Artificial Tax Avoidance: The English and American Approach' [1986] *BTR* 327; P Millett, 'The Secret History of Ramsay v IRC' (1999) *Trusts & Estates Tax Journal* 23; S Templeman, 'Tax and the Taxpayer' (2001) 117 *LQR* 575; S Templeman, 'Form and Substance' in J Getzler (ed), *Rationalising Property, Equity and Trusts: Essays in Honour of Edward Burn* (Oxford, Oxford University Press, 2003) 130–34; R Walker, 'Ramsay 25 Years On: Some Reflections on Tax Avoidance' (2004) 120 *LQR* 412; L Hoffmann, 'Tax Avoidance' [2005] *BTR* 197.

to change. Remarkably, it committed to going beyond the mere requirements of the law when tax planning.

BMBF contributes in these manifold ways to our understanding of avoidance and how to address it. On a personal note, *BMBF* was decided while I was writing my PhD thesis, largely on the judicial approach to tax avoidance, at the University of Cambridge. I attended the two-day hearing and reported back to Professor John Tiley – a doyen of tax avoidance scholarship – via email after each day. On 14 October 2004 – the day after the hearing ended – I wrote to John summarising the day's events. I started the email with: 'Tuesday's hearing started off with a real bang. Lord Nicholls and Lord Hoffmann asked for some clarifications from counsel for the Revenue and I got the impression that he was having some difficulty answering them satisfactorily'. I ended the email with: 'The impression I got was that the Revenue were substantially less upbeat than they were after the first day'. The Revenue's assessment – at least, as I perceived it – proved to be correct.

This chapter is organised as follows. Section II sets out the difficulties courts faced over the years in developing a judicial approach to counter avoidance. Section III focuses on the period immediately preceding *BMBF* and explains why the uncertainty surrounding the approach reached its peak then. Section IV discusses *BMBF*. After providing some context, it explains how the decision clarified the judicial approach to avoidance but at the same time illustrates the difficulties inherent in an approach based on purposive interpretation. Section V identifies some of the problems arising in the courts' use of the judicial approach to avoidance in the cases following *BMBF*. Section VI discusses the particular role played by the financial sector in the tax avoidance saga. Section VII concludes.

II. THE QUESTIONS ADDRESSED IN *BMBF v MAWSON*

The approach to tax avoidance developed by courts is generally known as the *Ramsay* approach after *WT Ramsay Ltd v CIR*[4] (*Ramsay*).[5] It was reasonably clear from its very beginnings that it allowed courts to look beyond the legal characterisation of transactions, for example to the economic effect of a composite transaction as a whole. However, in which circumstances, how and on what grounds this was to be done remained obscure. The approach was thus reformulated a number of times following *Ramsay* as judges sought to provide satisfactory answers to these questions.[6] The frequent reformulations

---

[4] *WT Ramsay Ltd v CIR* [1981] STC 174.

[5] Parts of this section are based on the analysis in J Vella, 'Shams, Tax Avoidance and a "Realistic View of the Facts"' in E Simpson and M Stewart (eds), *Sham Transactions* (Oxford, Oxford University Press, 2013).

[6] Whilst judges mostly sought to explain the differences in formulations away, some did hint at this shifting ground. In *Furniss v Dawson*, Lord Scarman thus warned that 'the law in this area is in

caused uncertainty, as they implied judicial approaches of differing natures and scope. This was indeed a period of 'struggle, experiment and semi-rational limitations'.[7] *BMBF* provided definitive answers to all three questions.

The starting point to understanding the courts' struggles in developing this approach is that UK courts characterise transactions in accordance with their 'legal substance'. This corresponds to their form, unless the transactions are shams.[8] Courts do not look beyond the legal substance of transactions on the grounds of artificiality,[9] an avoidance purpose,[10] or their economic effect.[11] Whilst developing the *Ramsay* approach, courts upheld this principle in the tax field: taxpayers are taxed according to the legal substance of their transactions, and not their economic effect. This principle is commonly associated with *CIR v The Duke of Westminster*,[12] 'the leading tax case on the substance of a transaction'.[13] Indeed, this principle has been said to express the true ratio[14] of the case.

Most judges who contributed to the development of the *Ramsay* approach grappled with *Duke of Westminster*. Although some expressed doubts or concerns at the outcome of the case,[15] many denied suggestions that the approach they were developing was in any way inconsistent with it.[16] Indeed, an approach which went against *Duke of Westminster* and allowed courts to look beyond the legal substance of transactions was generally thought to go against the constitutional principle that taxpayers are to be taxed by Parliament and not the courts.[17]

---

an early stage of development' [1984] STC 153, 156 b–c, and 20 years later, in *Collector of Stamp Revenue v Arrowtown Assets Limited*, Lord Millett could only modify the warning slightly when stating that the approach 'is still in course of development in the United Kingdom' [2003] HKFCA 46, para 104.

[7] J Tiley, 'Tax Avoidance Jurisprudence as Normal Law' [2004] *BTR* 304, 305.

[8] Shams arise if the form of the transaction differs from its legal substance: *Snook v London and West Riding Investments Ltd* [1967] 2 QB 786. For further detail see J Vella, 'Sham Transactions' [2008] *LMCLQ* 488.

[9] See, eg, *Belvedere Court Management Ltd v Frogmore Developments Ltd* [1997] QB 858, 876 E–F (Sir Thomas Bingham MR).

[10] See, eg, *Re George Inglefield Ltd* [1933] 1 Ch 1, 22–23 (Lord Hanworth) and 26 (Romer LJ).

[11] See, eg, *Welsh Development Agency v Export Finance Co Ltd* [1992] BCC 270, 300–01 (Staughton LJ) and 281 B (Dillon LJ).

[12] *CIR v The Duke of Westminster* [1936] AC 1. The House of Lords here unanimously rejected any suggestion that a taxpayer should be taxed according to the economic substance of the transactions he enters into.

[13] *Re Polly Peck International plc (in Administration)* [1992] 2 All ER 433, 446 g (Robert Walker J).

[14] See, eg, *Ramsay* (above n 4) 180 c and 191 c–e (Lord Wilberforce). See also the arguments conceded by the Crown [1982] AC 300, 316; and *CIR v McGuckian* [1997] STC 908, 915 a (Lord Steyn).

[15] See, eg, *Furniss v Dawson* (above n 6) 157 d–e (Lord Roskill); *McGuckian* (above n 14) 920 a and 921 b–c (Lord Cooke).

[16] See, eg, *Ramsay* (above n 4) 180 c–d (Lord Wilberforce) and at 191 d–e (Lord Fraser); and *MacNiven v Westmoreland* [2001] STC 237, paras 38 and 39 (Lord Hoffmann).

[17] Art 4, Bill of Rights 1689. This principle was conceded by the Crown in *Ramsay* (above n 4). See also *MacNiven* (above n 16) para 29 (Lord Hoffmann); *Arrowtown* (above n 6) para 105 (Lord

Whilst the courts did not expressly overturn the *Duke of Westminster* principle, in a number of cases – especially *Furniss v Dawson* and cases that followed it – they formulated and applied the *Ramsay* approach in a way which might well be thought to be contrary to it. Writing extra-judicially, Lord Hoffmann did not equivocate. He described the turn taken in *Furniss v Dawson* as stepping 'outside the meaning of the statute and develop[ing] a general anti-avoidance doctrine based upon whether the transaction or parts of the transaction had a business purpose'.[18]

There was, however, a way in which one could reconcile an approach which allowed courts to look beyond the legal substance of transactions, as the *Ramsay* approach appeared to do, with both the *Duke of Westminster* principle and the principle that tax must be imposed by Parliament and not the courts. This was expressly identified in *Craven v White*:

> [J]udges are not legislators and, if the result of a judicial decision is to contradict the express statutory consequences which have been declared by Parliament to attach to a particular transaction which has been found as a fact to have taken place, that can be justified only because, as a matter of *construction of the statute*, the court has ascertained that that which has taken place is not, within the meaning of the statute, the transaction to which those consequences attach.[19]

An inroad into the *Duke of Westminster* principle is provided by statutory interpretation – particularly purposive interpretation – since a court may interpret a statute as requiring it to look beyond the legal characterisation of a transaction. A statutory provision may be interpreted, for example, as imposing a tax on transactions viewed in accordance with their economic substance. On this analysis, the *Ramsay* approach can be seen as nothing but a matter of statutory construction. Although, Lord Hoffmann stated that '[e]veryone agrees that *Ramsay* is a principle of construction',[20] it took courts time to work out its full implications and apply it is as such. Lord Hoffmann noted that, in *Craven v White* itself, the approach was 'treated as a general extra-statutory rule'[21] and, similarly, in a number of cases statutory interpretation was used as an ill-fitting cover for a non-statutory based approach.[22] In 1994, Whitehouse answered

---

Millett). See, generally, RT Bartlett, 'The Constitutionality of the *Ramsay* Principle' [1985] *BTR* 338, esp the sources quoted at 353–54.

[18] Hoffmann (above n 3).

[19] *Craven v White* [1988] STC 476, 497 g–i (Lord Oliver) (emphasis added). See also Lord Goff, 511 b–f.

[20] *MacNiven* (above n 16) para 28. See also *Arrowtown* (above n 6) para 105 (Lord Millett); *Craven v White* (above n 19) 499 a (Lord Oliver); *Norglen Ltd v Reeds Rains Prudential Ltd* [1999] 2 AC 1, 13–14 (Lord Hoffmann).

[21] Hoffmann (above n 3) 202.

[22] An interesting example is found in Lord Browne-Wilkinson's speech in *McGuckian* (above n 14). See extra-judicial comments by Lord Oliver in P Oliver, 'A Judicial View of Modern Legislation' (1993) 14 *SLR* 1, 10 and comments in JF Avery Jones, 'MacNiven v Westmoreland: The Humpty Dumpty School of Judicial Anti-Avoidance' [2001] *Private Client Business* 381.

the question of the extent to which the *Ramsay* principle is a rule of statutory construction by saying: '[i]t cannot be. The rule recharacterises transactions and it is that recharacterisation which is then subject to taxation according to the terms of the legislation'.[23]

III. THE UNCERTAINTY IMMEDIATELY PRECEDING *BMBF*

In *MacNiven v Westmoreland*, Lord Hoffmann took the view that the *Ramsay* approach is a principle of statutory interpretation 'extremely seriously';[24] in other words, he took it to its logical conclusion. The judges in *Craven v White* and, with the exception of Lord Clyde, those in *McGuckian*, had noted that the *Ramsay* approach must be based on statutory interpretation but then stated that it allowed them to look at the substance of a composite transaction whenever certain factual requirements were met. But if the *Ramsay* approach is based on statutory interpretation it can only allow a court to look beyond the legal substance of composite transactions if the statutory provision at hand is interpreted as requiring it. This is the crucial point Lord Hoffmann kept returning to.[25] However, he then appeared to formulate the approach too narrowly, by suggesting that certain concepts used in statutes are 'commercial' rather than 'juristic' in nature.[26] If a court interpreted a concept as being 'juristic' it had to take the transaction according to its legal characterisation when applying the statutory provision to it. If, on the other hand, the concept is found to be 'commercial', 'the court was required to take a view of the facts which transcended the juristic individuality of the various parts of a pre-planned series of transactions'.[27]

In retrospect, one can argue that Lord Hoffmann used the juristic/commercial distinction to explain his conclusion rather than to reach it, but his speech certainly led many in the tax community to believe he had reformulated the *Ramsay* approach. This caused surprise, even bemusement. Tiley wrote, '[w]e now know that we have all misunderstood *Ramsay* for 20 years; we have been wrong about its basis and therefore wrong about its scope'[28] and that 'many of the old cases were correctly decided even if we have all misunderstood what they said – according to Lord Hoffmann anyway'. Tiley thus pleaded for

---

[23] C Whitehouse, 'Fitzwilliam – An End to Ramsay' [1994] *Private Client Business* 71, 82. This was just after *Fitzwilliam (Countess) v CIR* [1993] STC 502.

[24] J Tiley, 'First Thoughts on Westmoreland' [2001] *BTR* 153.

[25] *MacNiven* (above n 16) paras 44, 49, 58, 63 and 64.

[26] See, generally, B McFarlane and E Simpson, 'Tackling Avoidance' in J Getzler (ed) *Rationalising Property, Equity and Trusts: Essays in Honour of Edward Burn* (Oxford, Oxford University Press, 2003).

[27] *MacNiven* (above n 16) para 32.

[28] Tiley, 'First Thoughts on Westmoreland' (above n 24) 153.

the need to bring 'some intellectual cohesion to an area of law which is in danger of falling into disrepute'.[29]

The general sense of uncertainty following *MacNiven* was compounded by the intervention of two former Law Lords who had played critical roles in the development of the *Ramsay* approach. Templeman whose name – as Lord Walker wrote extra-judicially – 'has been associated with tax avoidance in the same sort of way as Lady Thatcher's was associated with enthusiasm for an ever-closer union with Europe',[30] wrote a critical article in the *Law Quarterly Review*[31] – which Hoffmann later described as 'brilliant'.[32] Templeman disagreed with Lord Hoffmann's 'diffuse' speech in no uncertain terms, arguing: '[t]he future is uncertain because of the attempt by Lord Hoffmann to distinguish that which cannot logically be distinguished' and that '[t]he argument of Lord Hoffmann … reflects ingenuity but not principle'.

Templeman clearly took umbrage at Lord Nicholls' suggestion in *MacNiven* that the *Ramsay* approach 'is no more than a useful aid':

> But the language of Lord Wilberforce, Lord Diplock and Lord Brightman, and the powerful supporting speeches of Lord Fraser of Tulleybelton, Lord Scarman, Lord Roskill and Lord Bridge of Harwich, do not permit this deduction. The three decisions and 15 speeches in *Ramsay, Burmah* and *Furniss*, the considered pronouncements of an eminent generation of modern Law Lords applying principles to tax avoidance schemes, cannot be downgraded to a mere useful aid.

Lord Millett also disapproved of *MacNiven* – and in particular Lord Hoffmann's speech – in a decision he handed down as a non-permanent member of the Court of Final Appeal of Hong Kong in *Arrowtown*. However, he did so in a more measured and analytic manner. Lord Millett was a recognised authority on tax avoidance; he wrote a number of articles on the matter, and, significantly, was counsel to the Crown in both *Ramsay* and *Furniss v Dawson*. He is on record saying that *Ramsay* is the case he is most proud of,[33] and has been referred to as 'the "midwife" of the *Ramsay* doctrine'.[34] In his speech, Lord Millett went through the main cases to show the difficulty in fitting them into Lord Hoffmann's analysis,[35] before concluding that the juristic/commercial distinction is hard to understand, its source is not discernible, and leads to questionable conclusions and 'arid debates' into which category a word fits.[36]

---

[29] J Tiley 'Composite Business Transactions: Business Transactions or Not?' (2003) 62 *CLJ* 272, 274.

[30] Walker (above n 3) 412.

[31] Templeman, 'Tax and the Taxpayer' (above n 3).

[32] Hoffmann (above n 3).

[33] Millett, 'Secret History' (above n 3) 23.

[34] R Venables, 'Tax Avoidance: Reflections on Lord Hoffmann's Lecture in Honour of Professor Sir Roy Goode' [2005] *Corporate Tax Review* 1.

[35] *Arrowtown* (above n 6) paras 145–47.

[36] ibid, paras 148–49.

It is hard to dismiss the thought that the Law Lords deciding *BMBF* – particularly Lord Hoffmann and Lord Nicholls – had the opinion of these two highly distinguished predecessors in mind when contributing to the decision in *BMBF*. Hoffmann took Templeman's criticism seriously enough to address them directly in a public lecture he gave at Queen Mary University of London soon after *BMBF*.[37]

IV. *BMBF v MAWSON*

A. Key Players in *BMBF*

Revisiting *BMBF* one is struck by the confluence of characters in and around the case who played significant roles in the tax avoidance drama over the years. In a topographic representation of the history of tax avoidance in the UK, many lines would lead to and from this case.

The members of the Judicial Committee of the House of Lords were Lord Nicholls, Lord Steyn, Lord Hoffmann, Lord Hope and Lord Walker. Lord Hoffmann played different roles in the tax avoidance drama over the years. He spoke and wrote extra-judicially on tax avoidance[38] and was the Chairman of the Financial Market Law Committee, which issued a critical and robust response to the 2009 HMRC Consultation Document on a Code of Practice for Banks, which as discussed below, sought to alter the tax planning behaviour of banks.[39] Most significantly, he was part of the advisory committee to Graham Aaronson QC on the GAAR. Aaronson QC was asked by the UK government to lead a study programme on the GAAR, and his report eventually led to its adoption in the UK. Arguably, this was the most important development in the fight against tax avoidance of the past few decades.

Aaronson QC is the clearest link between *BMBF* and the GAAR as he was lead counsel for the taxpayer in this case. Further links between the two can be traced. The two academics on the study group, Professor Judith Freedman of Oxford and Professor John Tiley of Cambridge wrote influentially on the *Ramsay* approach and *BMBF*;[40] and the latter had done his pupillage under Lord Nicholls.[41] Two other members of the GAAR advisory committee – Howard

---

[37] Hoffmann (above n 3).

[38] ibid.

[39] Financial Markets Law Committee, 'Response to the June 2009 HM Revenue & Customs Consultation Document on a Code of Practice for Banks', Issue 146 (October 2009).

[40] See, eg, Tiley, 'Tax Avoidance Jurisprudence as Normal Law' (above n 7); J Tiley, 'Barclays and Scottish Provident: Avoidance and Highest Courts; Less Chaos but More Uncertainty' [2005] *BTR* 272; and J Freedman, 'Defining Taxpayer Responsibility: In Support of a General Anti-Avoidance Principle' [2004] *BTR* 332.

[41] C Stebbings, *Biographical Memoirs of Fellows of the British Academy*, XVI, 219–236. Posted 25 April 2017. The British Academy 2017, available at www.britac.ac.uk/sites/default/files/12%20 Tiley%201837.pdf.

Nolan and Sir Lancelot Henderson – clashed over *BMBF* in later years. The former was a Special Commissioner and the latter a High Court judge in *HMRC v Tower MCashback LLP 1 and another*. The two cases concerned a claim for capital allowances under substantially similar provisions. Henderson J expressed amazement at Howard Nolan's conclusion that *BMBF* was not 'of any relevance to the facts of this case'.[42] Henderson J continued 'I can only conclude that he must have misunderstood, or at least failed to appreciate the significance of, the principles of law which were so clearly established by BMBF'.

It is also worth highlighting that the High Court judge in *BMBF* was Park J, a renowned tax expert. His experience and knowledge in these matters was explicitly noted both in the Court of Appeal[43] and the House of Lords.[44] He was lead counsel in many important cases before the House of Lords on the Ramsay Approach, including *Craven v White* (with David Goy QC, who was lead counsel for HMRC in *BMBF*) and *CIR v McGuckian* (with Lancelot Henderson). In later years, he wrote a report on commission from the National Audit Office on tax settlements following a controversy that – arguably – played a key role in catapulting tax avoidance to the front of international public and political concern.[45]

B. The *Ramsay* Approach in *BMBF*

The House of Lords expressly acknowledged the uncertainty at the time[46] and thus delivered a single speech in which it sought to provide clarity on the basic principles. It made it immediately clear that the *Ramsay* approach is nothing more than an approach to statutory construction.[47] It held:

> The essence of the new approach was to give the statutory provision a purposive construction *in order to determine the nature of the transaction to which it was intended to apply* and then to decide whether the actual transaction (which *might* involve considering the overall effect of a number of elements intended to operate together) answered to the statutory description.[48]

---

[42] *HMRC v Tower MCashback LLP 1 and another* [2008] EWHC 2387 (Ch); [2008] STC 3366, 3411, para 75.

[43] [2002] EWCA Civ 1853, [2003] STC 66, para 34 (Peter Gibson LJ). See also the praise levelled at him at para 16.

[44] *BMBF* (above n 2) para 19.

[45] This controversy was one of the factors which drew the attention of the Public Accounts Committee to tax matters under the chairmanship of Margaret Hodge MP. The subsequent forays of the PAC into tax matters played an important role in drawing and intensifying the public and political spotlight on tax avoidance. Perhaps it is not too far-fetched to speculate that the OECD's Base Erosion and Profit Shifting project would not have been undertaken were it not for the PAC's actions, or at least, the project would not have been undertaken at the same time and in the same manner.

[46] *BMBF* (above n 2) para 26.

[47] ibid, paras 26 and 27.

[48] ibid, para 32 (emphasis added).

The House of Lords thus explained that under the *Ramsay* approach, the facts can be looked at realistically, if and only if allowed by statute – '(which *might* involve'). There is no separate principle which allows a court to look at the facts realistically independently of statute, as was held in previous decisions and as suggested in Mr Justice Ribeiro PJ's speech in *Arrowtown*, which the House of Lords, regrettably, chose to quote favourably:

> The driving principle in the *Ramsay* line of cases continues to involve a general rule of statutory construction *and an unblinkered approach to the analysis of the facts.* The ultimate question is whether the relevant statutory provisions, construed purposively, were intended to apply to the transaction, *viewed realistically.*[49]

This formulation has acquired canonical status as a result of its frequent citation by courts. It risks error because it suggests that facts can be viewed realistically *independently* of the particular wording of the statute and, therefore, not if, and only if, the statute is interpreted as requiring such a view of the facts. As can be seen in *MacNiven* and *BMBF*, purposive interpretation in some instances may lead to the conclusion that the facts are not to be viewed realistically.

Another regrettable element in the House's speech is that it treated *Furniss v Dawson* as having been decided correctly. The House of Lords then bemoans the fact that cases such as *Furniss v Dawson*

> gave rise to a view that, in the application of *any* taxing statute, transactions or elements of transactions which had no commercial purpose were to be disregarded. But that is going too far. It elides the two steps which are necessary in the application of any statutory provision: first, to decide, on a purposive construction, exactly what transaction will answer to the statutory description and secondly, to decide whether the transaction in question does so.[50]

The House of Lords is absolutely correct both in stating that this view of the *Ramsay* approach was held and that it is wrong. This view was held, however, because that is the approach courts appeared to adopt!

Finally, we should note that the House of Lords took care to show that the approach it advocated in *BMBF* does not mean that a court cannot interpret a statute as requiring a transaction to have a business purpose if it is to fall within its ambit, along the lines of Lord Millett's approach in *Arrowtown*.[51] It also kept the legal/commercial dichotomy originating from Lord Hoffmann's speech in *MacNiven* alive. It dismissed, however, the notion that either of these two tests existed independently of statute and should thus be applied to any statutory provision blindly.[52]

---

[49] *Arrowtown* (above n 6) para 35 (emphasis added).
[50] *BMBF* (above n 2) para 36.
[51] ibid, paras 35 and 38.
[52] ibid, paras 36 and 38.

C. The Facts and Relevant Statutory Provisions in *BMBF*

BGE, an Irish statutory corporation, employed contractors to build a pipeline for the transport of natural gas. The funds were provided by an EEC grant and a consortium of banks. BGE later sold the pipeline to BMBF, a member of the Barclays group and the UK market leader in finance leasing, for £91 million.[53] BMBF borrowed the money to acquire the pipeline from Barclays Bank on commercial terms. BMBF leased the pipeline back to BGE for, in total, just under 33 years, at the expiration of which it could be renewed yearly. BGE formed a wholly owned UK subsidiary, BGE (UK) and sublet the pipeline to it for the same duration as the head lease. The parties agreed that BGE (UK) would pay the rent due to BMBF by BGE, thus discharging the payments due to BMBF by BGE and to BGE by BGE (UK). BGE (UK) and BGE then entered into a transportation and an ancillary licence agreement under which BGE (UK) undertook the obligation of transporting natural gas through the pipeline in consideration of payments which would ensure that BGE (UK) would be put in funds to meet the payment of rent due to BGE.

BMBF required security for the payment of the rent due to it. Security was given by means of a guarantee provided by Barclays Bank, which in turn required a counter-security in the form of a charge over the £91 million. BGE thus deposited the £91 million with Deepstream, a Jersey company managed by a company in the Barclays group. By a series of indemnities, assignments and charges, which also involved a Manx company within the Barclays group, BIoM, with which Deepstream deposited the £91 million, Barclays Bank took adequate security over the £91 million. BIoM kept its funds on deposit with Barclays Bank, and thus actually deposited this amount with the bank. So, at the end of this series of transactions the £91 million returned from where they originated, namely Barclays Bank.[54]

The attraction of this transaction, in which 'the £91m passed from [BB] to BMBF, from BMBF to BGE, from BGE to Deepstream, from Deepstream to BIoM and from BIoM back to [Barclays Bank] again',[55] was that BMBF could claim capital allowances under section 24(1)[56] of the Capital Allowances Act 1990 for the expenditure incurred on the acquisition of the pipeline.

---

[53] The exact amount was £91.292 million.

[54] Note that Barclays argued that the flow of funds was designed in this way for regulatory purposes. See Tiley, 'Composite Business Transactions' (above n 29) and Tiley, 'Less Chaos but More Uncertainty' (above n 40).

[55] *BMBF* (above n 2) para 17.

[56] 'Subject to the provisions of this Part, where –

  (a) a person carrying on a trade has incurred capital expenditure on the provision of machinery or plant wholly and exclusively for the purposes of the trade, and

  (b) in consequence of his incurring that expenditure, the machinery or plant belongs or has belonged to him, allowances and charges shall be made to and on him in accordance with the following provisions of this section'.

The outcome of this scheme was that the capital allowances less a margin kept by BMBF would find their way to BGE. Indeed, the House of Lords noted that 'the benefit obtained by BGE was entirely attributable to BMBF being able to pass on the benefit of its capital allowances'.[57]

D. The Decision in *BMBF*

HMRC accepted that had there been no security arrangements, BMBF would have been entitled to the capital allowances.[58] They contended however, that one should view the sale, leaseback and ancillary transactions, together with the security arrangements as one composite scheme. Thus viewed, they argued, this series of transactions, which was designed by BZW, yet another company in the Barclays group, acting as advisor to BGE, did not fall within the scope of section 24(1). Tiley, wrote that the Barclays team explained to him that their 'primary concern in drawing up arrangements was to ensure the bank met the capital adequacy rules laid down by the UK banking regulatory authorities'. If true, then the transactions would arguably have had a bona fide commercial purpose.[59]

The House of Lords – following the approach it advocated – did not start off by looking at the facts in a more realistic manner but looked to the statutory provision at hand – section 24 – to determine what was required of the transaction to qualify for the capital allowances. It found that it did not include any implicit business purpose test or a commercial concept that would have required it to view the series of transactions as a whole. It came to the conclusion that even on a purposive interpretation, all that it required was that 'a trader should have incurred capital expenditure on the provision of machinery or plant for the purposes of his trade'.[60] This requirement was satisfied and so the capital allowances were available.

E. Purposive Interpretation and *BMBF*

BMBF clarified the approach to be adopted when faced with avoidance arrangements – or indeed any arrangement. However, this does not mean that it is a straightforward approach to apply or that it became easier to predict the outcome of a given case.

First, the approach is based on purposive interpretation, a method of interpretation with a relatively short history in the tax field (and beyond, subject

[57] ibid.
[58] ibid, para 13.
[59] Tiley, 'Composite Business Transactions' (above n 29) and Tiley, 'Less Chaos but More Uncertainty' (above n 40).
[60] *BMBF* (above n 2) para 39. See also para 3.

to some qualification) in the UK. For many years literal interpretation was the dominant mode of interpretation,[61] and this was justified on various grounds, including that tax law was comparable to criminal law and to confiscation of property[62] and that tax statutes were said to have no purpose other than that of collecting revenue, a claim which Williams argues was historically justified.[63] By the time *BMBF* was decided there was no doubt that tax statutes should be interpreted purposively – as Lord Millett said a few years earlier 'of, course are all purposive constructivists now' – but the relative novelty of the approach helps us understand why UK judges at times struggled and continue to struggle with it. It is perhaps not entirely coincidental that two Law Lords who pushed forward purposive interpretation in the tax field – Lord Steyn[64] and Lord Hoffmann[65] – both of whom sat in the House of Lords in *BMBF* – had studied and practised law in South Africa.[66]

Second, purposive interpretation is simply difficult to apply in the context of tax statutes, given their notorious length, detail and complexity.[67] As a rule of thumb, the more detailed and complex the statute, the more difficult it is to interpret purposively.[68] Of course, as Mr Justice Vinelott pointed out, the complexity and detail of tax statutes 'does not mean that the courts are absolved from the task of endeavouring to ascertain the purpose of the legislation as a whole and to extract some rational and coherent scheme from it'.[69] However, this can be a thankless task; occasionally, it might even be impossible, as Staughton LJ found in *BP Oil Development Ltd v CIR:* 'In reaching these conclusions I have not attempted any purposive construction of the detailed provisions of the Act, since I am not sure what their purpose is'.[70]

Third, purposive interpretation is inherently uncertain. Uncertainty arises, for example, because a number of purposes can emerge when seeking to interpret

---

[61] See, eg, *Partington v A-G* (1869) LR 4 HL 100, 122 (Lord Cairns) and *Cape Brandy Syndicate v CIR* [1921] 1 KB 64, 71 (Rowlatt J).

[62] See the discussion in WD Popkin, 'Judicial Anti-Tax Avoidance Doctrine in England: A United States Perspective' [1991] *BTR* 283.

[63] DW Williams, 'Taxing Statutes Are Taxing Statutes: The Interpretation of Revenue Legislation' (1978) 41 *MLR* 404, 411.

[64] See 'Lord Steyn Obituary' *The Times* (1 December 2017).

[65] See P Davies and J Pila (eds), *The Jurisprudence of Lord Hoffmann* (Oxford, Hart Publishing, 2015).

[66] South Africa is a mixed jurisdiction with influences from both civil and common law traditions. Traditionally, lawyers from civilian jurisdictions appeared to be more comfortable with purposive interpretation than lawyers from common law jurisdictions.

[67] See, generally, Renton Committee, *The Preparation of Legislation*, Committee chaired by the Rt Hon Sir David Renton (Cmnd 6053, 1975) 110–20.

[68] See Lord Denning MR's comments on the difference in interpreting a legal instrument emanating from the EU and a UK statute in *HP Bulmer Ltd v J Bollinger SA* [1974] Ch 401, 425 (CA). See also K Diplock, 'The Courts as Legislators' in BW Harvey (ed), *The Lawyer and Justice* (London, Sweet & Maxwell, 1978) 273.

[69] J Vinelott, 'Interpretation of Fiscal Statutes' (1982) 3 *SLR* 78, 80.

[70] *BP Oil Development Ltd v CIR* 64 TC 498, 532B–D (Staughton LJ).

statutes purposively.[71] A number of purposes can emerge for a particular statutory provision, for the part of the statute containing the provision and also for the statute in general. In such a case, it is not clear which purpose should be used. What if the different purposes lead to different interpretations and hence different results on the facts? *BMBF* itself is a good example of this problem. The question of multiple purposes could be seen to be the real issue on which this case turned.

In *BMBF* HMRC conceded that acquisitions made for finance leasing purposes usually qualify for capital allowances but argued that this case was different. The reason being that, the acquisition price received in this case was used as security and therefore, the lessee (BGE) was unable to lay its hands on it. The money simply went around in a circle. Whether this difference was relevant or not depended entirely on section 24 of the Capital Allowances Act 1990 which granted capital allowances for expenditure incurred on the acquisition of plant for the purposes of the trade.

On a literal interpretation, this section grants capital allowances on the mere incurrence of expenditure on plant for the purposes of the trade; what the lessee does with the money received is irrelevant. If BGE's inability to lay its hands on the money was to be relevant, the meaning reached on a literal interpretation must have been contrary to the purpose of the provision. The resolution of this case thus revolved on the purpose of the provision.

The House of Lords identified the purpose behind section 24 as follows:

> The object of granting the allowance is, as we have said, to provide a tax equivalent to the normal accounting deduction from profits for the depreciation of machinery and plant used for the purposes of a trade. Consistently with this purpose, section 24(1) requires that a trader should have incurred capital expenditure on the provision of machinery or plant for the purposes of his trade. When the trade is finance leasing, this means that the capital expenditure should have been incurred to acquire the machinery or plant for the purpose of leasing it in the course of the trade. In such a case, it is the lessor as owner who suffers the depreciation in the value of the plant and is therefore entitled to an allowance against the profits of his trade.[72]

This purpose thus led the House of Lords to conclude that all that was required for an entitlement to a capital allowance to be obtained under section 24 is that the purchaser/lessor incurred capital expenditure on the acquisition of machinery to be used in its trade. BMBF did so and was entitled to a capital allowance. What BGE did with the money received was irrelevant.

---

[71] DR Miers and AC Page, *Legislation*, 2nd edn (London, Sweet & Maxwell, 1990) 188–91; J Bell and G Engle (eds), *Cross: Statutory Interpretation*, 3rd edn (London, Butterworths, 1995) 33 and 57; RS Summers, *Essays in Legal Theory* (Dordrecht, Kluwer, 2000) 240–41; F Bennion, *Statutory Interpretation*, 4th edn (London, Butterworths, 2002) 813.

[72] *BMBF* (above n 2) para 39. See also para 3 and *Richard Dale Peterson v The Commissioner of Inland Revenue* [2005] UKPC 5 [41], where Lord Millett approved the identification of the purpose behind capital allowances in *BMBF*.

This approach is purposive; however, other purposes can be identified. Park J did just that in the High Court:

> As regards finance leasing the underlying purpose of Parliament, in my view, is to enable capital allowances to be used so as to provide to lessees at attractive rates finance for them to use and to develop their real business activities. The underlying purpose of Parliament is not to enable cash payments to be made annually to third parties who are able to provide a major item of machinery or plant which satisfies one of the conditions for a finance lessor to claim the allowances. Nor is that in accordance with 'the purpose and spirit of the legislation.

If Park J's view is correct then one must conclude that a literal interpretation of the statutory provision (viz that all that is required for a purchaser/lessor to be entitled to capital allowances is that he incurs expenditure on machinery for the purposes of his trade) leads to a meaning that is contrary to the purpose of the statutory provision. A secondary meaning must thus be sought. Section 24 could then be interpreted as excluding the grant of a capital allowance if the expenditure is incurred as part of a series of transactions that simply provide tax benefits but do not provide one party with finance at attractive rates. To see if this was so the court would have to take into consideration the whole series of transactions, including the security arrangements, ie, what the lessee (BGE) did with the money received on the sale of the pipeline. This would be done however, only because the statute requires it, on this interpretation.

Was the purpose identified by Park J or that identified by the Court of Appeal and the House of Lords the 'correct' purpose? Could both be correct at some level? If so, which should be chosen? This is not the place to answer these questions. The divergence of opinion on the relevant purpose in *BMBF* simply illustrates the difficulties which flow from the possibility of finding multiple purposes when engaging in purposive interpretation. This is just one issue which makes it hard to predict the outcome of a case when an approach based on purposive interpretation is used.[73]

V. THE *RAMSAY* APPROACH POST-*BMBF*

In a number of cases following *BMBF* courts claimed they applied an approach based on statutory interpretation but their decision betrays little evidence of attention being given to the relevant statutory provision. *HMRC v Tower MCashback LLP 1 and another*[74] is perhaps the most instructive case because it involved Parts 1 and 2 of the Capital Allowances Act 2001 (CAA 2001) which, as noted, were in substantially similar term to the statutory provisions at

---

[73] See also *UBS AG v Revenue and Customs Commissioners* [2016] UKSC 13; [2016] 1 WLR 1005 (SC); noted in D de Cogan 'Defining Tax Avoidance: Flirting with Chaos, Again' (2016) 75 *CLJ* 474.

[74] *Tower MCashback* (above n 42).

play in *BMBF*.[75] In contrast to *BMBF*, the Supreme Court in this case interpreted the provisions as requiring a realistic view of the facts. One would have expected the Court to carefully examine these provisions and in particular the phrase 'capital expenditure incurred in the provision of plant and machinery wholly or partly for the purposes of the qualifying activity carried on by the person incurring the expenditure'.[76] This was necessary to establish 'what, on a purposive construction, the statute actually requires'.[77] In determining whether and how much expenditure was incurred, did the statute require the Court to look only at the acquisition of the items on which the allowances were claimed or also at the broader set of transactions?

Lord Walker, who also sat in the House of Lords in *BMBF* gave the main speech. He noted '[t]he need to recognise *Ramsay* as a principle of statutory construction, the application of which must always depend on the text of the taxing statute in question'.[78] However, the connection between this essential point and Lord Walker's eventual conclusion is far from clear. His largely concentrates on the *facts* before stating, only in the penultimate sentence of the judgment and without significant reasoning in support, that the test laid down by the CAA 2001 'requires *real* expenditure for the *real* purpose of acquiring plant for use in a trade'.[79] But why so? How did the purpose of the legislation lead to this conclusion?

In his brief speech, Lord Hope similarly held that '[p]urposively construed, [the statutory provision] requires it to be demonstrated in this case that the whole of the claimed expenditure of £27.5m was *actually incurred* on acquiring rights in the software'.[80] Again, Lord Hope does not explain how this conclusion was reached, despite acknowledging the need 'for a close analysis of what, on a purposive construction, the statute actually requires'.[81]

VI. AVOIDANCE AND THE FINANCIAL SECTOR

It is fitting that a landmark case on tax avoidance involved a company from the financial sector, because this sector played a particular role in the tax avoidance drama over the years. Anecdotal evidence suggests that certain

---

[75] The analysis of *Tower MCashback* in this section follows that in Vella, 'Shams, Tax Avoidance and a "Realistic View of the Facts"' (above n 5).

[76] CAA 2001, s 11(4).

[77] *BMBF* (above n 2) para 39.

[78] Lord Hope gave a separate speech, but this largely followed that of Lord Walker in its approach. The remaining judges agreed with these two speeches.

[79] *Tower MCashback* (above n 42) para 80 (emphasis added). Lord Hope does not add much analysis in his speech – at [88]. It is also interesting to contrast the arguments put forward by the taxpayer and HMRC. The former focused on the legislation, the latter on the facts (see para 25).

[80] ibid, para 88.

[81] ibid, para 87. Lord Hope was referring to the comment by the House of Lords in *BMBF* (above n 2) para 39.

banks – including Barclays – were particularly aggressive on this front. Furthermore, apart from using aggressive planning/avoidance to reduce their own tax bills or those of their employees, banks also facilitated aggressive planning/avoidance by others.[82] In 2009, the then Financial Secretary, Stephen Timms explained:

> [I]t is clear that some banks have been involved in tax avoidance that goes well beyond reasonable tax planning. Given their access to capital and financial markets as well as their range of contacts, banks are uniquely placed to enter into transactions designed to avoid tax, offer transactions of this sort to their customers, or simply to provide the very large amounts of funding and other financial instruments these transactions can require.[83]

HMRC similarly explained: 'Banks have historically promoted tax avoidance on their own account, for clients and for their staff. Their behaviour has been more aggressive than that of other sectors'.[84] As a result of these concerns, in 2009 the then Chancellor of the Exchequer, Alistair Darling, announced the introduction of a Code of Practice on Taxation for Banks.[85] The Code was said to be 'voluntary', although his successor, George Osborne, gave the major UK banks a deadline within which to sign up to it.[86] The Code has since been backed by legislation.[87]

The most controversial aspect of the Code relates to banks' tax planning.[88] The Code and its guidance have been 'refreshed' a number of times. The original Code explained that [t]he Government expects that banking groups, their subsidiaries, and their branches operating in the UK, will comply with the spirit, as well as the letter, of tax law, discerning and following the intentions of Parliament'. HMRC's guidance intimated that the Code enjoined banks to refrain from undertaking certain forms of tax planning/avoidance activities, even if they technically comply with the law:[89]

> In arriving at a view as to whether the transaction is contrary to the intentions of Parliament, the bank should *not only consider a purposive construction* of the

---

[82] See OECD, *Study into the Role of Intermediaries* (OECD, 2008); OECD, *Report on Building Transparent Tax Compliance by Banks* (OECD, 2009); and OECD, *Framework for a Voluntary Code of Conduct for Banks and Revenue Bodies* (OECD, 2010). See also, eg, J Sweeney, 'Tax inquiry into Lloyds offshore' (*BBC* 'Panorama', 21 September 2009).

[83] HC Deb 29 Jun 2009, cols 1–2WS.

[84] HMRC, *A Code of Practice on Taxation for Banks – Consultation Response Document* (9 December 2009) 8.

[85] HMRC, *A Code of Practice on Taxation for Banks* (December 2009). See also HMRC, *Strengthening the Code of Practice on Taxation for Banks* (31 May 2013).

[86] HM Treasury and the Rt Hon George Osborne MP, 'Top 15 banks Sign Code of Conduct', Press Release (30 November 2010) available at www.hm-treasury.gov.uk/press_66_10.htm.

[87] See R Collier, 'Intentions, Banks, Politics and the Law: The UK Code of Practice on Taxation for Banks' [2014] *BTR* 478.

[88] For criticism of the first draft of the Code, see Financial Markets Law Committee (above n 39). The Code has since been amended but part of the criticism still stands.

[89] HMRC, *HMRC Governance Protocol on Compliance with the Code of Practice on Taxation for Banks* (26 March 2012) 6 (emphasis added).

legislation but should also consider whether Parliament can realistically have intended to give the proposed result in circumstances that are very different from those that existed at the time (eg are loopholes being used to arrive at an unexpected result). The question of whether the tax results are contrary to the intentions of Parliament can be answered in practice by asking whether the tax consequences of a proposed transaction are too good to be true.[90]

Later HMRC documents referred to the Code's 'overall intent of constraining destabilising tax avoidance transactions *that are likely to trigger a need for Parliament to consider legislative change*'.[91] If there is a need to change the law, it is because the law is considered to be inapt to deal with the avoidance scheme, which presupposes that the avoidance scheme itself is within the law. The latest version of the Code and its guidance is less clear on this point.[92] However, it might still be argued that the Code requires banks to go beyond mere compliance with the law interpreted purposively on the ground that this would be tantamount to requiring banks to comply with their existing legal obligations. It is not clear what the point of such a Code would be.

As HMRC argued that the transaction in *BMBF* did not satisfy the requirements of the law, one assumes that had the Code been in existence HMRC would have also encouraged the taxpayer not to enter into the transaction on the basis of its commitment under the Code. The House of Lords finding that the transaction was effective should make us pause and reflect on the Code and similar regulatory strategies. On the other hand, one might ask whether BMBF would have engaged in this particular transaction in the current climate. Of course, one cannot know and perhaps planning of this level of 'aggressiveness' would still be undertaken, but it is clear that the Barclays group, of which BMBF formed part, has changed its general approach to tax planning since *BMBF* was decided.

Parts of the Barclays group were singled out by the press in the past for being particularly aggressive in their tax planning. Their Structured Capital Markets (SCM) division hit the headlines in 2009 as the *Guardian* ran a series of articles describing – what Nigel Lawson later called – 'industrial scale' tax avoidance.[93] In February 2012, HM Treasury intervened in a high-profile avoidance case involving Barclays by taking the uncommon step of introducing retrospective legislation to ensure that two transactions – which SCM had designed – would not be effecitve. This step was partly justified on the ground that Barclays had signed up to the Code.[94]

---

[90] HMRC, *A Code of Practice on Taxation for Banks – Supplementary Guidance Note* (9 December 2009) 4–5 (emphasis added). See also HMRC, *Consultation Response Document* (above n 84).

[91] HMRC, *HMRC Governance Protocol* (above n 89) 6 (emphasis added).

[92] HMRC, *The Code of Practice on Taxation for Banks – Consolidated Guidance* (8 November 2016).

[93] I Cobain, 'Fear, revenge and ingenious tax deals – life on the top floor at Barclays' *The Guardian* (16 March 2013).

[94] See, eg, *BBC*, 'Barclays Bank told by Treasury to pay £500m avoided tax' (29 February 2012) available at www.bbc.co.uk/news/business-17181213.

In July 2012 the board of directors of Barclays group announced that it had commissioned an independent external review of its business practices led by Anthony Salz.[95] The review was commissioned in the wake of the Libor-rigging scandal. It was wide-ranging and its overall mandate was to 'determine how Barclays can rebuild trust and develop business practices which make it a leader'. Its discussion of tax issues focuses on SCM and one should be careful not to automatically extend the conclusion it reaches to *all* parts of the group. However, it can provide useful context. After discussing the two avoidance schemes closed through retrospective legislation, the review concluded:

> Barclays appears to have been insensitive to changing political and public expectations around tax and to the UK regulators' expectations on openness and compliance with the spirit of the rules … We consider that this is another example of Barclays' failure to assess adequately the reputational damage of its actions, inclining to rationalise its behaviour on technical arguments rather than reaching a broader judgment of reasonable public expectations.[96]

Barclays' commitment to bringing change to its tax practices was signalled in 2013 through the voluntary publication of its tax principles and by shutting down SCM. The current version of the principles explain that Barclays believes that tax planning, for their clients and on their own account, must, inter alia, 'comply with generally accepted custom and practice, in addition to the law and the UK Code of Practice for Taxation for Banks'. It is remarkable that Barclays now clearly commits to going beyond the strict requirements of the law.

The move signalled by Barclays is in line with the change in public and political tolerance for tax avoidance. In turn, these broad changes in mood may also affect – at some level – the way cases are decided once they reach the courts. This must be kept in mind when reading *BMBF* and applying the approach clarified there, particularly given the interpretative room afforded by purposive interpretation.

VII. CONCLUSION

Memorably, and with characteristic brilliance, Tiley wrote that *BMBF* brought less chaos but more uncertainty.[97] *BMBF* did indeed address the chaos surrounding the judicial approach to avoidance, and it is regrettable that, at times, the directions given in *BMBF* are not followed. If the approach is based on purposive interpretation, courts can look beyond the legal substance of transactions, for example to the economic effect of a series of transactions, but only if the statute

---

[95] A Salz, *Salz Review – An Independent Review of Barclays' Business Practices* (April 2013) available at, online.wsj.com/public/resources/documents/SalzReview04032013.pdf.

[96] ibid, 74.

[97] Tiley, 'Barclays and Scottish Provident' (above n 40).

so requires. This necessitates a careful examination of the statute in question. It cannot be satisfied by brief and generic statements about the need to apply tax statutes to real transactions, or similar.

This process is difficult. It affords judges considerable interpretative space thus leading to uncertainty. *BMBF* itself illustrates the deep uncertainty that surrounds avoidance cases when approached through purposive interpretation. The question then follows whether uncertainty is significantly reduced through alternative approaches to avoidance – judicial or otherwise – that are also effective and respect the rule of law. Of course, *BMBF* cannot answer this intractable question, but the insights it offers lay bare some of the fundamental difficulties in finding such an approach.

19

Cadbury Schweppes and Cadbury Schweppes Overseas *(2006)* CFC Rules Under EU Tax Law

CHRISTIANA HJI PANAYI

THE *CADBURY SCHWEPPES* case[1] is undoubtedly one of the high water-marks of permissiveness and liberalism in the European Court of Justice (ECJ). Arguably, it reflects a romanticised view of EU corporate tax law at the time – a time when the ECJ gave full force to the EC Treaty's fundamental freedoms, with little consideration for concepts such as double non-taxation, low taxation, base erosion and profit shifting. All these concerns have been highlighted both by the Organisation for Economic Co-operation and Development's Base Erosion and Profit Shifting (BEPS) project and by the EU's own Anti-Tax Avoidance Directive (ATAD).[2] *Cadbury Schweppes* was very typical of the pre-BEPS age of innocence for some – and of aggressive tax planning for others.

In order to understand this landmark case and the implications of it in the wider context of EU corporate tax law, it is important to get back to basics and to look at the background issues at stake: tax planning (or tax avoid-ance) through controlled foreign companies (CFCs) and the response under international tax law. In this chapter, the author examines the case in the context in which it was decided at the time but also reviews the impact of later developments on the legacy of this important case. The last part considers the extent to which *Cadbury Schweppes* has been eroded by the provisions of the ATAD.

---

[1] Judgment of 12 July 2006, *Cadbury Schweppes and Cadbury Schweppes Overseas*, C-196/04, EU:C:2006:544. The contents of this chapter are based on materials available up to 1 September 2017.
[2] Directive 16/1164/EU [2016] OJ L193/1.

I. CFC RULES UNDER INTERNATIONAL TAX LAW
PRIOR TO *CADBURY SCHWEPPES*

Whilst most countries tax their residents on a worldwide basis, technically, a group company is not taxed on the profits of another group company, whether resident or not, each being separate legal entities.[3] Taxation is deferred until the subsidiary's profits are distributed to the parent company[4] or the parent company disposes of its shares in the subsidiary. If the non-resident subsidiary is controlled by the parent company, then the parent company can effectively avoid paying domestic corporation tax by diverting foreign-source profits to that subsidiary. The combined effect of these rules is that, if the non-resident subsidiary is located in a low tax jurisdiction or a tax haven, and is controlled by the parent company, then the parent company can effectively avoid paying domestic corporate income tax by diverting profits to that subsidiary.

As capital barriers and exchange controls were gradually removed over a period of 50 years, the need for legislation to prevent the sheltering of profits or the deferral of corporate income tax became apparent,[5] especially for capital-exporting industrial states.[6] Controlled foreign company regimes, sometimes called 'anti-deferral regimes', have often been put in place to prevent such arrangements by taxing resident shareholders of CFCs on their pro rata share of some or all of the undistributed income of the CFC.[7] A CFC is typically described as a non-resident company controlled by residents (individuals or companies), which is subject to a much lower level of taxation by being established offshore.[8] Therefore, the main focus of CFC rules is thought to be to prevent or limit the ability of residents of a country to use foreign companies in tax havens, in order to avoid or defer domestic tax (namely, protection of the tax base from tax haven deferral).[9]

---

[3] Some countries allow consolidation of profits between group companies for tax purposes.

[4] Upon distribution, the parent company state may tax the dividend but give a credit for foreign taxes paid or exempt the dividend (see OECD Model Convention, Arts 10 and 23).

[5] OECD, *Controlled Foreign Company Legislation* (Paris, 1996).

[6] Department of the Treasury, *The Deferral of Income Earned Through US Controlled Foreign Corporations – A Policy Study* (Washington DC, 2000) 61; G Kofler, 'CFC Rules' in M Lang (ed), *Common Consolidated Corporate Tax Base* (Vienna, Linde, 2008) 725, 727–28; BJ Arnold and PJ Dibout, 'General Report' in BJ Arnold and PJ Dibout (eds) *Limits on the Use of Low-Tax Regimes by Multinational Businesses Current Measures and Emerging Trends* (The Hague, Kluwer Law International, 2001) 21.

[7] OECD, *Controlled Foreign Company Legislation* (above n 5); BJ Arnold, *The Taxation of Controlled Foreign Corporations: An International Comparison* (Toronto, Canadian Tax Foundation, 1986) 1ff; J Malherbe et al, 'Controlled Foreign Corporations in the EU After *Cadbury Schweppes*' (2007) 36 *TMIJ* 607; M Lang et al (eds), *CFC Legislation, Tax Treaties and EC Law* (The Hague, Kluwer Law International, 2004); Arnold and Dibout (above n 6).

[8] Arnold and Dibout (above n 6) 38ff; Department of the Treasury (above n 6) chs 1–2; Commission, 'The Application of Anti-abuse Measures in the Area of Direct Taxation – Within the EU and in Relation to Third Countries' (Communication) COM (2007) 785 final, 7.

[9] Arnold and Dibout (above n 6); Department of the Treasury (above n 6) ch 3.

Originally, CFC rules were indeed devised to prevent moneybox companies. However, CFC rules are no longer limited to tax haven deferral. In fact, in recent years, their scope has been extended to include the deflection of income into jurisdictions that may not be tax havens, but which have preferential regimes for certain types of income. Controlled foreign company regimes are also a means through which tax audits can be facilitated in countries that are reluctant to exchange information or do not exchange information at all.

The importance of CFC rules in combating harmful tax competition was reiterated and emphasised by the OECD Committee on Fiscal Affairs in its 1996 report on harmful tax competition[10] and in subsequent reports. It was also considered more recently in the OECD/G20's BEPS project, under Action 3, which concentrated on the strengthening of CFC rules.[11] As discussed in that report, for most countries, CFC rules are used to prevent income shifting either from the parent jurisdiction or from the parent and other tax jurisdictions. However, some countries do not currently have CFC rules and others have rules that do not always counter BEPS situations in a comprehensive manner. For example, some countries which tax on the basis of territoriality do not currently apply CFC rules. For those countries, CFC rules would have to be limited to targeting profit shifting.[12] However, where countries have worldwide tax systems, they may also be concerned about long-term deferral rather than just preventing profit shifting and therefore their rules may have broader policy objectives.

Insofar as the technical details and the focus of CFC regimes are concerned, these vary across countries. There is a diversity of techniques for defining CFCs, encompassing criteria such as control, effective level of taxation, activity and type of income of the CFC. There is also a diversity of methods for the identi-fication of low-taxation regimes, ranging from objective criteria to a system of lists, or both.[13]

In essence, there are two (theoretical) approaches according to which countries frame their rules in taxing the parent company on the (sheltered) profits of its non-resident subsidiary. Under the first approach, the sheltered profits are deemed to have been distributed ('the fictive/deemed dividend approach'). Under the second approach, the profits are considered to have arisen in the hands of the shareholder/parent company ('the attribution of income approach').[14] Both approaches raise concerns as to the compatibility of CFC rules with double

---

[10] OECD, *Harmful Tax Competition – An Emerging Global Issue* (Paris, 1998) 40ff.

[11] OECD, *Public Discussion Draft, BEPS Action 3: Strengthening CFC Rules* (Paris, 2015) (*CFC Discussion Draft*), available at www.oecd.org/ctp/aggressive/discussion-draft-beps-action-3-strengthening-CFC-rules.pdf; OECD/G20, *Designing Effective Controlled Foreign Company Rules, Action 3 – 2015 Final Report* (Paris, 2015), available at dx.doi.org/10.1787/9789264241152-en.

[12] And see Kofler (above n 6) 727 for the difference between anti-exemption and anti-deferral.

[13] Arnold and Dibout (above n 6) 29–34.

[14] Also see OECD, 'Double Taxation Conventions and the Use of Base Companies' in *International Tax Avoidance and Evasion: Four Related Studies* (Paris, 1987), listing three approaches (para 24).

taxation agreements. One argument is that the attribution of income approach, insofar as business income is concerned, is contrary to Article 7 of the OECD Model, as it breaches the source country's exclusive right to tax the profits of the CFC. Another argument is that the fictive/deemed dividend approach is contrary to Article 10 of the OECD Model, as it leads to taxation of dividends before they are paid, contrary to paragraph 1 of that Article. Also, the taxation of a foreign subsidiary's undistributed profits in the hands of the shareholder is contrary to Article 10(5) of the OECD Model.

The OECD has long treated domestic CFC provisions as not being in conflict with the OECD Model.[15] The *Commentary* to the OECD Model states that CFC legislation, which is 'internationally recognised as a legitimate instrument to protect the domestic tax base',[16] is not contrary to the provisions of it.[17] As far as incompatibility with Article 7 is concerned, the official position of the OECD is that a contracting State is not restricted from taxing its own residents under domestic law, even though the CFC tax imposed is computed by reference to the profits of a non-resident enterprise that are attributable to the residents' participation in the enterprise.[18] Furthermore, the CFC tax levied by a State on its own residents is not considered as reducing the profits of the non-resident enterprise 'and may not, therefore, be said to have been levied on such profits'.[19] As far as incompatibility with the dividends Article is concerned, the OECD *Commentary* states that Article 10(5) of the Model is confined to taxation at source (namely, in the State of the CFC) and concerns the taxation of the company, having no bearing on the taxation in the country of residence of the shareholder and the taxation of the shareholder.[20]

The above arguments appear to be overtly technical and have been criticised.[21] Whilst in some jurisdictions the risk of conflict between domestic CFC rules and tax treaties has been avoided following judgments in national courts,[22] in other jurisdictions a finding of treaty override could not be avoided.[23] The question of compatibility of CFC regimes with tax treaties is, therefore, still unsettled.[24]

---

[15] OECD Model, *Commentary to Art 1*, para 9 (also para 7). CFC rules do not reduce the profits of the other State and cannot be said to have been levied on them (OECD Model, *Commentary to Art 7*, para 10.1). See also OECD Model, *Commentary to Art 10*, paras 37–39 (dividends).

[16] OECD Model, *Commentary to Art 1*, para 23.

[17] ibid.

[18] OECD Model, *Commentary to Art 7*, para 14.

[19] ibid.

[20] OECD Model, *Commentary to Art 10*, para 37.

[21] See eg, P Harris and D Oliver, *International Commercial Tax* (Cambridge, Cambridge University Press, 2010) 304–05; M Lang, 'CFC Regulations and Double Taxation Treaties' (2003) 57(2) *IBFD Bulletin* 51; Lang et al (above n 7); Arnold and Dibout (above n 6) 81ff.

[22] See *Bricom Holdings Ltd v CIR* [1997] STC 1179; Case KHO 596/2002/26 *Re A Oyi Abp* (2002) 4 ITL Rep 1009; Harris and Oliver (above n 21); M Helminen, 'National Report: Finland' in M Lang et al (eds), *CFC Legislation, Tax Treaties and EC Law* (The Hague, Kluwer Law International, 2004) 204ff.

[23] See *Société Schneider Electric* (Case No 232276) (2002) 4 ITL Rep 1077.

[24] Arnold and Dibout (above n 6) 81ff.

The question of compatibility of CFC regimes with EU law is, however, far more complex. To an extent, under CFC rules, the parent company may be seen as being penalised for having invested in foreign (low-tax) jurisdictions.[25] Under CFC rules, the advantage of investing in a low tax subsidiary is neutralised as profits are deemed to have arisen for the parent company (that will be taxed on them) when dividends have not yet been paid by the low tax subsidiary. Also, in effect, the parent company is treated detrimentally for investing in a non-resident (low tax) subsidiary, compared to investing in a domestic subsidiary. Whether this treatment is indeed compatible with EU law was first considered in a seminal case at the ECJ – the case of *Cadbury Schweppes*.[26]

II. THE *CADBURY SCHWEPPES* CASE

Cadbury Schweppes was the first important case which dealt with the CFC regime of an EU Member State. The focus was on the UK rules existing at the time, namely, sections 747–56 and Schedules 24–26 of the Income and Corporation Taxes Act 1988. According to this legislation, a resident company was subject to corporation tax on its worldwide profits, which at the time included the profits of a foreign branch but not the profits of a foreign subsidiary. In principle, a UK parent company was taxed on the profits of the foreign subsidiary only when they were distributed to it as dividends. Where the UK legislation applied, the profits of a foreign subsidiary were attributed to the UK parent company at the time when these profits arose and were taxed with a credit for the foreign tax paid by the subsidiary. If the subsidiary subsequently distributed a dividend, this tax could be credited against the tax payable by the parent company on the dividend.

Cadbury Schweppes was a UK company, which owned the shares of two Irish subsidiaries. Under the Irish tax rules at the time, these subsidiaries were subject to 10 per cent corporate tax.[27] As this tax rate was much lower than the UK tax rate, the UK CFC rules were triggered. There were a number of exceptions to the application of the UK's then CFC rules, such as: the 'acceptable distribution policy' exception, whereby 90 per cent of the subsidiary's profits were distributed to the parent within 18 months and taxed in the hands of the UK company; the 'exempt activities test', whereby certain specified activities, such as trading activities, were exempt from the application of the CFC rules; the 'de minimis test', whereby CFC rules did not apply to the profits of a subsidiary if profits did not exceed £50,000; the 'public quotation' requirement, whereby the subsidiary was quoted on a recognised stock exchange and 35 per cent of the

---

[25] C HJI Panayi, *European Union Corporate Tax Law* (Cambridge, Cambridge University Press, 2013) ch 8.

[26] C-196/04, EU:C:2006:544.

[27] This has now been phased out.

voting power had to be in the hands of the public; and, finally, the 'motive test'. Under the motive test, the taxpayer had to show that, if there was a reduction in UK tax as a result of the transactions with the foreign subsidiary, the reduction in UK tax was not the purpose, or one of the main purposes, of those transactions. The taxpayer also had to demonstrate that the diversion of profits from the UK to the subsidiary was not the main reason, or one of the main reasons, for the existence of the subsidiary.[28]

In the case at hand, none of these exemptions applied and as a result Cadbury Schweppes was taxed on the profits of its Irish subsidiaries. The taxpayer complained that this was in breach of the freedom of establishment, the freedom to provide services and the free movement of capital. Upon appeal to the Special Commissioners, who happened to be leading UK/EU tax scholars and lawyers, Dr John Avery Jones and Malcolm Gammie QC, the proceedings were stayed and the case was referred to the ECJ.[29] Perhaps their decision was influenced by the fact that, in an earlier case on cross-border loss relief, the now infamous *Marks and Spencer* case[30] where they again acted as Special Commissioners,[31] they did not refer, choosing instead to base their decision on grounds[32] which were subsequently not followed by the ECJ.

The Special Commissioners in *Cadbury Schweppes* set out important issues for which ECJ guidance was needed. One of the issues was whether the parent company (Cadbury Schweppes) was exercising its Treaty freedoms when it established subsidiaries in another Member State or whether this was instead an abuse of such freedoms, thus negating their scope of protection. Another issue was whether the UK's CFC rules restricted these freedoms and whether the fact that Cadbury Schweppes would pay no more tax than if the subsidiaries were established in the UK meant that there was no restriction. It was also questioned whether the UK CFC rules could be justified by the need to prevent tax avoidance and, in particular, in light of the opportunity provided by the motive test to Cadbury Schweppes, to show that it did not have a tax-avoiding motive. More specifically, the Special Commissioners referred the following, more general, question to the ECJ:

> Do Articles 43 [EC], 49 [EC] and 56 EC preclude national tax legislation such as that in issue in the main proceedings, which provides in specified circumstances for the imposition of a charge upon a company resident in that Member State in respect of the profits of a subsidiary company resident in another Member State and subject to a lower level of taxation?

[28] T O'Shea, 'The UK's CFC rules and the Freedom of Establishment: Cadbury Schweppes plc and its IFSC Subsidiaries – Tax avoidance or Tax Mitigation?' (2007) 1 *EC Tax Review* 13, 14–15.
[29] *Cadbury Schweppes plc and Another v CIR* (Order for Reference to the Court of Justice) [2004] STC (SCD) 342.
[30] Judgment of 13 December 2005, *Marks and Spencer plc v CIR*, C-446/03, EU:C:2005:763.
[31] [2003] Eu LR 46; [2003] STC (SCD) 70; 5 ITL Rep 536; [2003] SWTI 68.
[32] In *Marks and Spencer*, the Special Commissioners had found that residents and non-residents were not usually in a comparable position.

Arguably, by phrasing the main question so generally, the referring court intended to prevent the redrafting (by the ECJ) of the various questions and thus have more control over the process. On the other hand, this approach enabled the ECJ to focus its discussion on the more general issues, leaving various secondary questions unanswered.

Advocate General Léger's Opinion was released on 6 May 2006 and the decision of the ECJ on 12 September 2006. In delivering his Opinion, the Advocate General made several interesting points, most of which were confirmed in the ECJ's judgment. One such issue was that of the applicable fundamental freedom. The Advocate General argued that, in this case, only freedom of establishment was at the core of the proceedings. A resident company was dissuaded from establishing a subsidiary in another Member State. Although this had the result that the supply of services by such a subsidiary out of that Member State was prevented, that latter restriction was a consequence of the hindrance to establishment. In any case, the exclusion of the free movement of capital as the primarily relevant freedom would not have changed the result of the case as both the parent company and the subsidiary were established in EU Member States.[33]

In order to decide the case, the Advocate General thought that it was essential to address the following questions. First, whether the establishment by a parent company of a subsidiary in another Member State, for the purpose of enjoying a more favourable tax regime, was in itself an abuse of freedom of establishment. Secondly, whether the UK legislation restricted the exercise of that freedom and, if so, whether that restriction was justified. Regarding the question of Treaty abuse, the Advocate General argued that a Member State could not prevent a company from exercising its freedom of establishment in another Member State on the ground that such an operation entailed a reduction in tax revenue than if the company had pursued that activity in its Member State of origin.[34] Furthermore, the mere fact that a resident company established a secondary establishment in another Member State could not give rise to a general presumption of tax evasion or avoidance or justify a measure which compromised the exercise of a fundamental freedom guaranteed by the Treaty.[35] Without actually using the word 'abuse', the Advocate General concluded that a Member State could not hinder the exercise of the rights of freedom of movement in another Member State by using the pretext of a low level of taxation in that State.[36] In the absence of Community harmonisation, there was tax competition between Member States which led to disparities in the rates of taxation of company profits. This was a political matter which could not be resolved in the courts.[37]

---

[33] AG's Opinion of 2 May 2006, *Cadbury Schweppes and Cadbury Schweppes Overseas*, C-196/04, EU:C:2006:278, para 36.

[34] ibid, para 52.

[35] ibid, para 53.

[36] ibid, para 54.

[37] ibid, para 55.

Advocate General Léger concluded that the UK CFC rules were not incompatible with freedom of establishment, to the extent that these rules applied only to 'wholly artificial arrangements' intended to circumvent national law:[38]

> Such legislation must therefore enable the taxpayer to be exempted by providing proof that the controlled subsidiary was genuinely established in the State of establishment, and that the transactions which have resulted in a reduction in the taxation of the parent company reflected services which were actually carried out in that State and were not devoid of economic purpose with regard to that company's activities.[39]

The assessment of whether there was a 'wholly artificial arrangement' entailed a

> case-by-case examination of whether the subsidiary is genuinely established in the host State and carries on its activities in that State with regard to the services provided to the parent company, the payment for which has resulted in a reduction in the tax due by that company in the State of origin.[40]

Three criteria were relevant to this assessment:[41] the degree of physical presence of the subsidiary in the host State; the genuine nature of the activity provided by the subsidiary; and the economic value of that activity with regard to the parent company and the entire group.[42]

As far as the first criterion was concerned (the degree of physical presence of the subsidiary in the host State), this meant examining whether the subsidiary had the premises, staff and equipment necessary to carry out the services provided to the parent.[43] As far as the second criterion was concerned (the genuine nature of the subsidiary's services), this related to the competence of the subsidiary's staff in relation to the services provided and the level of decision-making in carrying out those services.[44] As for the third criterion (the value added by the subsidiary's activity), what needed to be assessed were the services provided by the subsidiary and their economic substance in light of the parent company's activities.[45] The motive for establishing a subsidiary was irrelevant to the analysis. According to the Advocate General, 'wholly artificial arrangements' could not be inferred from the parent company's purpose of obtaining a reduction of its taxation in the State of origin. In other words, a 'wholly artificial arrangement' intended to avoid national tax law could only be established on the basis of objective factors: the subjective reasons for which an economic operator had exercised the rights conferred on it by the Treaty could not call into question the protection it derived from those rights once the objective

---

[38] ibid, para 151.
[39] ibid.
[40] ibid, para 110.
[41] As argued by the UK government and the European Commission.
[42] C-196/04, EU:C:2006:278, para 110 (Opinion).
[43] ibid, para 112.
[44] ibid, para 113.
[45] ibid, para 114.

pursued by it was fulfilled.[46] The Advocate General emphatically reiterated that 'the fact that a parent company decided to relocate certain services necessary for the pursuit of its activities in a low-tax State for the purpose of reducing its tax burden is not relevant to a finding of tax avoidance'.[47]

The ECJ agreed with Advocate General Léger. Its reasoning was, however, less elaborate. The ECJ first dealt with the point of which freedom was applicable and agreed with the Advocate General that the UK legislation had to be examined in light of freedom of establishment only. The UK CFC rules applied to resident companies that had a controlling holding in their subsidiary established outside the UK. This gave the resident company definite influence on the subsidiary's decisions and allowed the resident companies to determine the subsidiary's activities.[48] Although the rules had restrictive effects on the free movement of services and the free movement of capital, such effects were an unavoidable consequence of a restriction on the freedom of establishment.[49]

As only profits of a non-resident low-taxed controlled company were attributed to the UK parent company and not profits of a UK resident controlled company,[50] the ECJ found the UK rules incompatible with the freedom of establishment. The focus was on whether the tax was substantially lower than the tax that would have been paid if the subsidiary had a UK tax residence – in other words, the focus was both on the rate and the base. Such a difference of treatment dissuaded UK resident companies from establishing, acquiring or maintaining a subsidiary in a Member State with such a lower level of taxation, and therefore constituted a restriction on the freedom of establishment.[51] In this case, although many freedoms were relevant, the question was decided on the basis of one freedom only: freedom of establishment. This point, whilst not crucial in the case, as it dealt with an EU scenario, could be very important when it came to CFCs set up in third countries.

Referring to settled case law, it was reiterated that

> any advantage resulting from the low taxation to which a subsidiary established in a Member State other than the one in which the parent company was incorporated is subject cannot by itself authorise that Member State to offset that advantage by less favourable tax treatment of the parent company.[52]

---

[46] ibid, paras 116–17.

[47] ibid, para 116.

[48] Technically, under UK company law, this is not the case, at least unless the company's articles so provide. The only legal power that the parent company has is to remove the directors of the subsidiary.

[49] C-196/04, EU:C:2006:544, paras 31–33 (CJEU).

[50] ibid, para 44.

[51] ibid, para 45.

[52] ibid, para 49. Citing, inter alia, *Commission v France*, C-270/83, EU:C:1986:37 and *Eurowings*, C-294/97, EU:C:999:524.

Moreover, such advantage could not give rise to 'a general presumption of tax evasion and justify a measure which compromises the exercise of a fundamental freedom guaranteed by the Treaty'.[53] Similarly, the need to prevent the reduction of tax revenue was not an acceptable justification.[54] More had to be shown. As the ECJ noted, 'a national measure restricting freedom of establishment may be justified where it specifically relates to wholly artificial arrangements aimed at circumventing the application of the legislation of the Member State concerned'.[55]

The UK CFC rules also had to be proportional. The fact that it was the intention to obtain tax relief which prompted the incorporation of the CFC did not suffice to conclude that there was a wholly artificial arrangement intended solely to escape that tax. In determining whether or not such an arrangement existed, subjective factors were to be taken into account (for instance, the intention to obtain a tax advantage), in addition to objective circumstances,[56] which were ascertainable by third parties (for instance, the extent to which the CFC physically existed in terms of premises, staff and equipment).[57] The ECJ mentioned 'letterbox' or 'front' subsidiary companies as examples of CFCs with the characteristics of a 'wholly artificial arrangement',[58] thus raising the bar of artificiality rather high. As the ECJ emphasised,

> the fact that the activities which correspond to the profits of the CFC could just as well have been carried out by a company established in the territory of the Member State in which the resident company is established does not warrant the conclusion that there is a wholly artificial arrangement.[59]

The resident company had to be given 'an opportunity to produce evidence that the CFC is actually established and that its activities are genuine'.[60] In this case, it was argued that the competent authorities had the opportunity, for the purposes of obtaining the necessary information on the CFC's real situation, of resorting to the procedures for collaboration and exchange of information under the then applicable Mutual Assistance Directive 77/799/EEC and the UK–Ireland double tax treaty of 1976.[61]

As regards the motive test, the ECJ was not as dismissive as the Advocate General had been. The ECJ held that it was for the national court to determine whether the UK motive test lent itself to an interpretation which enabled the UK CFC legislation to be restricted to 'wholly artificial arrangements', or whether

---

[53] C-196/04, EU:C:2006:544, para 50.
[54] ibid, para 49.
[55] ibid, para 51.
[56] ibid, paras 64–65.
[57] ibid, para 67.
[58] ibid, para 68, referring to *Eurofood IFSC*, C-341/04, EU:C:2006:281, paras 34 and 35.
[59] C-196/04, EU:C:2006:544, para 69.
[60] ibid, para 70.
[61] ibid, para 71.

it subjected resident parent companies to the CFC charge, despite the absence of objective evidence which indicated the existence of an arrangement of that nature.[62]

Taking all these factors into consideration, the ECJ's overall answer to the question referred was that freedom of establishment

> must be interpreted as precluding the inclusion in the tax base of a resident company established in a Member State of profits made by a CFC in another Member State, where those profits are subject in that State to a lower level of taxation than that applicable in the first State, unless such inclusion relates only to wholly artificial arrangements intended to escape the national tax normally payable. Accordingly, such a tax measure must be not be applied where it is proven, on the basis of objective factors which are ascertainable by third parties, that despite the existence of tax motives that CFC is actually established in the host Member State and carries on genuine economic activities there.[63]

Since the parties settled the case after the ECJ decision, the First-tier Tribunal never actually had the opportunity of applying the 'wholly artificial' test to the facts of the case. Nevertheless, *Cadbury Schweppes* is considered as a landmark case for several reasons, as analysed in the next section.

III. THE LEGACY OF *CADBURY SCHWEPPES*: RESPECTED OR TARNISHED?

One important impact of the *Cadbury Schweppes* case was the approach of the ECJ regarding the simultaneous application of fundamental freedoms. In previous decisions,[64] the ECJ had shown a readiness to accept that a certain activity could be covered (and protected) by more than one fundamental freedom. The *Cadbury Schweppes* case was one of the very first cases where the ECJ reversed this trend and eschewed the simultaneous application of many freedoms, choosing instead to base its decision on the freedom that was predominantly or primarily relevant. Restrictions under the other applicable freedoms were seen as an unavoidable or inevitable consequence of the restriction on that predominant freedom.

This approach was confirmed early in 2007, in the European Commission's Communication on the application of anti-abuse measures in the area of direct taxation – within the EU and in relation to third countries.[65] It is noteworthy that the Treaty on the Functioning of the European Union (TFEU) introduced further amendments which expressly permit the different tax treatment of third

---

[62] ibid, para 72.

[63] ibid, para 75.

[64] eg, Judgment of 11 November 1981, *Casati*, C-203/80, EU:C:1981:261; Judgment of 28 January 1992, *Bachmann v Belgian State*, C-204/90, EU:C:1992:35; Judgment of 13 April 2000, *Baars*, C-251/98, EU:C:2000:205; Judgment of 1 June 1999, *Konle*, C-302/97, EU:C:1999:271; Judgment of 18 November 1999, *X AB and Y AB*, C-200/98, EU:C:1999:566.

[65] Commission, COM (2007) 785 final (above n 8).

country nationals.[66] It should be pointed out that, in *Cadbury Schweppes*, the freedom that was subordinated was the free movement of capital. As already mentioned, in this case, having the freedom of establishment as the predominantly or primarily relevant freedom was not detrimental to the final result, since the setting up of the establishment was intra-EU. Therefore, even if the free movement of capital was not subordinated, the result would have likely been the same, as both the parent company and the CFC were EU companies. If, however, the CFC had been in a third country and the free movement of capital – which is the only freedom applicable to third-country nationals – was not the predominantly relevant freedom, then the parent company could not get any protection from EU law vis-a-vis its restrictive home-State CFC rules. Indeed, in subsequent cases with a third country element,[67] when the free movement of capital was subordinated in favour of the freedom of establishment or the freedom to provide services, none of which applied to third-country nationals, this had very important implications insofar as third-country nationals were concerned.[68]

A second important result of the *Cadbury Schweppes* case was the handling of the concept of abuse. The discussions of the Advocate General and of the ECJ were very illuminating. As already mentioned, it was stated both by the Advocate General and the ECJ that, as regards the question of abuse, a Member State could not prevent a company from exercising its freedom of establishment in another Member State on the ground that this operation led to tax revenue reduction as compared with if the company had pursued that activity in its Member State of origin. The mere fact that a resident company established a secondary establishment in another Member State could not give rise to a general presumption of tax evasion or avoidance or justify a measure which compromised the exercise of a fundamental freedom.[69] In other words, tax planning which led to tax savings, however substantial, was not thought of, by itself, as an instance of abuse precluding, *ab initio*, the protection of the fundamental freedoms, nor was it a blanket justification (the justification of prevention of tax evasion) against a restrictive rule.

This conclusion fits in well with judgments in other cases, which confirmed that EU law does not provide a general principle of abuse of rights in the field

---

[66] See new Art 65(4).

[67] Judgment of 13 March 2007, *Thin Cap Group Litigation*, C-524/04, EU:C:2007:161; Judgment of 25 October 2007, *Geurts and Vogten v Belgian State*, C-464/05, EU:C:2007:631, para 16; Order of the Court of 10 May 2007, *Skatteverket v A and B*, C-102/05, EU:C:2007:275; Judgment of 13 November 2012, *Test Claimants in the FII Group Litigation v CRC (formerly CIR) (No 3)*, C-35/11, EU:C:2012:707; Judgment of 28 February 2013, *Petersen and Petersen*, C-544/11, EU:C:2013:124; Judgment of 13 March 2014, *Bouanich v Directeur des Services Fiscaux de la Drôme*, C-375/12, EU:C:2104:138. See HJI Panayi, *European Union Corporate Tax Law* (above n 25) section 4.3.1.

[68] See A Cordewener, G Kofler and CP Schindler, 'Free Movement of Capital and Third Countries: Exploring the Outer Boundaries with *Lasertec, A and B and Holböck*' [2007] *European Taxation* 371.

[69] See C-196/04, EU:C:2006:278, paras 52–53 (Opinion) and C-196/04, EU:C:2006:544, paras 50–51 (CJEU).

of direct taxation. Whilst a principle of abuse of rights was deduced in some cases in the area of value added tax (VAT),[70] it was subsequently found that it did not apply in a non-harmonised area. In fact, aside from VAT cases, the idea of a general principle of abuse of tax law was first discussed in cases under the Merger Directive.[71] It was in *Kofoed*,[72] that the ECJ first toyed with the idea that the anti-abuse provision of the Merger Directive reflected the general Community law principle that abuse of rights was prohibited. Similar statements were made by Advocate General Kokott in her opinion in the same case[73] and also in *Zwijnenburg*.[74] The ECJ in *Zwijnenburg*, however, did not follow this approach, preferring instead a strict interpretation of the provision.[75] In *Foggia*,[76] another case on the Merger Directive, the ECJ followed *Kofoed*. Here, the ECJ was asked to delineate the contours of the anti-abuse provision of the Merger Directive and the extent to which tax savings from restructuring operations were caught. The ECJ repeated its statement in *Kofoed*, that there was a general principle of EU law that abuse of rights is prohibited.[77] Citing previous case law,[78] the ECJ reiterated that

> the application of EU legislation may not be extended to cover abusive practices, that is to say, transactions carried out not in the context of normal commercial operations, but solely for the purpose of wrongfully obtaining advantages provided for by that law.[79]

Although the ECJ's statements in *Kofoed* and *Foggia* suggested a free-standing principle of abuse of rights, it was still unclear whether these comments were restricted to cases in the context of a directive, which was effectively an area where there was harmonisation through ad hoc legislation. It was debated in a number of cases whether a general principle of abuse of rights applied to

---

[70] See Judgment of 21 February 2006, *Halifax plc Leeds Permanent Development Services Ltd v CCE*, C-255/02, EU:C:2006:121, paras 69, 74–75. See also the refinement of the test in Judgment of 21 February 2008, *Ministero dell'Economia e delle Finanze v Part Service Srl*, C-425/06, EU:C:2008:108, para 12 and Judgment of 20 June 2013, *Ocean Finance*, C-653/11, EU:C:2013:409. See analysis in HJI Panayi, *European Union Corporate Tax Law* (above n 25) ch 8, and C HJI Panayi, *Advanced Issues in International and EU Tax Law* (Oxford, Hart Publishing, 2015) ch 5.

[71] Directive 2009/133/EC [2009] OJ L310/34.

[72] Judgment of 5 July 207, *Kofoed v Skatteministeriet*, C-321/05, EU:C:2007:408, para 38. See K Petrosovich, 'Abuse under the Merger Directive' (2010) 12 *European Taxation* 558.

[73] See AG's Opinion of 8 February 2007, *Kofoed v Skatteministeriet*, C-321/05, EU:C:2007:86, para 57.

[74] AG's Opinion of 16 July 2009, *Modehuis A Zwijnenburg BV v Staatssecretaris van Financiën*, C-352/08, EU:C:2009:483, para 61.

[75] Judgment of 20 May 2010, *Modehuis A Zwijnenburg BV v Staatssecretaris van Financiën*, C-352/08, EU:C:2010:282, para 46.

[76] Judgment of 10 November 2011, *Foggia – Sociedade Gestora de Participacoes Sociais SA v Secretario de Estado dos Assuntos Fiscais*, C-126/10, EU:C:2011:718.

[77] ibid, para 50.

[78] Judgment of 9 March 1999, *Centros*, C-212/97, EU:C:1999:126, para 24; *Halifax* (above n 70) paras 68 and 69; and *Kofoed* (above n 72) para 38.

[79] *Foggia* (above n 76) para 50.

all tax areas, harmonised or not. In the *3M Italia* case,[80] the ECJ found that it did not. Here, what was at stake was the transfer of the right of usufruct over the shares in an Italian company (3M Italia) from a US company to another Italian company, in order to benefit from a lower withholding tax and a tax credit. The Italian tax authorities took the view that this was a sham transaction, designed to evade tax and that the dividends distributed by 3M Italia had in fact been received by the US company. The case was referred to the ECJ. One of the questions[81] asked was whether the principle of the prohibition of abuse of rights, as defined in VAT cases,[82] could only apply in the field of harmonised taxes and in matters governed by provisions of secondary EU law, or whether it extended, as a category of abuse of fundamental freedoms, to matters involving non-harmonised taxes, such as direct taxes.

In its judgment in the *3M Italia* case, the ECJ rejected the argument that the principle of prohibition of abuse of rights could be extended to the field of non-harmonised taxes. To the ECJ, it was clear that no general principle existed in EU law that might entail an obligation on Member States to combat abusive practices in the field of direct taxation.[83]

This decision confirms the proposition that tax planning per se, leading to reduction of the tax revenue collected by a Member State, is not by itself sufficient to preclude the application of a fundamental freedom (or freedoms, if there is no predominantly relevant freedom). Abuse, preferably 'rebranded' as tax evasion or tax avoidance, could be a relevant justification for the restriction of a freedom, but could not by itself prevent the application of the freedom *ab initio*. Furthermore, in assessing the legality of national anti-abuse rules, such as CFC regimes, the 'wholly artificial arrangements' test is an essential component of the justification of 'protecting against tax avoidance/evasion'.

This 'wholly artificial arrangements' test is, perhaps, the greatest legacy of the *Cadbury Schweppes* case. This test has become instrumental in delineating the benchmark for the compatibility of several national anti-abuse rules with EU law and has been followed in other cases looking at anti-deferral regimes. For example, the *Cadbury Schweppes* 'wholly artificial arrangements' test was followed in the *CFC GLO* case.[84] In this case, the ECJ again looked at the UK CFC rules.[85] An important feature of this case was that the ECJ found certain compliance requirements (where the resident company sought exemption from

---

[80] Judgment of 29 March 2012, *Ministero dell''Economia e delle Finanze, Agenzia delle Entrate v 3M Italia SpA*, C-417/10, EU:C:2012:184.

[81] See analysis in A Zalasinski, 'The Principle of Prevention of (Direct Tax) Abuse: Scope and Legal Nature – Remarks on the 3M Italia Case' (2012) 9 *European Taxation* 446.

[82] Above n 70.

[83] C-417/10, EU:C:2012:184, para 32.

[84] Judgment of 23 April 2008, *Test Claimants in the CFC and Dividend Group Litigation v CIR*, C-201/05, EU:C:2008:239.

[85] The ECJ also looked at the rules on the taxation of inbound dividends and followed established case law, which is not considered in this chapter.

taxes already paid on CFC profits) not to be prohibited, as long as their aim was to verify that the CFC was actually established and that its activities were genuine and such compliance requirements did not entail undue administrative constraints.[86] The ECJ also held that the resident company was best placed to establish that it had not entered into 'wholly artificial arrangements' which did not reflect economic reality.[87] It was up to the national court to determine whether the motive test of the UK CFC legislation lent itself to an interpretation which enabled the CFC charge to be restricted to 'wholly artificial arrangements'.

The 'wholly artificial arrangements' test has also been followed in cases scrutinising thin capitalisation rules.[88] Shortly after the *Cadbury Schweppes* case, the ECJ decided the *Thin Cap GLO* case,[89] which looked at the compatibility of the UK thin capitalisation rules with EU law. In this case, it was emphasised that companies had the right to structure their affairs as they wished, and they should be allowed to finance their subsidiaries by equity or debt. As in *Cadbury Schweppes*, the ECJ stated that a national measure restricting freedom of establishment might be justified where it specifically targeted 'wholly artificial arrangements' which did not reflect economic reality, in order to escape the legislation of the Member State concerned. A general presumption of abuse did not suffice to justify the restriction.[90]

Interestingly, in the *Thin Cap GLO* case, Advocate General Geelhoed dealt with the issue of abuse in a slightly different way from the ECJ in *Cadbury Schweppes*. He pointed out that the right of companies to structure their affairs as they wished 'reaches its limit when the company's choice amounts to abuse of law'.[91] The Advocate General pointed out that the arm's length principle, was 'in principle a valid starting point for assessing whether a transaction is abusive or not'.[92] The ECJ did not deal with the issue of abuse in this way, but rather amalgamated it with the question of 'wholly artificial arrangements' and justifications to a restriction. The reasoning of the ECJ was followed in subsequent thin capitalisation cases.[93]

In a later case, *Commission v UK*,[94] the ECJ followed the *Cadbury Schweppes* case. Here, infringement proceedings were brought against the UK on its rules on the transfer of assets abroad and the attribution of gains to members of non-UK resident companies – not directly related to CFC legislation but relevant to aspects of it.[95] The measures at issue provided that UK resident participators of a non-UK resident close company with at least a 10 per cent shareholding in

---

[86] C-201/05, EU:C:2008:239, paras 82 and 85.
[87] ibid, para 82.
[88] HJI Panayi, *European Union Corporate Tax Law* (above n 25) ch 8.
[89] C-524/04, EU:C:2007:161.
[90] ibid, paras 72–74.
[91] ibid, para 66.
[92] ibid.
[93] See Judgment of 17 January 2008, *NV Lammers and Van Cleeff*, C-105/07, EU:C:2008:24.
[94] Judgment of 13 November 2014, *Commission v UK*, C-112/14, EU:C:2014:2369.
[95] See Press Release IP/12/1147, 24 October 2012 and Press Release IP/12/1146, 24 October 2012.

that close company[96] were liable to immediate taxation on the capital gains realised on disposals of company assets, regardless of whether they actually received the proceeds.[97] Where a UK-resident close company disposed of assets and made taxable gains, tax was charged only in the event of a distribution of the gains to participators or if they disposed of their interests in the company. Furthermore, the tax was based on the amount actually received by the participator, not on the amount of the gains made by the company itself.

The ECJ, in *Commission v UK*, concluded that this difference in tax treatment discouraged UK resident taxpayers from investing in non-resident close companies and made it more difficult for such companies to attract capital.[98] There was a restriction to the free movement of capital which could be justified on the basis of combating tax evasion and tax avoidance. However, following *Cadbury Schweppes*, the national rule went beyond what was necessary to attain this objective.[99] This rule

> is not confined specifically to targeting wholly artificial arrangements which do not reflect economic reality and are carried out for tax purposes alone, but also affects conduct whose economic reality cannot be disputed. The section applies generally to gains made on the disposal of assets by companies not resident in the United Kingdom controlled by no more than five persons, in particular without taking into account whether or not the taxpayer resident in the United Kingdom to whom the gain resulting from such a disposal is to be attributed is one of those persons, with its application being excluded only in a few circumstances, such as the disposal of an asset used exclusively for the purposes of a trade carried on by that company outside the United Kingdom. Furthermore, the section does not allow the taxpayer concerned to provide evidence to show the economic reality of his participation in the company in question.[100]

The national legislation was therefore in breach of the free movement of capital. Although both this freedom and freedom of establishment were applicable (as the legislation applied to both), since the Commission sought primarily a declaration that the United Kingdom had failed to fulfil its obligations under Article 63 of the TFEU and Article 40 of the EEA Agreement, the ECJ confined itself to examining the case from the point of view of the free movement of capital, 'an examination from the point of view of freedom of establishment being necessary only if the failure to fulfil obligations alleged primarily is not established'.[101]

---

[96] Under UK law, a 'close' company was one under the direct (or indirect) control of a limited number of shareholders, or those with an interest in the company's capital or income.

[97] After the compatibility of this legislation with EU law was challenged, the legislation was amended by FA 2013 for disposals from 6 April 2012.

[98] C-112/14, EU:C:2014:2369, para 20.

[99] ibid, paras 26–29.

[100] ibid, para 28.

[101] ibid, para 17.

It is noteworthy that in its 2013 Finance Act, the UK introduced 'significant economic activity' and commercial justification exclusions applicable in relation to disposals on or after 6 April 2012. Arguably, unless the definition of these exclusions is broad enough to include all commercial business activities and, ultimately, the tax is only applicable where there are 'wholly artificial arrangements', then national legislation may still be incompatible with EU law. This development is not surprising, considering the Court of Appeal's decision in an earlier case. In *Vodafone 2 v HMRC*,[102] in the High Court, Evans-Lombe J found that the UK CFC legislation was incompatible with EU law because its motive test did not ensure that only 'wholly artificial arrangements' would be caught by the regime. Therefore, the UK CFC rules had to be disapplied. The Court of Appeal,[103] reversing this decision, held that the CFC rules should be interpreted as if there was a new additional exception applying with retrospective effect. This new exception would apply to companies that were actually established in the EU/EEA area and which carried on 'genuine economic activities' there. The concept of 'genuine economic activities' was not defined – though, arguably, neither was the concept of 'wholly artificial arrangements'. For companies established outside the EU/EEA area, and for companies established in the EU/EEA area but without genuine economic activities, the normal CFC rules would apply. It is understood that this case was subsequently settled.[104]

Therefore, in the UK, the idea that for the purposes of CFC legislation genuine economic activities are equivalent to 'wholly artificial arrangements' has long been established – rightly or wrongly – without being formally challenged. The view is that, if the CFC engages in genuine business activities, then the arrangement cannot be a 'wholly artificial' one. Although the two concepts are not identical, much depends on whether they are interpreted by national courts in the spirit of the *Cadbury Schweppes* judgment.

The guidance given by ECOFIN, in its resolution on the co-ordination of CFC and thin cap rules in the EU,[105] is helpful in deciding how to interpret any genuine activities test in the context of CFC rules. The guidelines included a non-exhaustive list of indicators suggesting that profits may have been artificially diverted to CFCs. The indicators included: whether there were insufficiently valid economic or commercial reasons for the profit attribution, which therefore did not reflect economic reality; whether incorporation did not essentially correspond with an actual establishment intended to carry on genuine economic activities; whether there was no proportionate correlation between the activities apparently carried on by the CFC and the extent to which it physically

---

[102] *Vodafone 2 v HMRC* [2008] EWHC 1569 (Ch).

[103] *Vodafone 2 v HMRC* [2009] EWCA Civ 446.

[104] See D Stewart, 'Vodafone Settles Dispute with HMRC Over Controlled Foreign Corporations' [2010] *WTD* 142. D Klass, 'Rereading UK Legislation to Reflect ECJ Decisions' (2010) 58 *Tax Notes International* 543.

[105] Draft Council resolution contained in 10597.10 FISC 58, dated 2 June 2010 (adopted by ECOFIN on 8 June 2010).

existed in terms of premises, staff and equipment; and whether the non-resident company had significantly more capital than it needed to carry on its activity. Another indicator was whether the taxpayer had entered into arrangements which were devoid of economic reality, or served little or no business purpose, or which might be contrary to general business interests, if not entered into for the purposes of avoiding tax. The guidance very much suggested a holistic substance-based analysis – certainly not partial artificiality.

It comes, therefore, as something of a surprise that the OECD in the context of BEPS Action 3 and its CFC Discussion Draft (2015),[106] which was confirmed in its CFC Final Report in October 2015,[107] described the previous case law of the ECJ in this area as suggesting that, on the basis of the *Thin Cap GLO* case, a CFC regime may not be limited to 'wholly artificial arrangements'. Broadly, the CFC Discussion Draft and the CFC Final Report considered all the constituent elements of CFC rules and put them into building blocks that were necessary for effective CFC rules. The categories would allow countries without CFC rules to implement recommended rules directly and would allow countries with existing CFC rules to modify their rules in order to align them more with the recommendations. The majority of these building blocks included recommendations.[108] It was conceded that there were different policy drivers for CFC regimes. Countries could permit a territorial approach to implementing CFC rules or a wider approach. It was emphasised that there was no 'one size fits all' solution.

It was thought at the time the report was finalised that countries with existing regimes were unlikely to introduce changes as a result of this report. It was acknowledged that, whilst recommendations developed under BEPS Action 3 needed to be broad enough to be effective in combating base erosion and profit shifting, they also had to be adaptable, where necessary, to enable Member States to comply with EU law.[109] The CFC Discussion Draft and, later, the CFC Final Report, referred to the *Cadbury Schweppes* case and the 'wholly artificial arrangements test', as 'the litmus test'.[110] It was also argued that on the basis of the *Thin Cap GLO* case,[111] a CFC rule in a Member State that targeted income earned by a CFC that was not itself 'wholly artificial' may nonetheless be justified, so long as the transaction giving rise to the income was at least partly artificial.

---

[106] OECD, *CFC Discussion Draft* (above n 11). In the *CFC Discussion Draft*, it was emphasised that this draft was not a consensus document. See HJI Panayi, *Advanced Issues in International and EU Tax Law* (above n 70) ch 2, section 2.

[107] OECD, *CFC Discussion Draft* (above n 11) 18.

[108] One building block, that on the definition of a CFC, did not include any recommendations, but there was a discussion of the possible options. Specific questions were identified for which input was required to advance the work on CFC rules.

[109] OECD, *CFC Discussion Draft* (above n 11) para 11.

[110] ibid, para 14.

[111] C-524/04, EU:C:2007:161.

The OECD's reliance on the language of 'partly artificial arrangement' in BEPS Action 3 is very suspicious, for a number of reasons. First, at the time of the publication of these reports, *Cadbury Schweppes* remained the main directly relevant authority for CFC rules, and not the *Thin Cap GLO* case, which dealt with rules restricting interest deductibility.[112] In fact, *Cadbury Schweppes* was the only authority on CFC rules since, at the time, the ATAD had not been proposed.[113] Secondly, the analysis in the CFC Discussion Draft and in the CFC Final Report completely ignored subsequent cases in which the 'wholly artificial arrangements' test was emphatically reiterated,[114] in particular in the context of CFC regimes.[115] Thirdly, while there was one reference in the *Thin Cap GLO* case to 'the transaction in question representing, in whole or in part, a purely artificial arrangement',[116] not much importance was placed on this point by the ECJ, nor by commentators since then. The 'wholly artificial arrangements' test of *Cadbury Schweppes* was repeated throughout the ECJ's judgment as being the guiding authority, not just on CFC rules but also on anti-abuse rules.

Arguably, in the *Thin Cap GLO* case, references to a transaction being in part a purely artificial arrangement were relevant to the specific transaction in question, namely, an excessive loan interest payment. Part of the payment was at arm's length, part of it was not at arm's length. Technically, the impact of the thin capitalisation legislation was on the non-arm's length amount. This is arguably why the ECJ referred to the transaction being, in part, a purely artificial arrangement. However, extrapolating a new interpretation of the artificial arrangements test from a brief passing remark in a relatively old judgment, in an ancillary area of law, is clearly intended to erode the importance of the *Cadbury Schweppes* test. It also appears to be slightly disingenuous for the OECD to argue that the relevant authority in a CFC context is a case on thin capitalisation rather than a case on CFC regimes, one which has hitherto been considered to be the main authority. As the author has argued elsewhere, to be compatible with EU law, any proposals made under BEPS Action 3 should follow the established understanding of the *Cadbury Schweppes* test and not the interpretation of it suggested under the CFC Discussion Draft and the CFC Final Report.[117]

---

[112] HJI Panayi, *European Union Corporate Tax Law* (above n 25) ch 8 (slight variations to the test in *Cadbury Schweppes* in different areas of the anti-abuse case law, especially in respect of transfer pricing).

[113] Part IV below.

[114] Judgment of 3 October 2013, *Itelcar – Automoveis de Aluguer Lda v Fazenda Publica*, C-282/12, EU:C:2013:629 and *Commission v UK* (above n 94).

[115] See *CFC GLO* (above n 84).

[116] C-524/04, EU:C:2007:161, para 81.

[117] HJI Panayi, *Advanced Issues in International and EU Tax Law* (above n 70) ch 6, section 3.

IV. THE ANTI-TAX AVOIDANCE DIRECTIVE'S CFC PROVISIONS: THE DEMISE OF *CADBURY SCHWEPPES*?

There is, potentially, a further threat to the legacy of *Cadbury Schweppes*: the CFC provisions of the ATAD. The ATAD was part of the Commission's Anti-Tax Avoidance Package, published in January 2016. This Package consisted of seven parts: a proposed Anti-Tax Avoidance Directive (the ATAD);[118] a Recommendation on the implementation of the OECD/G20 BEPS recommendations on tax treaty abuse and on permanent establishments; a proposed amendment to Directive 2011/16/EU[119] on mandatory automatic exchange of information to enable coordinated implementation of the BEPS country-by-country reporting requirements (Action 13); a general policy Communication on the ATAP and proposed way forward; a general policy Communication on an EU external strategy for effective taxation; a Commission Staff Working Document; and a Study on Aggressive Tax Planning.[120]

In the initial ATAD proposal, the Commission proposed action in three areas covered by the BEPS proposals, namely: hybrid mismatches (Action 2); interest restrictions (Action 4); and CFCs (Action 3). However, action was also proposed in three areas not reflected in the BEPS Action plan, namely: a general-anti-abuse rule; a switch-over clause; and exit taxation. Political agreement on the Directive was finally reached on 17 June 2016, after several amendments and the overall deletion of the switch-over clause from the Directive.[121]

The ATAD's CFC rules are set out in Articles 7–8. Article 7(1) lists two cumulative conditions – the ownership percentage test[122] and the difference in corporate tax paid test[123] – both of which must be satisfied for an entity or permanent establishment to be treated as a CFC. If indeed this entity or permanent establishment is a CFC, then there is a further stipulation in that the Member State of the taxpayer (that is, of the parent company) shall include the non-distributed income of the CFC either under an 'entity/categorical approach', or a 'transactional approach'. It is up to Member States to decide which approach to adopt in choosing how to tax the non-distributed income of the CFC.

Under the entity/categorical approach, several categories of passive income are listed which would qualify as non-distributed income for the purposes of Article 7(1). This approach does not apply 'where the controlled foreign company

---

[118] Commission, 'Proposal for a Council Directive laying down rules against tax avoidance practices that directly affect the functioning of the internal market' COM (2016) 26 final.

[119] Commission, 'Proposal for a Council Directive amending Directive 2011/16/EU as regards mandatory automatic exchange of information in the field of taxation' COM (2016) 25 final – 2016/010 (CNS).

[120] 'Study on Structures of Aggressive Tax Planning and Indicators, Final Report' (2015) Taxation Papers, Working Paper No 61.

[121] Directive 16/1164/EU.

[122] ATAD, Art 7(1)(a).

[123] ibid, Art 7(1)(b).

carries on a substantive economic activity supported by staff, equipment, assets and premises, as evidenced by relevant facts and circumstances'.[124] However, Member States may decide to refrain from applying this provision for CFCs that are resident or situated in a third country that is not party to the EEA Agreement. In such circumstances, the more mechanical entity/categorical approach will apply irrespective of the existence of substantive economic activities.

Under the transactional approach, the taxpayer's Member State must include in its tax base 'the non-distributed income of the entity or permanent establishment arising from non-genuine arrangements which have been put in place for the essential purpose of obtaining a tax advantage'.[125] As stated in the Directive:

> For the purposes of this point, an arrangement or a series thereof shall be regarded as non-genuine to the extent that the entity or permanent establishment would not own the assets or would not have undertaken the risks which generate all, or part of, its income if it were not controlled by a company where the significant people functions, which are relevant to those assets and risks, are carried out and are instrumental in generating the controlled company's income.[126]

Member States can choose to opt out from these rules under certain strictly prescribed circumstances.[127]

Under the computation rules set out in Article 8, 'the income to be included in the tax base of the taxpayer shall be calculated in accordance with the rules of the corporate tax law of the Member State where the taxpayer is resident for tax purposes or situated'.[128] Losses will not be included in the tax base but may be carried forward according to national law and taken into account in subsequent periods. Furthermore, the income to be included in the tax base is calculated in proportion to the taxpayer's participation in the CFC entity.[129] As stated immediately above,

> the income to be included in the tax base of the taxpayer shall be limited to amounts generated through assets and risks which are linked to significant people functions carried out by the controlling company. The attribution of controlled foreign company income shall be calculated in accordance with the arm's length principle.[130]

It is also stated that the income 'shall be included in the tax period of the taxpayer in which the tax year of the entity ends'.[131]

The main issue relating to the ATAD's CFC provisions is the extent to which it is aligned with EU law, and more specifically the established case law of the

---

[124] ibid, Art 7(2)(a).
[125] ibid, Art 7(2)(b).
[126] ibid, Art 7(2)(b).
[127] See ATAD, Art 7(3) (opt out under the entity/categorical approach) and ATAD, Art 7(4) (opt out under the transactional approach).
[128] ATAD, Art 8(1).
[129] ibid, Art 8(3).
[130] ibid, Art 8(2).
[131] ibid, Art 8(4).

ECJ and primarily the *Cadbury Schweppes* case. However, the ATAD's avowed goal was in fact alignment with the conclusions of the OECD on BEPS Action 3. As stated in the ECOFIN General Approach paper issued for the May 2016 ECOFIN meeting, 'the aim of this rule, which is based on the conclusions of OECD BEPS Action 3, is to tax companies resident in low tax jurisdictions when controlled by EU resident taxpayers'.[132] Compliance with the case law of the ECJ was, presumably, taken for granted.

Nevertheless, from a purely EU law perspective, several questions arise. First, the most obvious question: are the non-genuine arrangements to which ATAD refers the same as the 'wholly artificial arrangements' test established under *Cadbury Schweppes*? Furthermore, is an arrangement 'wholly artificial' if it follows, Article 7(2)(b) of the ATAD? This provision stipulates that

> the entity or permanent establishment would not own the assets or would not have undertaken the risks which generate all, or part of, its income if it were not controlled by a company where the significant people functions, which are relevant to those assets and risks, are carried out and are instrumental in generating the controlled company's income.

One could argue that the two are not the same. In the *Cadbury Schweppes* test, the threshold for finding that national CFC rules were compatible with freedom of establishment was very high. Only 'wholly artificial arrangements' could justify CFC rules which were restrictive in nature. Here, it would appear that the threshold is lower. Under the ATAD, non-genuine arrangements seem to be equated with arrangements where the parent company carries out 'significant people functions', relevant to the assets and risks generating the CFC income. There is no mention of artificiality or usurpation of power.

As mentioned above,[133] the UK has adopted the 'significant economic activity' test which appears to be a diluted test compared to the *Cadbury Schweppes* test. Whilst there is no formal recognition that this test is different from the test set out in the *Cadbury Schweppes* case, the fact that there is acceptance of that wording, and that the Commission has not issued any infringement proceedings on this point, suggests that it may not be disapproved. Much would of course depend on the judicial interpretation of any test and the extent to which there is a real search for artificiality.

Another related question is the following. Is the exclusion of 'the controlled foreign company [carrying] on a substantive economic activity supported by staff, equipment, assets and premises, as evidenced by relevant facts and circumstances' from the scope of the CFC provision according to Article 7(2)(a) of the ATAD, the same as excluding arrangements which are not wholly artificial arrangements under the *Cadbury Schweppes* test? In other words, is

---

[132] See the ECOFIN General Approach Paper (9432/16) of 24 May 2016, 5, available at data.consilium.europa.eu/doc/document/ST-9432-2016-INIT/en/pdf.
[133] Part III above.

artificiality the same as not carrying on a substantive economic activity? How about ancillary economic activities? These are issues which ought to have been addressed.

A further concern is whether the treatment of third countries under the CFC provisions of the ATAD is compatible with EU law. As mentioned, in Article 7(2)(a) of the ATAD, Member States are entitled to apply the entity/categorical approach without an exception for substantive economic activities when the CFC is in a third country. In fact, Member States could apply this approach only, since in taxing the parent company of the CFC, the Member State of the parent company has a choice between the entity/categorical approach and the transactional approach. One could argue that, as the ATAD legislation is intended to apply only to those shareholdings which enable the holder to exert a definite influence on a company's decisions, and to determine its activities, then freedom of establishment is the predominantly relevant freedom and not the free movement of capital. As freedom of establishment does not protect third-country nationals, then applying the CFC provisions to third-country nationals in a more restrictive way than to EU nationals is not in breach of EU law.

However, this last argument assumes that in this context, the predominantly relevant freedom will always be the freedom of establishment and never the free movement of capital. This argument ignores the fact that the ATAD provisions, themselves quite controversial, are considered to be *de minimis* harmonisation rules and that some Member States may opt for stricter rules that do not just focus on definite influence and control. Precluding a third-country CFC which engages in substantive economic activities (and, as a corollary, its parent company) from ever benefiting from the protection of EU law is an assumption that the ECJ never made in *Cadbury Schweppes*. The decision as to which freedom is the predominantly relevant one was to be made on a case-by-case basis, something confirmed in later cases.[134]

In any case, what is evident is the shift of emphasis since *Cadbury Schweppes* was decided. At the time, the appetite at the ECJ was very much one of scrutiny of CFC (and other anti-abuse) regimes rather than blanket permissiveness. A decade ago, the focus was very much on dismantling tax obstacles to cross-border movement and not on preserving or enhancing them.[135] CFC regimes at the time were seen as restricting freedom of establishment unless they complied with certain conditions, the most important of which was the 'wholly artificial arrangements' test. *Cadbury Schweppes* and the 'wholly artificial arrangements' test were for a long time considered to be the main precedent in this area.

With the advent of the OECD/G20's BEPS project – one Action item of which was devoted to the strengthening of CFC rules[136] – and the EU's overall

---

[134] Cordewener, Kofler and Schindler (above n 68) *passim*.

[135] On chronology, see HJI Panayi, *Advanced Issues in International and EU Tax Law* (above n 70) ch 5 and C HJI Panayi, 'International Tax Law following the OECD/G20 Base Erosion and Profit Shifting Project' (2016) 11 *Bulletin for International Taxation* 628.

[136] See OECD, *CFC Discussion Draft* (above n 11).

endorsement of the BEPS project and the final deliverables, it is not surprising that the EU's emphasis on CFCs has shifted from compliance-monitoring to norm-imposing. To an extent, the same analysis applies to most of the issues dealt with under the ATAD. Previous encounters with most of these rules in the EU jurisprudence were from the perspective of checking compliance (of the incumbent Member State) with the relevant fundamental freedoms. However, the shift of emphasis from compliance-monitoring to norm-imposition is all the more striking as regards CFC rules, as the *Cadbury Schweppes* case was the landmark and indisputably clear case which set out the EU law compatibility test for CFC regimes and other anti-abuse rules. The *Cadbury Schweppes* test and its 'wholly artificial arrangements' benchmark seem to be ignored in the ATAD provisions. What is also striking is the fact that, following the adoption of the ATAD, almost half of the Member States (namely, Ireland, Cyprus, Malta and more) were asked to enact (anti-abuse) tax legislation that they did not have at the time,[137] and not simply to check the compliance of their existing legislation with the principles of EU law. Conceptually, this is a huge normative shift, the impact of which is likely to be felt more extensively after the ATAD provisions are incorporated in Member States' tax systems and begin to affect taxpayers.

It should be pointed out that the CFC provisions in the ATAD may not even comply with the avowed aim of the Anti-Tax Avoidance Package, which was to reinforce the BEPS project, and to create a solid framework for Member States to deliver on their BEPS commitments. As mentioned in Part III, the CFC Final Report in fact left considerable leeway for countries to introduce or allow a territorial approach to implementing CFC rules or a wider approach. The CFC Final Report also recognised that there was no 'one size fits all' solution. By contrast, the CFC provisions of the ATAD force Member States to adopt a CFC regime with a 'one size fits all' approach that extends to arrangements with third countries.

One could question whether these developments, and the overall erosion of the *Cadbury Schweppes* case, are really about protecting the tax base of Member States or more about curbing tax competition. The fact that the EU is demanding that all Member States impose specific CFC rules evinces the EU's appetite for *de minimis* and uniform protection, rather than mere monitoring of existing national CFC regimes. This is notwithstanding a Member State's attitude towards CFC rules (or lack of). It is a shame that this landmark judgment and the relevant case law it has generated, have been effectively sacrificed in the name of the latest political initiatives to address aggressive tax planning.

Brexit is likely to add a further twist to this. At the time of writing, it is not entirely clear what kind of deal (if any) will be agreed between the UK and the

---

[137] See, eg, the Study on aggressive tax planning, produced in the context of the Anti-Tax Avoidance Package which recognised that many Member States have no CFC rules or have ineffective CFC rules. Also, see Commission, 'Communication on the Anti-Tax Avoidance Package: Next steps towards delivering effective taxation and greater tax transparency in the EU' COM (2016) 23 final.

EU and the extent to which the UK will be bound by fundamental freedoms and/or by the previous and/or the post-Brexit jurisprudence of the ECJ. If the UK leaves the EU without being bound by EU law and the ECJ, then, technically, after the end of the two-year period set out under the withdrawal clause of the Treaty of the European Union (Article 50 TEU) – or in fact, any transition period agreed – the UK is free to revert to stricter rules – that is, stricter than *Cadbury Schweppes* and the ATAD provisions. Such rules would go some way in securing the UK tax base from tax avoidance strategies. Conversely (and more likely) the UK may opt for more business/taxpayer-friendly CFC rules, severely limiting the ambit of such CFC rules, or abolishing them altogether.[138] This would help preserve the competitiveness of the UK tax system, without flagrantly contradicting the OECD/G20's BEPS recommendations on Action 3 which, let us not forget, deferred heavily to countries' choices. In other words, the UK's powers to follow taxpayer-friendly and liberal CFC rules in the spirit of *Cadbury Schweppes* will be unhinged. It is, therefore, rather ironic, that the legacy of this landmark case is likely to be respected more in case of a 'hard Brexit' rather than through the UK's continuing membership in the EU.

---

[138] It should perhaps be noted, though, that many consider that the FA 2012 CFC rules, enacted in the wake of *Cadbury Schweppes*, are already too liberal.

20

Jones v Garnett *(2007)*
Legal Form, Legal Problem

GLEN LOUTZENHISER

A T FIRST GLANCE *Jones v Garnett*[1] is not an obvious 'landmark' revenue case. At issue was the possible application of anti-avoidance rules known as the 'settlements provisions' to an alleged husband and wife income-splitting arrangement involving their small private company, Arctic Systems Ltd.[2] Her Majesty's Revenue and Customs alleged that the aim of the arrangement was to reduce the couple's overall tax liability by diverting income that would otherwise belong to Mr Jones – and subject to tax at his higher rate of income tax – to Mrs Jones, where it would be subject to her lower rates of tax and thus save the couple on tax overall. The settlements provisions, formerly in Income and Corporation Taxes Act 1988 (ICTA 1988) and now in Income Tax (Trading and Other Income) Act 2005 (ITTOIA 2005), were introduced in the 1920s and 1930s with the relatively narrow aim of targeting tax avoidance schemes using parental settlements on minor children or 'piggy bank' settlements aimed at reducing liability for 'surtax', which was then an additional income tax levied on high incomes.[3] The settlements provisions had generated

---

[1] *Jones v Garnett (Inspector of Taxes)* [2005] STC (SCD) 9 (Jones (SC)), aff'd [2005] EWHC 849 (Ch) (*Jones* (HC)), rev'd [2005] EWCA CIV 1553 (*Jones* (CA)), aff'd [2007] UKHL 35 (*Jones* (HL)). The case is also known as 'Arctic Systems', after the name of the Joneses company.

[2] A cautionary note: economists sometimes use the phrases 'income shifting' or 'income splitting' to describe the conversion of labour income into capital income or the shifting of profits from one country to another. In this chapter 'income shifting' and 'income splitting' are used interchangeably and have the meaning described above – moving income from one taxpayer to another (related) taxpayer to save on the overall combined tax charge.

[3] The surtax was introduced as 'super-tax' by Lloyd George in 1909 and repealed in 1973 when it was replaced by higher rates of income tax for those with high incomes. For more on the history of the setttlements provisions and surtax see DP Stopforth, 'The Background to the Anti-avoidance Provisions Concerning Settlements by Parents on their Minor Children' [1987] *BTR* 417; DP Stopforth, 'Settlements and the Avoidance of Tax on Income – The Period to 1920' [1990] *BTR* 225; DP Stopforth, 'The First Attack on Settlements Used for Income Tax Avoidance' [1991] *BTR* 86; DP Stopforth, 'The Pre-Legislative Battle over Parental Settlements on their Children' [1994] *BTR* 234; and DP Stopforth, 'The Legacy of the 1938 Attack on Settlements' [1997] *BTR* 276.

some litigation prior to *Jones v Garnett*, but nothing to suggest that they might apply to the Jones's situation or that the provisions might warrant a landmark decision. Moreover, the *Jones v Garnett* decision itself has been subsequently considered in only a handful of cases in the years since it was decided by the House of Lords in 2007.

When you dig a little further, however, the landmark nature of *Jones v Garnett* begins to emerge. Certainly, there were difficult and fascinating legal questions at stake. The legislation itself reads like a fiendish logic puzzle – 'if this and this, then that, except when, unless' – and the remarkably different judicial views as to whether the settlements provisions applied to the taxpayers and, if so, on what basis, makes the full case history a stimulating read. But what really cements *Jones v Garnett* as a landmark revenue decision is that it brought to the surface, and then left largely untouched, some fundamental, controversial and ultimately unsatisfactory tax design choices underpinning the UK's income tax legislation.

This chapter begins with an analysis of the pre-*Jones v Garnett* legal land-scape before turning its attention to the thorny legal issues raised in the case itself. This is followed by reflections on the aftermath of the case, focusing in particular on the continuing failure of policymakers to address the more favour-able tax and National Insurance Contribution (NIC) treatment of economic activity carried on through incorporated and unincorporated businesses as compared with employment – which in this writer's view was the prover-bial 'elephant in the room' in *Jones v Garnett*. This issue has received some much needed policy and public attention in recent years, including in the 2010 Mirrlees Review,[4] several reviews by the Office of Tax Simplification (OTS)[5] and also the Summer Budget 2015 announcement of a new system for taxing dividends aimed at reducing 'tax-motivated incorporations'.[6] It hit the front pages at Spring Budget 2017, when the Chancellor proposed,[7] and then quickly withdrew,[8] small increases in NICs on the self-employed. It was again high-lighted in Matthew Taylor's 2017 review of modern working practices.[9] But a comprehensive answer to the problem remains elusive.

---

[4] C Crawford and J Freedman, 'Small Business Taxation' in J Mirrlees et al (eds), *Dimensions of Tax Design: The Mirrlees Review* (Oxford, Oxford University Press, 2010); J Mirrlees et al (eds), *Tax by Design: The Mirrlees Review* (Oxford, Oxford University Press, 2011) ch 19.

[5] Office of Tax Simplification, *Tax and national insurance alignment*, available at www.gov.uk/government/collections/tax-and-national-insurance-alignment; *Small Company Taxation Review*, available at www.gov.uk/government/publications/small-company-taxation-review; and *Employment Status Review*, available at www.gov.uk/government/publications/employment-status-review.

[6] HM Treasury, *Summer Budget 2015* (HC 264, 2015) [1.184–1.189].

[7] HM Treasury, *Spring Budget 2017* (HC 1025, 2017) [3.5].

[8] *BBC News*, 'U-turn over Budget plan to increase National Insurance' (15 March 2017), available at www.bbc.co.uk/news/uk-politics-39278968.

[9] M Taylor et al (eds), *Good Work: The Taylor Review of Modern Working Practices* (July 2017) 66–73, available at www.gov.uk/government/publications/good-work-the-taylor-review-of-modern-working-practices. See also slides and materials from the Oxford University-led interdisciplinary

While much of the discussion on how best to deal with this problem has focused on closer alignment of tax/NIC rates on earning income through employment, self-employment and a company, it is argued here that, given the clear lack of political appetite for such reform combined with the difficulty in achieving and maintaining alignment, the focus should instead move to encouraging economic activity that is essentially personal services/labour income to be carried out as, and taxed as, employment income – and actively discouraging the use of unincorporated and incorporated 'business' forms for such activity. Finallly, it is argued that discouraging the use of companies or partnerships as vehicles for carrying on essentially personal services would have the added bonus of further restricting taxpayers' ability to split labour income with a spouse – thereby filling to some extent the gap left by the judges in *Jones v Garnett*.

I. THE PRE-*JONES v GARNETT* LANDSCAPE

A. The Settlements Provisions

It will be recalled that at issue in *Jones v Garnett* was the application of anti-avoidance legislation known as the 'settlements provisions' orginally in Part XV of ICTA 1988 and, from 6 April 2005, rewritten as Part 5 Chapter 5 of ITTOIA 2005. Very generally, the settlements provisions were introduced to prevent an individual diverting income to family members through a trust; a second aim was to restrict the use of entities such as trusts as 'piggy banks' where income is taxed at the entity's tax rate rather than the settlor's (higher) marginal tax rate.[10] The use of trusts in these ways has become less of a concern following the alignment of the income tax rate applicable to trusts and dividend trust rate with the top income tax rate for individuals.[11]

The current versions of the settlements provisions are found principally in ITTOIA 2005, sections 620–29, and are relatively unchanged from their ICTA 1988 predecessors (sections 660A–G). As the relevant sections are fairly brief they are set out next. Section 620 contains the key definitions:

620(1) In this Chapter –

'settlement' includes any disposition, trust, covenant, arrangement or transfer of assets ... and 'settlor', in relation to a settlement, means any person by whom the settlement was made.

conference Different ways of working – reforming employment law, tax and social security for the 21st century (15 June 2017), available at www.sbs.ox.ac.uk/faculty-research/tax/events/different-ways-working-reforming-employment-law-tax-and-social-security-21st-century, and in particular the presentation by H Miller, Institute for Fiscal Studies and B Freudenberg, Griffith Business School.

[10] P Whiteman et al, *Whiteman on Income Tax*, 3rd edn (London, Sweet & Maxwell, 1988) 994–95. A similar description can be found in Tax Law Rewrite Committee, 'Settlements' Paper CC(03)(16) (2003) [2]. See also the historical articles by Stopforth (above n 3).

[11] ITA 2007, ss 9, 479, 481 formerly ICTA 1988, ss 686(1)–(1A) as amended by FA 2004, s 29.

(2) A person is treated for the purposes of this Chapter as having made a settlement if the person has made or entered into the settlement directly or indirectly.

Section 624 is the main charging provision and its ambit is extended by section 625 in the case of settlors with spouses:[12]

624(1) Income which arises under a settlement is treated for income tax purposes as the income of the settlor and of the settlor alone if it arises (a) during the life of the settlor, and (b) from property in which the settlor has an interest.

625(1) A settlor is treated for the purposes of section 624 as having an interest in property if there are any circumstances in which the property or any related property (a) is payable to the settlor or the settlor's spouse, (b) is applicable for the benefit of the settlor or the settlor's spouse, or (c) will, or may, become so payable or applicable.

…

(5) In this section 'related property', in relation to any property, means income from that property or any other property directly or indirectly representing proceeds of, or of income from, that property or income from it.

Section 626 then provides an exception from the settlement provisions for 'outright gifts' between spouses:

626(1) The rule in section 624(1) does not apply in respect of an outright gift (a) of property from which income arises, (b) made by one spouse to the other, and (c) meeting conditions A and B.

(2) Condition A is that the gift carries a right to the whole of the income.

(3) Condition B is that the property is not wholly or substantially a right to income.

In summary, the settlements provisions provide that if income from property arises under a 'settlement', which includes an 'arrangement', and the 'settlor' has an interest in the property, then the income is treated for income tax purposes as the income of the settlor and not the income recipient. Further, the settlor is treated for this purpose as having an interest in the property where income from the property may become payable to his or her spouse. However, the income will not be treated as the settlor's income if it arises from an 'outright gift' of property between spouses so long as the property is not 'wholly or substantially a right to income'. Sounds simple enough!

B. The Facts in *Jones v Garnett*

Mr Jones was employed in the information technology (IT) field for many years until he was made redundant in 1992. Shortly thereafter, he and his wife decided

---

[12] In the settlements provisions references to 'spouses' includes married spouses and, from December 2005, registered civil partners: Tax and Civil Partnership Regulations, SI 2005/3229, regs 183, 187.

to start an IT consulting company. It appears that their choice of corporate form was driven at least in part by the prevailing industry practice – IT agencies and their clients preferred to contract with limited companies rather than unincorporated self-employed consultants, presumably to avoid possible arguments that the consultant was in substance an employee.[13] The couple viewed the decision to enter into the business as a joint marital decision and the ongoing business as very much a joint undertaking.[14]

Following their accountant's advice, Mr and Mrs Jones each acquired one of the two outstanding ordinary shares of an off-the-shelf company, Arctic Systems Limited (Arctic) for £1 per share. Mr Jones was sole director and the company offered his IT services to a small number of clients, through a small number of agencies, for fees.[15] Mrs Jones, a former catering manager, acted as company secretary and spent about five hours per week looking after the financial and administrative requirements of the company. According to Malcolm Gammie, who appeared as counsel for Mr Jones throughout in the case: 'In the event nobody doubted that Mrs Jones made a genuine contribution to the running of the business and nobody who met Diana Jones would have been left in any doubt of her managerial capabilities'.[16]

Further, on their accountant's advice, Mr and Mrs Jones decided to take their remuneration in the form of small salaries to meet their basic needs, with any excess profits distributed as dividends. The figures varied from year to year and there is some discrepancy between the figures used in the lower courts and the House of Lords, but for present purposes it is asssumed that Arctic's turnover was in the region of £80,000–£90,000 per annum. The company paid Mr Jones an annual salary of about £7,000, which clearly was far below the salary he could command in the market. Mrs Jones was paid a salary of around £4,000, which was assumed throughout the litigation to be adequate compensation for her administrative services. After allowing for the tax-deductible salaries paid to Mr and Mrs Jones, other deductions and corporation tax at the then small companies rate of 19–20 per cent, the company's net annual profit was about £60,000. In the tax year at issue (1999–2000) Arctic paid dividends of about £25,000 to each of Mr and Mrs Jones, with the dividend cheques deposited into the couple's joint bank account.

The couple's decision to take small salaries and the rest of the profits as dividends is hardly surprising given the risks and uncertainties in launching their new venture. It also was a tax-efficient way to structure their remuneration at that time – and, as will be discussed in more detail below, still is. Each

---

[13] *Jones* (HL) (above n 1) [2] (Lord Hoffmann).
[14] M Gammie, 'Reflections on *Jones v Garnett*' [2007] *BTR* 687.
[15] In a little more than a four-year period, Arctic provided Mr Jones's IT services to only three agencies and through them to only four clients.
[16] Gammie (above n 14) 687.

of their salaries would have been covered or mostly covered by the personal allowance (then £4,300). Each would have incurred a small NIC charge to the extent the salary amount exceeded the then employee threshold (about £3,500 per annum), but crucially this would have ensured each had an NIC contribution record for contributory benefit entitlement purposes. At the time dividends gave rise to a dividend tax credit, and since they were not higher-rate taxpayers they paid no additional tax on dividends received. Spreading the dividends between the spouses allowed the couple to utilise both of their basic rate bands, effectively doubling the amount of dividends that could be paid free of income tax. Further the dividends were not – and still are not – subject to employee or employer NICs.

C. The Possible Application of the Settlements Provisions to Mr and Mrs Jones

Although it is clear that the settlements provisions were not drafted with a situation like the Joneses in mind, in November 2004 the then Inland Revenue published a guide on their potential application in the small business context.[17] One of the main examples the Revenue used in the guide may sound familiar – a husband and wife who were equal shareholders in a small IT consulting company, with the husband responsible for earning the fees while the wife acted as company secretary. According to the Revenue, if the wife otherwise made no contribution to the business and income arising from the business was paid out equally between them as dividends then the settlements provisions would apply, and the dividends paid to the wife would be taxed as her husband's income.[18] Further, the Revenue suggested an arm's length test to assess whether the settlements provisions applied. Relevant factors would include whether an individual (ie, the husband) was drawing an uncommercially low salary in light of the going rate for the job and also the individual's previous earnings,[19] and whether someone (ie, his wife) was receiving a disproportionate return on capital investment (for example, a share purchased for £1).[20] While the Revenue asserted that their position had been in place since the early 1990s, their pronouncements were met with considerable surprise and opposition from the

---

[17] Inland Revenue, *A Guide to the Settlements Legislation for Small Business Advisors* (November 2004), available at webarchive.nationalarchives.gov.uk/20111005100347/http://www.hmrc.gov.uk/practitioners/guide_sba.pdf (*Settlements Guide*). The *Settlements Guide* incorporated and expanded upon previous guidance published in Inland Revenue Tax Bulletin 64 (April 2003) and Tax Bulletin 69 (February 2004), available at webarchive.nationalarchives.gov.uk/20110202145554; www.hmrc.gov.uk/bulletins.

[18] *Settlements Guide* (above n 17) Annex A, example 11.

[19] ibid [4.9.1].

[20] ibid [4.8.1]. By way of example, the Revenue viewed someone who invests £1 in an ordinary share and gets £35,000 a year in dividends as earning a disproportionate return since that £1 invested in the stock market or a bank would have generated a much lower return.

tax community.[21] Moreover, as Baroness Hale observed in *Jones v Garnett*, the Revenue's position was unprincipled as the Revenue decided to ignore other genuinely co-operative family ventures where spouses contributed unequally and sought to pick apart only situations in which one spouse contributed the work that generated the business turnover while the other contributed necessary but ancillary services that made the work possible but brought in no independent money from outside.[22]

The Revenue's controversial position soon came to be tested in the landmark *Jones v Garnett* litigation. HMRC reassessed Mr Jones under the settlements provisions for income tax on the full amount of the dividends Arctic paid to Mrs Jones. He appealed his assessment, and the appeal was heard by two Special Commissioners: Dr Brice, presiding, and Miss Powell, who disagreed on the outcome.[23] Dr Brice took the view that the settlements provisions applied; Miss Powell disagreed and was in favour of allowing Mr Jones's appeal.[24] Dr Brice exercised her casting vote, and the appeal was dismissed.[25] The result was confirmed on appeal to the High Court before Park J, but was reversed by a unanimous Court of Appeal. The Court of Appeal's decision (but not its reasoning) was eventually upheld unanimously on further appeal to the House of Lords. The case received considerable media attention across the UK throughout its run, with the press generally sympathetic to Mr and Mrs Jones and portraying their litigation with HMRC as a 'David versus Goliath battle'.[26] Mr and Mrs Jones were even named 'Tax Personality of the Year' at the 2006 Lexis-Nexis Butterworths tax awards.[27]

II. THE HOUSE OF LORDS DECISION IN *JONES v GARNETT*

Two main questions were at issue by the time *Jones v Garnett* reached the House of Lords: (1) was there a settlement, and if so (2) did the spousal outright gift

[21] F Lagerberg, 'Why We Should Not Settle for This' (29 April 2004) 153 *Taxation* 105; A Redston, 'The Settlement Saga' (25 November 2004) 154 *Taxation* 202 ('Act 1: The Revenue launches surprise attack on small businesses. Act 2: The professional bodies mount massed counter-attack').

[22] *Jones* (HL) (above n 1) [67–71] and Gammie (above n 14) 690. Baroness Hale would have preferred a year-by-year approach to determining if there had been a gratuitous transfer of income between husband and wife: 'This would be a practical way of catering for the uncertainties and vicissitudes of family life and family business, while meeting the policy objectives discussed earlier' [68].

[23] *Jones* (SC) (above n 1).

[24] For commentary on the Special Commissioners decision see M Robson, '*Jones v Garnett*: Settlements and All That' [2005] *BTR* 15.

[25] By regulation, in the event of such a deadlock, the Special Commissioner presiding at the hearing is entitled to exercise a second or casting vote: see Special Commissioners (Jurisdiction and Procedure) Regulations 1994 SI 1994/1811, Reg 18(2).

[26] See, eg, S Bain, 'Landmark tax ruling for small family firms' *Glasgow Post* (16 December 2005); J Griffin, 'Couple's red tape victory' *Birmingham Evening Mail* (20 December 2005); D Prosser, 'A victory for some married couples' *The Independent* (26 July 2007); Anon, 'Victory for the little man in Arctic Systems battle' *Express & Echo* (Exeter, 8 August 2007); and Anon, 'Couple take on the might of the taxman … And win' *Herald Express* (Torquay 10 August 2007).

[27] C Harris, 'Fighters Rewarded' *Financial Times* (25 May 2006) 12.

exception apply? As Lord Neuberger explained, the answers to these two questions were hardly straightforward:

> The senior special commissioner found for the Revenue on both issues; the junior commissioner found against the Revenue on both issues. Park J found for the Revenue on both issues but his main reason on the second one was different from that of the senior commissioner. The Court of Appeal found against the Revenue on the first issue, but would have been for the Revenue on the second issue, although disagreeing with the reason of the senior commissioner. Your Lordships agree with the Revenue on the first issue, but are against them on the second.[28]

A. Settlement?

Beginning with the first main issue, it will be recalled a settlement includes 'any disposition, trust, covenant, arrangement or transfer of assets'.[29] Pre-*Jones v Garnett* cases conclusively determined that a settlement could exist without a trust, such as where a corporate structure was involved.[30] Further, the 'settlor' of a settlement is any person by whom the settlement was made – and it was conceded that if there was a settlement then Mr Jones was the settlor.[31] Once it is established that a settlement exists, any income which arises under it is treated for income tax purposes as the income of the settlor and of the settlor alone if it arises (a) during the life of the settlor, and (b) from property in which the settlor has an interest. Further, a settlor is deemed to have an interest in property

> if there are any circumstances in which the property or any related property (a) is payable to the settlor or the settlor's spouse, (b) is applicable for the benefit of the settlor or the settlor's spouse, or (c) will, or may, become so payable or applicable.

Related property for this purpose means income from the property.

i. Arrangement

The broad scope of the definition of 'settlement', and in particular the meaning of the word 'arrangement' included in that definition, was confirmed by the House of Lords in *Jones v Garnett*. Lord Hoffmann (with whom all the other judges said that they agreed)[32] and Lord Walker (in separate reasons)[33]

---

[28] *Jones* (HL) (above n 1) [74].

[29] Then ICTA, s 660A, and now ITTOIA, s 620.

[30] Most notably *Copeman v Coleman* (1939) 22 TC 594 (KB); *Butler v Wildin* (1988) 61 TC 666 (Ch); and *Young v Pearce* (1996) 70 TC 331 (Ch).

[31] In *Jones* (HC) (above n 1) [17], the taxpayer's counsel had accepted that if Park J found there to be a settlement, Mr Jones would have been the settlor, and this point was not disputed in the Court of Appeal or in the House of Lords.

[32] *Jones* (HL) (above n 1) [13].

[33] ibid, [49].

specifically adopted a passage from *Crossland v Hawkins* where Donovan LJ concluded an arrangement merely required 'sufficient unity' to its components.[34] According to Lord Walker:

> The Court has been reluctant to try to lay down any precise test for identifying the components of an arrangement or for assessing the 'sufficient unity' to which Donovan LJ referre ... In my opinion the Court's caution has been well-advised. 'Arrangement' is a wide, imprecise word. It can (like 'settlement' or 'partnership' or indeed 'marriage') refer either to actions which establish some sort of legal structure (in this case, a corporate structure through which the taxpayer's income could be channelled) or those actions together with the whole sequence of what occurs through, or under, that legal structure, in accordance with a plan which existed when the structure was established. The planned result may be far from certain of attainment. It may be subject to all sorts of commercial contingencies over which the taxpayer has little or no control. But if the plan is successful and income flows through the structure which he has set up, it is 'income arising under the settlement'.[35]

Although Baroness Hale ultimately agreed with the other Lords, it was with some hesitation because the existence of the settlement rested on expectations about later events which were 'too uncertain and fluid' to be included as part of the intial arrangement.[36]

ii. Bounty

Although the broad scope of the word 'arrangement' was confirmed by the Lords, that is not the end of the matter because the cases also have established that before an arrangement can be within the definition of settlement an element of 'bounty' must be present.[37] The existence of bounty has been variously described as 'a taxpayer giving away a portion of his income, or of his assets', 'a flavour of donation' or 'the recipient benefits without any assumption by him of any correlative obligation'.[38] In *Chinn v Collins*, Lord Roskill cautioned that the word 'bounty' appears nowhere in the statute, and described it as 'a judicial gloss on the statute descriptive of those classes of cases which are caught by the section in contrast to those that are not'.[39] In *Jones v Garnett*, Lord Hoffmann described the 'bounty' requirement as follows:

> This old-fashioned phrase ... conjuring up the image of Lady Bountiful in *The Beaux'*
> *Stratagem*, is perhaps not the happiest way of describing a provision for a spouse or

---

[34] *Crossland v Hawkins* (1961) 39 TC 493 (CA), 549–50.

[35] *Jones* (HL) (above n 1) [50].

[36] ibid, [71].

[37] Most notably *Bulmer v CIR* (1966) 44 TC 1 (Ch) and *CIR v Plummer* [1980] AC 896 (HL).

[38] *Jones* (CA) (above n 1) [72], referring to *CIR v Plummer* (above n 37) and *Chinn v Collins* [1981] AC 533 (HL) 555.

[39] *Chinn v Collins* (above n 38) 555. Lord Wilberforce expressed a similar view in *CIR v Plummer* (above n 37) 912.

minor children. A donation to a spouse or child is traditionally expressed in a deed to be 'in consideration of natural love and affection' rather than the donor's bounty. It is nevertheless exactly the kind of thing at which the anti-avoidance provisions are aimed.[40]

Lord Hoffmann concluded that the general effect of the cases is that the settlor must provide a benefit under the arrangement that would not have been provided in a transaction at arm's length.[41] Further, and notwithstanding the Joneses view that their arrangement was commercial, all five of the Law Lords accepted that Mr and Mrs Jones had entered into a 'bounteous' arrangement. Lord Hoffmann (with whom all the other judges said that they agreed) rejected Carnwath LJ's finding that the Joneses arrangement was a normal commercial transaction without bounty, stating:

> I cannot agree that this was a 'normal commercial transaction between two adults'. It made sense only on the basis that the two adults were married to each other. If Mrs Jones had been a stranger offering her services as a book keeper, it would have been a most abnormal transaction. It would not have been an arrangement into which Mr Jones would ever have entered with someone with whom he was dealing at arms' length. It was only 'natural love and affection' which provided the consideration for the benefit he intended to confer upon his wife. That is sufficient to provide the necessary 'element of bounty'.[42]

For Lord Hoffmann, it was the allotment of the Arctic share to Mrs Jones with the expectation that dividends would be paid on the share out of the company's future profits that was the essence of the bounteous arrangement.[43] Lord Walker came to a similar conclusion, although he framed his description of the arrangement slightly differently, and more broadly, than Lord Hoffmann, stating:

> [T]he establishment of the corporate set-up, together with the common intention that Mr and Mrs Jones would use it to minimise tax in accordance with their accountants' advice, was the essential arrangement. What happened afterwards was that the arrangement was put to its intended use.[44]

Thus, the arrangement was made at the time the ordinary share in Arctic was transferred to Mrs Jones. Although later events could constitute part of the arrangement in other fact patterns, as Lord Hoffmann thought appeared to be the case in an earlier case *Crossland v Hawkins*,[45] in situations such as in *Jones v Garnett* they may be only factors to consider in determining whether

---

[40] *Jones* (HL) (above n 1) [70].
[41] *Jones* (HL) (above n 1) [7]. Baroness Hale, while agreeing with Lord Hoffmann, expressed even more displeasure with the 'patronising and inaccurate term "bounteous"' in her reasons, preferring instead to use the term 'gratuitous': [22].
[42] *Jones* (HL) (above n 1) [24].
[43] ibid, [29].
[44] ibid, [54].
[45] ibid, [22].

the arrangement has the necessary element of bounty to constitute a statutory settlement. Consequently, in *Jones v Garnett*, the events occurring after the allotment, namely the revenue Mr Jones was able to secure for Arctic from providing his services as an IT consultant for an artificially low salary, and the payment of dividends to Mr and Mrs Jones, were not part of the arrangement. However, that did not mean that these future events were to be disregarded entirely; they were relevant to the issue of whether the arrangement contained the necessary element of bounty. This is most clearly evident in Lord Neuberger's reasons (with whom all the other Lords except Lord Hoffmann also said that they agreed) when he stated:

> The essential point here is that, in the light of reasonable expectations as to what Mr Jones would achieve in terms of winning contracts for the company and would be prepared to accept by way of remuneration (*which expectations were in due course fully realised*), the value in 1992 to Mrs Jones of her share was considerably greater than the £1 which she paid. In those circumstances, there was indeed an element of bounty involved in her acquisition of the share, and that bounty was provided through the expectation of what Mr Jones would do (emphasis added).[46]

Thus, in Lord Neuberger's opinion, the bounty arose because the share allotted to Mrs Jones was worth substantially more than the £1 she paid for it given the expectations associated with the arrangement. Lord Hoffmann also observed that the value of a share depends upon expectations of future yield,[47] and that it was Mr Jones's consent to the transfer of a share with expectations of dividend to Mrs Jones for £1 which provided the element of bounty.[48]

In summary, following the House of Lords decision in *Jones v Garnett*, the meaning of 'arrangement' and thus 'settlement' is quite broad and the common law bounty requirement is not a difficult hurdle for HMRC to clear – so long as the arrangement at issue would have been entered into only by parties dealing otherwise than at arm's length.

B. Outright Gift

This brings us to the second main issue in the case – whether the exception for 'outright gifts' between spouses applied.[49] In order to qualify for this exception the gift from one spouse to another must (1) carry a right to the whole of the income and (2) the property must not be 'wholly or substantially a right to income'. Further, a gift is not an outright gift for the purposes of this section if (a) it is subject to conditions, or (b) there are any circumstances in which the

---

[46] ibid, [88].
[47] ibid, [20].
[48] ibid, [28].
[49] Then ICTA 1988, s 660A(6), now ITTOIA 2005, s 626.

property, or any related property (i) is payable to the giver, (ii) is applicable for the benefit of the giver, or (iii) will, or may become, so payable or applicable.

i. Meaning of 'Gift'

In *Berry v Warnett (Inspector of Taxes)*, Buckley LJ thought that the ordinary primary meaning of 'gift' was 'a voluntary transfer of property made without consideration'.[50] In *Jones v Garnett*, Park J in the High Court concluded that the arrangement involving Mr and Mrs Jones could not even be described properly as an 'outright gift' in the first place:

> There was far more comprised in [the] arrangement than would be covered by the expression 'an outright gift'. Indeed, the arrangement did not even include an element which could, even taken in isolation, be regarded as an outright gift. Mr Jones did not give to Mrs Jones her share.[51]

In the Court of Appeal, Morritt C agreed with Park J's reasoning and conclusion on this point,[52] but the Law Lords did not. Lord Hoffmann began his reasons on this point by noting that a gratuitous transfer of quoted shares from husband to wife, although obviously a settlement for the purposes of ICTA 1988, section 660A, is excluded from the section and the income is taxed as the wife's income.[53] He then considered the Revenue's arguments why this treatment did not apply in Mrs Jones's situation:

> First, [the Revenue] say there was no gift of the share by Mr Jones to Mrs Jones. He never owned the share which she took. It belonged to the formation agents and Mrs Jones bought it from them for £1.
>
> In my opinion this narrow analysis of the transaction would be inconsistent with the reasoning by which I think the transfer comes within section 660A in the first place. It was Mr Jones's consent to the transfer of a share with expectations of dividend to Mrs Jones for £1 which gave the transfer the 'element of bounty' for the purposes of section 660A. By the same token, I think it made the transfer a 'gift' for the purposes of subsection (6). And there is no dispute that, if it was a gift, it was outright.[54]

Having rejected the Revenue's first line of argument, Lord Hoffmann continued:

> The [Revenue's] second argument is that the transfer of the share was not the whole of the arrangement, which included the provision of services by Mr Jones, the dividend policy and so forth. Again, I think that would be inconsistent with the argument by which the Revenue have, in my opinion, succeeded on the first point. The transfer of the share was in my opinion the essence of the arrangement. The expectation of

---

[50] *Berry v Warnett (Inspector of Taxes)* [1980] 3 All ER 798 (CA) 811. Buckley LJ was considering the meaning of the phrase 'a gift in settlement' in FA 1965, s 25(2).
[51] *Jones* (HC) (above n 1) [44].
[52] *Jones* (CA) (above n 1), [91]–[93].
[53] *Jones* (HL) (above n 1) [26].
[54] ibid, [27–28].

other future events gave that transfer the necessary element of bounty but the events themselves did not form part of the arrangement.[55]

Similarly, Lord Walker concluded:

> Arctic was the chosen vehicle through which Mr Jones was to offer his valuable services as an IT consultant, and it was an act of bounty on his part to permit his wife to acquire half its equity for the nominal sum of £1. In my opinion that amounted to an outright gift of the share within the meaning of section 660A(6). I respectfully disagree with Park J's contrary conclusion because I think he took too expansive a view of the scope of the statutory settlement.[56]

Lord Neuberger found Park J's view 'formidable', as does this writer, but ultimately Lord Neuberger agreed with the other Lords – the reasons underlying the 'bounty' conclusion also support a finding that there was an 'outright gift'.[57] Thus, going forward once bounty has been established, it will not be difficult for a taxpayer to bring himself or herself within the outright gift exception. That is not the end of the matter, however, as the exception will not apply to gifts that are 'wholly or substantially a right to income'.

ii. Wholly or Substantially a Right to Income

Prior to *Jones v Garnett*, the leading settlements case on whether shares in a family business were 'wholly or substantially a right to income' was *Young v Pearce*.[58] In that case, preference shares were issued to the wives of the two ordinary shareholders and directors of a small company. The preference shares carried the right to a dividend equal to 30 per cent of the company's net profits for a year provided the company resolved to distribute any part of its profits for that year; the ordinary shares carried a right to a dividend in respect of any balance of the profits resolved to be distributed. Preference shareholders were entitled to attend and to speak, but not to vote, at the company's general meetings, and on liquidation the preference shareholders were entitled only to repayment of the nominal sums paid on the allotment of the shares. Dividends of £60,000, £40,000 and £36,000 were paid in the 1990, 1991 and 1992 tax years, respectively. The husbands were reassessed under the settlements provisions for tax on the dividends paid to their wives.

In the High Court in *Young v Pearce*, Sir John Vinelott found for the Revenue, holding that the creation of, application by each wife for, and allotment of the preference shares together constituted an arrangement or disposition and thus a statutory settlement.[59] Further, he held that the spousal outright gift exception

---

[55] ibid, [29].
[56] ibid, [55].
[57] ibid, [94].
[58] *Young v Pearce* (above n 30).
[59] ibid, 345.

did not apply because the property given (the preference shares) was wholly or substantially a right to income. Apart from the right to receive the preferential dividend if the taxpayers (the only directors) decided to distribute profits, the shares had only the limited rights described above. While as a matter of strict legal principle the preference shares were assets distinct from the income derived from them, Sir John Vinelott concluded that in reality they could never have been realised.[60]

In *Jones v Garnett*, the Law Lords were unanimous that the 'outright gift' exception applied. Lord Hoffmann distinguished Mrs Jones's ordinary share from the shares held by the taxpayers' wives in *Young v Pearce* as follows:

> The share [owned by Mrs Jones] was not wholly or even substantially a right to income. It was an ordinary share conferring a right to vote, to participate in the distribution of assets on a winding up, to block a special resolution, to complain under section 459 of the Companies Act 1985. These are all rights over and above the right to income. The ordinary share is different from the preference shares in *Young v Pearce* ... which conferred nothing except the right to 30% of the net profits before distribution of any other dividend and repayment on winding up of the nominal amount subscribed for their shares. Those shares were substantially a right to share in the income of the company.[61]

Lord Hope agreed, going so far as to conclude that ordinary shares could never fall within the carve-out for outright gifts that are wholly or substantially a right to income.[62] The views of the Law Lords on this point are convincing. As Peter Vaines argues, even though Mrs Jones was not a director, by virtue of owning 50 per cent of the ordinary shares with 50 per cent of the votes, Mrs Jones had the potential to exert considerable influence over the company's affairs, including the re-election of Mr Jones as sole director and the approval of each final dividend payment.[63] Moreover, the Arctic shares had capital value. If at the outset of their arrangement Mr and Mrs Jones were asked if there was a possibility they might at some point decide to sell their shares, or liquidate their holdings, the answer undoubtedly would be 'yes'. Admittedly her share need only be 'substantially' a right to income, but in these circumstances Mrs Jones's share was much more than that.

III. THE AFTERMATH OF *JONES v GARNETT*

A. The Legal Landscape After *Jones v Garnett*

Immediately after the taxpayer's win at the House of Lords in *Jones v Garnett*, the government responded with a bold announcement that it intended to

---

[60] ibid, 345–46.
[61] *Jones* (HL) (above n 1) [30].
[62] ibid, [38].
[63] P Vaines, 'Arctic Systems: Director or Dictator?' (28 October 2004) 154 *Taxation* 90–91.

introduce new legislation to 'clarify' the law and address the 'unfair outcome'.[64] A joint HM Treasury/HMRC consultation document was released, which included illustrative draft legislation introducing a new anti-income-shifting legislative scheme.[65] The proposed scheme was excessively long, complicated, fact dependent and heavily criticised; however,[66] and shortly thereafter the government decided to 'defer action' but keep this issue 'under review.'[67] At the time of writing no legislation has been issued, nor is there any indication it might be forthcoming.

Interestingly, the Canadian government recently issued new rules to address concerns over preferential tax treatment of private corporations in that country – including from family income-splitting arrangements.[68] The Canadian rules rely on extending an existing anti-avoidance rule aimed at income splitting with minors[69] to catch arrangements with adults where the split income is 'unreasonable' in the circumstances. Reasonability is to be assessed on the basis of factors such as capital contribution and duties performed[70] – very much along the lines of the 2004 Revenue guidance and the failed UK draft legislative proposals. On this point, in 2007 when the UK proposals were imminent, Anne Redston highlighted just a few examples of the difficulty in making such a determination in all but the most simple fact pattern, including balancing value of work with volume of work, assessing the value of individual contributions to joint decision-making, balancing work done with capital contributions, the difficulties caused by intangible property and risk exposure, the need to adapt to changing fact patterns over time, and the difficulty in expecting small business owners to accurately keep track of relevant factors including time spent by all concerned individuals on business matters.[71] At this early stage it remains to be seen how the Canadian rules will fare in practice but this writer is sceptical.

---

[64] Written statement to Parliament from the Exchequer Secretary to the Treasury, Angela Eagle, Hansard HC, cols 89–90 (26 July 2007 WS), available at www.publications.parliament.uk/pa/cm200607/cmhansrd/cm070726/wmstext/70726m0001.htm.

[65] HM Treasury and HMRC, *Income Shifting: A Consultation on Draft Legislation* (December 2007), available at webarchive.nationalarchives.gov.uk/+/http://www.hm-treasury.gov.uk/consultations_and_legislation/income_shifting/consult_income_shifting.cfm.

[66] Crawford and Freedman (above n 4) 1053–54; Chartered Institute of Taxation, *Income Shifting: A Consultation on Draft Legislation – Response by the Chartered Institute of Taxation* (28 February 2008) ('The legislation would be unworkable and have no semblance of practicality or certainty': [2.1]).

[67] HM Treasury, *Pre-Budget Report November 2008* (Cm 7484, 2008) [5.103].

[68] Department of Finance (Canada), *Tax Planning Using Private Corporations* (2017), available at www.fin.gc.ca/activty/consult/tppc-pfsp-eng.pdf.

[69] The 'Tax on Split Income' (TOSI) rules in Income Tax Act (Canada), s 120.4.

[70] Department of Finance (Canada) (above n 68) 25–26. The current and former Chief Justices of the Tax Court of Canada have warned that the highly subjective and situation-dependent nature of the reasonableness test could swamp the Canadian Revenue Agency and courts with a high volume of appeals (see J Snyder, 'Ottawa's tax changes threaten to swamp the court, chief justices warn' *Financial Post* (Toronto, 11 December 2017)).

[71] A Redston, 'Income Sharing: The Nelsonian Option' [2007] *BTR* 680, 683–85.

As briefly mentioned earlier, there have been very few cases since *Jones v Garnett* considering the decision – *Patmore* and *Bird* (applying),[72] *Buck* and *Donovan*[73] (distinguishing) and a brief mention in two others.[74] In *Buck*, Sir Stephen Oliver concluded that a husband's dividend waiver was not an outright gift to his then wife (the only other shareholder) both because the property given was wholly or substantially a right to income and also because the shares giving rise to the income were not transferred.[75] This result seems uncontroversial and very much consistent with *Young v Pearce* as explained in *Jones v Garnett*. *Patmore* sheds a little more light on both bounty and outright gift. The case involved a husband and wife shareholding in a large undertaking with many employees – not a personal services company like *Arctic*. The tribunal judge held that there was no bounty as Mrs Patmore provided consideration in return for her dividends, including assuming joint liability with her husband on a mortgage and another loan used to buy the company.[76] The tribunal judge also stated, in obiter, that had there been a settlement there was no 'outright' gift on the facts as the spouses' plan was that any dividends paid were to be applied at least in part for Mr Patmore's benefit in the form of repaying the joint mortgage used to buy the company and not to use the dividends for another purpose.[77]

B. Two Issues Left Unresolved

The Law Lords' decision in *Jones v Garnett* completely stopped HMRC in its tracks from attempting to use the settlements provisions as a sticking plaster to bandage over some fundamental tax design problems that the settlement provisions were never intended to address and were not capable of addressing in a coherent and complete way. The Lords effectively threw the ball back into the policymakers' court, and, as just seen, a legislative vacuum combined with a paucity of subsequent cases have left the legal landscape more or less undisturbed. However, there are indications that policymakers have at last begun to grapple, to a limited extent, with two big policy issues left outstanding after *Jones v Garnett*: (i) non-neutral taxation across business forms, and (ii) spousal labour income shifting.

---

[72] *Patmore v CRC* [2010] UKFTT 334 (TCC); *Bird v CRC* [2009] STC (SCD) 81 (dividends paid to the taxpayers' minor children was income arising under a settlement).

[73] *Buck v CRC* [2009] STC (SCD) 6. The taxpayer's waivers of any dividend that might be declared on his shares in a joinery business, with the result that substantial dividends were paid to the taxpayer's wife, was a bounteous arrangement but did not constitute an outright gift. A similar result occurred in another spousal dividend waiver case, *Donovan v CRC* [2014] UKFTT 48 (TC), where the First-tier Tribunal cited and applied the reasoning in *Buck*.

[74] *DR v GR (Financial Remedy: Variation of Overseas Trust)* [2013] EWHC 1196 (Fam); *Collins v CRC* [2008] STC (SCD).

[75] *Buck v CRC* (above n 73) [21]–[22].

[76] *Patmore v CRC* (above n 72) [54].

[77] ibid, [69].

i. Non-Neutral Taxation Across Business Forms

With all the focus in *Jones v Garnett* on income-splitting between spouses, it is easy to forget that the preferential tax/NIC treatment the Jones's accountants sought to achieve derived principally from the favourable taxation of small companies. The tax/NIC savings from income splitting were in many ways just the icing on a very tasty cake. As shown in the table below, the UK tax regime still remains decidedly more favourable towards carrying on personal service activity through a company rather than through employment or self-employment – and this situation seems unlikely to change any time soon.

Table 1 Tax/NICs Across Business Forms, including Husband and Wife Company

2017–18	£83,200 income/profits per annum [£1600 pw]			
	Employed	Self-employed	Incorporated	H+W Incorporated
Salary	74,101	83,200	8,164	16,328
Income tax	18,340	21,980	0	0
NICs				
Class 1 employee	5,228		0	0
Class 1 employer	9,099		0	0
Class 2 (£2.85 pw)		148		
Class 4		4,079		
Corporation tax (19%, on profits less salary)			14,257	12,706
Dividend tax		9,919	2,812	0
Total tax and NICs	32,668	26,207	24,176	15,518
Net receipts	50,532	56,993	59,024	67,682
Total tax and NICs as a % of gross profits/income	**39.26%**	**31.50%**	**29.06%**	**18.65%**
Increase in net receipts compared to employed		**6,460**	**8,492**	**17,150**
2015/16 – Total tax and NICs as a % of gross profits/income	39.76%	32.13%	26.84%	16.13%

Source: This table is based on Table 11C.1 in Crawford and Freedman (2010) with the addition of a fourth column for husband and wife companies. The figures have been updated by this writer to reflect the tax and NIC rates applicable for 2017-18, and assume no other taxable income. Figures in the column for the employee reflect Class 1 employee and employer NICs. Figures for the self-employed reflect Class 2 and 4 NICs.

The incorporated example in the third column of numbers assumes a salary of £8,164 paid to the owner-manager, which is the amount of salary at which an NIC contribution record is triggered but just below the level at which NICs must actually be paid. It also assumes all profits after the payment of salary and corporation tax are paid out as dividends. The final column of figures assumes a company with two equal shareholders (Husband and Wife), paid equal salaries of £8,164 each and paid equal dividends out of the entire amount of after-tax profits. As the table shows, at a level of profits/income of £83,200, an employee will pay total tax/NICS at 39.26 per cent, a self-employed person at 31.5 per cent, a single taxpayer working through a company at 29.06 per cent, and a husband and wife working through a company (as in *Jones v Garnett*) at a mere 18.65 per cent.

In 2010 the Mirrlees Review was very critical of this unsatisfactory situation – which had even back then been the situation for some time – and recommended that the tax system aim for neutral tax treatment of labour income across legal forms through aligning tax/NIC rates.[78] The Review editors argued that this would be economically more efficient and fairer as well as ensuring sustainable tax receipts.[79] Long overdue albeit small changes along those lines started to emerge five years later when the magnitude of the revenue at stake finally got politicians' attention. At Summer Budget 2015 the Chancellor introduced higher taxes on dividends in an attempt to tackle tax-motivated incorporations, citing Office for Budget Responsibility estimates that the increasing number of people working through their own company will cost the Exchequer an *additional* £3.5 billion a year by 2021/22 over and above the present £6 billion a year foregone.[80] The shaded figures in the bottom row and at the end of the dividend tax row in the above table show an increase in tax/NIC rates of about 2 per cent on both individuals and couples using companies on the comparable figures for 2015/16 under the former dividend tax regime (from 26.84 to 29.06 per cent and from 16.13 to 18.65 per cent, respectively).[81] Focusing on the two middle columns, it is evident that some progress has been made in aligning tax/NIC rates as between self-employed persons and one-person companies distributing their profits – but the employed still pay an additional 8–9 per cent.

Some small steps towards dealing with this differential with employees were attempted at Spring Budget 2017. The Chancellor proposed very modest

---

[78] Mirrlees, *Tax by Design* (above n 4) 463–64. For an earlier discussion of this non-neutral treatment see J Freedman, 'Personal Service Companies – "The Wrong Kind of Enterprise"' [2001] *BTR* 1.

[79] Mirrless, *Tax by Design* (above n 4) ch 19.

[80] Miller (above n 9); S Adam, H Miller and T Pope, 'Chapter 7: Tax, legal form and the gig economy' in C Emmerson, P Johnson and R Joyce, *IFS Green Budget 2017* (London, IFS, 2017), available at www.ifs.org.uk/uploads/publications/comms/R124_Green%20Budget_7.%20Tax%2C%20legal%20form%20and%20gig%20economy.pdf, 3–4; *Summer Budget* 2015 (above n 6).

[81] The amount of dividend tax paid has increased slightly from April 2018 when the Dividend Allowance dropped from £5,000 to £2,000 (see F(No 2)A 2017, s 8).

increases in self-employed NICs to stem the estimated £5.1 billion a year the Exchequer is losing from the lower rates of NICs paid by the self-employed, which is expected to rise to £6.1 billion by 2021/22.[82] The non-neutral NICs treatment of employed versus self-employed was exacerabated by the 2016 increases in state pension entitlement for the self-employed but which, for some unknown reason, was not accompanied by any increase in self-employed NICs. As a consequence there is now little difference in the contributory benefits available to the self-employed as compared with employees but big differences in the NICs paid by the two groups.[83] Unfortunately, the Chancellor's proposal to raise self-employed NICs fell afoul of the Conservative Party's manifesto pledge not to raise NICs and were quickly withdrawn.[84] It is also worth noting that although specific tax changes were formally outside its remit, the Taylor Review expressed support for the principles behind the Spring Budget 2017 proposals to raise NICs on the self-employed.[85]

Clearly, more needs to be done to address the non-neutral tax/NIC treatment of employees as compared with the self-employed and also those working through companies. The Mirrlees Review recommended tax/NIC rate alignment, and this is still the IFS position in Green Budget 2017.[86] Unfortunately the rate alignment approach suffers from obvious political difficulties, as witnessed by the Spring Budget 2017 u-turn. Moreover, the government responded to the Taylor Review with the announcement of a series of consultations on the Review's recommendations – except, remarkably, on the issue of rate alignment:

> While we agree with the review that the small differences in contributory benefit entitlement no longer justify the scale of difference in the rates of NI contributions paid in respect of employees and the self-employed, we are clear that we have no plans to revisit this issue.[87]

In any event, a rate alignment approach is unlikely to be a panacea in practice.[88] The primary difficulty with rate alignment is that there are too many moving parts to achieve and maintain alignment including, to name just the main ones, the rates of personal income tax on earnings, dividend tax, corporation tax, capital gains tax, employee and employer NICs, the dividend allowance, personal allowance and a host of tax-base factors and relief including entrepreneurs'

---

[82] Miller (above n 9); Adam, Miller and Pope (above n 80) 3–4; Spring Budget 2017 (above n 7).

[83] Miller (above n 9) 'Differences in benefits could justify less than 1 ppt difference in rates'; and Adam, Miller and Pope (above n 80) 26.

[84] *Spring Budget* 2017 (above n 7); and *BBC News* (above n 8).

[85] Taylor et al (above n 9) 9, 66-73.

[86] Adam, Miller and Pope (above n 80) 31.

[87] HM Government, *Good work: A response to the Taylor Review of Modern Working Practices* (February 2018), available at www.gov.uk/government/publications/government-response-to-the-taylor-review-of-modern-working-practices, 65.

[88] For a further discussion of the weaknesses of alignment see G Loutzenhiser, 'Where Next for Small Company Tax Reform in the UK?' [2016] *BTR* 674.

relief. Furthermore, politicians have a tendency to change rates and allowances without thinking of the bigger picture and knock-on effects. For example, the government enacted a reduction in the dividend allowance from 2018 plus a further reduction in the corporation tax rate to 17 per cent from 2020, and announced plans for further increases to the personal allowance.[89]

If rate alignment is not the silver bullet, what is? Crawford and Freedman and the OTS considered, and rejected, other possible reforms, including mandatory or optional look-through taxation of small companies, whereby a company's shareholders would pay income tax/NICs on the company's profits directly like partners in a partnership.[90] The OTS also suggested an entirely new legal entity for small business (the SEPA), which would be simpler to administer than a company and would combine the benefits of a degree of limited liability for business owners offered by a company with the look-through tax treatment of unincorporated partnerships and sole proprietorships.[91] It should also be noted that some including Redston have questioned whether it is even appropriate to compare employees with business owners:

> [T]he vast majority of family businesses depend on the contribution of the participating individuals. For example, a husband and wife business cannot normally operate without both parties playing a role, albeit that each make unequal contributions. Employees are not in the same position.[92]

This writer favours another, and in many ways easier, option towards addressing to some degree the unfairness and non-neutrality of business taxation – placing more reliance on an improved and expanded IR35 regime. The IR35 regime was introduced in 2001 with the aim of deterring taxpayers from carrying on economic activity that essentially amounts to providing the personal services/labour of the taxpayers to clients indirectly through the use of personal services companies (PSCs) and other intermediaries in the first place.[93] PSCs provide a mechanism for taxpayers to peform 'fiscal alchemy' by converting what would otherwise be highly taxed labour income (ie, employment or, to a lesser extent, self-employment income) into more lightly taxed income from capital (ie, dividends). Thus, Mr Jones was paid by Arctic for his services by way of small salary

---

[89] On the dividend allowance reduction see above n 81. On the 17% corporation tax rate from April 2020, see FA 2016 s 46. On the plan to increase the personal allowance to £12,500 – and the higher rate tax threshold to £50,000 – see HM Treasury, *Autumn Budget 2017* (HC 587, 2017) [3.5].

[90] Office of Tax Simplification, *Lookthrough Taxation, Final Report* (November 2016), available at www.gov.uk/government/uploads/system/uploads/attachment_data/file/564577/Lookthrough_paper_-_final.pdf, 3 and 13; Crawford and Freedman (above n 4) 1062–63.

[91] Office of Tax Simplification, *Sole Enterprise with Protected Assets (SEPA), Final Report* (November 2016), available at www.gov.uk/government/publications/ots-final-report-on-sole-enterprise-with-protected-assets-sepa.

[92] Redston, 'Income Sharing: The Nelsonian Option' (above n 71) 681.

[93] See also Freedman (above n 78); and G Loutzenhiser, 'Section 6 and Schedule 1: Workers' Services Provided to Public Sector through Intermediaries' [2017] *BTR* 201.

and large dividends – with the added tax advantage that an equal amount of dividends could be paid to Mrs Jones to further reduce the couple's combined tax charge.

It should be said that Crawford and Freedman[94] and also the IFS in Green Budget 2017[95] were against trying to write and police anti-avoidance rules such as IR35 that determine what should fall on each side of the employee/self-employed/company boundaries, preferring to tackle the underlying structural issue head-on with rate alignment. Much of their criticism of IR35 focuses on its reliance on the complicated case law on employment versus self-employment;[96] however, importantly, both the OTS[97] and the Taylor Review[98] have proposed ways to address the problems with the case law. The Taylor Review recommended the development of 'legislation and guidance that adequately sets out the tests that need to be met to establish employee or dependent contractor status', backed up by sophisticated online help tools – both of which strike this writer as positive and practical suggestions.[99]

In any event, in this writer's view an enlarged IR35 is much easier to pursue politically as just another in a long line of anti-avoidance rules – especially given that the government has ruled out pursuing rate alignment. FA 2017 saw an initial move in that direction with a shifting of the onus for IR35 compliance away from the PSC to public sector engagers;[100] indeed, one option would be to shift the onus from taxpayers to all engagers, which would match up with general obligations under ITEPA 2003 and PAYE and eliminate this newly created distortion favouring private sector work over public sector work.[101] Alternatively, or

---

[94] Crawford and Freedman (above n 4) 1050–53. IR35 is given only the briefest of attention in Mirrlees, *Tax by Design* (above n 4) 461, apparently because the Review editors did not wish to focus too heavily on UK-specific legislation.

[95] Adam, Miller and Pope (above n 80) 30–31.

[96] Crawford and Freedman (above n 4) 1051; and Freedman (above n 78).

[97] Office of Tax Simplification, *Employment Status Report* (March 2016), available at www.gov.uk/government/uploads/system/uploads/attachment_data/file/537432/OTS_Employment_Status_report_March_2016_u.pdf.

[98] Taylor et al (above n 9) 32.

[99] Taylor et al (above n 9) 40. See also Loutzenhiser, 'Section 6 and Schedule 1' (above n 93) 206. A new, enhanced online tool for checking employment status is available on the gov.uk website: www.gov.uk/guidance/check-employment-status-for-tax. For an indication of the future potential of IT solutions in this área readers are directed to the developing work of Professor Benjamin Alarie at the Faculty of Law, University of Toronto. Professor Alarie has experimented with teaching the IBM Watson supercomputer the Canadian tax case law on the employee/independent contractor distinction, with promising results: see A Scott, 'Elementary My Dear Watson' *Nexus* (Spring/Summer 2015), available at www.law.utoronto.ca/utfl_file/count/documents/Nexus/nxus_ss15_online.pdf, 18.

[100] FA 2017, s 6 and sch 1 and see Loutzenhiser, 'Section 6 and Schedule 1' (above n 93).

[101] At the time of writing the government has issued a consultation on off-payroll working in the private sector, which includes the possibility of shifting the IR35 compliance onus to private sector engagers: see www.gov.uk/government/consultations/off-payroll-working-in-the-private-sector. See also B Dodwell, 'Time for Change' *Tax Advisor* (1 July 2017); and Loutzenhiser, 'Section 6 and Schedule 1' (above n 93) 205 on the benefits, and almost certain likelihood, of extending the

additionally, the substantive scope of the provisions could be expanded with an Australian-type 'personal services income' (PSI) category, which represents income that is gained mainly as a reward for the personal efforts and skills of an individual.[102] This seems a well-targeted rule, as it is the mischief of essentially personal services carried on through small companies – such as Arctic – that is the primary concern in this area; it makes little sense to draw comparisons between employees, on the one hand, and companies with a significant capital base, on the other. The Australian rules may not be a perfect example to follow and resemble another fiendish logic puzzle[103] but they give some indication of a possible, targeted approach to this issue. Essentially, if a taxpayer has PSI earned through a company, for example, and is not otherwise taken out of these provisions on the basis of conditions including business hallmarks[104] and no more than 80 per cent of the PSI coming from one client (and associates), the PSI is attributed to the taxpayer with consequent income tax and payroll withholding obligations as well as limits on claiming deductions. In the UK context, a PSI-type test could be developed and added to the IR35 rules, with the result that PSI would be 'deemed employment income' under IR35.[105]

ii. Spousal Labour Income Shifting

In an income tax system that adopts the individual as the tax unit and has a progressive marginal rate structure, a high-rate paying taxpayer has an obvious incentive to 'shift' or 'split' income to a low- (or no-) rate paying spouse solely to minimise the family's total tax burden. When independent taxation was introduced in the late 1980s the then Financial Secretary to the Treasury (Norman Lamont) said that '[i]ndependent taxation is bound to mean that some couples will transfer assets between them with the result that their total tax bill will be reduced. This is an inevitable and acceptable consequence of taxing husbands and wives separately'.[106] Although recent times have seen some small moves away from the individual unit, most notably with the high income child benefit charge[107] and the ability for some married spouses/registered civil partners

---

responsibility for complying with IR35 to private sector engagers as well. See Freedman (above n 78) 8 for a discussion of the original proposals.

[102] Freudenberg (above n 9). See also Australian Taxation Office (ATO) website on PSI: www.ato.gov.au/Business/Personal-services-income.

[103] The ATO has helpfully prepared a flowchart to assist taxpayers in working out if the rules apply: www.ato.gov.au/uploadedFiles/Content/MEI/downloads/Working_out_if_the_PSI_rules_apply.pdf.

[104] eg, is the taxpayer paid for a specific result, required to provide his or her own equipment/tools *and* responsible for rectifying mistakes at his or her own expense? (the 'results test').

[105] ITEPA 2003, s 50.

[106] Standing Committee G (13 June 1989). Similar statements were made a year earlier: see Standing Committee A (23 June 1988) col 624. See also A Redston, 'Unsettled Business' (13 November 2003) 152 *Taxation* 162; and Redston, 'Income Sharing: The Nelsonian Option' (above n 71) 682–83.

[107] ITEPA 2003, s 681B *et seq*. For commentary see G Loutzenhiser, 'Finance Act Notes: Section 8 and Schedule 1: High Income Child Benefit Charge' [2012] *BTR* 370.

to transfer up to 10 per cent of their unused personal allowance to their basic-rate paying spouse/partner,[108] the individual unit remains central – and rightly so.[109] As Crawford and Freedman acknowledged, another disadvantage of their recommendation to align tax/NIC rates on earning income through different legal forms is that the ability to make full use of each spouse's personal allowance and basic rate band of income would still make income-splitting arrangements like that in *Jones v Garnett* worthwhile – further measures would be required.[110]

A secondary benefit from pursuing the expanded IR35 approach advocated above is that income-splitting arrangements like that in *Jones v Garnett* would become less of a concern. An expanded IR35 regime would lead to more PSI taxed under the employment regime, which has strong family income-shifting avoidance rules[111] – and these have been buttressed by the wide purposive interpretation approach adopted in the recent Supreme Court decisions *UBS/DB*[112] and especially *Rangers FC*.[113] Family income-splitting arrangements like *Jones v Garnett* could be further discouraged by adding a new rule to the spousal outright gifts exception to the settlements provisions, specifically excluding from that exception arrangements involving wholly or substantially PSI of the settlor. In commenting upon the Court of Appeal decision in *Jones v Garnett*, Professor John Tiley described the outright gift exclusion as a sensible exercise in line-drawing: the transfer of assets is permitted to be effective for income tax purposes between spouses living together but it must be real.[114] Introducing a statutory carve-out from the outright gift exception for PSI would further this reality.

IV. CONCLUSION

Since the Law Lords' decision in *Jones v Garnett* it is remarkable how little has changed in terms of the legal framework governing income-splitting arrangements and family companies. Some small developments are starting to take

---

[108] ITA 2007 s 55A et seq. For criticisms of the partial transferable allowance see G Loutzenhiser, 'Transferable Personal Allowances: A Small Step in the Wrong Direction' [2015] *BTR* 110. For an opposing view see L Beighton and D Draper, 'Transferable Personal Allowance: A Small step in the Right Direction' [2015] *BTR* 580.

[109] ITEPA 2003, s 681B *et seq*. For more on the arguments supporting independent taxation see Loutzenhiser, 'Finance Act Notes' (above n 107); and Loutzenhiser, 'Transferable Personal Allowances' (above n 108).

[110] Crawford and Freedman (above n 4) 1054. See also Adam, Miller and Pope (above n 80) 21.

[111] See eg ITEPA 2003, s 201, extending the employee benefit rules to 'family or household' members.

[112] *UBS AG v Revenue and Customs Comrs; DB Group Services (UK) Ltd v Revenue and Customs Comrs* [2016] UKSC 13; [2016] 1 WLR 1005.

[113] *Rangers FC and others v Advocate General for Scotland* [2017] UKSC 45; [2017] 1 WLR 2767.

[114] J Tiley, 'Tax, Marriage and the Family' (2006) 65 *CLJ* 289, 299.

place, but the government has firmly rejected pursuing closer alignment of tax rates across legal forms and putting more teeth in IR35 can only go so far in addressing the legal and political vacuum post-*Jones v Garnett*.

Looking to the future, the case also points to the need for a wider debate on the present mix of taxes overall, and in particular whether tax/NICs on labour income are too high relative to returns on capital. On this note, the Taylor Review was critical of taxes on employment such as the apprenticeship levy for increasing the 'employment wedge' – the additional, largely non-wage, costs associated with taking someone on as an employee.[115] Instead of seeking to raise NICs on the self-employed as attempted at Spring Budget 2017 – a politically difficult task and one that leaves the favourable position enjoyed by companies untouched – policymakers instead could look to reduce employee and employer NICs as a way of removing the employment wedge and look to make up the lost revenue elsewhere, for example, by raising VAT. This approach dovetails with work others are pursuing on corporate tax reform. At the 2017 Oxford University Centre for Business Taxation summer conference Professor Devereux outlined the destination-based cash flow tax (DBCFT) alternative to the present corporate tax regime.[116] Professor Devereux also suggested an alternative, less radical reform of the tax system that would achieve much of the benefits sought by the DBCFT and be revenue-neutral.[117] The key components of that approach were lowering the corporate tax rate to 12.5 per cent and increasing the bank levy to offset lower corporate tax on banks, increasing VAT by 4.5 per cent (and labelling it a 'VAT Business Surcharge' to make it more politically palatable), and decreasing employee NICs to 7.5 per cent.[118] Food for thought.

---

[115] Taylor et al (above n 9) 9.

[116] M Devereux, presentation at Oxford University Centre for Business Taxation Summer Conference (30 June 2017), available at www.sbs.ox.ac.uk/faculty-research/tax/events/summer-conference-2017.

[117] ibid.

[118] ibid.

Bibliography

PRIMARY SOURCES

Official Documents

Organisation for Economic Co-operation and Development (OECD)

OECD, *Model Tax Convention on Income and on Capital* (1963).
—— 'Double Taxation Conventions and the Use of Base Companies' in *International Tax Avoidance and Evasion: Four Related Studies* (Paris, 1987).
—— *Controlled Foreign Company Legislation* (Paris, 1996).
—— *Harmful Tax Competition – An Emerging Global Issue* (Paris, 1998).
—— *Policy Brief: Untying Aid to the Least Developed Countries* (OECD, 2001).
—— *Arrangement on Officially Supported Export Credits: Ex Ante Guidance for Tied Aid. 2005 Revision* (OECD, 2005).
—— *The Paris Declaration on Aid Effectiveness* (OECD, 2005).
—— *Study into the Role of Intermediaries* (OECD, 2008).
—— *Report on Building Transparent Tax Compliance by Banks* (OECD, 2009).
—— *Framework for a Voluntary Code of Conduct for Banks and Revenue Bodies* (OECD, 2010).
—— G20, *Designing Effective Controlled Foreign Company Rules, Action 3 – 2015 Final Report* (Paris, 2015).
—— *Public Discussion Draft, BEPS Action 3: Strengthening CFC Rules* (Paris, 2015).
—— *Model Tax Convention on Income and on Capital* (2017).

European Commission

Commission, 'The Application of Anti-abuse Measures in the Area of Direct Taxation – Within the EU and in Relation to Third Countries' (Communication) COM (2007) 785 final.
—— Press Release IP/12/1146 (24 October 2012).
—— Press Release IP/12/1147 ((24 October 2012).
—— ECOFIN, 'General Approach Paper (9432/16) (24 May 2016).
—— 'Communication on the Anti-Tax Avoidance Package: Next steps towards delivering effective taxation and greater tax transparency in the EU' COM (2016) 23 final.
—— 'Proposal for a Council Directive amending Directive 2011/16/EU as regards mandatory automatic exchange of information in the field of taxation' COM (2016) 25 final – 2016/010 (CNS).
—— 'Proposal for a Council Directive laying down rules against tax avoidance practices that directly affect the functioning of the internal market' COM (2016) 26 final.

UK Parliament

Joint Committee on Parliamentary Privilege, *Parliamentary Privilege* (first report) (1998–99, HL 43-1, HC 214-I).
Parliamentary Archives, *Appeal Cases, series 3 – 1906, D*, HL/PO/JU/4/3/541.

—— *Judicial Papers A-C 1-46*, HL/PO/JO/10/11/2057/427.

Report and Minutes of Evidence before the Select Committee on Medicine Stamp Duty (Cmd 54, 1937).

—— MP Devereux, J Freedman and J Vella, *Tax Avoidance* (Oxford University Centre for Business Taxation, 2012).

Seely, A, 'Capital Gains Tax: Background History', House of Commons Library, SN860 (2 June 2010).

—— 'Taxation in the Construction Industry', House of Commons Library, SN814 (20 May 2011).

HM Government

Board of Customs and Excise and Predecessor: Private Office Papers, The Medicine Stamp Duties 1783–1936, The National Archives CUST 118/366.

Board of Inland Revenue: *Precedents and Instructions*, 1904, The National Archives IR 78/60; IR 83/61.

Department for Constitutional Affairs, *Transforming Public Services: Complaints, Redress and Tribunals* (July 2004).

FA 1965 drafting papers, The National Archives, Public Record Office, file IR40/16688.

Good Work: A response to the Taylor Review of Modern Working Practices (February 2018).

HMRC, *A Code of Practice on Taxation for Banks* (December 2009).

—— *A Code of Practice on Taxation for Banks – Consultation Response Document* (9 December 2009).

—— *A Code of Practice on Taxation for Banks – Supplementary Guidance Note* (9 December 2009).

—— *HMRC Governance Protocol on Compliance with the Code of Practice on Taxation for Banks* (26 March 2012).

—— *Strengthening the Code of Practice on Taxation for Banks* (31 May 2013).

—— *The Code of Practice on Taxation for Banks – Consolidated Guidance* (8 November 2016).

HM Treasury, 'Finance Bill; report stage and third reading. Vol III', The National Archives, T 171/210 (1922).

—— *Treasury Minute on the seventeenth to twenty-first reports from the Committee of Public Accounts* (Cm 2602, 1993–94).

—— *Pre-Budget Report November 2008* (Cm 7484, 2008).

—— *Summer Budget 2015* (HC 264, 2015).

—— *Whole of Government Accounts: Year Ended 31 March 2016* (HC 2016–17, 254).

—— *Autumn Budget 2017* (HC 587, 2017).

—— *Spring Budget 2017* (HC 1025, 2017).

HM Treasury and HMRC, 'Income Shifting: A Consultation on Draft Legislation' (December 2007).

National Archives, T 172/1844, *Medicine Stamp Duty*, 1936.

—— T176/18, f17, undated and unsigned typescript on the tax privileges of various government loans.

Inland Revenue, 'Capital Gains Tax on Compensation and Damages; Zim Properties Ltd – Compensation and Damages', ESC D33.

—— *Forty-fifth Report of the Commissioners of His Majesty's Inland Revenue for the year ended 31st March 1902* (Cd 1216, 1902).

—— *Forty-seventh Annual Report of the Commissioners of Inland Revenue* (Cd 2228, 1904).

—— 'Second Budget: Inland Revenue memoranda (Part 2), The National Archives, T 171/120 (1915).

—— 'Finance Bill 1922: vol 2 memoranda', The National Archives, IR 63/101 (1921–22).

—— Finance Bill 1922: Parliamentary Papers', The National Archives IR 86/102.

—— '"Three Years Average" cases', The National Archives, IR 40/2708 (1921–22).

—— *Report of the Commissioners of Inland Revenue on the duties under their management for the years 1856 to 1869 Inclusive* (C 82, 1870).

—— *Sixty-seventh report of the Commissioners of His Majesty's Inland Revenue for the year ended 31st March 1924* (Cmd 2227, 1924).

—— *Seventy-first report of the Commissioners of His Majesty's Inland Revenue for the year ended 31st March 1928* (Cmd 3176, 1928).

—— *Seventy-second report of the Commissioners of His Majesty's Inland Revenue Commissioners of His Majesty's Inland Revenue for the year ended 31st March,1929* (Cmd 3500, 1929–30).

—— *Seventy-fourth report of the Commissioners of His Majesty's Inland Revenue for the year ended 31st March 1931* (Cmd 4027, 1932).

—— *Seventy-ninth report of the Commissioners of His Majesty's Inland Revenue for the year ended 31st March 1936* (Cmd 5297, 1937).

—— *Ninety-first report of the Commissioners of His Majesty's Inland Revenue for the year ended 31st March 1948* (Cmd 7738, 1949).

—— *Ninety-second report of the Commissioners of His Majesty's Inland Revenue for the year ended 31st March 1949* (Cmd 8052, 1950).

—— *Ninety-seventh report of the commissioners of Her Majesty's Inland Revenue for the year ended 31 March 1954* (Cmd 9351, 1954–55).

—— *Ninety-eighth Report of the Commissioners of Her Majesty's Inland Revenue for the year ended 31st March 1955* (Cmd 9667, 1956).

—— *One hundred and second report of the commissioners of Her Majesty's Inland Revenue* (Cmnd 922, 1959–60).

—— *Report of the Commissioners of Her Majesty's Inland Revenue for the year ended 31st March 1964: Hundred and Seventh Report* (Cmnd 2572, 1965).

—— Press Release (19 December 1988), available at [1988] *Simon's Tax Intelligence* 865.

—— *Tax Bulletin 64* (April 2003).

—— *Tax Bulletin 69* (February 2004).

—— *A Guide to the Settlements Legislation for Small Business Advisors* (November 2004).

Office of Tax Simplification, *Employment Status Report* (March 2016).

—— *Lookthrough Taxation, Final Report* (November 2016).

—— *Sole Enterprise with Protected Assets (SEPA), Final Report* (November 2016).

—— *Simplification of the Corporation Tax Computation* (July 2017).

—— *Accounting Depreciation or Capital Allowances?* (June 2018). Inland Revenue, *A Guide to the Settlements Legislation for Small Business Advisors* (November 2004).

Raithby, J (ed), *Statutes of the Realm* (Great Britain Record Commission, 1819).

Renton Committee, *The Preparation of Legislation* (Cmnd 6053, 1975).

Report of the Committee of Inquiry on Small Firms (Cmnd 4811, 1971–72).

Report of the Departmental Committee on Income Tax (Cd 2575, 1905).

Royal Commission on the Income Tax, *First Instalment of the Minutes of Evidence with Appendices* (Cmd 288, i–viii, 1919).

—— *Appendices and Index to the Minutes of Evidence* (HMSO, 1920).

—— *Report* (Cmd 615, 1920).

Royal Commission on the Press (Cmnd 1811, 1961–62).

—— *Minutes of Oral Evidence, Volume II* (Cmnd 1812-1, 1961–62).

—— *Industrial Relations in the National Newspaper Industry, a Report by ACAS* (Cmnd 6680, 1976–77).

Tax Law Rewrite Committee, 'Settlements' Paper CC(03)(16) (2003).

Judiciary of England and Wales

Judiciary of England and Wales, *Guide to Judicial Conduct* (March 2013).

Law Commission

Law Commission and Scottish Law Commission, *Partnership Law: A Joint Consultation Paper* (Law Com No 159 and Scottish Law Com No 111, 2003).

Other Governments

Attorney-General's Department, *Symposium on Statutory Interpretation* (Australian Government Publishing Service, 1983).
Department of Finance (Canada), *Tax Planning Using Private Corporations* (2017).
Department of the Treasury, *The Deferral of Income Earned Through US Controlled Foreign Corporations – A Policy Study* (Washington DC, 2000).
Internal Revenue Service, US Treasury, 26 CFR Part 301 (PS–43–95), *Simplification of Entity Classification Rules* 61: 93 Federal Register (10 May 1996) 21989, 21990.
New Zealand Law Commission, *A New Interpretation Act: To Avoid Prolixity and Tautology* (NZ Law Com No 17, 1990).

Philosophical and Literary Works

Aristotle, *The Nicomachean Ethics*, JAK Thomson, H Tredennick and J Barnes (eds and trans) (London, Penguin, 2004).
Berlin, I, 'Two Concepts of Liberty' in I Berlin, *Four Essays on Liberty* (Oxford, Oxford University Press, 1969).
Blackstone, W, *Commentaries on the Laws of England*, 4 vols (first published 1765; Oxford, Oxford University Press, 2016).
Chapman, G, *A Passionate Prodigality: Fragments of Autobiography* (London, MacGibbon & Kee, 1965).
Durkheim, E, *Professional Ethics and Civic Morals* (C Brookfield trans), 2nd edn (London, Routledge, 1992).
Hobbes, T, *Leviathan* [1651], M Oakeshott (ed) (Oxford, Basil Blackwell, 1955).
Hume, D, *A Treatise of Human Nature* (first published 1739–40; Oxford, Clarendon Press, 1978).
Locke, J, 'Of Civil Government. Book II: Second Treatise' in I Shapiro et al (eds), *Two Treatises of Government* and *A Letter Concerning Toleration* (New Haven, CT, Yale University Press, 2003).
Mendelson, E (ed), *WH Auden: Selected Poems* (London, Faber & Faber, 1979).
Murphy, L and Nagel, T, *The Myth of Ownership* (Oxford, Oxford University Press, 2000).
Nozick, R, *Anarchy, State, and Utopia* (New York, BasicBooks, 1974).
O'Shaughnessy, A, 'Ode' in A Quiller-Couch (ed), *The Oxford Book of English Verse 1250–1918*, 2nd edn (Oxford, Clarendon Press, 1939).
Plowden, E, *The Commentaries, or Reports* (first published 1548–79; London, Brooke, 1816).
Rattigan, T, *Collected Plays*, vol 1 (London, Hamish Hamilton, 1953).
Rushworth, J, *Historical Collections of Private Passages of State*, 8 vols (London, 1721 edn).
Smith, A, *An Inquiry into the Nature and Causes of the Wealth of Nations* (1776), RH Campbell et al (eds), 2 vols (Carmel, IN, Liberty Fund, 1981).
von Gierke, O, *Die Genossenschaftstheorie und die deutsche Rechtsprechung* (Frankfurt, Weidmann, 1887).
von Hayek, FA, *The Road to Serfdom* [1944] (London, Routledge, 1997).
—— *The Constitution of Liberty* (first published 1960; Abingdon, Routledge 2006).
von Savigny, FK, *Das Obligationenrecht als Theil des heutigen Römischen Rechts* Vol 2 (Berlin, Veit, 1853).
—— *System des heutigen römischen Rechts* Vol 8 (Berlin, Veit, 1849).

—— *A Treatise on the Conflict of Laws, and the Limits of their Operation in Respect of Place and Time*, vol 8, translation with notes by W Guthrie (Edinburgh, T & T Clark, 1869).

Wittgenstein, L, *Philosophical Investigations* (trans GEM Anscombe et al), 4th edn (Chichester, Wiley-Blackwell, 2009).

Private Archives

Charter of the British South Africa Company, *London Gazette* (20 December 1889).

Churchill Archives Centre, Cambridge, CHAR 2/3/34.

—— CHAR 2/18/86, Bowles to Churchill, 23 November 1904

—— CHAR 2/3/131, Bowles to Churchill, 14 December 1904.

De Beers Consolidated Mines Ltd *Minute Book No 1* (1885–24 April 1891, Kimberley).

—— *Minute Book No 2* (April 1891–August 1906, Kimberley).

—— *Minute Book No 3* (August 1897– May 1900, Kimberley).

—— *Minute Book No 4* (19 May 1900–23 June 1902, Kimberley).

—— *Minute Book No 6* (25 February 1904–1 June 1905, Kimberley).

—— *Minute Book No 7* (1 June 1906–17 January 1907, Kimberley).

—— *Minute Book No 8* (24 January 1907–24 June 1909, Kimberley).

Statute (or Charter) for the Berlin–Saxony (Anhalt) Railway Company 1839 (Statut der Berlin-Sächsischen (Anhaltischen) Eisenbahn-Gesellschaft) in (1839) 1 *Gesetzsammlung für die Königlich-Preußischen Staaten* 178.

Statute (or Charter) for the Berlin–Stettin Railway Company 1840 (Statut der Berlin-Stettiner Eisenbahn-Gesellschaft) in (1840) 1 *Gesetzsammlung für die Königlich-Preußischen Staaten* 306.

SECONDARY SOURCES

Books

Allen, CK, *Law in the Making*, 7th edn (Oxford, Clarendon Press, 1964).

Arnold, BJ, *The Taxation of Controlled Foreign Corporations: An International Comparison* (Toronto, Canadian Tax Foundation, 1986).

Ashworth, W, *An Economic History of England 1870–1939* (London, Methuen, 1960).

Bailey, D and Norbury, L, *Bennion on Statutory* Interpretation, 7th edn (London, Lexis Nexis, 2017).

Bank, SA and Stark, KJ (eds), *Business Tax Stories* (New York, Foundation Press, 2005).

Barnett, J, *Inside the Treasury* (London, André Deutsch, 1982).

Baum, L, *Ideology in the Supreme Court* (Princeton, NJ, Princeton University Press, 2017).

Bell, J and Engle, G (eds), *Cross: Statutory Interpretation*, 3rd edn (London, Butterworths, 1995).

Bennett, RJ, *Local Business Voice* (Oxford, Oxford University Press, 2011).

Bennion, F, *Statutory Interpretation*, 4th edn (London, Butterworths, 2002).

Bettsworth, M, *The Growth of a Business Pressure Group: Federation of Small Businesses 1974–1999* (NFSE, 1999).

Bingham, T, *Tax Evasion: The Law and the Practice* (London, Alexander Howden, 1980).

Blackett-Ord, M and Haren, S, *Partnership Law* (Haywards Heath, Bloomsbury, 2015).

Boucher, T, *Blatant, Artificial and Contrived: Tax Schemes of the 70s and 80s* (ATO, 2010).

Bowles, TG, *Defence of Paris; Narrated as it was Seen* (London, Sampson Low, Son and Marston, 1871).

—— *Maritime Warfare* (London, W Ridgway, 1877).

—— *The Declaration of Paris: Being an Account of the Maritime Rights of Great Britain, a Consideration of Their Importance; a History of Their Surrender by the Signature of the Declaration of Paris; and an Argument for their Resumption* (London, Sampson Low, Marston & Company, 1900).

—— *Gibraltar: A National Danger, being an Account of the Nature and Present State of Certain Works Now Being Constructed on the Western Side of Gibraltar; an Exposition of the Danger which These Will Create for Great Britain; An Argument for Certain Alterations Calculated to Diminish the Danger Attached to Them; and a Plea for the Suspension of the Works Until a Re-examination and Reconsideration Has Been Made of the Whole Matter* (London, Sampson Low, Marston & Company, 1901).

—— *National Finance: An Imminent Peril* (London, T Fisher Unwin, 1904).

—— *The Public Purse and the War Office. Being a Vindication of Parliamentary Control Over National Expenditure, and a Protest Against the Sacrifice of the Constitution to a Military Oligarchy* (London, T Fisher Unwin, 1907).

—— *National Finance in 1908 and After: Being a Review of the Past, a Forecast of the Future, and Appeal for True Accounts, a Plea for Retrenchment, a Protest Against Debt, and a Warning Against False Taxation* (London, T Fisher Unwin, 1908).

—— *Sea Law and Sea Power as They Would be Affected by Recent Proposals with Reasons Against the Proposals* (London, J Murray, 1910).

—— *Bowles v the Bank of England: The Proceedings in Court (from the shorthand writer's notes) and official court documents, with an introduction by T Gibson Bowles* (London, Butterworth, 1914).

Braddick, MJ, *The Nerves of State: Taxation and the Financing of the English State, 1558–1714* (Manchester, Manchester University Press, 1996).

——, *State Formation in Early Modern England c 1550–1700* (Cambridge, Cambridge University Press, 2000).

—— *The Common Freedom of the People: John Lilburne and the English Revolution* (Oxford, Oxford University Press, 2018).

Brooks, D (ed), *The Destruction of Lord Rosebery. From the Diary of Sir Edward Hamilton, 1894–1895* (London, The Historians' Press, 1986).

Brooks, R, *The Great Tax Robbery: How Britain Became a Tax Haven for Fat Cats and Big Business* (London, Oneworld Publications, 2013).

Burgess, G, *The Politics of the Ancient Constitution: An Introduction to English Political Thought* (Basingstoke, Macmillan, 1992).

Butler, D, Adonis, A and Travers, T, *Failure in British Government: The Politics of the Poll Tax* (Oxford, Oxford University Press, 1994).

Caron, PL (ed), *Tax Stories* (2nd edn, New York, Foundation Press, 2009).

Carroll, L, *Through the Looking Glass* (London, Macmillan, 1872).

Carter, RN, *Murray & Carter's Guide to Income-Tax Practice*, 11th edn (London, Gee & Co, 1927).

Chilvers, HA, *The Story of De Beers* (London, Cassell and Company, 1939).

Churchill, WS, *Liberalism and the Social Problem* (London, Hodder & Stoughton, 1909).

—— *My Early Life: A Roving Commission* (London, Butterworth, 1930).

Clarke, P, *Liberals and Social Democrats* (Cambridge, Cambridge University Press, 1978).

Conan Doyle, A, *The Great Boer War* (London, Smith, Elder & Co, 1900).

Courtney, LH, *The Working Constitution of the United Kingdom and its Outgrowths* (London, JM Dent & Co, 1905).

Dauber, N, *State and Commonwealth: The Theory of the State in Early Modern England, 1549–1640* (Princeton, NJ, Princeton University Press, 2016).

Daunton, M, *Trusting Leviathan: The Politics of Taxation in Britain, 1799–1914* (Cambridge, Cambridge University Press, 2001).

Davies, P and Pila, J (eds), *The Jurisprudence of Lord Hoffmann* (Oxford, Hart Publishing, 2015).

Davitt, M, *The Boer Fight for Freedom* (New York, Funk & Wagnalls, 1902).

Denning, A, *The Closing Chapter* (London, Butterworths, 1983).

Devlin, P, *Easing the Passing: The Trial of Dr John Bodkin Adams* (London, Faber & Faber, 1986).

Dicey, AV, *Introduction to the Study of the Law of the Constitution* (first published 1885; Carmel, IN, Liberty Fund 1982).

—— 'Lectures Introductory to the Study of the Law of the Constitution' in JWF Allison (ed), *The Oxford Edition of Dicey: Volume I*, rev edn (Oxford, Oxford University Press, 2013).

Douglas, R, *Taxation in Britain Since 1660* (Basingstoke, Macmillan, 1999).

Dromey, J and Taylor, G, *Grunwick: The Workers' Story*, 2nd edn (London, Lawrence & Wishart, 2016).

Dymond, R, Johns, RK and Greenfield, RR (eds), *Dymond's Capital Transfer Tax: A Companion Volume to the Fifteenth Edition of Dymond's Death Duties* (London, Oyez Publishing, 1977).

Ekins, R, *The Nature of Legislative Intent* (Oxford, Oxford University Press, 2012).

Elliott, M and Varuhas, J, *Administrative Law: Text and Materials*, 5th edn (Oxford, Oxford University Press, 2016).

Epp, CR, *The Rights Revolution: Lawyers, Activists, and Supreme Courts in Comparative Perspective* (Chicago, IL, University of Chicago Press, 1998).

Epstein, RA, *Design for Liberty: Private Property, Public Administration, and the Rule of Law* (Cambridge, MA, Harvard University Press, 2011).

Erskine May, T, *A Practical Treatise on the Law, Privileges, Proceedings and Usage of Parliament*, 2nd edn (London, Butterworths, 1851).

Fairpo, A and Salter, D, *Revenue Law: Principles and Practice*, 35th edn (London, Bloomsbury Professional, 2017).

Farnsworth, A, *Addington: Author of the Modern Income Tax* (London, Stevens & Sons, 1951).

Ferguson, N, *The World's Banker: The History of the House of Rothschild* (London, Weidenfeld & Nicolson, 1998).

Field, F, Meacher, M and Pond, C, *To Him Who Hath: A Study of Poverty and Taxation* (Harmondsworth, Penguin, 1977).

Fry, TH, *Income Tax: Its Return, Assessment, and Recovery* (London, Stevens & Sons, 1909).

Gardiner, SR (ed), *The Constitutional Document of the Puritan Revolution 1625–1660*, 3rd edn (Oxford, Oxford University Press, 1906).

Gill, M, *Accountant's Truth: Knowledge and Ethics in the Financial World* (Oxford, Oxford University Press, 2009).

Gillard, M, *In the Name of Charity: The Rossminster Affair* (London, Chatto & Windus, 1987).

Gourvish, TR and Wilson, RG, *The British Brewing Industry 1830–1980* (Cambridge, Cambridge University Press, 1994).

Grant, J, *A Practical Treatise on the Law of Corporations in General, As Well Aggregate as Sole* (London, Butterworths, 1850).

Grant, T, *Jeremy Hutchinson's Case Histories* (London, John Murray, 2015).

Gray, K and Gray, SF, *Elements of Land Law*, 5th edn (Oxford, Oxford University Press, 2009).

Griffith, JAG, *The Politics of the Judiciary* (London, Fontana, 1977).

Grigg, J, *The History of the Times: The Thomson Years 1966–1981* (London, Times Books, 1993).

Gross, DM, *We Won't Pay! A Tax Resistance Reader* (North Charleston, SC, Createspace, 2008).

Hackney, J, *Understanding Equity and Trusts* (London, Fontana Press, 1987).

Hague, W, *William Wilberforce: The Life of the Great Anti-Slave Trade Campaigner* (London, HarperPress, 2007).

Harlow, C and Rawlings, R, *Pressure Through Law* (Abingdon, Routledge, 1992).

Harris, P and Oliver, D, *International Commercial Tax* (Cambridge, Cambridge University Press, 2010).

Harris, P, *Corporate Tax Law: Structure, Policy and Practice* (Cambridge, Cambridge University Press, 2013).

Harrison, B, *Finding a Role? The United Kingdom, 1970–1990* (Oxford, Clarendon Press, 2010).

Hart, JS Jr, *The Rule of Law, 1603–1660* (Harlow, Pearson, 2003).

Healey, D, *The Time of My Life* (London, Michael Joseph, 1989).

Herbert, AP, *More Misleading Cases in the Common Law* (London, Methuen & Co, 1930).

Heuston, RFV, *Lives of the Lord Chancellors 1885–1940* (Oxford, Oxford University Press, 1964).

Heuston, RFV and Stevens, R 'Romer, Mark Lemon, Baron Romer (1866–1944)' in *Oxford Dictionary of National Biography* (Oxford, Oxford University Press, 2004).

Hirsch, A, *The Duke of Wellington Kidnapped: The Incredible True Story of the Art Heist That Shocked a Nation* (Berkeley CA, Counterpoint, 2016).

HJI Panayi, C, *European Union Corporate Tax Law* (Cambridge, Cambridge University Press, 2013).

—— *Advanced Issues in International and EU Tax Law* (Oxford, Hart Publishing, 2015).

Hocking, A, *Oppenheimer and Son* (New York, McGraw-Hill, 1973).

Hoyle, RW (ed), *The Estates of the English Crown 1558–1640* (Cambridge, Cambridge University Press, 1992).

Humphreys, S, *Theatre of the Rule of Law: Transnational Legal Intervention in Theory and Practice* (Cambridge, Cambridge University Press, 2010).

Huret, RD, *American Tax Resisters* (Cambridge, MA, Harvard University Press, 2014).

Hyde, E, Earl of Clarendon, *History of the Rebellion and Civil Wars in England* WD Macray (ed), 6 vols (first published 1702–04; Oxford, Oxford University Press, 1888).

Innes, D, *Anglo American and the Rise of Modern South Africa* (New York, Raven Press, 1984).

Janes, H, *Albion Brewery, 1808–1958: The Story of Mann, Crossman & Paulin Ltd* (London, Harley Publishing Company, 1958).

—— *The Red Barrel: A History of Watney Mann* (London, John Murray, 1963).

Johnston, A, *The Inland Revenue* (London, Allen & Unwin, 1965).

Jones, O, *Bennion on Statutory Interpretation*, 6th edn (London, Butterworths, 2013).

Judge, MH (ed), *Political Socialism: A Remonstrance. A Collection of Papers by Members of the British Constitution Association, with Presidential Addresses by Lord Balfour of Burleigh and Lord Hugh Cecil* (London, PS King, 1908).

Keenan, D and Bisacre, J, *Smith and Keenan's Company Law*, 13th edn, (Harlow, Pearson, 2005).

Kiesling, HJ, *Taxation and Public Goods: A Welfare-Economic Critique of Tax Policy Analysis* (Ann Arbor, MI, University of Michigan Press, 1992).

King, M and Thornhill, C, *Niklas Luhmann's Theory of Politics and Law* (Basingstoke, Palgrave Macmillan, 2003).

King, R and Nugent, N (eds), *Respectable Rebels* (London, Hodder & Stoughton, 1979).

Knightley, P, *The Rise and Fall of the House of Vestey* (London, Warner Books, 1993).

Knowles, E (ed), *Oxford Dictionary of Quotations*, 7th edn (Oxford, Oxford University Press, 2009).

Konstam, EM, *A Treatise on the Law of Income Tax* (London, Stevens & Sons, 1921).

Kray, R, *Our Story: London's Most Notorious Gangsters, in Their Own Words* (London, Pan Macmillan, 2015).

Lamb, M, et al (eds), *Taxation: An Interdisciplinary Approach to Research* (Oxford, Oxford University Press, 2005).

Lang, M et al (eds), *CFC Legislation, Tax Treaties and EC Law* (The Hague, Kluwer Law International, 2004).

Lankester, T, *The Politics and Economics of Britain's Foreign Aid* (Abingdon, Routledge, 2013).

Lavisse, E and Rambaud, A, *Histoire Générale du IVe siècle á nos jours, I* (Paris, Armand Colin, 1894).

Lentin, A, *The last Political Law Lord: Lord Sumner 1859–1934* (Newcastle, Cambridge Scholars Publishing, 2008).

Letwin, SR, *On the History of the Idea of Law*, NB Reynolds (ed) (Cambridge, Cambridge University Press, 2005).

Lindley, N, *A Treatise on the Law of Companies, Considered as a Branch of the Law of Partnerships* (London, Sweet & Maxwell, 1902).

Loughlin, M, *Public Law and Political Theory* (Oxford, Clarendon Press, 1992).

—— *Legality and Locality* (Oxford, Oxford University Press, 1996).

—— *The Idea of Public Law* (Oxford, Oxford University Press, 2003).

—— *Foundations of Public Law* (Oxford, Oxford University Press, 2010).

—— *The British Constitution: A Very Short Introduction* (Oxford, Oxford University Press, 2013).

Loutzenhiser, G, *Tiley's Revenue Law*, 8th edn (Oxford, Hart Publishing, 2016).

Lubbock, J, *Municipal and National Trading* (London, Macmillan, 1907).

Maitland, FW, *Equity*, 2nd edn (Cambridge, Cambridge University Press, 1936).

Mathias, P, *The Brewing Industry in England 1700–1830* (Cambridge, Cambridge University Press, 1959).

McBriar, AM, *An Edwardian Mixed Doubles: The Bosanquets versus the Webbs. A Study in British Social Policy, 1890–1929* (Oxford, Clarendon Press, 1987).

McCahery, JAM and Vermeulen, EPM, *Topics in Corporate Finance: Understanding (Un)incorporated Business Forms* (Amsterdam Center for Corporate Finance, 2005).

McGhee, J (ed), *Snell's Equity*, 33rd edn (London, Sweet & Maxell, 2017).

McKibbin, R, *Parties and People: England 1914–1951* (Oxford, Oxford University Press, 2010).

McNair, Lord, *The Law of Treaties* (Oxford, Clarendon Press, 1961).

Michell, L, *The Life and Times of the Right Honourable Cecil John Rhodes, 1853–1902* (New York, Mitchell Kennerley, 1912).

Miers, DR and Page, AC, *Legislation*, 2nd edn (London, Sweet & Maxwell, 1990).

Millett, P, *As in Memory Long* (London, Wildy, Simmonds & Hill Publishing, 2015).

Mirrlees, J et al (eds), *Tax by Design: The Mirrlees Review* (Oxford, Oxford University Press, 2011).

Monroe, HH, *Intolerable Inquisition? Reflections on the Law of Tax* (London, Stevens & Sons, 1981).

Moore, C, *Margaret Thatcher: The Authorized Biography: Volume One: Not for Turning* (London, Allen Lane, 2013).

Morrill, J, *Revolt in the Provinces: The People of England and the Tragedies of War 1630–1648*, 2nd edn (Harlow, Longman, 1999).

Murray, BK, *The People's Budget 1909/10: Lloyd George and Liberal Politics* (Oxford, Clarendon Press, 1980).

Naylor, LE, *The Irrepressible Victorian: The Story of Thomas Gibson Bowles, Journalist, Parliamentarian and Founder-Editor of the Original Vanity Fair* (London, Macdonald, 1965).

Newbury, C, *The Diamond Ring* (Oxford, Clarendon Press, 1989).

Oakeshott, M, *The Politics of Faith and the Politics of Scepticism*, T Fuller (ed) (New Haven, CT, Yale University Press, 1996).

Oats, L, Miller, A and Mulligan, E, *Principles of International Taxation*, 6th edn (London, Bloomsbury Professional, 2017).

Offer, A, *Property and Politics, 1870–1914: Landownership, Law, Ideology and Urban Development in England* (Cambridge, Cambridge University Press, 1981).

Picciotto, S, *Regulating Global Corporate Capitalism* (Cambridge, Cambridge University Press, 2011).

Piketty, T, *Capital in the Twenty-First Century* (A Goldhammer trans) (Cambridge, MA, Harvard University Press, 2014).

Pimlott, B, *Harold Wilson* (London, William Collins, 2016).

Pirie, M, *Think Tank: The Story of the Adam Smith Institute* (London, Biteback Publications, 2012).

Pocock, JGA, *The Ancient Constitution and the Feudal Law: A Study of English Historical Thought in the Seventeenth Century*, 2nd edn (Cambridge, Cambridge University Press, 1987).

Pontifical Council for Justice and Peace, *Compendium of the Social Doctrine of the Church* (London, Burns and Oates, 2004).

Porter, R, *London: A Social History* (Cambridge, MA, Harvard University Press, 1998).

Prosser, T, *Test Cases for the Poor* (London, CPAG, 1983).

—— *The Economic Constitution* (Oxford, Oxford University Press, 2014).

Ridgway, P, *Lecture Notes: Revenue Law* (Abingdon, Routledge-Cavendish, 1996).

Robb, G, *The Debateable Land: The Lost World Between Scotland and England* (London, Picador, 2018).

Roberts, B, *Kimberley: Turbulent City* (Cape Town, David Philip, 1976).

Rotberg, RI, *The Founder: Cecil Rhodes and the Pursuit of Power* (Oxford, Oxford University Press, 1988).

Russell, C, *Parliaments and English Politics 1621–1629* (Oxford, Oxford University Press, 1979).

—— *The Causes of the English Civil War* (Oxford, Oxford University Press, 1990).

Ryan, A, *On Politics: A History of Political Thought from Herodotus to the Present* (London, Allen Lane, 2012).

Sabine, BEV, *A History of Income Tax* (London, George Allen & Unwin, 1966).

Sandbrook, D, *State of Emergency: The Way We Were: Britain, 1970–1974* (London, Allen Lane, 2010).

—— *Seasons in the Sun: The Battle for Britain, 1974–1979* (London, Allen Lane, 2012).

Scott, AW et al, *Scott on Trusts*, 4th edn (New York, Aspen Publishers, 1998).

Seldon, A, Ilersic, AR and Myddelton, DR *et al*, *Tax Avoision* (IEA, 1979).

Seligman, ERA, *The Income Tax: A Study of the History, Theory and Practice of Income Taxation at Home and Abroad*, 2nd edn (New York, Macmillan, 1914).

Sharpe, K, *The Personal Rule of Charles I* (New Haven, CT, Yale University Press, 1990).

Shenfield, AA, *The Political Economy of Tax Avoidance* (London, IEA, 1968).

Sin, KF, *The Legal Nature of the Unit Trust* (Oxford, Clarendon Press, 1997).

Slater, J, *Return to Go: My Autobiography* (London, Weidenfeld & Nicolson, 1977).

Snape, J, *The Political Economy of Corporation Tax: Theory, Values and Law Reform* (Oxford, Hart Publishing, 2011).

Standing, G, *Basic Income: And How We Can Make It Happen* (London, Pelican Books, 2017).

Stanley, O, *Taxology* (London, Weidenfeld & Nicolson, 1972).

Stead, WT (ed), *The Last Will and Testament of Cecil John Rhodes with Elucidatory Notes to which are Added Some Chapters Describing the Political and Religious Ideas of the Testator* ('Review of Reviews' Office, 1902).

Stebbings, C, *The Victorian Taxpayer and the Law: A Study in Constitutional Conflict* (Cambridge, Cambridge University Press, 2009).

—— *Tax, Medicines and the Law: From Quackery to Pharmacy* (Cambridge, Cambridge University Press, 2017).

Stevens, R, *The English Judges: Their Role in the Changing Constitution* (Oxford, Hart Publishing, 2005).

Street, H, *Justice in the Welfare State*, 2nd edn (London, Stevens, 1975).

Summers, RS, *Essays in Legal Theory* (Dordrecht, Kluwer Law International, 2000).

Supperstone, M, QC, Walker, P, Goudie, J and Fenwick, H (eds), *Judicial Review*, 5th edn (LexisNexis UK, 2014).

Thomas, G and Hudson, A, *The Law of Trusts*, 2nd edn (Oxford, Oxford University Press, 2010).

Thuronyi, V, *Comparative Tax Law* (The Hague, Kluwer Law International, 2003).

Tilly, C, *Coercion, Capital and European States AD 990–1992* (Oxford, Blackwell, 1992).

Tomkins, A, *Public Law* (Oxford, Oxford University Press, 2003).

Turing, J, *Nothing Certain But Tax* (London, Hodder & Stoughton, 1966).

Tutt, N, *The Tax Raiders: The Rossminster Affair* (London, Financial Training, 1985).

—— *The History of Tax Avoidance* (London, Wisedene, 1989).

Walker, DM, *The Oxford Companion to Law* (Oxford, Oxford University Press, 1980).

Watt, G, *Equity Stirring: The Story of Justice Beyond Law* (Oxford, Hart Publishing, 2009).

Whiteman, P et al, *Whiteman on Income Tax*, 3rd edn (London, Sweet & Maxwell, 1988).

Whiting, RC, *The Labour Party and Taxation* (Cambridge, Cambridge University Press, 2000).

Wilberforce, S (ed), *Reflections on My Life* (Croydon, Privately Published, 2003).

Wilkinson, NJ, *Secrecy and the Media* (London, Routledge, 2009).

Woodworth, A, *Purveyance for the Royal Household in the Reign of Queen Elizabeth* (American Philosophical Society, 1945).

Young, H, *One of Us: A Biography of Margaret Thatcher*, 3rd edn (London, Pan, 1993).

Zagorin, P, *Hobbes and the Law of Nature* (Princeton, NJ, Princeton University Press, 2009).

Chapters in Edited Volumes

Adam, S, Browne, J and Heady, C, 'Taxation in the UK' in S Adam and T Besley et al (eds), *Dimensions of Tax Design: The Mirrlees Review* (Oxford, Oxford University Press, 2010).

Adam, S, Miller, H and Pope, T, 'Chapter 7: Tax, Legal Form and the Gig Economy' in C Emmerson, P Johnson and R Joyce, *IFS Green Budget 2017* (IFS, 2017).

Alborn, TL, 'Lubbock, John, first Baron Avebury (1834–1913)' in *Oxford Dictionary of National Biography* (Oxford, Oxford University Press, 2004).

Arnold, BJ and Dibout, PJ, 'General Report' in BJ Arnold and PJ Dibout (eds), *Limits on the Use of Low-Tax Regimes by Multinational Businesses: Current Measures and Emerging Trends* (The Hague, Kluwer Law International, 2001).

Ashton, R, 'From Cavalier to Roundhead Tyranny, 1642–49' in J Morrill (ed), *Reactions to the English Civil War 1642–1649* (Basingstoke, Macmillan, 1982).

Avery Jones, JF, 'Defining and Taxing Companies 1799 to 1965' in J Tiley (ed), *Studies in the History of Tax Law: Volume 5* (Oxford, Hart Publishing, 2011).

—— 'The Sources of Addington's Income Tax' in P Harris and D de Cogan (eds), *Studies in the History of Tax Law: Volume 7* (Oxford, Hart Publishing, 2015).

Bowles, TG, 'The British Constitution' in *Report of the Constitution Congress in Connection with the Franco-British Exhibition, Being a Special Number of 'Constitution Papers'* (British Constitution Association, 1908).

Braddick, MJ, 'The Rise of the Fiscal State' in B Coward (ed), *A Companion to Stuart Britain* (Malden, MA, Blackwell, 2003).

Briggs, A, 'Birmingham: The Making of a Civic Gospel' in A Briggs, *Victorian Cities* (London, Penguin, 1968).

Chance, W, 'Old Age Pensions: The Better Way. A Question for Friendly Societies' in MH Judge (ed), *Political Socialism: A Remonstrance. A Collection of Papers by Members of the British Constitution Association, with Presidential Addresses by Lord Balfour of Burleigh and Lord Hugh Cecil* (London, PS King, 1908).

Churchill, WS, 'The Royal College of Physicians. March 2, 1944' in R Rhodes James (ed), *Winston S. Churchill His Complete Speeches 1897–1963*, vol 7 (New York, Chelsea House Publishers, 1974).

Cochrane, A and Matthew, HCG, 'Bowles, Thomas Gibson (1842–1922)' in *Oxford Dictionary of National Biography* (Oxford, Oxford University Press, 2008).

Cosgrove, RA, 'Dicey, Albert Venn (1835–1922)' in *Oxford Dictionary of National Biography* (Oxford, Oxford University Press, 2004).

Crawford, C and Freedman, J, 'Small Business Taxation' in J Mirrlees et al (eds), *Dimensions of Tax Design: The Mirrlees Review* (Oxford, Oxford University Press, 2010).

Daly, S, 'The Life and Times of ESCs: A Defence?' in P Harris and D de Cogan (eds), *Studies in the History of Tax Law: Volume 8* (Oxford, Hart Publishing, 2017).

Daunton, M, 'Creating a Dynamic Society: The Tax Reforms of the Thatcher Government' in M Buggeln, M Daunton and A Nützenadel (eds), *The Political Economy of Public Finance: Taxation, State Spending and Debt since the 1970s* (Cambridge, Cambridge University Press, 2017).

Davenport-Hines, R, 'Rank (Joseph) Arthur, Baron Rank (1888–1972)' in *Oxford Dictionary of National Biography* (Oxford, Oxford University Press, 2004).

De-la-Noy, M, 'Shee, George Archer- (1895–1914), literary prototype' in *Oxford Dictionary of National Biography* (Oxford, Oxford University Press, 2014).

Dicey, AV, 'Address' in *Report of the Constitution Congress in Connection with the Franco-British Exhibition, Being a Special Number of 'Constitution Papers'* (London, British Constitution Association, 1908).

Diplock, K, 'The Courts as Legislators' in BW Harvey (ed), *The Lawyer and Justice* (London, Sweet & Maxwell, 1978).

Freedman, J, 'The Role of Realisation: Accounting, Company Law and Taxation' in International Fiscal Association Congress Seminar Series 21B, *The Influence of Corporate Law and Accounting Principles in Determining Taxable Income* (Alphen aan den Rijn, Kluwer Law International, 1997).

—— 'Financial and Tax Accounting: Transparency and "Truth"' in W Schön (ed), *Tax and Corporate Governance* (Berlin, Springer Science, 2008).

Gammie, M, 'The Origins of Fiscal Transparency in UK Income Tax' in J Tiley (ed), *Studies in the History of Tax Law: Volume 4* (Oxford, Hart Publishing, 2010).

—— 'The Relationship of *Situs* and Source Rules for Tax Purposes' in J Tiley (ed), *Studies in the History of Tax Law: Volume 6* (Oxford, Hart Publishing, 2013).

Hailsham, Lord, 'Richard Wilberforce: A Man for All Seasons' in M Bos and I Brownlie, *Liber Amicorum for Lord Wilberforce* (Oxford, Clarendon Press, 1987).

Hattingh, J, 'On The Origins of Model Tax Conventions: 19th Century German Tax Treaties and Laws concerned with the Avoidance of Double Taxation' in J Tiley (ed), *Studies in the History of Tax Law, Volume 6* (Oxford, Hart Publishing, 2013).

Helminen, M, 'National Report: Finland' in M Lang et al (eds), *CFC Legislation, Tax Treaties and EC Law* (The Hague, Kluwer Law International, 2004).

Heydon, JD, 'Equity and Statute' in M Godfrey (ed), *Law and Authority in British Legal History, 1200–1900* (Cambridge, Cambridge University Press, 2016).

Jalland, P, 'Irish Home Rule Finance: A Neglected Dimension of the Irish Question, 1910–1914' in A O'Day (ed), *Reactions to Irish Nationalism, 1865–1914* (London, Hambledon Press, 1987).

Jansen van Rensburg, E, 'The History of Income Taxation in the Cape Colony: A Story of Dangerous Beasts and Murderous Fathers' in J Hattingh, J Roeleveld and C West (eds), *Income Tax in South Africa The First 100 Years 1914–2014* (Cape Town, Juta & Co, 2016).

Kofler, G, 'CFC Rules' in M Lang (ed), *Common Consolidated Corporate Tax Base* (Vienna, Linde, 2008).

Kohli, M, 'Intergenerational Transfers and Inheritance: A Comparative View' in M Silverstein (ed), *Intergenerational Relations Across Time and Place: Annual Review of Gerontology and Geriatrics* (New York, Springer, 2004).

Lee, C, 'A Road not Taken: Select Committees and the Estimates, 1880–1904' in P Evans (ed), *Essays on the History of Parliamentary Procedure in Honour of Thomas Erskine May* (Oxford, Hart Publishing, 2017).

Likhovski, A, 'The Story of *Gregory*: How Are Tax Avoidance Case Decided?' in SA Bank and KJ Stark (eds), *Business Tax Stories* (New York, Foundation Press, 2005).

—— 'Tax Law and Public Opinion: Explaining *IRC v Duke of Westminster*' in J Tiley (ed), *Studies in the History of Tax Law: Volume 2* (Oxford, Hart Publishing, 2007).

Lubbock, J, 'Municipal and Government Trading' in MH Judge (ed), *Political Socialism: A Remonstrance. A Collection of Papers by Members of the British Constitution Association, with Presidential Addresses by Lord Balfour of Burleigh and Lord Hugh Cecil* (London, PS King, 1908).

McFarlane, B and Simpson, E, 'Tackling Avoidance' in J Getzler (ed), *Rationalising Property, Equity and Trusts: Essays in Honour of Edward Burn* (Oxford, Oxford University Press, 2003).

McHugh, J, 'The Self-Employed and the Small Independent Entrepreneur' in R King and N Nugent (eds), *Respectable Rebels* (London, Hodder & Stoughton, 1979).

Macmillan, Lord and Stevens R, 'Younger, Robert, Baron Blanesburgh (1861–1946), judge' in *Oxford Dictionary of National Biography* (Oxford, Oxford University Press, 2004).

Matthew, HCG, 'Courtney, Leonard Henry, Baron Courtney of Penwith (1832–1918)' in *Oxford Dictionary of National Biography* (Oxford, Oxford University Press, 2004).

—— 'Gibson, Thomas Milner (1806–1884)' in *Oxford Dictionary of National Biography* (Oxford, Oxford University Press, 2011).

Miller, P and Power, M, 'Accounting, Law and Economic Calculation' in M Bromwich and A Hopwood, *Accounting and the Law* (London, Prentice Hall, 1992).

Napier, C and Noke, C 'Accounting and Law: An Historical Overview of an Uneasy Relationship' in M Bromwich and A Hopwood, *Accounting and the Law* (London, Prentice Hall and ICAEW, 1992).

Neill, P, 'Wilberforce, Richard Orme, Baron Wilberforce (1907–2003)' in *Oxford Dictionary of National Biography* (Oxford, Oxford University Press, 2007).

Nugent, N, 'The National Association for Freedom' in R King and N Nugent (eds), *Respectable Rebels* (London, Hodder & Stoughton, 1979).

Poole, T, 'Hobbes on Law and Prerogative' in D Dyzenhaus and T Poole (eds), *Hobbes and the Law* (Cambridge, Cambridge University Press, 2012).

'Presidential Address of Lord Balfour of Burleigh' in MH Judge (ed), *Political Socialism: A Remonstrance. A Collection of Papers by Members of the British Constitution Association, with Presidential Addresses by Lord Balfour of Burleigh and Lord Hugh Cecil* (London, PS King, 1908).

'Presidential Address of Lord Hugh Cecil' in MH Judge (ed), *Political Socialism: A Remonstrance. A Collection of Papers by Members of the British Constitution Association, with Presidential Addresses by Lord Balfour of Burleigh and Lord Hugh Cecil* (London, PS King, 1908).

Propert, PSG, 'The Problem of Unemployment' in MH Judge (ed), *Political Socialism: A Remonstrance. A Collection of Papers by Members of the British Constitution Association, with Presidential Addresses by Lord Balfour of Burleigh and Lord Hugh Cecil* (London, PS King, 1908).

Ridd, P, 'Statutory Interpretation in Early Capital Gains Tax Cases' in P Harris and D de Cogan (eds), *Studies in the History of Tax Law: Volume 8* (Oxford, Hart Publishing, 2017).

Rose, K, 'Cecil, Hugh Richard Heathcote Gascoyne-, Baron Quickswood (1869–1956)' in *Oxford Dictionary of National Biography* (Oxford, Oxford University Press, 2004).

Rubin, GR, 'Finlay, Robert Bannatyne, first Viscount Finlay (1842–1929), Lord Chancellor' in *Oxford Dictionary of National Biography* (Oxford, Oxford University Press, 2004).

Shenfield, AA, 'Hayek on Law' in N Barry (ed), *Limited Government, Individual Liberty and the Rule of Law* (Cheltenham, Edward Elgar, 1998).

Snape, J, 'Corporate Income Tax Subjects in the United Kingdom' in D Gutmann (ed), *Corporate Income Tax Subjects* (IBFD, 2016).

—— 'Legal Interpretation of Tax Law: United Kingdom' in RF van Brederode and R Krever (eds), *Legal Interpretation of Tax Law*, 2nd edn (The Hague, Wolters Kluwer, 2017).

Stebbings, C, 'The Equity of the Executive: Fairness in Tax Law in Nineteenth-Century England' in M Godfrey (ed), *Law and Authority in British Legal History, 1200–1900* (Cambridge, Cambridge University Press, 2016).

Stopforth, D 'Restricting Tax Relief on Business Entertaining and Gifts: 1948–1965' in J Tiley (ed), *Studies in the History of Tax Law: Volume 5* (Oxford, Hart Publishing, 2011).

Templeman, S, 'Tackling Tax Avoidance' in A Shipwright (ed), *Tax Avoidance and the Law: Sham, Fraud or Mitigation* (Oxford, Key Haven Publications, 1997).

Templeman, S, 'Form and Substance' in J Getzler (ed), *Rationalising Property, Equity and Trusts: Essays in Honour of Edward Burn* (Oxford, Oxford University Press, 2003).

Tiley, J, 'An Academic Perspective on the Ramsay/Dawson Doctrine' in J Dyson (ed), *Recent Tax Problems: Current Legal Problems* (London, Stevens, 1985).

Tribe, K, 'Liberalism and Neoliberalism in Britain, 1930–1980' in P Mirowski and D Plehwe, *The Road from Mont Pèlerin: The Making of the Neoliberal Thought Collective* (Cambridge, MA, Harvard University Press, 2009).

Varuhas, J, 'The Public Interest Conception of Public Law' in J Bell, M Elliott, J Varuhas and P Murray (eds), *Public Law Adjudication in Common Law Systems* (Oxford, Hart Publishing, 2016).

Vella, J, 'Shams, Tax Avoidance and a "Realistic View of the Facts"' in E Simpson and M Stewart (eds), *Sham Transactions* (Oxford, Oxford University Press, 2013).

Venables, R, QC, 'Tax Avoidance – A Practitioner's Viewpoint' in A Shipwright (ed), *Tax Avoidance and the Law: Sham, Fraud or Mitigation?* (Oxford, Key Haven Publications, 1997).

Williams, I, 'Developing a Prerogative Theory for the Authority of the Chancery: The French Connection' in M Godfrey (ed), *Law and Authority in British Legal History, 1200–1900* (Cambridge, Cambridge University Press, 2016).

Journal Articles

Adams, R, 'Gray v IRC: Unnatural Units of Property' [1995] *BTR* 338.
AG, 'Inland Revenue v Mann; Same v Crossman' (1937) 1 *MLR* 82. Ch 7.
Ahmed, F and Perry, A, 'Constitutional Statutes' (2017) 37 *OJLS* 461.
Alder, J, 'The Legality of Extra-Statutory Concessions' (1980) 1 *New Law Journal* 180.
Avery Jones, JF, 'The Leedale Affair' [1983] *BTR* 70.
—— 'Further Thoughts on Zim' [1988] *BTR* 29, 32.
—— 'Bodies of Persons' [1991] *BTR* 453.
—— 'MacNiven v Westmoreland: The Humpty Dumpty School of Judicial Anti-Avoidance' [2001] *Private Client Business* 381.
Avery Jones, JF et al, 'Characterization of Other States' Partnerships for Income Tax' (2002) 56 *Bulletin for International Fiscal Documentation* 288; [2002] *BTR* 375.
—— 'The Origins of Concepts and Expressions used in the OECD Model and their Adoption by States' [2006] *BTR* 695.
Bartlett, RT, 'The Constitutionality of the *Ramsay* Principle' [1985] *BTR* 338.
Beighton, L and Draper, D, 'Transferable Personal Allowance: A Small Step in the Right Direction' [2015] *BTR* 580.
Bennion, F, 'Executive Estoppel: Pepper v Hart Revisited' [2007] *PL* 1.
Binder, AS, 'A Model of Inherited Wealth' (1973) 87 *Quarterly Journal of Economics* 608.
Bogenschneider, BN, 'Wittgenstein on Why Tax Law is Comprehensible' [2015] *BTR* 252.
—— 'The Taxing Power after *Sebelius*' (2016) 51 *Wake Forest Law Review* 941.
Brown, J, 'Unincorporated Associations: Property Holding, Charitable Purposes and Dissolution' (2009) 21 *Denning Law Journal* 107.
Brown, HG, 'Criteria for a Rational Tax System' (1961) 20 *American Journal of Economics and Sociology* 443.
Cane, P, 'Statutes, Standing and Representation' [1990] *PL* 307.
Carnwath, R, 'Tribunal Justice, A New Start' [2009] *PL* 48.
Cass, B, and Brennan, D, 'Taxing Women: The Politics of Gender in the Tax/Transfer System' (2003) 1 *eJournal of Tax Research* 37.
Collier, R, 'Intentions, Banks, Politics and the Law: The UK Code of Practice on Taxation for Banks' [2014] *BTR* 478.
Cordewener, A, Kofler, G and Schindler, CP, 'Free Movement of Capital and Third Countries: Exploring the Outer Boundaries with *Lasertec, A and B and Holböck*' [2007] *European Taxation* 371.
Cutts, T, 'The Nature of Equitable Property: A Functional Analysis' (2012) 6 *Journal of Equity* 44.
Cygan, A, 'Protecting the Interests of Civil Society in Community Decision-Making: The Limits of Article 230 EC' (2003) 52 *ICLQ* 995.
Davies, AG, 'The Tax Raiders: In the Name of Charity Review Article' [1988] *BTR* 311.
de Cogan, D, 'Defining Tax Avoidance: Flirting with Chaos, Again' [2016] *CLJ* 474.
Eden, S, 'The Mystical Art of Valuing Agricultural Tenancies' [1991] *BTR* 181.
Evans, RS, '"Assets" for Capital Gains Tax Purposes' (1988) 138 *New Law Journal* 275.
Feldman, D, 'Public Interest Litigation and Constitutional Theory in Comparative Perspective' (1992) 55(1) *MLR* 44.
Freedman, J, 'Profit and Prophets – Law and Accountancy Practice on the Timing of Receipts' (Part II) [1987] *BTR* 104.

—— 'Ordinary Principles of Commercial Accounting – Clear Guidance or a Mystery Tour?' [1993] *BTR* 468.

—— 'Personal Service Companies – "The Wrong Kind of Enterprise"' [2001] *BTR* 1.

—— 'Aligning Taxable Profits and Accounting Profits: Accounting Standards, Legislators and Judges' (2004) 2 *eJournal of Tax Research* 71.

—— 'Defining Taxpayer Responsibility: In Support of a General Anti-Avoidance Principle' [2004] *BTR* 332.

—— 'Interpreting Tax Statutes: Tax Avoidance and the Intention of Parliament' [2007] *LQR* 53.

Gammie, M, 'Extra-Statutory Concessions' [1980] *BTR* 308.

—— 'Reflections on *Jones v Garnett*' [2007] *BTR* 687.

Goldberg, D, '*Mars and Secan:* There Illusion and Here Truth; The Computation of Profit' (2008) 7 *GITC Review* 1.

Goodhart, AJ (ed), 'Notes' (1928) XLIV *LQR* 8.

Gordon, MD, 'The Collection of Ship-money in the Reign of Charles I' (1910) 4 *Transactions of the Royal Historical Society, Third Series* 141.

Gourvish, TR and Wilson, RG, 'Profitability in the Brewing Industry, 1885–1914' (1985) 27 *Business History* 146.

Gower, LCB, 'The English Private Company' (1953) 18 *Law and Contemporary Problems* 535.

Griffith, JAG, 'Comment' [1963] *PL* 401.

—— 'The Political Constitution' (1979) 42 *MLR* 1.

Gutzke, D, 'The Social Status of Landed Brewers in Britain since 1840' (1984) 17 *Social History/ Histoire Sociale* 93.

Hackney, J, 'The Politics of the Chancery' [1981] *CLP* 114.

Hanbury, HG, 'A Periodical Menace to Equitable Principles' (1928) XLIV *LQR* 468.

—— 'The Field of Modern Equity' (1929) 45 *LQR* 199.

Hand, Judge Learned, 'Thomas Walter Swan' (1947) 57 *Yale Law Journal* 167.

Hansmann, H and R Kraakman, 'Organizational Law Asset Partitioning' (2000) 44 *European Economic Review* 807.

Harden, I, 'Value for Money and Administrative Law' [1996] *PL* 661.

Harlow, C, 'Public Law and Popular Justice' (2002) 65 *MLR* 1.

Harris, JW, 'Towards Principles of Overruling – When Should a Final Court of Appeal Second Guess?' (1990) 10 *OJLS* 135.

Harris, R, 'The Bubble Act: Its Passage and Its Effects on Business Organization' (1994) 54 *Journal of Economic History* 610.

Harrison, B, 'Mrs Thatcher and the Intellectuals' (1994) 5 *Twentieth Century British History* 206.

Hoffmann, L, 'Tax Avoidance' [2005] *BTR* 197.

Hole, D, 'Withdrawal of the Cash Basis – sections 42 to 46 and Schedules 6 and 7' [1998] *BTR* 405.

Jackson, D, 'Thomas Hobbes' Theory of Taxation' (1973) 21 *Political Studies* 175.

Jaconelli, J, 'The "Bowles Act" – The Cornerstone of the Fiscal Constitution' (2010) 69 *CLJ* 582.

Jordan, G and Halpin, C, 'Cultivating Small Business Influence in the UK: The Federation of Small Businesses' Journey from Outsider to Insider' (2003) 3 *Journal of Public Affairs* 313.

Keedy, ER, 'A Petition of Right: Archer-Shee v The King' (1939) 87 *U Pa LR* 895.

Keir, DL, 'The Case of Ship-Money' (1936) 52 *LQR* 546.

Kerridge, R, 'The Taxation of Emoluments from Offices and Employments' (1992) 108 *LQR* 433.

Kynaston, D, 'The Long Life and Slow Death of Exchange Controls' (2000) 2 *Journal of International Financial Markets* 37.

Lang, M, 'CFC Regulations and Double Taxation Treaties' (2003) 57(2) *IBFD Bulletin* 51.

Langelüddeke, H, '"I finde all men & my officers all soe unwilling": The collection of Ship-money, 1635–1640' (2007) 46 *Journal of British Studies* 509.

Laws, J, 'Law and Fact' [1999] *BTR* 159.

Loutzenhiser, G, 'Finance Act Notes: Section 8 and Schedule 1: High Income Child Benefit Charge' [2012] *BTR* 370.

—— 'Transferable Personal Allowances: A Small Step in the Wrong Direction' [2015] *BTR* 110.

—— 'Where Next for Small Company Tax Reform in the UK?' [2016] *BTR* 674.

—— 'Section 6 and Schedule 1: Workers' Services Provided to Public Sector through Intermediaries' [2017] *BTR* 201.

Lustgarten, L, 'The Arms Trade and the Constitution: Beyond the Scott Report' (1998) 61 *MLR* 499, 507.

Lye, DN, 'Adult Child–Parent Relationships' (1996) 22 *Annual Review of Sociology* 79.

Lyell, N, '*Pepper v Hart*: The Government Perspective' (1994) 15 *Stat LR* 1.

McAuslan, P, 'The International Development Act, 2002: Benign Imperialism or a Missed Opportunity?' (2003) 66 *MLR* 563.

Macdonald, G, *HMRC v William Grant & Sons Distillers Ltd and Small (Inspector of Taxes) v Mars UK Ltd:* Accountancy Practice and the Computation of Profit' [2007] *BTR* 366.

Macfarlane, B and Stevens, R, 'The Nature of Equitable Property' (2010) 4 *Journal of Equity* 1.

Malherbe, J et al, 'Controlled Foreign Corporations in the EU After *Cadbury Schweppes*' (2007) 36 *TMIJ* 607.

Menchik, PL. 'Primogeniture, Equal Sharing, and the U.S. Distribution of Wealth' (1980) 94 *Quarterly Journal of Economics* 299.

Mendle, M, 'The Ship Money Case, *The Case of Shipmony*, and the Development of Henry Parker's Parliamentary Absolutism' (1989) 32 *Historical Journal* 513.

Miles, J, 'Standing under the Human Rights Act 1998' [2000] *CLJ* 133.

Miller, P and Power, M, 'Accounting, Organizing, and Economizing: Connecting Accounting Research and Organization Theory' (2013) 7 *The Academy of Management Annals* 557.

Millett, P, 'A New Approach to Tax Avoidance Schemes' (1982) 98 *LQR* 209.

—— 'Artificial Tax Avoidance: the English and American Approach' [1986] *BTR* 327.

—— 'Construing Statutes' (1999) *SLR* 107.

—— 'The Secret History of Ramsay v IRC' [1999] *Trusts & Estates Tax Journal* 23.

Monroe, HH, 'The Constitution in Danger' [1969] *BTR* 24.

—— 'Fiscal Statutes: A Drafting Disaster' [1979] *BTR* 265.

Montagu, G, 'Is a Foreign State a Body Corporate?' [2001] *BTR* 421.

—— 'Anson and Entity Classification Revisited in the Light of Brexit: Can an LLC Constitute a "Body Corporate?"' [2016] *BTR* 466.

Morgan, G, 'Accounting as Reality Construction: Towards a New Epistemology for Accounting Practice' (1988) 13 *Accounting, Organizations and Society* 477.

Morse, G, '*Grays Timber Products Ltd v Revenue and Customs Commissioners*: Valuing Employee Shares with Non-Assignable Rights' [2010] *BTR* 210.

—— 'Fiscal Statutes: A Drafting Disaster' [1979] *BTR* 265.

Murphy ME, 'Lord Plender: A Vignette of an Accountant and His Times, 1861–1948' (1953) 27 *Bulletin of the Business Historical Society* 1.

Odell, KA and Weidenmier, MD, 'Real Shock, Monetary Aftershock: The 1906 San Francisco Earthquake and the Panic of 1907' (2004) 64 *Journal of Economic History* 1002.

Oliver, JDB, 'Withholding Tax and Tax Credits, with some Reflections on Union Texas' [1991] *BTR* 245.

O'Shea, T, 'The UK's CFC Rules and the Freedom of Establishment: Cadbury Schweppes plc and its IFSC Subsidiaries – Tax Avoidance or Tax Mitigation?' (2007) 1 *EC Tax Review* 2007 13.

Oliver, P, 'A Judicial View of Modern Legislation' (1993) 14 *SLR* 1.

Panayi, CHJI, 'International Tax Law following the OECD/G20 Base Erosion and Profit Shifting Project' (2016) 11 *Bulletin for International Taxation* 628.

Park, A, 'Tax Law in and after the Wheatcroft Era' [1997] *BTR* 371.

Parrot, D and Avery Jones, JF, 'Seven Appeals and an Acquittal: The Singer Family and their Tax Cases' [2008] *BTR* 56.

Parry-Wingfield, M, 'Deprecation in Stock: Where Next?' [2007] *Tax Journal* 13.

Paterson, AA, 'Lord Reid's Unnoticed Legacy – A Jurisprudence of Overruling' (1981) 1 *OJLS* 375.

Peddle, DE, 'Long Cecil: The Gun made in Kimberley during the Siege' (1977) 4 *Military History Journal* 1.

Petrosovich, K, 'Abuse under the Merger Directive' (2010) 12 *European Taxation* 558.

Pleming, N, 'The Contribution of Public Interest Litigation to the Jurisprudence of JR' (1998) 3 *Judicial Review* 63.

Popkin, WD, 'Judicial Anti-Tax Avoidance Doctrine in England: A United States Perspective' [1991] *BTR* 283.

Prebble, J, 'Why Is Tax Law Incomprehensible?' [1994] *BTR* 380.

—— 'Ectopia, Tax Law and International Taxation' [1997] *BTR* 383.

Rawlings, R, 'Modelling Judicial Review' (2008) 61 *CLP* 95.

Redston, A, 'Income Sharing: The Nelsonian Option' [2007] *BTR* 680.

Reitan, EA, 'The Civil List in Eighteenth-Century British Politics: Parliamentary Supremacy Versus the Independence of the Crown' (1966) 9 *Historical Journal* 318.

Rix, MS, 'Company Law: 1844 and To-Day' (1945) 55 *The Economic Journal* 242.

Robson, M, '*Jones v Garnett*: Settlements and All That' [2005] *BTR* 15.

Rosefsky, KP, 'Tied Aid Credits and the New OECD Agreement' [1993] 14 *U Pa L Rev* 437.

Russell, C, 'The Ship-Money Judgments of Bramston and Davenport' (1962) 77 *English Historical Review* 303.

Sales, P, '*Pepper v Hart*: A footnote to Professor Vogenauer's Reply to Lord Steyn' (2006) 26 *OJLS* 585.

Salt, SP, 'Sir Simonds D'Ewes and the Levying of Ship-Money, 1635–1640' (1994) 37 *Historical Journal* 253.

Samuels, A, 'Permission for Judicial Review Out of Time: An Overview' (2002) 7 *Judicial Review* 216.

Sandler, D, 'Commerzbank – Fast Track to Harmonisation?' [1993] *BTR* 517.

Scott, AW, 'The Nature of the Rights of the "Cestui que trust"' (1917) 17 *Columbia Law Review* 269.

Seyedsayamdost, E, 'Development as End of Poverty: Reform or Reinvention?' (2015) 21 *Global Governance* 515.

Simpson, E, 'The Ramsay Principle: A Curious Incident of Judicial Reticence?' [2004] *BTR* 358.

Slesser, H, 'The Failure of Distributism' (1975) 1 *The Chesterton Review* 51.

Snape, J, 'Stability and its Significance in UK Tax Policy and Legislation' [2015] *BTR* 561.

Sparkes, P, 'The Derivation of Capital Sums' [1987] *BTR* 323.

Spencer, M and Spencer, J, 'The Judge as "Political Advisor": Behind the Scenes at the National Industrial Relations Court' (2006) 33 *Journal of Law and Society* 199.

Steyn, J, '*Pepper v Hart*; A Re-examination' (2001) 21 *OJLS* 59.

Stopforth, DP, 'The Background to the Anti-avoidance Provisions Concerning Settlements by Parents on their Minor Children' [1987] *BTR* 417.

—— 'Settlements and the Avoidance of Tax on Income – The Period to 1920' [1990] *BTR* 225.

—— 'The First Attack on Settlements Used for Income Tax Avoidance' [1991] *BTR* 86.

—— 'The Pre-Legislative Battle over Parental Settlements on their Children' [1994] *BTR* 234.

—— 'The Legacy of the 1938 Attack on Settlements' [1997] *BTR* 276.

—— 'The Birth of Capital Gains Tax – The Official View' [2005] *BTR* 584.

—— 'Getting Tough on Avoidance – Blocking Reverse Annuities' [2005] *BTR* 557.

Sumption, J, 'Judicial and Political Decision-making: The Uncertain Boundary' (2011) 16 *Judicial Review* 301.

Sutherland, B, 'The Valuation for Tax Purposes of Controlling Holdings of Unquoted Shares' [1996] *BTR* 397.

Teh, YK, 'The Future Fraud and Corruption Scenario in Developing and Developed Countries' (1997) 5 *Journal of Financial Crime* 58.

Templeman, S, 'Tax and the Taxpayer' (2001) 117 *LQR* 575.

Thomas, R, 'Sir Sidney and Sir John: The Rowlatts and Tax' [2011] *BTR* 210.

Thorne, SE, 'The Equity of a Statute and *Heydon's Case*' (1936–37) 31 *Illinois Law Review* 202.
Tiley, J, 'The Rescue Principle' (1967) 30 *MLR* 25.
—— 'First Thoughts on Westmoreland' [2001] *BTR* 153.
—— 'Composite Business Transactions: Business Transactions or Not?' (2003) 62 *CLJ* 272.
—— 'Tax Avoidance Jurisprudence as Normal Law' [2004] *BTR* 304.
—— 'Barclays and Scottish Provident: Avoidance and Highest Courts; Less Chaos but More Uncertainty' [2005] *BTR* 272.
—— 'Tax, Marriage and the Family' (2006) 65 *CLJ* 289.
Tomes, N, 'The Family, Inheritance, and the Intergenerational Transmission of Inequality' (1981) 89 *Journal of Political Economy* 928.
Tomkins, A, 'Judges Dam(n) the Government' (1996–97) 7 *Kings College Law Journal* 91.
Trautrims, C, 'Geschichte und Bedeutung von Sitz- und Gründungstheorie im deutschen Recht' (2012) 176 *Zeitschrift für das gesamte Handels- und Wirtschaftsrecht* 435.
Troup, E, 'Unacceptable Discretion: Countering Tax Avoidance and Preserving the Rights of the Individual' (1992) 13(4) *Fiscal Studies* 128.
Turrell, RV, 'Review Article: "Finance … The Governor of the Imperial Engine": Hobson and the Case of Rothschild and Rhodes' (1987) 13 *Journal of African Studies* 417.
Turrell, RV and van Hilten, JJ, 'The Rothschilds, the Exploration Company and Mining Finance' (1986) *Business History* 181.
Vella, J, 'Sham Transactions' [2008] *LMCLQ* 488.
Venables, R, QC, 'Tax Avoidance: Reflections on Lord Hoffmann's Lecture in Honour of Professor Sir Roy Goode' [2005] *Corporate Tax Review* 1.
Vineberg, PF, QC, 'The Ethics of Tax Planning' [1969] *BTR* 31.
Vinelott, J, 'Interpretation of Fiscal Statutes' (1982) 3 *SLR* 78.
Vogenauer, S, 'A Retreat from *Pepper v Hart*? A Reply to Lord Steyn' (2005) 25 *OJLS* 629.
Walker, R, 'Reflections on the Finance Act 1894' [1994] *BTR* 368.
—— 'Ramsay 25 Years On: Some Reflections on Tax Avoidance' (2004) 120 *LQR* 412.
Warren, T, 'Moving Beyond the Gender Wealth Gap: On Gender, Class, Ethnicity, and Wealth Inequalities in the United Kingdom' (2006) 12 *Feminist Economics* 195.
Waters, DWM, 'The Nature of the Trust Beneficiary's Interest' [1967] *Canadian Bar Review* 219.
Wheatcroft, GSA, 'The Law Shipping Rule Eroded' [1972] *BTR* 51.
Whitehouse, C, 'Fitzwilliam – An End to *Ramsay*' [1994] *Private Client Business* 71.
Whittington, G, 'Tax Policy and Accounting Standards' [1995] *BTR* 452.
Williams, D, 'Taxing Statutes Are Taxing Statutes: The Interpretation of Revenue Legislation' (1978) 41 *MLR* 404.
—— 'Extra-Statutory Concessions' [1979] *BTR* 137.
Williston, S, 'Uniform Partnership Act with Some Remarks on Other Uniform Commercial Laws' (1914–15) 63 *U Pa L Rev* 196.
Wooldridge, F, 'The General Partnership Under French Law' (2009) 77 *Amicus Curiae* 29.
Zalasinski, A, 'The Principle of Prevention of (Direct Tax) Abuse: Scope and Legal Nature – Remarks on the 3M Italia Case' (2012) 9 *European Taxation* 446.

Newspaper and Professional Articles

Anon, 'Review of Taxation, Revenue, Expenditure, Power, Statistics, and Debt of the Whole British Empire' (1833) 10 *The Eclectic Review: Third Series* 22.
—— *Poverty Bay Herald* (New Zealand, 8 January 1904) 4.
—— 'Sir Robert Younger's Title' *The Times* (17 November 1923).
—— 'Estate Duty: Valuation of Shares with Restricted Right of Transfer' (1934) 178 *Law Times* 83.
—— 'Estate Duty: Valuation of Shares with Restricted Right of Transfer' (1936) 81 *Law Times* 301.
—— 'Lord Blanesburgh: An Appreciation' *The Times* (27 August 1946).

—— 'Fleet Street hit' *The Guardian* (5 March 1979).

—— 'The Guardian' *The Guardian* (6 March 1979).

—— 'Print workers offered tax amnesty' *The Guardian* (8 March 1979).

—— 'Victory for the little man in Arctic Systems battle' *Express & Echo* (Exeter, 8 August 2007).

—— 'Couple take on the might of the taxman … And win' *Herald Express* (Torquay, 10 August 2007).

—— Death notice [Robert Ramsay], *Grimsby and Scunthorpe Telegraph* (15 December 2011).

—— 'Sir David Mitchell obituary' *The Telegraph* (31 August 2014).

—— 'Lord Steyn Obituary' *The Times* (1 December 2017).

Anonymous (*Pharmaceutical Journal* Editors), 'Legal Intelligence, Medicine Stamp Duty Acts' (1902) 68 *Pharmaceutical Journal* (series 4) 443, 523, 562.

—— 'Legal Intelligence, Medicine Stamp Duty Acts' (1902) 68 *Pharmaceutical Journal* (series 4) 561.

—— 'Legal Intelligence, Medicine Stamp Duty Acts' (1902) 68 *Pharmaceutical Journal* (series 4) 563.

—— 'Legal Intelligence, Medicine Stamp Duty Acts' (1902) 68 *Pharmaceutical Journal* (series 4) 524.

—— 'Medicine Stamp Duty Acts' (1903) 71 *Pharmaceutical Journal* (series 4) 8.

—— 'The Incidence of Medicine Stamp Duty' (1903) 71 *Pharmaceutical Journal* (series 4) 233–34.

—— 'Known, Admitted, and Approved' (1903) 71 *Pharmaceutical Journal* (series 4) 293.

—— 'Legal Intelligence, Medicine Stamp Duty Acts' (1903) 70 *Pharmaceutical Journal* (series 4) 503, 630.

—— 'Liability to Medicine Stamp Duty' (1903) 70 *Pharmaceutical Journal* (series 4) 828.

Aaronson, G, QC, 'The Swing of the Pendulum: Tax Avoidance in Modern Times' *Tax Journal* (30 September 2016) 6.

Andrews, J, 'Fleet Street tax amnesty faces High Court challenge' *The Guardian* (23 March 1979).

Avery Jones, JF, 'A New Approach to Tax Disputes' (1 November 2015) *Tax Adviser*.

Bailey, J 'Landlords! Is Your Buy to Let a "Cinema' or a "Ship"? – Repairs Before the First Letting' *Tax Insider* (July 2010).

Bain, S, 'Landmark tax ruling for small family firms' *Glasgow Post* (16 December 2005).

Blanchard, K, 'Entity Classification: The Significance of Legal Personality' *Business Entities* (March/April 2016) 4.

Bowes, D, 'Timber!' [2010] 165 *Taxation* 18.

Brinsmead-Stockham, J, 'Analysis – Tax Appeals: What is the "Point of Law"?' (26 September 2015) 1278 *Tax Journal* 14.

Cobain, I, 'Fear, revenge and ingenious tax deals – life on the top floor at Barclays' *The Guardian* (16 March 2013).

Cowe, R, 'Obituary of James Slater' *The Guardian* (22 November 2015).

'De Beers and the Politicians: Chairman's Reply to Attacks' *The Times* (16 December 1907) 5.

Dodwell, B, 'Time for Change' *Tax Advisor* (1 July 2017).

Editor, 'A Glance Back' (1903) 63 *Chemist and Druggist* 1051.

Editorial, 'A Leaky Umbrella' *The Times* (18 December 1979).

Ford, Jonathan and Plimmer, Gill, 'Public Service, Private Gain' *Financial Times* (23 January 2018).

Gladstone to Gwyn, 16 February 1860, quoted in *Morning Advertiser* (17 February 1860).

Gordon, K, 'Return of the Naïve' (December 2016) *Tax Adviser* 44.

Greene, C and Maddalena, C, 'Zim Reversed by Concession' (1989) 103 *Accountancy* 51–52.

Griffin, J, 'Couple's red tape victory' *Birmingham Evening Mail* (20 December 2005).

Harris, C, 'Fighters Rewarded' *Financial Times* (25 May 2006).

Heuston, RFV, 'Lord Wilberforce Obituary' *Independent* (19 February 2003).

Howard, P, 'HMRC's consultation on legislating ESC D33' (2014) 1228 *Tax Journal* 8 (29 August 2014).

'Ingenious Media clients face unenviable choice' *STEP Newsletter* (5 June 2017).

Kaye, F and Hodgson, M, 'The Taxman Cometh' (2014) 164 *New Law Journal* 31 (31 October 2014).

Kirby, CH, 'The Recent Medicine Stamp Duty Decisions' (1903) 71 *Pharmaceutical Journal* (series 4) 75–77.

Klass, D, 'Rereading UK Legislation to Reflect ECJ Decisions' (2010) 58 *Tax Notes International* 543.

Lagerberg, F, 'Why We Should Not Settle for This' (29 April 2004) 153 *Taxation* 105.

Langdon, J, 'Sir David Mitchell obituary' *The Guardian* (2 September 2014).

Lyon, 'Gallagher v Jones: The Revenue Loses by a Length' *Asset Finance and Leasing Digest* (April 1993) 14.

McKie & Co, 'Ensuring the Fair Administration of the Tax System' (2014) XVII *Rudge Revenue Review* 7.

Miles, G, 'The Taxation of Pay-outs under Buy-side Warranty and Indemnity Insurance Policies' (2016) 1334 *Tax Journal* 12 (2 December 2016).

Mount, F, 'A Time to Moan and Weep' *Spectator* (2 October 2010).

Pearce, E, 'Teresa Gorman obituary' *The Guardian* (28 August 2015).

Pickard, Jim, 'Is Britain Ready for John McDonnell?' *FT Weekend Magazine* (3/4 March 2018).

Pilling, David and Cotterill, Joseph, 'The Selling of South Africa' *FT Weekend Magazine* (2/3 December 2017).

Prosser, D, 'A victory for some married couples' *The Independent* (26 July 2007).

Redston, A, 'Unsettled Business' (13 November 2003) 152 *Taxation* 162.

—— 'The Settlement Saga' (25 November 2004) 154 *Taxation* 202 ('Act 1: The Revenue launches surprise attack on small businesses. Act 2: The professional bodies mount massed counter-attack').

Richards, G, 'Revenue concession on Zim' (1989) 86 *LSG* 28 (19 April 1989).

Ridd, P, 'Verdict by Misadventure' *Tax Journal* (16 July 2007).

Snyder, J, 'Ottawa's tax changes threaten to swamp the court, chief justices warn' *Financial Post* (Toronto, 11 December 2017).

Stewart, D, 'Vodafone Settles Dispute with HMRC Over Controlled Foreign Corporations' [2010] *WTD* 142.

'Study on Structures of Aggressive Tax Planning and Indicators, Final Report' (2015) Taxation Papers, Working Paper No 61.

Travis, A, 'Revealed: 1961 Goya "Theft" from National Gallery was a Family Affair' *The Guardian* (30 November 2012).

Tweedie, N, and Day, P, '1973: A Year of Conflict and Scandal' *Daily Telegraph* (1 January 2004).

Vaines, P, 'Arctic Systems: Director or Dictator?' (28 October 2004) 154 *Taxation* 90.

Walters, J, 'Taxation of Damages, Costs and Interest (3)' (2003) II(2) *GITC Review* 75.

Wiggins, HW, 'Leedale v Lewis – Revenue Law-Making' [1983] *LSG* 461.

Willetts, D, 'Quiet Hero of Thatcherism who became its nemesis' *Financial Times* (12 October 2015) 2.

Williams, R, 'Pergau Dam Affair: "Sweeteners" row sparked trade ban' *The Independent* (7 September 1994).

Wilson, D, 'Insuring M&A Tax Risk' (2016) 1319 *Tax Journal* 12 (29 July 2016).

Miscellaneous

BBC, 'Barclays Bank told by Treasury to pay £500m avoided tax' (29 February 2012).

Bowler, T, 'HMRC's Discretion: the Application of the Ultra Vires Rule and the Legitimate Expectation Doctrine', TLRC Discussion Paper no 10 (London, IFS, 2014),

Carnwath, R, 'From Judicial Outrage to Sliding Scales – Where Next for Wednesbury?', ALBA annual lecture (November 2013).

Catholic Church, *Catechism*, rev edn (London, Geoffrey Chapman, 1999).

Chartered Institute of Taxation, *Income Shifting: A Consultation on Draft Legislation – Response by the Chartered Institute of Taxation* (28 February 2008).

Financial Markets Law Committee, *Response to the June 2009 HM Revenue & Customs Consultation Document on a Code of Practice for Banks*, Issue 146 (October 2009).

Financial Reporting Council, 'Statement of Standard Accounting Practice 21 on accounting for leases and hire purchase contracts (SSAP 21)' (1984).

Gill, AAM, 'Ship-Money during the Rule of Charles I: Politics, Ideology and the Law' (PhD thesis, University of Sheffield, 1990).

Harris, P, 'A 200-page Income Tax Constitution for the UK?', presented at the conference 'Celebrating the End of the Rewrite', HM Treasury (October 2010).

Howe, G and Joseph, K et al, *The Right Approach to the Economy* (Conservative Central Office, 1977).

International Accounting Standards Board, 'Conceptual Framework for Financial Reporting' (2018).

National Federation of Self-Employed, *An Inspector at the Door* (Adam Smith Institute and NFSE, 1979).

Perkins, N, 'The Judiciary and the Defence of Property in the Law Courts during the Personal Rule of Charles I' (PhD thesis, University of Cambridge, 1997).

'Reports of Solicitor upon Legal Business', The National Archives, RAIL 250/522 (1919–20).

'Reports of Solicitor upon Legal Business', The National Archives, RAIL 250/523 (1921).

Southern, D, 'Changes to the taxation of compensation (ESC D33)', Chancery Bar Association / Revenue Bar Association (25 March 2015).

Special Committee of Tax Law Consultative Bodies, *Tax Law After Furniss v Dawson* (London, Law Society of England and Wales, 1988).

Sweeney, J, 'Tax inquiry into Lloyds offshore' (*BBC*, 'Panorama', 21 September 2009).

Taylor, M, and others (eds), *Good Work: The Taylor Review of Modern Working Practices* (July 2017).

Walters, RM, *Finance Act 1978: taxation changes/prepared for the Society of Company and Commercial Accountants* (Society of Company and Commercial Accountants, 1978).

Wilberforce, Lord, *Law and Economics: Presidential Address* (Holdsworth Club, 1966).

Index